THE INDIAN OCEAN

DUKE PRESS POLICY STUDIES

The Indian Ocean

Perspectives on a Strategic Arena

EDITED BY
William L. Dowdy
and Russell B. Trood

Duke University Press   Durham   1985

© 1985 Duke University Press
All rights reserved
Printed in the United States of America
on acid-free paper ∞

Library of Congress Cataloging in
Publication data appear on the
last printed page of this book.

Contents

     Regional Security   *Sheldon W. Simon*   377

PART FOUR   Interests of External Powers

     Introduction   397

22   Projection of Force by External Powers
     Michael MccGwire   400

23   The Indian Ocean: U.S. Military and Strategic Perspectives
     Larry W. Bowman and Jeffrey A. Lefebvre   413

24   Diego Garcia: The Military and Legal Limitations of
     America's Pivotal Base in the Indian Ocean   *Joel Larus*   435

25   Aspects of United States Naval Deployments in the
     Indian Ocean   *Alvin J. Cottrell*   451

26   Soviet Interests in the Persian/Arabian Gulf
     Oles M. Smolansky   458

27   Western European Interests in the Indian Ocean
     Ferenc A. Váli   478

28   Japanese Interests in Indian Ocean Security
     Taketsugu Tsurutani   494

29   The People's Republic of China: Perspectives
     on the Indian Ocean   *Russell B. Trood*   508

PART FIVE   Conclusion

30   Security in the Indian Ocean Arena: Trends and
     Prospects   *Ian Clark*   527

     Notes   539
     Index   597
     Contributors   611

Tables, Figures, and Maps

Abbreviations

ABM	Anti–ballistic missile
ANC	African National Congress
ANZAC	Australian–New Zealand Army Corps
ANZUS	Australia–New Zealand–United States alliance
ARMSCOR	Arms Corporation of South Africa
ASEAN	Association of South-East Asian Nations
ASW	Antisubmarine warfare
AWACS	Airborne Warning and Control System
BIOT	British Indian Ocean Territory
BOSS	Bureau of State Security (South Africa)
CD	Committee on Disarmament
CENTO	Central Treaty Organization
CIA	Central Intelligence Agency (U.S.)
COMECON	Council for Mutual Economic Assistance
COPWE	Conference Organizing the Peoples and Workers of Ethiopia
CPD	Comprehensive program of disarmament
CSCE	Conference on Security and Cooperation in Europe
CSOE	Capital-surplus oil exporter
CTB	Comprehensive test ban
CW	Chemical weapons
DCP	Defence Cooperation Program (Australia)
DOD	Department of Defense (U.S.)
EAC	East African Community
EEC	European Economic Community
EEZ	Exclusive economic zone
ELF	Eritrean Liberation Front
EPLF	Eritrean Popular Liberation Front

FAC	Fast attack craft
FDL	Fast deployment logistics
FLS	Frontline States
FMS	Foreign military sales
FRELIMO	Frente de Libertação de Moçambique
FY	Fiscal year
GCC	Gulf Cooperation Council
GDP	Gross domestic product
GNP	Gross national product
ICG	Indian Coast Guard
ICO	Islamic Conference Organization
IMF	International Monetary Fund
INF	Intermediate nuclear force
IOC	Indian Ocean Commission
IOR	Indian Ocean region
IOZP	Indian Ocean zone of peace
IRP	Iranian Republican party
JDA	Japan Defense Agency
KANU	Kenya African National Union
LDC	Less-developed country
MAB	Marine amphibious brigade
MAF	Marine amphibious force (U.S.)
MBFR	Mutual and balanced force reductions
MEDO	Middle East Defense Organization
MEF	Middle East Force (U.S.)
MFO	Multinational Force and Observers (in the Sinai)
MIDEASTFOR	Middle East Force (U.S.)
MMM	Mouvement Militant Mauricien
MNR	Mozambique National Resistance
MPLA	Movimento Popular de Libertação de Angola
MPS	Maritime pre-positioning ships
MRD	Movement for the Restoration of Democracy (Pakistan)
MSDF	Maritime Self-Defense Force (Japan)
MSM	Mouvement Socialiste Mauricien
NALT	Naval Arms Limitation Talks
NAM	Nonaligned movement

NATO	North Atlantic Treaty Organization
NDC	National Development Corporation (Tanzania)
NDF	National Democratic Front (North Yemen)
NIC	Newly industrializing country
NIS	National Intelligence Service (South Africa)
NLF	National Liberation Front (South Yemen)
NM	Nautical miles
NOSIS	Naval Ocean Surveillance Information System
NPT	Non-Proliferation Treaty
NSC	National Security Council (U.S.)
NWFZ	Nuclear-weapon-free zone
OAPEC	Organization of Arab Petroleum Exporting Countries
OAU	Organization of African Unity
ODA	Official development assistance
OEC	Oil-exporting country
OECD	Organization for Economic Cooperation and Development
OIC	Organization of the Islamic Conference
OPEC	Organization of Petroleum Exporting Countries
PAC	Pan-Africanist Conference
PDRY	People's Democratic Republic of Yemen (South Yemen)
PLO	Palestine Liberation Organization
POMCUS	Pre-positioning of material configured to unit size
PRC	People's Republic of China
PSDM	Parti Social Democrat Mauricien
PSM	Parti Socialiste Mauricien
RAN	Royal Australian Navy
RCD	Regional Cooperation for Development
RDF	Rapid Deployment Force
RSA	Republic of South Africa
SAA	South African Airways
SACEUR	Supreme allied commander, Europe
SACLANT	Supreme allied commander, Atlantic
SADCC	Southern African Development Coordination Conference
SADF	South African Defence Force
SAN	South African Navy
SAR	South African Railroads

SAR&H	South African Railway and Harbour Corporation
SATCC	South Africa Transport and Communications Commission
SEATO	South-East Asia Treaty Organization
SLBM	Sea-launched ballistic missile
SLOC	Sea lines of communication
SNF	Strategic nuclear force
SPPC	Security Policy Planning Committee (Japan)
SPPF	Seychelles Peoples' Progressive Front
SSM	Surface-to-surface missile
STANAVFORLANT	Standing Naval Force, Atlantic
SWAPO	South West African People's Organization
TANU	Tanganyika African National Union
TAZARA	Tanzania-Zambia Railway Authority
UAE	United Arab Emirates
UAR	United Arab Republic
UDI	Unilateral declaration of independence
UN	United Nations
UNCLOS	United Nations Conference on the Law of the Sea
UNITA	União Nacional para a Independência Total de Angola
UNSSOD	United Nations Special Session on Disarmament
USFJ	United States Forces, Japan
VLF	Very low frequency
WENELA	Witwatersrand Native Labor Agency
WEU	Western European Union
WSLF	Western Somali Liberation Front
YAR	Yemen Arab Republic (North Yemen)
ZANU	Zimbabwe African National Union
ZAPU	Zimbabwe African People's Union
ZIPRA	Zimbabwe People's Revolutionary Army
ZOPFAN	Zone of peace, freedom, and neutrality

Preface ◣

Less than twenty years ago the Indian Ocean was a relatively quiet, little-known strategic backwater. Oil cost less than two dollars a barrel. Haile Selassie and the shah of Iran were firmly ensconced on their respective thrones. Minority white regimes were ruling Angola, Mozambique, and Rhodesia, as well as South Africa. British military units were based in the Persian Gulf as they had been, with regularity, for over a century and a half. The United States and Australia were preoccupied with Vietnam, the Soviet Union with Czechoslovakia.

The 1970s, however, brought a succession of developments that thrust the Indian Ocean into the mainstream of international politics: the British withdrew from east of Suez; there was another Indo-Pakistani war and Bangladesh was born; the superpowers increased their naval intrusion; most of the remaining colonies/protectorates in the area came to independence; there was the oil embargo of 1973–74 and the ensuing energy crises; warfare occurred intermittently on the Horn of Africa; the Soweto riots took place, increasing racial conflict in South Africa; the Iranian revolution happened; the Soviet Union invaded Afghanistan; and Iraq and Iran went to war. The 1980s so far have seen a continuation of the prevailing pattern of instabilities, a trend likely to ensure that the Indian Ocean region will remain a major focus of international politics through this decade and beyond.

Most of the chapters in this book began life as papers prepared for a conference on "The Indian Ocean: Perspectives on a Strategic Arena." The conference was held in Halifax, Nova Scotia, Canada, 12–14 October 1982, and was sponsored by Dalhousie University's Centre for Foreign Policy Studies with collaboration of the Western Australian Institute of Technology. Participants included scholars and government officials with professional interests in the Indian Ocean region from Canada, the United States, Western Europe, and several Indian Ocean states. The conference was funded in large part by the Centre for Foreign Policy Studies, using funds provided by its five-year Military and Strategic Studies Programme grant from the Canadian Department of National

Defence, and by grants from the Social Sciences and Humanities Research Council of Canada and the Research and Development Fund administered by Dalhousie's Faculty of Graduate Studies. As organizers of the conference, we gratefully acknowledge the financial support provided by these institutions. Lee Dowdy also wishes to thank the Joseph Rowntree Foundation for his 1983–84 Visiting Fellowship at the University of Lancaster's Centre for the Study of Arms Control and International Security which supported him during most of the editorial period.

The format of this volume largely replicates the conference agenda. The papers were prepared in response to requests we directed to specific scholars. Each author was given minimal guidance as to how he should approach his subject. Generally we did little more than indicate the topic we wished to see addressed, specify our requirement for originality, and express our strong desire for papers that would be forward-looking and reflective of the overall conference theme of Indian Ocean security. From the outset we looked upon the conference and subsequent publication of the papers as one enterprise, and we encouraged participants to regard them in the same way. (For brief synopses of the presentations and of the discussions following the various conference panels, see Ken Booth, "The Indian Ocean: Perspectives on a Strategic Arena—A Conference Report," available from the Centre for Foreign Policy Studies, Dalhousie University, Halifax, Nova Scotia, Canada B3H 4H6.)

Each of the papers in this book has been revised, in some cases substantially, since the conference. Some revisions were undertaken by the authors themselves to reflect insights gained at the conference; others are the result of our own editorial efforts. For the most part, the latter were directed to ensuring that the book have as much thematic unity as possible, without unnecessarily constraining the subject matter. Four chapters did not originally appear as conference papers. The contributions of Colin Legum, Rouhollah Ramazani, Taketsugu Tsurutani, and Russell Trood were commissioned later to fill obvious gaps in the coverage of issues. Ian Clark's conference paper was expanded at our request to provide a suitable concluding chapter for the book.

This Duke Press volume, which represents the combined labors of nearly three dozen specialists, is, we believe, the most comprehensive collection of new writings on strategic issues in the Indian Ocean to appear since the publication over a dozen years ago of *The Indian Ocean: Its Political, Economic, and Military Importance*, edited by Alvin J. Cottrell and R. M. Burrell (Praeger, 1972). In the intervening period since the Cottrell-Burrell volume was published, a critical mass of experts—mostly political scientists—have remained in close touch with the rapid and significant developments in the Indian Ocean region and have maintained a degree of momentum in what some have called "Indian Ocean Studies." We are fortunate that most of the leading analysts of Indian Ocean affairs agreed to participate in the Dalhousie conference and to contribute to this book.

At the time of the conference and until August 1983 we were both members of Dalhousie's Centre for Foreign Policy Studies. Without the support and encouragement of our former colleagues there and the related Department of Political Science, the conference could not have taken place. In particular we gratefully acknowledge the unfailing assistance of the former director, Gilbert Winham, and his successor, the present director, Robert Boardman. Both offered active personal encouragement to the enterprise and were generous in providing access to Centre funds. We also acknowledge a considerable debt to Dan Middlemiss who tendered advice freely, but unintrusively, throughout the project.

Both during the conference and in the preparation of the manuscript Doris Boyle, the Centre's administrative secretary, gave her time and energy willingly to tasks too numerous to mention, but vital to the success of the whole enterprise. Our friend and colleague, Baljinder Dhillon, was always prepared to provide administrative assistance when we seemed to need it most. Lesley Adamson expertly typed much of the manuscript before we left Halifax, while Pat Martin, Susan Parkinson, and Valerie Robinson at the University of Lancaster and Ellen Ruffles, Barbara Atkinson, and Kerry Foran at the Australian National University all contributed their secretarial skills. Thanks are also due to Carolyn Bowlby of Acadia University for typing final portions of the manuscript. The maps were prepared by Dalhousie's Graphics Department under the guidance of Jane Lombard who expertly combined the need for cartographic precision with visual clarity.

Our editor at Duke University Press, Reynolds Smith, tendered sound advice, was a courteous critic, and showed infinite patience through all stages of publication. We are very grateful for his support and expert professional assistance.

Last but not least we thank our contributors, whose work constitutes much the greatest part of this book. Those who attended the conference helped to make it a stimulating, rewarding, and congenial meeting. Later, their strong commitment to publication of the conference papers made our work as editors much easier. For their encouragement, patience, and help throughout we are deeply indebted.

For reasons they know, this volume is dedicated to our wives.

William L. Dowdy
Russell B. Trood

PART ONE ☙

General Introduction

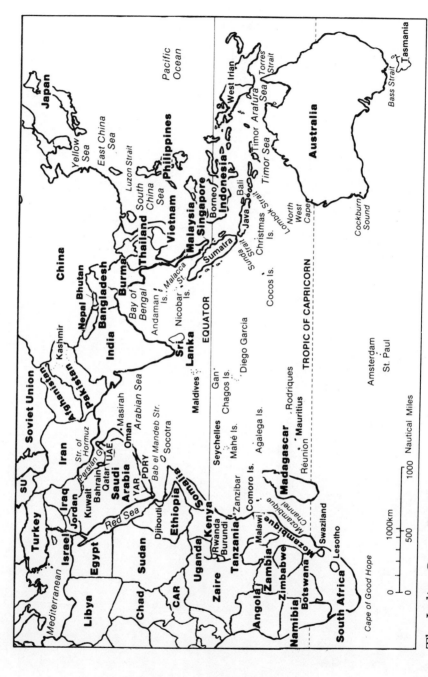

The Indian Ocean Region

1. The Indian Ocean Region as Concept and Reality ◾ William L. Dowdy

Responding to the increasing salience of Indian Ocean issues in international relations even while writing from different disciplinary perspectives within the social sciences and humanities, a sizable number of academics seem to have taken an "Indian Ocean region" as an a priori concept. It is the purpose of this chapter first to suggest theoretical bases and rationales for such a concept and, second, to explore "real world" perspectives—both external and indigenous—that suggest that it is not only academics, but also policy makers, who are increasingly thinking about the Indian Ocean in regional terms.

Theoretical Bases for the Concept of an Indian Ocean Region

The academic study of the international relations of regions is largely a post–World War II development. It may be traced in part to the emergence in the 1940s and 1950s of the "area studies" approach, inspired more by a particular interest in the affairs of a given locality than by a general interest in global affairs.[1] Western Europe achieved a modern regional identity during postwar rehabilitative efforts. The coming to independence in the fifties and sixties of large numbers of former colonies generated additional regional consciousness, with Southeast Asia and parts of Africa being added to Latin America and the Middle East as areas of study by regional experts. Furthermore, the "loosening of the bipolar world, moves toward autonomous policies by the middle range powers, and explicit efforts at fostering patterns of international collaboration in various areas of the world" all served to direct scholarly attention toward "regional foci of interaction."[2] Regions have also come to be seen as useful intermediate units of analysis at a level between individual nation-states and the world as a whole.

There is a modest body of literature on the international politics of regions that draws upon concepts of general systems theory and the research tradition of systems analysis. Working from the conception of the world as "the international system," a group of scholars has applied the systems perspective to analyses of geographically distinct (and otherwise distinct) groupings of states, variously called "subordinate systems," "subsystems," or "regional subsystems" of the international or global system.

Generally recognized as the first to attempt such an approach was Leonard Binder in a 1958 article on the Middle East.[3] Following from Binder's pioneering effort have been a number of works seeking to submit area data to systematic analysis. Michael Brecher has written about southern Asia;[4] William Zartman about Africa;[5] Larry Bowman about southern Africa;[6] Donald Hellmann about East Asia;[7] and Louis Cantori and Steven Spiegel have explored the subject generally, taking a comparative approach to the international politics of regions.[8]

Characteristically, these subsystem studies have considered both disintegrative and integrative developments—both conflict and cooperation.[9] They have gone beyond the area studies tradition of intense interest in one particular area for its own sake toward a "heightened interest in the relationships between the global system and regional subsystems," relationships virtually unexplored by area specialists.[10]

Writing in 1973, William R. Thompson surveyed the extant international relations literature that had used the subsystemic approach to the study of regions. He concluded his article with an explication of the concept of "regional subsystem" based on his analysis of twenty-two academic works in which the concept had been centrally applied. Thompson concluded that there were four necessary and sufficient conditions for identifying a regional subsystem: "(1) The actors' pattern of relations or interactions exhibit a particular degree of regularity and intensity to the extent that a change at one point in the subsystem affects other points. (2) The actors are generally proximate. (3) Internal and external observers and actors recognize the subsystem as a distinctive area or 'theatre of operation.' (4) The subsystem logically consists of at least two and quite probably more actors."[11]

It will be argued in this chapter that there is in the Indian Ocean a discernible "linkage of instabilities" such that "a change at one point . . . affects other points"—the first condition above. Furthermore, evidence will be cited for increasing levels of economic interaction and cooperation among Indian Ocean states, as well as for incipient security cooperation among various groups of states.

With respect to Thompson's third condition, it seems clear from both internal and external perspectives that the Indian Ocean is now recognized as a distinctive "theatre of operation." The superpowers, in particular, have increasingly approached the Indian Ocean area as a "strategic arena" for the multiplicity of reasons discussed in the second section of this chapter. For their part, the Indian Ocean states have become increasingly sensitive to external intrusions, both as threats and as opportunities. The Indian Ocean zone-of-peace and nuclear-free-zone initiatives and the existence and longevity of the United Nations Ad Hoc Committee on the Indian Ocean constitute some of the evidence of an indigenous perception that the Indian Ocean defines a distinctive area in international politics.

Thompson's fourth criterion of two or more actors is prima facie no obstacle to considering the Indian Ocean area a regional subsystem. Indeed, some critics may object that thirty-six actors are too many,[12] but Thompson set no upper limit and other widely accepted regional subsystems have even more "members."

Whether the Indian Ocean area meets Thompson's second definitional criterion for the existence of a regional subsystem is more problematic. Whether South Africa, Iran, and Australia can be said to be "generally proximate" is highly questionable by most standards. Indeed, most critics of the notion that the Indian Ocean defines a "region" argue that the area is simply too big for such a conception to be meaningful.

A solution to this dilemma of size and expanse is provided by Cantori and Spiegel's concept of "core sectors" within regional subsystems. A core sector "consists of a . . . group of states which form a central focus of the international politics within a given region. . . . There may be more than one core sector within a given subordinate system."[13] It is possible to identify at least five core sectors within the Indian Ocean regional subsystem: a Persian Gulf core, a South Asia core, a Red Sea core, a southern Africa core, and an Australasia core.

Some state actors may usefully be considered as members of more than one core. Saudi Arabia, for example, is clearly a principal Persian Gulf actor but it has also from time to time been heavily involved in the Red Sea core, defined as the two Yemens, the Horn of Africa (Ethiopia, Somalia, Djibouti), and, on some issues, Sudan and Egypt. To take another example of multiple core membership, Pakistan—a "natural" member of the South Asia core—has become increasingly involved in affairs in the Persian Gulf, in the spirit of Islamic solidarity and for the reality of balance-of-payments benefits.

An East Africa core was apparent in the late 1960s during the most successful period in the life of the East African Community. Kenya recently has been drawn more into the affairs of the Horn of Africa; Tanzania, a "Frontline State," into the affairs of southern Africa. It is not inconceivable, however, that an East Africa core will some day reemerge when political and economic factors are once again conducive to higher levels of interaction in that sector of the Indian Ocean littoral.

So what? What is the rationale for such a conception of an Indian

Ocean regional subsystem with multiple core sectors—that is, what purpose does it serve? It is potentially useful in at least two ways: first, to assist the analyst (and maybe even the policy maker) in thinking about international politics and security issues in that part of the world and, second, to aid in the description of reality.

Of course, those two potential benefits of a regional systems perspective on Indian Ocean affairs are not mutually exclusive. To the contrary, thinking about the world and describing the world (or portions and aspects of it) are really sequential occupations on a continuum familiar to all those who aspire in some sense to be "scientists." The next two steps are explanation and prediction.

With regard to the first potential benefit of a region/cores conceptualization, namely, its use in thinking about the politics and security of the Indian Ocean area, the systems-analytical approach advocated here is neither magical nor mysterious (despite the efforts of some of its jargonistic exponents to shroud it in mystery—or obfuscation).[14] Systems analysis, according to Michael Banks, is simply "a more formalized version of clear thinking about complicated problems. . . . We divide a large problem into sections, concentrate our attention separately and singly on each section in turn or on a group of sections, and we explain each part to ourselves, rebuild[ing] the whole piece-by-piece in order to reconstruct the phenomenon mentally in a form in which we feel we can understand it."[15]

As Richard Little points out, "There is no body of rules indicating how a systems approach should be implemented. There is, therefore, no formal methodological procedure associated with the approach. Nevertheless, there is a systems perspective and it is normally quite clear when analysis is being written from this perspective."[16]

Characteristic of the systems perspective advocated in this chapter are the following assumptions:

1. A system (or regional subsystem) is more than simply the sum of its parts.[17] It is both a "structure" (construct) consisting of its components (e.g., the Indian Ocean nation-states) *and* the transactions among and between those parts. Much of the essence of international politics consists of linkages, interactions, reactions, and interdependence—more than the simple sum of all relevant national foreign policies.

2. Various actors (individual decision makers, nation-states, multinational corporations, international organizations, etc.) are assumed to be conditioned and constrained by the characteristics of the system

in which they operate. In other words, "systems-level forces seem to be at work."[18] Therefore some part of the explanation of international behavior and of policy outcomes is to be found in the characteristics of the system. Furthermore, influences and constraints are assumed to flow in both directions: just as the structure of the system affects interacting units, so too do the actions of the units affect the system's structure. The interrelationship is dynamic and reciprocal.

3. The examination of patterns of international relations on various levels (e.g., subnational, national, regional levels) contributes to an understanding of politics at the global level.

4. Even in the field of international relations, there are areas of coherence and orderliness in the midst of apparent randomness and diversity. "[A system] is a means of organizing apparently chaotic behavior between entities."[19] Systems thinking is meant to be "an attack on the problem of complexity."[20]

5. Finally, systems thinking can be used as a bridge to insights from other social science disciplines, such as political geography. "Political geographers have been accustomed to thinking in terms of system relationships almost from the beginning of their field. Thus a system framework . . . will be easily understood by the political geographer, and his work easily adapted to it."[21]

The second potential usefulness of the regional systems perspective, namely, to abet description (and to contribute toward explanation) of the reality of international relations in the Indian Ocean region, arises from the suggestiveness of systems thinking. It inspires propositions that can be tested against reality. For example, the definitional assumption that systems are dynamic (not static) entities suggests questions about the nature of system transformation. Is the system becoming more cohesive or is it disintegrating? Are its interactions becoming more cooperative or more conflictual? Operationalizing degrees of cohesiveness and levels of cooperation is not easy but it is possible.[22]

More controversial has been research into the issue of stability within a system, particularly as it relates to the structure and distribution of power. For example, an interesting question with respect to the Indian Ocean subsystem, or its various cores ("sub-subsystems"), is whether stability is increased by the concentration and hierarchical distribution of power *or* by the diffusion and roughly equal distribution of power. The first proposition is intuitively more appealing. The Persian Gulf core was a more stable place when the shah's Iran dominated (or was perceived by other core actors to dominate) the power hierarchy. In

South Asia, the clear predominance of India may have contributed to a more stable core area than might otherwise have been the case (particularly since Indian predominance became so clearly apparent after the birth of Bangladesh). The southern Africa core is another case in point with a dominant South Africa. The work of David Singer and various associates provides potentially useful operational techniques for research into the question of power distribution versus stability in the Indian Ocean region.[23]

The multilevel characteristics of the systems perspective suggest and abet inquiry into additional issues such as: the opportunities for subsystem dominance (e.g., Persian Gulf oil producers versus "dominant system" consumers); Islamic revivalism (e.g., in Iran, in the Persian Gulf core, in the Indian Ocean generally); and the politics of ethnicity (e.g., Kurdish insurgency in subnational areas of Iraq and Iran, liberation movements in the southern Africa core).

Finally, systemwide problems suggest the need to search for systemic solutions. Such problems as the preservation and management of migratory fish stocks, the necessity for joint action against sources of undesirable levels of air or ocean pollution, and the curtailment of militarization or nuclearization are likely to lead to (and, indeed, have led to) a convergence between the concept and the reality of an Indian Ocean regional system. It is to an examination of such an emerging reality that we now direct our attention.

Real World Bases for the Concept of an Indian Ocean Region

One reason why scholars—particularly those specializing in international relations, strategic studies, and foreign policy—have increasingly begun to think in terms of an Indian Ocean region is because both external and indigenous policy makers have themselves been approaching issues in that area in a more comprehensive fashion.

External perspectives

Current superpower rivalry in the Indian Ocean arena is, in a sense, business as usual. Only the players have changed, and the stakes. The "post-Gaman" history of that part of the world has witnessed successive hegemonies by external (European) powers.[24] Since 1498, the Indian Ocean has had a sort of strategic unity or coherence imposed from the outside by, successively, Portugal, Holland, and Britain, with France,

Germany, and Italy challenging British predominance in certain sectors at certain times with limited success.

The Portuguese empire in the Indian Ocean was established in accordance with the strategic plan of Alfonso d'Albuquerque. His strategy included capturing the approaches to the ocean, sealing off entrances to foreign shipping, and establishing bases along the littoral. Albuquerque secured the cape route by occupying key points along the East African coast and he controlled the entrance to the Red Sea by capturing Socotra Island. Hormuz was taken in order to dominate the Persian Gulf, and Malacca to command access to the spice islands (Malaysia and Indonesia). The same "choke points" were objectives of subsequent imperial contestants, with the Suez Canal added to the list in 1869. The contemporary "base race" of the superpowers, seeking friends and real estate near the same choke points, is not unfamiliar against this historical background.

Holland ended Portugal's predominance in 1641 by capturing Malacca. In 1652, the Dutch established the first European settlement on the Cape of Good Hope, a possibility that, curiously, the Portuguese had overlooked. According to Auguste Toussaint, "The period from the fall of Malacca [to the Dutch in 1641] to the completion of the British conquests in 1815 was really one long interregnum during which no single power controlled the ocean."[25] During that period, the principal struggle for control was between the British and the French. But for over 150 years after the Congress of Vienna, the Indian Ocean was essentially a "British lake." While other European powers obtained or maintained footholds at various locations in the region, Britain held all the most strategic points and tied them together with the Royal Navy.

The explosion of nationalist sentiment in the wake of World War II precipitated a rapid and sometimes cataclysmic decolonization process in the area. Beginning with the partition of India in 1947, it had largely run its course by the early 1960s. The British announcement in 1968 of withdrawal from "east of Suez" by the end of 1971 marked the end of the era of British hegemony in the Indian Ocean.

The superpower competition in the area that has escalated since the British withdrawal can be seen in historical perspective as yet another attempt by external powers to establish a strategic condominium over the Indian Ocean, albeit for different reasons and in a substantially transformed environment. Washington and Moscow, and a few other major capitals, have developed de facto Indian Ocean policies, though not always explicit ones. Indeed, if the case for the contemporary strategic coherence of the Indian Ocean area depended on the existence of

Indian Ocean desks and sections in foreign ministries and defense bureaucracies, there would be little if anything more to say. That is, in the governments of external powers the responsibility for Indian Ocean policy is shared, usually among policy makers working on Africa, the Middle East, South Asia, and Oceania, with no single office having overall authority for policy development toward the region per se. Of course there is nothing particularly unusual about this situation. Policy making is invariably a fragmented process in which the burden of formulation is distributed among and within different departments of government. This reality of bureaucratic life therefore suggests that we direct our attention away from policy formulation to policy outputs and their focus. What policies have external powers actually pursued toward the region? The policies of the two superpowers are naturally of primary concern. Their immediate interests in the area have merged with the broader conduct of their global rivalry so that the Indian Ocean has become a strategic arena of considerable importance to both.

The interests of the United States revolve around the need to ensure access to Persian Gulf oil for itself and its allies. American dependence on gulf oil has never been as great as that of Western Europe and Japan (which received approximately 75 percent and 90 percent of their oil, respectively, from the gulf at the time of the 1973–74 embargo). The most portentous result of the embargo was not the damage to Western economies (which was considerable), but the serious bickering and back stabbing in the Atlantic alliance as member states scrambled for favored access to unembargoed oil and for future access to Arab oil. A sustained denial of Persian Gulf oil to the West is an eventuality that the United States is therefore keen to avoid for reasons of alliance solidarity as well as economic health, a fact underlined by the Carter Doctrine and the development of the Rapid Deployment Force (RDF). Despite the recent glut in worldwide oil supplies and falling prices, Persian Gulf oil—about 55 percent of the world's proven reserves—will remain of vital strategic importance to the West through the end of this century. A distinct but related interest is the concern of the United States to maintain sea lines of communication (SLOC), particularly through vital choke points such as the Straits of Malacca, Bab el Mandeb, and Hormuz.

For years the United States, consistent with the Nixon Doctrine, depended upon local surrogates to defend its core political, economic, and strategic interests in the Indian Ocean area. But in the wake of the events that began to shake the region in the late 1970s Washington developed a new approach to its security interests there. By actively seeking to enhance its access to naval, air, and communications facilities throughout the area, by improving the operational capability of British-owned Diego Garcia, by increasing the level of Indian Ocean naval deployments, and by creating the RDF, the United States has substantially improved its capacity to project power into the Indian Ocean and has thereby declared its intention to take a more active role in the region's affairs. Whether these military responses are appropriate to what many see as essentially political and social problems in the area is a question of profound importance but it is beyond the scope of this chapter. The question at hand is whether the actions of American policy makers evince a coherent strategic approach to the region.[26]

Members of the Reagan administration certainly have argued that they do present a unified approach to policy. In 1981, for example, the secretary of state noted that "our broad strategic view of the Middle East recognizes the intimate connections between the region and adjacent areas: Afghanistan and South Asia, northern Africa and the Horn, and the Mediterranean and the Indian Ocean." Similarly the deputy assistant secretary of state for Near Eastern and South Asian Affairs testified that "our approach takes into account threats and developments in contiguous areas. We will carry out a coherent and consistent policy in full awareness of the interrelationships between tensions in different regions and theaters."[27] The claims of any government to be acting consistently on the basis of a coherent policy should, of course, be treated with utmost caution. Nevertheless, there does appear to be a relatively high degree of coherence, at least in American declaratory policy, toward the Indian Ocean.

The efforts of the United States to improve its position in the area are focused, not surprisingly, on the Persian Gulf, but it would be a mistake to conclude that the policy is exclusively gulf-centered. The concentration of efforts in the northwest quadrant of the Indian Ocean reflects the high priority that Washington attaches to its interests in the gulf and an overall emphasis on the stability of that core sector. However, Washington has not overlooked its political and military concerns in other parts of the region. Thus, in the last few years it has sought to improve its military dispositions in the eastern approaches to the Indian Ocean by, among other things, securing landing rights for B-52 bombers in Australia. In the political sphere, areawide policy concerns have been reflected in assiduous attempts to secure better relations with India and in closer contacts with South Africa. Despite some inconsistencies, American policy makers convey both by their words and their deeds an overall perception of the interdependence of events in the Indian Ocean region. There is a recognizable framework for American policy in the area that, while arguably inappropriate to the political forces at work in the region, nevertheless suggests a coherent and comprehensive approach to the protection of American interests. Finally, it is noteworthy that the Soviet Union appears to recognize a certain coherence in American policy. In April 1979, *Pravda* referred to "the defense line being created by the Pentagon along the Egypt-Israeli, Persian Gulf, Diego Garcia, Australian perimeter."

In contrast, the policies of the USSR itself exhibit a more inconsistent quality. Much of this appears to be attributable to its general inability to gain support for its policies rather than to an absence of any clearly defined interests in the region. In fact, the Soviet Union's proximity to the region has produced a certain continuity of interests that continues to dictate the course of Soviet policy as it has in the past.[28]

Foremost among those interests is Moscow's preoccupation with the maintenance of stability on its borders and of a measure of influence, if not control, over its neighbors. This standard dimension of Soviet policy is most clearly manifested in its relations with the states of Eastern Europe but it also has relevance throughout Soviet Asia where ancient cultural and ethnic traditions tend to undermine Moscow's political authority and create natural communities of interest with peoples outside the Soviet Union. The Iranian revolution and the Iraq-Iran war are particularly worrisome to Moscow because they could give rise to unstable or anti-Soviet regimes on its borders. At least the shah was predictable.

Apart from the proximate territory to the south, the Indian Ocean itself is of importance to Soviet security. It offers one alternative means of linking Soviet Europe with Soviet Asia should the trans-Siberian railroad be rendered inoperable in peace or war. The Indian Ocean also offers a back door to China by which the Soviet Union could relieve military pressure along their common central Asian border if necessary. Thus, like the United States, the Soviet Union has an abiding interest in maintaining sea lines of communication throughout the region. Moscow also sees the ocean as a potential operational area for American strategic missile submarines that should not be allowed to move about unchallenged. Finally, the Indian Ocean is an arena in which the Soviet Union competes for influence with the United States as part of the global search for strategic advantage. It has discovered that in addition to hunting submarines, warships can be used to reassure friends and to discourage potential enemies.

This catalogue of interests continues to provide a foundation for Soviet policies in the Indian Ocean region. From the Chinese perspective at least, these policies have been seen as exhibiting a regional coherence, a view that lends support to the notion of a Soviet Indian Ocean policy. According to the Chinese, "Moscow is stepping up its strategic dispositions along the arc from Africa through West Asia to Southeast Asia."[29] Beijing is hardly an objective observer; even so, there appears to be substance to the Chinese analysis. Over the past decade the Soviet Union has attempted to expand its influence throughout Africa, the Middle East, and Asia, while maintaining a relatively high level of naval deployment in the Indian Ocean. In the early 1970s its objective was a collective security regime that would embrace much of the region. This failed, however, to attract the support of local states and is recognized, even by Soviet analysts, as unattainable at present. Moscow also has suffered setbacks in its bilateral relations in the region, having been ejected from Somalia and Egypt and "forced" to intervene in Afghanistan.

Overall, the pattern of Soviet activity in the region is fragmented but care should be taken in suggesting that Soviet policies are similarly fragmented. The internally inconsistent features of Soviet policies are probably more a reflection of their mixed success than the consequence of a basic lack of coherence in overall design. The Soviet Union is characteristically opportunistic in the conduct of its foreign policy. This is always likely to create uncertainty among observers about policy objectives. But this opportunism is arguably more closely related to the tactical than to the strategic side of Soviet security policy. The latter gains its coherence from the constancy of Soviet interests in the region.

Besides the superpowers, France, Britain, Japan, and China have substantial interests in the Indian Ocean area.[30] The diversity and relative importance of these interests is reflected in the varying degrees of coherence that is apparent in the policies of these nations toward the region. Of the four, French policy perhaps exhibits the greatest cogency. The French remain quite active in the Indian Ocean, maintaining the largest naval presence after that of the United States and the Soviet Union. Réunion, near Mauritius, and the island of Mayotte (Mahoré) in the Comoros are administratively parts of France, and Paris continues to station army and air forces in Djibouti. Britain's former status as the principal colonial power has left it with a range of political, economic, and strategic concerns in the region that remain of considerable importance despite its formal withdrawal from east of Suez. Britain lacks the resources to protect independently all of its interests in the Indian Ocean and therefore has to rely heavily on the United States for this purpose. Nevertheless, the British government, drawing on a rich bureaucratic memory, appears to retain a clear conception of the complicated relationships that characterize the region's affairs.

While the evidence may be inconclusive, it does seem that the external powers with the greatest interests in the Indian Ocean region look upon events in one core area as having implications for others. On balance, their policies toward the region reflect a perception of the ocean's strategic integrity.

Internal perspectives

If the last decade or so has brought a heightened awareness of Indian Ocean challenges and interests to the capitals of major external powers, particularly the superpowers, it also has resulted in greater apparent understanding of their common dangers and opportunities on the part of indigenous leaderships in the region itself. This is reinforced by a sense of shared identity, based in part on the common historical experience of European imperialism.

However, long before the age of imperialism the ocean itself had become a medium of contact, of movement, of exchange, bringing together peoples and cultures that otherwise would have remained isolated from each other. As A. P. S. Bindra writes, "Milleniums before Columbus traversed the Atlantic . . . and before Magellan circled the globe, the Indian Ocean had become a . . . cultural highway."[31] The present residents of Madagascar are believed to have originated principally in the Indonesian islands, having arrived in the western ocean in a series of migratory waves. There are large populations of people in eastern and southern Africa whose ethnic roots can be traced back to the Indian subcontinent and the Malay Peninsula. Arabs and other Muslims historically established themselves along the Red Sea and East African coasts and eventually in the Indian subcontinent and Indonesian archipelago as well. The Hindus themselves had established a sort of "greater India" to the east before being supplanted by the Muslims.

The islands in the middle of the Indian Ocean also have served as meeting grounds. Blacks from the African coast have mixed with south Asians to produce the Creole populations of Mauritius, the Seychelles, etc. The people of the Comoros speak a Bantu-like language with Arab borrowings. The Swahili dialect of East Africa is said to have clear affinities with the Arabic of the Persian Gulf. In short, there has clearly been extensive contact among the littoral and island peoples of the Indian Ocean. Whole populations have cultural memories and cultural reminders of other Indian Ocean lands. Assimilated island populations are composed more of "Indian Ocean people" than of blacks or Indians or Arabs.[32]

Against this historical and cultural backdrop, contemporary strategic and economic relationships are emerging. The proliferation of regional strategic linkages underlines the increasing interrelatedness of events in the Indian Ocean area. Ian Clark has pointed out that events may be connected in two ways.[33] The first is by means of a "linkage of instabilities," a notion posited by Ferenc Váli in one of the few single-author books on the Indian Ocean. According to Váli, the "instabilities and unbalanced situations which prevail in one subregion not only radiate into the neighboring countries but may also reach out into more distant parts of the region [to form] a 'linkage of instabilities' which extends throughout the area."[34] Situations may "radiate" and "reach out" in a variety of ways, not necessarily uniformly. The impact of a situation on events near its place of occurrence is likely to be different from that which is felt further afield but, while different, the implications may be highly significant for all parties. Thus, the Vietnamese invasion of Kampuchea created a massive refugee problem and an apprehension of direct threat to security in Thailand, while in places like Indonesia and Australia the invasion was seen as an unwelcome and dangerous manifestation of regional instability. Similarly, the Soviet invasion of Afghanistan raised the specter of a direct Soviet threat to Pakistan and to Persian Gulf oil fields while raising fears in the more distant parts of the region over the means and ends of Soviet policy. Ill treatment by East African regimes of their citizens of South Asian extraction has periodically caused considerable consternation in the Indian subcontinent. As a consequence of these and other developments over the past decade, it is now unlikely that any event threatening the interests and security of even the smallest states in the Indian Ocean will be dismissed as of no consequence to other states of the area.

In the second place, Clark suggests that "linkages are created between [sub]regions when individual states, or groups of states, consciously pursue security policies on a wider than subregional basis."[35] One example is the concerted effort of the black states of southern Africa, together with other Indian Ocean countries, to isolate and place pressure on white-ruled South Africa. A second example is Saudi Arabia's policy of seeking "to integrate security postures from the Red Sea through the Gulf and to the extremities of the Indian subcontinent."[36] However, the linkage process is a fragmentary one at present. The states of one core of the Indian Ocean region have not generally sought security by concerted actions with those of other cores. Security linkages heretofore have been largely extraregional, involving a local state and an outside power: Australia with the United States, India with the Soviet Union,

Pakistan with China and the United States. But there are precedents for states of one core joining a formal alliance with those of another. Although both have included outside powers, the South-East Asia Treaty Organization (SEATO) and the Central Treaty Organization (CENTO) were alliances of this character. Their success, however limited, suggests that more formal core coalitions may be possible in the future. The recently established Gulf Cooperation Council (GCC), ostensibly a co-operative economic initiative, is evolving in the direction of a security alliance in the context of the Iraq-Iran war, and there are indications that Islamic Pakistan may someday formalize its present de facto involvement in the security of the Arabian peninsula.

Another criterion that can be used to assess internal perceptions of the strategic coherence of the Indian Ocean region is the character of regional responses to external intrusions. Have local states *as a group* adopted common policies and positions in an effort either to deny or to accommodate external (mainly superpower) activities in the region?

Among the issues that offer some insight into this matter is the proposal that the Indian Ocean be declared a zone of peace. This idea was originally advocated by Sri Lanka during the twenty-sixth session of the United Nations General Assembly in 1971. The UN adopted a resolution supporting the proposal and called upon the interested states to enter into consultations to implement it. Since then, all efforts to resolve the problems confronting the proposal have proved fruitless and, accordingly, it remains no closer to reality than it was in 1971.

The significant point for this analysis, however, is the initiative itself which demonstrated a collective identity and a collective concern among the Indian Ocean states. The vision behind the proposal was provided by Prime Minister Bandaranaike of Sri Lanka, who told a Commonwealth heads-of-government meeting in Singapore in January 1971: "The Indian Ocean is a region of low solidarities or community of interests. Although it forms a geographical and historical entity, there are few cooperative links between countries in the region, and these are either bilateral or sub-regional. A Peace Zone in the Indian Ocean will provide countries of this region with time to develop trends toward integration and cooperation so that in course of time the Indian Ocean region could move from an area of low solidarity to an area of high solidarity."[37] In 1972, the UN General Assembly appointed an Ad Hoc Committee on the Indian Ocean to consider ways of implementing the zone-of-peace resolution. The committee has become the principal focus for work on the issue, expanding its membership to forty-eight by 1985. Its efforts have been paralleled by informal meetings of the representatives of Indian Ocean states, initiated by Sri Lanka in 1973 and culminating in a general meeting of littoral and hinterland states in July 1979.[38] Another is in prospect in 1986.

Whatever the ultimate fate of the zone-of-peace concept and a companion proposal for an Indian Ocean nuclear-weapons-free zone put forward by Pakistan in 1974, such initiatives have contributed to a perception of the Indian Ocean region as a distinctive geostrategic zone. Indeed, such a perception can even be said to have been institutionalized in the UN Ad Hoc Committee, which continues to meet annually.

Although the Indian Ocean area is one of considerable economic diversity, various aspects of its economic life also lend a measure of support to the notion of emerging regionality. Here three of these characteristics are examined: the similar economic profiles of most of the states of the area, the movements toward subregional economic cooperation, and the trend toward expansion of intraregional trade.

Over half of the states of the Third World are located on the littoral or in the hinterland of the Indian Ocean. Recent World Bank statistics describe thirty of the thirty-six Indian Ocean states as less-developed countries (LDCS) with per capita gross national products (GNPS) of less than $4,830.[39] Only one of the remaining nations, Australia, is regarded as industrialized by the World Bank.[40] The others—Iraq, Kuwait, Qatar, Saudi Arabia, and the United Arab Emirates—are categorized as "capital-surplus oil exporters" (CSOES). This economic profile has had a profound effect on the economic life of the region. Indeed, it can be argued that the comparative economic homogeneity of the Indian Ocean states gives the whole region a degree of coherence as an area of underdevelopment.

At first glance this homogeneity of the LDCS of the Indian Ocean is not readily apparent. There is considerable diversity and disparity among such economic indicators as level of income, rate of economic growth, and size of gross national product. Bangladesh, the poorest country of the region, has a per capita GNP of only $90, while that of Singapore, a near neighbor, is $3,830. Similarly, India's gross domestic product (GDP) of $112 billion is many times higher than Somalia's at $1 billion.[41] Such statistics, however, tend to obscure some underlying similarities in the structures of the region's economies. About two-thirds of the LDCS and CSOES of the region have either one-crop or two-crop economies. That is to say, in excess of half—and in most cases much more—of their income is derived from the export of one or two commodities. Of the LDCS that remain, most depend on only three or four major exports.

The absence of diversity in the economies of the LDCS and CSOES means that they have limited flexibility and are subject to similar stresses and strains. For most LDCs, the agricultural sector of the economy makes the largest contribution to GDP. In some countries, such as Somalia, this can be as high as 60 percent but for most the figure is around 30 percent. The service, industrial, and manufacturing sectors follow in roughly that order. The CSOEs, with their dependence on crude oil production, are in an analogous situation.[42] In their case, the level of dependence on one sector of the economy is around 75 percent and, in some cases, even higher.

In the picture that emerges of the Indian Ocean region, most of the countries have narrowly based economies, highly vulnerable to the vicissitudes of the international economic system. Whether the single "crop" is oil, copper, coffee, sugar, cotton, or some other product, these countries share common concerns regarding access to reliable markets, maintenance of high prices, and sustaining demand for their products. The problems they confront in attempting to achieve these goals could hardly be more evident than at present. In a period of long-term global recession, both the single-crop agricultural economies of countries such as Mauritius and Somalia and those of the oil-exporting countries have been similarly afflicted with economic decline. In the latter case, these countries now confront conditions thought to have been left behind with the phenomenal oil price increases of 1973 and beyond.

These economic realities have significant policy implications, frequently affecting the positions that LDCs have taken on a range of international economic matters. Thus, on issues of international finance, the transfer of technology, trade liberalization, and, of course, the creation of a "new international economic order," they have similar attitudes and have adopted similar negotiating positions. In sum, the LDCs and, to a lesser extent, the CSOEs of the Indian Ocean region share a set of affinities that are partly obscured by conventional economic indicators. Their governments face similar problems, have similar interests, and aspire to similar objectives in the international system. These shared economic concerns and imperatives, it is argued, lend a measure of economic coherence to the Indian Ocean area.

Another indication of that emerging economic coherence is to be found in the attempts at economic cooperation within various cores of the region. This has been most evident in Southeast Asia where the states of ASEAN have achieved an impressive degree of economic cooperation since the formation of their organization in 1967.[43] Despite numerous problems, the association has made a significant contribution to economic development in the area. At the same time, the perceived advantages of association have given impetus to the settlement of some regional political issues such as the long-standing territorial dispute between Malaysia and Indonesia over the Malacca Strait.

Another systematic attempt to form an integrated economic association, the East African Community, established by Kenya, Tanzania, and Uganda in 1965, has failed to achieve the expectations of its founders. Between 1971 and 1979, while Idi Amin was in power in Uganda, it virtually ceased to function. While there are now signs that the founding members of the community are reviving their interest in it, differing economic ideologies, particularly evident between socialist-oriented Tanzania and free-market-inclined Kenya, could well prove to be an insurmountable impediment to the integration process.

A more recent experiment in economic cooperation is the Gulf Cooperation Council formed in the spring of 1981. Consisting of Bahrain, Kuwait, Oman, Qatar, Saudi Arabia, and the United Arab Emirates, the GCC has established administrative headquarters in Riyadh and is touted as a first step toward the economic, social, political, and military integration of member states. The GCC is being built on a pattern of cooperation among Persian Gulf states which emerged during the 1970s, largely as a result of British withdrawal. Such cooperation has taken the form of jointly owned and operated airline and shipping companies, multilateral financial aid institutions, trade liberalization agreements, and joint industrial and service ventures. When its formation was announced, heavy emphasis was placed on economic objectives as the raison d'être of the GCC's existence. These economic aims were rapidly eclipsed, however, by the urgent security concerns created by the Iranian revolution and the Iraq-Iran war. When the security environment becomes less threatening, the GCC may be expected to emphasize its economic agenda once again. What role, if any, Iraq and Iran might ultimately play in the organization remains to be seen.[44]

A venture in expanded economic cooperation also has been launched in southern Africa. In April 1980 the black states of southern Africa signed the Lusaka declaration to establish the Southern African Development Coordination Conference (SADCC). Among the stated aims of the conference were the reduction of economic dependence generally (and not merely with regard to South Africa) and the forging of links to create genuine, equitable, regional integration. Neither of these objectives will be easy to achieve in the circumstances prevailing in southern Africa. The economies of the Frontline States (Angola, Botswana, Mozambique, Tanzania, Zambia, and Zimbabwe) rely heavily on trade with and access routes through South Africa. This dependent relationship is one that the South African government will not wish to see changed and Pretoria can be expected to continue to pursue policies that will make the black states' tasks of reducing dependence and increasing economic cooperation among themselves extremely difficult. In the longer term, however, a South Africa with a majority government would be a natural partner in any subregional economic organization.

In the South Asia core, where instability and conflicts have hitherto foreclosed all avenues to closer relations, there is both potential for and an indication of growing economic cooperation. The decline in tensions between India and Pakistan, partly as a result of the Soviet invasion of Afghanistan in December 1979, has given impetus to the expansion of the trade relations that had begun to develop between the two countries after the rapprochement of 1973. Similarly, there has been an increase in trade relations between India and Bangladesh. India's economy will likely dominate any regional economic association in South Asia, a factor that clearly poses a major obstacle to cooperation. And Indo-Pakistani relations will undoubtedly continue to have their ups and downs. But the diversity of the Indian economy with its expanding industrial and manufacturing sectors complements others in the area and provides a basis for cooperation.

The sector of the Indian Ocean littoral where economic cooperation is largely nonexistent is on the Horn of Africa. Somalia and Ethiopia, the area's two principal states, are among its poorest. In recent years their wars against each other, together with a sustained period of drought and famine, have caused major economic disruption. There appears to be little prospect that either of these blights will disappear from the horn in the near future.

The various efforts at economic integration in the Indian Ocean have obviously had mixed success. Yet it seems clear that the area's LDCs are aware of the need to accelerate their development and that they see economic cooperation as a useful vehicle for abetting the process. Although the more distant consequences are uncertain, it is likely that the evolution of regional economic organizations would improve the LDCs' trading performance, both within and outside the region. Such organizations might also prove to be useful instruments for the management of common resources such as fish and common problems such as pollution which overlap the jurisdictions of the extant subregional organizations. Whether the scope of these organizations will broaden to match the scope of regionwide problems remains to be seen.

The third dimension of economic activity bearing on the issue of cohesion in the Indian Ocean is the state of intraregional trade. Generally, developing countries provide poor markets for each other's exports. To ensure economic survival, they must rely on export markets in developed countries outside the region. In turn, those countries have provided the industrial equipment and expertise necessary for development and the manufactured goods to help meet rising consumer demand. The predominant place of developed countries in the trade activity of LDCS in the Indian Ocean region is reflected in their profiles, with LDCS and CSOES still looking to developed countries outside the region as their principal trading partners.

Yet, despite the continuing importance of extraregional trade, for most of these countries the value of intraregional trade flows has increased significantly over the past decade. Substantial increases have taken place in exports from Australia to Southeast Asia (especially Indonesia), South Asia (India and Pakistan) to the Persian Gulf (Saudi Arabia, Iran, and the United Arab Emirates), the Persian Gulf (Saudi Arabia) to Southeast Asia (Singapore and Indonesia), and Southeast Asia (Singapore) to South Asia (Pakistan). Other less significant gains have been recorded between the Persian Gulf (Bahrain) and East Africa (Kenya) and between South Asia (India) and Southeast Asia (Indonesia).[45] These increases in part reflect developments that have had a worldwide impact on trade, namely, several years of inflation and a substantial increase in the price of oil as a result of the activities of the Organization of Petroleum Exporting Countries (OPEC).[46] Beyond these factors, however, the increases reflect changes taking place within the region: an acceleration in the pace of development in some LDCS; a concerted effort on the part of one industrialized country of the region, Australia, to expand its markets in the area;[47] and a diversification in the economies of several of the larger states (such as India) which has improved levels of complementarity.

However, the increase in intraregional trade is not uniform. For example, countries of Southeast Asia and Australia (the Australasia core) still have only small export markets in Africa. Similarly, only a few African states have found extensive markets in the Persian Gulf core or in Australasia. While an array of factors specific to each case has contributed to this situation, the lack of complementarity among the economies of many of the countries has been an important underlying factor.

Given the continuing efforts toward subregional economic integration and the likelihood that intraregional trade will continue to expand as area economies diversify, it is likely that the trend toward greater economic interaction in the Indian Ocean will persist. At this stage, however, regionwide economic integration along the lines of that in Western

Europe, or even the more modest core model of ASEAN, will be beyond the capability of most governments in the area. The lack of complementarity in LDC economies, incompatible economic systems, and the persistence of widespread political instability all act as restraints on economic interaction. The economic life of the Indian Ocean will be characterized by diversity and a relatively low level of cohesion for the foreseeable future but there are unmistakable signs that the long-term trend is toward greater economic interaction.

Conclusion

The concept of an Indian Ocean region is not without its critics. Barry Buzan is one of the more articulate: "As things stand, the attempt to conjure up an Indian Ocean region tends to detract more from understanding than it adds. The problems of omission and superficiality which arise from the scale and diversity of the area, are not offset by the weak and tentative linkage which the Indian Ocean framework provides."[48]

This chapter has been an attempt to examine both theoretical and empirical bases for viewing the Indian Ocean as a regional subsystem of the global political system. The systems-analytical perspective has been suggested as a tool for coping with "the scale and diversity of the area," as a tool for bringing some structure to thinking, some order to description, and some inspiration to research. Furthermore, it has been suggested that the conceptual abstraction of an Indian Ocean region has an empirical basis in the "real world" of indigenous and external policy makers, reflected both in their rhetoric and in their actions. Indeed, it has been argued that the empirical case for the concept of an Indian Ocean regional subsystem is becoming stronger over time.

Buzan is right to inveigh against potential sins of omission and superficiality. The Indian Ocean region is undeniably large and diverse but so too are Latin America, the Middle East, the North Atlantic community, the Commonwealth, the Far East, the Mediterranean, and other geographic and conceptual generalizations commonly used in international political analysis.

The key question here is whether the concept of an Indian Ocean region is a useful one, whether on balance it adds to or detracts from our understanding of political and strategic reality. The consensus among contributors to this volume clearly appears to be that the concept adds to understanding. (This book should also go some distance in meeting Buzan's point about superficiality.)

Analysis from the perspective of an Indian Ocean region is not intended to replace the labors of country specialists or of traditional area specialists. It is also not being touted as the best approach toward enlightenment on all the questions worth asking about the international politics of the Indian Ocean area. Rather, the regional perspective is meant to complement, supplement, and incorporate insights from more traditional analysis. The objective is the advancement of overall knowledge of an increasingly strategic area of the world.

PART TWO

Areawide Perspectives

Introduction ☙

One test of the efficacy of the concept of an Indian Ocean region is its usefulness in the analysis of international politics. All five chapters in this part are implicitly or explicitly based on the assumption that taking an "areawide" view of certain international issues helps to provide insights that more narrow perspectives may fail to reveal.

In chapter 2 Mohammed Ayoob undertakes an analysis of the ideologies that have recently dominated the Indian Ocean region and its constituent subregions, "for only by studying the central motivations of the region's elites (and, quite often, its masses) in the recent past, can one hope to predict how they will behave in the future." A central question in Ayoob's analysis is whether the prevalent Indian Ocean ideologies have affinities with each other: "Can it be said that they are manifestations of the same basic motivational force?" The answer to that central question is yes according to Ayoob: nationalism, nonalignment, and Islamic reassertion—the predominant ideologies of the Indian Ocean region—"in many ways are variations on the same 'autonomy' theme" which itself "embraces the subcategories of autonomous political action, autonomous economic growth, and autonomous cultural development." Iran, Ayoob observes, has lately "demonstrated the compatibility, indeed the merger, of the three ideologies" and is therefore a potent symbol in the region.

Raju Thomas in chapter 3 examines the relationship in the Indian Ocean "between regional security issues on the one hand and the growth of regional economic cooperation and integration on the other." He sees promising signs of increased two-way flows of goods and services within the Indian Ocean, both within certain of its constituent subregions and between countries in different subregions. The Association of South-East Asian Nations is the leading example of the former pattern of exchange; trade between South Asian and Persian Gulf states of the latter. Over the long run Thomas sees "a strategy of peace through economic interdependence" as more efficacious than balancing military forces or establishing a nuclear-weapons-free zone in the Indian Ocean region.

Ashok Kapur, on the other hand, sees certain salutary effects of militarization in the Indian Ocean region. Viewing the area from a North-South perspective, he argues that the development of military capabilities (and even the use of military force) may be instrumental to the establishment of regional order, as well as to regional institution-development and consensus-development, with the desirable effect of minimizing the involvement of extraregional powers. The "middle powers" of the Indian Ocean have especially important roles to play, according to Kapur, because only they have sufficient "weight" to thwart the extension of superpower condominium over the Indian Ocean region, to escape forcible intervention or diplomatic isolation by external powers. "The constructive use by middle powers of militarization and even nuclearization" is clearly seen by Kapur as a natural and desirable realization of the ideology of autonomy identified by Ayoob as the prevailing ideology in the Indian Ocean region.

Ken Booth and Lee Dowdy in chapter 5 examine the naval dimension of the Indian Ocean militarization process. It is the middle powers or potential middle powers of the region that also show signs of becoming the naval powers of the area. India is now the premier naval power of the Indian Ocean and likely to remain so. But even the small and weak states of the region can be expected to equip and operate modest naval forces given recent change in the law of the sea. Not only has it created the two-hundred-mile exclusive economic zone with all this entails by way of new naval tasks but it has also raised the level of consciousness of the international community regarding the maritime environment. "Around the Indian Ocean in the years ahead, warships will continue to be acquired as badges of sovereignty, as instruments of order, and as cost raisers to deter potential troublemakers," conclude Booth and Dowdy. Such acquisition of naval forces may be seen as part of the process of normal and irreversible modernization but also as one dimension of the quest for autonomy noted by Ayoob.

In the final chapter of part 1, Rod Byers reviews and evaluates the prospects for arms limitation measures in the Indian Ocean region and confirms what the previous two chapters have suggested. The trend is in the opposite direction, i.e., toward militarization and even nuclearization. Ironically, the Indian Ocean zone-of-peace and nuclear-free-zone initiatives of the early 1970s were among the first factors contributing to regional consciousness among Indian Ocean states (also leading to formation of the United Nations Ad Hoc Committee on the Indian

Ocean). Even though General Assembly Resolution 38/185 calls for a 1985 conference in Colombo, Sri Lanka, to consider implementation of the zone-of-peace resolution, Byers is pessimistic concerning immediate prospects for "any form of arms limitation agreement. . . . The diversity of regional security interests and the concerns of both the major external powers and the IOR [Indian Ocean region] states themselves suggest that comprehensive regional arms limitation options will not be agreed upon."

2. The Quest for Autonomy: Ideologies in the Indian Ocean Region ◪ Mohammed Ayoob

To assess the impact of ideologies on an area as vast and as diverse as the Indian Ocean region is, to put it mildly, an extremely difficult job. The task becomes even more difficult when account is taken of the proliferation of officially sponsored "ideologies" ranging from the "National Resilience" of Suharto's Indonesia, through the "Self Reliance" of Rajiv Gandhi's India, to the "Islamic ideology" of Zia ul-Haq's Pakistan.

It is necessary, therefore, to be clear about two things when discussing the role or impact of ideologies in our area of concern. First, the definition of ideology must be distinguished both from philosophy and world view on the one hand, and from mere slogans on the other. Second, it should be possible to extract the essence or the central element of an ideological system and separate it analytically from the trappings within which it is encased. This is very important because it is usually this central element of the ideological system that determines the relevance of that ideology within a particular social and historical context. This element also provides the ideology with an appeal that goes beyond narrow and well-defined sectional limits, thereby turning it into a mobilizational force that can move in the same direction segments or strata of society with widely diverse and sometimes conflicting interests. It is essential to be able to pinpoint this central element to avoid explanations of phenomena that either have no connection with reality or, what is worse, distort reality itself.[1]

The Meaning of Ideology

How is ideology to be distinguished from philosophy or world view? In this context Apter's definition of the term "ideology" is very apt. According to him:

"Ideology" refers to more than doctrine. It links particular actions and mundane practices with a wider set of meanings and, by doing so, lends a more honorable and dignified complexion to social conduct. . . . "Ideology" is a generic term applied to general ideas potent in specific situations of conduct. . . . Because it is the link between action and fundamental belief, ideology helps to make more explicit the moral basis of action. . . . That is why the role of ideology is central to the thinking of revolutionaries. Working out an ideology is for them a way of stipulating the moral superiority of new ideas.[2]

It is the link between ideas (or "pure thought") and action that gives the term ideology that crucial dynamic element best expressed by Clifford Geertz in his statement that "whatever else ideologies may be . . . they are, most distinctively, maps of problematic social reality and matrices for the creation of collective conscience."[3]

An ideology by definition is action-oriented (otherwise it would become a mere outlook or a world view or, to give it more intellectual respectability, a philosophy), and its success or failure is judged by its ability to influence, indeed determine, the actions of people. What distinguishes it from the other categories we have been talking about is, in the words of Edward Shils, "its greater *explicitness*, its greater *internal integration* or *systematization*, its greater *comprehensiveness*, the greater *urgency* of its application, and its much higher *intensity of concentration* focused on certain propositions or evaluations."[4] Shils carries this discussion further by pointing out that ideologies cannot "avoid being political except by the extreme reaction-formation of complete withdrawal from society." He argues that this is so because ideologies are invariably concerned with "authority," whether transcendental or earthly, and once the concept of authority becomes the central focus of any intellectual exercise, the latter is bound to become political in character. He goes on to say that "this is true of Marxism, despite the fact that it is reputed to have made everything dependent on economic relationships. In Marxist ideology the relations of production are property relations—i.e., relationships of authority supported by the power of the state."[5] Any perceptive observer of the Iranian scene would easily see that Shils's prescription about Marxism is equally relevant to the Islamic republic's ideology, although in the revolutionary rhetoric politics is supposed to be subsidiary to religion as in the case of Marxism it was supposed to play second fiddle to economics. However, Shils's own ideological bias prevents him from ascribing the term ideology to what he calls "prevailing outlooks," in other words, the ideology or ideologies of the status quo. This bias is made explicit in his comment that "all ideologies . . . entail an aggressive alienation from the existing society,"[6] thus making the definition unduly restrictive and, by implication, pejorative in character.

Possibly the most accurate and least value-laden definition of ideology has been provided by Peter Willetts. According to him, "An ideology is a programmatic assertion of political values, which are held to be of universal validity for their proclaimed domain." He goes on to explain that "an ideology has to be political to distinguish it from personal moral values, though it will be noted that almost any moral value may become political when it is no longer considered personal but universal. . . . It is the fact that the political values have been translated into proposals for action that transforms the values into an ideology. . . . Finally, it is the strength of the assertion of the programme that makes us recognise it as an ideology. The more passionate the assertion, the more quickly it is recognised as ideology."[7]

Indian Ocean Ideologies

Having determined the distinction between ideologies on the one hand and world views and philosophies on the other, and having also identified the primarily political nature and content of ideologies, it is now time to turn our attention to the Indian Ocean region. This chapter will analyze the ideologies that have dominated the region or parts of it within the last few decades, particularly in the post–Second World War era. It will also attempt to see if there is a common thread that runs through these ideologies both in terms of time and space. It is only by doing so that this chapter can be made relevant to the current problems facing the Indian Ocean region and its constituent subregions, for only by studying the central motivations of the region's elites (and, quite often, its masses) in the recent past, can one hope to predict how they will behave in the future. Also, the following pages will offer insight into the second issue raised earlier, namely, the question of determining the essence or central element of an ideology. One of the main questions we hope to answer in this chapter is, what are the central elements in the ideologies that have dominated the Indian Ocean region and do their central concerns have any affinity with each other? Indeed, could it be said that they are different manifestations of the same basic motivational force?

If one looks closely at the ideologies in the Indian Ocean region over the last fifty years that have adequately performed the principal task a successful ideology is supposed to perform—to mobilize people and to direct their energies toward specific political ends—one would be struck by the fact that all of them revolve around one central concept, namely, autonomy, including the subcategories of autonomous political action, autonomous economic growth, and autonomous cultural development. This is a phenomenon that is not difficult to explain but which is often lost sight of in the debates, often acrimonious and partisan, carried on about the relevance of particular ideologies like nationalism or socialism to the concrete political and socioeconomic conditions of the region.

This quest for autonomy is directly related to the similar if not identical experiences that the countries of the region have undergone in terms of European colonial domination and its corollaries of economic exploitation and cultural denigration. While at first this quest had remained largely elitist in character, the new "native" elites that emerged in the colonies and semicolonies soon realized that they could not achieve their objective unless they were able to mobilize the masses in this anticolonial undertaking. Beginning with Mahatma Gandhi, they therefore self-consciously became leaders of *movements*, commonly called nationalist movements. The very term movement signifies dynamism and popular mobilization; with these nationalist movements one enters the era of mass-based politics in Asia and, to a lesser extent, Africa. The more successful a particular movement (or its ideology or leadership) in mobilizing the masses, the greater its chances of wresting autonomy or control of its own affairs from its colonial masters.

Out of these separate struggles for national autonomy—independence, if you will—emerged the consciousness among the nationalist leadership that while "nationalism in each empire might be directed against a single Western power . . . the nationalism in Asia [and in Africa] was part of a wider concern with restoring all non-Western peoples to political equality in the new world order."[8]

It was the combination of the individual country's search for national independence, together with the awareness that this was a pan-Asian (later Afro-Asian) struggle, that led to the emergence of the concept that later came to be dubbed the "Third World." This feeling (with the concept of autonomy as its central concern) was eloquently given voice by Jawaharlal Nehru at the First Asian Relations Conference held in New Delhi in 1947 when he declared that "far too long have we in Asia been petitioners in Western courts and chancelleries. . . . That story must now belong to the past. We propose to stand on our own legs. . . . We do not intend to be the plaything of others."[9]

The development and success of socialist or, more explicitly, Marxist ideology in parts of the Indian Ocean region (indeed in the Third

World as a whole) was basically a variation on the same theme of autonomy, an attempt to become the master of one's own destiny. Both the Chinese and Vietnamese experiences bear this out, the latter even more than the former. Hanoi's ability to mobilize its population against a succession of dominant foreign powers and against extremely heavy odds could not have been sustained for such a prolonged period had not its combination of Marxism and nationalism—national Marxism—appealed to the Vietnamese instinct for national independence. The same theme was repeated in Africa whenever the colonial powers delayed their departures for too long and in countries where tremendous sacrifices in terms of human lives had to be made to achieve national independence. In such cases the "national struggle" and the "social struggle," as Basil Davidson has termed them,[10] tended to become enmeshed, and the divisions within colonial societies tended to break through the surface of national unity. Often this succeeded in transforming the nature of nationalist politics from one of mass mobilization for the support of the leadership to one of mass participation.[11]

While this is an important distinction in the history of national movements, for our purpose the graduation of a movement from the stage of mass mobilization to mass participation does not change the essential thrust of the movement, at least until the colonizer or the occupying power has been expelled. It is true, however, that thereafter the shape of the newly independent countries is determined to a large extent by whether the national and social struggles have been carried on simultaneously during the colonial period—or at least in its last stages—or whether independence has been achieved before the issues around which a social struggle could be waged have been properly crystallized. But, even in those societies where the latter is the case, twentieth-century national movements could not possibly remain completely immune to the pressures of social and economic demands. This is why there exists an increasing preoccupation, partly genuine and partly contrived, with socioeconomic issues on the part of nationalist leaderships that have been turned into Third World ruling elites. In the prevailing international ethos of the last quarter of the twentieth century this concern (whether apparent or real) is considered to be an essential part of the strategy aimed at legitimizing the rule of the nationalist elites (or their successors) in their respective countries. In this sense the concern with the social question (and the consequent rhetoric of populism and socialism) is a continuation of the search for autonomy—the ability to run their own lives and make their own decisions—on the part of the peoples of the Third World, which includes the Indian Ocean region. It is basically an attempt to extend the principle of self-determination from the nationalist elite to the constituencies these elites claim to represent. In the context of the social and economic inequalities prevalent in most Third World societies, it is no wonder that this ideology, namely, the socialist variation on the nationalist theme, assumes such potency.

The ideology of nonalignment

In the field of postcolonial international relations, this quest for autonomy was operationalized through the strategy of "nonalignment" and, later, institutionalized in what has come to be called the Nonaligned Movement (NAM).

Whether one considers "nonalignment" an ideology or not, it is obvious that at least as far as the initiators of this strategy (Nehru, Sukarno) and the moving spirits behind the NAM (Nehru, Nasser, Tito) were concerned, they looked upon the concept of nonalignment, at least in substantial part, as an extension of their respective movements for national independence. This attitude was succinctly summed up by Nehru when, speaking in the Indian constituent assembly in 1949, he posed the rhetorical question, "What does independence consist of?" and supplied the following answer: "It consists fundamentally and basically of foreign relations. That is the test of independence. All else is local autonomy. Once foreign relations go out of our hand into the charge of somebody else, to that extent and to that measure you are not independent."[12]

Nonalignment was viewed as the logical corollary of political freedom and as a suitable strategy to operationalize this freedom of action in foreign affairs, particularly in the context of a bipolar world. It was this essential bipolarity of the post-1945 international system that determined the nomenclature for this strategy in foreign affairs; had the power configuration in the postwar world been different, the term used to describe the essence of nonalignment, namely, autonomy of action, may well have been different. The validity of this proposition is borne out by the fact that despite the erosion of bipolarity—in political and economic, though not in strategic, terms—the concept of nonalignment has not faded from the vocabulary of contemporary international politics. In fact, during the very years when this erosion was taking place as a result of the twin processes of loosening of alliance blocs and the emergence of détente between the superpowers, nonalignment was being institutionalized in the NAM and the organizational base of the movement was being strengthened.

It was during the same years, particularly in the 1960s when the NAM was emerging in a viable form, that the Afro-Asian movement that had been launched with such fanfare at Bandung in 1955 was being laid to rest. The rift between the Soviet Union and China had become apparent, producing an effort on the part of the former to enter the Afro-Asian movement and on the part of the latter to prevent this occurrence. The NAM, on the other hand, by definition excluded those states that had pretensions about being "poles" of power themselves, thus disqualifying both Moscow and Peking. Writing as early as the mid-1960s, a perceptive scholar of the Afro-Asian scene predicted that this would happen. According to Jansen, "Despite appearances to the contrary, and the temporary upsurge of the Afro-Asians at the expense of the non-aligned, the policy of non-alignment will outlive the Afro-Asian feeling because it is based on a solid and useful principle and not merely on geography."[13] The concept and the movement have been able to survive the changes that have taken place in the international system through the 1960s and the 1970s because nonalignment and the NAM are an expression of the desire of the vast majority of Third World states to act autonomously of the dominant powers in international affairs, both political and economic.

Ali Mazrui has referred to nonalignment, and particularly to the NAM, as "a solidarity of the less powerful in global affairs." He goes on to say:

> It is possible to identify in non-alignment a solidarity of protest, a movement for moderation in East-West relations, and a commitment to global reform in North-South relations. The solidarity of protest is a continuing theme. But historically, there has been a change of focus from a preoccupation with reducing the level of conflict in East-West relations to a more pronounced emphasis on transforming the basis of North-South relations.
>
> An examination of the issues that have preoccupied the non-aligned states over the years reveals anti-colonialism as a persistent theme of *protest*. In the days of Jawaharlal Nehru non-alignment was also anxious to *moderate* the tensions of the Cold War and prevent too sharp a polarization of the world. But the 1970s especially have witnessed in non-alignment a clearer focus on a basic *restructuring of the global system* in the direction of greater equity in North-South relations.[14]

This shift in the NAM's preoccupation from questions of superpower relations per se to questions of North-South economic relations has been combined with what Mazrui calls "the persistent theme" of protest in the form of anticolonialism. More and more, as decolonization has proceeded, anti–settler colonialism (southern Africa, Palestine) has given a sharp anti-Western edge to the main thrust of the movement, reflected in its resolutions and generally in the rhetoric of its leadership. This has not resulted from any success on the part of the "radicals" within the NAM in capturing its leadership (as some Western analysts had argued when Havana was chosen as the site for the 1979 NAM summit), but from a general leftward shift of the movement that occurred in the 1970s as a result of changes in the movement's preoccupations. This point has been well argued by William LeoGrande in an article assessing the Havana summit. According to him, "The anti-Western (as distinct from pro-Soviet) consensus which has existed [in the NAM] since 1973 is rooted in realities that John Foster Dulles recognized two decades ago: the issues of decolonization and international economics, even when expressed in bloc-neutral terms, tend to be inherently anti-Western in nature. As long as these issues dominate the priorities of the nonaligned movement, it is unlikely to become much more moderate."[15]

Theoretically, one could argue that the Third World's sense of economic grievance against developed states should apply equally to the advanced capitalist and socialist countries but since "most of the Third World's economic linkages are in fact with the West . . . the real antagonisms generated by international economic issues have tended to be between the nonaligned nations and the developed *capitalist* ones."[16] However, increasing Soviet involvement, both military and economic, in Third World affairs, a process that has been considerably accelerated during the 1970s, is bound to produce—as is already evident—a set of Third World grievances against Moscow. This process, however, will not change the reality of the anti-Western thrust of the nonaligned movement; it will only add a new dimension to that thrust.

This brings us to the question of whether the NAM has an ideology or, in other words, can nonalignment be considered to be an ideology in the same sense as nationalism could be so considered. While there has been considerable debate about nonalignment as a strategy versus nonalignment as a principle governing action (something akin to ideology), a great deal of this debate has resulted from the confusion between two concepts: nonalignment as a strategy in the foreign policy of a particular country versus nonalignment as a movement, with certain core considerations around which such a movement is organized and increasingly institutionalized. It is in the latter sense—and the evolution of the NAM has demonstrated this—that nonalignment can be considered an ideology, or at least something approximating an ideology.

The major difference between nonalignment and other ideologies that one is commonly used to dealing with lies in the constituency to which nonalignment addresses itself. As Peter Willetts has pointed out, while

> an ideology is usually concerned with the role of individuals in society . . . nonalignment is concerned with the role of states in the international system. The ideology arises from the need for identification for new states entering a complex and demanding system; as a counter-ideology to the pressures from the "free-world" and the "socialist system"; and in many cases as a result of specific situations of stress, that some of the states were facing. Particularly in relation to economic needs the ideology serves the purpose of interest articulation. Just as with ideologies concerning man and society, the origins of nonalignment lie in identification, stress and interest.[17]

The relevance of the NAM and its ideology to the Indian Ocean region is self-evident on two counts. First, the overwhelming majority of the states of the Indian Ocean littoral and its hinterland are developing countries that belong to and identify with the Third World. Nonalignment is an ideology that aims to maximize the capacity of Third World states to act autonomously, in economic and political terms, of the dominant powers within the international system. It has become (on the basis of a simple statistical head count of Third World states within and outside the NAM) the ideology that dominates the Third World's pattern of interaction with the developed countries. Its relevance to and its impact upon the actions of the states of the Indian Ocean region vis-à-vis the dominant powers therefore needs no further elaboration. Second, on a rough count made by this author, approximately forty of the ninety-two full members of the NAM represented at the sixth summit in Havana in 1979 belong to the Indian Ocean region (defined to include the Persian Gulf and Red Sea littorals and landlocked countries in the hinterland, e.g., Afghanistan, Bhutan, Malawi, Nepal, Zambia, Zimbabwe).[18] No matter how one defines the Indian Ocean region, an impressive proportion of the countries of the NAM is included.

Islam as ideology

If some controversy still surrounds the use of the term ideology to describe the concept of nonalignment, there is much greater consensus—

among both its supporters and opponents—on the issue that Islam has of late emerged as a very potent ideology in the northwestern quadrant of the Indian Ocean region. It is also widely acknowledged that it is an ideology that affects the behavior of individuals and groups within certain states and one that has the potential to influence in a major way the external behavior of states in this area as well.

This consensus is the result of the combination of several factors. These include the strategic importance of the northwestern quadrant of the Indian Ocean (the Persian Gulf) in terms of the concentration of proven and exportable oil reserves, the linkage of the politics of the gulf (and, therefore, the politics of oil) with the central issues of Middle East politics, and the effect of the Islamic Revolution in Iran on the rest of the Muslim world, particularly on the Arab populations of the gulf and its parent Middle East region.[19]

As far as the Iranian Revolution is concerned, experts on the Iranian polity and economy have told us, and rightly so, that it was the result of many political and economic factors ranging from the oppression of the shah's regime, and the near-total decimation of the secular opposition, to the critical downturn in the Iranian economy in the last years of Pahlavi rule. But the most important lesson of the Iranian experience for the Third World, for its Muslim component, and especially for Iran's neighbors, lies in the fact that it demonstrated that a revolution, in both its internal and external dimensions—namely, the restructuring of the domestic order and the rejection of foreign domination—could take place in authentically "native" terms and without the help of external legitimizing agents or ideologies. This, one can reasonably expect, has had far-reaching effects on the ethos of the region, not only in the gulf but in the Middle East as a whole. Fouad Ajami, speaking of its impact on the Arab world, has summed up this phenomenon very aptly in the following words: "For the Arab world, the drama of Iran was the spectacle of men and women in the street making and remaking their own history. Win or lose, they were out there, demanding to be counted or heard. All the Arab elite's attempts to say that Iran's troubles were peculiar to that society and to point out the detailed (and legitimate) differences between their own countries and Iran were beside the point."[20]

It is precisely this use of Islam as an ideology of protest that provides the essential relevance of the Iranian Revolution to the majority of the people in the Muslim world, indeed to the Third World in general. Islam, as an ideology of protest, is very much akin to the essential components of both the nationalist and nonaligned ideologies. In the Iranian context, it succeeded in overthrowing an iniquitous domestic order underwritten by one of the superpowers and its allies and in the process demonstrated Iran's autonomy in its external relations as well. The combination of authenticity, autonomy, and radical social transformation is a very potent ideological mixture in a region where regimes either lack legitimacy or are themselves engaged in using some form of anti–status quo rhetoric to bolster their legitimacy.

Implications of ideological Islam.   What does all this portend as far as the wider Indian Ocean region is concerned? What kind of impact is this use of Islamic ideology for anti–status quo and antihegemonic ends expected to have on other countries of the region, particularly those that are predominantly Muslim in character?

It would not be wrong to say that of the five subregions into which the larger Indian Ocean region can be divided, namely, Australasia, South Asia, the Persian Gulf, the Red Sea, and southern Africa, Muslims are demographically preponderant in three. Southern Asia, because of India's predominantly non-Muslim population, and the African littoral provide the exceptions. But even in South Asia, if we put the Muslim populations of the subcontinent together, they add up to close to 300 million, almost three times the population of the Arab world. Moreover, Bangladesh, India, and Pakistan rank as the second, third, and fourth largest Muslim countries respectively in terms of population (Indonesia being the largest), and, of course, in both Bangladesh and Pakistan the overwhelming majority of the population is Muslim. The countries of East Africa, particularly Tanzania, also have substantial Muslim populations.

In this vast region Islam has been used of late for various ends ranging from the legitimation of a particular status quo, however iniquitous it might be, to the extension of legitimacy to revolutionary and/or autonomist-secessionist activity.[21] Moreover, it is true, as I have argued elsewhere, that "Islam, like any other religion or dogma, is open to various and varied interpretations. These interpretations, which in terms of political action can be called the operationalization of the concept of Islamic polity, differ greatly depending upon the political and social contexts in and the historical juncture at which they are so operationalized. They also vary depending upon who—person or party—is the medium through which such operationalization takes place."[22]

Nonetheless, the appeal of the Islamic Revolution in Iran seems to have transcended geographic and political boundaries, particularly as far as the mass of the people is concerned. In this sense, Khomeini's appeal in the Muslim world in the 1980s parallels that of Nasser in the 1950s and the early 1960s and for the same reason. Like Nasser, he has become the symbol of the reassertion of the dignity of Muslim peoples. While some of the excesses and the infighting of the revolutionary process may be deplored, and while the popularity of the revolutionary regime may have been eroded as a result of its inability to find adequate answers to Iran's economic problems, the fund of sympathy at the popular level for the Iranian Revolution—particularly for its political rather than exclusively religious dimension—is still considerable. What is more, this sympathy transcends the traditional Sunni-Shia divide.

The seriousness with which Khomeini's word is taken in the Muslim world was demonstrated in November 1979 when, following seizure by Muslim fundamentalist fanatics of the Grand Mosque in Mecca, Iranian Radio broadcast a statement blaming the Americans and the Israelis for this violation of the *Kaabah*'s sanctity. This set off a wave of anti-American rioting in the Muslim world, culminating in the burning down of the American embassy in Islamabad, at a time when the Pakistani rulers were assiduously courting the U.S. government for major arms supplies. The Khomeini phenomenon, as this incident demonstrated, derives a substantial part of its popularity from a high degree of anti-Westernism, particularly anti-Americanism, scarcely below the surface at the mass level in the Muslim world.

A major reason for this anti-American feeling is related to the American support for Israel in the latter's continuing effort to deny the Palestinians a homeland. Without going into details of the Arab-Israeli conflict, it would suffice to say that in the Muslim world Israel is considered to be the product of a European ideology (Zionism). It is viewed as a settler-colonial state because of its European origin and its predominantly European ethos and because Jewish settlement in Palestine took place under the British mandate. The whole record relating to Western, particularly American, support for Zionism and later for Israel is viewed as an attempt by the Christian West to assuage its guilty conscience regarding its own (European) Jews at the expense of the Arab and predominantly Muslim people of Palestine. American policy since 1967, which is perceived as underwriting not merely Israeli security but Israeli expansionism as well, adds greater salience to this image of a hostile West (particularly the United States) out to undermine every Muslim (or Arab) expression of political autonomy.

To this aspect of the appeal of "political Khomeinism" is added its capacity for mass mobilization and the fact that it symbolizes popular revolt against a tyrannical order underwritten by the United States. Last, but not least, its authenticity as an indigenous ideology adds tremendously to its appeal. It is an ideology that, while reactive to the phenomenon of Western domination, does not formulate its response in terms borrowed from Western ideological frameworks, either of the liberal-capitalist or the Marxist-socialist variety. Bernard Lewis's statement with regard to Islamic movements in general applies to the Khomeinist ideology with particular force. According to Lewis, "Of all the great movements that have shaken the Middle East during the last century and a half, the Islamic movements alone are authentically Middle Eastern in inspiration. Liberalism and fascism, patriotism and nationalism, communism and socialism, are all European in origin, however much transformed by Middle Eastern disciples. The religious orders alone spring from the native soil, and express the passions of the submerged masses of the population. Though they have all, so far, been defeated [this was written before Iran], they have not spoken their last word."[23]

At a time when imported models of political and economic systems have been tried and found wanting, the appeal of the indigenous, authentic model is enhanced. This appeal is further augmented because of the lack of legitimacy and popular identification from which most governments in the Muslim world suffer today. In short, in most Muslim countries, "the basic rightness of leaders, regimes and political systems is not widely and deeply accepted."[24] Most of these regimes draw upon non-Islamic ideologies for their legitimacy (e.g., Baath socialism in Iraq and Syria, of the Takriti and Alawite varieties respectively) or have appropriated Islam and turned it into an official, establishment ideology without popular content (e.g., in Pakistan and Saudi Arabia). As a consequence, revolutionary Islam as a movement of protest has great potential for popular mobilization in these countries, a lesson driven home by the Iranian example. This is particularly true of the Arab world where the crisis of legitimacy for regimes has been made acute as a result of the continuing conflict with Israel and the inability of Arab regimes to bring this conflict to a successful conclusion. The recent Israeli invasion of Lebanon, the enforced withdrawal of the Palestinian resistance from Beirut, and the subsequent massacre of noncombatant Palestinian men, women, and children by assorted Christian militias with Israeli connivance, clearly demonstrated the impotence of conservative as well as radical Arab regimes to meet this challenge from a source considered a Western surrogate. This impotence, above all, has been demonstrated to the populations in the Arab countries themselves, and the point has been driven home that there was something so radically wrong about the political structures over which these regimes presided that it prevented their combined potential strength—in demographic and economic terms—from being translated into actual political and military capabilities.

This demonstration of impotence, coming as it did not merely on the heels of the Iranian Revolution but in the context of the Iranian expulsion of the Iraqi invading armies, the bloody uprising against the Assad regime in Hama staged by the Muslim Brotherhood, the assassination of Egyptian President Anwar Sadat by Muslim "fundamentalists" (they termed it "execution"), and above all the capture of the Grand Mosque in Mecca in 1979 by another group of Muslim "fundamentalists," served as sharp reminders of the internal as well as the external weaknesses of the Arab regimes.

Since the issues of regime legitimacy and the question of Palestine are intimately connected with the future of the Indian Ocean littoral's strategically most important subregion, the Persian Gulf, they form an integral part of this discussion of the impact of ideology on the Indian Ocean region. The question of Palestine is as important as the problem of legitimacy, because the Israeli military successes against Nasser's Egypt (the leader of pan-Arab nationalism) and recently against the Palestinian Liberation Organization (the symbol of Palestinian nationalism) seems to have led many in the Arab world to conclude that secular nationalist ideologies are incapable of mobilizing the resources of the Arab world for a successful struggle against the Zionist enemy.

The alternative yet to be tried in the Arab world is radical, politicized Islam. Moreover, despite the picture that may have been painted by recent apologists of Arab nationalism, influenced as they have been by the form rather than the content of European nationalisms, there is no basic contradiction between Islam and Arabism. Viewed in the historical context it is clear that it was Islam that made the Arabs great and vice-versa. In fact, it was Islam that provided the solidarity (*asabiya*) to Arab tribes of the peninsula on which their initial victories were based and which laid the foundations of the great Arab-Islamic civilization that flourished for centuries. Thus, according to Zeine N. Zeine, "The Arab nation, *al-Ummah al-'Arabiyyah*, was . . . a nation originally born out of Islam. Islam was the prime creator of the national life and political unity to the Muslim Arabs. This 'religious nationalism' remains an indelible part of the hearts and minds of Arabs."[25]

In the nineteenth century when the concept of the Arab *umma* was in the process of evolving out of the womb of the Islamic *umma*, most ideologues of Arab nationalism stressed the intimate link between the two. In fact, Al-Kawakibi (1849–1902), who, according to Sylvia Haim, "may be considered as the first true intellectual precursor of modern secular pan-Arabism,"[26] while attacking the Ottoman Empire, based his arguments on the assertion that because of its tyranny the empire was unfit to preserve Islam and, further, that Islamic regeneration should be the work of the Arabs who should supply a caliph, residing in Mecca, to be the spiritual head of an Islamic union. It was in that context that Al-Kawakibi provided a list of twenty-six reasons to demonstrate the superiority of the Arabs over other Muslims and to justify why the caliphate should devolve upon them.[27] Even the Christian Arab ideologues of secular Arab nationalism, like Qustantin Zuraiq, Nabih Amin Faris, and Michel Aflaq, unequivocally propounded the view that Islam is inseparable from Arab nationalism, although Aflaq went to the extent of explicitly representing Islam "not as a divine revelation but in part as a response to Arab needs at the time of Muhammad and in part as a foundation of Arabism."[28]

As far as the Arab-Muslim masses are concerned—and, in an area of increasing mass mobilization, it is the masses that will count increasingly—the two terms, Islam and Arabism, are virtually indistinguishable. The attempts over the last century by the Christians of Mount Lebanon to opt out of the mainstream of Arabism (or Arab nationalism)—a trend recently symbolized by the late Bashir Gemayel and his Phalange on the one hand and the renegade Major Saad Haddad on the other—and the Christians' more recent cooperation with the Arabs' Zionist enemy further entrench this identification in the popular Arab mind. The Phalange have seen to it that the Christian Arab minority will for a long time to come remain largely irrelevant to the development of an Arab ideological response to the problems facing the Arab world today.

The linkage between Arabism and Islam has, if anything, been strengthened by the examples of Zionist and Israeli successes. Nineteenth-century Zionism was essentially politicized Judaism with its energies primarily directed toward secular ends. The parallel with Jamal al-Din Afghani's attempt to use Islam for similar purposes during the same period is both interesting and instructive.[29] The post-1948 military successes of Israel, its ability to construct a modern state and master advanced technology, have further enhanced the demonstration effect of the Zionist-Israeli experience. One major lesson drawn in the Arab world from the Israeli example is that its military and political successes are based on its capacity to create solidarity based on religious nationalism. Therefore, the obvious question posed is, Cannot one beat the Zionist enemy at its own game? If this religious nationalism of 3 million Jews in Israel (backed by a few million more elsewhere) can achieve such miracles, why can an Arab-Islamic religious nationalism with its vastly superior demographic resources not achieve similar ends? As Fouad Ajami has pointed out, "The principal lesson that the religiously inclined Arabs drew from Israel's victory was that people can both go to the laboratory and worship. Israel combined what an entire generation of liberals and secularists had assumed to be incompatible things. It was both more religious and more scientific than the Arab states. Israel had demolished the easy superficial distinction that the scientific state is built on the debris of an extinguished religion."[30]

Therefore, the Arab world is likely to be under increasing and parallel pressure both from Khomeini's Iran and from Israel to try to achieve temporal—political and military—success on the basis of a solidarity founded on politicized religion and mass participation and mobilization. It is this dual pressure that will to a large extent determine the contours of the dominant ideology in the Arab world in the 1980s and the 1990s.

Three ideologies and the Gulf

As stated earlier, the Arab world includes within it a substantial portion of the strategically most important part of the Indian Ocean region: the Persian Gulf. Therefore, the ideological climate in the Arab world as a whole is bound to influence what goes on in the Arab littoral of the gulf. In some ways, given the character of the gulf regimes—conservative, monarchical, and pro-American, with their legitimacy based at least in part on their Islamic credentials—the challenge of a radical, populist Islamic ideology could be much more severe and potentially much more destabilizing than it would be for the rest of the Arab world.[31] Among other things, this could trigger off a process of direct external military intervention aimed at the appropriation of the oil wells on which so much of Western industrial development depends, even in these days of oil glut. This, however, is a subject that cannot be addressed in this chapter although I have done so, at least partially, elsewhere.[32] Suffice it to say that in that event the gulf would come to epitomize, even more than it does already, the problems and confrontations in the Third World between indigenous forces and external powers regarding issues of economic independence, cultural autonomy, and political self-determination.

Meanwhile, the ideological quest for autonomy in the gulf, as in other parts of the Indian Ocean region, will continue. Nationalism, non-alignment, and Islamic (or Muslim) reassertion in many ways are variations on the same autonomy theme. In fact, they may be viewed as different points on the same continuum, moving in an often erratic but nevertheless unilinear fashion. In recent years in the Indian Ocean region it has been Iran that has demonstrated the compatibility, indeed the merger, of the three ideologies during and after the revolutionary process. A highly nationalist population using Islam as a vehicle for political mobilization was able not only to overthrow a well-entrenched order with the most advanced instruments of repression at its command, but also to demonstrate its independence of the superpowers by declaring that its foreign policy would be determined by the criterion "Neither East Nor West!" This is why, despite the sometimes apparently unsavory behavior of the revolutionary regime in Tehran over the last few years, the demonstration effect of Iran's example on the Indian Ocean region, particularly on its Muslim-Arab component, remains so strong. The essence of this effect was summed up by a remark made to me by an Egyptian journalist who, for obvious reasons, will have to remain unnamed: "Even if Khomeini is a disaster—and I don't say he is—he is at least our homegrown disaster. He is not a disaster . . . imposed upon us by foreign powers and interests or their regional surrogates."

3. The Economic and Strategic Interdependence of the Indian Ocean Region ☜ Raju G. C. Thomas

The recent buildup of Soviet and American military forces in the Indian Ocean, following the gradual withdrawal of British forces east of Suez in the early 1970s, has once again raised the interrelated aspirations of promoting regional security arrangements and regional economic cooperation among the littoral and hinterland states of the Indian Ocean. As with the earlier nebulous notions of Afro-Asian solidarity, nonalignment, and peaceful coexistence in response to the cold war, efforts to establish the Indian Ocean as a zone of peace have proved so far to be less than successful. Various Asian and African states have perceived the intrusion of the great power military forces into the Indian Ocean as either enhancing or eroding their security and the continued military presence of the superpowers in the Indian Ocean has had the overall effect of linking great power security concerns with regional security issues.[1]

The failure to establish the Indian Ocean as a zone of peace is not merely due to a lack of consensus among the African and Asian states on how to eliminate the great power military presence, but is also due to several and often conflicting interpretations on what the term means and how it is to be achieved. Interpretations have included the establishment of a nuclear-free zone, the maintenance of a balance of military forces in the region that would include some external forces, and the promotion of regional economic cooperation and development.[2]

This chapter examines the nature of the last interpretation as evident in the Indian Ocean region, namely, the relationship between regional security issues on the one hand and the growth of regional economic cooperation and integration on the other. Despite the severe hurdles and failures of the past, the assessment here will suggest that the pursuit of intraregional economic cooperation may precede the resolution of traditional issues of conflict in the Indian Ocean. States do not usually trade with their enemies. However, states could trade with the friends of their enemies provided there is no direct conflict of interest between the two. Thus, for instance, India conducted a great deal of trade with the shah's Iran during a time when Iran and Pakistan were partners in the Central Treaty Organization (CENTO) military alliance and the Regional Cooperation for Development (RCD).

The Nature of Regional Economic Cooperation and Integration

While the terms regional economic cooperation and regional economic integration are sometimes used conjunctively, interchangeably, or even sequentially, they need not always be synonymous or sequential. Economic cooperation means the promotion of trade and investment that carry mutual benefit. Economic integration suggests the promotion of an economic free trade zone with the objective of broadening the internal economic base of production and distribution.[3] Under the latter circumstances, the entire region would constitute a greater single domestic market and might lead to economies of scale in production and the increasing competitiveness of regional manufacturing firms outside the free trade zone. However, as another consequence of the integration process and the removal of trade barriers, certain firms in some countries of the customs union may prove uncompetitive when faced with the production and services provided by other members within the group. This may cause certain production units to be driven out of business once the free trade zone is established. The resistance during the 1960s of British dairy farmers to Britain's membership in the European Economic Community (EEC) is a good example of some of the domestic political and economic consequences of regional economic integration.

On the other hand, trade or economic cooperation within a regional group of countries suggests some form of tariffs, although the overall flow of goods and services is expected to provide mutual benefit. The growth of trade may be expected to lead to economic interdependence among nations. However, there could be domestic resistance to virtually unrestricted external trade, especially when such trade leads to the elimination of domestic manufacturers and to unemployment. The impact of Japanese automobile sales in the U.S. market on American auto manufacturers and on general unemployment levels is illustrative. But among most countries trade is pursued in goods and services not entirely available in the domestic market. Where imports constitute a major threat to domestic industries, some form of direct or indirect protection is usually attempted.

For most less-developed countries (LDCs), trade within the region only becomes possible if the nations of the group carry the relevant goods and services that can satisfy the needs of others within the group. If all states produce coffee, for example, the scope for economic cooperation would be negligible. On the other hand, if all the members produce coffee *and* create an integrated economy, then rather than competing for the overseas market among themselves, as well as with other coffee producers, the broad-based production arrangements might enable the group of countries to lower their costs and compete more effectively against the other exporters of the same products. Additionally, integration could lead to the growth of more diversified economies within the region because of the larger and broader-based market available. Economic integration, therefore, suggests both regional efficiency and self-sufficiency.

The arguments that are being advanced here are not merely relevant to the states of the Indian Ocean region but to all developing countries. Peace through economic interdependence of the Indian Ocean states constitutes merely a step toward peace everywhere through economic interdependence. This analysis therefore merely represents a regional focus in the overall North-South negotiating strategy. To propose that the LDCs of the Indian Ocean region should pursue greater economic cooperation for mutual benefit, or should attempt to foster regional free trade zones, does not necessarily preclude the promotion of such economic cooperation between the Indian Ocean states and other parts of Africa and Asia, as well as Latin America.

However, the concept of *peace* through economic cooperation and integration suggests the interaction of security and economic relationships. As against cooperation with other parts of the Third World, the countries of the Indian Ocean may be perceived to share greater common cause because their security problems are becoming increasingly interrelated. Superpower military rivalry in the Indian Ocean and the revival of the cold war in the region, which tend to draw in the littoral and hinterland states of Asia and Africa, indicate the commonality of security themes in the Indian Ocean. On the other hand, to the extent that such security problems are less regional and more universal—for example, policies and problems regarding the development of nuclear energy among the Third World states and the potential diversion to nuclear weapons purposes—they may give rise to economic cooperation of all Third World states, including those beyond the Indian Ocean, that are affected.

Constraints on Economic Interdependence

The rationale underlying this chapter may be summarized by suggesting three sets of conditions that are perceived to restrict or preclude regional economic cooperation and integration. Conversely, the following observations imply that the resolution or mitigation of these adverse conditions would tend to advance the overall objective of peace through economic interdependence.

Power and ideology

Power. The existence of uneven power capabilities within a region makes weaker states fear a neighboring dominant state and may motivate them to draw on external support. The uneven regional distribution of power has often been one of the main sources of regional instability. Relations between a dominant state and its weaker neighbors, especially where there are unresolved territorial, ethnic, or ideological issues, precludes any form of cooperation, economic or otherwise. Such conditions may be found in the relationships at various times between India and Pakistan, India and Bangladesh, Indonesia (under Sukarno) and Malaysia, China and Vietnam, Iran (under the shah) and Iraq, and South Africa and its neighbors.

Where no such political issues exist, unequal economic capabilities may still carry political undertones. If trading and economic bargaining relationships are uneven, the weaker state may fear being pressured into disadvantageous economic agreements, becoming the dumping ground for the manufacturers of the dominant state, and may fear conditions in which the dominant state may take control of much of its domestic investments. Such fears of becoming the economic satellite of the dominant state, a problem that may be found in the relationship between Canada and the United States, may also be seen in concerns about a dominant Indonesia within the Association of South-East Asian Nations (ASEAN), or a dominant India in South Asian economic cooperation schemes. Under such circumstances, unequal military, political, or economic capabilities sometimes tend to push weaker states into a search for military or political support and for trading partners outside the region. This undermines the prospect of promoting peace through economic interdependence.

Ideology. The other component at this level of constaints is ideology. The prevalence of competing political ideologies and incompatible economic systems—communism or state-owned enterprises versus capitalism or private enterprises operating in market economies—makes economic integration difficult, if not impossible. The main examples here would be the question of Vietnam's entry into ASEAN, and the different development approaches adopted by states within the East African economic community. In the former case, it is difficult to see how the economy of communist Vietnam could exist alongside the free market economies of ASEAN countries within a customs-free and unrestricted trading zone. In the latter case, no doubt one of the major obstacles to the development of the East African Community (EAC) was posed by Idi Amin's erratic and irrational regime in Uganda. But a more basic problem in East Africa may be found in Julius Nyerere's decision to adapt and adopt the Chinese model of development which emphasizes socialist economic planning at the agricultural and grass roots level. In contrast, Kenya under Jomo Kenyatta and lately under Daniel Moi has promoted a free enterprise economy and encouraged foreign investments.

The main problems under such conditions may prove to arise from the lack of fairness of state-controlled and subsidized enterprises competing with the private firms of the free-market economies in an enlarged free trade zone. Conversely, there may be fears in the socialist state of more efficient private enterprises eliminating state-controlled enterprises, thereby defeating socialist policies at home. The socialist state may be tempted to introduce tariffs to protect its controlled and subsidized enterprises, thereby defeating the objective of establishing a customs union.

There would also be basic security fears within a group of states with radically different ideological systems if respective members are perceived to be supported by external like-minded superpowers. For example, reservations expressed by some ASEAN states about Vietnam's entry into their regional economic arrangement go beyond economic reasons to suspicions of Vietnam's ultimate political objectives in Southeast Asia with the possible collusion of the Soviet Union.

Internal and external security

Internal security. Internal political strife and violence, separatist movements, and civil wars are often supported by bordering states or tend to spill over into them. The result is friction among these states and the destabilization of the region. Frequent domestic revolutions, coups, and countercoups also make for volatile and inconsistent foreign policies. As a consequence, the pursuit of regional economic cooperation becomes difficult. This has been one of the basic reasons why economic cooperation has made little headway among states within the subregions of southern Asia, the Middle East, and much of sub-Saharan Africa.

In Pakistan, for instance, there have been insurgencies and/or secessionist movements in Baluchistan, Pushtunistan, and the former East Pakistan province; Kashmir, Nagaland, and Mizoram in India have experienced similar problems. Such volatile internal conditions have attracted outside diplomatic and/or material support from the hostile governments in India and Pakistan, respectively. Similar examples may be seen in the Kurdish nationalist problem that straddles Iran and Iraq, the problem of the large Shia Arab population in Iraq susceptible to incitement by Persian Shias in Iran, and the Eritrean and Ogaden issues between Ethiopia and Somalia. The situation in southern Africa appears to be comparable. The rise of the African National Congress (ANC) and the Pan-Africanist Congress (PAC) in reaction to South Africa's internal apartheid policies has been supported and assisted by the surrounding states. All of this can hardly be considered conducive to economic cooperation.

External security.   The potential for conflict in the region arising from unresolved territorial or ideological disputes as well as from the domestic political conditions described above constitutes the most obvious obstacle to regional economic cooperation. Where such regional conflicts persist, the great powers tend to become involved. The degree to which the great powers are drawn into regional issues usually depends on the strategic value of the region or on the importance of the respective states to the global balance of power. Almost all the subregions of the Indian Ocean have been under the cloud of war in recent years.

The structure of economic production and trade

Structure of production.   As discussed earlier, there generally exists a lack of economic compatibility among the states of the Indian Ocean region. The production profiles of individual states tend to be heavily agricultural with the prevalence of either subsistence agricultural output or the surplus production of one or two primary commodities. Such goods carry a limited or specialized overseas market mainly in the industrialized world with much less prospect in other less-developed countries. Thus, for example, the markets for Persian Gulf oil, South Asian textiles, tea, and jute, East African coffee and agricultural commodities, and the minerals of southern Africa lie mainly outside these particular areas and usually outside the Indian Ocean region as well. It is the West, Japan, and the Soviet bloc that promise the most lucrative markets for the Indian Ocean countries. Consequently, countries within these areas find themselves in competition among themselves. Persian Gulf oil exporters have been an exception by managing, at least for the time being, to avoid competition through price fixing in the Organization of Petroleum Exporting Countries (OPEC).

Structure of trade.   The problem here arises from the undiversified structure of production and is usually characterized by a lack of complementarity in the needed imports and available exports of the LDCs. The major import needs of almost all the states of the Indian Ocean region are finished alloy steels, heavy machine tools and other engineering goods, chemical products, and similar goods normally associated with highly industrialized states. As with the structure of production, LDC export capabilities are usually limited to certain primary commodities for which there is little demand in other LDCs. This trade profile implies a dependent relationship whereby LDC exports of primary commodities, as in the cases of East Africa and the horn, are subject to extreme market fluctuations. Even where manufactured goods now constitute a significant portion of exports, as in the case of southern Asia, the level of total export value continues to remain considerably lower than the cost of importing badly needed capital goods for development programs. These states possess weak external bargaining capabilities and are faced with a perpetual foreign exchange crisis.

The above three sets of characteristics inhibit regional economic cooperation and development. It may be noted that of the five constituent subregions of the composite Indian Ocean region—Australasia, South Asia, the Persian Gulf, the Red Sea/Horn of Africa, and eastern/ southern Africa—conditions in Australasia appear to be the most favorable for economic cooperation and integration. Indeed, considerable progress has been made in the promotion and development of ASEAN despite the fact that the states of Indochina, Burma, and Australia continue to remain outside the organization for ideological, cultural, and security reasons. For the other subregions, most or all of the characteristics suggested above have been prevalent in varying degrees, preventing significant trading ties. Within them prospects for economic integration appear to be remote. However, this has not prevented substantial trade from occurring across the various Indian Ocean subregions, such as that among South Asia, the Persian Gulf, and Australasia.

The preceding analysis suggests two approaches toward establishing peace through economic interdependence:

1.   Where the above constraining factors within a region are at a comparatively low level, *intra*regional economic cooperation may be pursued. This could begin with a core group and steadily be expanded outward until the organization includes all states in a subregion, together with some states from across other traditionally conceived subregions. Two possible examples are to expand ASEAN to include Burma, as well as to provide associate membership for Sri Lanka and Bangladesh, both of which have expressed interest in joining the ASEAN economic community; and, second, to expand the East African Community to include states further north and south of it, such as Somalia or Zambia. While the prospects for economic integration that includes communist Vietnam in ASEAN or Marxist Ethiopia in an EAC may appear highly problematical, the promotion of trading ties with these states would appear both feasible and desirable.

2.   Where the above constraining factors within a region are at a comparatively high level, subregional trade is best promoted through outside ties that may eventually push states within subregions of traditionally high conflict into some form of cooperation among themselves. The main experience here has been the increasing trade between the countries of South Asia (containing the hostile states of India and Pakistan) and the Persian Gulf (containing the warring states of Iran and Iraq), although the level of economic cooperation within these subregions continues to be low. However, it is noteworthy that in recent years increasing trade has been evident between India and Pakistan, a fact perhaps partly due to the growth of economic ties between South Asia and the Persian Gulf.

The objective of both approaches would be to expand the basis for economic cooperation and integration so as to encompass ultimately much of the entire Indian Ocean region. The problems raised in this analytical framework are discussed further in the sections that follow.

The Interaction of Economic and Security Issues

The analysis thus far suggests linkages between economic and strategic interdependence. However, rather than furthering peace, economic interdependence among nations may tend at times to make ethnic and territorial conflicts in one subregion of relevance to another since it may lead to the disruption of growing economic ties between the states of two subregions. Conflict in one subregion may even entangle the states of the other who may feel compelled to support their economic partners. The economic effect of the Iraq-Iran war on the newly established economic ties between the states of the Persian Gulf and the Indian subcontinent is suggestive, although the conflict has largely been confined to the original two combatants. While economic issues are less likely to provoke war among states, they may aggravate existing territorial and ethnic issues. The degree to which economic cooperation will diffuse traditional security concerns is uncertain.

First, conflict may occur if economic access to a critical commodity becomes difficult or impossible. This situation is exemplified by the American threat in 1974 (by then Secretary of State Kissinger and Secretary of Defense Schlesinger) to intervene militarily in the Middle East if OPEC pricing policies were to "strangulate" the Western industrialized economies.[4] It is important to remember that the adverse economic conditions faced by the Western powers in the mid-1970s were also confronted by the developing countries. Indeed, one Western report at the time suggested that a large and relatively powerful state such as India could well resolve its domestic economic plight arising from higher oil prices by seizing one or two of the smaller Persian Gulf shaikhdoms. However preposterous this scenario may seem, it was nevertheless within the realm of possibility.

As it happened, the response of India and other LDCs to the international oil crisis was to minimize the "security" problems arising from their costly economic access to oil. Instead, the strategy of many of the states of South and Southeast Asia and black Africa has been to lend support to the pricing policies of OPEC, to emphasize the need to maintain Third World solidarity against past and present economic exploitation by the Western colonial powers, and to seek concessional borrowing terms and developmental assistance from the capital-surplus OPEC states of the Middle East.

Second, conflict within the oil-producing area of the Middle East among the oil exporters themselves could lead to political alignments or even to military entanglement of other nearby Indian Ocean states heavily dependent on the flow of oil from one of the combatants. As noted earlier, the Iraq-Iran war has the potential to create such a situation. That it has not resulted in conflict or subsidiary military entanglements spilling over from one subregion to another may have been due partly to the fortuitous timing of the war: the outbreak of hostilities occurred when the international oil crisis had eased and alternative supplies of oil were becoming available. However, future conflict scenarios in which, for instance, the Saudi Arabian monarchy is overthrown (as was the Pahlavi dynasty in Iran), or in which conflict occurs between Saudi Arabia and Syria, point to the economic vulnerability of all states dependent on Middle East oil. What remains portentous for the Indian Ocean LDCs adjacent to the oil-producing Middle East—India, Pakistan, Afghanistan, Somalia, Ethiopia, Egypt—is that such conditions could jeopardize not merely their economic security but could also embroil them in conflicts involving the oil-producing states and the great powers.

Third, the accumulation of petrodollars by the Middle East oil-exporting states has generally resulted in the large-scale infusion of Western and Soviet military arms into the region. Economic rather than security considerations tend to be the primary rationale for such arms transfers. Reversing the flow of petrodollars through arms sales enables the Soviet Union and Western arms-producing states either to enhance their hard currency reserves or to resolve their adverse balance-of-payments problems. But military sales aside, the management of adverse trade balances by the Western powers and Japan has been largely accomplished through the much more substantial sales of a variety of consumer goods and services to the capital-surplus oil exporters (CSOES) of the Persian Gulf. Indeed, arms imports by Saudi Arabia, Iran, Iraq, and Kuwait between 1970 and 1979 constituted just 3 to 15 percent of their total imports, with the exception of Iraq which imported arms worth almost 30 percent of its total imports. This is no cause for optimism for the LDCs of the Indian Ocean since the bulk of the civilian imports of the oil-exporting countries are also bought from the industrialized states. Some of the LDCs are therefore not only faced with the aggravated problems of security arising from the flow of arms into the Middle East but are also unable to resolve their economic plight at home through increased civilian exports to the oil-exporting states.

Among the more serious security concerns of the LDCs is the fact that the Middle East arms buildup with petrodollar surpluses has adversely affected military balances in the adjacent areas of the Indian subcontinent and the Horn of Africa where several conflicts have occurred over the last four decades. The weaker Islamic states of Pakistan and Somalia have sought to establish military links with the Persian Gulf states to offset the military superiority of their rivals, India and Ethiopia. Economic and military power possessed by the oil-exporting states additionally constitute the potential for upsetting security relationships farther south and east in the Indian Ocean region in southern Africa and Southeast Asia. Libya has already demonstrated the potential and the inclination for political and military interference among the central African states. The prospect for such intrusions by the Arab states with their surplus of weapons into the more distant areas of the Indian Ocean region, although much less likely, cannot be entirely discounted.

Note, however, that direct arms transfers are less likely to be the mode of intrusion among the Indian Ocean states. Instead, as development assistance in hard currency is increased to select (usually Islamic) states of southern and southeastern Asia and Africa, the ability of these states to import greater quantities of arms is also thereby increased. For instance, the American sale of $2.5 billion worth of arms to Pakistan, including F-16 fighters, M-48A tanks, and TOW antitank missiles, was expected to be underwritten through Saudi economic assistance. Similarly in Somalia, Saudi economic assistance and a liberal Saudi import trade policy (Saudi Arabia now constitutes more than 85 percent of the Somali export market) have enabled Somalia to import much needed arms to conduct the hostilities with Ethiopia.

Fourth, the costly dependence of some of the LDCs such as India and Pakistan on oil imports from the Middle East has prompted these states to embark on major nuclear energy programs at home. These nuclear energy programs have been repeatedly justified for peaceful civilian purposes. Yet, at the same time, the setting up of enrichment and reprocessing facilities in these countries for the declared purpose of controlling the nuclear fuel cycle and asserting the independence of the nuclear energy program at home, carries with it the potential for diversion to a nuclear weapons program. An Indo-Pakistani nuclear arms race stemming indirectly from their nuclear energy program may have implications for the Middle East. Both Islamabad and New Delhi may compete for economic favors among the CSOEs of the Middle East in return for the transfer of Indian or Pakistani nuclear technology and equipment.[5] It may be recalled that in the mid-1970s, Colonel Qadhafy of Libya offered financial support in exchange for a shared nuclear weapons program with India. When the government of India declined the offer, Libya then turned to Pakistan where, reportedly, a nuclear weapons program is currently being financed directly or indirectly by Libya, with uranium from Niger also being supplied indirectly via Libya.

Peace through Economic Interdependence

The preceding discussion suggests how certain economic conditions within, and growing economic interdependence among, the CSOEs and the LDCs of the rest of the Indian Ocean region foster varying levels of strategic interdependence and security concerns.[6] Such interregional security spillover effects tend to arise mainly from two conditions. First, they result from the *net* economic dependence of the LDCs on the oil exporting states. Where such dependence is high—as in the cases of the Indian subcontinent and the Horn of Africa—the security spillover effect is also high. Conversely, where such net dependency is low—in southeastern Asia and southern Africa—the security spillover effect also tends to be low. Second, the spillover effect is clearly also due to the proximity of these areas to the oil-producing regions of the Persian Gulf and Arab North Africa.

Efforts by the LDCs to reduce their economic dependence by increasing their exports to the CSOEs so as to produce a greater balance in their trade relationship, also tend to reduce tension and to advance regional economic cooperation. In other words, the promotion of genuine economic interdependence in the Indian Ocean region through a two-way flow of goods and services shows signs of furthering regional peace and security. This has been particularly evident in South Asia and the Persian Gulf. Although the immediate aftermath of the international oil crisis made the South Asian states acutely dependent on the Persian Gulf states, this economic dependency has been steadily reduced over the last few years. This was accomplished through an increasing flow of Indian, Pakistani, and Bangladeshi manufactures, labor, and professional services, to the Persian Gulf.

Nevertheless, the situation is not entirely satisfactory since the export of South Asian goods and services remains hostage to international market conditions and to potential conflict in the Middle East. South Asia must continue to compete with Japan and the advanced industrialized states of the West and even with some of the middle income countries of East Asia, notably South Korea and Taiwan. The West continues to enjoy a greater technological advantage compared to the less significant advantage of cheaper labor costs maintained by the South Asian states. The CSOEs are much too rich to seek marginally lower prices offered by South Asia for their goods and services. Quality and high technology rather than price tend to be their main criteria for purchase. The major trading partners of the CSOEs continue to be the industrialized West, including Japan. Additionally, the vulnerability of the South Asian export market to conflict in the Persian Gulf is exemplified by the effects of the Iraq-Iran war; much of the substantial and budding trade between the two subregions has been disrupted.

While there have been signs of growing trade between the LDC subregions of the Red Sea/Horn of Africa (mainly Somalia and Sudan) and South Asia on the one hand, and the Persian Gulf on the other, there have been no major developments in the growth of trade *within* these three subregions. Most of the imports and exports of the states within the Indian subcontinent, the Persian Gulf, and Horn of Africa have been with states outside of their own areas of the Indian Ocean. Not unexpectedly, this has been due to the climate of tensions and conflicts that has prevailed within these subregions in the post–Second World War and postcolonial eras. These conflicts have included the Ethiopian revolution that resulted in the overthrow of Emperor Haile Selassie by the present Marxist regime; the Somalian-Ethiopian war; civil war in Sudan in the 1960s; four Arab-Israeli wars; the Kurdish rebellion and separatist movement in Iraq and Iran; civil wars and revolutions in Lebanon, Iran, and Iraq; the Iraq-Iran war; four Indo-Pakistani wars; separatist movements in Nagaland and Mizoram in India supported by Pakistan; and similar movements in Baluchistan and Pushtunistan in Pakistan supported by India.

Significant attempts at regional economic cooperation by the states of these three subregions have usually transcended traditional subregional boundaries, for example, the RCD among Pakistan, Iran, and Turkey, and the OPEC cartel, which includes states outside the Middle East in Southeast Asia, West Africa, and South America.[7] Even these economic cooperative efforts have been the unintended outgrowth of military alliances or other responses to war conditions. Thus, the RCD was basically the outgrowth of the CENTO security alliance sponsored by the West against the communist bloc. Similarly, OPEC in its present form (it was founded much earlier in the 1960s but remained largely ineffective) was initially a reaction by the Organization of Arab Petroleum Exporting Countries (OAPEC) to the Arab-Israeli war of October 1973. The new OPEC strategy commenced as an attempt by Arab oil-exporting states to pressure the West into reducing or eliminating their support for Israel over the Palestinian issue. Political and security reasons underlying the oil embargo of October 1973 subsequently gave way to mainly economic motives when Ecuador, Gabon, Indonesia, Iran, Nigeria, and Venezuela coordinated efforts with the Arab oil exporters to fix prices so as to maximize the profits of all members.

In contrast to such cross-regional economic collaboration in the RCD and OPEC, there have been more systematic efforts made to bring about subregional economic cooperation and integration in Southeast Asia and East Africa. Both ASEAN and the EAC were initiated and promoted along the lines of the EEC. No doubt even the origins of the EEC carried security undertones, namely, the realization among the sponsors of the Treaty of Rome of the loss of West European power and the need to establish countervailing power in Europe against the rise of Soviet (and, to an extent, American) military and economic capability.

Similar motives may have been present in the initiation of ASEAN and, to a lesser extent, the EAC. The prolonged war in Indochina and the confrontation over north Borneo between Tunku Abdul Rahman's newly created state of Malaysia and Sukarno's Indonesia in the early 1960s were clearly obstacles to the promotion of regional economic cooperation in Southeast Asia. However, they also provided the impetus for seeking closer economic and political ties by some of the states in the area. Subsequently, the fall of Sukarno in 1966 facilitated the setting up of ASEAN. Unlike Sukarno, who attempted to establish Indonesia as the leader of the Southeast Asian nations and as a major Asian power, his successor, President Suharto, has sought to maintain a low profile both in the region and in world affairs. This has been a deliberate policy to encourage the development of ASEAN that might have otherwise produced fears of a dominant Indonesia within the group.[8] Also recognizing the interrelationship between regional economic cooperation and regional security, Indonesia and its ASEAN partners have sponsored and promoted the establishment of the zone of peace, freedom, and neutrality (ZOPFAN) in Southeast Asia. Today ASEAN includes all the states of Southeast Asia except Burma, Kampuchea, Laos, and Vietnam. Even these states have shown interest in joining ASEAN, although there is resistance among the more conservative members—Malaysia, Singapore, and Thailand—to admitting them. Other bordering states of the region that are traditionally considered to be part of South Asia, Sri Lanka and Bangladesh, have also expressed interest in joining this economic free trade zone.

In many ways, the latter situation represents the failure of the South Asian states—Afghanistan, Bangladesh, Bhutan, India, Nepal, Pakistan, and Sri Lanka—to seek a similar regional economic community. Nevertheless, there have been some encouraging signs in South Asia in recent years. Since the Simla Agreement of 1973 between India and Pakistan in which both sides declared their intention to resolve bilateral issues through peaceful means, moderate trade has grown between the two countries.[9] Similarly, despite occasional friction over the Farrakha Dam between India and Bangladesh, trade between those two countries today is substantially greater than during the time when Bangladesh was part of Pakistan. While one of the major obstacles to cooperation in South Asia is the size and dominance of India and the security and economic apprehensions caused thereby, geography indicates both the practicality and necessity of economic cooperation. For instance, planning irrigation schemes in all three countries cannot be undertaken without reference to the other states since the rivers of the northern subcontinent flow through all three countries. There is also a greater complementarity of goods and services available in South Asia than elsewhere in the Indian Ocean. The diversified economy of India is capable of supplying some of the heavy engineering and manufactured goods needed by the other states in the subregion, and India may be willing to absorb some of the primary commodities and manufactures available for export by the smaller states of South Asia.

The experience of the EAC thus far has been somewhat different.[10] First started in 1963 among Kenya, Tanzania, and Uganda (the last being the union of Tanganyika and Zanzibar), it virtually ceased to function during the rule of Idi Amin in Uganda from 1971 to 1979. Since all these states were once ruled by Britain and therefore had common economic and political institutions and an integrated network of communications, the potential for economic cooperation was good from the start. Existing trading privileges in the decolonized British Commonwealth of Nations provided the basis for similar preferred trading arrangements among these three states. Most of these conditions were also true for South Asian states that were all once part of the British Indian Empire. But unlike South Asia, where the outbreak of the Indo-Pakistani war and continuing conflict between the two states after independence in 1947 made a discourse on economic issues nearly impossible, conditions were more conducive to economic cooperation in East Africa. The East African states are comparatively more uniform in size and need not fear the economic domination of one major state as in the case of India in South Asia.

Reasons for the failure thus far to establish firmly an integrated East African community go beyond Idi Amin's policies. It is primarily economic considerations that have slowed the integration process. As noted earlier, Julius Nyerere embarked on his own brand of socialism in Tanzania, while Kenya pursued economic policies that emphasized a free-market economy and an acquisitive society. The comparative lack of progress in East African economic cooperation also arose from the domestic production and import-export structure of these states. No doubt, if economic integration were achieved in the EAC, this would produce a broad-based economy providing economies of scale in production and creating a subregional basis for a sizable and profitable trade policy beyond the EAC. However, the interim phase toward such integration poses a major problem. When each of the three members of the EAC emphasize production in certain basic primary commodities, it results in a trade structure within the area where there is little complementarity in the goods and services available for export. Consequently, the great majority of the trading partners of the individual EAC members are the advanced industrialized nations who are able to provide the advanced technology and the heavy capital goods needed for development.

Economic cooperation in the Horn of Africa is complicated by conditions that are similar to those in South Asia. Tensions and conflict over ethnic, religious, ideological, and territorial issues color the relationship between Marxist Ethiopia and Muslim Somalia. Conflict over the disputed Ogaden territory has distorted trading priorities in both countries. In 1979, arms imports constituted 75 percent and 89 percent of the total export earnings of Ethiopia and Somalia, respectively. Even assuming that disputes over the Ogaden and other issues are eventually resolved, there is little scope for economic cooperation in the Horn of Africa. Neither country produces much that the other country needs. However, as in the case of South Asia, both Somalia and Ethiopia conduct a fair amount of trade with the Persian Gulf countries. Saudi Arabia and, to a lesser extent, Kuwait represent common trading partners for both states and the prospect of peace through economic interdependence may necessarily have to come through cross-regional trade between the Horn of Africa and the other subregions of the Indian Ocean.

The presence of a white-ruled and economically dominant South Africa makes overt economic cooperation difficult in southern Africa. Pretoria's internal apartheid policy continues to exacerbate differences—often indirectly caused by East-West tensions or the economic policies of the West—among the surrounding states of Angola, Botswana, Mozambique, Zambia, and Zimbabwe on the political and economic policies to be pursued toward South Africa. White-dominated South Africa's own strategy of survival indeed rests on maintaining such differences among the various states of southern Africa. However, unlike East Africa and the Horn of Africa, the economic resources and the complementary structure of production of the states of southern Africa indicate considerable scope for increasing trade and economic cooperation within that subregion.

Developments in the Persian Gulf have produced one of the major sources of economic troubles for the LDCs in recent years and at the same time may provide the best hope for economic cooperation and development in the Indian Ocean. The phenomenal rise in OPEC oil prices from about $4 per barrel in 1973 to the range of about $32 to $42 per barrel in 1982 has over these years wreaked havoc on the economies of the LDCs. For example, in the case of India the cost of oil imports rose from about 10 percent of the total import bill in 1973 to about 50 percent in 1981 and consumed about 80 percent of India's export earnings that year. Despite increasing Indian exports of manufactures and engineering goods to the Persian Gulf countries since the mid-1970s, this has by no means resolved the crippling Indian trade imbalance. No doubt some of the cost of the oil import bill has been met through foreign exchange remittances by Indian nationals working in the Persian Gulf countries, notably in Kuwait and the United Arab Emirates. But this has been comparatively insubstantial and quite unlike the Pakistani experience where almost the entire cost of Pakistani oil imports was met through the remittances of foreign exchange by Pakistani nationals working in the Persian Gulf. The Iraq-Iran war has further cut into this source of foreign exchange for all the countries of South Asia. The demand for Indian, Pakistani, and Bangladeshi labor has been reduced considerably as the economies of these two belligerent states of the Persian Gulf continue to be devastated by war.

Ironically, the economic hopes of the LDCs of the Indian Ocean may rest with the Middle Eastern members of OPEC if much of the petrodollar surpluses can be diverted from the West. Despite their much lower level of oil import and consumption than the industrialized West, the overall trade deficit of the LDCs was almost $60 billion in 1980. In the same year the trade surplus of the OPEC countries was $120 billion.[11] Moreover, even after assessing the extravagant civilian and military imports of the OPEC countries, approximately $70–80 billion has been estimated as the petrodollar surplus available for overseas investment and development assistance. Yet over 85 percent of this amount flows back to the Western industrialized nations in the form of federal and commercial bank deposits, investments, and purchases of bonds and treasury bills. Bilateral development assistance—almost exclusively in the form of low-interest loans—was less than 15 percent, while indirect multilateral assistance to developing countries through international agencies such as the World Bank and its affiliates was negligible.

Most of the Persian Gulf oil-exporting countries, and in particular Saudi Arabia, are reluctant to channel aid through multilateral agencies since they cannot control the destination, terms, and flow of such aid. Saudi economic aid has mainly benefited other Islamic states, especially Pakistan, Somalia, Sudan, North Yemen, and, until President Sadat entered the Camp David negotiations, Egypt. Although the Persian Gulf CSOEs, such as Saudi Arabia and Kuwait, have claimed that they provide more aid per capita than members of the Organization for Economic Cooperation and Development (OECD), this assertion obscures the true capacity of the gulf states to assist the LDCs and to foster more equitable and beneficial trade relationships with the poorer developing countries. OECD members usually need to squeeze their own populations through extra taxation in order to provide development assistance. On the other hand, most of the OPEC states carry enormous (and basically "unearned") petrodollar surpluses without even the capacity to absorb these amounts into their own national development plans. Present OPEC investment and development assistance may prove to be based on a certain short-sightedness. Whereas petrodollar investments in the OECD nations may be more profitable in the short run, the investment potential of the LDCs of the Indian Ocean may be well worth exploring. The resources of sub-Saharan Africa remain mainly untapped, while the large markets of populous southern and Southeast Asia may provide rich dividends for CSOE investments.[12]

Prospects

There is now a greater consciousness among the LDCs of the Indian Ocean of the need to accelerate development within their own countries and of the prospects for such development through regional economic cooperation and integration. While traditional issues of conflict over territory, ethnicity, and nationalism are likely to persist for several years to come, in some cases these have shown signs of ameliorating. Clearly, the Kashmir dispute appears no longer as volatile as it did some fifteen years ago. Territorial issues among the ASEAN states have been virtually resolved and the acceptance of Burma into the organization may not be far away. The case of Vietnam and the other states of Indochina poses special problems. The end of the Vietnam war has left Hanoi with an accumulated arsenal of weapons. This was further increased following the 1979 Sino-Vietnamese war. Since then, there has been a slowdown in the arms buildup in Indochina. Nevertheless, Vietnam remains the most powerful military force in Southeast Asia and is perceived by the other states of the area as a continuing threat. The problem of integrating the communist systems of Indochina into the ASEAN system will continue to pose another complicated problem. But, meanwhile, this need not prevent the promotion of trade between Vietnam and the ASEAN group of nations so as to ease tensions within Southeast Asia.

The wars of attrition in the Persian Gulf between Iraq and Iran, and in the Horn of Africa between Ethiopia and Somalia, are likely to burn out over the next year or two as the resources of the antagonists are steadily exhausted. Even in those subregions the conflicts have not prevented the conduct of limited trade by these countries both with neighboring states and with states in other subregions of the Indian Ocean. Furthermore, with the overthrow of Idi Amin of Uganda, conditions are more conducive at present for the former EAC members to plan new strategies of economic cooperation and integration in the future.

Economic and political developments in the Indian Ocean have always carried global implications because, after all, the littoral and hinterland states constitute a large proportion of the Third World. They represent a multiplicity of regional strategic interests with a variety of internal economic problems. But if a strategy of peace through economic interdependence could be generated and sustained until the turn of the century, the economic condition of the region would be transformed and, with it, a measure of stability contributed to global politics in general.

4. A Challenge to Superpower Global Condominium: Middle Powers and Militarization in the Indian Ocean Region ✎ Ashok Kapur

A critic of Indian Ocean studies has questioned the validity and utility of treating the ocean area as a coherent region. He asks why such studies cannot be dealt with in a conventional framework and quite properly suggests that "coherent historical, geopolitical, economic, and conceptual justification" is needed to rationalize Indian Ocean studies.[1]

This chapter addresses this concern not by arguing that the diverse people, societies, and political regimes in Africa, the Middle East, and South and Southeast Asia constitute a region, either in the sense that there is a significant level of regional cooperation between or among them, or that regional institutions or organizations are taking shape. There is some evidence in favor of both propositions but clearly regional cohesion is difficult to achieve when the dominant features of the Indian Ocean littoral and hinterland states are diversity, regime instability, conflict-involvement, and ethnic unrest. Yet there is some utility and value in recognizing the existence of an Indian Ocean region. It is to be found in the realization that the leaders of the major regional powers of the area pursue policies having a significant impact on global strategic thinking; and, second, that these policies also have an impact on regional power politics, with implications for the distribution of power in the world beyond the central place of superpower competition, namely Europe.

The principal focuses of international military relations today are to be found in the northern strategic cores: North America, the North Atlantic, Europe, the Soviet Union, China, and northeast Asia. These areas constitute part of the central military balance, with military relations in the rest of the world being largely peripheral. My hypothesis is that the Indian Ocean region (or its various subregions) is emerging as the principal secondary zone of international military relations and conflict, and that it is becoming increasingly important in shaping the global power structure.

This contention rests on the fact that several Indian Ocean littoral and hinterland states, particularly the major regional/middle powers, such as India, Egypt, Israel, and South Africa play roles as strategic buffers of the "stronger" powers; they act as "trimmers" (see discussion below) playing the stronger powers against one another.[2] At the same time they are continually increasing their internal might and economic weight and are generally able to escape forcible superpower military intervention and diplomatic isolation. These buffers represent the frontiers of the superpowers' influence and pose barriers to the globalization of superpower condominium.

In their quest for economic and military development and in their international behavior, these buffer states/middle powers resist policies that would cause their own disarmament, neutralization, or non-nuclearization, while simultaneously advocating reduced armament and nuclearization for the stronger northern powers. The regional managers of secondary international conflict zones seek to formulate attitudes and policies that combine strategy and culture and they seek a balance among strategy, culture, and material means that can cope with domestic, regional, and wider international environments.[3] This objective does not require that the secondary zone buffer powers catch up militarily and economically with the superpowers but only that they have enough capabilities to safeguard their vital interests.

The absence of formally agreed and publicly acknowledged policy coordination among the security managers of regional power politics does not mean that their individual and collective actions are without impact on the stronger powers of the northern world. Indeed, to the extent the conflict/buffer zone actors are able to engage the stronger powers, and to do so from positions of increasing military strength, they will be able increasingly to frustrate the superpowers' policy objectives and decision-making establishments and to prevent the worldwide acceptance of superpower norms. If the indigenous actors can develop new concepts of regional power and middle power roles that challenge the superpowers' definitions of regional and international security, then new patterns of international relations with global ramifications may well emerge from the Indian Ocean region during the remainder of this century.

The first section of this chapter examines the distinction between great and middle powers and the implications that flow from it. The concept of a buffer zone is then briefly discussed, with special reference to the Indian Ocean region as an international buffer zone, with the unique features of that region being noted to emphasize its conceptual unity. The distinctive Indian Ocean setting points to the importance of buffer states and of middle powers as strategic catalysts. Finally, the meaning and significance of militarization of the Indian Ocean world will be assessed in terms of the unique features of that area.

Middle Powers and Great Powers

Middle powers are active participants in regional and international life, frequently practicing buffer zone diplomacy in their respective conflict zones. Their conduct has international and regional impact, even though the crises in the secondary conflict zones may be described as "low"- or "middle"-level crises (for example, the 1971 South Asia crisis or the 1973 Middle East crisis) compared with those in the northern strategic core (for example, the Cuban missile crisis). Such low- or middle-level crises nevertheless involve the power and prestige of the superpowers and the major powers, and their outcomes have both immediate and long-term consequences.

The concepts of "middle power" and "strategic buffer" are usually neglected in post-1945 international relations studies, particularly by American scholars. Before applying these concepts to the Indian Ocean world, it will be helpful to define them. Martin Wight, one of the few scholars to take the concept of middle power seriously, is worth quoting at some length. According to Wight:

> Two kinds of minor power achieve an eminence which distinguishes them from the common run: regional great powers, and middle powers. Political pressures do not operate uniformly throughout the states-system, and in certain regions which are culturally united but politically divided, a subordinate international society comes into being, with a states-system reproducing in miniature the features of the general states-system. . . . In such sub-systems . . . there will be some states with general interests relative to the limited region and a capacity to act alone, which gives them the appearance of local great powers. Egypt, Iraq and perhaps Saudi Arabia have been great powers in the Arab world. . . . Similarly, South Africa may be regarded as a great power relative to Black Africa. Such regional great powers will probably be candidates, in the states-system at large, for the rank of middle power.
>
> With more precision, it might be argued that a middle power is a power with such military strength, resources and

strategic position that in peacetime the great powers bid for its support, and in wartime, while it has no hope of winning a war against a great power, it can hope to inflict costs on a great power out of proportion to what the great power can hope to gain by attacking it.

There is usually a greater gulf between great powers and minor powers (middle powers included) than there is between middle powers and other minor powers. Minor powers (middle powers included) have the means of defending only limited interests. . . . They have territorial or maritime disputes with their neighbours . . . or their livelihood depends on fisheries . . . or they have to sell their raw materials. . . . But they cannot unify continents, or rule the high seas, or control the international market.[4]

My usage of the term "middle power" is adapted from Wight's treatment of the subject. To avoid confusion, it is necessary to explain that Wight's hierarchy of power in descending order includes dominant power, world power, great power, and minor power, with middle powers and regional great powers in the minor power category. In the world today, according to Wight's criteria, there is neither a dominant power nor a world power. Furthermore, not a single great power actually measures up to Wight's standards or, at least, their qualifications are debatable. According to Wight, great powers have a tendency to "club together as a kind of directorate and impose their will on the states-system. They usually justify their actions as enforcing peace and security."[5] Furthermore, great powers tend to claim that they are more restrained and responsible than minor powers but the test of a great power is the ability to wage successful war against another great power. Great power status is won or lost by violence. In 1919, great powers asserted at the Paris Peace Conference that they were the "great responsibles" because they had wider interests and greater resources than the minor powers and, hence, a duty to pacify the world. The right of veto later accorded to various states in the League of Nations and subsequently in the United Nations Security Council was taken as a sign of great power status.[6]

The various respects in which the superpowers fall short of Wight's criteria do not mean that the United States and the Soviet Union are no longer great powers. Rather, because of the superpowers' lack of "clubbiness," their irresponsibility, their self-preserving reluctance in the nuclear age to test each other militarily except by proxy warfare, and the lack of efficacy of their vetoes in determining the outcome of real-world dilemmas, the contemporary essence of great power status must reside in the existence of wide interests and great resources for influencing the states-system as a whole. However, even those residual qualifications appear to be deteriorating. While wide interests remain, the power to promote such interests in various parts of the world has arguably decreased in recent years.

The qualifications of middle powers, on the other hand, if measured in terms of their impact on the states-system, are contemporaneously being upgraded. It can be argued that the emergence of middle powers in the post-1945 world is not a consequence of the weakening of the great powers but the result of several other factors: the middle powers have been developing attitudes and policies since 1945 that are intended to give their concerns a place on the international agenda. Their diplomatic, economic, and military strategies are intended not only to increase their intrinsic capabilities (their "internal weight") but also to increase their weight in the international system. Their strategies are responsive to their definitions of their respective cultures. The middle powers are engaging the great powers (the United States, the Soviet Union, and others) under adverse conditions: outside of existing alliance structures, from a position of material weakness, while stressing the norm of economic and military development, and by rejecting the United States and the Soviet Union as role models while using them as suppliers of aid.

"Middle-powerism" originated in the mid-1940s and was manifest in the policies of states at the San Francisco Conference in 1945, precisely when the great power status of the United States and the Soviet Union was not in dispute, indeed, when the world was described as bipolar and the two powers were indisputably the "superpowers" (see second column, table 4-1). The great power category was then a hardened category and, moreover, the atomic bomb had just nuclearized military strategy and frozen the international military structure. The middle power outlook, as an attitude and as a policy, was, and remains, significant as a reaction to the world views of the two superpowers. The reaction was in part to adopt the policy instruments of the two great powers by accepting industrialism, statism, and militarization as the elements of power. But at the same time the notion that these two great powers in any way represented the wider interests of the world community or the states-system was rejected. This creative adaptation was meant simultaneously to engage and to challenge the power structure of the two international giants. In sum, the effect of the rise of middle powers was to avoid the hierarchical, integrative, and dependency implications of a world of military alliances. Middle powers reject the spurious claims

Table 4-1 Three States-Systems: Motivations, Institutions, and Consequences

European states-system	Bipolar system	Third World
Strategic motivations of great powers	**Strategic motivations of superpowers**	**Strategic motivations of weak states/weaker powers**
1. expand national power	1. items 1, 2, and 3 in column 1	1. develop national economic and military weight
2. create and maintain a balance of power	2. freeze existing distribution of world power relations; keep international power divided	2. avoid dependent alignment/seek nonaligned status
3. improve methods of self-help	3. achieve alliance cohesion	3. challenge the international position of both superpowers; question their right to formulate international regimes; use them as aid-givers
weak states/lesser powers	4. preserve international position of the superpowers	4. challenge the utility of military alliances and the norm of military security in the definition of international and regional security
1. self-defense	5. preserve superpowers' military balance	5. seek the development of weak powers' status as trimmers in the secondary zones of international conflict; avoid satellite and neutral status
2. survival	6. freeze strategic conflict that threatens superpowers' balance	6. seek to enforce rejection of superpower-organized regional crisis management
3. improve methods of self-help	7. establish buffers where superpowers' conflict can be "played out"	7. use military force and propaganda to develop and
Institutions	8. develop conventions of superpower-organized crisis management	
1. war	9. ensure that arms racing is a competitive, not a distributive activity	
2. alliances	10. develop images of international enemies that help create a clear public identification with elite goals, that generate domestic social support for elite policies	
3. diplomacy		
4. trade	**Institutions**	
5. "great-powerism"	1. two superpowers preferable to several great powers to organize/stabilize world power relations	
6. belief in balance of power	2. nuclearized military strategy to freeze strategic conflict	
7. arms racing as mobilization toward war	3. mistrust and antagonistic political values as the basis of superpowers' propaganda, threatening posture, and arms racing	
8. acquisition of overseas empires for strategic, economic, and cultural reasons	4. alliances to reinforce bipolarity	
9. belief in international		

law and European culture in organizing world power relations
10. use of buffers for strategic reasons
11. avoidance of world empire, world federation, or a central international political authority

Consequences
1. States-system sought peaceful exchange through diplomacy and trade but recognized alliances and war as the ultimate methods to settle political disputes. Wars had distributive
2. Wars had distributive consequences (e.g., wars of gain/colonial conquest) or had doctrinal aims (e.g., holy/just wars).
3. There was some sort of cultural unity in the European states-system.
4. A distinction existed between traditional diplomacy defined as peaceful exchange by negotiation and compromise, and diplomacy as communi-

5. decolonialism verbally supported as ties with the Third World help reinforce bipolarity
6. informal empires preferable to formal colonial empires (too costly in economic and political terms). Informal empires provide access and control over decision making regarding the mobilization of resources without the cost of maintaining physical control over foreign territories.
7. coercive diplomacy replacing traditional peacetime diplomacy
8. peaceful exchange/international trade conducted under rules and norms of Western, particularly U.S., industrial powers. International financial institutions promote aims of Western capitalism (e.g., the World Bank).
9. international law and cultural unity less important than power in organizing international relations
10. arms racing to promote war preparation and arms trade, not war; war fighting is to be avoided because it would destroy the international system physically

Consequences
1. There is rank concordance between various indicators of power.
2. The fear of imminent nuclear conflict is heightened. Fear cements alliance ties and polarizes international relations.
3. Mistrust reinforces arms racing and arms racing reinforces mistrust.
4. To the extent that commitment to bipolarity is irrevocable, it is anti–Third World nationalism, and thus the superpowers and Third World states are on a collision path strategically.

establish regional order, institutions, and consensus so as to minimize the involvement of extraregional powers.
8. use force to unfreeze regional social and strategic conflict
9. mobilize Third World cultures in support of strategic objectives and to strengthen the social base of diplomatic-military policy
10. try to achieve a balance among culture, material means, and strategy in relation to the international environment

Institutions
1. political diplomacy, viz., opposition to the cold war, the danger of nuclear war, the need for global and particularly superpower disarmament, the need to democratize international security debates
2. economic diplomacy, viz., quest for new international economic order, North-South dialogue to achieve equitable distribution of

Table 4-1   Continued

European states-system	Bipolar system	Third World
cation of propaganda and threat in a world of nonnegotiable values. 5. There was no psychological limit against escalation of conventional wars.	5. The replacement of formal empires with informal ones means that the vertical pattern of management and exploitation of the South/Third World/Indian Ocean countries is retained. Unequal exchange remains the norm, as in European approach to international relations in the colonial context. 6. The bipolar world is anticulture and anti-intuition inasmuch as big organization and expertise (technocracy) are regarded as the basic sources of management and direction of world affairs.	global resources, and use of resources diplomacy 3. militarization of Third World countries, particularly of the middle powers in the Indian Ocean area 4. nuclearization of Third World countries, particularly of the middle powers in the Indian Ocean area Consequences 1. The international position of the superpowers is under attack. 2. The internal weight of Indian Ocean middle powers is gradually growing, and these powers are able to escape forcible intervention and diplomatic isolation in crisis situations. 3. The cultural basis of Third World military strategies is being defined, reflecting a previously latent tendency in Indian Ocean power politics.

of the United States and the Soviet Union that their intention is to pacify and to stabilize world relationships. Instead, middle powers prefer a world of horizontal relationships among semiequals.

Middle powers benefit by the existence of buffers. The relationship between them may be one of two kinds. First, the middle power itself may be the buffer zone, or a part of a larger buffer zone in the politics of the great/superpowers. Alternatively, the middle power may be able to regulate its relationship with the greater powers while seeking its own buffers in neighboring countries. In the latter case, the middle power successfully works the system as a trimmer. Having enhanced its intrinsic capabilities in the international system, it is able to create its own outside buffers to insulate itself from external forces. Both dimensions of the middle power–buffer zone relationship are implicit in this essay.

The Concept of a Buffer Zone

Wight argues that

> a buffer state is a weak power between two or more stronger ones, maintained or even created with the purpose of reducing conflict between them. A *buffer zone* is a region occupied by one or more weaker powers between two or more stronger powers; it is sometimes described as a "power vacuum." Each stronger power will generally have a vital interest in preventing the other from controlling the buffer zone, and will pursue this interest in one of two ways, according to its strength. It will seek either to maintain the buffer zone as neutral and independent, or to establish its own control, which may lead in the long run to its annexing the buffer zone and converting it into a frontier province. Buffer states may therefore be roughly divided into trimmers, neutrals and satellites. Trimmers are states whose policy is prudently to play off their mighty neighbours against one another. . . . Neutrals are states without an active foreign policy at all; their hope is to lie low and escape notice. Satellites are states whose foreign policy is controlled by another power.[7]

Buffers can be studied from three angles. First, from the perspective of a great power that seeks and maintains buffers; second, from the perspective of a weak power (trimmer) that plays off mighty neighbors against one another; and third, from the perspective of a weaker power in circumstances where the characteristics of a greater power, and of particular great powers, are changing or are in dispute. Wight studies the buffer state in the first and second senses. The intention here is to try to shift the discussion to the third perspective, the middle power perspective, but first let us briefly consider Wight's discussion of the subject.

From the point of view of a great power, the creation and maintenance of buffers serve several purposes: to prevent the other great power from controlling a buffer zone, that is, to prevent the enemy from transforming a buffer into a satellite; to increase territory and influence, if possible and desirable, by making a buffer into one's own satellite; and to reduce conflict between itself and other great powers. Here great power conflict is diverted to buffer areas, extending great power conflict in other regions and on other issues. In this sense, great power military, political, and commercial/economic diplomacy in buffer areas may require some sort of arms control. Within a buffer area the great powers achieve coexistence between themselves; their collective policies (as practiced, not merely as declared) help to reduce conflict in the international system. Great power buffer diplomacy is important not only for what it reveals about their attitudes, interests, and policies with regard to the buffer area itself, but also for what it reveals of their attitudes, interests, and policies internationally in relation to each other. From the point of view of the great power, the "weak power" is essentially a weak state, an arena rather than a factor that could conceivably alter the distribution of power and the pattern of relationships in a particular region. If a buffer is essentially a plaything of the great powers, it is a weak state, not a weaker power.

Whereas the first perspective from which buffers may be studied is in terms of a great power/weak state relationship, the second one can be characterized as that of a great power/weak power relationship. Wight himself does not make the distinction between the first and the second perspectives. Furthermore, although he distinguishes among buffer states as satellites, neutrals, and trimmers, he does not explain that it is only in the sense of a trimmer that a buffer can call itself a weak power. In the context of a great power/weak power relationship—where the great powers have a vested interest in creating and maintaining a buffer—the weak power succeeds as a trimmer to the extent that it finds for itself a limited area of negotiability with one or the other great power. There is limited maneuverability and limited negotiability in great power/weak power relations and they do not result in a redistribution of power or strength in the buffer area. Furthermore, a weak power's internal military and economic weight does not grow.

A weak power seeking trimmer status succeeds because at least two great powers want this weak state to be a satellite, to be neutral, or to be a trimmer. Its role as a trimmer in a great power/weak power relationship will persist while the great powers continue their involvement. A trimmer (as defined by Wight) does not induce great power involvement but rather benefits from it. In a great power/weak power context, a trimmer enjoys limited benefit from great power competition but it does not enjoy a veto over the framework of great power relationships in the buffer area.

As regards the existence of trimmers and buffer zones in the Indian Ocean region, several important observations need to be made. First, the character and influence of "greater" power and of particular great powers—some call them superpowers—are changing or are in dispute. Power (as capabilities) is undoubtedly unevenly divided, hence the reference to greater power in the hands of one "superpower" today. But power is not necessarily strength. Second, present-day trimmers are not simply beneficiaries of limited opportunities and limited influence in circumstances where the great powers enjoy predominant influence, or where those powers have sought to create and to maintain buffer zones, or where their competition is the predominant element in the power relations in a buffer zone. Trimmers today induce great powers' involvement even when the great powers are not inclined to seek involvement in a particular zone of conflict. Third, the framework of power relationships in a buffer area depends not only on great powers' attitudes, interests, and policies, but also on the attitudes, interests, and policies of the trimmers. The middle powers in the Indian Ocean region induce great power involvement and, furthermore, manipulate the development of the framework of regional power relations in a manner that promotes the internal weight and the policy concerns of the middle powers themselves while increasing the costs to the great powers of their involvement. Damned if you do intervene, damned if you don't, is the consequence of middle powers' manipulation of the great powers. Hence, Indian Ocean trimmers not only benefit from great power involvement in military, economic, and political diplomacy of buffer zones, but the trimmers also retain something of the initiative and a veto over the nature, scope, and effectiveness of regional crisis and noncrisis diplomacy.

The Distinctiveness of the Indian Ocean Region

What kinds of attitudes and policies distinguish the Indian Ocean region as a secondary zone of international conflict, as a buffer area in which certain powers have roles as trimmers? Put another way, why cannot the Indian Ocean be studied in conventional Western terms or in the context of modern industrialism, statism, and the militarization of political and economic life?

Table 4-1 outlines the general motivations, institutions, and consequences of three different systems of states and power politics. A movement from the first to the second type of system is evident by comparing the world before and after 1945. In the contemporary international system a strategic and cultural encounter is currently in progress between the second and the third type of system. In the Indian Ocean region this encounter is manifest in two broad movements that, taken together, lend distinctiveness to the region in contemporary international politics. First, historically and culturally, most Indian Ocean states were victims of colonialism, suffering racial and cultural humiliation as well as an identity crisis. The colonial period lasted from the seventeenth century through the twentieth century and created a memory of an ugly past that still permeates elite and popular thinking in Third World countries. To the extent that European colonialism was in part a product of European culture and its mission to "civilize" the natives (the other motives were economic and strategic), the colonial experience continues to evoke counterracism and a countercultural response to Western norms. For instance, militant Islam in recent decades may be studied as a political, military, and cultural reaction to Western imperalism of recent centuries.[8]

During the past three hundred years the encounter between West and East (and South) matched superior Western military organization, firepower, and information against Eastern faith in its cultural superiority, its traditional political authority, and its self-sufficiency. In this encounter, the West's firepower and political cunning won. The contest occurred in different circumstances in China, India, Africa, and in other parts of the Indian Ocean region. To the extent that past experiences shape present thinking, the lesson in Third World thinking is that the encounter is a continuing one; it did not end with the dismantling of European empires and the emergence of new states. Its impact continues in the postindependence, decolonization process. For Third World elites, the lessons are basically of two kinds: first, if the Third World is to successfully engage Westerners (including the Soviet Union) in this continuing encounter, the material basis of Third World power must be developed, hence the emphasis on economic and military development as the twin pillars of security; and, second, to the extent that local rivals and local power struggles (e.g., in India from the 1600s to the middle of this century) facilitated European intervention, the social/cultural/domestic base of power and policy must also be developed to limit the opportunities for external interference. So, even though the

Third World/Indian Ocean states are obviously copying some of the forms of Western statism, industrialism, and military development, the policy objectives and the underlying political and cultural values are different, indeed hostile, to those of the first (capitalist) and the second (socialist) worlds.

Strategically, the Indian Ocean countries are responding to—that is, challenging and engaging—the northern powers. The responses appear in situations of crisis and noncrisis. This emerging pattern of interactions has led an American political geographer, Saul Cohen, to anticipate the growing geostrategic significance of the Indian Ocean world.[9] Using the notions of "place" (location of population, economic cores, etc.) and "movement" (trade orientation, ideological/cultural bonds, etc.), he perceives the world to be divided into two geostrategic regions that possess "globe-influencing characteristics": "the Trade-Dependent Maritime World" and "the Eurasian Continental World." Cohen sees the Indian Ocean area as a potential third geostrategic region; he believes that if "the European foothold in Central and South Africa should be lost, then the entire eastern half of the continent might gravitate geostrategically to South Asia."[10] On present evidence this is a development unlikely to take place soon. South Africa is likely to remain intact, at least during the 1980s, both because of Pretoria's determination and because the black African states have not yet achieved consensus about how to influence the future of the white regime. In this connection, if the Arab resort to war against Israel since the late 1940s provides a lesson for African elites, it is that even with all the financing in the world, the military option cannot buy a change in the regional power equation as long as the Arab (black) regimes suffer from internal regime instability and inter-Arab (black) divisiveness. In the same way, ambitious talk that lacks a well-planned, long-term strategy will not result in a change in the regional power equation. If the African states are waiting for future Sowetos to destroy the confidence and the ability of the white regime, they may well be disappointed. Pretoria's slow quest for internal labor and constitutional reform is probably calculated to create a black middle class in South Africa that will "listen to reason" and will be content with slow accommodation and change rather than resorting to revolutionary upheaval. Furthermore, Pretoria's program to develop a southern African economic community may slowly create economic incentives against revolution by the Frontline States (Angola, Botswana, Mozambique, Tanzania, Zambia, and Zimbabwe). Finally, there is no sign that Western economic, political, and cultural connections with South Africa are disintegrating. Accordingly, South Africa is likely to emerge as a power unit in its own right; indeed, it is arguable that it already is a power unit inasmuch as the South African "pariah" can tell Washington, "this much and no more."

America's inability to dictate terms to Pretoria is symptomatic of the emergence of the third states-system portrayed in table 1. This state of affairs is mirrored throughout the Indian Ocean region where the great powers are increasingly unable to enforce their preferred policies (for example, the Non-Proliferation Treaty/International Atomic Energy Agency regime, the Law of the Sea) on their own terms. When the key regional states or trend setters in the Indian Ocean are able to act on their own (e.g., regional crisis diplomacy by India in 1971; Egypt's war initiative in 1973; Israel's bombing of the Iraqi nuclear reactor in 1981 and its invasion of Lebanon in 1982) despite the opposition of the great powers, or the "superpowers," the need is clear to study middle power–great power/superpower interactions, and to study the upward flow of influence from the Indian Ocean periphery to the international power center. This new pattern of influence is generally expressed by a number of activities: resources diplomacy, militarization, and nuclearization, as well as multilateral diplomacy, such as nonaligned and Islamic conferences, meant to evoke debate and consensus development at the international and regional levels.

A distinction should be made at this point concerning the characteristics of the Indian Ocean countries in contrast to the status of South America and Latin America in the international system. The Indian Ocean world, unlike most of the southern Americas (with the exception of Cuba and small parts of Central America), coexists not only with American power but also with Soviet power; the Indian Ocean countries have been subjected since the mid-1950s to the diplomatic and economic influence and presence of the Soviet Union and to its outward military pressure. In contrast, the south Americas have been U.S. backyards for over one hundred years; Moscow has respected the Western hemisphere as a U.S. sphere of influence.[11] Apart from grain imports from Argentina and a few fishing agreements (which evoke negative comments from the host countries in South America as in Africa), and apart from the relationship with Cuba, which is costly economically, the Soviet Union is not an active participant in Western hemispheric relations. In the Indian Ocean by contrast, the Soviet Union is a trader, military arms supplier, diplomatic supporter, troublemaker, and strategic threat, at least to some countries as the situation in Afghanistan makes clear. The duality of Soviet involvement in the Indian Ocean—as a partner to local regimes and as a threat to regional life—underlines the vitality and the complexity of middle power–superpower interactions in this incipient third geostrategic region of the international system.

Overall, the extension of superpower competition into the Indian Ocean world, particularly since the mid-1970s, provides the challenges and the opportunities for the Indian Ocean middle powers to play trimmer roles: to play the superpowers against each other; to improve the internal economic and military weight of the middle powers; and to gradually transform the region (or subregions) into semiautonomous units with some inherent strategic unity and a power structure. This appears to be the pattern of development in South Asia, the Middle East, and southern Africa.

"Third-Worldism" is being promoted by the Indian Ocean states in contrast to superpowerism. In this regard, Horowitz refers to the "essential integrity and autonomy of the Third World."[12] This point deserves careful study because it is easy to regard post-1945 political and military relationships between Third World/Indian Ocean states and the superpowers in the framework of only two power blocs, the bipolar model of table 1 above. The overt interstate relationships between Third World/Indian Ocean states and the United States and the Soviet Union obscures the deep, non-negotiable hostility between the world views of the two superpowers and the Third World. America and the Soviet Union use different language but agree that international relations are essentially a struggle between two opposing systems. Much as Moscow tries to portray itself as a guardian of the Third World, it cannot hide the fact that Soviet support for nonalignment and peaceful coexistence makes no sense to Soviet authorities except in the context of the Third World as an ally in the struggle against imperialism, meaning the West. The Third World/Indian Ocean states accept this neither as a practical strategy nor as the intellectual and moral basis of their foreign policy and military strategy.

To optimize their role as trimmers—to facilitate emergence of the new pattern of influence characteristic of the third state system in the table—and to confront the dangers inherent in their own region, Indian Ocean states have in recent years undertaken steady programs of militarization. We shall conclude our consideration of the Indian Ocean region as a geostrategic buffer area resisting great power condominium by examining that principal instrument of resistance.

The Meaning and Significance of Militarization in the Indian Ocean Context

Militarization in the Indian Ocean may be studied from several angles. The growing militarism of states in the area is measured by signs of internal repressiveness of regimes in South Asia, the Middle East, and

Africa; the growth in the size and quality of the region's military forces that are used externally in local and regional conflicts; the shift in the incidence of conflict from the North to the South (the world beyond the North Atlantic Treaty Organization and the Warsaw Treaty Organization areas)—all these are indicators of militarization.[13] The use of military force by the regional great powers or middle powers in a manner calculated to develop a viable power structure in their respective regions is yet another sign of militarization. In this instance, the use of force is creative. It is intended to shape a regional order. The use of force is deplorable in any circumstance, and the massacre of civilians deserves particular condemnation, but the use of force is necessary to shift conflict relationships from a condition of anarchy to one of organized conflict. The latter is preferable because it yields distinct enemies who are capable of negotiating and delivering on promises. The existence of enmities is not the essential problem in this scheme of things. Rather, strong enemies are needed as potential negotiators and partners in hostile pairs. Enemies are essential actors, for instance, Pakistan in Indian thinking, the Arabs in Israeli thinking, and the black African states in South African thinking. The norm is that organized conflict is to be preferred to unorganized killing which does not reflect a long-term strategy or offer prospects for informal arms control and some sort of conflict resolution and reduction. The ability to shape regional power structures, the creative use of military force to unfreeze frozen social and strategic conflict, the capability of escaping forcible intervention by the superpowers, and the ability to shape the strategic agenda, its timing, and the nature of the participants—these are the important attributes of middle-powerism in the Indian Ocean world.

In the northwest sector of the region, increased Arab wealth has helped remilitarization for a variety of purposes: internal policing of suspected populations, management of hostile neighbors, increasing the costs of extraregional intervention and thereby increasing the uncertainty in Washington's and Moscow's decision-making processes, and the achievement of tactical surprise, using modern arms as Sadat did in 1973. The remilitarization is a consequence of mobilized wealth, not vice versa.

Fear of enemies remains relevant in the Third World/Indian Ocean countries as a cause of militarization and regional wars. The threat of war and the use of limited war remain efficacious methods to introduce fear of punishment into the hearts of stubborn and fiery enemies. The use of controlled force, the fear of military punishment and of preemptive strike, and the fear of latent nuclearization are methods to induce caution between enemies. The fear of punishment induces moderation in the Idi Amins, the Syrian Assads, and the Iraqi Hussains, and even in the faceless generals in Washington and Moscow.

There is both militarism and militarization in the Indian Ocean world. This is accented by the shift in the incidence of military conflict to the Third World. To make sense of the data concerning the relentless growth of the Third World's military expenditures,[14] the growth in the size and quality of Third World military forces, and the growth in the incidence of regional conflict,[15] an attempt should be made to distinguish between different functions of the growth of militarization in the Indian Ocean area. First, militarization helps internal policing by fostering domestic social control until domestic power structures are stabilized and a desirable level of nation building can occur. Second, because of the fear of hostile neighbors—some of whom are proxies and clients of foreign powers—militarization helps fight and win local and regional wars; it provides instruments of self-defense. Third, militarization enables the middle powers (e.g., Egypt, India, Israel, and South Africa) to manage the danger of direct or indirect superpower or extraregional military intervention that might disadvantage the middle powers' regional and international position. Here the middle power tries to redistribute regional power and to restructure the power relationships between the region and extraregional states. Fourth, by the use of controlled and limited force and military threats, militarization enables the middle powers to establish regional power structures that force "historical enemies" to rethink their strategies for the future. Here the middle power alters the power relationships within the region. The logic is that arms control must of necessity be preceded by a good fight engineered by a regionally satisfied (but probably internationally dissatisfied) middle power vis-à-vis a regionally dissatisfied state within the same region. Fights provide test cases, and test cases are required to establish patterns of behavior in crises, to suggest precedents, and to formulate limits of acceptable interstate behavior. Only when a regionally dissatisfied state recognizes the desirability and the costs of inconclusive military encounters can a basis for a meaningful dialogue emerge, that is, dead ends must be reached militarily before strategic rethinking occurs. From this perspective, regional arms racing, local crises, and wars are functional and a step toward the peace process.

Given a world of historical rivalries in the Indian Ocean, arms control and crisis management under superpower auspices is a prescription to freeze—or to extend—existing social and strategic conflicts. That helps the northern industrial strategy players but it does not bring peace (defined as harmony) to the Third World. In fact, it is a prescription for continued anarchy in the Indian Ocean world. Whatever the precise regional outcome in the 1980s may be, the constructive use by middle powers of militarization and even nuclearization to induce rethinking and caution among enemies can no longer be ignored as a subject of study.[16]

5. Structure and Strategy in Indian Ocean Naval Developments: Taking Stock ☎ Ken Booth and William L. Dowdy

Students of international politics are familiar with the phenomenon of learning about the geology of an area after the volcano has erupted. Crises regularly occur in faraway places about which little is known; by the time they do occur, it is too late for us to become experts. Consequently, because of the global diffusion of military power, the Western powers should have a growing interest in trying to understand strategic developments in all parts of the world. This need was brought home rather forcefully—and at great cost—to the British at the beginning of 1982, when Argentina invaded the Falkland Islands. Up to that point few analysts in Britain, or in the West in general, had shown any interest in the characteristics of Argentinian air or naval forces. Virtually overnight, those who expressed any knowledge of the subject were at a premium. Instant experts proliferated. This war was an uncomfortable warning that no part of the globe is now so remote or so militarily primitive that the major powers can afford to ignore the local trends and prospects. One day the volcano may splutter, or even erupt, in any region.

The Indian Ocean Region: An "Insecurity Community"

Of all the regions within the Third World, the Indian Ocean needs the least justification for detailed strategic analysis for, as other chapters in this book testify, the Indian Ocean region is a strategic arena of considerable importance and complexity. While economic development in the region as a whole remains ponderous, this is not the case when it comes to the development of military potential, whether measured in terms of the amount of money spent, the quantity and quality of arms transferred, or the numbers of men in uniform. The Middle East obviously remains the sector of this strategic arena with the greatest expansion of military potential but no subregion is without some degree of arms modernization or militarization in one form or other. Given the domestic and international sources of instability that exist throughout most of the Indian Ocean region, and the rather traditional attitudes toward the utility of force that generally still prevail, the process of military modernization could obviously have serious consequences in the event of war. Meanwhile, in peacetime, the growing market for arms gives the industrial powers capable of supplying them an opportunity for influence and profit, but it also entails the risk of being dragged into local quarrels.

Anyone who examines the Indian Ocean region as a strategic arena will be struck by the extent to which security problems exist in so many aspects of life; as a result, the region might be dubbed a kaleidoscope of crisis, and not merely an "arc." Within the region there is military, political, economic, religious, and racial insecurity. Threats are felt by individuals in some states as well as by groups—religious, national, and ethnic. At the international level insecurities are felt between some states and between some groups of states and even the extraregional superpowers perceive themselves under challenge. Given this manifold interaction of security problems and multilayered threats—none of which seems likely to go away in the foreseeable future—the strategic arena of the Indian Ocean can perhaps best be conceived not so much as a region in the conventional geographical sense but as what might be termed, in international politics, an "insecurity community."

To date, most of the attention in Indian Ocean naval affairs has been focused on the superpowers and their interactions. In contrast, the aim of this chapter is to take stock of the much less familiar naval developments of the indigenous states.[1] This will be accomplished by applying Samuel Huntington's distinction between the *strategic* and *structural* worlds of military policy.[2] According to this distinction, decisions made in the category or currency of international politics may be described as strategic in character. They are of two types: "program decisions" concerning the strength, composition, and readiness of forces, and the number, type, and rate of development of their weapons; and "use decisions" concerning the deployment, commitment, and employment of military force, as manifested in alliances, war plans, declarations of war, force movements, and so on. In short, "strategy concerns the units and use of force." Structural decisions, in Huntington's formulation, are made in the currency of domestic politics. They deal with the procurement, allocation, and organization of the men, money, and material that go into the strategic units and uses of force.

On first sight it might seem unwise to attempt an overview encompassing countries as different in size and development as South Yemen and Australia, and India and Mozambique. However, valid generalizations are possible in the field of naval developments since in all the countries under consideration problems and constraints are the dominating themes of any examination of their trends and prospects. Indeed, a number of the generalizations that will be made are also valid for some of the larger and more capable navies of richer countries, as well as for Third World navies in Latin America, West Africa, and the Far East. The problem of technological modernization, the constraints posed by escalating costs, and the uncertainties facing doctrinal evolution are issues that dominate the in-trays of all navies in the late twentieth century.

Structural Context of Naval Policy

Defense policy, like charity, begins at home, and so it is appropriate to begin with an examination of structural trends, namely those developments made in the context of domestic politics.[3]

Modernization

The most obvious trend in the naval procurement policies of Indian Ocean states is the steady progress in modernization that has been taking place. Most, if not all, countries in the region have some new naval asset that they have just bought, are buying, or are planning to buy.

In many cases the new warships are additions to, rather than replacements of, existing warships. This in itself is not a sign of a region-wide arms race, since in all cases there is no surplus of capability over requirements. Instead, the navies of the region are generally struggling to meet some fairly basic needs. States within the region are not engaged in intense and direct competitions in naval arms procurement with others as a result of a conviction that national security and diplomatic strength can only be ensured by striving to get ahead, or keep ahead, in warship acquisition. An increase in armaments of itself is not proof of an arms race, even when the increase involves a number of countries in the same region. The term "race" can only properly be applied if there is clear evidence of what Robert McNamara called the "action-reaction phenomenon." This has not so far been the case in the Indian Ocean region. The local navies have been attempting to meet minimal requirements rather than achieve supremacy over some neighboring naval adversary. What is happening, therefore, can best be described as an arms buildup rather than a race as such. This distinction is important, among other reasons, because of the danger of self-fulfilling analyses in strategic affairs. One sure way of bringing about an arms race is to spread the conviction that such a race is already under way.

In addition to navies modernizing their inventories to meet new requirements, the replacement of existing warships has become an urgent matter for some countries. This is either to replace the larger ships that are the legacies of the colonial era or to replace some of the warships acquired as components of the off-the-shelf mininavies of the 1960s. Examples of the former include the need for the replacement of the forty-year-old Indian aircraft carrier, the *Vikrant*,[4] or the need to replace Pakistan's aging (formerly British) destroyers, which were laid down in World War II.[5] The major examples of obsolete mininavy vessels are Indonesia's (former Soviet) fast attack craft (FAC), the Komars and P6s. Most of these were transferred to Indonesia during 1961–63, and now need replacing.

Types of ship

There is a mixed trend in the types of warships being procured by the Indian Ocean navies, according to the type of navy concerned. In the case of embryonic navies, such as those in East Africa, Southeast Asia, or the Persian Gulf, the characteristic recent, new, or proposed purchase is one of the wide variety of FAC available, armed with missiles, guns, or torpedoes—or some combination of these—and in the 100–500-ton range. Malaysia, for example, has six FAC on order, with fourteen in its inventory, including eight with surface-to-surface missiles (SSMS). Similarly, Oman has three FAC on order with six already in its inventory. The three on order will be armed with Exocet; it already possesses two boats with this particular weapon.

The more established navies in the region are less concerned with ships at the lower end of the spectrum than with replacing or adding to some of their bigger vessels. India has recently taken delivery of two Kashin-class guided-missile destroyers from the Soviet Union. A third was delivered in 1983 and three more are reported to have been ordered. Australia has two frigates on order and, until the election of the Labour government at the start of 1983, was looking for a carrier to replace the *Melbourne*.

Overall, the one common characteristic among the navies of the region—the Australian decision against carrier replacement being the big exception—has been the step-up in warship capability both in terms of size and punch. There has been a tendency for a navy with one frigate to order more, such as Iraq's, or to move from corvettes to frigates, such as Saudi Arabia's, or for a basically FAC-armed navy to develop corvettes (the Italian 560-tonners, the Lupo-class, being a popular choice), and for even embryonic navies to invest more in missiles.

Unbalanced navies

In comparison with the major navies of the Northern hemisphere, a notable general feature of the Indian Ocean navies is the low priority given to air defense, submarines, and antisubmarine warfare (ASW). However, there are signs that more attention is now being given to air defense and ASW.

In terms of the threats posed to each other by Indian Ocean states, the lack of attention paid to ASW activities is not very surprising. So far the indigenous submarine capability is minimal, especially if one considers the vast distances involved and the very limited potential on-station time that small numbers allow. As a result, the relative inattention given to ASW activities is entirely understandable. However, this does mean that some targets will remain vulnerable to submarines. This "window of opportunity" has not encouraged the local navies to invest in submarines. Great distances, technical difficulties, and expense continue to result in only small submarine inventories. India has eight (with few on order), Australia and Pakistan have six each, Indonesia has four, South Africa has three, and Bangladesh has one; Egypt and Israel also operate submarines, though probably almost exclusively in the Mediterranean. In addition, the operational readiness of the Pakistani and Indonesian boats can be questioned. The mediocre performance of Argentinian submarines during the Falklands War of 1982 suggests the limited capabilities of middle power or regional navies in submarine operations when they confront a developed naval power.

Clearly the limited ASW development of the Indian Ocean navies is of greater significance if they confront extraregional powers with significant submarine fleets than if they face another regional power. In addition to the superpowers, Britain, China, France, and Japan each have powerful submarine capabilities. Several countries in the region depend for their prosperity upon continuing stability in international trade, including maritime transportation. Consequently, the disruption of such trade has to be regarded as a potential target for adversaries; submarines are a primary means of effecting such disruption. The countries that are particularly dependent upon maritime traffic are the Persian Gulf states, Australia, Singapore, and South Africa.

If the indigenous submarine threat in the Indian Ocean is presently limited, and does not require extensive ASW, the same is definitely not true of the air threat to warships, for in any war in the region the potential threat to surface shipping from neighboring land-based aircraft will be extensive. In this regard, it is important to keep in mind that in the Falklands War of 1982 fourteen British warships were either sunk or damaged by rather outdated 1950s-style aircraft operating at the limit of their range, using old-fashioned bombs of which only about half detonated.[6] Airpower will be a major factor in determining the outcome of any naval conflict in the region, as it will be in any war on land. Typically, the order books of national air forces are fuller, and are given a higher priority, than those of the navies of the countries of the region.

Manpower problems

For the navies of the Indian Ocean littoral states, as well as for their air forces, there is one problem that is shared to a greater or lesser extent by all: the shortage of trained manpower. This, of course, is a problem also faced by the world's major navies, though in their cases the problem is usually that of retaining trained manpower in the service, as opposed to not having a big enough pool in the first place. For the nonindustrialized states in the region, the demands on their relatively small pool of technically trained personnel is particularly telling.

It is difficult to generalize about the quality of the naval manpower in particular countries of the region. There is some anecdotal evidence about the poor quality of some countries' navies regarding the handling and maintenance of ships but it is always difficult to know how much significance to attach to such stories. However, there are clearly strains on trained manpower. That having been noted, it is also evident that some of the new navies have been making serious efforts within their limited capabilities to improve the technical quality of their personnel. The ten-year United States–designed Saudi Naval Expansion Program, for example, is attempting to improve training (it involves the development of a naval academy) as well as seeking to develop a logistic and servicing infrastructure. At a less ambitious level, Kuwait is said to be developing a core of naval, as opposed to coast guard, personnel. Typifying the improvement in the skills of embryonic navies has been the progress that Omani officers have made in taking over posts of responsibility from foreign, mainly British, personnel.

Due to the undeveloped technical skills of some of the local navies, foreign officers sometimes play a big part in their development. The case of Britain and Oman has just been mentioned.[7] Less well known, but of at least equal interest, has been the important role played by Pakistani officers and petty officers in the development of the navies of several of the smaller gulf states. Such arrangements may develop between other countries as the demands on technical skill increase with the acquisition of new technology.

Sources of warship procurement

A recurrent problem for Third World countries in general, not only in their warship procurement, is the tension between their desire for independence and the reality of their dependence on the industrialized world for advanced technology and skills. Not surprisingly, the unwilling dependence suffered by Third World governments, and the opportunities for manipulation offered to the industrialized powers, result in periodic stresses and strains in arms transfer relationships.

In the case of warship procurement, the countries surrounding the Indian Ocean place nearly all of their orders abroad. But the desire for freedom from such dependence is strong, since no state chooses to be beholden to another. One worry for the arms consumer is the scope for leverage that the arms transfer relationship gives to the arms supplier. This worry is certainly justified, for military aid diplomacy—particularly on the part of the superpowers—is pursued with the specific intention of turning arms into influence. Another worry for the arms consumer is the possibility that supplies might be interrupted. This may be the result of a range of uncontrollable factors, including changes in the political orientation of the supplying state or changes in the fortunes of the supplying government: South Africa has been a notable victim of the vagaries of the international arms trade. In its case, supplies have been interrupted when foreign governments have used this means of registering their disapproval of South Africa's almost universally detested laws on racial segregation. But supplies can also be interrupted as a result of unpredictable occurrences affecting the supplier, such as happened with Britain after the Falklands War. Because of the reevaluation of British defense needs following the war, London changed the arrangements it had made with Australia regarding the sale of the minicarrier HMS *Invincible*. While new arrangements were being contemplated by both governments, there was a general election in Australia that resulted in the fall of the Fraser administration. The new Labour government scrapped the idea of any new carrier.[8]

The obvious response of arms recipients to the inevitable uncertainty of the marketplace is to diversify the sources that supply them. Several states in the region have in fact done this. Iraq, for example, diversified away from Soviet technology after 1979, and even Kenya, not one of the region's more noteworthy naval nations, has been slowly moving away from its sole reliance on British weaponry, as shown by its purchase of Israeli antiship missiles. But even diversification is not a solution, for the possession of a hodgepodge of equipment complicates training, the receipt of replacements, and so on. Thus, one commentator has described African military forces as "a storekeeper's nightmare and an arms merchant's delight."[9] The Indian navy has had something of a dual personality with its British legacy and weaponry and its Soviet legacy and weaponry. Diversification has some advantages but it cannot be allowed to go too far or it will interfere with efficiency.

The problems caused by a dependent relationship have impelled some states in the region to look toward at least a degree of independence. As a result, a number of countries have built lighter vessels for themselves. These include Indonesia, Malaysia, Singapore, and Thailand, and even the gulf states may get into the business.[10] Some of the lighter vessels produced within the region are potentially very effective. One significant development has been the South African Minister-class, Pretoria's version of the Israeli Reshef FAC (missile). The first three of these came from Haifa shipyard in Israel but five more have subsequently been launched in South Africa itself.[11] These ships form part of a major effort by South African industry over the past few years to beat the effects of the arms embargo imposed by the United Nations Security Council in 1977. Another state that has been keen to "go it alone" has been India, though for less urgent reasons. With aspirations to produce its own submarines, or at least manufacture them under license, India has been the region's most ambitious naval builder. After prolonged delays, progress was finally achieved as a result of a contract in 1982 to procure four submarines from West Germany. Two are to be built in Bombay. Meanwhile, there has been progress in surface ship development. In 1981 the last of a series of modified British Leander-class frigates was commissioned in Bombay, while speculation persists about the possibility of an Indian-built replacement of—or addition to—the *Vikrant*.[12] But this dream, like others among the economically overburdened countries of the region, is likely to go unfulfilled. In practice, the appetite of many countries of the Third World for modern weaponry—of which warships are relatively low in priority—will largely be met by the enthusiastic arms salesmen of the competing superpowers, some of the former colonial powers, and a number of the newly industrializing countries (NICS). Of particular significance among the NICS are Israel and South Korea; the latter is fast becoming the naval shipyard of Asia.

Strategic Context of Naval Policy

Turning from structural matters to strategic, the naval trends in the region are not as apparent. This should be the cause for some satisfaction, since strategy flourishes alongside trouble.

Operational developments

For the most part in recent years, it has been a case of business as usual as far as operations are concerned in the Indian Ocean region. The major exception is the Iraq-Iran war, which has involved a series of violent exchanges at sea: ship versus ship early in the war and aircraft versus ship during later phases. It is still too soon to draw definite naval lessons from this war, particularly given the dearth of unbiased eyewitness accounts and the grossly inflated claims of the belligerents, but the following points seem to emerge from the media reports: the relative unavailability of Iran's large warships, the reliance of Iraq on land-based air power, the importance of missiles, the rapid attrition when naval forces do engage, and the flexibility of merchant traffic in adjusting to the prolonged crisis.[13]

With the exception of this one open war at sea, the navies of the region have been carrying out their routine peacetime tasks: coastal defense, adjusting to changing technology, and training. War at sea, for the most part, has seemed a distant prospect. Indeed, one of the problems for naval planners in this region—particularly for relatively secure Australia—has been defining a national naval strategy in a low-threat environment. In Australia's case, for example, its most likely military threat will be from across the sea, but in practice it is difficult to propose a reasonably plausible scenario, let alone cast it. In such circumstances, national naval planners are reduced to consoling themselves with their conviction about the place of the unpredictable in international relations, and the consequent need for prudence in national defense efforts.

A low-threat naval environment is common, to a greater or lesser extent, across the region. The main military problems faced by the littoral countries are from the possibility of land and air attack from neighbors. But most of the countries do face some naval threats of a worst-case variety. South Africa and Australia have to make some provision for the safety of their harbors and merchant shipping, given the importance of overseas trade to them and their vulnerability in the event of being faced by a determined adversary. In addition, South Africa has to contemplate the prospect of some future UN sanctions being backed by a naval blockade, while the empty island continent of Australia has to face the possibility that it might one day be the destination for a massive influx of "boat people" following a crisis in a country to the north. Some littoral states, more urgently, have need to consider the implications of superpower naval diplomacy and the requirement, if not to counter superpower forces in some future crisis, at least to be able to increase the risks and costs to any superpower that might want to "tilt" against them. Such prospects should play a part in the contingency planning of the Indian navy, particularly after its experience in the war with Pakistan in 1971.[14] Diplomacy has been one way most states of the region have tried to deal with the dangers of superpower naval rivalry, that is, by trying to exclude superpower forces under an Indian Ocean zone-of-peace arrangement. However, so far this idea has made little progress and the obstacles to its achievement appear formidable.[15]

Sea-based disputes

Despite the points made in the previous section about the low-threat maritime environment, there are several disputes in the region that are both sea-based and may have naval implications. The possibility that one of these disputes might erupt will be enhanced during the period while the 1982 UN Convention on the Law of the Sea settles. Until that time one might expect several contending national claims to be backed by naval power. And, as one spokesman for an extraregional naval power has put it, "The clearest interpretation of the ambiguous language of the treaty will be the actual operational practices of those who base their navigational rights on its provisions."[16] In short, those with naval power will underline their legal opinions with warship demonstrations.

For the most part, however, it is not likely that major conflicts will arise in the Indian Ocean as a result of law-of-the-sea disputes. The most likely scenario would be a repeat of the relatively minor naval confrontation that took place in 1981 between Indian and Bangladeshi warships over the ownership of an uninhabited island. Nevertheless, the likelihood of such minor confrontations does appear to be growing in the opinion of some authorities, mainly because "island grabbing" has proved to be successful in the recent past. According to one writer, this "fashionable trend" began in the Indian Ocean region, with the seizure by the Iranian navy in 1971 of the strategically important islands of Greater and Lesser Tumb at the mouth of the gulf.[17]

Although the general expectation is that maritime-based disputes will be few and will involve only low levels of violence—a considerable number of boundaries have already been demarcated by negotiation[18]—

the fact remains that several disputes do exist and that there is some potential for others to arise.

Since the UN Conference on the Law of the Sea began at Caracas in 1974, major maritime demarcation disputes have taken place between Iran and Iraq, Iraq and Kuwait, Iran and the United Arab Emirates, Somalia and Kenya, India and Sri Lanka, and Thailand and Burma; in addition, major fishing disputes have involved India and Taiwan, India and Japan, Thailand and Taiwan, and Australia and Taiwan. Therefore, to some extent, the Indian Ocean is a "troubled sea," but Barry Buzan's sensible prognosis in the mid-1970s still remains valid, namely that with the exception of navigation rights through the Red Sea and ports of Southeast Asia, "this region does not seem to contain much potential on law-of-the-sea matters. . . . This is not to say that maritime relations in the region are entirely happy. Many local states have expressed resentment at the intrusion of outside fishing, shipping, and naval activities, and this resentment seems likely to increase. For the most part, however, there is very little they can do about it."[19]

In sum, the potential for trouble at sea is present but the dangers do not seem to be ominous. Having said that, who can be at ease in the aftermath of the unpredicted 1982 Falklands War? If nothing else, that war was a reminder to those who had grown complacent about such matters that nations do feel strongly about sovereignty and about historic claims, and that they will sometimes act violently upon those feelings and claims. This is especially likely to be the case if other states are foolish enough not to show that they are willing to fight to defend what they believe is rightly theirs.

Mission structure

There is enough maritime uncertainty in the Indian Ocean region, therefore, to justify the possession of at least a minimal naval capability on the part of most, if not all, littoral states. Warships have utility in demonstrating a nation's determination to defend its rights and to push up the costs to those who might interfere with those rights. In addition, most nations in the region need to improve their prospects for enforcing their authority in the larger areas of national maritime jurisdiction that have been legitimized by the 1982 UN Convention on the Law of the Sea (UNCLOS). As a result of this codification process, particularly the legitimization of the twelve-mile territorial sea and the concept of the exclusive economic zone (EEZ), those organizations that were formerly little more than coast guard services are having to think more like "real" navies, hence the trend toward modernization and the step-up in warship capability. At present, the new enforcement tasks appear not to have seriously overburdened the littoral navies, and the word "efficient" has been applied to the naval forces of such diverse countries as Singapore and Kenya, while Oman's navy has been said to be meeting its heavy traffic control tasks at the entrance to the gulf with growing skill.[20]

"Mission structure" is perhaps too grand a phrase to describe what most of the navies of the region plan to do, but whatever phrase is used, it is clear that their raison d'être is far from archetypal Mahanian, with a "command of the sea doctrine" at its core. For the most part, the mission of Indian Ocean navies is to enforce order in contiguous waters and to pose at least a minimal sea denial threat to potential intruders. In short, these forces intend to have some capability of stopping others from using contiguous waters in a hostile fashion. By so doing, they also hope to provide themselves with some diplomatic leverage. Even a small force can have disproportionate results in some circumstances. In the mid-1970s, for example, Iceland gained considerable diplomatic mileage out of the possession of only a handful of gunboats in its confrontation with Britain over fishing zones. In Iceland's case, as with countries around the Indian Ocean, maritime forces are a badge of national sovereignty. All states require such a badge, however hard up they are, and however small. "We fight therefore we are," as Begin once put it.[21]

Requirements and capabilities

In relation to their missions, the navies of the Indian Ocean region are not "balanced" in the traditional Anglo-American sense; they do not have sufficient capability to discharge the widest variety of tasks. They are becoming more balanced, however, in relation to the limited range of tasks they have chosen. This is the optimum position for a navy to achieve, as long as the correct tasks have been chosen in the first place. That said, few if any of the navies concerned feel that they have achieved a satisfactory balance between capabilities and requirements. While such dissatisfaction is to be expected from all naval establishments, it is likely to be especially pronounced in a region where ships are few and distances are considerable.

Alliances

A traditional method by which weak states attempt to meet their security problems is by sharing the burden (or even "free riding") in an alliance. As far as naval cooperation in the Indian Ocean is concerned, there has been only a limited trend in this direction. The two most interesting developments in the region concern the Gulf Cooperation Council (GCC) and the Association of South-East Asian Nations (ASEAN).

One observer has described naval cooperation as a logical step for the GCC, in view of its members' interest in joint security measures. To date, however, no consensus has emerged regarding appropriate action. A major problem facing the GCC members is that of their future relationship, if any, with Western naval powers. The ASEAN countries are similarly aware of their common security interests but in their case maritime problems figure more prominently than for the GCC members. These problems include an awareness of an increased Soviet maritime presence in the region and a recognition of the naval burdens caused by the creation of EEZs. As far as the Soviet threat is concerned, the ASEAN nations hope that the United States will continue to maintain a strong presence in the western Pacific, while in the case of EEZ duties the individual nations seem determined to look after their interests unilaterally. Nevertheless, the ASEAN nations do recognize the advantages of cooperation and they have participated in combined naval operations.[22]

Great hopes cannot be invested in regional alliances as a means of distributing maritime burdens among relatively weak states. Even the history of such an integrated instrument as NATO suggests that one's perspective should be minimalist. The Australia–New Zealand–United States alliance (ANZUS), it might be added, is concerned with the Pacific area rather than the Indian Ocean, although with the 1962–64 "confrontation" between Malaysia and Indonesia, Australia received assurances from the United States that article 5 of the treaty would be applicable in the Borneo area, outside the Pacific.[23] In the present globalist mood of the White House, the administration might not be adverse to extending the scope of the ANZUS treaty, should the perceived need arise.

Quick fixes

For overcoming problems of the Third World navies in the region, various "quick fixes" have been suggested.[24] Some of these are technical, such as making better use of shore-based radar for surveillance, but in theory the most promising approach involves the coordination of surveillance and enforcement efforts between neighboring coastal states. However, the chances of such a development materializing are low, since all the potential coordinators are themselves overstretched, and many neighboring countries have mistrustful relations. A more likely way of overcoming weaknesses in this area would be for greater assistance to be provided by the developed naval states. The latter would probably be keen to step in to help, since they are always seeking the magic formula by which they might turn military aid into diplomatic gold. The Soviet navy's "West Africa Patrol" off the coast of Guinea is a model for such a development.[25]

In their efforts to improve capabilities, some of the developing states have begun to create a naval infrastructure of their own, such as the better facilities being built by Malaysia and Kuwait. These efforts will have relatively minor impact on the strategic environment of the region, however, when compared with the extensive interest of the superpowers in building up their own global strategic infrastructure. The latter has resulted in a base race for the region's scarce strategic real estate.[26]

Trends and Prospects

There is always a tendency in foreign policy or strategic analysis to convert every "trend" (or general tendency) into a "prospect" (or probability); today's perceptions easily slip into tomorrow's predictions. On the matter of Indian Ocean naval developments, however, there is likely to be a close congruence between trends and prospects because of the objective conditions in which the countries surrounding the Indian Ocean find themselves. Within the next ten to fifteen years it is unlikely that there will be any radical discontinuities in the naval environment. Consequently, it is possible to identify the following range of prospects with a degree of confidence.

First, economic constraints will continue to limit the development of regional naval forces. Great resources will not suddenly be released for the expansion of naval power and what resources are made available will have to face competition from more pressing national priorities. The inability of many Indian Ocean countries to meet their manifold national problems and achieve both economic development and political stability will continue to be much more prevalent than any surplus of resources for significant naval expansion.

Second, navies will continue to be relatively unimportant in the overall scheme of things for all Indian Ocean littoral states. As a result, the bulk of national appropriations and the bulk of arms transfers from overseas will continue to be channeled into the development of national armies and air forces. A partial exception to this is India, where the navy's share of the defense budget rose from 4 percent in 1971–72 to 7 percent in 1977–78.[27] But even this amount, in absolute terms, is miniscule compared with expenditures for a superpower's navy.[28] Even if the region were to enter a new season of military intervention, the instruments would be land and air forces rather than navies and marines. Even threats from extraregional powers will tend to be met by land-based systems. This is partly the result of bureaucratic factors; when a country does not have a naval tradition it does not automatically think of naval power as the natural counter to threats from the sea. But whatever mix of land- and sea-based coastal defense is organized, the military costs of intervention from the sea are bound to be pushed up.

Third, there will be no quick fixes to naval power. In World War II, Lord Cunningham said that it took a navy three years to build a ship but three hundred years to rebuild a tradition.[29] Traditions come somewhat more quickly than that but there was an important grain of truth in Cunningham's remark. The problem he referred to was clearly revealed by the Indonesian navy in the 1960s, which proved unable to turn the modern warships it had acquired from the Soviet Union into a modern and effective fighting force. Off-the-shelf warships do not make an off-the-shelf navy.

Fourth, although the phrase "arms race" has sometimes been used to describe naval developments in the Indian Ocean and elsewhere in the Third World, what is occurring cannot accurately be called a race, nor would a race appear likely in the immediate future. To the extent any racing is going on, it will be on land and in the air rather than at sea, since the former environments are where the threats to national security will be most urgent and where the potential payoffs will be the greatest. What is happening at sea can more accurately be called a naval buildup or, simply, modernization. Warship procurement is certainly proceeding but what is involved in many cases is an effort to meet fairly minimal requirements with the best technology that can be afforded. We are not witnessing a process of warship building explicitly involving particular pairs of adversaries in classic action-reaction fashion. An arms buildup might turn into a race, but equally it might settle into a comfortable or at least acceptable balance. Whether it becomes a race or a balance will depend in part on the degree of stability that exists in the maritime environment in general, which in turn will partly depend on the future character of the regime resulting from the changing law of the sea. If, as was suggested earlier, the maritime environment for most of the countries of the region continues to be one of low-threat, with disputes rather than conflicts,[30] then the likelihood of naval arms racing is greatly reduced. At the same time, however, the expanded requirements resulting from the changing law of the sea will continue to generate a steady buildup.

Fifth, since a continuing process of modernization is projected, rather than one of naval arms racing, it is thought unlikely that there will be any significant change in the constellation of regional naval power. Iran's bid under the shah to become the dominant power at sea in the northwest quadrant of the Indian Ocean does not look like it is being repeated; the present regime's route to power is spiritual rather than military. Indonesia is one possible contender to change its naval status—as it promised in the 1960s—but the past should encourage caution. In all likelihood, India will retain its lead as the premier naval power in the region, although in most circumstances outside contiguous waters this will not represent usable power. For India, and even less so for many other littoral countries, a big navy cannot be created overnight. If any state wishes to achieve naval preeminence, there will be plenty of warning.

Sixth, as the navies of the Indian Ocean struggle to meet their requirements, there will be a continuation of the tension between their nationalistic desire for independence and their inability to avoid a degree of dependence on the industrialized powers. Military aid diplomacy will continue unabated on the part of several industrialized states, particularly the superpowers, as they continue to search for ways to control a not-very-pliant world. Military aid in the future, as in the recent past, will not prove to be a panacea for the problems of superpower foreign policy, but it will remain a useful diplomatic instrument. Because some, if not most, of the states in the region are concerned about being manipulated by the superpowers, or being drawn into superpower confrontations, it is likely that they will seek when possible to diversify their arms suppliers. This will open a commercial gap for countries such as Brazil and South Korea to supply weapons platforms, particularly in the FAC range.[31] The supplying of major warships, however, will presumably remain the business of the principal naval powers, while diversification will always be restrained by the organizational advantages of having a single supplier.

Seventh, it seems unlikely that all the maritime disputes in the region will be permanently settled. Nevertheless, the interests and limited capabilities of the countries concerned would seem to suggest that these disputes will not blow up into open conflict. Even so, one should never underestimate the improbable in international politics, especially if the international environment of the 1980s and 1990s proves to be rather more militant than that of the 1970s. The unlikely and unwanted war between Britain and Argentina over the Falkland Islands in 1982 was a costly warning of the uncertainty of our times. Much more dangerous tension spots already exist around the Indian Ocean. In the maritime sphere the potentially most serious problems would be challenges to access through the gulf or through Southeast Asia. These strategic water-ways are the focuses of both regional problems and the core interests of extraregional powers.

If fighting were to break out at sea, high attrition rates are to be expected, as the Iraq-Iran war has shown. Aircraft and missiles will play a major part in the outcome of war at sea but the naval skills and readiness of the local powers will always be difficult to forecast in ad-vance of war. This is particularly the case in the Indian Ocean region since observers have only limited knowledge about the local forces and there are few lessons of experience. Again, the Falklands War offers a cautionary note. Who, before the event, knew that the Argentinian air force would come through their test with such skill and panache, while the country's navy would effectively disappear from sight?

Eighth, it can be expected that Indian Ocean navies will remain "unbalanced" as fighting instruments with serious deficiencies in some areas, particularly ASW and air defense. However, it can be expected that they will become better balanced in relation to their routine enforce-ment tasks within national EEZs.

Finally, despite the shortfalls in capability experienced by several Indian Ocean states, little progress can be expected to develop from multilateral alliance cooperation in naval affairs. The basis for long-term integrated alliance cooperation does not seem to exist in the various subregions of the Indian Ocean littoral. Better results are likely to be achieved if specific states make bilateral arrangements with suitable countries, such as those that have already occurred between Saudi Ara-bia and the United States, Oman and Britain, and the gulf states and Pakistan.

Conclusion

Overall, it might be concluded that the naval prospects for the Indian Ocean region might be described as "the same only more so." Navies of even modest size are expensive, and will remain so, but for many states they are no longer the luxury that they formerly were. UNCLOS III, and its 1982 convention, will have lasting effect in this regard. Not only has it created the EEZ, with all this entails by way of new naval tasks, but it has also raised the level of consciousness of the international com-munity regarding the maritime environment. As a result, more states want to use the sea for more purposes than ever before.[32]

Around the Indian Ocean in the years ahead, warships will con-tinue to be acquired as badges of sovereignty, as instruments of order, and as cost raisers to deter potential troublemakers. Consequently, a steady process of naval modernization will continue. Sometimes this process will be competitive but it is unlikely to deserve the label "naval race" or "new navalism," whereby national power is conceived and measured—and perhaps even tested—in maritime terms. What we have seen in this region, and will continue to see, is a large number of nations going through the first stage of development as powers with some capability to exercise some force at sea. Those observers who have grown up accustomed to seeing the global naval map dominated by a Western monopoly—and who believe that such a pattern should still be the natural order of things—are tempted to ring alarm bells about the diffusion of naval power into different parts of the world. Such an attitude should be resisted. Certainly the developments—and in some cases threats— should be noted and studied but alarmist conclusions should not be drawn from a process of normal and irreversible modernization.

6. The Indian Ocean Region and Arms Limitation: Prospects for the Future ≈ R. B. Byers

From both a global and a regional perspective the Indian Ocean region (IOR) will continue to be an arena of increased economic, political, and strategic significance during the 1980s. It seems highly likely that regional conflicts and political instabilities will continue to be a hallmark of significant parts of the region, especially in Africa, the Persian Gulf area, and probably in South Asia. At the same time, economic, political, and military rivalry between the superpowers will persist and in all probability become more intense. The major external powers will continue to demand some form of military presence in the region, given perceptions of their security interests.

Under these circumstances it is important to assess whether or not various arms limitation options can enhance regional security and reduce the probability of armed conflict. To that end this chapter is divided into two sections. The first addresses the strategic environment, taking into account various arms limitation perspectives, while the second section focuses on options and prospects for arms limitation in the 1980s and beyond.

The Strategic Environment and Arms Limitation

Prior to assessing the feasibility of various arms limitation options, it is necessary to link such considerations to the current strategic environment. It is therefore useful to address three sets of issues: the security concerns of the region, military-strategic developments that could affect the IOR, and the current state of arms limitation negotiations.

Security concerns

Three groups of forces have interests of importance to the Indian Ocean region. The security concerns can be placed within the context of the interests and objectives of the Soviet Union, the United States and the West, and the indigenous states.

From a Western perspective no consensus exists regarding ultimate Soviet interests and objectives in the region. Nevertheless, the USSR is a military superpower that will continue to attempt to expand its influence, to acquire allies, and to gain access to military facilities within the IOR. By these activities Moscow expects to enhance its own position and frustrate Western states in the pursuit of their own concerns. In furthering these objectives, the Soviet leadership appears to have adopted a policy of ad hoc opportunism, as shown by events such as the shift of Soviet support from Somalia to Ethiopia and attempts to influence Indian policy. In short, during the 1980s and perhaps beyond, the IOR will become increasingly important to the USSR and be a major arena for Soviet policy initiatives.

For the West, access to gulf oil remains essential for the maintenance of economic and military security. Yet among Western powers there is no consensus on the priority that should be given to securing oil supplies or the means by which these can best be achieved. The irony is that the states most dependent on gulf oil appear the least interested in taking concrete steps to guarantee supplies, while states like the United States and Britain, with good indigenous reserves of oil, search for appropriate protective strategies.

American policy, as reflected in the Carter Doctrine, constitutes a reaffirmation of containment as the main response to the dangers of further Soviet intervention. The Reagan administration has also followed this course. At the same time, American policy reflects the perceived need to ensure access to vital resources by maintaining sea lines of communication (SLOC) and guaranteeing the nondisruption of seaborne trade and commerce. For these reasons it is essential for the West to maintain naval forces and military facilities in the region.

On balance, then, the IOR is of greater economic, strategic, and political importance for the United States and the West than it is for the USSR. Given increased superpower competition in the region, it would be naive for the IOR states to assume the major powers will withdraw from the area.

From the perspective of the IOR states at least four other security concerns must be taken into account: the pervasiveness of force as an instrument of policy within the region; the political instability of specific states (for example, India, Saudi Arabia, South Africa, and Thailand); the impact of nuclear proliferation, given that India, Iran, Iraq, Pakistan, and South Africa are nuclear threshold states; and, finally, the diversity of political alignments within the region, whether with external powers or related to the ideal of genuine nonalignment.

Within the broader political-military context the impact of wars outside the region must also be taken into account. While the Arab-Israeli conflict in the Middle East has focused attention primarily on the eastern Mediterranean, it hinders the possibility of reaching arms limitation agreements in the Indian Ocean. In addition, the impact of the Falklands War has increased Western (and probably Soviet) perceptions of the need to project power abroad, especially seapower. External powers are less likely to agree to arms limitation agreements that could hinder their ability to project power into the region.

There are also major difficulties for arms limitation in the IOR stemming from the geopolitical and geostrategic environment. With respect to the former, the divergent security interests of the major regional actors—especially Australia, India, Pakistan, and South Africa—tend to complicate any comprehensive approach to arms limitation. Geostrategic issues, on the other hand, focus on asymmetries between the United States and the Soviet Union. Even with reasonable access to base facilities, the United States and the West must necessarily operate on extended lines of communication and support compared with the Soviet Union. Consequently the USSR retains greater flexibility in projecting land and air power into the IOR. Here the Soviet Union should be able to retain regional superiority, even though Western capabilities to project sea power partially offset Soviet land and air capabilities. This situation could, of course, change over time if Soviet naval capabilities are allowed to outstrip those of the West.

Military-strategic developments

Security developments in the IOR are likely to be affected by changes in American strategic doctrine, by enhanced capabilities to fight nuclear war on the part of both superpowers, and by increased conventional military capabilities.

From a strategic doctrinal perspective, the 8 February 1982 Annual Report of the Department of Defense (DOD) to Congress by Secretary of Defense Caspar Weinberger indicated a shift toward the adoption of a nuclear war–fighting doctrine. In addition to possessing nuclear weapons for deterrence purposes within the NATO region, the report indicated that nuclear weapons could be employed to impose the termination of a major war and/or to negate possible Soviet blackmail. This was followed by the Fiscal Year (FY) 1984–88 Defense Guidance Plan which advocated a "protracted nuclear war strategy."[1] When placed within the context of limited nuclear options, the possible implications for the IOR become obvious.

At the global level the IOR states could perceive a less stable strategic environment where the possibilities of nuclear war have been enhanced. From a regional perspective, the doctrinal shift could be interpreted to mean that the use of nuclear weapons in the IOR is now more likely than in the past. The more firmly "limited nuclear options" become rooted in American strategic doctrine, the more likely American decision makers will lean in the direction of applying these considerations to the IOR. This is particularly true in a military-strategic environment where the United States and the West could be at a disadvantage with respect to conventional military capabilities. The statement by then Secretary of State Vance regarding the possible use of nuclear weapons in the gulf region at the time of the Soviet invasion of Afghanistan reflected the difficulty involved.

A second set of nuclear issues concerns the possible future deployment of new systems, especially cruise missiles and the neutron bomb. The expansion of landing facilities at Diego Garcia suggests that air-launched cruise missiles could be introduced into the region. Similarly, if the United States proceeds with deployment plans for sea-launched cruise missiles, the IOR will probably be involved. Such developments would result in similar Soviet capabilities being introduced into the region. The production of the neutron bomb could result in its introduction into the IOR some time in the future and, again, the Soviet Union would have to respond in one form or another.

On balance, nuclear technological developments are such that the superpowers will, in the future, have enhanced strategic, intermediate range, and battlefield nuclear war–fighting capabilities unless there is agreement to limit these developments. Irrespective of the arguments over deterrence credibility and the linkage of capabilities to doctrine, the implications suggest that strategic stability in the IOR could be adversely affected. This in turn will increase fears of nuclear weapons use within the region should a superpower conflict arise.

Within the conventional military context the arguments pro and con regarding the American Rapid Deployment Force (RDF) are discussed elsewhere in this book. However, the attempt to develop a credible RDF takes on added significance in terms of the FY 1984–88 Defense Guidance Plan, inasmuch as the Persian Gulf and Asia have been designated as priority regions after the United States and Western Europe. Similarly, the FY 1983 DOD Report to Congress clearly indicates that the United States is, in principle, committed to defend militarily the gulf region against Soviet intervention. It may be, however, that a strong continuing Western naval presence is the most viable approach to cope with Western security concerns. Such a presence could reduce the concerns expressed by some Indian Ocean states regarding possible uses of an RDF. (It should also be remembered that these developments are occurring in an environment where Soviet conventional capabilities—land, sea, and air—will be enhanced during the 1980s.)

When enhanced superpower conventional military capabilities are considered in light of the attrition rates and lethality of the Falklands and Lebanon wars, the implications of modern warfare for the IOR can be readily envisaged. In addition, of course, the war-fighting capabilities of some of the Indian Ocean states—Australia, India, Iran, Pakistan, and South Africa, for example—are by themselves such that some of their neighbors have cause to be concerned.

Last, but no less significant, are the security implications for the IOR of chemical weapons. This issue will be discussed in some detail in the second part of this chapter.

Current state of arms limitation negotiations

It is difficult to be optimistic about the prospects for either Soviet-American or more generally East-West arms limitation agreements, given the current international climate. Mutual suspicion and lack of trust have returned as the major characteristics of relations between Washington and Moscow. With the breakdown of detente, no ground rules have been agreed upon for the management of the relationship. One indication of present difficulties is to be found in the state of the intermediate nuclear force (INF) and the strategic nuclear force (SNF) talks, neither of which show signs of an early breakthrough. More broadly, the poor repair of East-West relations is reflected in the lack of progress at the Mutual and Balanced Force Reductions (MBFR) Talks in Vienna and the difficulties that accompanied the reaching of an agreement at the Conference on Security and Cooperation in Europe (CSCE) Review Conference. In addition, there has been no progress with negotiations taking place within the United Nations system. The Second Special Session on Disarmament (UNSSOD II) ended in failure, while discussions within the Committee on Disarmament have reached a stalemate.

On other issues that affect regional security and stability, the second Non-Proliferation Treaty (NPT) Review Conference indicated the increased inability of non-nuclear powers to affect the policy and posture of the nuclear powers, especially the superpowers. Linkages between vertical proliferation and horizontal proliferation will thus remain an important issue for many Third World states. At a minimum, the nuclear threshold states will be able to argue increasingly that the nuclear powers have not lived up to the 1968 treaty. This will tend to decrease the legal and moral constraints on the threshold states on proliferation-related issues.

Despite the problems and difficulties, there are a number of more optimistic trends that could have a positive impact for arms limitation. First, the peace movements of Europe and North America could have the effect of increasing the possibility of eventual Soviet-American agreements on nuclear arms. As discussed below, this could have an indirect benefit for the IOR. At a minimum, the peace movement will keep arms limitation issues on the political agenda in both Europe and North America. This could raise the consciousness of political decision makers regarding the need for more comprehensive and/or regional approaches to arms limitation that could also benefit the Indian Ocean region.

Second, the impact of the 1984 American presidential election must be taken into account. Despite President Reagan's hard-line approach to the Soviet Union during his first term, he moderated his arms control positions during his reelection campaign. Political pressures within the United States, together with Reagan's own concern over his historical legacy, should increase the probability of reaching some form of accommodation with the USSR during his second term. While this may not have a direct impact on the IOR, it could produce an arms limitation environment that could benefit the region.

Finally, the majority of littoral and hinterland states of the region will continue to demand that arms limitation talks on the IOR remain a priority. Thus, despite the current position that has been adopted by the superpowers, such pressures eventually are bound to have an impact on regional arms control issues.

Arms Limitation Options

Three categories of arms limitation negotiations/agreements can be identified that would have some impact on the IOR. The first consists of the bilateral superpower negotiations and agreements: the INF and SNF talks and, theoretically, the Naval Arms Limitation Talks (NALT) on the Indian Ocean, should they be resumed. The second category is global negotiations within the context of the United Nations: UNSSOD II and the Committee on Disarmament. The final option is regional negotiations that, generally, would be conducted within the context of the United Nations, for example, the establishment of the IOR as a zone of peace and/or nuclear-free zone.

Soviet-American negotiations

Any agreement at the SNF talks would have a positive, although indirect, impact on the Indian Ocean region. At a minimum it would indicate a willingness by the United States and the Soviet Union to negotiate agreements and that could lead to greater flexibility regarding negotiations in other issue areas, possibly involving regional perspectives. It would also indicate a reduction in East-West and superpower political and military tensions. This would be particularly true with respect to reducing fears of a nuclear war. Finally, there could be a positive spillover to the NPT. An SNF agreement would indicate to the Third World a more serious approach on the part of the superpowers with respect to their NPT obligation to reduce their own nuclear arsenals. The nuclear powers might, as a result, have greater leverage on the threshold states.

With respect to the substance of an SNF agreement, a reduction in force levels—especially if the cuts are substantial and coupled with emphasis on destabilizing systems—could alter perceptions regarding attempts by the two superpowers to acquire a first strike capability. This would have the effect of reducing fears that either superpower could acquire a credible nuclear war–fighting capability. Thus, the global strategic environment would become more stable and, one would hope, the next round in the strategic nuclear arms race could be avoided. Needless to say, this could have a positive impact on the Indian Ocean region.

Similarly, a successful conclusion of the INF talks could affect the Indian Ocean security environment in several ways. For example, a "zero option" arrangement, even though it appears highly unlikely, would involve the withdrawal and/or dismantling of Soviet SS-20s and the cancellation of NATO's nuclear modernization program. If an INF agreement involved only the withdrawal of Soviet SS-20s targeted on Western Europe, the IOR could be adversely affected as presumably the Soviet Union could then target a larger number of SS-20s on China and other states (if desired) in the Indian Ocean and hinterland regions. The dismantling of all NATO and Soviet INF forces, on the other hand, would remove a potential security threat to the northern part of the IOR. This being the case, it is in the security interests of states within the region to actively encourage an INF solution that would move in the direction of the zero option, and thereby reduce the INF threat to Indian Ocean countries to the greatest possible extent.

If the scope for the INF talks is expanded, which will have to be the case if the superpowers negotiate seriously, the results could also be beneficial for the Indian Ocean. Limitations and/or reductions on the number of dual purpose (nuclear and conventional) land-based and carrier-based aircraft within an INF framework could have the effect of reducing the capabilities of the superpowers to conduct nuclear strikes against IOR states. In addition, even though they are not subject to negotiations at this particular time, there is increasing pressure within Western circles for arms talks to include battlefield nuclear weapons. Should this situation arise, the United States would presumably halt production of the neutron bomb and thus reduce the possibility that battlefield nuclear weapons could be deployed into the Indian Ocean region.

There are two related issues that in effect cut across the SNF and INF talks: first, the question of a nuclear freeze and, second, declarations regarding no first use of nuclear weapons. In both cases the initiative has been taken by the Soviet Union. This has had the effect of increasing skepticism within the West regarding the military and strategic viability of these proposals and has made it more difficult for NATO and the United States to respond in a positive fashion. While the Reagan administration and NATO have rejected both proposals there are considerable differences within the Western alliance regarding how to approach these issues.

It would appear to be in the security interests of the IOR states to address seriously the questions of a nuclear freeze and no first use and to develop strategic rationales that will support their views regarding extension of such security guarantees to the region. Yet it should be acknowledged that this could create a major debate within the West. For example, it remains highly unlikely that the West will perceive that it can protect its security interests in the Indian Ocean region by relying exclusively on conventional capabilities. This issue in itself deserves further and detailed consideration.

Efforts to reach some form of consensus regarding the reduction of military competition in the IOR must also be placed within the context of the ill-fated superpower bilateral naval arms limitation talks. In 1977 and 1978, the United States and the Soviet Union held a series of four discussions on possible ways to pursue mutual military restraint within the region. The range of possible alternatives focused on the 1977 level of naval deployments including ship days in the region, number of ships, and the possibility of limiting base facilities by means of balancing Diego Garcia against Soviet access to the naval base at Berbera. No agreement was reached concerning the issue of naval deployment patterns and, once the Soviet Union was expelled by Somalia, there was no incentive on the part of the United States to agree on base facility limitations. By early 1979 NALT was suspended. International and regional events made it increasingly clear that no agreement could be reached. Despite pressure from a number of the IOR states for resumption of the negotiations, it is clear that the Reagan administration has no intention of moving in this direction.

In retrospect it can be argued that NALT was ill-conceived, not in the security interests of the West, and detracted from the prospects that the IOR states themselves might reach some form of agreement on regional approaches to arms limitation. With respect to the conceptual basis of NALT, negotiations to limit base facilities could, at least in theory, be viable. But it also remains clear that the West must have access to adequate facilities given their sea power requirements. Furthermore, to attempt to negotiate limitations by reference to ship days, number of ships, ship types, tonnage levels, and so on, would appear to reflect a misunderstanding of the asymmetrical nature of Soviet and American naval capabilities. More important, such an approach fails to take into account that from both economic and security perspectives the IOR is of greater strategic significance to the West than it is to the Soviet Union.

The desire of Indian Ocean states for a NALT agreement can be appreciated. However, the bilateral negotiations had the effect of allowing the initiative for regional arms limitation to reside too exclusively within the purview of the superpowers. The impact was twofold: first, the IOR states were excluded from the negotiations and, second, NALT tended to direct attention away from multilateral efforts at regional arms limitation.

Global negotiations

The second category of arms limitation negotiations that could have an impact on the security of the Indian Ocean region involves global multilateral issues within the United Nations framework, that is to say, UNSSOD and the work of the Committee on Disarmament in Geneva.

From 23 May to 1 July 1978, the UN held its first Special Session on Disarmament (UNSSOD I). The main accomplishment of the special session was consensus on a final document that spelled out a comprehensive program of action for arms limitation. The priorities outlined in the program focused on disarmament negotiations related to nuclear weapons, other weapons of mass destruction (including chemical weapons), conventional weapons, and the reduction of armed forces. In each of these areas the program of action indicated in considerable detail how international security could be enhanced via disarmament measures. At the same time, many delegates to UNSSOD I were relatively optimistic that some substantive progress could be made in various arms limitation forums, especially in areas that involved the strategic nuclear arms race. Unfortunately the optimism of the day gave way to the reality of the breakdown in East-West relations and the corresponding cessation of progress in any arms control forum.

In many respects, therefore, the holding of UNSSOD II from 7 June to 10 July 1982 took place in a much different atmosphere, one devoid of any real prospect for success. The delegates to UNSSOD II had to admit defeat when, unlike UNSSOD I, they were unable to unanimously endorse another comprehensive program of disarmament (CPD). This failure was also marked by the lack of new initiatives, given the chilly rhetoric and public denunciation exchanged by the superpowers. President Brezhnev through Foreign Minister Andrei Gromyko, accused the United States of trying to change the strategic military balance and condemned the Reagan administration for its "spirit of militarism." For his part, President Reagan ignored the Soviet proposal on non–first use and instead focused on previously publicized American proposals. At the same time President Reagan referred to the Soviet Union's "record of tyranny" within the context of Afghanistan and Poland as well as the situation in Central and Latin America. On balance, therefore, it is easy to conclude that the general political climate prevented the superpowers from offering any mutually agreeable initiatives within the UNSSOD context. In addition, many delegations from the Third World used the conference to express their dissatisfaction with regional issues. Consequently, the concluding document did not attempt to hide the deep differences that had made agreement improbable from the outset. Nevertheless, the General Assembly reaffirmed its commitment to the 1978 program of action and there was some glimmer of hope that the disarmament cause could benefit from the agreement at UNSSOD II to launch a world disarmament campaign.

At both UNSSOD I and UNSSOD II the work of the Committee on Disarmament emerged as a focus for discussions. Unfortunately, the committee, like other arms control forums, has not been isolated from the general international political climate. Consequently, there has been no progress on two major agenda items: the comprehensive test ban (CTB) and chemical weapons (cw) treaties. The three major parties involved in the test ban negotiations—the United States, the Soviet Union, and Great Britain—all remain committed in principle. However, the position of the Reagan administration is that the time is not now "propitious." American officials have argued that verification remains a problem, but it could be argued that American reluctance to conclude a CTB treaty stems from its determination to close the perceived "window of vulnerability." Similarly prospects for a cw treaty are highly unlikely given American statements of the need to close the capability gap with the Soviet Union, as well as the new binary program that has been advocated by the administration. Even if the United States agreed to proceed with these two proposals, it is conceivable that the Soviet Union could then find objections.

For the Indian Ocean region, treaties banning nuclear tests and chemical weapons could have significant implications. The latter would obviously decrease the probability of chemical weapons being used by littoral and hinterland states within the region. Given allegations that they are already in use in Afghanistan and Southeast Asia, it is certainly in the interests of the IOR states to do their utmost to urge the United States and USSR to reach agreement on a cw treaty. In the absence of such a treaty the United States will probably proceed with its binary program, and the USSR will undoubtedly follow suit. By itself, a treaty may not prevent the introduction of chemical weapons into future conflicts but it could constitute an impediment and therefore be a useful step.

Of greater import than a cw treaty, however, is the desirability of a comprehensive test ban agreement. This would be an important step in halting the nuclear arms race and could indirectly and directly affect the Indian Ocean region. Indirectly, a CTB treaty would mean that its signatories—presumably the United States, the Soviet Union, and Great Britain at first—would have lost some of their ability to test successfully future generations of nuclear warheads. That is, the qualitative aspect of the nuclear arms race would be affected. Second, it would put greater pressure on France and China to abide by such a treaty. For the IOR, the leverage that could be applied to China could be of particular significance. Third, there would be greater pressure for nuclear threshold states to abide by the 1968 NPT which, in turn, might have a beneficial impact on the establishment of nuclear-free zones in the Indian Ocean. It is this latter issue that can most appropriately be discussed from the regional perspective. At this time, therefore, the IOR states who participate in the Committee on Disarmament should actively advocate treaties banning chemical weapons and nuclear tests. If the deadlock between the United States and the Soviet Union cannot be satisfactorily resolved, it may even be in the IOR states' interest to have the committee itself file treaties for signature with the United Nations.

Regional perspectives

The possibility of the IOR becoming a zone of peace has been on the security agenda of the United Nations for more than a decade. At the twenty-sixth session of the General Assembly, the UN adopted Resolution 2832 (XXVI) that advocated designation of the Indian Ocean as a zone of peace.

The major thrust of efforts to establish a zone of peace in the region has been, from the outset, primarily directed at the great powers, especially the superpowers. This remains the case today but the prospects for implementation remain even less likely now than they were during the 1970s.

The 1971 resolution called on the great powers to "enter into consultation with the littoral States of the Indian Ocean with the view to halting the further expansion of the military presence in the Indian Ocean and eliminating from the area all bases, military installations and logistical supply facilities, nuclear weapons and weapons of mass destruction and any manifestation of great-Power rivalry." It also called upon the littoral and hinterland states of the Indian Ocean, the permanent members of the Security Council, and other major maritime users of the Indian Ocean to

> enter into consultations aimed at the implementation of the Declaration by taking necessary action to ensure that: a) warships and military aircraft might not use the Indian Ocean for any threat or use of force against . . . any littoral or hinterland States . . . ; b) subject to the foregoing and to the norms and principles of international law, the right to free and unimpeded use of the zone by vessels of all nations was unaffected; and c) appropriate arrangements were made to give effect to any international agreement that might ultimately be reached.[2]

This was followed at the twenty-seventh General Assembly in 1972 by the adoption of a resolution that established an Ad Hoc Committee on the Indian Ocean for the purpose of harmonizing views regarding possible implementation of the 1971 resolution. Since 1972 the ad hoc committee has expanded from its original fifteen members to forty-eight member states. By the end of 1981 the committee had held almost two hundred meetings in its attempt to reach some form of agreement relating to the IOR as a zone of peace, and it continues to meet regularly.

During the period of discussion both procedural and substantive issues have dominated the committee's deliberations. Procedurally, the committee has spent more than a decade trying to establish firm dates for an international conference on the Indian Ocean for the purposes of establishing a zone of peace. In the late 1970s it appeared as though the conference would be held in 1981 but the Soviet invasion of Afghanistan intervened. Now, the continuation of the Soviet presence causes Western members of the committee to be even more leery of the value of a conference.

As to substance, the following points should be taken into account. At the more general level, the majority of states in the IOR perceive the zone of peace as a means to halt and then eliminate great power military presence in the region. Historically, this has been a major rationale for the proposal though a minority of IOR states have always argued that a zone of peace can only be viable if external and indigenous security issues are integrated into a comprehensive package. For these states, a region free of the presence of great powers, but dominated by regional military powers, is hardly a welcome alternative. Further, the discussion of issues related to external-indigenous military linkages has taken place in a global environment where the IOR has become increasingly important to the great powers, especially the United States. Under current circumstances, the prospects for harmonization of views prior to the holding of a conference are nonexistent.

It should be appreciated, however, that world opinion, at least as reflected in the 1978 consensual final document of UNSSOD I, agrees in principle that zones of peace can enhance regional security. Paragraph 64 of the final document notes that "the establishment of zones of peace in various regions of the world, under appropriate conditions, to be clearly defined and determined freely by the States concerned in the zone, taking into account the characteristics of the zone and the principles of the Charter of the United Nations, and in conformity with international law, can contribute to strengthening the security of States within such zones and to international peace and security as a whole."[3]

Nevertheless, in the case of the IOR the following specific disagreements must be kept in mind. First, there is the underlying issue of great power military rivalry. A number of littoral and hinterland states have argued that the escalation of great power rivalry and the ensuing buildup of external forces have constituted a major factor inhibiting progress. The Western members of the ad hoc committee tend to share this view, particularly since the Soviet invasion of Afghanistan. As already noted, they see little point in proceeding with the conference unless the Soviet Union withdraws from that country. For their part, the Soviets continue to argue that they have never been, and are not presently, responsible for the state of tensions within the region. For them, Afghanistan constitutes a legitimate call for assistance on the part of the Afghan government and Soviet troops will be required as long as external powers continue to provide military aid to the rebels.

In reality, the security interests of both the West and the Soviet Union suggest that states of the IOR should not anticipate the elimination of military-strategic rivalry in the area. Rather than focus on this issue as a major problem it might be more productive to accept that some form of external military presence will continue to be the norm. Thus, a more fruitful focus would be to emphasize those aspects of regional security that can have the effect of reducing the possibility for great power military intervention.

A second issue relates to the establishment of military installations and bases in the region. Several IOR states relate the general to the specific and point out that great power military installations and bases have been a continuing problem. Iraq, Madagascar, Mozambique, the Seychelles, South Yemen, and Tanzania have been particularly vociferous on this point. Since the Soviet Union lost access to Berbera, Somalia, it has joined with the littoral states on this particular issue. Nevertheless, should the Soviet Union be able to obtain base facilities elsewhere in the region its position could well change.

The current debate focuses primarily on the leasing by Britain to the United States of base facilities at Diego Garcia. The United States is in the process of investing a substantial sum to upgrade military facilities on the island, including the extension of the runway to handle B-52s. Furthermore, the island is to be the main staging area for the American RDF should it be required in the region (thus, the pre-positioning of equipment as well as container ships being kept on station). Despite current efforts by the new government of Mauritius to assert sovereignty over the island, the British and the Americans are standing firm. Given current perceptions in Washington, it is unrealistic for the IOR states to expect that the United States would willingly agree to forego base facilities in the region. Again, this is an issue that will remain unresolved and progress should not be expected even if an international conference is held.

A third issue involves the question of regional cooperation and security. In the longer term it may be that a more positive approach for the IOR states would be to place greater emphasis on the need to strengthen regional ties. A number of states in the region—Bangladesh, Bhutan, Indonesia, Madagascar, Malaysia, Nepal, and Pakistan—have argued that "a common position" should be forged in dealing with external powers. Other states, such as Australia, have agreed in principle but point to the diverse nature of security interests within the region as constituting an almost insurmountable problem.

The fourth issue involves the question of nuclear proliferation. States such as Indonesia have argued that a prerequisite for a zone of peace is a commitment by the states of the region to uphold the NPT and to reaffirm their convictions not to acquire nuclear weapons. Pakistan shares this view and has argued that a zone of peace could not be created unless all states within the region make an unambiguous joint commitment to keep the region denuclearized. Clearly this poses problems for both China and India. In the latter case, there is no agreement from India regarding the issue of denuclearization.

The other aspect of this particular issue regards the introduction of nuclear weapons into the region by nuclear powers. For example, the United States has argued, at least in the past, that it would be prepared under appropriate conditions—to offer security assurances. At the same time, however, the United States has stated that such a prohibition would not apply to naval vessels. The Soviet Union has adopted the view that no nuclear power should introduce nuclear weapons or other weapons of mass destruction into the region. This policy proposal has to be seen within the broader context of the Soviet proposal for the conclusion of an international convention regarding the guarantee of security for non-nuclear states. Thus, the USSR has stated that it will guarantee not to use nuclear weapons against non-nuclear states and this would apply to the Indian Ocean region. But the real difficulty, as will be discussed below, is that the nuclear threshold states are not willing to commit themselves to denuclearization.

Given the range of factors and disagreements relating to the establishment of a zone of peace in the Indian Ocean, it would be unrealistic to hold out the view that such a zone can be established, at least in the foreseeable future. The combination of divergent superpower security interests and objectives, coupled with the inability of the IOR states themselves to reach a consensus on how to solve indigenous security problems, support the view that the pursuit of a zone of peace in the region will not produce tangible results. Even so, it is likely that the regional approach to arms limitation via a zone of peace will continue to remain on the agenda.

From a regional perspective the most concrete disarmament measure under active consideration is the establishment of nuclear-weapon-free zones (NWFZ) in the region. The concept has been developed over the years within the framework of the United Nations with the view of halting the spread of nuclear weapons. The issue was a major agenda item at UNSSOD I and at that time the comprehensive program on disarmament stated that "the establishment of nuclear-weapon-free-zones on the basis of arrangements freely arrived at among the States of the region concerned, constitutes an important disarmament measure. The process of establishing such zones in different parts of the world should be encouraged with the ultimate objective of achieving a world entirely free of nuclear weapons."[4] Unfortunately, there has been no progress with respect to the establishment of such zones since the treaty for the prohibition of nuclear weapons in Latin America was opened for signature in 1967. The only other zone of its kind resulted from the Antarctic Treaty of 1961. Since then, however, there have been numerous proposals for the creation of additional zones in other areas of the world.

In the case of the IOR, one of the difficulties confronting the establishment of such zones is that no one proposal covers the entire region. That is, three specific proposals covering different parts of the region (the Middle East, Africa, and South Asia) have been under consideration. These three proposals have been discussed within the Committee on Disarmament, by the General Assembly, and also by the Disarmament Commission established as a result of UNSSOD I. It hardly need be pointed out that, from the perspective of the establishment of nuclear-free zones, the fact that the IOR has not been considered as a distinct geographic region has both its advantages and disadvantages. With respect to the former it may be more realistic to consider the establishment of such zones in geographically distinct regions. For example, it may be that, given the diverse nature of security interests and the large number of states involved with the IOR, it is completely unrealistic to think of a nuclear-free zone covering all of the region. Similarly, if it is possible to establish a nuclear-free zone in one of the three areas currently under consideration, there could be a positive spillover into the other areas of the region. With respect to disadvantages, however, it should also be noted that in one sense the region is geographically integrated around the Indian Ocean itself and in this sense there are some grounds to argue that states, for example, in South Asia would not be willing to proceed with the establishment of such a zone unless there was a corresponding move in the Middle East. The same type of argument could also apply for some of the African states vis-à-vis the Middle East.

With respect to the practicality of the establishment of such zones, the major stumbling block becomes, in all instances, the reality that in each one of the subregions the threshold states involved have not been willing to support their establishment. For example, it is well known that South Africa will not limit its nuclear development program; the real fear on the part of African states is that South Africa already has a nuclear capability. As long as the members of the UN continue to try to isolate South Africa from the deliberations within the UN, it remains unlikely that they will get any form of cooperation. Further, as long as South Africa continues to pursue its current policies and perceives its security to be threatened by the frontline black African states, the possibility of agreeing upon a nuclear-weapon-free zone in Africa remains nil. Finally, there are difficulties relating to the transfer of nuclear technology to South Africa by other states. For example, in the General Assembly on 9 December 1981, France, Israel, the United Kingdom, and the United States voted against Resolution 36-86A (regarding the implementation of the declaration on the denuclearization of Africa). In part, these votes reflected the importance that some Western states attach to South Africa's position as a state strongly opposed to Soviet policies in the Indian Ocean region. At the same time, the United States has argued that, rather than serving their intended purposes, UN declarations regarding South Africa actually discourage Pretoria from implementing a nonproliferation policy.

The situation in the Middle East has been increasingly complicated by the Israeli attack on the nuclear reactor in Iraq, as well as by the reluctance of both the United States and Israel to support the establishment of a nuclear-weapon-free zone in that region of the world. Once again it should be acknowledged that the likelihood of establishing such a zone in the Middle East remains out of the question as long as the general political situation remains unresolved. Thus, until the Palestinian question and the final borders of Israel are settled in a manner satisfactory to all parties, it serves little purpose to advocate the establishment of a nuclear-weapon-free zone in the Middle East.

The situation with respect to proposals for a zone in South Asia raises a different set of issues. Pakistan is considered to be a threshold state and could develop a nuclear capability in the foreseeable future. Nevertheless, Islamabad has taken various initiatives to promote nonproliferation within the region. Thus on 12 November 1981 Pakistan submitted a draft resolution regarding the establishment of a nuclear-weapon-free zone in South Asia. The draft resolution was based on Pakistan's commitment to nuclear nonproliferation and its acknowledged concern that other states within the region should advocate a commitment to nuclear nonproliferation.

The Indian situation complicates the establishment of such a zone within South Asia. India has adopted the view that any such initiatives must be taken within the context of a broader nuclear disarmament program. Second, India states that such proposals must emanate from the countries within the region concerned and involve well-defined geographical and political units. Not surprisingly, therefore, when the General Assembly voted on 9 December 1981 on a resolution relating to the establishment of a nuclear-weapon-free zone in Asia, India was one of three recorded votes opposed to the resolution.

Another dimension involves the attitudes of the nuclear powers toward the establishment of such zones. For its part, the Soviet Union has generally argued that the creation of nuclear-weapon-free zones could constitute one measure to reduce the threat of nuclear war as well as to strengthen the nonproliferation regime and regional military detente. Thus, the USSR has supported the establishment of such zones in Africa and the Middle East.

The United States has, in principle, tended to support the concept but has then gone on to reiterate specific criteria to judge the effectiveness of such zones. For example, American statements have generally stated: the initiative must come from the states of the region, all states must participate to effect the implementation of the zone, adequate verification must exist, the existing security arrangements must not be disturbed to the detriment of regional and international security, no nuclear explosive devices should be developed, the arrangement should not impose restrictions on the rights of other states recognized under international law, and, finally, the establishment of a zone should not affect transit privileges for other states including overflights and ports of call.

The other actor of some significance is, of course, China. The Chinese position seems to be based on the view that the establishment of such zones has to be reconciled with the reality that superpower rivalry and military expansion in various regions of the world constitute major obstacles.

On balance, therefore, it would appear highly unlikely that any of the three proposals for the establishment of such zones in the IOR will come to fruition in the foreseeable future.

Conclusions

The foregoing analysis suggests the following conclusions:

1. Given the current international climate, prospects for any form of arms limitation agreement that could enhance IOR security are virtually nonexistent.

2. Even if the current international climate should improve, the prospects for regional arms limitation options, such as either a zone of peace or a nuclear-weapon-free zone in the IOR, appear highly unlikely. The diversity of regional security interests and the concerns of both the major external powers and the IOR states themselves suggest that comprehensive regional arms limitation options will not be agreed upon.

3. Nevertheless, it is in the security interests of the IOR states to advocate the successful conclusion of the chemical weapons treaty and a comprehensive test ban treaty within the framework of the Committee on Disarmament. Agreement on these two issues could have a beneficial impact on IOR security.

4. The IOR states should actively encourage the superpowers to reach agreements in the SNF and INF negotiations. In both cases, agreements could indirectly enhance IOR security. This would be particularly true if a comprehensive nuclear freeze could be agreed upon in conjunction with substantial reductions in counterforce nuclear systems. This would reduce the probability of strategic nuclear war and also reduce the probability of expanding the nuclear arms race into the IOR with new generations of nuclear systems.

5. The Indian Ocean states should continue to urge the nuclear powers to provide negative security assurances for the region, that is, declarations of nonintroduction and nonuse of nuclear weapons. Such declarations are, of course, primarily confidence-building measures but could enhance perceptions of regional security.

6. While nuclear issues have been the primary focus for arms limitation negotiations within the IOR context, it is also important that the transfer of conventional arms be addressed.

As a final observation, it is ironic that the regional proposals for arms limitation offer little prospect for enhancing security and that, in the final analysis, the IOR states must turn to the major external powers for arms limitation options to enhance their own security. In these circumstances, it becomes increasingly important for both the external powers and the Indian Ocean states themselves to search for political solutions rather than to rely upon military solutions to resolve differences. If this can be accomplished, then more valuable and comprehensive regional arms limitation arrangements could have some prospect for success. In the meantime, unfortunately, arms limitation proposals offer no real scope for solving the security problems of the region.

PART THREE ▰

Subregional Perspectives

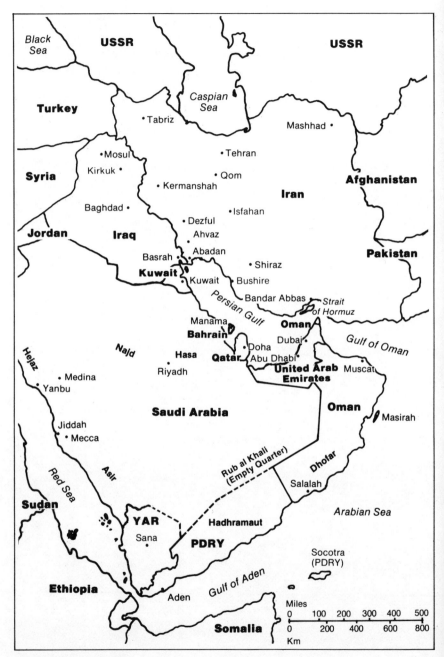

The Persian Gulf

The Persian Gulf

Much of the strategic character of the Indian Ocean region can be attributed directly or indirectly to the fact that nearly three-fifths of the world's proven (and most easily exploitable) oil reserves lie in and around the Persian Gulf. Add to that the gulf's proximity to one of the superpowers and the area's prevailing and potential levels of instability, and one has accounted for much of the explanation for the gulf's salience in late twentieth-century international politics.

In the first of five subregional surveys, we here present the analyses of four distinguished observers of Persian Gulf affairs. In the first essay, Mike Burrell focuses on the implications of the Iran Revolution for security in the gulf. After arguing that recent events in Iran can indeed be described as "revolutionary," Burrell then examines two fundamental questions: whether the Tehran regime has the *desire* to export revolution and whether it has the *ability* to do so. The first question is answered unconditionally in the affirmative; the answer to the second is more problematical. Tehran's success or failure in disseminating Islamic radicalism "will probably rest on factors that are beyond Iran's control." It will depend on "the circumstances that prevail in each individual country. . . . The balance of forces is a delicate one," according to Burrell, "and it would be foolish to offer an optimistic forecast." It would also be unwise to assume that the Iranian revolution is only a short-term challenge: "Although some kind of collective leadership may well emerge" when Ayatollah Khomeini passes from the scene, "the policies followed by the government are unlikely to undergo major or rapid change" in Burrell's judgment. An eventual end to the Iraq-Iran war may cut two ways. On the one hand, the Tehran regime will no longer be able to use the war as the rallying cause for religious zealots or as an excuse for the regime's domestic shortcomings. On the other hand, "a cessation of hostilities would allow Iran to turn its attention and efforts to other areas of the gulf and to indulge even more actively in the dissemination of revolution." The overall prospect in the gulf, therefore, is for continued instability.

Jim Bill's analysis lends support to the notion that the Iranian Revolution is here to stay and that its period of extremism is likely to be prolonged. In a revealing case study, Bill compares the Iranian Revolution to the great revolutions of the past by applying the analytical framework developed by Crane Brinton in his classic study, *Anatomy of Revolution*. In Brinton's terms, the Iranian Revolution is an unfinished one; indeed, it remains in the third stage—the period of extremism— having passed through the fall of the *ancien* regime and the rule of the moderates. Bill finds the explanation for the prolonged period of extremism in the Iranian case in its most striking departure from the Brintonian model: its religion-inspired extremism is an "extremism of the many" rather than the "extremism of the few" that was typical of Brinton's classical revolutions. In the latter part of his essay, Bill undertakes a detailed inventory and analysis of the strengths and weaknesses of the Iranian Revolution, concluding that "there are six major factors that explain the survivability of the new social and political systems that have developed in Iran after the fall of the Shah." At the time this book goes to press, the six factors identified by Bill remain operative: the shrewd, charismatic leadership of Khomeini; the widespread support of the masses; the fervor of Shi'i Islam; the support of the regime by the military; the growing experience of the clerics in governing; and the unifying effect of external threats. Bill predicts that "the Iranian Thermidor will one day appear," that is, the period of a convalescent swing back to moderate politics. This next stage may conceivably be ushered in by Khomeini's death, a loss of military support, or the lessening of external threat by, for example, an end to the war with Iraq. Brinton's final stage of revolution is the rise of a new form of authoritarianism to succeed the period of Thermidor. Will the new authoritarianism arise from the right or from the left? Neither Bill nor we are incautious enough to attempt to answer that question.

Tareq Ismael takes us from Bill's realm of microanalysis to the macroanalysis of the systems perspective. He conducts the reader through three transformations of the Middle East subsystem in an attempt to trace the evolution of events that led to the Iraq-Iran war. Tracking the successive transformations of the "Arab cooperative core" and the "Arab-Israeli conflict core" and the changing role of the "intrusive system" (external power participation in the affairs of the region), Ismael makes a case for the proposition that events in the gulf have over time more tightly integrated the Arab gulf states into the Arab cooperative core.

The threat of Iran's Islamic expansionism, together with Israel's increased militancy in Lebanon and on the West Bank, has, according to Ismael, promoted greater solidarity within the Arab cooperative core and reduced the significance of ideological divisions within the Arab world. Whether one agrees or not with the proposition that the Iraq-Iran war has promoted Arab solidarity is perhaps less important than Ismael's reminder that events in the gulf are inextricably linked to the Arab-Israeli conflict.

Ruhi Ramazani offers one of the first authoritative analyses of the origins and prospects of the Gulf Cooperation Council (GCC). Noting that the original raison d'être of the GCC was mutual economic benefit, Ramazani points out that the course of events in the gulf quickly shifted the focus of the organization to security and defense cooperation. "The all-important reason for the fear of the six monarchical regimes for their survival was, and continues to be, the perceived threat of contagion of the antimonarchical Iranian Revolution. Against the background of this greater concern, fear of the spread of the gulf war appears to have been more the catalyst than the cause of the creation of the GCC." Ramazani identifies three other factors that were influential in the creation of the GCC: the Soviet invasion of Afghanistan, the search for an alternative to a too-close association with the United States; and the Saudi Arabian desire to exploit the preoccupation of Iraq and Iran with each other in order to bolster Riyadh's own position in the gulf. Returning to discussion of the Iranian Revolution as the single most important explanation of GCC solidarity, Ramazani argues that it is Saudi Arabia that "perceives the threat of Iranian agitation . . . most vividly." Indeed, he discusses at some length what he calls the "Riyadh-Tehran cold war" that has as its basis the Saudis' support for the shah, the objectionable behavior of Iranian pilgrims to Mecca, the diametrically opposed relationships of the two capitals with the United States, the more radical stance of the Iranians toward Israel, and the long-running differences between Tehran and Riyadh over oil prices and production levels. As for the future prospects of the GCC, Ramazani discounts three alternative GCC options (military buildup, military partnership with Iraq, close military association with the United States) in favor of a fourth policy line. "Future security and stability of the gulf region and that of the GCC and its members will depend less on military muscle than on political and diplomatic consensus. That is the single most important lesson of an objective study of the GCC's experiences over its early life." For the future success of its objectives, the GCC will have to develop a consensus within the organization over the nature and extent of its relationship with Iraq and Iran and with the superpowers. Furthermore, Ramazani counsels, the GCC states should accord their relationship with Iran the highest priority, setting as their minimal goal damage limitation in GCC-Iran relations.

7. Implications of the Iranian Revolution for the Security of the Persian Gulf ⚓ R. M. Burrell

The title of this chapter conceals at least two presuppositions: that there has been a revolution in Iran and that the revolutionary process has already had important consequences for the stability of the gulf region. The title may also appear to suggest that those implications are now both evident and certain, a conclusion in no way justified by events. Both of the presuppositions merit brief review before the central theme can be discussed.

Those who use the term "revolution" lay themselves open to the close scrutiny of political scientists who have devoted much effort to the definition of that term, and to the construction of comparative typologies. For purposes of this discussion it is assumed that revolutions are characterized by a violent shift in the location of political power accompanied by changes in both the ideology of the state and in the institutions of government. Using those criteria, and adding the further observation that such violent changes tend to reject, and sometimes even to devour, their own children, then the recent history of Iran can indeed be described as revolutionary.[1] The precise nature of that revolution is more difficult to define but it requires careful clarification because the avowed aims of Ayatollah Khomeini and his supporters have undeniable consequences for other states of the region, as well as for Iran.

The political views of Khomeini are complex and his expression of them is often intricate and obscure, at least to the non-Muslim reader.[2] At heart what he has said is that the role of the religious classes should be a more dynamic one and that whereas in the past they acted as the guardians of the community of believers, they should now take upon themselves the tasks of government. In earlier times their function was to act as "holders of the political ring," as the means whereby political legitimacy was conferred upon, or possibly withdrawn from, the ruler of the day. This theoretical position was not always achieved in practice for strong and determined shahs could, and did, challenge the authority of the religious leaders, but the latters' power and influence were both considerable and enduring.

Some earlier Muslim writers had indeed expressed the belief that if mortal danger were ever to threaten the Islamic community then the religious leaders themselves should direct the affairs of state.[3] What Khomeini has argued is that this ought to happen in normal and ordinary circumstances and that, in the absence of the Hidden Imam, political power in Iran should rest in the hands of those who are learned in Islamic law.[4]

It would, however, be a mistake to imagine that Khomeini's theories apply exclusively to the Shi'ite Muslim community, for many of his views appeal with equal force to adherents of the majority Sunni branch of that faith. The importance of the Ayatollah's writings lies not only in the activist role that he seeks for the religious leaders, but also in his forceful reassertion of traditional views concerning the origins of political sovereignty and the nature of law. On both matters he is uncompromising: political sovereignty belongs exclusively to God, and he alone can make law. Such views are difficult, if not impossible, to reconcile with theories that regard man as a political animal who has the right to govern his own affairs. In Khomeini's world the burdens laid upon government are strictly defined. They involve nothing more, or less, than the preservation and the enforcement of Islamic law.[5] The law of God is preexistent, immutable, and all-embracing. It must not be modified or abrogated, and its rigorous implementation will assuredly lead to the emergence of a better world. The danger of arbitrary, corrupt, or despotic rule—against which democracies have tried to create a series of institutionalized checks and balances—should not arise, for what an Islamic government has to do is already laid down and widely known. Any deviations from the set path will therefore be obvious. Moreover, justice and tranquility are guaranteed if divine law is implemented in full, for they are essential features of God's universe.

According to Khomeini's view, the government's functions are therefore limited (because they have been divinely prescribed), but its tasks will not be light or easy, for Islamic values have been weakened by both the onslaught of alien secular ideas and by the blandishments of material prosperity. In offering his solution to the problems now faced by the whole Islamic community Khomeini stands apart from one of the most striking trends to have emerged during the last hundred years, namely the desire to learn from the West. He is, of course, even more strongly opposed to its corollary, the urge to imitate.[6]

In rejecting the ways of the foreigner Khomeini can evoke a powerful emotional response among those Muslims who feel that their religion has been enfeebled, and their sense of community undermined, by a slavish copying of secular ways and by the importation of alien institutions. By reverting to traditional teachings, the Ayatollah can therefore appeal to those Muslims who have embraced new ideologies and found them wanting, as well as to those who have never succumbed to such delusory attractions. The number of people in those two categories is by no means inconsiderable.

In discussing the possible consequences of Ayatollah Khomeini's political theories for the future stability of the gulf, there are two matters that require close attention: the desire of the Tehran regime to "export" revolution and its ability to do so. The first issue is relatively simple and can be dealt with quite quickly, but the other is more complex. Neither would be of more than academic interest were it not for the fact that the economies of the Western industrialized world will depend on oil supplies from the gulf until well into the twenty-first century.

On the issue of Ayatollah Khomeini's desire to expand the influence of the Iranian Revolution there can be little doubt. He has lost no opportunity to inspire suitable audiences with his wish to see other states adopt a system of government similar to that which now prevails in Tehran. Iranian students, diplomats, and, most important, pilgrims have been repeatedly told of the need to encourage other Muslims to return to the path of righteousness and to seek a renewal of traditional values. If Khomeini's political theories have received less attention from Western commentators than they have deserved, then his views of international relations have languished in even greater obscurity. What the Ayatollah seeks is nothing less than the triumph of Islam and he therefore rejects the present system of nation-states and of international relations. His view is both messianic and global; Iran's destiny is to lead the revival of Islam and to show the rest of the world the error of its ways. His messages to Iranian pilgrims departing for the annual journey to Mecca and Medina have been of considerable significance in this respect. Ever since he came to power in 1979 Khomeini has repeated the view that the pilgrimage is an event of political as well as of religious importance.[7] In his address to the departing pilgrims in September 1980, for example, the Iranian leader laid down the four conditions for the release of the American hostages that ultimately formed the basis of negotiations. In 1981 and again in September 1982, his exhortations to the outward-bound pilgrims were politically inflammatory. When those individuals held marches and demonstrations in Mecca and Medina, at which photographs of Khomeini were prominently displayed, the Saudi authorities were quick to arrest the most vocal of their leaders—including some members of the Iranian parliament—and even to deport some of those who were seized. To act in such a way against pilgrims in Islam's most revered cities is a matter of no little concern and sensitivity and Tehran was quick to condemn the "brutal and repressive behavior" of the Saudi security forces.[8] It would therefore be foolish to underestimate Khomeini's desire to disseminate the principles of Iran's revolution, for in his eyes the Islamic community is an indissoluble whole and Tehran's leadership will soon be cherished and emulated by Muslims everywhere.

What is more questionable is the ability of Iran to impose its views on its neighbors. History reveals that relations between the Persians and the Arabs have often been marked by deep, mutual suspicion. Since September 1980, for example, Iran and Iraq have been at war.[9] The origins of that conflict are many and varied; the immediate cause was a long-standing border dispute but it must be emphasized that the overthrow of the shah and the establishment of a new revolutionary regime in Tehran were also factors of considerable importance. It is difficult to imagine that Iraq, with a population only one third that of its eastern neighbor, would have opened hostilities with Iran if the Pahlavi monarch had remained firmly on the throne. The late shah's determination to preserve and to defend the interests of his country was obvious to all; the chaos and confusion that followed in the wake of his downfall may well have prompted the Iraqi regime to reevaluate its chances of achieving a military victory. The fact that so many senior officers had been executed, while others had fled into exile, together with the scale of desertions from the ranks of the army, meant that the morale and the command structure of the Iranian armed forces were seriously weakened. The Iraqi president, Saddam Hussein, certainly did not view those events with any sense of regret. While Baghdad may have welcomed the disintegration of the Iranian armed forces that occurred during and after the fall of the shah, it could not adopt the same attitude toward the new policies being pursued by Tehran. The majority of Iraq's population consists of Shi'ites and the appeal of Ayatollah Khomeini to them was not inconsiderable.

The installation of an Islamic government in Iran had therefore two consequences for Iraq. On the one hand the regime of Ayatollah Khomeini was believed to be militarily much weaker than the shah's had been, but at the same time the revolutionary fervor of Tehran was seen as a considerable threat to the stability of the government in Baghdad. In other words, the opportunity for inflicting military defeat on Iran appeared to be greater at the very time when the reasons for taking such action against that country were increasing. It has also been suggested that Baghdad may have been encouraged in its belief that the regime in Tehran was weak by exiled Iranian politicians who saw an Iraqi attack as a possible means of toppling the government and of regaining office themselves. What is certain is that throughout 1979 and the early months of 1980 Iranian-Iraqi relations were steadily deteriorating.

Other factors were also at work, for the border dispute between Iran and Iraq has deep historical roots. The Ottoman Empire and Safavid Persia fought many battles to assert control over the frontier zone between the two states. In the nineteenth and early twentieth centuries British and Russian diplomats strove to achieve a satisfactory demarcation of the border. In 1975 Iraq and Iran signed a new agreement in Algiers that, in theory, resolved the dispute. In fact, the regime in Baghdad resented that settlement, claiming that it had been negotiated under duress. Iran was, at that time, assisting Kurdish guerrilla operations in northern Iraq, and the shah insisted on all Iran's demands being met before he would cease to provide that support. One of the leading figures in the 1975 negotiations was Saddam Hussein. It has been suggested that the substantial concessions Iraq was required to make served to undermine his political position. To abrogate the unpopular treaty would therefore help him in the task of consolidating his control over the regime.

International as well as domestic circumstances also appear to have played a part in Iraq's decision to denounce the 1975 treaty and to seek a military solution to its dispute with Iran. The Camp David agreements of 1978 had resulted in the isolation of Egypt from its Arab neighbors. This meant that the Arab world was, in effect, left without an obvious leader. Under normal circumstances, and for many reasons, Cairo is the political center of the Arab bloc and there is no clear alternative candidate. Libyan pretensions are well known but equally widely scorned, and Saudi Arabia has yet to learn how to convert its massive financial strength into sustained political influence. Iraq, however, with its relatively large population and a potentially rich economy, can advance a good claim to be considered as the representative of the Arab world if Egypt is, for any reason, unable to perform that task. There is little doubt that Saddam Hussein coveted such a role, and establishing Iraq's military prowess by defeating Iran would certainly have helped him to assert his claim. It has also been pointed out that Baghdad was due to act as the host city for a nonaligned summit conference to be held in 1982; Iraq's standing in that body too would have been enhanced if it had been able to gain a victory over Iran.

The prevailing nature of great power relations with the Middle East may also have influenced Iraq's decision to go to war in the autumn of 1980. Washington was still locked in its bitter dispute with Tehran over the continued incarceration of the diplomatic hostages, and it was therefore most unlikely that the United States would give any aid to its former ally, Iran, if hostilities were to occur. At the same time the Soviet Union was heavily engaged in trying to assert its control over Afghanistan and Moscow would probably be very reluctant to get involved in any other dispute in the region. In other words Iraq could proceed to plan a war with few fears that the great powers would unite to prevent hostilities.

The background to the current fighting between Iran and Iraq is therefore a very complex one but the most important factor would appear to have been the belief of Saddam Hussein that his regime was threatened by the revolutionary fervor and appeal of Tehran. Ayatollah Khomeini had spent several years in exile in Iraq and his message on coming to power was unmistakable: the Baathist regime in Baghdad was not a legitimate one and its removal was both desirable and necessary. The clandestine Shi'ite organizations within Iraq were therefore given greater support and they became increasingly active.[10] In April 1980 Baghdad accused Tehran of being responsible for an attempt to assassinate Vice President Tariq Aziz. Later that month a leading Iraqi Shi'ite figure, Muhammad Baqir al Sadr, was arrested and summarily executed. Ayatollah Khomeini, who was a close friend of al Sadr, regarded that death as an act of murder, and this greatly increased his resolve to destroy the regime in Baghdad. Propaganda broadcasts from Tehran began to call openly for the violent overthrow of Saddam Hussein. Baghdad responded by expelling several thousand Iraqis of Iranian origin and in mid-July the Iraqi leader made a virulent public attack on Iran's "expansionism."

When the war began in September 1980, initial Iraqi successes appeared to confirm Baghdad's view that a quick and decisive victory was possible. Khorramshahr was soon captured and Abadan was besieged, but it could not be taken. Iran started to mount effective air attacks against oil installations in southern Iraq, thereby forcing Baghdad to rely exclusively on pipelines to the Mediterranean for the export of its petroleum. Winter brought a lull in the fighting but Iran began slowly to regain the military initiative during 1981, and the siege of Abadan was lifted in the autumn of that year. In May 1982 Khorramshahr was recaptured and in July Iranian forces—including units of the regular army and members of the Revolutionary Guards—crossed into Iraq. Tehran has not, however, been able to achieve the decisive victory it has sought and promised its people. It has failed, for example, to cut the vital road linking Baghdad with Basra and Kuwait, and both armies have shown greater fighting ability when defending their own territory than when attacking that of their neighbor. All attempts at mediation by bodies as diverse as the United Nations, the Islamic Conference, and the non-aligned movement have failed to produce any result, and the prospects of an early end to the war do not appear to be very good. The most obvious effects of the war have been an increase in the xenophobia of Iran and a revival in the ability of its armed forces. This latter factor has led some commentators to speculate that this may have hastened the day when an officer might seek to challenge the political authority of the government in Tehran. The Iranian regime is certainly well aware of the existence of a potential military threat and it continues to view the regular army with some suspicion. Even if the war were to end, however, the government could certainly keep its troops occupied in maintaining, or in some cases reestablishing, law and order in remote and turbulent provinces such as Kurdistan.

Iran's success in retaking the territories invaded by Iraq, and the fact that its economy has not collapsed into the ruin so confidently and repeatedly predicted by many economists and financial experts, have recently induced the governments of some of the smaller gulf states to reconsider their relations with Tehran. While none of those rulers has any cause to welcome Khomeini's Islamic fervor, the considerable cost of providing financial support for Iraq is beginning to prove very burdensome, particularly at a time when oil income has failed to reach predicted, and expected, levels. There is therefore a realistic desire, particularly in the United Arab Emirates, to try to reestablish better relations with their powerful northern neighbor. This wish is tempered, however, by the knowledge that Iran has already shown its willingness to aid and to support dissident groups opposed to incumbent gulf regimes.

The most spectacular example of this occurred in December 1981 when the security authorities in Bahrain arrested a total of seventy-three young men who were later charged with a series of offenses, including attempting to overthrow the government. Details of the affair remain few but the discovery of the plot owed much to the sharp eyes of immigration officials in Dubai who noticed suspicious, and probably forged, entries in the passports of a number of young men in transit to Bahrain. The group that was responsible for the plot, the Islamic Front for the Liberation of Bahrain, has its headquarters in Iran, and a considerable quantity of small arms were smuggled from there into Bahrain by both air and sea. It would appear that those arrested did not include the most senior members of the organization who were supposed to arrive in

Bahrain just before the coup was mounted. During the subsequent investigations it was alleged that some of those arrested had received training in weaponry and sabotage from Palestinian instructors at camps in southern Iran, and some of the plotters showed that they had been taught sophisticated techniques of resisting interrogation.

This incident prompted some rather frantic discussions on security cooperation among the Arab littoral states, and it led to the signing of bilateral treaties of protection between Saudi Arabia and both Bahrain and Qatar. This reaction has, however, given rise to further problems because some of the inhabitants of the smaller states—particularly the United Arab Emirates—have seen the treaties as yet another step toward Riyadh's alleged goal of seeking to exercise hegemony over the whole peninsula. Furthermore, Tehran has condemned the rulers of Bahrain and Qatar for seeking the protection of a power that is in league with "the great Satan." The closeness of the links between Riyadh and Washington is a powerful weapon in the hands of revolutionary Muslims of all political hues, and Tehran has not been slow to criticize the regime that has trust of Islam's most sacred shrines as treacherous and traitorous. When the death of King Khalid was announced in June 1982, radio Tehran stated that the Saudi monarch had "ruled for eight years as the head of a dynasty which placed all the human and material resources of the Arabian Islamic land at the disposal of western imperialism. May he get what he deserves from God."[11]

Although, as noted, much of Khomeini's thinking appeals to Sunni as well as to Shi'ite Muslims, it is the latter group that provides the most fertile ground for the dissemination of his views. Those states, or areas, with sizable Shi'ite populations are therefore the most obvious targets for action. The largest such group is in Iraq where, as noted above, Shi'ites account for over half the total population, and Tehran has given sustained support to clandestine Shi'ite groups such as Al Dawa (The Call) and Al Mujahidin (The Warriors).

Other important Shi'ite communities exist in Kuwait, Bahrain, and Dubai, and perhaps the most sensitive group of all is that in the eastern province of Saudi Arabia. There are no reliable figures for the size of that population but its numbers are less important than the fact that the group lives in the very heart of the oil-producing region.[12] There was quite serious unrest among that community in November 1979, at the same time as the attack on the Great Mosque in Mecca. The Saudi authorities then promised to rectify some of the long-standing grievances of the Shi'ites, in particular to improve the quality of local administration and to offer them greater opportunities in government service. Little appears to have been done and there were renewed violent disturbances in both 1981 and the spring of 1982. On several occasions public buildings and banks were attacked and communication links were disrupted. There is no evidence to suggest that Tehran's efforts to encourage dissidence among the Saudi Shi'ites are likely to diminish. Both the royal regimes of the Arabian peninsula and the secular Baathist government in Iraq therefore have genuine cause for alarm about the future intentions of Tehran. Its willingness to support radical terrorist groups of various political complexions is a matter of growing concern.

If Khomeini's desire to export revolution cannot be gainsaid, and while Tehran's ability to disseminate Islamic radicalism may be increasing, the success or failure of such ventures will probably rest on factors that are beyond Iran's control. To put the matter briefly, the extent to which the Ayatollah's ideology will attract other Muslims will depend upon the circumstances that prevail in each individual country. In lands where corruption, injustice, and inequality flourish, and in which religious values are publicly embraced but privately flouted by the ruling regime, the appeal of Islamic revolution may well be considerable. Under such circumstances the support, both material and ideological, of Tehran could be of great importance. In states where the sources of public discontent are less serious and provocative, then political opposition, despite the encouragement of Tehran, may not reach revolutionary dimensions.

The balance of forces is certainly a delicate one and it would be foolish to offer an optimistic forecast because the problems faced by the states of the Arab littoral are growing rather than diminishing. Perhaps the most serious long-term issue is the fact that oil incomes are now failing to match expectations. In the absence of a marked revival in global economic activity, oil sales would appear unlikely to increase in the foreseeable future. Iran's need to raise revenue from petroleum exports has led it to market its oil production at prices well below the agreed OPEC level. If hostilities with Iraq were to end, then both Baghdad and Tehran would immediately take the opportunity to try to increase the volume of their sales. This might, in turn, have a further depressant effect on the level of oil prices.

The impact of declining revenues obviously varies from country to country, and those most seriously affected are outside the gulf. But even the small wealthy emirates are now experiencing a degree of difficulty and the omens are far from reassuring. The fact that oil incomes have ceased to rise, together with the effects of their recent sharp fluctuations, have already begun to stimulate criticism of past economic policies. Some of the proud and nationalistic students from the gulf states who were sent to colleges and universities in Europe and North

America are now beginning to return home, and they find that there are diminishing opportunities to demonstrate their newly acquired skills. In some cases this is because of the resistance and opposition of older, established, officials and bureaucrats; in others, it is because investment funds are now greatly reduced in volume and new projects cannot be started. The returning graduates are therefore looking at their societies with a critical eye and sometimes in a mood of bitter disappointment. The fact that existing expensive industrial ventures have often failed to show profits—except to their Western suppliers, and not infrequently to those officials responsible for awarding the construction contracts—is increasingly a matter of debate. Some of those students now use the phrase "the economics of the treadmill." This somber judgment, which also reveals a measure of desperation, reflects the view that planning decisions made over the last decade when oil incomes were constantly rising have left the producing states with no alternative but to go on exporting their single vital commodity; almost all attempts at diversification have proved to be inadequate. The massive industrial schemes need constant subsidies to survive, while the indigenous economy—poor and fragile though it may have been—has been allowed to fall into total disrepair. Agriculture and fishing have received little careful attention say such critics, and oil income is therefore diverted from investment in order to pay for greater and greater food imports. The hope that revenues from petroleum would generate real and sustained growth, and that this would ensure both prosperity and economic independence, is now seen to be a snare and a delusion.

When such critical attitudes prevail, the appeal of Khomeini's views, which describe the states of the industrialized West as imperialist exploiters of the Muslim world, can appear attractive and even realistic. The fact that oil incomes are falling in value and that hard economic decisions will have to be made in many, if not all, of the producing states, may well allow the rhetoric of the Iranian Revolution to reach a larger number of ears, ears that will surely be more receptive than they would have been in conditions of rising prosperity.

Such considerations are of a long-term nature and more immediate problems now confront the Arab states of the gulf, perhaps the most serious of which is the continuation of Iraq's very expensive war with Iran. The other states of the region are becoming increasingly reluctant to supply funds to Baghdad, yet they cannot afford to see Iraq defeated.[13] The possibility of having to provide help with the heavy war reparations now demanded by Tehran is also an alarming prospect.[14] It is, however, Iraq that stands to lose most from the war, for that conflict has drained Baghdad of both men and money. The recent imposition of harsh economic policies by the government in Baghdad has finally brought home to the population the heavy costs involved and the almost total absence of any compensating success.

It has been argued that Saddam Hussein's position may now be less secure than it was at the start of the war. His political opponents may well wait for him to incur the odium of making peace with Iran on unfavorable terms before they attempt to unseat him. Meanwhile, the opportunities provided for Tehran to make political mischief are considerable and they are not being ignored. The possibility of a general Shi'ite uprising in Iraq is sometimes raised—and it would certainly be a terrible event—but the security forces will make every effort to prevent such an occurrence, and the Shi'ite organizations are probably not sufficiently strong or well coordinated to launch such an insurrection. A more realistic possibility would appear to be a sequence of bloody riots in towns and cities that have a large Shi'ite population; the religious centers of Najaf and Karbala are the most sensitive of all. Iran would certainly encourage—even if it had not already instigated—such turbulence. In other words, the threat from revolutionary Iran to the security of Iraq is likely to be a persistent one and it will endure beyond any possible cessation of military hostilities.

The expulsion of the Palestinian guerrillas from Beirut has also provided Tehran with another stick with which to beat incumbent Arab regimes. In the future, as the Palestinian organizations take stock of their new position, it seems likely that there will be much bitter and rancorous criticism of established regimes—particularly of the wealthy monarchical ones—for their failure to "save" the Palestinians. Indeed there are already signs that this process has begun.[15] Again Tehran will probably feel tempted to take an active part in the argument and it will likely lend its weight to those who are most violent in their condemnation of existing royal governments. Tehran's vocal support for the Palestinians has not, however, prevented it from accepting military supplies from Israel for its war with Iraq.

The major source of Khomeini's appeal to radical political groups is, of course, his role as the agent of the shah's destruction. There is still much wonderment in the gulf, and elsewhere, that a monarch who looked so powerful and confident could be toppled with such speed and ease. Appearances are, however, deceptive, and the reasons for the downfall of the shah extend far beyond the political counterattractions offered by a fundamentalist religious leader. Nevertheless Khomeini is seen as the man who brought about the end of the Pahlavi dynasty and as such he is an enormously attractive figure to those who seek a similar fate for other royal houses in the region. The fact that Iran is a sovereign state and can therefore offer tangible assistance in many and varied forms, serves only to enhance the value of his patronage.

As several Iranian political groups have learned—and are still learning at a bloody cost—the objectives of Khomeini and his supporters are by no means similar to those of the radicals.[16] Foreign groups that look to him for support are either blind to his acts of political repression at home or they have chosen to ignore them. In this respect it is worth considering, albeit very briefly, the attitude adopted by some Iranian groups toward the revolutionary regime. The initial, and shared, euphoria over the downfall of the shah did not endure for long before traditional liberal nationalists began to despair of the new regime. Politicians of an older generation—men such as Amini and Bazargan—quickly recognized that their aspirations, the creation of representative and responsible popular government, had little part in Khomeini's plan for Iran. Other groups, which shared the Ayatollah's authoritarian view of government but not his conception of its purpose, were happy to remain in alliance with him. But many of the religious leaders around Khomeini are men of considerable political ability and over the last few years they have gradually, and relentlessly, strengthened their grip on power. The reaction of the various leftist groups to this process is of considerable interest and it may help to illuminate the possible future nature of Tehran's relations with non-Iranian extremist groups.

The response of some Iranian radicals has been to condemn the Ayatollah's regime as both brutal and reactionary while they also claim that he came to power "along the broad road built by the Left," a view that is as spurious as it is simplistic. Some groups, however, have conducted a more rigorous analysis of the Iranian political situation and their views are both unusual and challenging.[17] What Khomeini regards as the greatest strength of the new regime—the active role given to the religious leaders—is seen by some radicals as its greatest potential weakness. They argue that by seeking the political limelight, by putting themselves forward as the very agents of government, the men of God have now laid themselves open to the charge of incompetence and ineptitude. In the past the political role of the religious classes was an indirect one and this meant that when policies failed and popular discontent grew the blame could be put elsewhere than on them: on the monarch, on his ministers, on foreign powers. Now that the religious leaders have both claimed, and begun to exercise, political power in their own right, many of those previous scapegoats have been removed and political censure will largely fall upon them alone. According to this analysis, what Khomeini has done is to make possible, for the first time ever, the political discrediting of Islam.

It is interesting to note that this is precisely the fear of some of Khomeini's religious opponents, of whom Ayatollah Shariatmadari is perhaps the best known. They recognize the great perils that will arise from being involved in the day-to-day conduct of affairs. Such religious figures have argued that it is very dangerous for their colleagues to take such a dominant and public part in government, and they have urged a return to the earlier situation in which the religious leaders had a much less prominent, but nevertheless very influential, role as guardians of the community of believers.

In keeping with this analysis some Iranian radicals now appear to take the view that Khomeini and his supporters should be "left to dig their own political graves," and that the energies of the radical organizations should be conserved for use in the struggle for power that will emerge as the current regime begins to collapse. It is, perhaps, pertinent here to suggest that the actual death of Khomeini is not necessarily foreseen by all Iranian radicals as heralding a suitable opportunity to seek office. For some of them have realized that although there is no single individual who could assume his mantle, many of those around him—who are often his former students—are deeply committed to his views. Although some kind of collective leadership may well emerge (and that process, while secret, would probably be marked by some bitter struggles and wrangling), the policies followed by the government are unlikely to undergo major or rapid change.

There is an extension of the above rather unusual view of Iran's political future that is relevant to the region as a whole, for it suggests that what we are observing is not a revival or a resurgence of Islam, but rather the final convulsive death throes of that religion as a political and social force. Adherents of this view argue that the regime in Iran will prove totally incapable of running a modern state and of planning a developing economy and that their failure will be obvious and catastrophic. This will in turn convince Muslims that while their religion can be a powerful source of moral guidance and of spiritual solace, it cannot hope to provide all-embracing solutions to every contemporary problem. The only answer, according to such an analysis, is for the Muslim states to follow the path of the West, i.e., to view Islam as a matter for the conscience of each individual believer. While the state should respect such values, it is in no way required to formulate its policies with the precepts of religion in mind nor should its actions be judged against those criteria.

Such views may appear attractive, and might even offer a measure of comfort, to those who are currently excluded from political power in Iran and who are suffering under a campaign of intense repression, but they remain somewhat fanciful. The essential reason why Islam is such a powerful political force is that many millions of people continue to believe deeply in its teachings and are obedient in following its precepts. If they ever begin to find their religion inadequate, if it can no longer provide them with both moral guidance and a sense of identity, then the above changes may begin to occur. But there are few, if any, signs of such a weakening in the mass appeal of Islam and while the faith endures its political role is unlikely to diminish.

More than five years after the downfall of the shah, the revolutionary regime in Iran has gone a long way toward consolidating its political position. New institutions have been created and old ones have been modified in such a way that theocratic rule has been established. This fact may be unpalatable for those whose attitudes are democratic and secular but our analysis will not be improved by pretending that the situation is other than it is. The new regime in Tehran obviously cannot fulfill the grandiose promises made by the late monarch, but the question then arises, and it merits careful attention: what do the Iranian people expect of their government? In the industrialized states the demands made on government are very great and the shah's attempts to modernize his country would almost certainly have led in a similar direction. But Khomeini's view is the traditional one that government should be minimal: defending the borders of Islam, propagating its values, maintaining internal tranquility, and administering impartial justice. The question raised by the radicals—how well can Islam cope with the affairs of state?—should perhaps be rephrased and put in the form, with what affairs of state will Islam have to cope? Only time will tell whether the Ayatollah's views are an accurate reflection of current Iranian perceptions. The fact that the population of Iran is so youthful— more than half the people are aged sixteen or under—may well have an important influence on this matter.

Another relevant question in considering the efficacy, and therefore the potential longevity, of the revolutionary regime is that of political legitimacy. The point at which discontent is transformed into open hostility and rebellion is greatly influenced by the degree of legitimacy attached to that government, and the current Iranian one can certainly lay greater claim to that attribute than could the Pahlavi dynasty. If Khomeini's views are well founded, then the fact that the regime is clearly Islamic in both composition and ideology may well help to compensate for a considerable degree of inefficiency. We might note too that a review of Islamic literature reveals that traditional rulers were often far from ignorant of the skills of statecraft.

The fact that the new regime lacks even the outward trappings of a democracy has also prompted some observers to cast doubts on both its domestic appeal and its possible durability. But, as noted, the traditional political philosophy of Islam is quietist and it is not one that emphasizes the desirability, let alone the necessity, of popular political participation. Experience in recent years of so-called "democratic" institutions in Iran, and elsewhere in the gulf, has been neither extensive nor propitious.

The outbreak of the war with Iraq has helped the revolutionary regime to strengthen its grip on power; in the organization of rationing, for example, it has shown itself to be both astute and competent. The fact that military defeat has been avoided, the opportunity to channel religious zeal against an external enemy, and the enthusiastic surge of xenophobia—these are factors that have combined to increase the prestige and the influence of the government in Tehran. There would seem to be few pressing reasons for Iran to seek an immediate end to the hostilities, but the incapacitation of the oil-loading facilities at Kharg Island could serve to alter that situation. If hostilities were to be terminated, then paradoxically the economic problems facing the regime would probably increase, for reconstruction of the devastated areas would then be necessary and it would no longer be possible to use the continuation of the war as an excuse for delaying that task. At the same time a cessation of hostilities would allow Iran to turn its attention and efforts to other areas of the gulf, and to indulge even more actively in the dissemination of revolution.[18]

In attempting to do so, however, the government in Tehran would be aware that it too is vulnerable to externally inspired subversion. The late shah's claim to be an imperial monarch was not merely a manifestation of royal grandeur. It was rather an accurate reflection of the fact that the Iranian population is a mixture, but not a blend, of diverse groups. Many of the country's border regions are inhabited by people who are not Persians and the opportunities thereby offered for the encouragement of separatist movements are far from inconsiderable. The most obvious example is that of the Kurds but when Iran and Iraq are at war the group's freedom for political maneuver is severely restricted; in Azarbaijan, northern Khurasan, and Baluchistan Iran is also vulnerable to a degree of fragmentation. Should the regime fail to maintain an adequate degree of central control and should separatist movements arise and pose a serious threat to the territorial integrity of the country, then Iran's northern neighbor would probably not stand idly by. However, an analysis of such great power involvement is beyond the scope of this chapter.

Barring a sudden and unexpected change in the nature of the regime in Iran it would, therefore, be true to say that the stability of the gulf is unlikely to increase in the near future. The Tehran government lacks for nothing in its desire to export revolution and its abilities to accomplish that end are not inconsiderable, for the political causes of violent unrest are already manifest in several states of the region. Many of the local Arab rulers were alarmed by the late shah's portrayal of himself as the "policeman of the gulf"; they can hardly be less comforted by his successor's desire to act as its harbinger of revolution. They must hope that there is truth in the Persian proverb that says, "The hollower the drum, the greater its sound."

8. Political Stability and the Future of the Islamic Republic of Iran ◼ James A. Bill

The continuing existence of the Islamic Republic of Iran has confounded the predictions of many observers and analysts who have forecast its demise ever since the revolution that overthrew the shah in 1978–79. Although personal insecurity, social upheaval, economic hardship, political conflict, and internal and external violence have shaken Iran ever since 1978, the system survives. Extremist religious leaders continue to direct the regime which continues in power despite numerous challenges and obstacles: a full-scale war against an invading neighbor on the western front, approximately 1.5 million refugees within its borders to the west and to the east, a struggling economy increasingly lacking resources and financial reserves, a political leadership that has suffered unprecedented losses in lives through assassinations and bombings, the flight and opposition (passive and active) of nearly one million members of the educated, professional, middle class who once provided the backbone of the technocracy, the constant threat of well-organized and dedicated guerrilla forces committed to the destruction of the regime, and the intermittent pressures of international ostracization.

Given these facts, it is time that political analysts began to reassess and to reevaluate as objectively as possible the social and political systems that exist in revolutionary Iran. In so doing, both weaknesses and strengths, problems and successes must be recognized and evaluated. On the whole, observers have tended to take polemical positions based on biased preconceptions, slanted sources, or superficial understandings. As a result, we have only a primitive understanding of the social and political processes at work in post-Pahlavi Iran.

Revolutions are highly disruptive and painful social and political events. Violence is an integral part of such movements; political incoherence and personal suffering often follow for years in the wake of revolutions. Revolutions tear their ways through and across societies and remain unfinished for years, even decades. There is no reason to believe that the revolution in Iran will be any different in this respect from the other great revolutions that have transformed society and changed the course of history. In fact, there are good reasons to believe that the Iranian case can be expected to be even more violent and disruptive than those that occurred in Western and Asiatic contexts.

Despite these facts of history, observers profess surprise at what has been occurring in Iran since 1978. Some are especially shocked because they either held vested interests in the *ancien* regime or had a stake in the establishment of some particular type of new system. Others have been genuinely stunned and upset by the ugly violence, cruel executions, and extremist politics that have marked Iran over the past few years. This revolution, like many others before it, has managed to convert high expectations into disillusionment and despair among many who supported it in its initial stages. As a result, these later casualties have joined hands with the members of the old regime who were the early losers, and together they have made it difficult for outsiders to develop a serious understanding of the social and political dynamics that energize the new system.

This situation has been aggravated by the extreme xenophobia and paranoia of the new regime that has only crudely sought to communicate its goals and realities to the world outside. At the center of this confusion and chaos in understanding has been a continuing bitter and bloody war of survival that has gone on between the new government and those groups dedicated to its destruction, as well as between the Iranian nation and outside powers such as Iraq. In these circumstances, it is little wonder that rhetoric triumphs over realism and reason, while emotion clouds and twists objectivity.

Finally, even before the revolution, Iranian society and politics were highly resistant to the understanding of outsiders. The subtlety of the culture, the evasiveness of the political process, and the complexities of Shi'i Islam always made the study of Iran a special challenge. It was something akin to attempting to view a constantly changing mosaic through a makeshift and shaking kaleidoscope. Since the revolution, the mosaic has been in a state of explosion while the lens in the wobbling kaleidoscope has become clouded both by the smoke from the explosion and by the ministrations of the viewer. Meanwhile, the viewer seems to have lost the discerning eye and tends to see precisely what it is he or she wants to see. And whispering into the viewer's ear are many who profess to have special knowledge, experience, and insight into what is happening to the mosaic. Most members of this crowd have suffered one way or another from recent events in Iran while the others speak as apologists for the new system.

This chapter attempts to analyze the political system of revolutionary Iran as objectively as possible and seeks in particular to avoid the danger of wishful thinking based upon the temptation to either praise or to condemn. Nothing can be done to change the situation of the exploding mosaic. All the analyst can or should do is to attempt to use the least distorting lens possible when studying the situation. Although it is surely impossible to succeed in providing a completely unbiased understanding of these realities, it is possible to make the attempt.

Here the Iranian Revolution will be placed in historical perspective and analyzed in the context of other great revolutions that have occurred in world history. In this way, it may be possible to rise above a particular time and place and thus to minimize the emotionalism inherent in the proximity and specificity of this event. The intellectual process of comparison in itself promotes objectivity in two ways. First, it forces observers to give up their preoccupations with the subjective by calling other events and models to their attention. This in itself often helps to break the cycle whereby scholars remain hung up in an analytical world dominated either by congratulations or condemnations. Second, it provides other contexts alongside of which observers can place the particular case study that they are primarily interested in explaining. The similarities and the differences that such comparison calls to mind also enable one to gain perspective and to make a more informed evaluation of the events under investigation.

Also, in this chapter an attempt will be made to analyze both the weaknesses and the strengths of the contemporary political system of revolutionary Iran. By presenting both sides of this issue, it is hoped that this study will enable the reader to make a better judgment about the political future of Iran. Finally, the first and second parts of the study will be related to one another by linking the conclusions of the section on the comparative study of revolution to those concerning the balance of weaknesses and strengths. The chapter will end with a political prognosis centering on the most likely political systems to dominate Iran over the next several years. These conclusions will, I hope, follow logically from the analysis and conclusions that have gone before.

Iran and the Stages of Revolution

A study of the dynamics of revolution through history reveals that such movements contain a number of similar patterns and uniformities. These uniformities are particularly evident with respect to the "classic" revolutions such as those that occurred in France in the 1790s and in Russia in the years following 1917. Although it is quite clear that each revolution is shaped by the particular context in which it occurs and that there are fundamental differences among societies across time and geographical location, it is also true that there are discernible similarities and recognizable patterns transcending cultural and spatial peculiarities. In this sense, one must generalize with care and with special sensitivity to the fact that differences are often at least as important as similarities. There is no reason why one cannot include both in the comparative analysis. The search here is for uniformities, not identities; to be similar is not to coincide.

In his seminal study, *The Anatomy of Revolution*, Crane Brinton presents a typology that describes the stages through which revolutions pass. In developing his model, Brinton draws in detail upon four case studies of revolution: England in the 1640s, America in the 1770s, France in the 1790s, and Russia during 1917 and afterward. Although Brinton's model does not fit Iran's case exactly, it is most suggestive in helping us to develop a better understanding of revolutionary Iran.[1]

According to Brinton, the roots of revolution are located in the policies of the *ancien* regime. After a dramatic takeover when the old system is overthrown, the new revolutionary government is directed at first by liberals and moderates. This rule is usually short-lived and is replaced by a government of extremists whose fanaticism and lack of concern for liberal democratic values enable them to defeat the moderates rather easily. As the extremists face continued resistance from political opponents, including both sympathizers of the old system and the newly alienated moderates, the rule of the extremists hardens into what Brinton terms the "reign of terror and virtue." This is the crisis of the revolution as violence and repression reign supreme. Ultimately, a national reaction to this period of brutality sets in and the time of the extremists gives way to a period of Thermidor, or convalescence, which involves a swing back to moderate politics.[2] An authoritarian leader then appears and puts an end to the threatening anarchy. Brinton summarizes the process of revolution as follows: "All are begun in hope and moderation, all reach a crisis in a reign of Terror, and all end in something like dictatorship" (p. 24).

In brief, Crane Brinton has presented a five-stage model that purports to describe the process through which all classic revolutions pass. These are (1) the fall of the *ancien* regime, (2) the rise of the moderates, (3) the period of extremism, (4) the appearance of the Thermidor, and (5) the rise of a new form of authoritarianism. The application of this model to the Iranian case study indicates that the Iranian revolution has not yet completed the process. Thus, if the Brinton analysis is accurate and relevant, the Iranian Revolution remains an unfinished one.

Brinton's model traces the roots of the revolution to three major problem areas that characterize the last years of the *ancien* regime. These are severe economic difficulties, ineffective and inefficient government, and accelerating opposition activity. Revolutions do not occur in societies "with declining economies, or in societies undergoing widespread and long-term economic misery or depression" (p. 29) but rather "during economic depressions which follow on periods of generally rising standards of living" (p. 30). Also, the wealth present in prerevolutionary societies is unevenly shared and income distribution gaps continue to grow rather than to shrink. Governmental and administrative inefficiency prevails prior to revolutions. There is usually a drive for centralization accompanied by an attempt to "modernize." These kinds of programs are stalled by administrative chaos and uncertainty. This gives rise in part to a series of dramatic reform programs in which the leaders of *ancien* regimes attempt improvements that are "carried out in a series of advances and retreats, cajolings and menaces, blowings-hot and blowings-cold" (p. 38). The ruling elite itself is often decadent, corrupt, and effete. Finally, opposition group activity intensifies significantly prior to the outbreak of revolution. This is marked by what Brinton and Lyford Edwards term "the transfer of the allegiance of the intellectuals" (p. 42), the growing alienation of the middle classes, and deepening class conflict throughout the society. "These class struggles are by no means simple; there are groups within groups, currents within currents" (p. 50). This view of the prerevolutionary situation is certainly not unlike that which existed in Iran in the years prior to 1978–79.

As the shah fell, the moderates rushed into positions of power. A major hypothesis of the Brinton model is that "those who had directly taken over the mechanism of government were in all four of our societies men of the kind usually called moderates" (p. 122). The moderates are individuals of relative tolerance and with a commitment to civil liberties and to the concept of liberal democracy. In England, they were represented by the Presbyterians and leaders such as Denzil Hollis; in France by the Feuillants and Girondins and individuals such as Comte de Mirabeau; in Russia, by the Social Revolutionaries, the Narodniks, Kadets, and especially the Mensheviks and figures such as Alexander

Kerensky. In revolutionary times, their very moderation is this group's critical weakness.[3]

In Iran, the rule of the moderates began with the premiership of Shapour Bakhtiar (of five weeks duration), passed through the prime ministership of Mehdi Bazargan (nine months), and ended with the presidency of Abol Hassan Bani Sadr (seventeen months). In the twenty-seven months of moderate rule, each of the moderate governments became progressively more radical as it fought for survival in an atmosphere of extremism. The fact that Bani Sadr was in many ways more radical than moderate helped him to survive as long as he did. He was one of those moderates who "often behave quite immoderately" (p. 123). The recruiting ground of the Iranian moderates was the professional middle class who formed organizations such as the National Front and the National Democratic Front, groupings not unlike the French Girondins or the Russian Mensheviks. In describing Alexander Kerensky, Brinton may very well have written the epitaph for the political career of Bani Sadr: "The eloquent compromisist leader seems to us a man of words, an orator who could move crowds but could not guide them, an impractical and incompetent person in the field of action" (p. 145).

The collapse of the moderates in these times seems inevitable and quite complete. Immediately upon their assumption of power, they find themselves on the defensive. "They were also confronted very soon with armed enemies, and found themselves engaged in a foreign or civil war, or in both together. They found against them an increasingly strong and intransigent group of radicals or extremists who insisted that the moderates were trying to stop the revolution, that they had betrayed it, that they were as bad as the rulers of the old regime—indeed, much worse, since they were traitors as well as fools and scoundrels" (p. 122). After a period of alternating phases of hope and despair, the harassed moderates find themselves driven from power. Brinton describes it well: "The moderates by definition are not great haters, are not endowed with the effective blindness which keeps men like Robespierre and Lenin [or Khomeini] undistracted in their rise to power. In normal times, ordinary men are not capable of feeling for groups of their fellow men hatred as intense, continuous, and uncomfortable as that preached by the extremists in revolution. Such hatred is a heroic emotion, and heroic emotions are exhausting" (p. 146).

In revolutionary Iran, the time of the Bakhtiars, Bazargans, Yazdis, Amir-Entezams, Ghotbzadehs, and Bani Sadrs gave way to the time of the Beheshtis, Raja'is, Kho'inihas, Khamene'is, Hashemi-Rafsanjanis, Nateq-Nuris, and Mo'adikhahs. Behind these figures rests the dedicated, charismatic, and overpowering figure of Ayatollah Ruhollah Khomeini.

It is Khomeini who is the closest Iranian equivalent to Robespierre in France and Lenin in Russia. In France, the extremist takeover occurred with the final overthrow of the monarchy on 10 August 1792, while in Russia it can be dated to the October Revolution of 1917. In Iran, it can be traced to the dismissal of Bani Sadr on 22 June 1981; with his defeat, the force of the moderate center was crushed. Ever since this time, the Iranian Revolution has been locked in its period of extremism.

History reveals that the extremists will use any means at their disposal to preserve their power and to protect their new system of government. In Brintonian terms, "Once the extremists are in power, there is no more finicky regard for the liberties of the individual or for the forms of legality. The extremists, after clamoring for liberty and toleration while they were in opposition, turn very authoritarian when they reach power. There is no need for us to sigh over this, or grow indignant, or talk of hypocrisy. We are attempting to discern uniformities in the behavior of men during certain revolutions in specific social systems, and this seems to be one of the uniformities" (p. 164). Brinton may have been describing the leaders of the Islamic Republican party in general and Ayatollah Khomeini in particular when he wrote, "Our orthodox and successful extremists, then, are crusaders, fanatics, ascetics, men who seek to bring heaven to earth" (p. 191). A careful reading of chapters six and seven of *Anatomy of Revolution* indicates the existence of twelve major hypotheses that describe the period of extremism. Since Iran is currently witnessing this revolutionary stage, it is instructive to examine each of these propositions.

1. *The extremists are fanatically devoted to their cause.* They display "a willingness to work hard, to sacrifice their peace and security, to submit to discipline, to submerge their personalities in the group" (p. 155). This has certainly been the case in Iran where the Islamic revolutionaries exhibit a mind set of martyrdom. Tens of thousands have proven their commitment by giving their lives. In a February 1982 speech, Ayatollah Khomeini described revolutionary Iran as "a nation whose love of martyrdom boils in the hearts of its men, women and young and old who compete with each other for martyrdom. . . . All have seen that each martyrdom has endowed our valiant nation with a remarkable growth, to the extent that each successive martyrdom guarantees the immunity of the Islamic Republic from any harm."[4] President Muhammad Ali Raja'i gave a speech on 15 August 1981 in which he stated, "I beseech God to grant us the honor of the survival of the revolution along with martyrdom for the revolution as a blessing and a favor."[5] Two weeks later Raja'i was assassinated. His widow indicated afterward that her husband had awaited "martyrdom for years."[6]

2. *The extremists will act ruthlessly to achieve their goals.* Once in power, the extremists are careful to distinguish "between liberty for those who deserve it, and liberty for those who don't" (p. 166). Arrests, imprisonments, torture, and executions make a comeback during these times. In Iran, there has been an atmosphere of violence not unlike that which existed in France and Russia during the reigns of terror there. In Iran, the prisons are overflowing and the executions have numbered in the thousands. In France, during one short period of "the Terror," 40,000 were killed and another 300,000 were arrested. In Russia, the November 1917 coup took place with relatively few deaths but after the Cheka was established there were 6,300 executions in 1918 alone.[7] Unlike the moderates, the extremists will utilize any means available to accomplish their goals. In September 1981, Iranian prosecutor Hojjat ol-Islam Musavi-Tabrizi put it in the following stark terms: "Anyone taking a stand against the Islamic Republican order and the Muslim's Just Imam must be killed. Under these circumstances, those captured must be killed and those wounded must be further wounded so they die."[8] In Brinton's words, "Only a sincere extremist in a revolution can kill men because he loves man, attain peace through violence, and free men by enslaving them" (pp. 159–60).

3. *The revolutionary extremism carries the fervor of a religious faith.* The parallel between the ideology of extremism during the height of revolution and a system of religious beliefs has been emphasized by Brinton and other observers of revolutionary movements. Both the Jacobins and the Bolsheviks were in principle opposed to human crime, laxness, and excesses. Their leaders tended to be ascetics and avoided lavish displays of wealth and luxury in their lifestyles. Their extremist attitudes toward social and political matters extended to their views of personal lifestyles. The Bolsheviks "felt that the ordinary vices and weaknesses of human beings are disgusting, that the good life cannot be led until these weaknesses are eliminated" (p. 188). In the early days of their rule, they even forbade the consumption of the Russian national drink, vodka. Lenin himself was "notably austere and contemptuous of ordinary comfort, and at the height of his power his apartments in the Kremlin were of barracklike simplicity" (pp. 187–88). In Iran, of course, the confluence of Shi'i Islam with the politics of the revolution has magnified the intensity of religious fervor. This in turn has reinforced the fanatic devotion and political ruthlessness of the extremist regime. In the Iranian instance, there have been numerous reports of the arrest, imprisonment, and even execution of prostitutes and petty criminals. Similarly, "petty thieves and in several instances even prostitutes were summarily disposed of by what amounts to lynch law during the French Revolution,

and similar instances can be found in England and Russia" (p. 174). In the French and Russian cases, many similarities to a religious movement were present while in the Iranian case the powerful influence of Shi'i Islam itself has dominated the revolution.

4. *The extremist regime establishes a new system of justice along with a new secret police and security apparatus.* In France, Russia, and England, the extremists organized a new and extraordinary system of justice complete with secret police apparatus. Brinton writes that the old legal system is "supplanted by extraordinary courts, revolutionary tribunals, or are wholly transformed by new appointments and by special jurisdictions. Finally, a special revolutionary police appears" (p. 172). In Russia, France, and England, that special police was the Cheka, the Comité de Sureté Generale, and the independent parish clergy, respectively. In Iran, it has been the SAVAMA backed by the *Pasdaran* (Revolutionary Guards). The old court system has been dismantled in Iran and a new system, more closely in tune with the Shi'i interpretation of law and the *shari'ah*, has been organized. Heading this system has been a special chief justice of considerable power while throughout the organization mullahs hold key positions of influence and are the major interpreters of the law. A visible example of this system in action was provided by Sadeq Khalkhali, a religious leader who dispensed instant justice in the immediate post-Pahlavi period.

5. *The extremist regime emphasizes centralized power and government by committee.* Crane Brinton discusses what he calls "rough-and-ready centralization" and asserts that the characteristic form of authority "is that of a committee. The government of the Terror is a dictatorship in commission" (p. 171). In both revolutionary France and Russia, councils, committees, commissions, and conventions were active everywhere. The same has been true in Iran where the extremist government has been dominated by a system of powerful *komitehs* and special commissions appointed throughout the country by Ayatollah Khomeini. In the autumn of 1982, for example, the regime established a network of purging and reconstruction committees that were charged with the task of identifying any antirevolutionaries still working in the administrative system. Khomeini also has his own personal representatives located in all major towns and cities of Iran. The Majlis and mosques are other important organizations that have played a major role in directing Iranian affairs during the rule of the extremists.

6. *The government of the extremists is marked by ineffective and inefficient administrative practices.* During the period of extremism, administrative upheaval and chaos is commonplace as ideological qualifications take precedence over professional competence. Inexperience is

the dominant characteristic of the new bureaucracy. In revolutionary England, France, and Russia, "the actual administrators were usually inexperienced, were often petty fanatics, often incompetent blowhards who had risen to prominence in politics of the New Model Army, in the clubs or the party" (p. 173). In Iran, inexperienced clerics have moved into key positions in political, economic, military, and diplomatic organizations. Young people whose main credentials have been their commitment to Islam, Khomeini, and the revolution have been receiving on-the-job training in a wide variety of sensitive positions. Obviously, there have been numerous costly mistakes and professional and organizational chaos. This situation has been particularly pronounced in Iran as the most extreme and hard-line faction among the clerics, the *maktabis*, have come to dominate the power structure.

7. *Extremists have an unusually strong willingness to follow their leaders.* During the extremist phase of revolutions, the leaders of the movement have a strong, almost mesmerizing influence over their followers. Brinton writes that "the extremists follow their leaders with a devotion and a unanimity not to be found among the moderates. . . . This magnifying of the principle of leadership runs right through the organization, from the subalterns up to the great national heroes— Cromwell, Robespierre, Lenin" (p. 157). In Iran, this has certainly been the case of the various leaders of the Islamic Republican party, although the overriding example has been Ayatollah Khomeini himself. This principle has been particularly relevant in the Iranian Revolution due to the concept of the imamate in Shi'i Islam whereby practicing Shi'ites relate themselves to their religious leaders in extended chains of emanation.[9] The masses act as the extension of the personality of Imam Khomeini and thus are better able to pursue his wishes and policies whether in the countryside as part of the Reconstruction Crusade (*Jehad-e Sazandegi*) or on the western front in the war with Iraq.

8. *The period of extremism witnesses the presence and pressure of foreign and civil war.* The French and Russian revolutions were soon accompanied by external warfare against foreign armies while "in America and England the crisis period was accompanied by a formal war, largely a civil war" (p. 199). In Iran, extremist politics have been reinforced and intensified by the long war with Iraq as well as by continual disturbances in the form of rebellion in Kurdistan and terrorism in the urban areas. "War necessities help explain the rapid centralization of the government of the Terror, the hostility to dissenters within the group—they now seem deserters—the widespread excitement which our generation now knows well enough by the cant term 'war psychosis'" (p. 199). There is little doubt that the war with Iraq has been used as

a rallying point for the revolution and a major justification for the call for all Iranians to pull in ranks behind the revolutionary government.

9. *The period of extremism is marked by severe economic crisis.* The acute economic crisis comes about to a large extent because of the disruption that accompanies the revolution. It begins with massive capital flight; much of the industrial structure crumbles and collapses; transformations of the agricultural system impede the production of foodstuffs; the new regime fails to develop coherent fiscal policy; and "then comes the war with its demand for men and munitions" (p. 200). In Iran, the economic difficulties have been very pronounced both because of the precedence given ideological considerations over sound economic realities and because of the tight international noose that has involved the partial boycott and embargo of key goods, materiel, and spare parts. High unemployment and runaway inflation have also been present in Iran.

10. *Deep and disruptive class conflict marks the extremist stage of revolution.* By the time that extremist politics harden into reality, "the different antagonistic groups within the society have polarized into the orthodox revolutionists in power and the somewhat mixed bloc of their enemies" (p. 201). In Iran, the extremist Islamic Republican party has faced off against such opponents as the Mujahedin-e Khalq, the Fedayan-e Khalq, the Peykar, the Ranjbaran, and many other opposition splinter groups. "Heightened like all other tensions and conflicts by the course of the revolution, these class antagonisms now take on a sharpness they normally possess only in the writings and speeches of intellectuals and agitators" (p. 201). The extremist leaders in Iran stress the fact that their revolution is for the lower and lower-middle classes against the upper-middle and upper classes in society. Khomeini himself constantly speaks in class terms.

11. *Once in power, the extremists begin to compete among themselves and begin internecine conflict.* In France, the extremist Montagnards divided into three distinct factions headed by Robespierre, Danton, and Hebert. The Iranian case has not yet witnessed division of this kind partially because of the overpowering personality of Ayatollah Khomeini. Nonetheless, a close examination of the composition of the Islamic Republican party (IRP) does reveal three groups, each with quite different perspectives: the Maktabis, the Hojjatiyeh, and the Jammiyat-e Ulema-ye Mujahedin.[10] The Maktabi group consists of the hard-line extremists while the Hojjatiyeh faction is composed of individuals who are more flexibly fundamentalist. The Jammiyat has as its members mullahs who float back and forth between the two primary groupings. When Khomeini disappears from the scene, it is quite possible that the under-

lying fissures in the extremist leadership structure will break wide open.

12. *The extremists are few in number.* Crane Brinton argues that in the great revolutions through history the extremists have been relatively few in number. This is presented as a major strength because it enables them to hold on to their deep emotional commitment while providing them with the ability to act quickly when necessary. "You cannot maintain the fever of fanaticism in large numbers of people long enough to secure the ultimate victory" (p. 154). This particular hypothesis appears not to stand up with respect to the Iranian Revolution. Important factors peculiar to the Iranian case intervene at this point. The role of Shi'i Islam, the fundamentalist flavor of the revolution, and the style and role of Ayatollah Khomeini are among the factors that have replaced Brinton's extremism of the few by the extremism of the many of the Iranian Revolution. Crowds and masses of people described by such Persian expressions as *hezbollahis, pasdaran, basij,* and more loosely, *mostaza'fin* are terms that refer in differing manner and context to very large groups whose members hold extremist sentiments.

These twelve principles of extremism in time of revolution help describe and explain post-Pahlavi and post-Bani Sadr Iran. The first ten propositions fit the Iranian case very closely, the eleventh point only partially; the final principle does not describe revolutionary Iran at all. Iran has not yet witnessed the deep internecine conflict among the extremists themselves. Thus far, it has been confined to the struggle between moderates and extremists as the 1982 demise of Ayatollah Kazem Shariatmadari indicates. In this sense, the success of extremism in Iran has been greatly furthered by the fact that the leadership of the regime has remained united in the face of numerous personal, political, and ideological challenges. This has been especially true in the case of the mullahs who do have documentable differences but who have managed to keep these differences from breaking out into any form of serious conflict.

The fact that revolutionary Iran is dominated by an extremism of the many rather than an extremism of the few represents a major departure from Brinton's calculations. The cleric-style extremism in Iran involves a large mass of lower and lower-middle class adherents who are totally committed to the goals of their extremist leaders. This has served to give the extremist movement in Iran a mass anchor that provides this system with an unusual form of stability not present in the other revolutions. Partly in recognition of this fact, the moderate opposition leaders in exile criticize not only Khomeini but in 1982 began to attack his followers as well. Former Prime Minister Shapour Bakhtiar, for example, charged that revolutionary Iran "is suffering from mass insanity."[11]

The Iranian version of the Terror reflects a two-winged extremism as fanaticism prevails on both the left and the right. The guerrilla fighters of the Mujahedin-e Khalq, for example, are just as zealous and dedicated to their particular cause as are the IRP fundamentalists to theirs. They also are willing to sacrifice their lives for their beliefs. This phenomenon of two-winged extremism will ultimately contribute to the extension of the period of extremism in three ways. First, the existence of a dedicated, fanatic opposition group provides a threat serious enough to keep the extremist-fundamentalists united and committed. Second, the existence of this challenging wing on the left will enable the cleric leaders to protect the environment of emotion so essential to any continuation of the period of extremism. Third, the fact that neither side has the coercive power to annihilate the other promises a particularly brutal and extended period of Terror in Iran. Although the extremist regime has been able to cripple severely the opposition guerrilla movements, it will not be able to destroy them. These groups are accomplished in the arts of terrorism having fought a war of survival with the shah's secret police for over a decade. They also have a ready source of recruitment in the moderate and middle classes who have tired of the general climate of violence and of the regime repression.

Although it must inevitably arrive, the Thermidor is not yet in sight in Iran. This was demonstrated clearly by the 15 September 1982 execution of former revolutionary foreign minister and Khomeini confidant, Sadegh Ghotbzadeh. In France, the reaction to the intense extremism began with the fall and death of Robespierre on 27 July 1794; in Russia, it can be traced to the establishment of the New Economic Policy of 1921. Most citizens cannot exist forever in a state of personal, social, economic, and political incoherence. Although Iranians are surely no different, there are special reasons to believe that the period of extremism in that country may extend for several more years. Some of the systemic reasons for this have been given above, but the first serious challenge will occur when Ayatollah Khomeini passes from the scene.

The Dialectics of Disintegration and Persistence of the Islamic Republic

A close examination of the extremist political system of the Islamic Republic of Iran reveals many serious problems, acknowledged by the leadership,[12] that could lead to the disintegration of the system. These include personal rivalry, economic malaise, ethnic divisions, alienation of the professionals, governmental inexperience, social insecurity, continuing class conflict, a costly war with a neighboring state, and a noticeable degree of international ostracization. The opposition within Iran continues to deepen and to grow as the brutal and ruthless dimensions of extremist politics remain a visible and threatening challenge to people throughout the country. Many of these problems are interrelated and act to reinforce one another. For example, the tenuous state of the economy is aggravated by the costs of the war with Iraq which steadily drains badly needed human and financial resources. This, in turn, promotes social insecurity and political rivalry as individuals and groups differ significantly in their views concerning the economic system as well as concerning the conduct of the war.

Despite great elasticity and resiliency, the Iranian economy was in dire straits during the first three years of the revolution. The foreign reserves of nearly $15 billion at the time of the shah's fall dwindled to less than $1 billion by 1982. Oil revenues fell from over $21 billion in 1978 to $11.8 billion in 1980 and to $10 billion in 1981. Even though revenues are expected to rise, Iran carries a serious monetary deficit. The lack of adequate financial resources has been only one part of the problem. Unemployment is high and inflation may approach 40 percent. Iranian planners have failed to develop a coherent and consistent fiscal policy. Large sections of the industrial infrastructure have collapsed and there has been very little increase in agricultural production. Although there have as yet been no major incidents of the bazaars closing down or initiating antigovernment activities, there is increasing disaffection and unrest in the bazaar. Finally, the lack of experience of the new managers and administrators has resulted in costly mistakes and considerable mismanagement.[13]

The stresses and strains in the system of revolutionary Iran will not necessarily lead to the collapse and destruction of that system. Much depends upon the presence and power of opposition forces. There are three major organizations that have the capacity to threaten seriously the regime of clerics, either in the short or in the longer run. These are the Fedayan-e Khalq, the Tudeh party, and the Mujahedin-e Khalq. Although there are numerous smaller opposition groups and organizations representing a multitude of ideological positions, only these three have the organization and constituency necessary to mount any kind of credible threat to the rule of the IRP.

The least threatening of the three is the Fedayan-e Khalq, a nationalist, Marxist group composed largely of students and the more radical members of the intelligentsia. The members of the Fedayan condemn capitalist and imperialist exploitation of all kinds, although there is a noticeable and marked special aversion in their platform to the West and to the United States in particular. This organization wants to build a radical socialist state in Iran and is not Islamic in orientation. In 1980, the Fedayan splintered into three main factions, including the Fedayan Guerrillas (*Cherikha*), the Minority (*Aqaliyyat*), and the Majority (*Aksariyyat*).[14] The reason for the division was tactical in nature as the Majority group decided to compromise and to form a front with the extremist ruling IRP. This was done in the face of unrelenting pressure from the regime and was determined to be necessary for survival. This bitter split hurt the Fedayan very badly and the Majority was condemned by many for its opportunistic tactics. Meanwhile, the more radical Fedayan Guerrillas have been constantly hunted and attacked by the *Pasdaran*. As a result, the Fedayan remains very active abroad but has sustained crippling blows back in Iran. They do have a limited capacity to carry out isolated incidents of anarchic violence and do remain totally committed to radical, socialist goals.

The Tudeh party adopted the strategy of the Majority faction of the Fedayan very early, that is, it sought to protect its interests by entering into an accommodation with Khomeini and the IRP. The Tudeh is a communist organization with direct ties to the Soviet Union. It is composed of middle-aged Iranians who are well financed and well organized. It is seriously weakened, however, by its position of compromise with the regime as well as by its associations with the Soviet Union. Talented members of the Tudeh party hold positions in the bureaucracy of the government, but they are watched and controlled by the regime. During 1982, the government carried out several purges of the Tudeh. The attitude of the extremist regime toward the Tudeh party can best be understood by quoting from a February 1982 newspaper editorial representing the official position of the IRP. Entitled "Which Is the Most Cunning Political Group in Iran," the article stated that the Tudeh "must be viewed as the most dangerous and cunning force operating within the country and if vigilance is not exercised and strong measures taken to prevent such an eventuality, it will create many more problems for Islamic Iran than other leftist parties did. . . . In addition to the vast knowledge that the party's leaders possess of Marxist ideology, it will no doubt seek help from the Russian secret services, adopt any hypocritical or opportunistic tactic that accords with Marxist-Leninist theorems in order to establish a Moscow-oriented puppet regime in Iran."[15]

Unlike the Fedayan-e Khalq and the Tudeh party, the Mujahedin-e Khalq is a radical opposition group with an important Islamic component. A major principle of the Mujahedin is the concept of *towhid*, which refers to "a divinely-integrated classless society, a society with total equity."[16] In this ideal society, there will purportedly be an end to the exploitation of man by man. To the Mujahedin, the true Islamic

Republic "must contain anti-imperialist, anti-reactionary, and anti-dicta-torial characteristics. . . . If these characteristics are not involved, it is fruitless to pretend that Islam in the true sense is being applied."[17] The Mujahedin have fought the regime with a fierce fanaticism of their own and have been responsible for numerous acts of violence and sabotage in the society. Despite the government's ruthless campaign against the Mu-jahedin, the latter have continued to survive and to increase their mem-bership base. They, in fact, have drawn from both the Fedayan-e Khalq and the Tudeh party and especially from the large, alienated middle class. These moderates have been driven to the Mujahedin out of des-peration born of self-defense against the extremist regime. By pursuing a policy of brutal repression, the IRP ruling elite is providing the Muja-hedin with an image of martyrdom of its own. Also, the religious ruling elite has forced this radical Islamic group underground where it is able to practice the guerrilla tactics it pursued so effectively against the Pahlavi regime in the 1960s and 1970s.

With the leader of the Mujahedin, Massoud Rajavi, in exile in Paris and with the violent death of Musa Khiabani, the second in com-mand, the Mujahedin are without charismatic leadership. Thousands of other leading members of their cadre have been arrested, jailed, and ex-ecuted by the *Pasdaran*. Violence begets violence and extremism creates extremism. As long as the period of extremism prevails, this organiza-tion will have excellent opportunities for recruitment among those alien-ated by the actions of the religious regime. The Mujahedin will be a factor in the future of Iranian politics.

Despite the existence of these dedicated opposition groups within the context of the severe social, political, and economic difficulties briefly listed above, the revolutionary Islamic regime in Iran is not without fun-damental strengths. Somehow, the system continues to survive and to protect and promote its own interests both in the country and in the region. There are six major factors that combine to explain the surviv-ability of the new social and political systems that have developed in Iran after the fall of the shah. These are the leadership of Ayatollah Ruhollah Khomeini, the support of the lower-class masses for the Is-lamic Republic, the significance of the ideology of Shi'i Islam, the es-tablishment of a new and powerful military support base, the growing experience of the clerics as statesmen, and the external catalysts that, by threatening and attacking Iran from without, actually promote unity within.

Ayatollah Khomeini has acted as a shrewd and effective political tac-tician in the context of revolutionary Iran. As the charismatic symbol of the revolution, he has placed himself above the everyday infighting and from there he has played the various extremist and radical groups off against one another. In the process, he has lived a simple lifestyle, has refused to compromise with his interpretation of Islamic principles, and has presented himself as the champion of the downtrodden and the oppressed (*mostaza'fin*). Khomeini also has ceaselessly attacked the superpowers of both East and West and has taken a position as defender of the Iranian people, of the nation-state of Iran, and of Islam. Khomeini is the primary reason why the natural competition and divisiveness that exist among the extremist revolutionary leaders have not yet led to debilitating internecine political conflict. He also has worked consistently to promote the politics of extremism in an atmosphere of deep national emotion. In late 1982, therefore, he continued to launch strong attacks against a variety of outside targets such as the United States, the Soviet Union, Iraq, Israel, and the Arab countries for their failure to come to the aid of the Palestinians in Lebanon. At the same time, he sent one of the most ideological of his followers to lead the Iranian pilgrims on the *hajj* to Mecca and sat on the sidelines while the regime tried and executed his old supporter, Sadegh Ghotbzadeh. Khomeini's presence, personage, and politics are major buttressing forces for the persistence of the Islamic Republic.[18]

While devouring significant groups of its own initial supporters (e.g., the middle classes), the revolution still maintains a solid base of popular support. The Shi'i leaders recognize the *mostaza'fin* as their major constituency and seek to meet the demands of the masses before all others. In continuing to take (often brutally) from the rich in order to give to the poor, the Shi'i political elite works hard to ensure the support of the masses. It is from the masses that the regime has recruited the young men who have fought and died for the revolution on the western front. In this context, Khomeini himself has regularly spoken in class terms about the commitment of the *mostaza'fin* to the revolution. "To which class of society do these heroic fighters of the battlefields belong? Do you find even one person among all of them who is related to persons who have large capital or had some power in the past? If you find one, we will give you a prize. But you won't."[19] On the third anniversary of the revolution, Khomeini warned high-ranking government officials that "whenever the people consider that one of you is climbing to the upper rungs from the middle classes or are seeking power or wealth for yourselves, they must throw you out of their ranks." He went on to observe that "it was Hezrat-e Ali who said that his torn shoes were more valuable than a position in government."[20] In September 1982, Khomeini indicated the continuing nature of his campaign for the masses when he stated, "We must all make efforts to serve the *mostaza'fin* who have been deprived throughout history and the government should always give priority to them."[21] Other Shi'i clerics and political leaders such as Ali Hussein Khamene'i and Ali Akbar Hashemi-Rafsanjani echo Khomeini's words in their own speeches in which they praise and defend the interests of the *mostaza'fin*. As long as this leadership is able to meet the demands of this large base of popular support, it has an extremely important foundation of power.

The ideology of Islam permeates revolutionary Iran. All programs and policies are justified in terms of Islam as indicated by the official name of the country, Islamic Republic of Iran. This ideology is very potent both in the breadth and depth of its appeal. Much of the attraction of Shi'i Islam resides in its ideological populism which is seen in the figure and life of Imam Ali. All systems by which an Iranian organizes his life are guided and influenced by Shi'i Islam. All Iranians, regardless of class membership or tribal affiliation, must come to grips with Islam. Since Shi'ism carries within itself the flavor of martyrdom, its adherents are often willing to make the ultimate sacrifice in defense of their country, their religion, and their revolution. Since January 1978, there have been tens of thousands of examples of this commitment; it has been most dramatically revealed during the fighting in the war with Iraq.

The religious revolutionary leadership in Iran has also survived because of the support of the military. With the fall of the shah, Khomeini and others such as Mustapha Chamran (later assassinated) carried out two major purges of the officer corps thus decapitating the shah's military organization. At the same time, the clerics created their own parallel force, the *Pasdaran*, and by the spring of 1982 had succeeded in blending the two organizations into one fighting unit. After years of fighting internal guerrillas and years of battle against an outside invader, this military force has become battle-hardened and experienced. A number of important victories in the war with Iraq document this record. In the process of this continual conflict, the Iranian military forces have developed a deeper commitment to the cause for which they have fought.

During the existence of the Islamic Republic, the clerics have come to a better understanding of the realities of politics. They have gathered some momentum as political leaders. Already, several dozen of them have traveled internationally where they have engaged in sensitive diplomatic and economic missions. The extremist *ulema* have managed to build a complex system of institutions that enables them to direct the society. These include the branches of the IRP that stretch throughout the country, the national network of mosques, the *Pasdaran* organization, the Reconstruction Crusade, the Islamic Komiteh system, the

Foundation of the Oppressed (*Bonyad-e Mostazafan*), and numerous other councils, committees, and corps. Although their mistakes have been many and the costs thereof very high, there is evidence that the cleric-rulers have learned a few lessons. One of the most expensive of these was the government's insistence on keeping oil prices unrealistically high throughout 1980, thereby driving away many customers while suffering a major loss in market and revenues. In 1981, Iran had to offer sharp discounts and shave prices in the face of a situation of economic desperation.

A final factor strengthening the revolutionary system in Iran is negative in character. The Iranian Revolution, like many revolutions in history, has found itself consistently attacked and threatened by external forces. Financial, psychological, and political pressure from both the traditional Arab countries and Western nations such as the United States has been linked to direct military invasion by the Iraqis. The activities of counterrevolutionary groups and exile organizations formed by wealthy members of the *ancien* regime are constant reminders of serious threats to the revolution. In the face of this, the various groups in Iran have had to close ranks and to cooperate against a common foe. In this sense, the outside powers who seek to destroy the revolution are ironically contributing to its strength and longevity. Ayatollah Khomeini recognizes well the political value of external pressure and his speeches reflect this. In the summer of 1982, for example, he told his people that "today it seems we are left alone as almost all of the West and the East are either directly opposing us or indirectly working against us."[22] Khomeini went on to say that Iran would fight these forces "with our bare hands and the weapons of faith."[23] After the Israeli invasion of Lebanon and the Phalangist massacre of Palestinians in August 1982, the Ayatollah sharply attacked the external enemies of Iran and Islam. In a speech in September 1982, his words were particularly inflammatory: "The *hajj* pilgrims should never consider this year the same as former years because the claws of the superpowers have driven deeper into the flesh of Islamic countries and the world's oppressed, and the blood of Muslim youth drips from their bloodied claws."[24]

The six forces promoting the persistence of the Islamic Republic are all closely entwined. Khomeini's own personal strategy has stressed special support for the *mostaza'fin* and has emphasized the overarching and sacred ideology of Islam. The relationship here is mutually reinforcing in nature. Khomeini uses Islam to solidify his support with the masses while the masses deepen their Islamic beliefs through their devotion to the charismatic symbol of the revolution, Ayatollah Khomeini. The cadre of political and military leaders that direct the affairs of the

Islamic Republic generally are sprung from the masses and hold special relationships with both Islam and Khomeini. The sixth factor—the external challenge—acts to buttress all of these reinforcing strengths and relationships by applying constant pressure from without. These threats from outside are also utilized by the leading regime actors to strengthen the resolve of their supporters along with their fierce commitment to Khomeini and to Islam.

A comparison of the interrelationships of both weaknesses and strengths provides a better understanding of the persistence of the system. Each point of weakness is confronted and transformed into the idiom of the ongoing system. For example, the deep economic difficulty is used both as an offensive and a defensive political weapon. The believers are asked to sacrifice for Islam and to share what they do have with needy neighbors. Also, the suffering and inconvenience caused by economic deprivation is blamed on external enemies such as the United States who are allegedly engaged in a campaign to destroy Iran and to strangle Islam. Actual economic hardship is at the same time softened by the commitment of the leaders to distribute what is available to the masses. The organization specifically designed to implement this distribution is the *Bonyad-e Mostazafan* via the network of mosques that stretches throughout the country.

The same general mechanism prevails with respect to the major internal opposition groups and organizations. The political elite of the Islamic Republic work hard to convert deep disadvantage into political advantage. Here, the dedicated opposition force of the Mujahedin-e Khalq is used by the regime to promote internal political coherence, Islamic fervor, and system support. The Mujahedin, for example, are seldom referred to as anything other than *Monafaghin*, a term that refers to dangerous enemies of Islam, usually translated as "hypocrites." The remnants of the old Pahlavi regime are *taghutis* (anti-Islamic idolators). All opposition organizations are portrayed as the tools and clients of outside powers who seek to destroy Iran's revolution. The regime links the Mujahedin with the "satanic" United States while at the same time stressing the Tudeh party's connection with the "atheistic" Soviet Union.

When Iraq invaded Iran, it provided both an ideal target and a catalyst of domestic stability in Iran. In this context, it is not accidental that Ayatollah Khomeini asked the following question in a September 1982 speech: "What shall we do with such a corrupt man as Saddam, who is destroying Iraq and thinks he is doing the same to Iran?" Khomeini went on to say, "From the very beginning Saddam said that he is fighting a regime which is Zoroastrian while our Iranian government is an Islamic regime under the banner of God who smacked him in the mouth."[25] Even the "successful" acts of terrorism carried out by the radical opposition are immediately converted into the advantage of the Islamic regime. The victims are mourned as martyrs whose deaths rally mass support to the system. Meanwhile, this provides the regime with strong justification to resort to terrorism of its own. In this way, the actions of the opposition result in immediate regime reaction which only reinforces the control of the leaders of the Islamic Republic.

The six forces that promote the strength and stability of the Islamic Republic are all intimately related to Crane Brinton's extremist stage of revolution. They exacerbate the climate of extremism and serve to extend this period beyond what occurred in past revolutions. Khomeini's role in this process has already been discussed; his uncompromising and fiery speeches have remained consistent since he returned to Iran in February 1979. Most important, whenever he has been forced to take a stand with respect to an extremist-moderate confrontation, he has consistently thrown his weight to the extremist position. In so doing, he has not hesitated to turn on former associates such as Bani Sadr and Ghotbzadeh. He has even acted against his son, Ahmad, and grandson, Hussein, both of whom have preferred a more moderate political style.

The fact that the extremism of Iran is an extremism of the masses who remain committed to their Shi'i guardians is quite different from the extremism of the few analyzed by Brinton. The ideology of Shi'i Islam and its commandment of total commitment via martyrdom is the cement that solidifies this mass anchor and binds it to the leadership. The rank and file of the army and *Pasdaran*, along with both civil and military leaders, are imbued with this attitude and mind set. External political, economic, and military pressures only contribute to the longevity of the period of Terror and Virtue.

The first genuine crisis period of extremist rule will occur when Ayatollah Khomeini passes from the scene since the major symbol and force for unity will then be gone. Also, in more general terms, the revolutionary Islamic regime will have lost the unrelenting and uncompromising voice that has prevented the period of extremism from slipping into the time of the Iranian Thermidor. Since Khomeini has played a major role in promoting the other five factors that have supported the Islamic Republic, his disappearance could lead to the subsequent weakening of these factors, causing the system to begin to unravel from the center.

On the other hand, it is certainly possible that the extremist Shi'i political elite will be able to protect and reinforce the system even without Khomeini. If they are able to maintain the support of the masses of *mostaza'fin* along with the loyalty of the military, the present system may remain in place after Khomeini. In order to guarantee this support, the members of the *ulema* who replace Khomeini must succeed in accomplishing two important tasks. First, they will have to maintain political cohesion and avoid the internecine conflict that could deeply divide their own ranks. Second, they must have the capacity to develop an economy healthy enough to enable them to meet the needs and demands of their mass constituency, the *mostaza'fin*. If they are able to succeed in these important political tasks, the system of religious rule in revolutionary Iran could continue for some time to come.

The Iranian Revolution remains locked in its period of extremism and the Reign of Terror and Virtue prevails. The Iranian Thermidor will one day appear, but, given the religious, social, and political forces at work in the country today, there is little reason to believe that the environment of extremist politics will recede any time soon. This scenario is one that all Persian Gulf and Indian Ocean countries would do well to understand. In the process, they may be better able to devise prudent and realistic policy with respect to the dynamic challenges generated by the Iranian Revolution.

9. The Iraq-Iran Conflict in Regional Perspective: A Systems Approach ⚫ Tareq Y. Ismael

Border disputes have been a major theme in the relations between Iraq and Iran in the post-World War II era.[1] While these disputes have been nominally a bilateral issue between the countries for most of this period, this chapter argues that the matter has never really been bilateral at all. Rather, it has been an issue particularly sensitive to the systemic qualities of the Middle East as a subsystem in international politics. This perspective is used to examine the issue at three critical points—1958, 1969, and 1980—and to forecast its emergence as a central one in Middle East politics, closely related to the Arab-Israeli conflict.

1958

Following the revolution in Iraq, on 14 July 1958, that toppled the Hashemite monarchy and brought to power a nationalist government, the border dispute between Iraq and Iran heated up significantly. In November 1959 the shah demanded adjustments in the frontier. In effect,

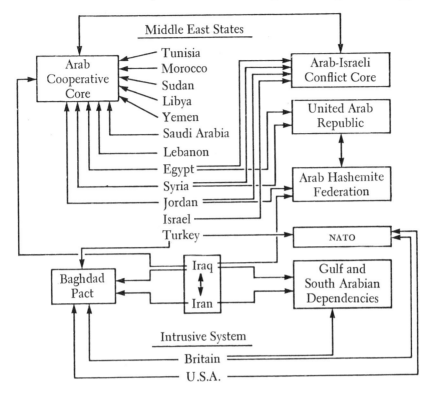

Figure 9-1 1958 systemic linkages in the Middle East subsystem (prior to the Iraqi Revolution).

he challenged the Frontier Treaty of 1937 between Iraq and Iran that had effectively stabilized the dispute for more than twenty years. A systems perspective of the sudden inflammation of an old issue suggests that systemic changes in the Middle East rather than only situational changes in bilateral relations between Iraq and Iran were at the root of the matter. Figure 9-1 identifies the systemic linkages in the Middle East just prior to the Iraqi Revolution.

The figure reflects the fact that Britain and the United States were the two dominant external powers involved with the Middle East at this time. The American presence was exercised through two channels: its bilateral relations with individual countries in the region (not reflected in the figure) and its informal though powerful role in the Baghdad Pact alliance, of which both Iraq and Iran were members. British influence was more direct. Not only was Britain a member of the Baghdad Pact, it was also involved in the Saadabad Entente (a British-sponsored alliance of Iraq, Iran, and Afghanistan organized in 1937 against the Soviet Union). This alliance was essentially superceded by the Baghdad Pact as the West's strategy against Soviet competition in the region. More significant in terms of the Iraq-Iran border dispute, Britain was still the colonial power in the Persian Gulf. Although Oman was formally independent, it was in effect one of the British gulf dependencies. It was also peripheral to the Arab world politically, socially, and economically in the sense that it was isolated and isolationist. Iraq, Iran, and Saudi Arabia were, in effect, the only formally independent gulf states at that time.

Within the intrusive system (referring to external power participation in the affairs of the region), the shift from Britain to the United States as the dominant external power active in the region had been an ongoing process since the end of the Second World War. The U.S. Central Intelligence Agency's involvement in the toppling of the nationalist government of Mohammed Mossadegh in Iran and the subsequent restoration of the shah in 1953, followed by the declaration of the Eisenhower Doctrine in 1957 signaled two important changes in the external system. First, dominance was transferred from Britain to America in Iran in particular and in the Middle East in general and, second, regional strategy was exercised increasingly through bilateral relations with national governments that, in effect, represented American client states in the Middle East subsystem, such as the shah's regime in Iran.

As the figure indicates, both Iraq and Iran were directly involved with the intrusive system through systemic linkages. This is not the case with the two subsystem cores: the Arab cooperative core and the Arab-Israeli conflict core. The Arab cooperative core, composed at that time of the Arab League and pan-Arab political groups and parties, included all of the independent Arab states of the region. Thus, it does not only refer to the efforts at cooperation by the Arab states, it signifies a supranational structural pattern of cooperative interaction, a pattern imposed by the necessity of common action. Iraq and Saudi Arabia were the only gulf states involved in the Arab cooperative core.

The Arab-Israeli conflict system, the second Middle East core, did not directly involve any gulf state. In fact, it only directly involved four states in the area. The profound regional magnitude of the issue is explained by the systemic linkage between the Arab cooperative core and this conflict core. Three of the states involved in the conflict core— Egypt, Jordan, and Syria—were also members of the cooperative core. Furthermore, by 1958, Egypt (involved in both regional cores) was the undisputed leader of the pan-Arab movement and had in fact forged a union with Syria and created the United Arab Republic (UAR) on 1

February 1958, realizing, if only temporarily, major progress toward the goal of Arab nationalism. Reflecting the impact of this, the Hashemite monarchies of Iraq and Jordan united to form the Arab Federation on 14 February in reaction to the nationalist challenge of the UAR.

The 1958 Iraqi Revolution directly effected a major change in the structure of state relations. With Iraq's withdrawal from the Baghdad Pact as one of the first acts of the revolutionary government, the alliance fell apart. While the other members remained allied under the Central Treaty Organization (CENTO) agreement, with no Arab member a key linkage of the intrusive system with the Arab cooperative core was lost. Thereafter, American strategy emphasized bilateral arrangements with the remaining CENTO members for military and economic aid. Furthermore, the Iraqi Revolution highlighted both the increasing alienation of the members of the Arab cooperative core from the dominant external powers and the emerging role of the Soviet Union as a significant competitor for external influence. It was in this setting that the Iraq-Iran border dispute flared up. Table 9-1 summarizes these changes.

The reduction of Western influence in Iraq—as reflected by the toppling of the pro-British government, withdrawal from the Baghdad Pact, and development of relations with the Soviet bloc—corresponded with increasing Western influence in Iran, especially increased bilateral arrangements between Iran and the United States. The reduction of influence in Iraq, however, was part of the larger process of diminishing Western influence going on in the Arab world generally. The Western powers had no direct linkages with the Arab cooperative core although there were some indirect connections through bilateral relations with some member states. During this period the United States intensified bilateral arrangements with Saudi Arabia and Jordan, for example, along the same lines but not on the same scale as with Iran. At the same time, the Soviet bloc was increasing bilateral relations with core members in direct competition with the United States, although this competition in effect nullified the efforts of each. In addition, any Western influence that may have been effected through the client states was offset by American support for Israel in the Arab-Israeli conflict core. The drift toward the reduction of the role of Western influence in the Arab world was in fact enhanced by Soviet-American competition and the American role in the Arab-Israeli conflict.

What, in fact, did this have to do with the 1958 flare-up of the Iraq-Iran border dispute? First, it intensified during a time of significant systemic changes in intrusive system linkages in the region, changes precipitated by the Iraqi Revolution. As figure 9-1 shows, both Iraq and

Table 9-1   Iraq and Iran's systemic linkages

	Iraq	Iran
Before 1958 Iraqi Revolution		
Bilateral/regional	Arab states, Turkey, Iran	Arab states, Turkey, Israel
Regional core	Arab Cooperative	None
Regional subcore	Arab Federation	None
Gulf	No gulf core as such. Iraq and Iran shared the geographic position of the gulf states. The other countries of the gulf, except Saudi Arabia, were still British dependencies. Power, of course, was in British hands.	
External big powers (bilateral)	Great Britain, United States	United States, USSR, Great Britain
Intrusive system	Baghdad Pact	Baghdad Pact
After 1958 Iraqi Revolution		
Bilateral/regional	Arab states, Turkey, Iran	Arab states, Turkey, Israel
Regional core	Arab Cooperative	None
Regional subcore	None	None
Gulf	Same as before 1958 Iraqi Revolution	
External big powers (bilateral)	USSR, Great Britain, United States	United States, Great Britain, USSR
Intrusive system	None	CENTO

Iran had been central to these linkages. Furthermore, Iraq was the only Arab state that was directly connected to the intrusive system. With this relation broken, the intrusive system did not only lose its direct link with the Arab cooperative core, indeed, the revolutionary nationalist government in Iraq became a strong antagonist of British and American power in the region within that core.

Second, the border dispute flared up at a time of impending systemic changes in the Persian Gulf. Gulf countries were inexorably moving toward independence as Britain finished dismantling its colonial empire. Iran was preparing for a surrogate role in the impending gulf power vacuum. With Iraq controlled by a nationalist government, Britain and Iran had reason to fear Iraq's influence on Arab nationalism in the gulf.

Finally, Iraq and Saudi Arabia were the only gulf states with membership in the Arab cooperative core. This was probably insufficient representation in the core to transform the issue from a bilateral to a regional one. Furthermore, the core itself was weak and lacked cohesion. The Arab League and the pan-Arab political groupings were mutually suspicious and antagonistic. The core, in other words, represented the Arab world's weakness and fragmentation. It was no more capable at that time of dealing with the Iraq-Iran border issue than it was of dealing with the Arab-Israeli issue.

1969

In April 1969, Iran unilaterally abrogated the Frontier Treaty of 1937, demanding that the thalweg (mid-channel) line be recognized as the boundary along the entire length of the Shatt al-Arab River. This was really the culmination of the dispute initiated in 1958. During the intervening period, the systemic structure of the Middle East had undergone considerable change (see figure 9-2).

One of the most profound changes was in the size and scope of the Arab cooperative core. Not only had the number of Arab states increased but so had the number of Arab League agencies. The political parties and groupings that made up the core had also changed. The focus of these movements had become the Palestine resistance struggle. Reflecting this, between 1961 and 1963 about forty Arab Palestinian organizations appeared. These were closely aligned and often directly associated with the pan-Arab parties and groups.[2] Furthermore, the pan-Arab Baath party was now in control of Syria and Iraq.

In addition to the core that had existed in 1958, there were several new components.

1 The Palestine Liberation Organization (PLO) was created by the first summit conference of Arab heads of state in January 1964 as the official representative of the Palestinians. The Palestine resistance movement became a powerful force in the Arab world in the aftermath of the 1967 Arab-Israeli war; by 1969, the PLO had become the umbrella organization of the entire movement.
2 Arab unity experiments, initiated with the formation of the UAR in 1958, were an important manifestation of core interaction in the sixties. The tripartite federal union of Egypt, Iraq, and Syria in 1963 and the Iraq-Egypt (UAR) union of 1964 reflected an ideological commitment to unity and a significant level of interaction within the system.

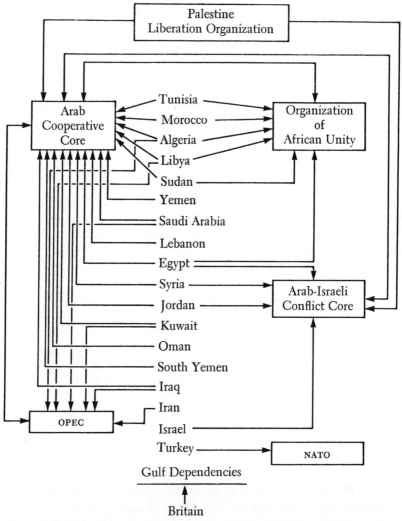

Figure 9-2   1969 systemic structure of the Middle East subsystem.

3 Heads-of-state summit conferences were initiated in January 1964 and convened three more times in the decade—September 1964, September 1965, and August 1967—reflecting the regional approach to major issues. The major issue, of course, was the Arab-Israeli conflict; except for the September 1965 meeting (convened over the Yemen civil war), all of the meetings focused on the Arab-Israeli situation.

4   The Organization of Arab Petroleum Exporting Countries (OAPEC) was organized in 1968.

The growth of the Arab cooperative core indicates that, from a systems perspective, linkages have developed among the Arab countries reflecting both a consistent perception among Arab leaders of common problems that cannot be resolved independently and a consistent push toward cooperation in solving these problems. This commonality of interests is manifested in spite of the significant ideological, economic, political, and social differences among the Arab states. One of the most salient characteristics of the growth of the core has been its consistent attempts to bring under control external influences and hence to reduce the impact of external powers on the course of Middle East developments. This has paralleled the tide of political transformation within Arab states that has swept out traditionalist regimes set up by colonial administrations as puppet or client governments and swept in nationalist regimes strongly opposed to foreign interference. By 1969, half of the Arab states were governed by revolutionary nationalist regimes and only five states were left with traditional monarchies: Jordan, Kuwait, Morocco, Oman, and Saudi Arabia. These monarchies have feared for their survival against the nationalist tide, a fear that both makes them more dependent on external alignments and forces them to compromise with nationalist sentiment. Like the dialectical nature of the link between the cooperative and conflict cores, these states maintain a dialectical position within the Arab cooperative core.

The overriding common problem facing the Arab world has been the Arab-Israeli conflict and the conflict core also has experienced expansion since 1958. The emergence of the Palestinian resistance movement and the PLO as significant forces in the two regional core systems was a direct outcome of the centrality of the Palestine issue to Arab political development. From the perspective of the Arab world, the Arab-Israeli conflict more than any other issue demonstrates the impact of foreign interference on the region. That the United States is responsible for sustaining Israeli militarism is perhaps the most consistent and persistent perception among Arabs, particularly since the 1967 war.

This points up another significant dimension of regional systemic development: the strengthening of the connection between the Arab cooperative core and the Arab-Israeli conflict core. The nature of that linkage is essentially dialectical, manifested in the role of the PLO as a significant actor in each core. Indeed, the PLO is the product of the interaction between the two cores.

Another profound change in systemic structure has been in the nature of the intrusive system. By 1969, the formal symbols of great power involvement in the Middle East had almost completely disappeared. Gone were the military alliance systems that had dominated the region in the fifties. The only formal vestige of great power influence was the remaining British gulf dependencies, although they too were on the threshold of independence. In fact, by 1969 the shift in the American regional strategy from formal military alliance systems to bilateral relations was essentially complete. This shift, of course, was necessitated by the strong hostility in the Arab world toward military alliances and it reflected the role of the Arab core in seeking a reduction of external influence. The surrogates for a military alliance system were Israel, Iran, and Saudi Arabia, built up through American military aid to regional power status.

In place of the alliance systems that had constituted the intrusive system in 1958, by 1969 the system was largely composed of formal linkages of the Arab cooperative core and/or member states with the Organization of African Unity (OAU), the Organization of Petroleum Exporting Countries (OPEC), and the nonaligned movement (NAM). These linkages with other Third World countries were effective forums for the Arab world to put forth its position on the Arab-Israeli conflict. While many Western forums were adamantly committed to Israel and essentially closed to the Arabs, by 1969 the Arabs had made significant headway among African and Asian countries in gaining support for the Arab position.

These changes in the systemic structure of the Middle East were reflected in Iraq. The Baath had taken power in 1968 and, as a pan-Arab party, the Baath had maintained a strong nationalist orientation and a central concern with the Arab-Israeli conflict, making it a key actor in the Arab cooperative core. However, the political instability in Iraq and the Kurdish rebellion that the Baath inherited served to preoccupy the government with internal issues. Iran was already aiding the Kurdish rebels. With the abrogation of the 1937 Frontier Treaty, Iran effectively deflected Iraq's attention from the gulf and from Arab cooperative core issues in general. In effect, Iran's actions forestalled Iraq's efforts to make the issue of imperialism in the gulf an Arab issue (as indicated by the substantial attention to this in Baath party literature during this period).

1980

Following Iran's abrogation of the 1937 Frontier Treaty in 1969, Iran continued pressure on the Iraq-Iran borders, occupied three gulf islands in 1971, and stepped up aid to the Kurdish rebels in Iraq. By 1973, the Kurdish rebellion constituted a civil war in northern Iraq and was a serious drain on Iraqi military and economic capabilities. In February 1973, Iraq took the border dispute to the United Nations Security Council, in effect initiating negotiations to settle the dispute. On 6 March 1975, a new agreement was signed between Iraq and Iran (the so-called Algiers Accord) based on the following terms: first, Iran would cease its support for the Kurdish rebellion; second, the frontier between Iraq and Iran would be adjusted, including the following of the thalweg along the entire length of the Shatt al-Arab; third, the propaganda war between the two countries would cease, along with Iraq's active opposition to Iran's occupation of the three gulf islands and any interference in each other's internal affairs.

Despite the Algiers Accord, full-scale war erupted between Iraq and Iran in early September 1980. Following the outbreak of war, Arab governments were indirectly drawn into the conflict, variously supporting one side or the other. The neutral role Arab states had taken with regard to the recurring border disputes between Iraq and Iran in the past broke down. Cleavages within the Arab world were manifested as countries declared themselves pro-Iraq or pro-Iran. The issue had become an Arab issue. The Fez Heads of State Summit Conference in September 1982 attempted to resolve these inter-Arab cleavages by giving strong support to Iraq in the war with Iran. Of course, this did not resolve the differences among the Arab states in terms of their individual positions on the Iraq-Iran conflict. As a summit, the Fez conference was a manifestation of the Arab cooperative core. It signified that the Iraq-Iran conflict had not only become an Arab issue, it had become an issue that motivated common action, even in the atmosphere of disagreement and dispute.

What had occurred in the Middle East system to explain the transformation of the conflict from a bilateral to a regional matter? While the structure of the system in 1980 was essentially as outlined in figure 9-2, significant changes had occurred within the core and intrusive system that are not reflected in the figure.

Within the core, the gulf states of the United Arab Emirates, Bahrain, and Qatar had joined the family of Arab states that constituted the Arab cooperative core. These states had achieved independence in the early seventies under British tutelage and Iranian stewardship of American interests in the gulf. They joined the conservative faction in the core, significantly strengthening it. The strength of this faction derived mostly from the great transformation in international affairs that resulted from the oil shortages of the seventies and the subsequent transfer of sovereignty from the Western-owned oil companies to the oil-producing states. The wealth of the oil-producing states greatly magnified their role in international affairs and their power in the core. Manifesting this power was the emergence of funds—the Kuwait Fund, the Saudi Fund, the Islamic Bank, etc.—for financing regional and Third World development with petrodollars. The new gulf states lined up with Saudi Arabia and Kuwait to represent conservative oil politics and conservative Arab policies against the nationalist oil politics and nationalist Arab policies of Algeria, Iraq, and Libya. In this, the conservative faction had a strong regional ally in Iran who effectively represented Western strategic interests in the gulf. Thus, the internal structure of the Arab cooperative core was modified.

The conservative states, furthermore, consolidated conservative interests through the Islamic movement. Just as the nationalist interests had increased interaction with the Third World countries through the OAU and the NAM, the conservative interests now increased them through the Islamic Congress and the Islamic Heads of State summit conferences. In effect, the intrusive system consisting of formal linkages with Third World states no longer represented the purely nationalist Arab interests but was extended to represent traditionalist interests as well. By the early seventies, then, the conservative forces in the region were indeed consolidating against the nationalist tide that had threatened to overwhelm them at the end of the sixties.

In spite of the strains of conservative-nationalist competition that marked the Arab cooperative core, the common problems of continued Israeli occupation of Arab territory, Israel's annexation of Jerusalem in 1967, the plight of the Palestinians, and Israel's settler colonization of the West Bank maintained the essential cohesiveness of the core. The 1973 Arab-Israeli war served to heighten the centrality of this problem to all Arab governments and served to deepen the perception in the Arab world of external influence as the root of the problem. Even the conservative regimes closely aligned with the United States perceive American support of Israel as the central problem in the Arab-Israeli dispute.

Egypt's isolation from the cooperative core as a result of its withdrawal from the conflict core through the Camp David Accords reflects the fundamental commonality of interests and orientation among the other Arab states. Israel's subsequent incursions into southern Lebanon—a state closely aligned with the United States—has heightened the dilemma of the conservative states and increased their participation in the strengthening of core structures. The Arab-Israeli conflict thus has cut across ideological divisions within the Arab world, reflected in the almost universal support given to the PLO. In 1974, the PLO achieved observer status at the United Nations and in 1975 the UN passed a resolution condemning Zionism as a form of racism. Israel had been effectively isolated from the Third World through concerted Arab cooperation.

The fall of the shah of Iran in 1979 changed the nature of the conservative alliance within the Arab core. The Islamic fundamentalism of Iran's new government threatened conservative and nationalist interests alike in the Arab cooperative core. Because of Iran's special role in the gulf—a role that had been supported by Saudi Arabia and Kuwait—the gulf was particularly vulnerable to Iran's new Islamic expansionism. In May 1981, the Gulf Cooperation Council (GCC) was formed by Bahrain, Kuwait, Oman, Qatar, Saudi Arabia, and the United Arab Emirates as a mutual security and defense arrangement directed primarily against the threat of Iranian-sponsored Islamic revolutions. The danger was highlighted by an Iranian-sponsored coup attempt in Bahrain in December 1981.

Iraq's claims of encirclement of the Arab world by Israel on one side and Iran on the other made in 1974 in the Political Report of the Eighth Congress of the Baath Party took on new meaning with the revelations that the Iranian government was receiving military supplies through Israel.[3] The conservative states of the Arab world were the first to support Iraq in the war against Iran, and the gulf states and Saudi Arabia have provided substantial economic support. Another issue has cut across ideological lines.

Conclusion

Israel's invasion of Lebanon and increased settler colonization of the West Bank and the threat to the gulf from Iran are regional issues of common concern to the Arab world irrespective of ideological, political, economic, and social divisions. These events heighten the common concern among Arabs over the role of external forces in fomenting attacks against the Arab world. The Iraq-Iran war represents the emergence of another conflict core in the region. This conflict core has direct linkages with the Arab cooperative core and indirect linkages with the Arab-Israeli conflict core (through Israel's role of arms supplier to Iran). Whatever the outcome, the Iraq-Iran war has precipitated the integration of the gulf region into the Arab cooperative core.

10. The Gulf Cooperation Council: A Search for Security ✒ R. K. Ramazani

In May 1984 the Gulf Cooperation Council celebrated its third anniversary. This chapter represents the first attempt to address several basic questions about this nascent regional organization. Why was it created? How was it formed? How has it tried to cope with the perceived challenges of the war between Iraq and Iran on the one hand, and with the Iranian Revolution on the other? And, finally, how will it be able to cope with future problems of security and stability in the Persian Gulf region? It should be obvious from these questions that the scope of this study is limited to an analysis of issues related to the security and stability of the gulf region; it is not an examination of efforts aimed at cooperation among its members in all fields.

Beginnings and Official Objectives

On 4 February 1981 in Riyadh, Saudi Arabia, the foreign ministers of six states of the Persian Gulf region agreed to establish the Cooperation Council of the Arab Gulf States (*Majlis at-Ta'awn li Duwal al-Khalij al-'Arabiyah*) or what is known in the West as the Gulf Cooperation Council (GCC). The foreign ministers of Bahrain, Kuwait, Oman, Qatar, Saudi Arabia, and the United Arab Emirates (UAE) were in fact following up their previous discussions in a side meeting of the Islamic Conference summit held earlier in Taif, Saudi Arabia. A committee of experts was entrusted with the task of working on the "basic statute" of the organization with a view to its approval by the foreign ministers of the member states and its subsequent ratification, during their first summit meeting, by the heads of the six states. The committee's work was completed during several meetings, beginning on 24 February. The organization's constitution was initialed by the six foreign ministers on 9 March at Muscat in Oman.

The first summit meeting of the GCC was held in Abu Dhabi on 25–26 May 1981 when the heads of state approved, in a closed meeting, what they called the Bylaws of the Supreme Council of the Arab Gulf Cooperation Council, containing the rules governing the meeting of the GCC and the performance of its functions. Besides the Supreme Council, which is the highest authority of the organization, the six states established the Ministerial Council (which is in fact the council of foreign ministers) and the General Secretariat.

A second summit was held on 10–11 November 1981. Since the initial idea of holding two summit meetings a year was subsequently abandoned, the third summit was held in Manama, Bahrain, on 9–11 November 1982. Apart from these three summit meetings during 1981–82, the foreign ministers of the GCC states held a number of meetings both of an "ordinary" and an "emergency" nature during that period. Furthermore, a large number of other meetings were held during 1981–82 by other GCC officials, including defense ministers, chiefs of staff, and economic and planning ministers, partly in efforts to realize the broad objectives of the new organization.

These objectives were stated at the end of the first summit on 26 May 1981 to include the promotion of "cooperation," "coordination," and "integration" among the six states in a variety of nonmilitary fields "in order to serve their interests and strengthen their ability to hold on to their beliefs and values." The leaders of the GCC states also declared that the "region's security and stability are the responsibility of its peoples and countries and that this council expresses the will of these countries and their right to defend their security and independence." Furthermore, they affirmed their "absolute rejection of foreign interference in the region from any source" and called for keeping "the entire region free of international conflicts, particularly the presence of military fleets and foreign bases, in order to safeguard their interests and the interests of the world." Finally, they stated categorically that guaranteeing "stability in the Gulf is linked to the achievement of peace in the Middle East, and this underlies the need to achieve a just solution for the Palestinian question," through the establishment of a "Palestinian state" and "Israeli withdrawal from all the occupied Arab territories, the foremost of which is Jerusalem."[1]

Two preliminary and related questions lie beneath these official pronouncements. First, what kind of an organization is the GCC? Second, why was it created in the first place? No definitive answer to either question is possible at this writing. The GCC is an embryonic organization that is in the process of formation largely in response to the dynamics of domestic, regional, and international circumstances as well as to the intentions and objectives of its founding fathers. Nevertheless, it is necessary to address these two preliminary questions before going any further. Besides the dearth of reliable information on the GCC, misguided assertions of its avowed supporters as well as of hostile detractors render more difficult an objective understanding of this new organization. One of its presumed supporters, for example, speaks of the raison d'être of the GCC as if it were created primarily as an anti-Israeli alliance, while many of its detractors have characterized it variously as an "arm of

NATO," as a "tool of the United States," as a "stalking horse of Saudi Arabia," and as a "latter-day Central Treaty Organization" (CENTO).

Let us begin with what its founders seem to say it is. First, they insist that the GCC is not an "alliance" or an "axis" created against any state. They say it is part of the "Arab nation"; it belongs to the "Islamic nation"; it is a grouping within the gulf region; and it is an influential segment of the Third World. As such, the GCC has an "organic link" with the Arab League, with the Islamic Conference Organization (ICO), with the Organization of Petroleum Exporting Countries (OPEC), with the Organization of Arab Petroleum Exporting Countries (OAPEC), and with the nonaligned movement (NAM). In the language of its founders, the GCC was created "in response to the historical, social, cultural, political and strategic reality through which the Gulf region passed and is passing" or, a bit more concretely: "We constitute part of an ethnicity which has one religion, a joint civilization, and joint values and customs. Moreover, our geographical location and oil resources make us vulnerable to international and political designs which almost amount to blackmail."[2]

Second, the GCC officials claim that they are a group of pragmatic states. The GCC Secretary General, Abdallah Bisharah, for example, says, "We don't adopt steps or resolutions that cannot be implemented; we actually avoid doing so." Finally, the officials of the GCC admit that the organization's initial emphasis on nonmilitary cooperation, particularly "economic integration," shifted to security and defense cooperation in response to changing circumstances without abandoning nonmilitary goals.

The multiplicity of stated principles that presumably underlie the creation and evolution of the GCC may aid its officials to relate the new organization to various states and other organizations when it is expedient for them to do so, but it creates problems of logic for them as well. For example, if Arabism is a constitutional principle of the organization, why not include Iraq as a member? Or if Islam is a basic founding principle, why not include Iran as a member as well? Or if regionalism is a fundamental principle, then why not include North Yemen, for example, as well as all the states of the gulf region proper?

The Saudis Take the Initiative

Stripped of rhetoric, the GCC was created by its six member states partly in response to the outbreak of the war between Iran and Iraq in September 1980. The exclusion of Iraq from membership—a question that in fact delayed the announcement until 4 February 1981 of the intention of its prospective members to create the GCC—was partly a reflection of the fact that Iraq was a belligerent power. However, it was also a sign of the continuing mistrust of the perceived subversiveness of the regime of Saddam Hussein and its bid for hegemony in the gulf. Mistrust prevailed despite a marked improvement in the relations of the conservative Arab states of the gulf with Baghdad, especially after the Egyptian signing of the Camp David Accords and the peace treaty with Israel.

As later explicated, the six GCC states (particularly Saudi Arabia) were at the time no less concerned with the perceived threat of the Iranian Revolution. The fact that it was Iraq that launched an armed attack against Iran, and that at first Iraq appeared to be winning, alarmed Saudi and other gulf leaders. Once the Iranians seemed to be resisting the Iraqi military advances effectively, however, concern over the Iranian revolutionary regime began to mount.[3]

Fear that the gulf war would adversely affect the security of Saudi Arabia no doubt propelled that country into leading the formation of the GCC, but more than external security was perceived to be at stake. The House of Saud, and similarly the royal families in the five other conservative regimes, believed that their very survival was at stake. This basic underlying, but unspoken, truth about the creation of the GCC has been underplayed by the GCC and the Western media. Seldom have observers described honestly the nature of the GCC and, when they have, they seem to be more condescending than realistic.[4] The all-important reason for the fear of the six monarchical regimes for their survival was, and continues to be, the perceived threat of contagion of the antimonarchical Iranian Revolution. Against the background of this greater concern, fear of the spread of the gulf war appears to have been more the catalyst than the cause of the creation of the GCC.

To leave the matter there, however, may still hide other key factors that underpin the creation of the GCC. Besides the perceived threats of the gulf war and the Iranian Revolution, three other factors were influential. First, the anticommunist conservative regimes were deeply alarmed by the Soviet invasion of Afghanistan, which Saudi Arabia took a lead in condemning in ICO meetings. The Soviet threat to their stability and security now seemed all the more imminent.

Second, the American reaction to the twin crises of Iran and Afghanistan was unwelcome to the Saudis for two main reasons. One was the new American commitment, under the Carter Doctrine, to defend the gulf oil supplies, even by military means; this seemed to increase the chances of superpower military confrontation in the gulf region. The other was that after the fall of the shah, Saudi Arabia felt greater American pressure to participate in a "consultative security framework." While such pressure was successfully resisted in 1979, it had to be resisted again after the Iraq-Iran war began, when in September 1980 the Saudis sought and received aid for defense against threatened Iranian air strikes on Saudi oil fields. Some American military officials wanted, for example, to use the crisis opportunity to push the Saudis into long-range commitments such as allowing stockpiling of equipment at Saudi air bases for American use in the event of a major war in the region.[5] These experiences convinced Saudi leaders that the formation of an indigenous security arrangement in the gulf might bolster Saudi resistance to such American pressures in the future. The Carter administration's decision to deploy four Airborne Warning and Control System (AWACS) planes was welcome largely as a sign of U.S. diplomatic support for the royal family, but militarily the Saudi leaders wished to avoid too close an association with the United States.

The third additional factor influencing creation of the GCC was the Saudi intention of using the gulf war as an opportunity to project its own power in the region. One way of doing that without being too obvious was through regional cooperation with like-minded regimes. As viewed from Riyadh, the distraction of Iran and Iraq from their traditional bid for hegemony in the gulf region could be used by Saudi Arabia and its friends as an opportunity to "get their act together" in order to fill the power vacuum themselves. The GCC officials have not been shy in speaking publicly about their "intrinsic power," a claim that seems justified, at least in terms of the combined putative power of their countries. Although their total population of about 12 million is less than that of Iraq alone, and less than one-third the size of Iran, the GCC states enjoy other ingredients of power. For example, they had the financial capability in 1982 to budget about $30 billion for military purposes. Saudi Arabia alone ranked fourth in world military spending after the United States, the Soviet Union, and Britain. Furthermore, the area covered by the six states constitutes the "oil heartland" of the world not only by virtue of containing the world's largest oil reserves, but also in terms of oil production. The six produce more than 40 percent of all oil produced by OPEC nations and account, together, for more than 20 percent of U.S. oil imports, 56 percent of Western Europe's, and nearly 70 percent of Japan's.

The Saudi bid for collective security in the gulf region through the formation of an indigenous mechanism in 1981 was by no means unprecedented. The shah's regime subscribed to the principle of regional security by gulf states as early as 1968 when the British announced their intention to withdraw their forces from the area "east of Suez."[6] No progress was made, however, as long as the Shatt al-Arab dispute between Tehran and Baghdad continued. Once this dispute and other bilateral issues were settled in 1975, Iraq and Iran took the initiative to press for regional cooperation. By 1978, when Baghdad-Moscow relations had begun to deteriorate over a wide variety of issues, the prospects of an Iraqi-Iranian initiative for leading regional security cooperation seemed to have improved unprecedentedly. More important, Saudi Arabia was also becoming interested in holding regular "security consultations" with the other two major gulf powers.[7] At the time, it appeared that the three traditional rivals for power and influence in the gulf region were prepared to cooperate in the face of a commonly perceived threat from the Soviet Union. It also appeared that they were confident they could persuade the smaller gulf states to join them eventually in a collective security arrangement. But the Iranian Revolution seemed to take Iran out of the game and Saddam Hussein's unsuccessful war seemed to squash his own bid for preeminent power and influence. As seen from Riyadh, the circumstances in 1981 could not have been any more favorable for a Saudi bid for superiority in the gulf region. The Saudis' two main rivals seemed wholly preoccupied with an inconclusive war. If the five smaller and more or less like-minded conservative regimes joined Saudi Arabia in an organization such as the GCC, Riyadh's preeminence in the gulf might be established.

The GCC and the Iraq-Iran War

In their efforts to achieve the stated objectives of security and stability in the gulf region, the GCC member states have had to cope with the war between Iraq and Iran on the one hand, and the Iranian Revolution on the other. A word of caution is in order. The GCC states do not constitute a monolithic bloc. They differ significantly in perceptions and policies in dealing with problems of security and stability. In order to understand where their interests converge and diverge, it is necessary to take note of their behavior both as members of an organization and as individual sovereign actors. Let us first take up their response to the war between Iraq and Iran.

The GCC states have been caught on the horns of a dilemma both militarily and diplomatically in trying to grapple with the problems of the war between Iraq and Iran. They have not been willing to commit troops as a means of supporting Iraqi war efforts. Clearly they do not seem to favor a decisive Iraqi victory regardless of all the talk about

Arab fraternity. They do not welcome a clear Iranian success either. A postwar preponderance of power in favor of either Iraq or Iran is envisaged as detrimental to the interests of the GCC states.

The unwillingness of the GCC states to join the Iraqis in actual combat against Iran is realistically coupled with a painful recognition of their lack of military capability for producing a successful and acceptable outcome. They realize that their ground forces, totaling some 133,000 troops, are too heterogeneous in national origin, training, and equipment to perform effectively against Iranian arms. Furthermore, their air power is incapable of inflicting heavy losses on Iran without inviting unacceptable costs to themselves. In order to fight a war to the finish against Iran, the GCC states would have to be able to cripple, for example, the gigantic oil terminal at Kharg Island. This they would not be able to do, judging by the demonstrated inability of Iraq to do so despite its superior air power and repeated but unwarranted claims to the contrary. The Iranians have massed almost their entire anti-aircraft missile armory in and around the vital island.[8] No such armory at the moment seems to protect the GCC's own oil terminals and facilities against an Iranian retaliation, despite the American deployment of four AWACS planes. The deployment of these planes in Saudi Arabia has so far been more important as a demonstration of U.S. diplomatic support of the Saudi regime than anything else. In March 1982, for example, these planes failed to spot a Phantom jet piloted by a defecting Iranian until it was about to land at Dhahran airport in Saudi Arabia.[9] Even if a decisive Iraqi victory were politically acceptable, which it is not, the GCC states are deeply conscious of the sheer technical and military difficulties involved in creating a joint control and command system that would do them any good at the present time in combat against Iran. Quite apart from the gulf war, they have decided to "coordinate" rather than "integrate" their defense forces, beginning with their ground forces, with an eye to increasing their military capability in the future. The unwillingness and inability of the GCC states to enter armed hostilities on the side of Iraq against Iran, however, have not prevented them from providing financial and logistical support. Logistically, Jordan has joined the Saudis and the Kuwaitis in aiding Iraq. But even the varying degrees of logistical and financial aid by the GCC states have been extended grudgingly. Not surprisingly, Iraq has resented this.

After April 1981 Iraq began to encounter serious financial difficulties. The Syrians closed down—perhaps as a bonus to Iran for signing a barter agreement with them—the trans-Syrian oil pipeline from the northern Iraqi oil fields to the Mediterranean. With its Khor al Amaya oil terminal near Fao on the gulf already crippled by Iran in 1980, the

Iraqi oil exports dwindled to less than a million barrels a day after the closure of the trans-Syrian pipeline. Iraqi oil could be exported then only through the Kurdish-threatened trans-Turkey oil pipeline.

From the start of the war Iraq had received substantial financial aid from the GCC states, perhaps as much as $25–35 billion worth, according to some Western accounts. But then, according to a complaint by Iraqi Deputy Prime Minister Tariq Aziz in January 1983, Iraq's "Arab brothers" had virtually ceased to help Iraq over the previous year. He also said that they had loaned Iraq "less than $20 billion," instead of the much higher figures reported by the Western press.[10] In all probability, the Saudis did want to extend further aid to the Iraqis. They tried hard to get their GCC partners to go along with them during the third summit meeting of the GCC leaders in November 1982 but they refused to do so. The Kuwaitis in particular must have been reluctant to extend more financial aid to Iraq, considering the fact that they alone had advanced Iraq three loans of $2 billion each in 1981. Furthermore, Kuwait had had to dig into its own capital reserves to meet Iraqi demands during an oil glut and in the context of diminishing Kuwaiti oil production and revenues.[11]

Kuwait's logistical support for its big Iraqi neighbor has also at times been generous, but it too has been costly. Since the start of the war the Kuwaitis have complained bitterly about Iranian air attacks, including two on their customs post bordering Iraq, one attack in November 1980 and another in June 1981. Kuwait also protested an alleged Iranian air attack on an oil installation at Umm Al-'Aish which was partially destroyed on 1 October 1981. Iran has vehemently denied all charges of attacking Kuwait. But the fact remains that about one-third of Kuwait's port capacity is taken up by supplies for Iraq, which at night include arms as well as the normal daytime traffic in nonmilitary goods.[12]

Diplomatically no less than militarily the GCC states have been caught on the horns of a dilemma. They have collectively been "a party" to the Iraq-Iran conflict, as the GCC Secretary General has more than once admitted,[13] and at the same time they have tried to urge the two warring powers to make peace. Before discussing major examples of their collective strategy, it is essential to realize that individually the GCC states have pursued divergent diplomatic courses of action. For example, while Kuwait and the UAE have managed to aid Iraq and simultaneously maintain a dialogue with Iran, Saudi Arabia has ended up in a bitter confrontation with Iran and tried hard to aid Iraq in various ways. As a case in point, Riyadh has tried to use its financial leverage with Syria, especially since the outbreak of the Lebanon war, to persuade Damascus to reopen the trans-Syrian oil pipeline and to persuade Hafiz Assad to nudge Iran toward a peace settlement with Iraq. Riyadh has also sought to use its "special relationship" with the United States to persuade Washington to be more receptive toward meeting Iraqi economic needs. It is possible that Washington's decision to grant $210 million in credit guarantees to finance food sales to Iraq by private American banks was a result of Riyadh's pleading for aid to the financially hard-pressed Iraqis.

The GCC's collective diplomatic strategy tries to use the carrot and stick indirectly as well as directly. Indirectly, for example, the GCC managed to get the Arab League during its September 1982 summit meeting at Fez to adopt a "Gulf War Resolution," presumably as a means of warning Tehran that its invasion of Iraq could be viewed as an act of war against the "Arab Nation."[14]

More directly, GCC leaders, in the final communiqué at the end of their third summit meeting in Manama on 11 November 1982, criticized Iran for "crossing its international border with Iraq and the great threat which these developments pose to the safety and security of the Arab nation." They also asked Iran to respond to the peacemaking efforts of the Islamic Conference Organization, the nonaligned countries, and the United Nations.[15] This was quite a soft attempt at pressuring Iran considering the report of An-Nahar Al-'Arabi Wa Ad-Duwali of 15–21 November 1982 to the effect that some Arab leaders had pushed at this meeting for the recall of the GCC ambassadors from Tehran. It has not been possible to verify that report, but it is not implausible that such a suggestion may have been made.

The conciliatory side of the GCC collective strategy in the gulf war has included two major aspects. First, there has been at least a hint that the GCC states are prepared to contribute to compensation for the losses and reconstruction projects of "vital establishments" of the two warring nations, despite public denials. Second, besides supporting the peacemaking efforts of the organizations mentioned before, the GCC decided to support more vigorously the mediation efforts of Algeria and Syria and, more importantly, to initiate mediation efforts of its own.

The GCC and the Iranian Revolution

The same basic power and ideological conflict between Saudi Arabia and Iran that significantly shapes the GCC attitude toward the gulf war also influences the organization's attitude toward the Iranian Revolution. As seen by the GCC states, the threat of the Iranian Revolution to their security and stability stems from Iranian attempts at subversion, or what they call "sabotage," on the one hand, and acts of "agitation" on the other. Let us first take up the perceived threat of sabotage.

There is no doubt that the dominant elements within the Iranian revolutionary regime today are ideologically committed to what they call the export of the "Islamic" (not "Iranian") revolution. Since this subject has been treated in depth elsewhere,[16] it will be sufficient simply to list some basic propositions before taking up the GCC's response to the perceived Iranian subversion and agitation.

1. Contrary to the view of most statesmen and scholars, including one contributor to this volume, the world view of Ayatollah Khomeini is *not* pan-Islamic, like that of Jamal al-Din Afghani or any other Muslim political thinker or activist. Khomeini's ideology does not call for the unity of the existing Muslim states. Rather, it calls for the establishment of what may be called an "Islamic world order." In this sense it is both a universalistic and revolutionary ideology. It rejects the Westphalia notion of the territorial nation-state and the modern political and legal order that is presumably based on it. As such, it requires the vouchsafing of Islam to *the entire world*, and it also rejects all regimes, Muslim-populated or otherwise, that are believed to be based on the will of the "privileged few" (*mostakbarin*) rather than the "underprivileged masses" (*mostaza'fin*). From such a revolutionary world perspective, the Saudi royalty, for example, represents "Islamic heresy."

2. The export of the Islamic Revolution is incumbent on Iran. The rationale is that Iran is the only country in the world in which the rule of the *faghih* (Islamic jurisprudence) has been actually established for the first time in history. That rule is claimed to be based on the *Sharia'h* (Islamic law) and is presumably supported by the underprivileged masses.

3. The export of the Islamic Revolution must take place peacefully or, as Khomeini puts it, "not by the sword," but mainly by the example of the Islamic behavior of Iranians and by means of propaganda. The Iranian crossing of the Iraqi borders in July 1982, for example, was not, according to this ideology, an attempt to export the revolution; it was to defend "Islam."

Looking at this brand of Islamic revolutionary ideology from the other side of the gulf, the GCC states in general, and Saudi Arabia in particular, believe that the shah's prerevolutionary bid for dominance in the gulf region was, by contrast, child's play. As such, the Iranian threat today is regarded as a crusade against the very existence of every gulf regime. The challenge to the GCC states, therefore, is perceived to require in response not only the containment of Iranian power but also the containment of Iranian revolutionary ideology.

Against the backdrop of such a view, the GCC states' panic-stricken reaction to the discovery of the alleged Iranian-backed plot in Bahrain may be better understood. Briefly, the Bahraini government announced on 13 December 1981 that it had arrested a group of "saboteurs," allegedly trained by Iran. Subsequently, the Bahraini interior minister charged that the group had planned to assassinate Bahraini officials; that it belonged to the "Islamic Front for the Liberation of Bahrain," headquartered in Tehran; and that all its "sixty" members were Shi'i Muslims. The actual number turned out to be seventy-three, sixty Bahraini and eleven Saudi dissidents and one Omani and one Kuwaiti national; there were no Iranians among the group. They were tried and sentenced in May 1982 in Bahrain, receiving jail sentences ranging from seven years to life.

The reaction of the GCC countries as a whole was not as vehement as that of Saudi Arabia. Saudi Interior Minister Prince Nayif ibn 'Abd al-'Aziz called on Iran to stop supporting "sabotage activities" in the gulf and asserted that while the Iranians had said at the beginning of their revolution that they would not act as the gulf's "policeman," they had now become "the Gulf's terrorists."[17] More important, Saudi Arabia rushed to sign four bilateral security agreements with Bahrain, Oman, Qatar, and the UAE. Kuwait refused to sign any agreement.

Beyond these bilateral agreements, the GCC as a whole began to devote increasing attention to security issues. Saudi Arabia took the lead to impress on its partners the need for a single, collective, internal security agreement among all the GCC members. The foreign ministers of the GCC states held their first emergency meeting in Manama 6–7 February 1982. In the words of the GCC secretary general, "what happened in Bahrain was not directed against one part of this body but against the whole body."[18] The final statement of the GCC foreign ministers declared the organization's "full support" for Bahrain's safety, stability, and sovereignty and its "determination to resist the acts of sabotage that are carried out by Iran with the aim of undermining security and stability, spreading chaos and confusion and threatening the interests of citizens."[19]

Saudi Arabia finally succeeded in convincing its GCC partners to agree in principle to sign a collective internal security agreement. This goal was achieved during the first meeting of the interior ministers of the GCC, held in Riyadh 24–25 February 1982; they reviewed "the plot" and stressed that "intervention by any country in the internal affairs of one of the member states is considered to be intervention in the internal affairs of all of the GCC states."[20]

Despite the agreement of the GCC states on the principle of collective domestic security, Saudi optimism faded in the months following the interior ministers' meeting. Even six months after that meeting it was clear that the Kuwaitis were dragging their feet in consenting to

sign a bilateral agreement with Saudi Arabia, let alone in signing a collective internal security agreement. Although Saudi Interior Minister
Prince Nayif underplayed the Saudi-Kuwaiti disagreement, the subsequent delays and finally the postponement of the signing of an agreement revealed the continued difficulties involved. A thirty-nine-article
draft agreement was reviewed finally by the leaders of the GCC states during their third summit meeting in Manama in November 1982, but it
was not adopted.[21] This setback was considered to signify Saudi failure,
given the fact that Riyadh had all along pressed for the signing of such
an agreement. The official explanation was that the matter, after almost
a year, still needed study; the formal explanation was that the Kuwaitis
did not accept the draft agreement's provisions regarding the extradi-
tion of criminals; and the real reason was that the Kuwaitis were reluctant to be sucked into the Saudi security orbit and the Saudi-Iranian
"cold war."

This brings us to an analysis of the GCC reaction to the perceived
threat of Iranian agitation. The GCC states feel this threat in varying degrees, but again Saudi Arabia perceives it most vividly. For this important reason, Saudi-Iranian relations will be emphasized.

The Riyadh-Tehran cold war did not happen overnight. It began
with the very start of the Iranian Revolution. When the revolution began, Saudi leaders strongly supported the shah's regime. For example,
the Saudi minister of defense and aviation, Prince Sultan, told the Kuwaiti *Al-Siyasah* in an interview in August 1978 that all the Arab countries should support the shah's regime against the forces of opposition.[22]
To cite another example, Prince Fahd told the *Al-Jazirah* in an interview in January 1979 that Saudi Arabia supported the shah's regime because it was based on "Islamic law" (*Sharia'h*). One can imagine what
Khomeini and his supporters thought about such assertions. The real
reasons for supporting the shah's regime were based partly on the Saudi
fear that the atheistic communists of Iran might seize control of the
Iranian government. This, of course, turned out to be a misperception
of the Iranian situation, but Prince Sultan and others are said to have
believed it possible.

After the seizure of power by the revolutionary forces in Iran (11
February 1979), Saudi leaders hoped to be able to maintain at least correct relations with the Bazargan government. The Saudis seemed to believe that there might still be a chance for control of the government by
moderate elements in Iran. On the day of the formal establishment of
the Islamic Republic of Iran (11 April 1979), King Khalid congratu-
lated Ayatollah Khomeini in a message and prayed "to the Almighty to
guide you [Khomeini] to the forefront of those who strive for upholding

of Islam and Muslims."[23] But as Muslim extremists took control of the Iranian government, Riyadh-Tehran relations began to deteriorate. Saudi-Iranian differences over four major issues reflect the underlying power and ideological conflict that has emerged since revolutionary forces took control in Iran. Let us examine these below.

First, the Saudi-Iranian cold war was sparked, for all practical purposes, by the behavior of the Iranian pilgrims in Saudi Arabia in the fall of 1981. The facts of the incidents involved are differently reported by the conflicting parties, but apparently Iranian pilgrims took posters of Ayatollah Khomeini and revolutionary tracts to Mecca and engaged in political demonstrations. The crisis finally led to an exchange of letters between the Ayatollah and King Khalid on 10 October, revealing clashing perspectives on the very meaning and purpose of the *hajj*, or pilgrimage, in Islam. In a nutshell, the king considered pilgrimage as a religious act, while Khomeini contended sternly that it was a "religio-political" duty.

Another *hajj* crisis broke out during the annual pilgrimage in September 1982. The Iranian revolutionaries in effect challenged the religious and political leadership of Saudi Arabia for the second time. This time Hojatoleslam Sayed Muhammad Musavi Khoiniha, who had led the Iranian seizure of the American embassy in Tehran, headed the Iranian pilgrims as a representative of Khomeini. Before his departure for Saudi Arabia, he expounded in detail Khomeini's religio-political view of the pilgrimage with every indication that once again the Iranian pilgrims would attempt to use the *hajj* opportunity in September to proselytize the Khomeini brand of Islam among some 2 million Muslims.[24] After a series of violent clashes in September, the Saudi authorities finally expelled one hundred Iranians, including their leader. The chasm between Riyadh and Tehran deepened farther.

Second, besides the *hajj* issue, Iran and Saudi Arabia clash over their diametrically opposed relationships with the United States. The shah's "special relationship" with the United States partly contributed to the Iranian Revolution, which for all practical purposes destroyed the decades-old friendly relations between Tehran and Washington.[25] Anti-Americanism has been an engine of revolutionary legitimacy in Iran, and hostility toward the United States continues to color Iranian views of almost anything. The United States is regarded as the godfather of both "imperialism and Zionism," and Saudi Arabia's "special relationship" with Washington makes the royal family "corrupt," "decadent," and an "agent" of the United States in the gulf region. The more extremist elements of the Iranian elite such as Ayatollah Montazari perceive the GCC in the same light by virtue of the Saudi-American connection, while the Hojatoleslam Hashemi Rafsanjani, speaker of the Iranian parliament, seems to oppose the GCC when it serves the "interests of the United States."[26]

A third issue that reveals the underlying hostility between Tehran and Riyadh is the Arab-Israeli conflict. Contrary to the general impression, the fall of the pro-Israeli shah's regime and the emergence of the anti-Israeli revolutionary regime have not necessarily meant an identity of views between Tehran and Riyadh on the Arab-Israeli conflict or, for that matter, between Iran and most Arab states. The current revolutionary views in Iran are closer to those of the radical group known as the "Steadfastness Front," which includes Algeria, Libya, South Yemen, Syria, and the Palestinian Liberation Organization (PLO). As such, the revolutionary regime has opposed all pleace plans that seem to recognize implicitly or otherwise the state of Israel, including the Fahd, Fez, and Reagan plans. Furthermore, the Khomeini regime condemned the "deadly silence" of the Arab world during the Lebanon war, called for an oil embargo, and dispatched Iranian volunteers to fight Israel in Lebanon. The reports of about $27 million in Israeli arms sales to Iran have been vehemently denied by the revolutionary regime but, denied or not, the fact remains that no such small-scale purchases could make any significant difference in the basic hostility of the present revolutionary regime toward Israel. Against such a backdrop, the GCC's endorsement of the peace plans mentioned above would make it an "agent" of the "Great Satan" in the eyes of the Iranian revolutionary zealots.

Fourth, and finally, the Saudi-Iranian conflict is revealed in their differences over oil issues. The differences are old, but the ideological overlay is new. The Iranian challenge to the Saudi preeminence in OPEC is now cast in terms of the Iranian protection of the oil-producing underdogs, or "underprivileged" (*mostaza'fin*) members of the organization. Furthermore, the Saudi Arabian use of the GCC forum to caucus its partners puts them too on the side of the "privileged" (*mostakbarin*) members of OPEC in the eyes of Iranian revolutionaries. The most vivid example of all this was the OPEC crisis during its Geneva meeting in January 1983. The meeting collapsed in disarray on 24 January because the oil ministers could not agree on a package of production levels and prices. Iranian Oil Minister Mohammad Gharazi lost no opportunity to state triumphantly that "Saudi Arabia has lost its major role in OPEC," adding that "Iran's political strength has forced Saudi Arabia to cut its oil production from 5 to nearly 4 million barrels a day. Any reduction in Saudi production that is added to ours means a victory."[27] He also did not lose the opportunity to use the revolutionary theme of the "under-privileged" versus the "privileged" on this occasion as a means of trying to align such indebted oil producers as Nigeria and Venezuela, with the help of Algeria and Libya, on the side of Iran against the GCC oil producers. He vowed that his government "will defend these oppressed peoples."[28]

The battle lines over oil issues for this subsequently unsuccessful OPEC emergency meeting had been drawn on both sides of the gulf, in Tehran and Manama. In Tehran the Iranian oil minister expounded the criteria for fixing production quotas in OPEC while Iran had already increased its own production unilaterally from the assigned 1.2 million barrels a day to 3.2 million, and had also sold its oil—not unlike some other OPEC members—way below the OPEC official price of $34 a barrel. The oil production, the minister hoped, would be fixed "logically," proportionate to populations, resources, and material needs of each country,[29] meaning, of course, that Iran's production allocation should be increased and those of Saudi Arabia and other gulf producers decreased, particularly given the Iranian need for revenues to finance its war with Iraq.

The GCC countries, led by Saudi Arabia, had prepared themselves for the OPEC Geneva meeting in an "extraordinary meeting" of their oil ministers on 15 January after five of them had met informally the night before. Although gas, oil, and petroleum terminal facilities and other issues of internal concern to the GCC members were discussed, there is little doubt that this meeting was to insure a common stance of the GCC oil producers within OPEC with which, according to *Ash-Sharq Al-Awsat*, the GCC has an "organic link." The Iranian oil and price challenge to the other gulf producers was fully discussed, although the Libyan production and price challenge was also of obvious concern.[30] As it turned out, however, Saudi Arabia's apparent success in the first phase of the OPEC meeting in reaching a quid pro quo with Iran was wiped out in the second phase of the meeting. In this latter phase, it was Saudi disagreement mainly with the African states that broke up the meeting, but the Saudi-Iranian oil battle was also in evidence as an aspect of the larger Riyadh-Tehran cold war.

Conclusion

If power and influence simply grew out of the barrels of guns and, in this case, also out of barrels of oil, then it would be possible to speculate about the future security and stability of the Persian Gulf region purely in those terms. One could argue that the GCC countries in the long run can win the oil war with Iran because they produce about 40 percent of the OPEC output and hence can, in effect, make or break oil production and prices in the world market. One could also argue, given the primacy of financial power of the GCC states, next only to the industrial world, that they in the long run can build up a formidable military arsenal based on high technology and sophisticated weaponry far superior to anything that Iran or Iraq can afford. Or, if this seems to claim too much for the GCC states even in terms of the long run, one could advocate, as some indeed have, membership of Iraq in the GCC as a means of maintaining an effective balance of power in the region between the Arab gulf states and Iran.

Even if such a membership seems to be too much to expect, then one could argue for the strengthening of GCC military power by hooking it up with the American Rapid Deployment Force (RDF), as indeed some Pentagon circles have been itching to do ever since the inception of the GCC. At least some American defense officials believe, for example, that the AWACS aircraft and their ground environment system will afford the capability to link the air defense network of these states into a unified system backed by the United States.

Furthermore, one could argue that any one of these three options, that is, the military buildup of the GCC, its military partnership with Iraq, or its close military association with the United States, could do more than just counterbalance Iranian power; it could also contain the Iranian Revolution. One could even think in terms of a mixture of these options or a modification of them. For example, former Secretary of State Henry Kissinger believes that as a result of the Lebanon war the potential for a de facto coalition between all moderate governments of the entire Middle East and the United States has emerged, and such a coalition must aim not only at containing Soviet imperialism, but also Shi'ite radicalism, Muslim fundamentalism, and Iranian revolutionary agitation.

However, since power and influence do not simply grow out of the barrels of guns and oil, it is clear that the ability of the GCC to maintain future security and stability in the gulf region will depend more on other factors. To suggest this proposition does not necessarily mean that the strengthening of the GCC military capability is not needed or is unimportant. Rather, it seems to be of secondary importance, given the nature of the deeper problems that beset the GCC as a whole and its members individually. For this important reason the future security and stability of the gulf region and of the GCC and its members will depend less on military muscle than on political and diplomatic consensus. That is the single most important lesson of an objective study of the GCC's experiences over its early life.

Consensus among the GCC member states must develop with respect to the nature and extent of their relationships with Iraq and Iran on the one hand, and with the superpowers on the other. Without such a consensus all the military muscle that the GCC can develop, whether independently or through some kind of a coalition, will hardly insure either the survival of the individual regimes or the future security and stability of the gulf region. As a matter of fact, without such a consensus the future viability of the organization itself may be placed in jeopardy. In bringing this chapter to a close, I will quickly outline the challenges to the GCC of these two sets of relationships.

First, with respect to the GCC's future relationship with Iran and Iraq, the immediate challenge, of course, is the war between them. The GCC's anomalous strategy of simultaneously being and not being a party to the conflict has so far avoided involvement in armed hostilities. As long as it continues this strategy it might avoid Iranian retaliation. The permission of the Saudis, for example, to allow some Iraqi planes to land on their airfields and to other Iraqi planes to fly through their airspace to Oman early in the gulf war nearly triggered an Iranian retaliation. The withdrawal of those planes defused the threat of the spread of armed hostilities. Because of its partiality in the gulf conflict, the GCC's influence in making peace between Iran and Iraq will continue to be nil. It is highly doubtful that even the more conciliatory members of the GCC such as Kuwait and the UAE can make any headway in peacemaking. If it is true that the GCC is indeed willing and able to contribute to the reconstruction of both Iranian and Iraqi "vital establishments" after the war, this may go some way toward assuaging the Iranian anger at the logistical and financial aid that has been extended to Iraq in the past. To some Iranian ears GCC disapprobation and admonition in whatever form sound hollow while to others they are "provocative," if not an outright instigation to settling scores with the hawkish members of the GCC after the war. In short, the GCC has next to no influence on the peacemaking process either directly or indirectly through the Islamic Conference Organization or any other mediatory party.

A more profound and long-range problem in the relationship of the GCC with Iran and Iraq, however, is the question of their eventual membership. So far, whenever GCC leaders and officials have been asked this question, they have either evaded it altogether or have fallen back on ambiguous rhetoric that only confirms the supposition that this basic question has not really ever been carefully considered by the founders of the organization. Whether or not it has been, the fact remains that the exclusion of those two gulf countries seems to cast doubt on the repeated claim of GCC officials that it is not an alliance *against* anyone. Still worse, it is one of those questions that reveals a deep lack of consensus within the GCC; some members may wish to leave the door open to the eventual membership of one or perhaps even both non-GCC gulf states, while others may be utterly opposed to it.

With respect to Iran, however, the question of membership is ultimately entwined with the much deeper problem of the GCC attitude toward the perceived threat of the Iranian Revolution. There is nothing wrong with Saudi Arabia's signing of four bilateral agreements with Bahrain, Oman, Qatar, and the UAE to protect themselves against "sabotage." Nor is anything wrong with a collective internal security agreement among all GCC states if they can develop a real consensus to that effect. But the fact that Kuwait has refused to sign a bilateral agreement, and has so far opposed a multilateral one, speaks for the problem of consensus within the GCC. Their inability to reach a consensus in this case is at least as important as their ability to mediate successfully in the chronic conflict between South Yemen and Oman or, even more significant, in the extant dispute between Bahrain and Qatar, two GCC fellow members.

What is important for GCC members to note in meeting the challenge of the Iranian Revolution in the future is threefold. First, they should realize that Iranian foreign policy is still in the process of revolutionary change. As such, it is often difficult, and sometimes impossible, to distinguish between official and unofficial policies of Iran. Furthermore, the power struggle between hawks and doves also continues in Iranian revolutionary politics.

Second, despite the undeniable disturbances of Shi'i Muslim groups in various gulf states, some GCC states have overreacted to them. The receptivity to the Iranian model has been at best mixed, and even negative in some instances. For example, the Shi'i Muslims of Iraq did not rise up to embrace the Iranians and overthrow Saddam Hussein when Khomeini called on them to do so the day after the invasion of Iraq, just as the Arabic-speaking Iranians did not rise up to embrace the Iraqi invaders in September 1980.

Third, and most important, the best way to contain the Iranian Revolution is to address those basic social, economic, and political problems of the GCC societies that alienate Sunni and Shi'i Muslims alike from their own governments. Neither hostile defiance nor expedient obsequiousness will work. The panicky reaction of the GCC leaders to the quixotic "Bahrain plot" has tended to blur the most important facts of the case. Some 30 percent of the Shi'i dissidents who were arrested were

Arab students and about 17 percent of them were unemployed workers. The point is that deeply felt sociopolitical dissatisfaction with their governments probably had more to do with their plot than their Shi'i identities.

Finally, the problem of consensus within the GCC relates to its relationship with the superpowers. The GCC has officially committed itself to a policy of nonalignment and self-reliance, and has rejected both American pressures for closer military association and Soviet proposals for the "neutralization" of the gulf region. However, in practice asymmetry in perception and performance vis-à-vis the superpowers does exist. Kuwait is the only GCC state that has diplomatic relations with the Soviet Union. Oman is the only GCC country that has signed an agreement for American access to its military facilities and engages in military maneuvers with the United States. Saudi Arabia is the only GCC member that has a "special relationship" with the United States, etc.

Obviously, identical perception and performance toward these basic challenges cannot be expected but the central point is the necessity of greater efforts at consensus building among the GCC members on these and other fundamental questions. In meeting this basic need for greater political and diplomatic cohesion, the GCC states should accord their relationship with Iran the highest priority. I am well aware that the complexity, fluidity, and unpredictability of the Iranian revolutionary situation would make that country enormously difficult to deal with successfully. But it is possible to set an objective of at least damage limitation in GCC-Iran relations between now and whenever the Iranian revolutionary process stabilizes. Such an objective would require, above all else, the avoidance of pushing the GCC as a whole into an unnecessary confrontational stance vis-à-vis Iran. There are elements within the revolutionary government in Iran, to be sure, that believe that everyone is out to get them, and hence the prospects of accommodation with them are minimal. But there are other elements that do seek a more restrained approach toward the GCC. For example, the Iranian goodwill mission to the UAE and Qatar in June 1982 was encouraged by the Iranian foreign minister.

A dialogue between Saudi Arabia and Iran is urgently needed. To date, ideologues on both sides have tended to aggravate the conflict between the two countries, but the situation requires the encouragement of dialogists on both sides. The present course of bitter mutual recriminations between Riyadh and Tehran threatens, rather than promotes, future security and stability in the gulf region. Some Iranian officials have said repeatedly that Iran will not interfere in the internal affairs of any state, that it will not commit aggression against anyone, and that it will accord the highest priority to its relationship with neighboring Muslim countries. Has not the time come for the Saudis and Iranians to sit together and ask how to achieve these principles of nonaggression and noninterference within the gulf region, and how each side can stick to its own brand of Islam? After all, both sides can start with the Koranic injunction, "In religion there is no compulsion."

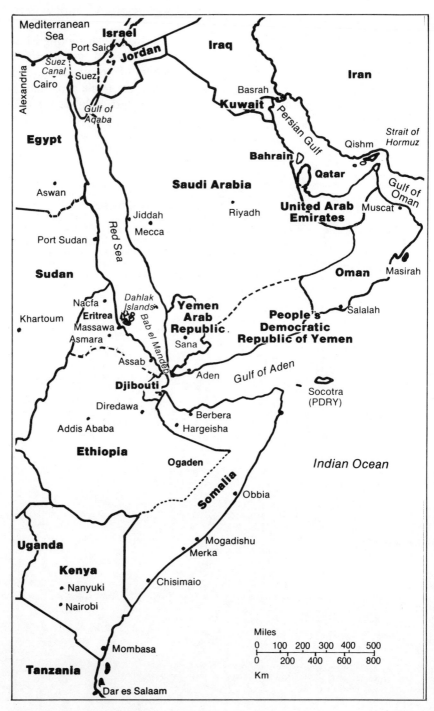

The Red Sea and Horn of Africa

The Red Sea and Horn of Africa

Colin Legum begins his chapter with the observation that the Red Sea has long been a vital maritime route, a fact reflected by the worldwide attention directed in the summer of 1984 to the damage caused to nearly two dozen merchant ships by naval mines planted in that stretch of water in the northwest quadrant of the Indian Ocean.

At the time this volume was going to press, no definitive evidence was available concerning the party or parties perpetrating the mining campaign or the motive, though a pro-Iranian terrorist organization claimed responsibility and President Mubarak of Egypt initially accused both the Libyan and Iranian governments of complicity. The original mine-clearing operation involving American, British, and Egyptian naval forces was joined by French, Italian, and Soviet assets, reflecting widespread concern over the safety of navigation in the area.

Whatever the eventual explanation, the episode served to underscore the strategic character of the Red Sea, particularly when the Suez Canal is open to its normal heavy traffic flow. Add to that factor the Saudi and Egyptian oil pipelines which have terminals on the Red Sea (and the prospective Iraqi terminal in Jordan), the potential mineral bounty on the floor of the sea, and the superpower "facilities" and staging areas on the Red Sea or near its entrances, and the strategic salience of political developments on the Horn of Africa and the littoral of the Red Sea are self-evident.

Legum, drawing on his decades of experience in visiting the area, observing and reporting developments there, and conversing with its political leaders, provides the reader with a comprehensive overview. He discusses the roles of the various subregional actors and the major external powers whose actions together largely determine the course of continuing issues on the Horn of Africa, including Somali and Eritrean nationalisms, the ongoing Ethiopian Revolution, instability in the Sudan, and superpower access. Stressing linkages with other parts of the Indian Ocean region, Legum concludes with the assertion that "it is inconceivable that any serious troubles in the Middle East or the gulf region would not spill over into the Red Sea area because of their overlapping interests and interconnections, and because of the sharply competing interests of the Soviet bloc and the NATO powers in that part of the world."

John Peterson, author of book-length studies of the two Yemens, describes in his chapter here the complicated domestic and international relationships that influence the two states, their neighbors, and the superpowers as all maneuver for advantage at the southern entrance to the Red Sea. Peterson's analysis goes to the heart of the approach-avoidance dilemma with which successive leaderships of the two Yemens have had to grapple: the intense emotional pressures for unification of their one nation into one state, combined with the ideological and functional incompatibility of their two political systems. Together these have produced several merger attempts on the one hand, but instability, rivalry, and periodic warfare on the other. Peterson foresees a continuation of domestic instability in both Yemens but with slightly improved prospects for progress toward eventual unification, perhaps initially through federation. Such progress might be expected to diminish the degree of interference in North Yemen's and South Yemen's affairs, respectively, by Saudi Arabia and the Soviet Union. Meanwhile, the United States, according to Peterson, should accept the fact that the Soviet Union is an established player in that corner of the Arabian peninsula and deal with both Yemens on a strictly bilateral basis, "involving neither subordination to the interests of intermediaries [the Saudis] nor counterproductive concentration on . . . a wider . . . superpower rivalry."

As this volume goes to press, two additional developments in the Red Sea area require mention, both of which significantly affect prospects for stability in the area. The more auspicious development is one foreshadowed by John Peterson: the normalization of relations between South Yemen and Oman, achieved through the good offices of Kuwait and the United Arab Emirates. If it lasts, the normalization should result in a less isolated South Yemen, perhaps, in turn, less dependent on the Soviet Union. Reignition of the quiescent Dhofari rebellion on the countries' mutual border also becomes less likely and external meddling consequently less tempting. The more recent development is the overthrow of President Nimeiry of the Sudan in a military-led coup on 6 April 1985. The events in Khartoum testify to the prescience of Colin Legum's observation of "disturbing signs of a revival of the north-south cleavage" in the Sudan. Head of the Transitional Military Council, General Abdul Swar al-Dahab has promised to hold elections within a year and is attempting to reconcile the southern Christians to his new government. Whether the military can hold the country together or whether Sudan will descend into the morass of civil war is an open question at this writing.

11. The Red Sea and the Horn of Africa in International Perspective ✎ Colin Legum

Throughout history the Red Sea has been one of the most pacific of the world's vital maritime routes, offering safe passage to ships taking the short route from west to east through the Indian Ocean or down the African east coast, to Arab and Israeli ships traveling south through the Bab el-Mandeb Strait or north to the Suez Canal, to tankers from the oil-producing Persian Gulf states coming through the Strait of Hormuz, to Soviet and other East European marine traffic coming out of the Black Sea en route to the Far East or Africa, and to the dhows plying between Africa's Indian Ocean ports and the Middle East.[1] Fully 30 percent of all Indian Ocean maritime trade with Western Europe passes through the Red Sea as do over 90 percent of all the oil tankers from the Arab gulf states and Iran.[2] Eighteen percent of the Soviet Union's maritime fleet of twenty-four hundred ships and a considerable part of its huge fishing fleet (which nets 20 percent of its catch in the Indian Ocean) transits the Red Sea.

Until the last decade the Red Sea was relatively free from warships, except for those in passage to other waters and, more important, it was free of rival foreign naval fleets and virtually free of military bases. Only France had a small army and naval base at Djibouti, and the British had a bunkering station at Aden and an air base at Khormaksar. This situation began to change in the 1950s with the onset of the Arab-Israeli conflict, the sharpening of inter-Arab rivalries, the retreat of Western colonialism from the region, and the developing competition among the major powers in the region. These parallel sets of rivalries—international and local—powerfully reinforced each other; it is with this interplay of forces that this chapter is mainly concerned.

The Red Sea basin is formed by Israel, Jordan, and the Egyptian Sinai on its northern rim; Egypt, Sudan, Djibouti, and Ethiopia on the African rim; Saudi Arabia, the Yemen Arab Republic (North Yemen), and the People's Democratic Republic of Yemen (South Yemen, or Aden) on the Arabian rim. The basin funnels through the Bab el-Mandeb Strait into the Arabian Sea to the north, and into the Indian Ocean to the south and east. Protruding into this network of international waterways at the southern exit of the Red Sea is the Horn of Africa, made up of four political entities: Djibouti, Ethiopia, Somalia, and Sudan.

Although the Horn has never been an entirely quiescent part of the world, it has known considerable stability over the centuries thanks to the supremacy of the Abyssinian kings and the largely unchanged nature of the colonial occupation of the coastal plains: France in Djibouti; Italy in Eritrea and southern Somalia; and Britain in Sudan, Egypt, and northern Somalia. Unusually, the colonial powers rarely came into actual conflict with one another in the region (the brief exception was in World War II when the British drove the Italians out of the area). There were, though, other kinds of wars and internal conflict. In 1867–68 the British sent an expeditionary force to Magdala to punish Emperor Theodore and the Italians twice invaded Ethiopia. The first attempt ended in a heavy defeat at Adowa in 1896 but the second secured Mussolini's conquest of Ethiopia in 1936, and lasted until 1941. There was also a period of unusual turbulence when the Sudanese Mahdia came into revolt against alien influences in the late nineteenth century and spread their campaigns into the Red Sea hills and down through Ethiopia into modern Somalia along the Red Sea coast.[3]

The radical, even revolutionary, changes that have swept across the Red Sea basin and the Horn of Africa since the 1970s are still far from having run their course. In Ethiopia, the passing of the last feudal emperor in 1974 plunged that ancient empire into a revolution led by Marxist-minded soldiers; they have formed a close alliance with the Soviet bloc and committed themselves to participating in "the national democratic revolution" of the Third World and to active cooperation with the international communist movement.[4] A state of affairs bordering on open warfare has grown up between Ethiopia and its eastern neighbor, Somalia, over national rights and border disputes, involving the Somali inhabitants of the Ogaden, a conflict that has drawn Somalia's southern neighbor, Kenya, onto the side of Ethiopia. Other "national democratic revolutions," led mainly by Marxists in opposition to the revolution proclaimed by the military rulers of Addis Ababa, are being pursued by force of arms in several parts of Ethiopia, notably in Eritrea, where the armed struggle for independence has gone on for over twenty years, but also in Tigray and Oromo provinces.[5]

Sudan, the back door to Ethiopia, has passed through a rapid, erratic political change under the leadership of President Jaafar Nimeiry. Since he took power in 1970, through a left-wing military coup pledged to an alliance with the Soviet bloc, his ruling Sudan Socialist Union has made a 180-degree shift from its original position and has now formed alliances with the anti-Soviet elements in the Arab world and become tied by arms treaties to the United States. The country's economy, despite promising oil finds, has continued to deteriorate, producing a climate of considerable uncertainty, and the peaceful detente with the southerners achieved through a federal constitutional agreement established by the Addis Ababa agreement of 1977 has shown ominous signs of failing to hold up. The Sudan's northern neighbor and close ally, the Egypt of Sadat and now of Mubarak, became the first Arab state to make a formal peace with Israel, thereby securing the return of the Sinai province on the northern rim of the Red Sea, but also resulting in its becoming largely isolated in the Arab world. Egypt is in chronic confrontation with its messianic revolutionary neighbor, Colonel Qadhafy's Libya, which is tied in a tripartite alliance with Ethiopia and South Yemen.

The situation in South Yemen has also been completely changed due to the rise of a Marxist leadership within the army; this has conferred on their country the distinction of becoming the first "people's democracy" in the Arab world. Like Ethiopia, South Yemen is tied by treaties of friendship and cooperation to the Soviet Union. The Marxist government in Aden has made it more difficult to fulfill the old dream of linking the two Yemens, North and South, to create a single nation-state down the east bank of the Red Sea. The rise of Soviet-allied states in the Red Sea has been seen as a menacing threat by the Kingdom of Saudi Arabia, whose leaders also view with suspicion the rise of Islamic fundamentalist movements, especially that of the Shi'as inspired by Ayatollah Khomeini. Also threatening are the pressures being brought by the forces of modernization within the kingdom itself. Throughout this large arc of change and instability, the only relatively calm oasis is the diminutive Republic of Djibouti, built almost entirely around a single port.

This brief survey of the political position in the Red Sea basin and the Horn of Africa conveys the picture of a region in a state of rapid evolution after centuries of relatively few changes in its traditional patterns of social and political order. The following is an attempt to identify the various local and foreign factors involved in the seminal changes of political and social systems, as well as changes of national alliances.

The Role of the Regional Actors

Ethiopia

A feature of the rise, growth, and survival of the Abyssinian Empire, and of the modern Ethiopian state that it spawned, was its assertive Christian character in an area totally dominated by Islamic societies. The only serious Islamic attempt to storm the Christian highlands, led by Mohammed Granye in the late fifteenth century, was successfully resisted.

Over two millenia, until the end of Haile Selassie's rule, the Muslims continued to be treated as second-class citizens, although not really any worse off than most of the other subjects under imperial rule. There is no certainty about the number of Muslims but they were estimated in the 1960s to have constituted anything between 25 and 40 percent of the total population, concentrated largely in the coastal and peripheral areas: Eritrea, the Danakil plains, the Ogaden, and part of the southeastern Oromo lands.

Although there was always evidence of Muslim resentment, these feelings counted for little in an empire where few citizens enjoyed many rights and where the Christian kingdom felt itself constantly embattled against the Islamic world. The passivity among the Muslims began to change during the period of the Italian occupation when alien conquest and rule led to a number of conflicting developments: a more assertive sense of Eritrean nationalism, a keener spirit of Ethiopian patriotism, a rekindling of traditional xenophobic feelings, more pronounced fissiparous tendencies, and a heightened antipathy to Shoan rule. These internal changes (except for the xenophobia) grew more pronounced after the restoration of Emperor Haile Selassie to the throne in 1941. With the end of World War II other, modern pressures were added. From the west and south, ancient Ethiopia found itself buffeted by the rise of the modern forces of African nationalism; from the north and east, it began to feel the pressures coming from the new tide of Arab nationalism and a radicalized Islam; and on the international front it found itself pulled between the conflicting forces of the West and the East.

The emperor chose the side of the West against the East and embraced pan-Africanism, but made no concessions to modern nationalism. He pressed ahead with modernization but left his imperial rule intact. The emperor was particularly concerned about a new threat from Islam, not only that coming from the modern forces unleashed by Nasserism but also that coming from his twin, the feudal Kingdom of Saudi Arabia across the Red Sea. This fear of Arabs and Islam led Selassie to take the side of Israel against the Arabs, a decision made easier by the Solomonic myth about the origins of the Amharic line of kings.

By embracing pan-Africanism and becoming the first chairman of the Organization of African Unity (OAU) in 1963, the emperor won considerable support from sub-Saharan Africa. However, by aligning himself with the West and Israel, he drove the Arabs and other Muslim nations into open hostility and sent the Soviets looking for other allies in the region.

Although the nature of Ethiopia's regime changed radically after Haile Selassie's fall, and its new foreign policy orientation meant supplanting one superpower's influence with another, little in fact was changed in the relations among the domestic forces or the regional powers. The Eritreans and Somalis continued to push their nationalist claims, now much more vigorously than before, and they were joined by other local forces, notably the Tigreans and Oromos. The Arabs (except for Libya and South Yemen) continued to be seen as enemies by the revolutionary regime, as they had been by their imperial predecessors; Israel continued as an ally until 1978 when the contradictions within Addis Ababa's alliance system became too difficult to manage.

The reasons for the changes in Ethiopia's allies had less to do with the altered nature of the regime than with the reluctance of the country's traditional allies in the West and, more recently, the United States, to provide the new regime with the massive military support it was demanding. By 1975–76 Ethiopia was alight with violent insurrection from one end of the country to the other: internal security was at a premium; in the capital, different Marxist groups were pitted against each other; the Eritrean revolt had reached a new pitch of intensity; in the Ogaden and the neighboring Oromo provinces of Bale, Sidamo, and Arssi, the administration had all but disintegrated; the Danakil had taken up arms; and Djibouti looked to be ripe for Somali picking. However, the biggest immediate threat was that a full-scale Somali offensive, making use of its Soviet-supported army, would swallow up the Ogaden. It was a perilous moment for Addis Ababa to find the United States limiting its arms supplies and qualifying the use of future supplies; there could have been little surprise that the military regime leapt at the offer held out by the Soviet bloc and Cuba to change sides and to become the strategic ally of Ethiopia instead of Somalia. The only element of surprise was that Moscow changed sides so readily.

It was this change of foreign allies that determined the new direction of the Ethiopian revolution, rather than the initial political orientation of Haile Selassie's successors. Their first choice, after all, had been the United States, and it was Washington's reluctance to be drawn into wars of local repression that led Colonel Mengistu Haile Mariam and his supporters to embrace Moscow and Havana.

For Ethiopia, two issues of national concern, irrespective of who rules over the country, remain at the center of Addis Ababa's policy making: the need to prevent the country from becoming landlocked by the loss of its corridor to the Red Sea ports of Assab and Massawa through Eritrea or by the interruption of rail traffic through Djibouti; and maintaining the country's territorial unity that, it is felt, would be jeopardized if any of the peripheral areas, notably Eritrea and the Ogaden, were ever lopped off.

Eritrea, Tigray, and Somalia

The roots of Eritrean nationalism are deep and tenacious.[6] Its armed struggle, begun in 1962, has survived the scorched-earth policy pursued by Haile Selassie as well as seven major military offensives, backed by the most modern weapons and helped by Warsaw Pact officers, launched by the Mengistu regime since 1975. Although the Eritrean struggle has been hampered because of three competing fronts within the liberation movement (pace the Palestine Liberation Organization), the skill, dedication, and endurance of its guerrilla fighters entitle them to a preeminent place among such movements in the Third World.

The dominant faction, the Eritrean Popular Liberation Front (EPLF), demands independence but has offered to negotiate a future relationship with Addis Ababa that will guarantee Ethiopia's free access to the Red Sea. However, the Mengistu regime is totally opposed to any such idea. Its position, as stated by Mengistu, is that "the territorial integrity of the motherland shall not be broken in the time of this revolutionary generation. . . . It is a historic fact and a proof of the unity of the people that we have paid dearly to repulse attacks made against us through the northern region. We cannot have peace until complete peace is restored in this region and the people are truly united."[7]

While the actual level of Arab support for the Eritrean struggle is small, its political support is a complicating factor because of traditional Ethiopian suspicions of Muslim ambitions in the area. The Eritrean people are themselves divided almost equally between Muslims and Christians, but the Eritrean revolt was called out by the Eritrean Liberation Front (ELF) under Muslim leadership. As a means of attracting Arab support, the ELF declared its struggle to be in the cause of liberating oppressed Muslims from a Christian tyranny. Opportunistically it was a shrewd tactic but once Christian Eritreans fully identified themselves with the struggle, the emphasis on a Muslim cause became a divisive issue.

Economic assistance and weapons for the Eritrean fighters initially came from Nasser's Egypt and later from Syria, Iraq, Saudi Arabia, the Gulf Emirates, and, until their switch of policy, from Libya and South Yemen. (In the emperor's time the Soviet Union and Cuba also gave some support to the Eritreans.) The Arab League and the Islamic Con-

ference Organization (ICO) both support the Eritrean struggle. However, the most important aid has been supplied by Sudan, which provides communications links to the outside world through Port Sudan,
places of retreat for guerrillas under heavy pressure (though that right
has now been extinguished), and sanctuary for a half million Eritrean
refugees. However, for reasons of national interest (see below), Sudan
has in recent years limited its support to the Eritreans. President Nimeiry, who has never favored complete Eritrean secession because of
the risk of encouraging a similar movement among southern Sudanese,
has actively engaged in the role of mediator.

Ethiopia's sensitive hostility toward Arab policies is reflected in a
statement issued by the Foreign Ministry protesting against the Arab
League hosting an international conference of support for the Eritreans
in Tunis.

> In spite of the Ethiopian government's repeated reminders to
> the Arab League to stop its sinister deeds and, despite its strong
> condemnation of the Arab League for interfering in the inter-
> nal affairs of the country, it had, in collaboration with inter-
> national imperialism, continued with its anti-Ethiopian out-
> cry. . . . If the Arab League secretariat refused to listen to
> this reminder (to stop meddling in Ethiopia's domestic affairs),
> Ethiopia would be compelled to re-examine its policies regard-
> ing the Arab League, in particular, and the Middle East in
> general.[8]

After more than twenty years, the situation in Eritrea has become
deadlocked. Not all the arms at Ethiopia's command nor the overwhelming number of troops put into the field in Eritrea—up to 120,000 in two
of the campaigns—has enabled the Ethiopian authorities to break the
revolt. On the other side, not all the tenacity, skill, and fighting qualities
of the Eritreans have been enough to force successive regimes in Addis
Ababa to negotiate, not even with the help of the Soviet bloc and Cuba
who have tried to influence a negotiated settlement. The future of this
crucial Red Sea province remains as unclear as ever.

The Eritrean threat on Ethiopia's northern flank is matched by a
different kind of threat on its eastern flank, in the Ogaden. There, the
Somali Republic has contributed to maintaining a warlike situation
since 1976, when the Somali army began to cross the border in support
of an insurrection by Ogadeni Somalis. The Ethiopian regime reversed
this process in mid-1982 when its army and air force crossed the Somali
border in support of an armed opposition movement to President Siad
Barre.

The birth of the Somali Republic in 1960 was not the culmination but only the start of a period of intensive Somali nationalism. Having united the former British Somaliland protectorate and the Italian Somalia colony, the new republic's flag of independence bore a five-point star proclaiming its ambition to add the missing parts of the Somali nation: Djibouti, the Ogaden, and the Northeast Frontier Province of Kenya. When Djibouti became independent in 1976, Mogadishu accepted this as a satisfactory compromise but, perhaps, not as a final solution. A brief skirmishing campaign on the Kenya border in the early 1960s produced only the negative result of drawing Kenya into a tight alliance with Ethiopia in common defense of their borders against Somali irredentism. The Ogaden claim led to the war just mentioned.

Somali nationalism, pitted against such powerful adversaries as Ethiopia and Kenya and running counter to the OAU Charter's prohibition of border changes except by agreement, led its leaders to seek out strong external allies. Their first choice was China, but in the end they gave in to Khrushchev's wooing. The Soviet Union agreed to train a Somali army of ten thousand men in exchange for naval facilities at the Red Sea port of Berbera and naval and air facilities at Mogadishu. The ardent striving after a united Somali nation therefore led its leaders into a deal that introduced the Soviet Union into the Red Sea area, a move that, at the time, they could hardly have foreseen as likely to boomerang so heavily against them.

Although Somalia's aggressive pursuit of its nationalist goals does not have the support of its colleagues in the Arab League, the Muslim world has tended to take the Somalis' side against Ethiopia. However, Somalia is not supported in its conflicts with Kenya, a country that few Third World countries wish to offend despite its formerly intimate ties with Israel.

When Moscow decided to change allies in 1975, the Somalis were left to find a replacement. This they did by copying the Ethiopian example of exchanging one superpower for another. Their treaty with the United States in 1980 gave the Americans the naval and air facilities at Berbera and Mogadishu, recently vacated by the Soviets, in exchange for arms and economic aid.

The divided Arabs

The break up of the old power relations in the Middle East after the birth of Israel in 1948 and the rise of the new Arab nationalism led by Gamal Abdel Nasser made the Red Sea a new focal point of local and international rivalries. Nasser was the first to propose turning the Red

Sea into what he called an "Arab sea" as part of his plan to tighten the blockade around Israel by impeding its southern exit from Eilat through Sharm-el-Sheikh. Later, there was an attempt to halt Israeli shipping by an artillery attack across the narrow Bab el-Mandeb Strait. Nasser's idea alarmed Saudi Arabia, which feared an Arab world dominated by Nasser's philosophy and Egypt's then budding alliance with Moscow. When the Soviet Union acquired a naval base in Alexandria and showed an active interest in also acquiring naval facilities in the North Yemen port of Hodeida, Saudi fears mounted. These were justified in the eyes of the Saudi rulers when Moscow acquired military facilities at Berbera and Mogadishu and, subsequently, also in Aden. A Saudi interest in promoting a regional naval defense alliance attracted the support of the shah of Iran.

Nothing ever came of either the Iranian/Saudi idea for a Red Sea naval alliance or Nasser's plan to turn the Red Sea into an "Arab sea." However, the mere suggestion of these two aims was sufficient to alarm both Ethiopia and Israel. While they shared a wish to exclude the Soviets from the region, neither wanted the Red Sea to come under Arab domination, irrespective of whether the guiding spirit was Egypt or the Saudis. This fear brought Ethiopia and Israel together in close military cooperation; it also did much to stoke up the old Ethiopian suspicions of the Arab/Islamic world. Since Nasser was the first foreign supporter of the Eritrean liberation movement—which broadcast from Cairo and had an exile headquarters there—Haile Selassie saw the movement for the province's independence as being directly linked to a strategy of depriving Ethiopia of its two Red Sea ports. The emperor's successors, as previously noted, have shared this old concern. While Ethiopia's relations with the major powers have changed, its perceptions about the nature of the "Arab threat" to Eritrea have not altered in the least.

There have, though, been other changes in the system of regional alliances that have affected the Mengistu regime's relations with two Arab nations, South Yemen and Libya. The South Yemen connection is a direct result of the separate alliances of Aden and Addis Ababa with Moscow. The Libyan connection was forged in the mid-1970s and arose from a shared enmity toward President Nimeiry's regime in Sudan. Ethiopian hostility was due to Nimeiry's open support, at the time, for the Eritrean cause and its (much more reserved) support for the Somali cause. Libya's hostility sprang from Nimeiry's close alliance with Egypt's President Sadat, a bitter personal foe of Qadhafy's. Qadhafy was openly committed to overthrowing Nimeiry's regime, a goal he hoped to achieve in the mid-1970s by arming the exile forces of the Sudan National Front, led by al-Mahdi al-Saddiq and Sharif Husayn al-Mahdi. They had military bases in both Libya and Ethiopia, from where they launched an abortive military coup in July 1976. Although Ethiopian-Sudanese relations began to improve in 1978, the Addis Ababa–Tripoli axis has survived because of a new point of common interest in opposition to the American Rapid Deployment Force (RDF). A triple alliance was formally established among Ethiopia, Libya, and South Yemen in Aden on 19 August 1981. Its raison d'être was: "A firm response to the emerging American axis, which now threatens to divide territorially the Arab homeland as part of Washington's overall strategy to force the Arab nation to submit to its hegemony. This American axis embraces the Zionist state in Palestine, Egypt, the Sudan and Somalia."[9] The treaty was described by Tripoli as marking "an important realignment by Ethiopia with the progressive Arab movement. Ethiopia is a non-Arab country, despite being geographically surrounded by the Arab states of Egypt, Sudan and Somalia, all of which align with the United States against the Arab movement."[10]

Although the tripartite alliance identifies Sudan as one of the target regimes to be eliminated (the others are Egypt, Somalia, and Israel) in a campaign to combat the American military presence in the region, this has not prevented Mengistu from promoting improved relations with Nimeiry. Another glaring contradiction in this triple alliance relationship is that none of the parties identifies the Kenyan government of Daniel Arap Moi as a target for destruction despite its entrance into an agreement with the United States that, like those of Egypt, Sudan, Somalia, and Oman, provides the RDF with military facilities. In Ethiopia's case, these two contradictions are explained by its national interest in wishing to strengthen its border security through establishing good relations with its neighbors, to discourage Sudan's support for the Eritreans, and to promote its common interest with Kenya in resisting Somali "expansionism."

Israel

Israel's paramount interest in wishing to prevent any obstruction of its free passage through the Red Sea is obvious. An important part of its maritime traffic with Asia and Africa originates in Eilat. The Israelis are also extremely concerned with the buildup of Soviet naval power in the Red Sea, the Indian Ocean, and the Mediterranean. Close military and economic ties were maintained with Ethiopia until 1978, that is, until four years after Selassie's fall from power. Israeli naval ships frequently traveled through the Red Sea to Assab and Massawa. The formal break with Addis Ababa was occasioned by an incautious speech by Israel's then foreign minister, Moshe Dayan, in which he bragged of his country's relations with the Mengistu regime. Such a public admission made it impossible for Mengistu to continue balancing his contradictory regional alliance system that, apart from the Israelis, included the Libyans and the South Yemenis. Since 1978, Israel has been virtually frozen out of any active role in the region; it must rely for the security of its shipping in the Red Sea on the presence of American and French naval forces.

Djibouti

This tiny republic, with its 220,000 inhabitants, achieved its independence from France in 1976. Until then its future had been closely fought over by Ethiopia and Somalia. Djibouti's population consists almost entirely of Afars, who are ethnically related to Ethiopians, and Issas, who belong to a Somali clan. Rather than go to war over Djibouti (as seemed possible at one time), both neighbors have allowed it to remain in the hands of a regime that maintains an even-handed policy toward both sides. This arrangement is particularly important to Ethiopia, whose only railway access to the Red Sea has its terminal in Djibouti. As the status quo suits both of its neighbors, no complaint has been leveled against the Djibouti regime's military treaty allowing France to keep 2,150 troops there and to use its port for the French naval force in the Indian Ocean.

The Role of the Major External Powers

The Red Sea basin was traditionally dominated by Britain, France, and Italy, the three colonial powers in the region. Although, as just described, France still maintains its residual role in Djibouti, Italy's role ended during World War II, while Britain largely disengaged itself when it adopted its policy of ending its "east of Suez" commitments in the 1960s. The Western military interest in the region has since passed almost entirely into the keeping of the United States. The Soviet Union's presence has greatly expanded since the middle of the 1960s.

United States

The United States became the dominant Western military power in the region in the 1950s, although for the next twenty years its role remained relatively small. The American interest was initially determined by five factors: its military communications facility at Kagnew, near Asmara, the capital of Eritrea; its wish to buttress a strongly pro-Western ruler, Haile Selassie, in the region; its military concerns with the security of Israel, Saudi Arabia, and Iran; the importance it attached to ensuring the unobstructed passage of oil tankers coming from the gulf states; and its desire to keep the Soviets from penetrating the area militarily. However, the Kagnew facilities had ceased to have any value in 1973 and, with the changed situation in both Egypt and Israel, American interest in the region declined to the point where the Nixon administration reduced its arms aid to Haile Selassie, and the Carter administration showed no desire to remain Ethiopia's principal arms supplier when it was offered that role by the emperor's successors. Nevertheless, the Pentagon, especially, kept an anxious eye on the Soviet Union's developing interest in the area as it concluded its defense treaty with Somalia and as Soviet naval forces began in 1972 to develop the facilities offered to them at Berbera and Mogadishu.

A series of events beginning in 1977 led to a major reappraisal of American interests in the region. The first of these events was the arrival of about twenty thousand Cuban combat troops in May 1977 and their deployment in the Ogaden. This was followed in December by a massive airlift of Soviet arms to Ethiopia.[11] A more dramatic event was the overthrow of the shah of Iran in January 1979 which raised the specter in the West of the destabilization of the entire gulf area with a serious potential danger to Saudi Arabia. Finally, there was the Soviet military intervention in Afghanistan in December 1979.

The collapse of the shah's regime led the Carter administration to formulate its plans for a Rapid Deployment Force (RDF) that, inter alia, called for a greater Western naval force in the Red Sea and the Indian Ocean; the enlargement of the military base at Diego Garcia; increased numbers of naval and air facilities in the region; and strengthening regimes friendly to the West. As part of the new security framework, Washington signed an agreement with Somalia for the use of naval and air facilities in Berbera and Mogadishu, and with Kenya for the use of naval facilities in Mombasa harbor and air facilities at the Nanyuki air base. There were also substantial increases in the supply of arms to Sudan and Saudi Arabia, including the sale of three Airborne Warning and Control System (AWACS) reconnaissance aircraft.

This sharp and rapid transformation of Washington's policy in the region over a period of about two years made highly visible the American military and political presence. Although Washington insisted that its agreements with Somalia were strictly limited to the supply of relatively small quantities of defensive weapons, this did nothing at all to assuage the serious fears of Ethiopia that the American role in Somalia would be to launch an "imperialist" campaign to impede its revolution by assisting the Barre regime to restart its war in the Ogaden. The war had been ended in April 1978, after the routing of the Somali forces with the help of the Cuban combat troops, thanks in large part to American mediation in arranging for the withdrawal of the Somali army. The Mengistu regime's new fear of an American-led offensive to bring it down has had a seriously disturbing effect—so disturbing, that in July 1982 it decided to carry the war onto Somali soil. However, this was soon halted once it became clear that the Somali population was not waiting to join, as predicted, in the uprising against an unpopular regime.

Soviet bloc and Cuba

Russian interest in the Red Sea goes back to the seventeenth century when Tsar Alexis and Peter the Great first conceived an interest in establishing "blue sea ports" in the Mediterranean and the Red Sea.[12] This need to find alternatives to Russia's northern ports, icebound for a large part of the year, was considered vital to the expansion of Russian influence. These ideas were pursued until the middle of the eighteenth century by Paul I and Catherine the Great, but the need for such ports stopped being the dream of expansion-minded tsars and tsarinas and became a prime necessity after the Soviet Union committed itself to the objective set by Admiral Sergei Gorshkov to create "a modern navy capable of dealing with the latest innovations in the enemy camp . . . in any part of the globe."[13] The importance attached to the Red Sea region was clearly expressed by V. Sofinskiy, head of the Press Department of the Soviet Foreign Ministry, in a televised speech in Moscow on 3 February 1978: "The Horn of Africa is first and foremost of military, political and economic significance. The importance of the area lies in its location at the link-up of the two continents of Asia and Africa. There are a lot of good sea ports in the Persian Gulf and the Indian Ocean. Moreover, there are sea lanes which link oil-producing countries with America and Europe." Such statements about Soviet interests in acquiring naval and air facilities in the Red Sea basin show them to be no different from those of any other major sea power throughout history. The only difference is that the Soviet navy appeared on the horizon at a time when the Western navies had begun their retreat from east of Suez.

Additional impetus was given to Moscow's desire for naval and air facilities in the Red Sea by the deployment in the 1960s of United States submarines with nuclear warheads targeted on South Russia—a temporary deployment pending the development of the North Atlantic Treaty Organization's (NATO) larger nuclear strategy. Nevertheless, it was naturally of sufficient concern to make Moscow want to take preventive action. Moreover, in its role as a rival superpower, the Soviet Union also wished to be in a position to counteract the growing American strength in the area arising from its development of the important base in Diego Garcia, and to be able to intervene, if necessary, in the gulf area. Yet another major aspect of Soviet interest in the region is its wish to expand its military delivery system to Asia and sub-Saharan Africa. Here Moscow's perennial concern is the possibility of a future military confrontation with China and the need to be in a position to face up to such a challenge at any point on the Asian continent. Meanwhile, the Soviet Union has major commitments in Afghanistan, Cambodia, and Vietnam. For all these reasons, the passage through the Red Sea and military facilities in the area are indispensable to the Soviet Union's role as an expanding world power. By 1983, Moscow could count on the following military facilities in the region: Dahlak Islands (Ethiopia), including helicopter pads, ship repair and resupply facilities, and a sheltered anchorage; Asmara (Ethiopia), airfield facilities; Assab and Massawa (Ethiopia), naval facilities; Aden (South Yemen), port facilities, a communications center, and use of the international airfield at Khormaksar; Socotra (South Yemen), sheltered anchorage.

The USSR has also developed a major base at Shindand in western Afghanistan, about six hundred miles distant from the Strait of Hormuz. Its air force more or less continuously patrols the Strait of Hormuz and the Bab el-Mandeb Strait, paralleling similar air reconnaissance by the United States Navy and Air Force. The Soviet navy maintains a network of mooring buoys in the Indian Ocean as rendezvous points for its warships, all of which transit the Red Sea. Soviet IL-38 "May" aircraft based at Aden and Asmara conduct regular maritime aerial reconnaissance. At times of tension in the region (as during the invasion of Afghanistan in 1979–80), the Soviet Indian Ocean fleet is capable of being rapidly expanded from its normal complement of about thirty warships including nuclear submarines.

Apart from its military/strategic interest in the region, the USSR is also interested in expanding its influence through the building up of Marxist regimes loyal to Moscow's ideas of "the unity of the international proletariat." With South Yemen as the first fruit of such a policy in the region, the hope is for something much more substantial through the successful consolidation of the revolution in Ethiopia, hailed by Fidel Castro and others as "Africa's first genuine Marxist revolution."[14] A communist Ethiopia would obviously have a tremendously important impact on future political developments in the region and, possibly, over a much larger part of the continent as well. But although Colonel Mengistu has proved himself to be a survivor and a substantial political figure, it is not yet possible to predict the future course of the revolution. It will certainly not get very far unless it finds ways—either military or political—of dealing with the challenges coming from the Eritreans and Tigreans, among others.

Cuba's interest in the Red Sea region springs from three separate involvements: support for the South Yemen regime through Cuban military training units and technical assistance, training for the Eritrean People's Liberation Front during the emperor's time, and technical aid for Somalia during the period of its friendship treaty with Moscow. Fidel Castro arrived in Addis Ababa on 14 March 1977 with a specific proposal to promote a "progressive alliance" of Red Sea states to embrace Ethiopia, Somalia, South Yemen, Djibouti, and, separately, Eritrea. He envisaged it as an alliance strong enough to confront the other Red Sea regional powers: Sudan, Egypt, and Saudi Arabia. Nothing came of this plan. Instead, Castro agreed in May 1977 to send between eleven and twenty thousand Cuban combat troops to assist the Ethiopian army in its campaign against the Somalis in the Ogaden. However, once that objective had been fulfilled, Castro adamantly refused to allow his troops to be used against the Eritreans on the grounds that the fighting there did not involve any infringement of Ethiopia's sovereign border and that it was a problem requiring a political, not a military solution.[15]

The Future

The Red Sea basin and the Horn of Africa are natural extensions of the so-called arc of instability lying to the south of the Soviet borders. Two ancient empires have already tumbled in that area, ushering in periods of revolutionary ferment—the one in Ethiopia threw up a leadership strongly oriented toward Moscow; the other in Iran produced an atavistic Islamic revival movement equally opposed to both superpowers. Between these two fallen empires still stands the uncertain Kingdom of Saudi Arabia, which can hardly hope to remain unchanged by the forces that undermined the thrones in Ethiopia and Iran; yet its fate need not resemble either of them.

Somali nationalism, tempered by defeat in war, is by no means quiescent. The nationalist revolts in Eritrea, Tigray, and the Oromo provinces show no sign of slackening; there is no evidence that military force is capable of suppressing them; and there is, as yet, no tangible hope of a political settlement. However, the schisms of Ethiopia are not unbridgeable, at least no more than those of the Sudan (where it took a fourteen-year-long civil war between the southerners and the northerners to produce a settlement). A solution for the nationality issues of Ethiopia could either transmute the Marxist revolution into a more truly indigenously based revolution or it could give an immense fillip to the creation of a full-blooded people's democracy. Neither can be ruled out.

The political system in the Sudan shows little sign of providing a stable form of government in the near future, although President Nimeiry's basic objective of creating a decentralized system of government seems to be ideally suited to a country as large as the Sudan, and with so many distinctive regional personae. There are also disturbing signs of a revival of the north-south cleavage.

It is inconceivable that any serious troubles in the Middle East or the gulf region would not spill over into the Red Sea area because of their overlapping interests and interconnections, and because of the sharply competing interests of the Soviet bloc and the NATO powers in that part of the world.

Apart from the political and military rivalries among the local powers, there is also the question of the opportunities for development of the important economic resources of the Red Sea bed. Whether the plans for exploiting these will open up new areas of disagreement or whether they will offer the region new opportunities for cooperation depends largely on the compatibility of the political systems that will finally evolve out of the present period of change and transformation in societies that had largely escaped the modernization process until the current generation.

12. The Two Yemens and the International Impact of Inter-Yemeni Relations ⋈ J. E. Peterson

For many observers, the southwest corner of the Arabian peninsula is not only terra incognita but a source of hopeless confusion when events there break into the world's headlines. Why are there two Yemen republics, and why do they persist in fighting each other? How do you tell North from South when they are actually east and west of each other? How do you distinguish friends from foes?

A successful revolution in 1962 against the old imamate or monarchy in North Yemen created the Yemen Arab Republic (YAR) with its capital at Sana. In the south, the People's Democratic Republic of Yemen (PDRY) emerged in 1967 after a long and violent struggle to evict the British from their colony at Aden and protectorate over the surrounding hinterland. (Britain's preoccupation with Aden itself, directly south of Sana, and only later concern with the eastern territories of South Yemen helps to explain the North-South characterization.) While there remains only one Yemeni nation, the different historical experiences of its constituent parts over recent centuries has been the principal factor in the appearance of two Yemeni states.[1]

There exists an intense rivalry between the two states (or regions, *shatr*, as they refer to themselves) for leadership of all Yemen. Intense emotional pressures for unity, combined with the ideological and functional incompatibility of the two political systems, have produced a situation of chronic instability.[2] The impact of this rivalry, the weakness of the two states, and their basic lack of legitimacy have all contributed to a situation in which Saudi Arabia has come to exercise preponderant influence in North Yemen while the Soviet Union holds similar sway in South Yemen.

Two Yemens

Geographically and culturally, the two Yemens essentially form a single unit, bounded on the west and south by the Red Sea and the Gulf of Aden, and inland by Saudi Arabia and Oman. Both are characterized by rugged landscapes, extreme economic underdevelopment, heavy dependence on traditional agriculture, and predominantly Arab Muslim populations that historically have journeyed to diverse parts of the world in search of employment. Politically, however, substantial divergence has taken place over the last century or two, prompted by both internal changes and outside influences, resulting in the creation of two separate states with distinct political systems, forms of government, and elite structures.

The two governments share one basic problem: legitimacy. To a large extent, this is because their political systems are based predominantly on new or "modern" concepts and institutions, theoretically derived in a rational manner, and heavily dependent on Western influences. At the same time, these systems have been uncertainly superimposed on societies whose primary allegiance is to traditional goals and institutions. Consequently, both governments are characterized by pervasive weakness, domination by small insecure cliques, political fragmentation into many competing ideologies and elite groups, and the absence of any widespread popular identification with and/or support for the central government.

Both states are caught in a very real and basic dilemma. There exists throughout Yemen a strong feeling of a common identity and a long-held sense of "nation," which contributes emotional pressure toward political unity. At the same time, neither of the two states is able to exercise more than rudimentary authority domestically and therefore neither is able to speak clearly and decisively for its own people. The most fundamental priority in both North and South Yemen must be the creation and inculcation of the idea of a "nation-state." This goes hand in hand with the development of a "national" political consciousness and the establishment of a basis for the legitimacy of the two existing states. To accomplish this, however, both states must first overcome the predominant identities of a local, tribal, or sectarian nature that have always played the central role in the determination of political loyalties.

Greater Yemen's rugged topography provides one major obstacle to national cohesion. The heartland of geographical Yemen is the mountainous spine dividing the arid coastal plains from the even more barren deserts of the interior. It is the highland that defines the distinctive character of Yemeni lifestyles, economy, and culture. Undoubtedly, the physical fragmentation of the country has been a principal factor in the continued strength and independence of the tribes. Even today, many of the northern tribes owe no loyalty to the central government and do not tolerate the intrusion of its agents or the conduct of activities in their autonomous territories. The major shaikhs, or leaders, have always been important at the level of tribal confederations and even nationally. Their role greatly diminished with the independence of South Yemen but they remain very strong in the YAR.

Another divisive factor in Yemeni politics is the sectarian cleavage between the Zaydis (a moderate branch of the Shi'i sect of Islam) and the Shafi'i school of Islamic law within the Sunni sect. Zaydis predominate in the northern half of greater Yemen and the Shafi'is in the southern half. Thus, the Zaydi and Shafi'i populations of the YAR are nearly equal while the PDRY is almost entirely Shafi'i. In terms of belief and ritual, there is little difference between Zaydis and Sunnis. The distinction is mainly political with the Zaydis having dominated national politics in the North for nearly a thousand years. Until 1962, North Yemen was a Zaydi imamate, a very loose political entity based on an elected imam, a semihereditary leader drawn from the ranks of those Zaydi religious scholars descended from the prophet Muhammad, whose political leadership depended on the personal allegiance given to him

by the various tribes. Naturally, the foundations of support for the imamate came from the Zaydi tribes; the extension of the imamate to Shafi'i
regions depended on its ability to muster superior force and secondarily
on its success in providing a stable and orderly environment for everyday
life. Not surprisingly, Shafi'is have been less resistant to outside penetration of Yemen and tended to cooperate with the Ottomans and the
British against the Zaydi imamate, a factor that has partially contributed
to the political dichotimization of the Yemeni nation.

The division of Yemen into two distinct political entities is a recent
phenomenon, as well as a largely artificial one. Historically, all Yemenis
share the legacy of the intrinsically Yemeni civilizations that have existed in southwest Arabia since the seventh century B.C.; the memories
and names associated with the Queen of Sheba and Ma'rib Dam remain
alive today even in areas far beyond Yemen. This common bond was
strengthened with the conversion of Yemen to Islam and the pivotal
role of Yemenis in the expansion of the early Islamic state outside
Arabia. Frequent periods of political unity through the centuries have
further enhanced the natural geographic and cultural unity of the
Yemeni nation. The beginning of a political division between North
and South dates only from the disintegration within the last several
centuries of any effective authority over all of Yemen.

What began as essentially an internal process of disintegration was
given additional impetus by the entry of external forces, particularly the
Portuguese, the Ottomans, and the British. The British occupation of
Aden in 1839 constituted the first step in the permanent separation of
Aden settlement and its hinterland from the remainder of Yemen.
Gradually through the course of the nineteenth and twentieth centuries,
treaties were concluded with the numerous petty rulers and some measure of British responsibility was assumed for all the territory of what
was before 1967 the Aden protectorate. After 1918 and the Ottoman
departure from Yemen and Arabia, a definite though imprecise frontier
existed between the independent Zaydi imamate in the north, with its
capital at the ancient city of Sana, and the British-administered territories of the Aden colony and protectorate. This division was never accepted as legitimate by the imams or by many Yemenis on either side of
the border.

Consequently, by the middle of the twentieth century, politically
activist Yemenis, influenced by modern nationalist ideas, viewed the
ouster of both the imamate in the North and the British in the South as
prerequisites to the creation of a modern, constitutional, and unified
Yemeni state. In the opinion of this admittedly narrow sector of the
population, the establishment of a republic in 1962 and its successful

struggle against the royalist supporters of the imamate in a long civil war (1962–70) constituted only the first phase in a wider contest that continued with the equally long struggle in South Yemen for liberation from the British. Southerners were prominent in the defense of Sana during the royalist siege of 1967–68; the embryonic YAR provided refuge and logistical assistance to the guerrillas operating against Aden up until its independence in 1967.

It was a shock to many in the North when the victorious southerners proclaimed a separate state in November 1967, rather than immediately declaring the South to be part of the Yemen Arab Republic. Since unification had been a primary goal of both republics from their respective inceptions, why was such an emotional as well as pragmatic goal denied fruition? Simply put, the seemingly superficial divisions of past centuries had actually accentuated existing social, cultural, and religious differences between the two halves of Yemen, and they were responsible for the erection of new demographic, economic, and political barriers.

A significant dichotomy had appeared in South Yemen. Aden colony was urbanized, an ethnic and racial melting pot, and economically relatively highly developed. The protectorate, however, remained politically fossilized into a myriad of tribal entities, economically no more advanced than it had been a thousand years before. In the North, the establishment of an Egyptian-dominated republic in Sana and eventual reconciliation with the royalist forces years later resulted in a weak and conservative state that held little sway over most of its countryside and whose ineffective leaders were consumed by fratricidal infighting.

Thus, by the end of the 1960s, Yemen was faced with the dilemma of two Yemeni states, one overwhelmingly fractionalized into many interests operating at cross-purposes and hopelessly under the thumb of neighboring Saudi Arabia, the other straitjacketed into a doctrinaire Marxist structure with its energy continually dissipated in nonproductive internal ideological battles. Two states, at opposite ends of the spectrum in terms of ideology and effectiveness, were in direct competition for the loyalty of a single Yemeni nation. While the proclaimed goal of unity was genuinely embraced in both Sana and Aden, outbursts of violence seemed to point in the opposite direction to that of peaceful negotiation between fraternal twins. With neither state having the ability to impose its political orientation on the other—and with both continuing to hope to do so—the Yemens have been trapped in a cycle of sporadic border clashes followed by incomplete attempts at merger and subsequent frustration.

Inter-Yemeni Relations

Simply put, it is unfortunately true that the two halves of Yemen have not been able to get along for a considerable length of time. Until the mid-1960s, a principal reason was the refusal of the Zaydi imams to accept the British occupation of the South as legitimate. The consequence was a fifty-year "forward policy" probing the British will to remain in the protectorate and taking advantage of every opportunity to advance into British-held territory. The turmoil engulfing both Yemens during the 1962–67 period also produced considerable cross-border activity when the British, unwilling to see President Nasser's expansionism succeed, more or less surreptitiously backed the royalists against the Egyptian-dominated republic. Meanwhile, the republicans in Sana were supported by, and in turn supported, various anti-British activists in the South. To many republicans, the reactionary royalists and colonial British were equal evils from which all of Yemen needed to be liberated.

With the denouement of the revolutionary struggle in both the North and the South there was no welcome surcease of inter-Yemen rivalry. The northern republic became solidly conservative (and thereby was able to effect a reconciliation with the royalists) and its radicals were forced into southern exile. At the same time, the Marxist National Liberation Front's (NLF) complete victory in the South meant that relatively more moderate groups were frozen out of any power in the new state and many activists went North, some of them subsequently attaining high positions in the YAR government. The five years following the emergence of two independent Yemens saw relations between the two new republics steadily worsen. Finally, by mid-1972 sporadic clashes escalated into open warfare.

By this time, the politics of the Sana government had moved steadily to the right, partially as a result of the growing strength of Saudi Arabia in North Yemen. The trend was aptly symbolized by the YAR's resumption of diplomatic relations with the United States in July, well over a year before many other Arab states took the same step. At the same time, the PDRY was lurching in the opposite direction. The moderate wing of the NLF, which had held power since independence, was ousted in 1969 by the radical wing. But the latter group also displayed serious internal divisions on several levels, one of these being the debate between the "unity at all costs" adherents (largely of northern origin) and their opponents who favored a more gradual approach. This difference appears to have produced the decision to assassinate a number of YAR shaikhs early in 1972, which in turn hardened the stand of the conservatives prevailing in the North. Another destabilizing factor was the opposition groups on both sides of the border who stepped up their activities during the early part of the year and eventually embroiled the respective armies in the fray.

Although the hostilities were drawn out over a period of months, the actual extent of the fighting was limited. Nevertheless, it took Arab League mediation and the efforts of Muammar al-Qadhafy at a summit conference in Tripoli to turn the mutual recriminations into an agreement for merger—certainly a novel way to end a war. The temporary euphoria provoked by this solution unsurprisingly gave way before the ideological incompatibility and internal divisions of the two states, and before long the situation deteriorated to its pre-1972 status.

Even as the Adeni struggle between the radicals and the ultraradicals continued indecisively through the next few years, significant realignments were appearing in the North. The political system forged out of national reconciliation in 1970 was disintegrating under the weight of national fractiousness and the inherent weakness of its conciliatory approach among a welter of basically incompatible forces. The collapse of the regime in early 1974 saw the emergence of a military government under the leadership of Colonel Ibrahim al-Hamdi. Because of Hamdi's developing charisma and vision, the initial hold of the Saudi conservatives and shaikhs on the YAR government was steadily loosened. But Hamdi's attempt to reduce his heavy dependence on Saudi Arabia and to create a viable modus vivendi with the PDRY leadership created a right-wing backlash and fed Saudi paranoia. The outcome was his assassination in October 1977.[3] His successor, Colonel Ahmad al-Ghashmi, had little of Hamdi's national standing and popular respect; he was the brother of a Zaydi shaikh, unknown and uneducated, and widely believed to have had a part in Hamdi's death.

Ghashmi's subservience to Saudi Arabia and strong ties to the northern shaikhs were considerable handicaps in either promoting national cohesion in the YAR or easing suspicions in Aden. His moves to consolidate his position by casting off Hamdi supporters and maneuvering key Shafi'i army officers out of their political positions gained him valuable time but also alienated large sectors of the population. Apparently at Riyadh's urging, he initiated a surreptitious channel of communications to Salim Rubayyi Ali, the PDRY president and leader of the "moderate" radicals in Aden. This connection was the immediate cause of the bizarre sequence of events of late June 1978.

It is impossible to know exactly what happened during those few days or why. The most plausible explanation seems to be that Salim Rubayyi Ali attempted to send a messenger to Ahmad al-Ghashmi and that Ali's opponents, among them Abd al-Fattah Ismail, the ultraradical secretary of the Yemeni Socialist party, were aware of this and changed messengers. Whether or not he knew it, the new messenger carried a briefcase enclosing a bomb into Ghashmi's Sana office; the resulting explosion killed them both. This act touched off a violent power struggle in the South. Ismail and his followers convened a meeting of the party's central committee that ordered Ali's arrest. Instead of complying, however, Ali gathered his supporters and barricaded himself in the presidential palace until the superior firepower of the ultraradical faction forced his surrender; shortly thereafter, Ali was sentenced to death and executed.

Surprisingly, the subsequent transition in power was smoothest in Sana where, after a short time, Lieutenant Colonel Ali Abdullah Salih was elected president by the People's Constituent Assembly. Like his predecessor and mentor Ghashmi, Salih was a Zaydi tribesman, uneducated and inexperienced, heavily dependent on the Saudis, and he had also been implicated by public opinion in Hamdi's death. There was considerable speculation both within and outside North Yemen as to how long the new president would last. Similar speculation also surrounded the new president in the South. There, Ismail had moved to strengthen his superior position by claiming the office of president in addition to party secretary. Seemingly, the ultraradicals had emerged victorious; in actuality, they still had to overcome considerable overt opposition from the late Ali's sympathizers in various areas of the country and covert dissent over the extremist tilt of the new ruling clique.

Just as the 1972 war had been provoked by the two governments' swings in opposite directions and the provocations of uncontrolled guerrilla groups along the border, so was the outbreak of fighting in early 1979. There were, however, two major differences this time. PDRY forces were much better organized than their opponents and more prepared for their advance deep into the YAR. The PDRY's forward movement was stopped only through a counterthrust provided by large numbers of Zaydi tribesmen who filled the gap left by the hasty retreat of the YAR army. Once again, an end to the fighting and PDRY withdrawal was accomplished through mediation by other Arab states, principally Iraq, Syria, and Kuwait, and a ceasefire was quickly followed by reaffirmation of the 1972 commitment to merger. Like the earlier example, however, the false optimism provided by this brotherly embrace soon dissipated into a more-to-be-expected distance.

In the years since 1979, the outward preparations for unity have proceeded steadily forward; actual commitment to full unity, however, seems to have remained as nebulous as ever. Nevertheless, there is some cause for limited optimism, since the factors providing momentum toward renewed conflict have diminished. In early 1980, Ismail was pressured into resigning all his positions and Ali Nasir Muhammad, earlier the balancer between Ismail and Ali, and between the left and the far left, assumed all three key positions: president, prime minister, and party secretary.[4] In both domestic and foreign policy, the Aden regime seemed for the first time to have taken a step back from its periodic lurches to the left and thus gained a welcome respite.

In Sana, the shock of defeat in 1979 failed to unseat Salih and in fact may have strengthened his low popular standing. Despite the shortcomings mentioned earlier, Salih proved himself to be politically astute, capable of taking sound advice, and clearly adept at shrewd maneuvering through the mine fields of YAR politics. Gradually, Salih was able to relax the Saudi grip while holding the conservatives and traditionalists at bay. Even though difficult circumstances and personal shortcomings did not allow him to pursue the same long-range goals as Hamdi had embraced, Salih was able to enter into a dialogue with the National Democratic Front (NDF) while resisting their inclusion in a coalition government.[5] By 1982, he was able to go on the offensive and partially evict the NDF from de facto control of substantial tracts of YAR territory and at the same time prevent a PDRY counterresponse.

This unusually quiescent or cooperative phase in inter-Yemeni politics resulted in a favorable environment for the announcement in late 1981 that a draft constitution had been produced for the unified Yemeni state. According to this document's provisions, agreed at a joint presidential conference in Aden, an executive council for both countries was to be established, along with joint ministerial committees, a joint legislative body, and a unified secretariat to supervise the transition into a single state with its capital at Sana.

In spite of the promulgation of this new agreement for unification, the prospects of its acceptance by referendum and particularly its adoption remain slim. The basic ideological differences between the Yemeni states have not been resolved and the stability of the two governments remains just as transitory as ever. Indeed, the factors that had propelled North and South into two wars in the last decade remain potent, even though relatively quiescent. The potential for damaging setbacks in inter-Yemeni relations as the result of negative developments in northern and/or southern domestic politics remains as likely as ever. From a broader point of view, this also means that the potentially destabilizing effect of discord between the Yemens on regional affairs and superpower politics in the area remains just as relevant.

Regional and International Politics

The principal foreign policy concern of both Yemens is the other Yemen. Other areas of focus, regardless of the degree of their central importance to the YAR or PDRY, are inevitably filtered through the prism of that primary concern. Thus, Yemeni involvement in regional issues is conditioned by inter-Yemeni rivalry, domestic pressures, regional identification beyond the Yemens (as on pan-Arab or Red Sea issues), ideological considerations, and superpower influence. The interrelationship of all these factors can best be elucidated by examining each state's relations with its neighbors, other regional powers, and the superpowers.

The regional relations that matter the most for the YAR lie within the Arab world. By far, the closest ties are with Saudi Arabia; these are also the most one-sided. There are essentially two major reasons for Riyadh's determination to influence North Yemeni affairs. First, Egyptian President Nasser's expansionist move into the Arabian peninsula through the use of the Yemeni revolution was an uncomfortable lesson in Saudi vulnerability; to Riyadh, the threat remains alive in the form of the Arab world's only Marxist state, South Yemen. Second, Saudis tend to consider Yemen as legitimately their "backyard"; it is thought that if not for some accident of history, Yemen could well be and perhaps should be a part of Saudi Arabia. Consequently, Riyadh maintains paramount influence in the YAR through official subsidies to the Sana government and keeps up its pressure for full Yemeni cooperation by providing numerous individuals in the government, army, and tribes with regular subventions.

The effect of Saudi interference on Yemeni public opinion has been disastrous. Nearly all Yemenis resent both the extent of Riyadh's influence and the frequently heavy-handed way in which it is maintained. This resentment is exacerbated by the treatment given Yemeni workers in Saudi Arabia and by the sincere belief throughout the YAR that the Saudis stole three Yemeni provinces as a result of the 1934 Saudi-Yemeni war.[6] As a consequence, Saudi policy toward North Yemen is confronted with a paradox. On the one hand, the Saudis want a North Yemen that is sufficiently strong and stable to keep the PDRY pinned down, while on the other, Riyadh fears the emergence of a cohesive, self-reliant state that contains not only the largest population in the Arabian peninsula but also the one that is perhaps the most fiercely independent and ambitious.[7]

Apart from Saudi Arabia and South Yemen, the YAR's relations with the rest of the Arab world are largely subsumed under the category of pan-Arab concerns, such as supporting the Palestinian cause or seeking aid from the oil-producing states of the gulf. In particular, Iraq has been a welcome donor and served as an important mediator during the 1979 inter-Yemen war. Because of this mediation and perhaps because of its influence on some of the more progressive political figures in Sana, Iraq was able to convince the Salih government to drop the ex-Adeni conservatives from their ministerial positions.

It is rather surprising that the YAR has taken little substantive interest in relations with neighbors across the Red Sea, given their geographical proximity and the extensive cross-migration of thousands of Yemeni workers and businessmen to Somalia, Djibouti, Ethiopia, and Sudan over the last century. It may well be that the twentieth-century percolation of ideologies into Yemen has firmly oriented the country's worldview toward the Arab world and that the continuing cycles of instability and intense rivalry with the South have severely restricted the YAR's horizons. Whatever the reason, the African states along the Red Sea have not played anywhere near the role in YAR foreign policy that they have in that of the PDRY.

Undoubtedly, the fundamental reason for the PDRY's relatively broader foreign policy concerns has been its Marxist ideology. Within the Arab world, the radical stance of the South Yemen regime has solidly allied it with the Rejection Front including Libya and Syria on Arab-Israeli issues. Closer to home, Aden's rigid adherence to ideological principles has cut it off from any potential aid donors and has embroiled it since independence with all three immediate neighbors. Despite the equivocal relationship with North Yemen there is no such ambiguity in Aden's relationship with Saudi Arabia and Oman.

To Saudi Arabia, South Yemen represents a continuation of the explicit radical threat to the gulf monarchies first articulated during the Arab cold war of the 1950s and 1960s. From Riyadh's viewpoint, there is little difference between Nasser's presence in North Yemen and the indigenous Marxists' in South Yemen; their common goal has been perceived as fomenting revolution throughout the monarchies of the peninsula. The strident rhetoric emanating from Aden and its dependence on Soviet bloc assistance have further enforced Saudi suspicions of a communist conspiracy.

Consequently, the Saudis have employed a three-pronged strategy to counter the PDRY threat. First, they have exercised predominant influence in the YAR in order to maintain a buffer between themselves and Aden. On South Yemen's other side, they have staunchly supported Oman in its attempts to defeat the PDRY-backed Marxist rebels in its southern province of Dhofar. The third prong has been direct confrontation; South Yemeni opposition groups have been maintained on Saudi soil, just as they have been in North Yemen. Furthermore, in the last half-dozen years, the Saudis have built up a major military base at Sharura, in the Rub' al-Khali desert near the PDRY border.

The PDRY leadership naturally has a radically different view on the sources of the two countries' mutual antagonism. Rather than being an expansionist power, South Yemen sees itself as a weak, beleaguered country surrounded by hostile enemies. Saudi Arabia has imposed its will on the YAR since the end of the civil war there and has intrigued continuously against the South. Riyadh's hostile designs on the PDRY are amply demonstrated by its anti-PDRY rhetoric, the help provided for subversive organizations against South Yemen, and its military build-up adjacent to PDRY territory.

As regards South Yemen's eastern frontier with Oman, the rebellion in Dhofar began long before South Yemen's independence and Oman's attitude toward the new government in Aden was biased from the first because of the predominant British position in Muscat. Consequently, the South Yemenis see Oman, with its British, Iranian, Jordanian, and now American "advisers," troops, and arms transfers, as the aggressor over an extremely volatile border, rather than Oman being on the defensive against a PDRY supported by the Chinese, Soviets, Cubans, and East Germans.

South Yemen's few friends in the region have been those states espousing similar ideologies or radical stances in international affairs. Among the Arab states, the two principal allies have been Iraq and Libya. Partly because of its good relations with both Yemens, Iraq was instrumental in the mediation ending the 1979 war. Shortly afterward, however, Iraqi-PDRY relations worsened considerably. South Yemen cooperated fully with Ethiopia in the Ogaden campaign and in Eritrea as well, providing not only its Soviet-made military equipment but also its pilots. Iraq, on the other hand, refused to allow the Soviet Union to transfer equipment from Iraq to the Horn or to use Iraq for airlift overflights. Iraqi efforts to persuade Aden to end its cooperation with a non-Arab state in operations against fellow Arabs were futile and only drove a wedge between the two states. This was followed by Iraq's kidnapping of an Iraqi communist lecturer at Aden University and the subsequent storming of the Iraq embassy by South Yemen police to rescue him; in return, Iraq invited the leaders of all the South Yemen exile groups to Baghdad for the establishment of a unified anti-PDRY front. While the situation has improved more recently, serious divisions still remain.

Libya's influence in South Yemen, as in North Yemen and various other states, has been both mercurial and marginal. PDRY cooperation with Qadhafy seems to have been based on the expectation of financial aid and on reaction to perceived increases in hostility from an alliance of Western and conservative gulf states. One clear illustration of the pragmatic—and even defensive—nature of the ties between these radical states of the region was the signing of the Tripartite Pact among the PDRY, Libya, and Ethiopia as a response to the formation of the Gulf Cooperation Council.

In contrast, the PDRY-Ethiopia relationship appears to have far more substantial roots. Rather than being essentially pragmatic and therefore transitory in nature, the close ties between the Marxist states of the Red Sea region were forged out of similar ideological outlooks, common external allies, and perceptions of themselves as islands surrounded by seas of hostility. A major factor in the loan of PDRY matériel and combatants to Ethiopia for use in the latter's internal battles undoubtedly was the conviction that Aden had played its part in helping to ensure the survival of the Marxist regime in Addis Ababa and that the Dergue would provide similar assistance to the PDRY if required.

Ideology, regional isolation, and extreme underdevelopment are the principal reasons for the PDRY's dependence on the Soviet Union and other communist bloc nations. While instrumental in economic and other infrastructural assistance, Moscow's role in the PDRY has been most clearly seen in military development. The trend toward cooperation in this sphere has quickened in recent years with the removal of China as a significant rival, the shifts to the left in internal PDRY politics, the transfer of Soviet equipment from Berbera to Aden in late 1977, and the emergence of common interests in supporting the Ethiopian Revolution. The strengthening of ties with Cuba, including the latter's provision of development experts and instructors for the PDRY militia, is more directly based on a common Third World Marxist identity and shared interests in the Horn. Additional significant assistance has come from East Germany, particularly in supervision of Aden's security and intelligence network.

Despite the preponderance of communist bloc aid and influence in South Yemen, it cannot be assumed simplistically that the PDRY is a Soviet puppet. The Arab and, in a cultural sense, Islamic identity of South Yemen remains intact, even with the thorough political, social, and economic reorientation of the country since 1967. Those who hold power in the PDRY are the remaining members of the innermost cadres of the old NLF, which fought a long and violent war against the British to gain independence. They are nationalists foremost and realize that granting bases to the Soviet Union would be no more palatable to other

Middle Eastern and Third World states than would be American bases in South Yemen's neighbors.

The often heavy hand of the Soviet Union has already contributed to the removal of Ismail from power in 1980, against Soviet wishes, and his subsequent exile to Moscow. In the following several years, Soviet bloc influence in the PDRY slackened noticeably, as shown particularly in the formerly tight security apparatus run by the East Germans. At the same time, Aden began a new and potentially more fruitful rapprochement with Saudi Arabia, invited Western commercial establishments to participate in development projects, and finally agreed to sit down at the negotiating table with Oman.

The YAR's relations with the superpowers are much more complicated. Here, this Yemeni state is caught in the middle; externally, it must play the politics of balance just as it must internally. The North's ties to the United States extend back to the imamate and the provision of development aid in the 1950s. These were strengthened by American recognition of the new republic in late 1962, the resumption of diplomatic relations prior to the October 1973 Arab-Israeli war, and the provision of some American military assistance during the 1979 fighting. Nevertheless, American interests in North Yemen suffer greatly from their subordination to Saudi direction.

The principal reason for the full-blown American reaction to the inter-Yemeni war in 1979 seems to have been the Carter administration's need to produce an aggressive response to presumed Soviet and Cuban advances in Africa and to counter charges of inactivity in face of the "loss" of Iran. But the immediate decision to provide the YAR with sophisticated military equipment (including F-5E fighters, C-130 transports, M-60 tanks, and armored personnel carriers) appears to have been due to Saudi Arabia's insistence and willingness to pay for it. Once the fighting died down, however, Riyadh was faced again with the other element in its paradoxical Yemeni policy: a strengthened YAR presumably would be able to threaten Saudi Arabia. Consequently, payment for the American arms was abruptly canceled and much of what had been promised never arrived in Sana. Not surprisingly, North Yemenis were not impressed by either Saudi or American behavior in this instance, and the government went ahead with a previously arranged arms deal at rock-bottom prices with the Soviet Union.

The alleged insistence of Washington (once again at Saudi instigation) that the YAR sever its relations with the Soviet Union only served to worsen the American position in Sana. Such a demand is completely unrealistic. The Soviet Union has provided development assistance to North Yemen for as long as the United States has, as well as military equipment and training since the time of the imamate. Furthermore, following the departure of Egyptian troops from Yemen in late 1967, the YAR was saved from extinction during the subsequent royalist siege of Sana in large part thanks to Soviet airlifts.

To cut the long and productive tie with the Soviet Union would serve to make the YAR much more dependent on Saudi Arabia—a highly unpopular move for any North Yemeni leader to contemplate—and would in effect send a hostile signal to both Moscow and Aden. Finally, it would run against the grain of a successful Yemeni tradition of playing one outside force off against another. For example, the three main cities of the YAR are connected by three paved roads: one built by the Americans, one by the Soviets, and one by the Chinese. An ideal policy for the Sana government would be a continuation of the policy of balance, extracting financial aid from the Saudis (and development assistance from the United States) but keeping Riyadh at arm's length, while simultaneously allowing the Soviet Union to maintain a small military training team and procuring cheap Soviet military supplies but not providing Moscow with access to the inner circles of YAR policy making. It is an awkward and dangerous game to play, but then North Yemen has little choice.

Prospects for the Future

While it would be foolish to make any prognostications, it may be worthwhile (and perhaps even safe) to point out some possible developments in the near future and the likely consequences they may have for the Yemens, their neighbors, and the superpowers. These developments may be grouped broadly into three categories: domestic developments in one or both Yemens, shifts in inter-Yemeni relations, and alterations in Yemen-superpower relations.

Given the record of political instability in both Yemeni republics and their lack of political development since independence, there is considerable likelihood of continuing power struggles and coups d'état, whether violent or not. The durability of the Salih regime in Sana has surprised most observers, both inside and outside the country. Nevertheless, the regime continues to be uncertainly balanced on the brink of disaster, and its energies are overwhelmingly devoted to simple survival. There are few capabilities or spare resources available to focus on the necessary corollary of political development: moving beyond regime maintenance to the creation of a national consensus and thus legitimacy for the existing YAR government. Salih is not able to live up to the legacy of the late President Hamdi, whether measured by the latter's personal charisma, neutral background acceptable to all Yemenis, or competence and vision.

It seems very probable that if a successful coup were staged tomorrow, Salih's successor would also be a Zaydi tribal officer of undistinguished background, possibly less skillful than Salih in political manipulation. Such a successor would be more vulnerable to traditionalist and Saudi pressures and thus more likely to provoke personal, sectarian, and ideological conflict. Internationally, the impact of such a development would be largely negative. Relations with South Yemen would deteriorate and the upsurge in Saudi influence would provoke a nationalist and possibly leftist backlash (and thereby redound to Washington's disadvantage). Such a new and inevitably weak regime would also invite successive coup attempts, thus exacerbating the country's political instability.

It is far more difficult to contemplate accurately the direction of any shift in the PDRY. The secrecy in which Adeni politics are habitually shrouded makes interpretation of what has already happened a matter of guesswork. The elevation of Ali Nasir Muhammad to the pinnacle of power was not foreseen by most observers; his continuation in power and even growing strength and confidence have also been something of a surprise. The principal factors contributing to this success story include recent improvements in the economy, welcome restraints on the security apparatus and therefore lessened Soviet influence, the promising advances toward Yemen unity, and perhaps a recognition of the universally felt need to suspend damaging fratricidal struggles within the diminishing core of the country and party's "founding fathers." Consequently, a reasonable guess would be that any change in regime in the short-term is unlikely; if one should occur, there is little indication in which direction PDRY politics would be shifted.

Another potential development that should not be overlooked is a deviation in inter-Yemeni relations independent of domestic regime changes. An unpredictable series of minor events could easily draw both countries into internecine warfare, just as happened in 1972 and 1979. The possibility of this happening would seem relatively remote, however, unless accompanied by more substantial fluctuations in either or both states. Slightly more likely is the prospect of substantive progress in unification. While complete merger seems incomprehensible in the foreseeable future, some sort of federation cannot be ruled out. It is not farfetched to imagine the evolution of a mutually-agreed-upon pan-Yemen foreign policy.

The advantages of such a venture would presumably encompass some diminution of direct foreign interference in Yemeni affairs, affecting both Saudi Arabia and the Soviet Union. It would also seem to present an opportunity for both superpowers to deal directly and productively with both Yemens and simultaneously reduce the inherently volatile nature of local superpower competition through Yemeni clients. The coordination of foreign policy should not prove too difficult to arrange on pan-Arab concerns; as regards the Horn, the probable result would be some moderation of the PDRY's ties to Ethiopia and some reorientation of the YAR toward regional concerns in the Red Sea.

The nature of Yemeni-superpower relations can of course be affected considerably by both domestic Yemeni developments and by superpower reaction to regional or extraregional occurrences that bear no direct relation to the Yemens. The impact of such events depends on the events themselves and thus any discussion is best left alone. However, speculation on deliberate changes in bilateral relations between various of the four states involved may prove more worthwhile.

Any improvement in YAR-U.S. relations depends on American willingness to deal directly with Sana, even if that incurs Saudi displeasure. Such a development is to be welcomed given the nearly one hundred thousand Yemenis working in the United States (and consequently large numbers of American citizens in the YAR), the modest but constructive American role in North Yemen's socioeconomic development, and the potential gain in promoting political development by reducing the likelihood of more unstable, Saudi-dominated governments. The strengthening of YAR-USSR relations may result from either reaction to unwelcome Saudi cum American interference in internal affairs or as a consequence of the formulation of a unified foreign policy. In either case, the YAR is not likely to rush unreservedly into a Soviet embrace unless there is no possibility for an open and constructive dialogue with the United States.

For reasons discussed earlier, any expectation of a rupture in Soviet ties to either Yemen is completely unrealistic. At the same time, the probability of any intensification in PDRY-USSR relations seems rather remote in the near future. The direction of events in South Yemen in the last few years has indicated a lessening of Aden's dependence on Moscow and this trend seems likely to continue barring unforeseen complications. This is not to suggest that the PDRY can be weaned away from communist bloc ties, but a much more limited policy objective seems attainable for the United States and the West. The establishment of diplomatic relations between Washington and Aden—begun in 1978 but aborted by the June events—would at least reduce the misperceptions and suspicions held by both sides. At the very least it could show American goodwill, provide Aden with an alternative source for development assistance, and possibly pay dividends in the moderation of PDRY foreign policy toward American friends in the region.

Finally, it seems only sensible that superpower policies in regard to the Yemens recognize the limitations and needs of these two states. Any policy built solely upon the assumption that the Yemens are interchangeable pawns of international politics will surely go awry, sooner or later. A more constructive alternative would appear to be dealing with both Yemens on a strictly bilateral basis, involving neither subordination to the interests of intermediaries nor counterproductive concentration on the possible ramifications of a wider and often irrelevant superpower rivalry.

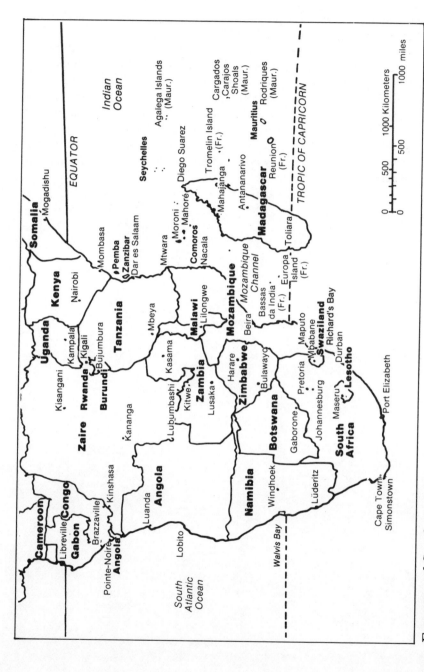

Eastern and Southern Africa

SECTION THREE ◣

Eastern and Southern Africa

The issue that pervades the politics of eastern and southern Africa is the confrontation between the black African states and the Republic of South Africa. As Douglas Anglin notes in his contribution to this section, for the Frontline States South Africa is a daily obsession. Pretoria's policies acutely affect their economic and political interests while the issues that are being contested influence all calculations of security in the area. Until very recently the apparent unwillingness of any of the parties to disputes in South Africa and Namibia to compromise their positions seemed to ensure that the problems of the region would only persist and probably deepen. The event that offers the most promise of a change in this singularly unpromising scenario is the signing in March 1984 of the Nkomati accord between Pretoria and Maputo. The obligations undertaken involve little more than each side refraining from providing sanctuary to guerrillas opposed to the policies of the respective governments. Nevertheless this agreement, along with signs of movement in Pretoria's position on Namibia, holds out hope, according to some observers, of a change in the pattern of violence that is such an endemic part of southern African politics. Others view Pretoria's moves with justifiable cynicism.

While political confrontation has long characterized relations between South Africa and the black African states, it has always been mixed with a strong element of economic pragmatism, a phenomenon also evident, as Peter Vale and Michael Spicer point out, in relations between the offshore island states and Pretoria. The black governments in particular are conscious of the extent to which their economic dependence on Pretoria restricts political options. By forming the strongly economics-oriented Southern African Development Coordination Conference in 1981 they took an important step toward trying to break this nexus. A similar experiment in regional cooperation is also under way among the island-states of Mauritius, the Seychelles, and Madagascar following the formation of the Indian Ocean Commission in July 1982.

One of the persistent dangers of the situation in southern Africa is that the periodic military encounters, which are already part of life there, will escalate, perhaps to the point where outside powers become involved. Insofar as superpowers might be tempted to intervene, the reasons are more likely to be broadly strategic than narrowly or overtly racial. As Jim Roherty's account of the "contemporary school" of South African strategy makes clear, Pretoria is certainly anxious to encourage a closer defense relationship with Washington as a counter to the perceived threat of communism. While the Reagan administration appears to have some sympathy for South Africa's concerns, it has been wary of closer ties. Still, the strategic imperatives for developing closer relations with the republic remain strong. The Simonstown naval facility that once helped to sustain Royal Navy operations in the Indian Ocean could well serve a similar purpose for the U.S. Navy. In particular, use of the facility would greatly enhance that navy's ability to protect the vital sea lanes that pass along the east African coast and around the Cape of Good Hope as a major route to Europe. At present such logistic support as is available for short-term deployments, and as would be necessary for more sustained operations, comes from facilities at Diego Garcia in the Chagos Archipelago and Mombasa in Kenya. In neither case can the United States be confident of long-term access to these facilities. The case of Diego Garcia is dealt with by Joel Larus elsewhere in this volume. But as George Shepherd discusses in the lead chapter of this section, there is growing opposition in Kenya to the policies of the present government. The opposition has its roots in economic disparities, but there are also overtones of anti-Americanism in the positions taken by the government's critics. If President Moi's government should fall, it is not certain that the United States would be able or, indeed, anxious to retain access to its presently expanding air and naval facilities in the country.

Whatever the prospects for closer defense cooperation between Washington and Pretoria, the Frontline States would certainly be unsettled by any such development, seeing it both as a potential threat to their own security and as evidence of Washington's contempt for the justice of the black cause. Their response would depend on a range of complex factors prevailing at the time. Certainly it is not obvious that they would attempt to encourage the Soviet Union to take a more active part in the region's affairs. Though Maputo already has close relations with Moscow, other Frontline States are more wary of such an association. As Shepherd and Anglin both observe, Tanzania in particular would be uneasy about the Kremlin's role, seeing it as likely to compromise President Nyerere's aspirations of self-reliance both for his country and its neighbors and as posing another obstacle to the creation of an Indian Ocean zone of peace of which Tanzania has been one of the strongest supporters. Given the widespread respect the Tanzanian president now commands in southern Africa (somewhat akin to the leadership role once fulfilled by Jomo Kenyatta), it is conceivable that, if pressed, other Frontline States could be encouraged to follow Tanzania's policy lead, whichever direction it took.

As signs of movement away from the political confrontation that has characterized southern Africa for so long are only embryonic, the region must continue to be regarded as one of chronic instability and therefore likely to affect the security concerns of the other states of the Indian Ocean region. Being preoccupied with local problems, the governments of southern Africa, particularly those of the Frontline States, find their attention deflected away from the Indian Ocean as an issue arena. Yet it is apparent that no state is fully able to insulate itself from the impact of wider regional developments. In altogether different ways, Kenya and South Africa have been drawn into the issues that constitute the region's security agenda. The Frontline States have adopted a rather lower profile. Yet even they, through their support of Sri Lanka's proposal that the region be declared a zone of peace and as a result of closer contacts with the oil-producing states of the Persian Gulf, have become parties to the wider dimensions of the region's political life. It remains unclear whether this is indicative of a trend that will see the Frontline presidents more actively involved in issues beyond southern Africa. Anglin may be correct that this is a luxury they can ill afford. On the other hand, with limited options and a restricted area for maneuver they may not be able to exercise a choice.

13. *Global and Indian Ocean Influences on the East African States* ☛ *George W. Shepherd, Jr.*

Since the 1960s East Africa has emerged as a highly important strategic area within the Indian Ocean system, developing important connections with the Middle East, the Persian Gulf, and southern Africa. The rivalry of the superpowers has spilled over from the Middle East into the East African region, introducing the conflicts of the Arab world into the politics of Kenya and Uganda. The struggle between South Africa and the Frontline States (Angola, Botswana, Mozambique, Tanzania, Zambia, and Zimbabwe) has involved Tanzania directly in a number of the major issues and new relationships of southern Africa. The failure of the East African Community (EAC) has left the separate states of East Africa to drift apart in increased and often intensive rivalry and conflict. These crises have been intensified especially by the Indian Ocean arms race and the competition between the superpowers that are prone to exploit differences when it benefits their own interests within the wider arena of conflict. Thus, global and regional issues are constantly interacting with and complicating the problems of individual East African states.

These developments can best be explained by acknowledging that the East African states, like most African states, have become postcolonial "tributary states" at different stages of development. They have obtained flag independence, but their political economies are still primarily under the control of other states and agencies of the international system in ways that have been well described by such dependency analysts as Amin, Wallerstein, and Frank.[1] However, the tributary states are not simply on the periphery of the international capitalist system, they are an integral part of the international security system of hegemonic superpowers that has replaced the colonial system.

The tributary state is characterized by high levels of economic penetration by the financial networks and corporate structures of the West (dominated by the United States), and by linkages to the superpowers covering the supply of military equipment and training, as well as base support systems.[2] This is not to argue that the tributary state does not have some autonomy or indeed that there is not considerable interdependence between important tributary states and hegemonic powers. There is substantial mutual interest and exchange but the essence of the relationship is unequal because the subordinate states operate within narrow limits of choice like a ship sailing through narrow straits. Regional cultural and economic conditions have a great bearing on their decisions but the major direction is charted by the intrusive powers who stand outside the region and control the decisive factors such as military supplies, banking loans, and technology transfers. In addition, there is a transnational tributary elite that serves the interests of the intrusive powers in a comprador relationship. In some cases this elite is well established as a ruling class, while in others it clings to power with the support of the superpowers and their allies.

The East African states are at various stages of this tributary relationship. When Idi Amin was at the height of his power, Uganda was a Soviet tributary, having a considerable degree of military dependence on Soviet supplies, primarily for the air force, while also receiving training and support from radical Arab states. Since the defeat of Amin by Tanzania and the restoration of Milton Obote as president, Uganda has extricated itself from this Soviet network and sought to reenter the Anglo-American hegemonic system. However, a high level of internal conflict has made this transition very difficult. Kenya has exemplified the well-developed Western tributary state since the days of President Jomo Kenyatta. There the ruling ethno-class has accepted close economic and military links with Britain, the United States, and their allies. Tanzania, in contrast, has been a tributary that has struggled to extricate itself from Western dependency through a program aimed at building self-reliance. However, global and regional rivalries, as well as internal conflicts, have made this transition very difficult.

This chapter focuses primarily on the experiences of Kenya and Tanzania as they have faced the problems of development, regional conflict, and superpower rivalry within the Indian Ocean security (tributary) system.

Kenya

From a Western viewpoint, Kenya is the most important country in East Africa. Once viewed as a model for colonial transition, Kenya's early rapid development has now given way to a series of military insurrections, tribal conflicts, and the growing repression of students and opposition leaders. Kenya's relations with South Africa, its ambivalence toward neighboring African states, and its growing association with American Indian Ocean policy suggest that Kenya's role in the Indian Ocean region is best defined and understood within the context of an unfolding tributary relationship.

The new tributary class

A small group of neobourgeoisie teachers, lawyers, trade union leaders, and tradesmen were the backbone of the Kenyan revolution. They successfully took power from the white settlers whose fear of the growing power of Kenyatta and his friends made Mau Mau much more significant than it would otherwise have been. Fortunately, the British Labour government of the period recognized and was prepared to negotiate with men such as Jomo Kenyatta and Tom Mboya. Kenyatta and Mboya were middle-class African nationalists, influenced by Fabian socialism and pan-Africanism, and disinclined to disturb fundamentally the basic economic and Western-oriented structure of Kenya.[3] These Africans were not racist like most of the settlers and were much more capable of leading a new and independent Kenya in cooperation with other groups than were the settlers.

The Kenya African National Union (KANU) movement that gained independence for Kenya was based on a peasant rebellion, but the leaders who took power with Kenyatta in 1962 were petit bourgeoisie. They very quickly used their power to Africanize the sources of wealth and created a new privileged class. Within a decade there emerged a comprador bourgeoisie that held political power and shared economic power with expatriates, mostly English Kenyans, who controlled the major companies and financial enterprises. With substantial incomes from profitable enterprises in farming and exporting, and even political payoffs, this bourgeoisie came to constitute a small but very wealthy group within Kenyan society. Primarily Kikuyu, and often closely associated with the Kiambu district of Kenyatta, Mbiyu Koinange, Charles Njonjo, and Njoroge Mungai, it has been argued they are a separate class functioning differently in Africa from the European bourgeoisie in Marxian terminology. According to Amey and Leonard, they repress rival groups and accumulate wealth through the use of tribal links and their ability to control the state.[4] The English-speaking members of the upper levels of the bureaucracy have joined this class. Like Peter Kenyatta, son of Jomo Kenyatta, who became very wealthy, they thrive on their contacts and close tribal or family ties to the source of contracts and patronage. They are, in short, a tributary class with overseas links through business and cultural ties to Western countries, especially the United States and Britain. At the same time they have a domestic power base in the bureaucracy, in business, and in tribal politics.[5] A Swahili term has been applied to this new class: *Matajiri*, meaning literally, the rich. A struggle for power goes on between the *Matajiri* and rival groups who have been denied both power and wealth. This is the key to the nature of the Kenyan political process that manifests itself in a competition for positions on the executive of KANU and for parliamentary seats in the central legislature.

Matajiri politics and the tributary economy

In the late 1970s, Kenya appeared to be a model of African capitalism and prosperity; it was not only profitable to foreign corporations but also provided a major point of access to the wider markets of East Africa, the Horn, and, to some extent, Central Africa. The multinational corporations had become an integral part of the Kenyan economy and were embraced by the *Matajiri* because they meant not only managerial jobs but also positions on boards of local subsidiaries.[6] To some, such as the Kenyatta family, the corporations offered opportunities to purchase substantial stock in return for favors in contracts and protection. Thus, a small capital-owning class emerged among Africans who controlled political power although at most they owned modest agriculture-processing facilities and manufacturing subsidiaries.[7] The foreign-owned corporations such as Lonhroes, East African Industries, J. Warren Africa, and General Motors remained the primary decision makers on investment, technology, and pricing.

Despite the importance of these foreign corporations African socialism in Kenya has meant a partnership between the state and foreign and domestic enterprise. Nationalization of industry has been rejected in favor of government-run boards, such as the Agriculture Finance Corporation, established to aid farming, and the Industrial and Commercial Development Corporation, which offers assistance to industry.[8] African participation was, of course, encouraged but in practice the *Matajiri* received the opportunities and formed the core of the comprador bourgeoisie.[9] Initially, this resulted in rapid expansion; "dependent development" appeared to be providing general prosperity, as Kenyatta had envisioned. However, inherent problems existed.

In the 1960s and early 1970s, Kenya's economy was healthy, showing growth rates that stimulated appreciable economic development. However the prosperity was inequitably shared with substantially greater benefits going to the ethno–ruling class. The effect has been the entrenchment of a pattern of wealth distribution that is one of the most inequitable in Africa. Although an International Labour Organization report first drew attention to this trend in 1972, little has been done to correct the situation.[10] In fact, the decline in Kenya's economic performance has only served to exacerbate the problem and to create a volatile political situation.

A major slump in Kenya's balance of payments began in 1979, resulting from the high cost of oil and the worldwide decline in coffee prices. This, together with the necessity for food imports following a decline in agricultural productivity and a continuing high demand for luxury goods for the tourist economy, has forced Kenya to borrow heavily. At the same time, the economy has been hit by high levels of inflation and growing unemployment as school leavers flock to urban centers at the rate of 150,000 per year. These economic difficulties have been aggravated by the worldwide recession, with the result that income and opportunity gaps have widened rapidly since the mid-1970s. With population growth unrestricted, with the *Matajiri* preserving their privileged position by increased repression of the petit bourgeoisie and the working class, and with increasing peasant tribal protest, the internal economic and political pressures in Kenya have become enormous.[11]

It is now evident that the position of President Moi, who succeeded Kenyatta in 1978, is becoming increasingly unstable.[12] His shaky regime has already had to defend itself against several concerted attempts at overthrow. Thus the abortive coup of August 1982, by the air force, stemmed from broad-based dissatisfaction with Moi's leadership and the state of the economy. It was an attempt by a rival *Matajiri* faction to guarantee its position of privilege more securely in the face of growing instability.[13]

While the *Matajiri* is firmly in power, its leaders have begun to bicker with one another. In these circumstances it is not inconceivable that the armed forces will emerge as the final arbiter. If the military does replace the civilian government it is unlikely to resolve any of the entrenched economic or social problems. The usual role of the military in Africa has been to constrain rebellion and maintain the position of the tributary class. This could be expected to occur in Kenya with the consequence that military rule will be even more intolerant of challenges to *Matajiri* rule.

Trend toward militarization

Toward the end of the 1970s Kenya had great prestige among other states in Africa, mainly because of the pan-African role of Jomo Kenyatta. It was also anticommunist and willing to provide facilities for U.S. air and naval operations in the northwest quadrant of the Indian Ocean. In recent years the increasing emphasis on the second of these roles has drawn Kenya toward becoming the center of hegemonic Western interest in northeastern Africa. Thus, the prominence already accorded to Western economic interests is being complemented by a recognition of strategic imperatives.

The increasing militarization of Kenya can therefore be seen as primarily the result of extension of the strategic zones of rivalry between the superpowers from the Persian Gulf and the northeast quadrant of the Indian Ocean to the northwest. Soviet bases in Eritrea and Aden have been countered by American "facilities" in Berbera and Mombasa. Extensive naval and air activity has grown steadily during the seventies. The Arabian Sea reputedly has been a key point for sea-launched ballistic missile (SLBM) submarine deployment by the U.S. Navy while the Soviets have intensified their shipping through the Suez Canal and the Red Sea. The United States' search for secure bases for the Rapid Deployment Force (RDF) has led them to identify Mombasa as being of central importance because of its facilities for carriers and inland air base backup.

Soviet influence in this region has grown rapidly since 1969 when Siad Barre seized power in Somalia. Kenya's opposition to Soviet intrusions predates even this period and can be traced back to 1964 when Kenyatta became angered by Moscow's role in the 1964 Congo crisis (which he had attempted to mediate). Since then the presence of the Soviet fleet in Indian Ocean waters has continued to disturb Kenya and has been the reason for Nairobi's support of the resolutions of the United Nations Ad Hoc Committee on the Indian Ocean seeking big power withdrawal from the region. Kenya's fear of the Soviet Union has been further aroused by signs that neighboring states might use Soviet arms to suppress internal opposition. At one time Idi Amin in Uganda sought to import Soviet arms, and later Milton Obote's new government became suspect when it invited the North Koreans, along with a small contingent of British officers, to help train the Ugandan army.

Kenya's opposition to communism has been manifested in other ways. For instance, the curious role Kenya played in a series of coup attempts in the Seychelles against Albert René's regime appears to be related to Kenyan officials' fear of "communism." René has accused Kenya of giving support to the two 1981 coup attempts against him and of working directly with South Africa to overthrow him.[14] The Seychelles' "leftist" politics are disliked in Nairobi and rumors that a Soviet base, comparable to the U.S. base on Diego Garcia, might be established on one of the Seychelles islands have unsettled Kenya as much as its patron powers, Britain and the United States.

Middle Eastern Arab politics have been mixed with the politics of the arms race in Kenyan Indian Ocean policy. Saudi Arabia has sought to build a conservative bloc against the radicalism of Libya, Ethiopia, and South Yemen and the backwash of the Iranian Revolution. In doing so the Saudis have been generous in providing aid to Indian Ocean countries, like Kenya, that have been prepared to take a strong stand against the spread of Soviet influence in the region. This aid has taken the form of both money and arms. Thus, a road is being built between Somalia and Kenya with a Saudi loan of $23.5 million.[15] The trade between these two East African states has always been quite small, so it seems likely that military value is being attached to the opening of a supply line from Mogadishu to the south to support the Somalis against an Ethiopian-Soviet expansion.

In its rivalry with the Soviet Union in the Indian Ocean, and in its efforts to expand trade and investment in Africa, the United States has found Kenya to be an important and receptive tributary. This tributary relationship can be seen more clearly in Kenya than most other states in the region, including the oil producers of the Persian Gulf. It has been encouraged by the *Matajiri* ruling class and is the result of combining economic expansion with military intrusion. The relationship is easily traced and has been well documented. It is tributary in the sense of neocolonial dependency and by virtue of the obvious and growing strategic role Kenya is playing in American efforts to project force into the Indian Ocean. Kenya's government has entered this new relationship willingly, while maintaining all the nominal trappings of independence. The United States protects Kenya against perceived threats from the Soviet Union, at a cost that may appear to be minimal, but that in reality is no less than the enormous cost of maintaining the Indian Ocean fleet and the RDF. However, without facilities such as the Mombasa port, these forces would be further from the "crescent of crisis" and arguably less able to fulfill their role.

Early in 1980, the United States reached a preliminary agreement with Kenya for the upgrading of naval facilities at Kalindini harbor in Mombasa.[16] The work is likely to cost the U.S. $50 million and when completed the harbor will be adequate for the servicing of the largest American carriers and battleships. The scope of the agreement is classified, but suspicions have been aroused that Kenya has become a central base in plans for RDF operations. Corroboration can be found in the fact that the United States has leased territory thirty miles inland at Mariakoni and is building large underground shelters. The United States is also building two new airfields.

While willing to provide these facilities, the Kenyans have pressed Washington for a range of military supplies. Their success in this endeavor has turned Kenya into the largest recipient of American military aid in non-Arab Africa. Thus a recent agreement provides for the upgrading of the ten F-5 Tiger aircraft that were supplied in 1976.[17] Kenya has utilized other Western sources of military supply, but between 1975 and 1979 U.S. sources have predominated with a total of $90.2 million being provided. Canada was second with $30 million, while Britain provided only $10 million. Generally, America has supplied advanced weapons and training to the air force, with Britain and Canada being the major source of expertise for training and the supply of less sophisticated weapons, such as tanks and armored cars.[18] This diversity is also reflected in the backgrounds of officers in the Kenyan military, many of whom have trained at either Sandhurst or Mons. Both the United States and Israel have training units in Kenya and the latter country is reported to have provided President Moi with protection during the August coup attempt.[19]

Issues of national security involving the American presence in Kenya, or even questions of Somalia's possible rearmament, are not debated in Parliament nor is the press allowed to comment on them in any detail. By using his power, President Moi has been able to curb expressions of opposition to his policies. However, there is considerable dissatisfaction and fear that Kenya may be caught in a war between the superpowers or may simply become a target for Soviet intrigue because of the U.S. presence in the country.

There is no concrete evidence that the Soviet Union or indigenous communists were behind the coup attempt of August 1982, and it was not apparently anti-American in character or origins. However, as the fighting progressed, it took on an anti-American theme as university students and members of the working classes joined in. When reasserting his authority after the failure of the coup, Moi imprisoned virtually all his left-wing opponents at the universities, in the party, and in the press.[20] By doing so he defined the coup as left-wing and anti-American and further identified the *Matajiri* with U.S. interests in the country.

This highlights one of the inescapable internal weaknesses of the tributary state: the tendency for the domestic opposition of the ruling class to be directed against its external support. In Kenya, the intellectuals have turned left and become more anti-American because U.S. power is blamed for the continuing repressive rule of Moi and the *Matajiri*. While this is not the full story, it is the tale that is told in the bazaars and coffee shops. Just as colonialism bred nationalism, the new tributary system breeds revolution, making it highly unlikely that Moi or the *Matajiri* can long survive in power. Before long the United States may find that Kenya has become another Iran and may seek to extricate itself prior to the collapse. At that point, Kenya's economic and political systems will break down and the *Matajiri* will be engulfed by the revolution.

Tanzania

Self-reliance is a method or strategy for accomplishing political and economic development goals. Its proponents are not utopian or necessarily advocates of a classless society. They propose a method of democratic political control over the major sectors of the production system and an equitable redistribution of the benefits to all classes and groups.[21] There are many forms that democratic political control can take—multiparty or single party—and there are many ways in which the levels of production can be controlled, especially in former colonial countries. These control methods are determined by historical conditions of culture, patterns of trade, the security framework, and the class system of production. The last is in turn influenced by levels of technology and the distribution of resources and population between rural and urban areas. Self-reliance is the realization of freedom through the provision of basic human rights for all citizens. These human rights are more than nineteenth-century liberal objectives. They can be defined in terms of basic human needs such as minimal levels of food and health care, as well as in terms of basic political freedoms.[22] Tanzania has become a major experiment in the application of these principles under Third World and African conditions. It is also a leading example of a country attempting to break out of a tributary relationship with great powers.

The idea of independent development through self-reliance, expounded by Tanzania's President Julius Nyerere, is more than ideology. It has become a strategy of economic and political activity calculated to build up the internal resources and self-confidence of the people of Tanzania so that they can determine their own pattern of African political life.[23] While no man or nation is an island free from the impact of events elsewhere in the world, Nyerere and his associates take the small nation-state seriously. They believe it is possible to establish sufficient internal strength, in cooperation with other self-reliant states, to free themselves from external control and exploitation.

Self-reliance as a concept

The concept of self-reliance as a strategy for the optimum development of Tanzania's resources was first articulated in the Arusha Declaration of 1967 and was the product of the frustration and failures of the first few years of Tanzanian independence. This was a period of growing conflict with Western powers, highlighted by controversies with the British over Rhodesia's unilateral declaration of independence and with the Americans over embassy spying charges. The idea of self-reliance is not autarky or even self-sufficiency; the idea is to utilize and build the country's own resources and strength to the point where it is no longer dependent upon the goodwill or the financial and technical ability of foreign powers.

During the first years of independence Tanzania's leaders came to realize that a policy of nonalignment and working with different great powers did not free their country from dependence.[24] Nyerere saw self-reliance as a means to counteract this and argued that it was "a positive affirmation that we shall depend upon ourselves for the development of Tanzania, and that we shall use the resources we have for that purpose. . . . We are not saying to other people: Please come and develop our country for us, and if you insist, we will stop being socialist or believing in equality."[25] Later, as the recipient of the Third World Prize, Nyerere stressed the idea of south-south cooperation as the alternative to north-south dependence. This was not based upon catching up with the north, but rather upon building collective self-reliance with all Third World nations.[26]

Thus, self-reliant socialism, according to Nyerere, is based upon the following principles:

1. Traditional African ethics, which provide the basic needs for all members of "the family," with none having more than they need;
2. Tanzania having control over and responsibility for the development of its own national resources, excluding external development;
3. The establishment of external trade and aid linkages with foreign powers prepared to accept Tanzanian self-reliance;
4. The struggle for self-reliant development throughout Africa, particularly with those who oppose neocolonial and racial rule.

The self-reliant political economy

Both from within and from outside Tanzania there has been a great deal of criticism of self-reliance.[27] But the suggestion that Tanzania has failed as an African socialist and self-reliant system is based more on ideological preference than on a careful empirical examination of the changes that have been introduced.

Nyerere and the Tanganyika African National Union (TANU) set out to prevent the emergence of a privileged class. From the time of the Arusha Declaration they initiated a program of deliberate economic redistribution to prevent inequities from becoming too great. This policy has been criticized for preventing growth by destroying incentives to produce. While there is some evidence that this has happened, especially in the agriculture sector, the Tanzanians have succeeded in preventing the emergence of an African comprador bourgeoisie. Many inequities exist, but even Nyerere's critics agree he has redistributed wealth with greater success than most other African leaders and has greatly reduced sharp class differences.[28] As a consequence, the comprador bourgeoisie has not gained control.[29] Instead, the major struggle has been between the privileged members of the bureaucracy and the party leaders (who have tributary tendencies) and a petit bourgeoisie comprised of the progressive peasants, workers, and unassimilated intellectuals whose commitment is to self-reliance development. In this struggle it is the latter who have generally prevailed. Tanzania's ruling class is a self-reliant, progressive group; it has limited corruption and dealt severely with the comprador black market.[30] No one tribal group has been permitted to emerge as the predominant beneficiary of the system although differences resulting from historical location and cultural habits (the nomadic Masai are a case in point) obviously make for inequities in adaptation to modern life.

Economically the application of self-reliance has produced mixed results. In agriculture the controversial attempt to achieve self-sufficient food production through the *"Ujama* villagization" (cooperative villages) campaign is acknowledged by critics and proponents alike to have been a failure.[31] Even so, the campaign does provide a means toward greater equity and has laid the foundation for a "green revolution" in Tanzania. Hybrid seed and mechanized production techniques now being developed with the assistance of the World Bank and the United Nations Food and Agriculture Organization are well suited to the village life that is the essence of *Ujama*.[32] Moreover, the campaign has accomplished several secondary goals in the building of a new way of life that could, in the long run, turn out to be as important in self-reliance development as increased agricultural production. In the small manufacturing and industrial sectors of the Tanzanian economy, expansion has taken place under the direction of the state and in cooperation with external private and state enterprises. The model of socialism is the mixed economy of northern Europe, rather than the total state enterprise of Eastern Europe and China under Mao.

Central control over the economic system was obtained by establishing the National Development Corporation (NDC) in 1965 and through the 1967 nationalization of the banking and financial system. Following the Arusha Declaration of 1967 the NDC became the central agency of development as the private sector waned in importance. Through the NDC and other government boards, the state has participated in and controlled many other enterprises.[33] Private industry has been required to work within the framework of this system. When they have deviated from government policy, private corporations have been nationalized with minimal compensation as in the case of the British company Lonhroes.

In certain sectors and industries Tanzania's achievements have been considerable. The financial reforms have enabled the country to minimize profit transfer pricing as well as other means for profit flight abroad, and have helped the state to utilize capital internally. New industries have been begun in textiles and motor vehicles. The industrial sector has grown under the leadership of the NDC, rather than foreign enterprise, though the private sector has also expanded. A conscious spread of industry outside of Dar es Salaam has broadened urban employment and eased the pressures of shantytown slums in the major seaport.

Cranford Pratt concluded that the first decade of socialism in Tanzania had successfully established a new model for socialist development in Africa.[34] While this is too optimistic, it does seem as though the progressive petit bourgeoisie has gained the upper hand in the power struggle within the ruling elites. Thus Nnoli has observed that "the power struggle has been broadened to involve more than the narrow ruling groups. As a result, the growing power of opponents of socialism is now countered by the growing strength of pro-Socialist forces, an alliance of the revolutionary elite and the politically conscious workers and peasants."[35] Nnoli concludes that self-reliance is the only alternative to the "slavish dependence advocated by the right wing," or to the "dignified martyrdom" that would inevitably follow a left-wing program. The question still remains, can it succeed?

Self-reliance and Tanzania's security

There are security dimensions both to the practice of and the prospects for self-reliance. Nyerere recognizes that the concept will fail to take root if it does not gain the support of other African and Third World countries. To be successful, self-reliance must be collective. Accordingly, he has sought to build security and economic ties with neighboring states in southern Africa and has become one of the primary advocates of south-south cooperation in the Indian Ocean region.[36] Nyerere's approach to these matters has won him the respect of other southern African leaders and he has established Tanzania as a leader in confronting the problems of the region, especially those relating to South Africa. Thus Tanzania played an important part in helping to found the Southern African Development Coordination Conference (SADCC) in 1979 and continues to take a significant part in leading the nine member states in a program of economic and security independence from South Africa. This is a long-shot commitment with progress being slow and difficult, as Douglas Anglin discusses in the next chapter. But eventually it may well provide the basis for collective self-reliance in East and Central Africa.

As the recognized leader of the Frontline States, Nyerere played a major role in the negotiations over the Zimbabwe settlement. At one point he prevented Cuban and Soviet intrusion into the fighting and, at another stage, forestalled the acceptance of a deal between Smith and Nkomo that would have prolonged the war. Together Nyerere and President Kaunda of Zambia succeeded in turning Margaret Thatcher against the internal settlement with Bishop Muzorewa and in turn persuaded the Patriotic Front to accept an all-parties conference. As Robert Jaster has noted, "Nyerere was seen as more or less neutral as well as being a strong supporter of the Patriotic Front."[37] He was therefore able to work toward a final settlement with both sides, one that is generally recognized as a remarkable outcome.

Tanzania has also played an important leadership and mediating role in the situation in Namibia. The Frontline States have backed the South West African People's Organization (SWAPO) and Angola from the outset. They pushed SWAPO to accept an electoral settlement under United Nations auspices in 1978, and they have kept the pressure on the five "contact states," who have sought a settlement by negotiation with South Africa. Nyerere has backed Angola and SWAPO in their opposition to President Reagan's proposal for a Cuban linkage to the agreement. While Kaunda has been a channel of contact with South African Prime Minister Botha and has supported a negotiated outcome, others, such as Nyerere, have gone back to the United Nations to seek a full-scale economic boycott. The effects of this on SADCC countries like Zimbabwe would be drastic but they have not opposed United Nations measures. Yet if the Frontline States have their way and sanctions are adopted, enforcement will become an issue both for them as well as for the superpowers. The direction events will take may well depend upon the leadership of Tanzania.

Within the region, the greatest danger to Tanzania lies in a possible clash with South Africa. This could be the result of an escalating conflict over an issue such as Namibia, one in which South Africa takes retaliatory action, as it has done against Angola and Mozambique. This has become more likely since Nyerere provided a home base for the South African Pan-Africanist Congress (PAC). PAC has regrouped under D. K. Leballo (who served a term on Robben Island) and is poised for increased action inside South Africa. Although South African strikes are likely to be limited to punishment rather than all-out war, the situation could get out of hand if the Africans, backed by the Soviet Union, were to begin retaliatory strikes. To date South Africa's raids like the ones on Cuamato (Angola) and Matola (Mozambique) in January 1981 have taken place without a commensurate response. This could change if the Soviets decide to intervene seriously and supply African states with sophisticated communications equipment and defensive weapons, such as more advanced aircraft and missiles. The warning of the Soviet Union to South Africa after the Matola raid, invoking its treaty with Mozambique, cannot be simply dismissed. Moscow could use the threat of South Africa to place weapons and technicians in Tanzania and southern Africa. With increased Western backing for South Africa the probability of a confrontation is heightened, although the Soviet Union could follow precedent and act indirectly with Cuban or other tributary forces.

African leaders like Mugabe and Machel are cautious about giving too much away to the Soviet Union. However, the direct attacks on Mozambique and Angola have forced these countries to consider their own defenses first. If this means superpower tributary protection in order to survive, they will move in that direction. Zimbabwe and Zambia could decide overnight to place Soviet-manned "defensive units" on their soil, in much the same way as Kenya and Somalia have provided military bases and facilities for the Americans.

Tanzania is in the most fortunate position and would be very wary about inviting Soviet military assistance. Nyerere has consistently reiterated the importance of attempting to control and limit superpower activity in the Indian Ocean, as well as within his own boundaries. Consistent with this stand, Tanzania has backed the Indian Ocean zone-of-peace proposal and the Ad Hoc Committee of the United Nations in the hope that they might dampen the arms race and lessen superpower presence. In the context of superpower rivalry the American buildup in Kenya and Somalia bothers Tanzania a great deal, as does the increasing Soviet presence in Mozambique, especially the use of port facilities by the Soviet navy. Nyerere has long maintained that direct use of Soviet aid in the liberation struggle was counterproductive as it gave the Western powers a stronger incentive to intervene through South Africa on the side of colonialism and racism.[38]

Given Tanzania's skepticism toward superpower activities in the Indian Ocean, it is perhaps not surprising that its bilateral relations with Washington and Moscow are somewhat strained. Relations with the former were harmed in 1982 when the United States refused to support Ambassador Salim Salim's bid for the post of secretary general of the United Nations. From Washington's perspective, this unduly complicated a relationship in which U.S. leverage has always been circumscribed. Such influence as it can exert comes largely through the provision of technical and economic aid. Yet even this has declined in recent years, a reflection of the Reagan administration's resentment of Nyerere's opposition to American policy in southern Africa. Nor are Tanzania's relations with the Soviet Union particularly close. Although Tanzania's military capability has largely been built around Soviet weapons systems this has not led to a softening of Nyerere's apprehensive attitude toward Soviet policies in the Indian Ocean region. A delegation from the Supreme Soviet did visit Tanzania in March 1982, and a communiqué was signed in which both countries reiterated their support for liberation in Namibia and South Africa and criticized the existing international economic system.[39] Despite such common ideological convictions it seems unlikely that there will be any breakthrough toward substantially closer relations in the foreseeable future.

Tanzania, like Kenya, is a part of the northwest quadrant security zone of superpower rivalry. Its place as the political leader of southern Africa causes the superpowers to take Nyerere very seriously, despite his country's poverty and lack of military strength. Thus there is considerable indirect rivalry to influence Tanzanian policy through third parties, such as Machel in Mozambique and Kaunda in Zambia. Yet neither superpower expects self-reliance to last beyond Nyerere's rule and both are eager to provide for the succession.

It has not been to the superpowers but to the People's Republic of China that Tanzania has traditionally looked for a model. Nyerere admires the Chinese achievement and much of the concept of self-reliance has been derived from Mao's philosophy of rejecting foreign domination. Chinese aid has declined appreciably since the completion of the TAZARA railway, but the Chinese connection is a firm one that continues to block Soviet inroads. Nyerere's frequent visits to Beijing in recent years attest to the strength of the relationship. China has now agreed to a new loan for repair and modernization of the TAZARA railway line, and recently completed a new textile mill for children's clothing, as well as cigarette and sugar manufacturing works.[40] China remains Tanzania's largest export customer after Europe. Insofar as China has become an Indian Ocean power, Tanzania and Mozambique have been its two major points of interest for trade, arms supply, and diplomatic support. While those who prefer the Soviet model find this very frustrating,[41] there is little doubt that China's interest in the region offers an alternative to superpower dominance.

Tanzania's determination not to affirm this dominance can also be seen in policies regarding the receipt of foreign aid. Although the recipient of more external economic assistance per capita than any other country in Africa, most of it has come from multilateral aid agencies. In recent years an increasing amount has come from European and United Nations sources. The Tanzanians have not been reluctant to refuse loans from the World Bank and the International Monetary Fund that attempted to push the economy away from government industry toward a free market system and that required devaluation and limiting of social expenditures.[42]

With regard to economic assistance, Tanzania's links to the Western nations are greater and of a more dependent character than elsewhere. Economic and military aid from Canada, Great Britain, West Germany, and the Scandinavian countries clearly has sustained the Tanzanian economy over difficult years in the 1970s.[43] When one adds to this the European Economic Community's (EEC) trade and investment in Tanzania, the reality of a continuing tributary dependence emerges into focus. This has changed little despite the policy of diversification for self-reliance. What this EEC plus Scandinavian and Canadian aid indicates is an interest on the part of some in retaining Tanzania within the Western sphere of influence and, on the part of others, a genuine interest in the success of self-reliance as a Third World alternative. The latter believe self-reliance does not threaten trade or Western capitalism but that it is a way of preserving contact and enhancing human rights in new African states and is a model they would like to see prevail.

Despite the self-reliance policy, Tanzania is still in transition from its tributary status. Nyerere has found it difficult to cut military and economic ties that have bound his country to the West. Arms are needed as well as financial and technical aid. The process of reducing this dependence is a long-term one, fraught with controversy and opposed by the two major powers and some internal groups. If it were to succeed, then a Third World alternative to tributary subservience would have been proven to exist.

Conclusion

Continuing escalation of the arms race in East Africa will end any chance of Tanzania becoming fully self-reliant. In Kenya, the conflicts are likely to increase as the *Matajiri* try to hold onto Western support and their own political power. The two East African countries are moving along separate tracks and, if Tanzania and other Frontline States become active bases for anti-apartheid arms and support, the superpower rivalry could become as fierce as in the Persian Gulf, or in the Middle East more generally. It would be most unfortunate for all concerned if Western power were to be deployed more directly in support of South Africa. This would only serve to further define the line of conflict that is already being drawn by virtue of the Soviet Union's support of the armed liberation struggle and its protection of black state independence. So far a widened, fiercer conflict has been little more than a prospect but it could become the reality if the United States and the West fail to back Tanzanian self-reliance and the Frontline States against an increasingly aggressive South Africa. To further divide Africa would be to in-

246 SUBREGIONAL PERSPECTIVES

troduce the arms race directly to the continent. To side with South Africa against African independence would be folly and would only serve to alienate the West from Africa for decades to come.

14. The Frontline States and the Future of Southern Africa ☛ Douglas G. Anglin

Southern African Perspectives on the Indian Ocean Arena

Of the six Frontline States (FLS) only Tanzania and Mozambique front on the Indian Ocean, although Zambia, Zimbabwe, and Botswana, designated "Indian Ocean hinterland states," are heavily dependent on east coast ports, notably Durban and Port Elizabeth (in South Africa), Maputo, Beira, and Nacala (in Mozambique), and Dar es Salaam (in Tanzania). Only Angola is clearly outside the region. Similarly, all but Angola have significant Asian minorities in their populations and, historically, Tanzania and Mozambique at least can look back on centuries-old trade ties with the Asian littoral states.[1] Overall, these six states scarcely perceive themselves as Indian Ocean powers and they do not feel any strong sense of belonging to an Indian Ocean community of nations. The stretch of sea separating southern Africa from Asia and distant Australia serves more as a barrier than a bridge.[2]

Both before and since independence, the international political and economic orientations of the Frontline States have been predominantly north toward Europe and south toward South Africa. Even when FLS leaders have conferred at summit venues along the Indian Ocean coast, their gaze has invariably been directed inward to the concerns of the subcontinent rather than outward to distant neighbors across the sea. In none of their numerous communiqués have oceanic issues found a mention. Instead, the constant preoccupation of summit deliberations has been the liberation of Rhodesia and then Namibia, and increasingly the overpowering presence of a hostile regime in Pretoria.

These were the imperatives that led to the emergence in 1974 of the Frontline States as an informal consultative forum of the presidents most directly involved in supporting the armed struggles in neighboring minority-ruled states.[3] The charter members were Julius Nyerere of Tanzania (who came to assume the permanent chairmanship), Kenneth Kaunda of Zambia, Sir Seretse Khama of Botswana, and Samora Machel of Mozambique; Machel was accepted as a full member from the outset even though Mozambique was not finally independent until June 1975.[4]

Subsequently, with the independence of Angola in November 1975 and Zimbabwe in April 1980, Agostinho Neto and Robert Mugabe took their places around the council table.[5]

One measure of the relative lack of interest the Indian Ocean area has evoked within the Frontline States is their limited diplomatic contact with the littoral states outside Africa. Only Zambia and Tanzania have maintained resident missions in the vast land mass between Cairo and Beijing; both states have high commissioners in New Delhi and in 1979 Zambia opened an embassy in Jiddah. As for reciprocal representation by the Asian maritime states and Australia, their diplomatic presence in the Frontline States is considerably greater: six countries have established a total of sixteen resident missions in four of the FLS capitals, all but Luanda and Gaborone. As most of these states acquired independence a good deal earlier than any in southern Africa, the imbalance is not surprising. Nevertheless, it does add some credence to the contention that southern Africa assumes greater salience for non-African states around the rim of the Indian Ocean than vice versa.

Although the Indian Ocean region has not loomed large in the consciousness of the Frontline presidents, it would be misleading to suggest that they have been completely oblivious to their interests in the area. On the contrary, there is mounting evidence of a growing recognition of its potential importance, a trend that can be expected to become more pronounced to the extent that progress is made in resolving the Namibian and South African conflicts. Developments up the East African coast, especially in the Horn of Africa, and challenges to the independence and stability of the offshore islands have occasioned some concern among FLS leaders, especially Nyerere. Tanzania has forged close political and military ties with the "progressive" governments in Madagascar and especially the Seychelles (where a detachment of Tanzanian troops is stationed).[6] For the other Frontline States, interest in east coast security has been marginal. There are, however, three issues that have led them into a heightened awareness of their shared interests with other Indian Ocean states. These are the pursuit of nonalignment, the international oil crises, and, especially, great power naval rivalry in the region.

Among Asian littoral states, India is the one with which southern African states, especially Zambia and Tanzania, have had the longest and closest personal and political links. For many years, the Indian National Congress served as an inspiration, as well as a source of material support, for African nationalists.[7] This association has been reinforced by Indian leadership of the nonaligned movement and, in the case of four of the Frontline States, by shared membership in the Commonwealth. The Indian government is also respected for having been among

248 SUBREGIONAL PERSPECTIVES

the first to champion the cause of African independence at the United Nations. Moreover, a number of nationalist leaders, notably Kaunda,[8] served their political apprenticeships in India, in many cases on Government of India scholarships. This, along with modest Indian technical and military assistance and growing investment in industry, has helped to cement the existing strong personal relationships. Prime Minister Indira Gandhi, in particular, was a frequent and honored visitor to Zambia and Tanzania for over twenty years. And, despite the powerful appeal of China, Kaunda and Nyerere, and more recently Mugabe, have made regular pilgrimages to New Delhi.[9] It is somewhat surprising, therefore, that the existence of these close personal ties of friendship have not had a greater spillover effect in arousing a more sustained interest in the affairs of the Indian Ocean region.

More important in policy terms has been the marked increase in FLS interest in establishing cordial relations with the oil-rich states in and around the Arabian peninsula. Although the impact on external behavior has been principally to draw the Frontline States more deeply into the maelstrom of Middle East politics, it has also focused their attention more sharply on the Indian Ocean littoral generally. Three related aspects of the developing relationship can be distinguished. In the first place, three of the Frontline States—Mozambique, Tanzania, and Zambia—are heavily dependent on Saudi Arabian oil,[10] while Botswana and, to a diminishing degree, Zimbabwe still rely on supplies imported through South Africa. Angola, as a major oil producer though not yet a member of the Organization of Petroleum Exporting Countries (OPEC), is self-reliant in this respect.

Second, the havoc caused to the balance of payments and foreign exchange reserves of the Frontline States by the quintupling of their oil bills has reduced them to penury. In desperation, they have been compelled in the interests of survival to turn to the Arab states to beg for financial relief in the form of concessionary prices and massive loans on favorable terms. The results have been meager in comparison with their needs and expectations and the effort expended. Although, by global standards, the "capital surplus" countries of the Middle East have been remarkably generous in sharing their wealth, the sums that have trickled down to southern Africa have been modest (see table 14-1). In the eight years from 1974 to 1981, less than $240 million has been made available to the Frontline States and only 30 percent of this represented genuine "aid." These crumbs have, however, been received with genuine gratitude and have often been repaid with political favors. Zambia, for instance, which has twice benefited from Iraqi loans and grants, has been strongly supportive of Baghdad in its invasion of Iran, despite Zambian

Table 14-1 Frontline States: Net financial receipts from OPEC countries[a]
(in U.S. $ million)

	Tanzania	Zambia	Mozam-bique	Angola	Botswana	Zimbabwe	Total
1973	0.0	0.0	0.0	0.0	0.0	0.0	0.0
1974	7.1	2.1	0.0	0.0	0.0	0.0	9.2
1975	7.3	13.9	2.1	20.6	5.4	0.0	49.3
1976	0.0	1.1	27.6	0.0	0.0	0.0	28.7
1977	12.8	0.3	4.4	13.2	0.0	0.0	30.7
1978	8.0	0.1	3.3	0.0	0.1	0.0	11.5
1979	6.3	9.5	15.0	0.0	0.6	0.1	31.5
1980	12.1	2.7	12.1	0.6	2.7	13.0	43.2
1981	14.9	9.8	2.7	0.0	0.4	8.0	35.8
Total	$68.5	$39.5	$67.2	$34.4	$9.2	$21.1	$239.9
	28.6%	16.5%	28.0%	14.3%	3.8%	8.8%	100%

Source: OECD, *Geographical Distribution of Financial Flows to Developing Countries.*

[a] Includes bilateral (from OPEC members) and multilateral (through Arab OPEC agencies) official development assistance (grants and loans) plus private investment, bank loans, export credits, etc.

membership in the mediation committee of nonaligned states attempting (unsuccessfully so far) to effect a resolution of the conflict.[11] The Lusaka government, in its present dire economic straits, can only hope to escape the necessity of swallowing the International Monetary Fund's (IMF) bitter medicine by securing an alternative source of financial salvation.[12] This may help to explain why Zambia—more than any other Frontline State—has been so solicitous of Arab sensibilities. In May 1982, President Kaunda undertook state visits to Iraq (the third within thirty months), Bahrain, and Kuwait; in June, on the occasion of the death of King Khalid of Saudi Arabia, he dispatched his prime minister to the funeral and proclaimed two days of national mourning.[13] Concerted efforts are also being made to interest the Arabs in supporting the Frontline States through aid to the Southern African Development Coordination Conference (SADCC).[14]

The incentive that has led the Frontline States to appease the Arab oil barons has not been solely the hope of recouping some of their massive losses at the hands of their prospective benefactors. They have also been exceedingly anxious—once again, especially Zambia—to commit the oil exporters finally and unequivocally to enforcing an effective embargo on the supply of oil to South Africa, directly or indirectly. One of the earliest missions to sell the case for sanctions was President Kaunda's personal appeal to the shah of Iran, in November 1974, to end his close collaboration with Pretoria and to join in applying sustained economic pressure on the apartheid regime. The expedition generated some Iranian aid and investment but little in the way of concrete action to interrupt the flow of oil.[15] The reaction of Arab producers has been similar. Until 1973, they simply ignored Organization of African Unity (OAU) pleas; since then, there have been endless assurances but little evidence of a serious intent to impose an effective embargo by, for instance, insisting on "end-use" clauses in all their contracts. The costs of oil to South Africa have risen sharply, but supplies continue to filter through without any great difficulty.[16]

Neither the established links with India nor the blossoming friendship with the Arab nouveau riche has succeeded in developing in the Frontline States much of a sense of common destiny with their neighbors in the Indian Ocean community. The only issue to excite any real interest in the region as a whole has been the growing menace of superpower intrusion and competition.[17] FLS objections to the escalating militarization of the region have reflected two fundamental convictions: opposition on principle to the presence of foreign military bases anywhere and an ingrained suspicion of self-serving South African warnings concerning the perceived Soviet naval threat to the cape sea route and the West's vital oil supplies. These sentiments found expression in the Declaration of the Indian Ocean as a Zone of Peace. Initially proposed by Sri Lanka and endorsed by the Third Conference of Non-Aligned Nations in Lusaka in September 1970, it was subsequently adopted by the UN General Assembly in December 1971 and has been routinely reiterated annually ever since.[18]

The provocation that sparked this initiative was Prime Minister Heath's declared intention in 1970 to counter the growing Soviet naval presence in the Indian Ocean by resuming arms sales to South Africa. The focus of African outrage, therefore, was more the arming of Africa's enemy than defense of the Indian Ocean, though Nyerere did argue that "Tanzania has a great interest in the Indian Ocean." He added, however, that "our interests cannot be served by the arming of South Africa—they are harmed by it."[19]

Throughout much of the 1970s, support for the zone-of-peace project among Frontline States remained largely rhetorical and ritualistic, partly as a result of reluctant recognition that it was probably an unrealizable ideal. More recently, however, there has been a revival of interest in the concept, especially with the emergence of a more militant government in Mauritius and the reference of its claim to Diego Garcia to the United Nations. The presence of a major American base on that island atoll, rather than the even more extensive Soviet facilities in Eritrea, South Yemen, and elsewhere, is the occasion for renewed concern. For this reason, it cannot be expected that the superpowers will receive even-handed treatment as targets of criticism. In assessing responsibility for the mounting militarization of the Indian Ocean basin, the Frontline States clearly perceive the United States to be the principal villain and the greater threat to the security of the region.[20] Yet, despite the increased salience of Indian Ocean issues for FLS decision makers,[21] neither the zone-of-peace proposal in general nor Diego Garcia in particular can hope to compete with the deteriorating southern African situation as a focus of Frontline attention. The Indian Ocean is an occasional diversion; South Africa is a daily obsession.

The South African Colossus

By almost every measure of economic and military capability (except size), the immense disparity between the poverty and weakness of the Frontline States and the wealth and power of their southern neighbor is starkly drawn (see table 14-2). This striking imbalance has largely—though not exclusively—been geographically and historically determined. Yet, what we have here is much more than a classic center-periphery relationship in which an underdeveloped hinterland is economically subordinated to a regional subimperial power; many underdogs in asymmetrical dyads find it uncomfortable "sleeping with an elephant" (to quote a common Canadian analogy). What distinguishes the plight of the Frontline States from most cases of severe dependency is that South Africa is a rogue elephant—a restless and reckless beast as well as ruthless and relentless in pursuit of its perceived national interests. It is scarcely surprising, therefore, that FLS foreign policy makers are consumed with coping with Pretoria's belligerent proclivities and that their preoccupation overshadows all other issues, including relations with the rest of Africa.

Attempting to divine South Africa's precise intentions toward black Africa—assuming Pretoria has clearly defined goals and a well-articulated strategy to achieve them—is far from easy. Apologists for the regime accept at face value South Africa's oft-declared desire to establish good neighborly relations based on noninterference in each other's domestic affairs and close collaboration in the interests of peace and prosperity in the region.[22] Certainly, coexistence rather than conflict would appear

Table 14-2 Frontline States and South Africa: Comparative indicators

	Area (sq. mi.)	Production (1981) U.S.$				Military (1981)	
		Population (1981) (millions)	Total GDP (millions)	GNP per capita	Energy consumption per capita[a] (1980)	Armed forces	Defense budget (U.S.$ m)
South Africa	471,000	29.5	74,670	2,770	3,204	81,400	2,760
Frontline States	1,809,000	53.3	19,240	420	c.290	178,700	c.1,700
Tanzania	362,000	19.1	4,350	280	69	40,350	180
Mozambique	303,000	12.5	c.2,360	c.230	103	21,600	192
Zimbabwe	150,000	7.2	6,010	870	778	63,000	555
Zambia	291,000	5.8	3,430	600	733	14,300	617
Angola	481,000	7.8	c.2,500	c.470	255	37,500	—
Botswana	222,000	0.9	590	1,010	—	2,000	22
Ratios (FLS : SA)	1 : 0.26	1 : 0.6	1 : 3.9	1 : 6.5	1 : 11.1	1 : 0.5	1 : 1.6

Sources: World Bank, *World Development Report*, 1983; International Institute of Strategic Studies, *The Military Balance, 1982–1983.*
[a] Kilograms of coal equivalent.

to be very much in Pretoria's economic as well as security interests. In practice, however, its actions have belied its soothing assurances. In its paranoia at the presence, however insignificant, of political exiles in neighboring states and its perception of the hand of Moscow behind every nationalist, the South African government has resorted to a variety of overt and covert preemptive measures to eliminate the alleged threats. Not satisfied with attacking African National Congress (ANC) and Pan-Africanist Conference (PAC) targets, Pretoria has demonstrated an increasing propensity to indulge in swift retributive action against the host states themselves, with the express intention of deterring them from according the "terrorists" continued support.[23] The scale of exemplary punishment administered, however, has frequently and deliberately exceeded anything the actual threat would justify. The South Africa government appears incapable of resisting the temptation to take advantage of its undoubted economic leverage and military superiority to create trouble and to dominate its dependent neighbors. This would explain its evident determination to destabilize, if not destroy, virtually every regime on its border. Certainly, the perception of the FLS target states is that Pretoria will never be content with coexistence among equals. Since its black neighbors are unwilling to resign themselves to subordinate status, they must be compelled to submit.

The spectrum of measures South Africa has employed to enforce its hegemony over the region has ranged from "final warnings" and economic sanctions to systematic subversion and direct military intervention. Outright territorial occupation (except in Namibia and certain border areas in Angola) appears not to have been contemplated. Although the South Africa Defence Force (SADF) is undoubtedly capable of overrunning any neighboring state, physical control is not deemed necessary and could prove counterproductive in terms of international opinion. Certainly, there is no evidence that this is an option that the Frontline States particularly fear. None of Zimbabwe's five army brigades, for instance, is deployed along the Limpopo facing South Africa, though in 1982, following an "unauthorized" South African raid, border patrols were instituted. The same cannot be said of assassination as a political weapon. As with the Portuguese and Rhodesians earlier, the use of parcel bombs to remove opponents is now an established practice with the South African security services. In recent years, ANC officials in Botswana, Mozambique, and Zambia have all fallen victim to skillfully concealed devices.[24]

More commonly, South African power has been asserted through direct military action. This has been demonstrated with devastating effect, most notably in Angola but also in other Frontline States. Only

Tanzania has escaped South Africa's wrath. Since 1971, South African garrisons in the Caprivi Strip have repeatedly launched "retaliatory" raids against alleged South West African People's Organization (SWAPO) bases in Zambia's exposed western province. On occasion, mechanized units have roamed more or less at will through vast stretches of Zambian territory, terrorizing villages and wreaking destruction indiscriminately.[25] In Mozambique in January 1981, a daring commando operation destroyed three ANC residences in Matola on the outskirts of Maputo;[26] in May 1983 it was savagely attacked from the air. Even Botswana, despite its obvious helplessness, has been a target of military attention; in April 1981, President Masire went so far as to accuse Pretoria of trying to turn his country into "another Lebanon."[27] In July 1982, a quarter of the aircraft in the Zimbabwe air force was destroyed at the Gweru air base in what was almost certainly the work of South African agents; in August, three whites in a South African army patrol were killed in an ambush inside Zimbabwe in the course of what the head of the SADF claimed, without much conviction, was an "unauthorized raid."[28]

Cross-border incursions into southern Angola have been a regular and increasingly menacing feature of South Africa's counterinsurgency strategy. What began ostensibly as "hot pursuit" raids (which, however understandable, are nevertheless illegal) have escalated dangerously into a pattern of almost continuous "reprisals" by ground and air forces combined with periodic full-scale invasions involving ever larger and more heavily equipped units striking into the interior more boldly and more deeply for more extended periods of time, inflicting more severe damage and casualties. In July 1982, for instance, a sizable South African armored column with ample air support penetrated more than 150 miles from the border in a major search-and-destroy mission; it lasted several weeks and claimed hundreds of lives.[29] Initially, attacks were confined to assumed SWAPO bases but, increasingly, local Movimento Popular de Libertação de Angola (MPLA) forces, Cuban troops, and ordinary villagers unfortunate enough to be caught in the path of the intruders have come to be regarded as legitimate targets since their mere presence is considered a constraint on South African freedom of action. In practice, any attempt to discriminate between guerrillas and refugees or between Namibians and Angolans has been abandoned. Moreover, the timing of the attacks reveals a further transparent South African motive. As the *Economist* commented, following the July 1982 assault, "For the umpteenth time South Africa has launched a major military operation into southern Angola just when the Namibia negotiations have reached a sensitive stage."[30]

It is now abundantly clear that South Africa's objectives are political as well as military. It is pursuing a calculated policy deliberately designed to subvert and destabilize—if not actually to overthrow—FLS governments. The intention is evidently to keep the pressure and publicity off its troubles at home by diverting attention to the supposed unpopularity and instability of ruling parties in neighboring states. Pretoria's purposes are most obvious in the case of the Marxist-oriented regimes in Angola and Mozambique, but are also evident with respect to the popularly elected governments in Harare, Lusaka, and Gaborone. Although South African–engineered coup attempts (such as the botched effort in the Seychelles), with or without reliance on mercenaries, cannot be ruled out,[31] Pretoria's preferred technique has been to instigate the emergence, or exploit the presence, of disaffected elements within the target states. This strategy has been employed with alarming consistency and some measure of success through support for União Nacional para a Independência Total de Angola (UNITA), the Mozambique National Resistance (MNR),[32] former Muzorewa auxiliaries (and possibly former Zimbabwe People's Revolutionary Army [ZIPRA] cadres) and unreconciled whites in Zimbabwe, and the Mushala gang and assorted dissidents in Zambia.[33] The MNR has been particularly effective in sabotaging strategic targets, notably roads, railways, bridges, ports, power lines, and the oil pipeline.[34]

South Africa's destabilization campaign in neighboring states has had an important economic dimension in addition to its political and military manifestations. The legacy of dependence that Botswana, Zambia, and Zimbabwe have inherited, coupled with their continued underdevelopment and landlocked geographical condition, have left them as well as Mozambique highly vulnerable to South African economic pressure (see table 14-3). Pretoria is fully aware of the political opportunities for exercising influence that its immense economic leverage offers. Certainly, it has had no scruples in seeking—admittedly not always successfully—to exploit its dominant position of power to maintain and extend its hegemony over the subcontinent and, in particular, to promote its dream of a southern African constellation of states with South Africa at its center.[35] The principal economic instruments available to Pretoria to constrain and coerce the black states on its borders have been its control of their access to ocean ports; the threat to withhold essential imports, especially emergency food supplies; curtailed recruitment of migrant labor for the south; and manipulation of industrial and commercial policies through investment and management practices.

Perhaps the most effective, and certainly the most subtle and frequently employed lever of power in South Africa's armory, at least with respect to the three landlocked Frontline States, is its stranglehold over

Table 14-3 Indicators of Frontline States' economic cooperation with South Africa

Frontline States	Trade with SA (1980)		Trade and transit traffic		Labor migration (1981)	Air service with SA (flights/week) (1982)	Major SA investments and interests
	% imports from SA	% exports to SA	% imports from and through SA	% exports to and through SA			
Botswana	89	15	94	93	29,200	32	copper, nickel, diamonds
Zimbabwe	25	22	78	46	17,000	49	mining, finance, manufacturing, farming (23%)
Zambia	28	4	50	30	1,700	10	copper
Mozambique	14	3	20[a]	20[a]	59,400	4	construction
Angola	11	2	0	0	70	0	diamonds
Tanzania	—		0	0	0	0	diamonds

Sources: A variety of sources have been used, not all of which are completely comparable or necessarily reliable.

[a] Estimated percentage of Mozambique's imports/exports in transit to/from South Africa.

their major rail outlets to the sea. Currently, between 40 and 90 percent of their trade passes through South Africa's road, rail, and port systems. Until reliable alternative routes with adequate capacity become available, this vulnerability to pressure by Pretoria will persist. At the time of this writing, the Benguela railway west to Lobito was still out of commission, the Tanzania-Zambia railway (TAZARA) northeast to Dar es Salaam was operating at only a third of planned capacity,[36] and the rail lines southeast through Mozambique to Beira and Maputo were only beginning to recover from years of war and neglect. Even if these rail routes were fully restored, there would still be the problem of congestion at the terminal ports as a consequence of inefficient management and limited capacity.

It is in Pretoria's interest to perpetuate this unhappy state of affairs as long as possible. Accordingly, it has pursued a two-pronged policy of dangling the carrot and wielding the stick. Through the skillful exercise of "transport diplomacy,"[37] it has sought to drive home to the hinterland states both their critical dependence on South African goodwill and the benefits to be derived from cooperation rather than confrontation. At the same time, the practice of assisting other railways in the region through the loan of locomotives, railway trucks, and other equipment, as well as technical and operational personnel, gives Pretoria—in the power to withdraw support at will—an additional weapon against states that incur its displeasure. This power has, in fact, been exercised, most blatantly in Zimbabwe in mid-1981, with devastating consequences for its economy.[38] Even more damaging has been the sustained campaign of economic sabotage that South Africa has conducted with a view to ensuring that competing routes are incapable of successfully challenging its dominance of the southern African transport network. Central to this strategy of denial has been the role of the internal dissidents in each country. UNITA has frustrated efforts to reopen the Benguela railway to international traffic, while the MNR regularly disrupts Mozambique's rail links with Zimbabwe and Malawi, systematically crippling Beira as a port and thereby deterring customers from diverting business to this route.[39] The scope for South African trouble making through sanctions and subversion appears almost unlimited.

The situation Mozambique has faced is somewhat different in that its economic survival is closely tied to the use that inland states, notably South Africa, continue to make of its ports and railways. For the present, South Africa's service is reasonably assured. Although the Mozambique Convention of 1909, which guaranteed Maputo nearly half the overseas traffic of the Witwatersrand, lapsed in 1977, the rail outlet through Maputo is still the most economical route for much of South

Africa's foreign trade. On the other hand, with the development of Richard's Bay in Natal, Pretoria is now in a position to divert at least its bulk cargo to its own port when other forms of pressure on Mozambique prove inadequate.[40]

A second major instrument for the perpetuation of South Africa's hegemony over its hinterland is trade. All the Frontline States maintain commercial relations with Pretoria, directly or indirectly. Moreover, the volume of goods exchanged is seemingly increasing, as is the balance in favor of South Africa. Ties of dependency are particularly strong in the case of Botswana, Zambia, and Zimbabwe, with their heavy reliance on mining equipment and spares. Also, Botswana is a member of the South Africa–dominated Southern African Customs Union, while Zimbabwe has, with obvious relief, succeeded in renewing its preferential trade agreement with Pretoria.[41]

Among South Africa's exports, the most politically strategic is food. Since the late 1970s the opportunities to exploit this "ultimate bargaining lever" have increased sharply with the recurring severe droughts in neighboring countries, the exodus of commercial (white) farmers, and the absence of adequate incentives for peasant producers.[42] The greater the food deficits in the Frontline States, the greater their degree of dependence on South Africa's emergency food reserves. Botswana, Mozambique, and Zambia have at times all felt compelled, albeit reluctantly, to turn in desperation to Pretoria for urgently needed supplies of maize, the staple diet of the urban masses. Although efforts have been made to tap surplus supplies in Zimbabwe and from overseas sources, South Africa continues to enjoy a competitive advantage with respect to price, credit terms, transportation costs and capacity, and delivery time, and continues to exploit these to the full.

Since early this century, the Frontline States have served as labor reserves for South African mines and farms, and Mozambique, Botswana, and, to a limited extent, Zimbabwe still do. This influx of cheap labor has contributed enormously to white prosperity. In recent years, however, South Africa has shifted its focus of recruitment to the bantustans, and has even expelled some foreign, mainly Zimbabwean labor.[43] This has had a significant adverse impact on employment and incomes in the states affected, in addition to cutting into their tax revenues and foreign exchange earnings from migrants' remittances. Similarly, South Africa has succeeded in reducing its reliance on Cahora Bassa power from 10 percent of national consumption to 7 percent.[44]

Thus, as with its patronage of Maputo port and its recruitment of foreign migrant workers, so in the case of electricity supplies, South Africa has sent the Frontline States and especially Botswana, Mozambique, and Zimbabwe an unmistakable signal reminding them that their need for South Africa is greater than its need for them. Pretoria has also served notice that it is not only quite capable of dispensing with their services but fully prepared to do so should they fail to cooperate. In this sense, therefore, South Africa's immediate neighbors, through no action of their own, find themselves becoming more vulnerable than ever to reprisals as the constraints on Pretoria's retributive instincts are eased. At the same time, a renewed awareness among the Frontline States of their disadvantaged position has kindled a fresh determination to secure greater control, individually and collectively, over their own destinies.

Frontline States' Response

Despite much rhetoric to the contrary, the South African government has found it difficult to accept the emergence of independently minded black states on its borders as equals. Quite apart from its obvious economic interest in maintaining its subimperial domination of the subcontinent, Pretoria is preoccupied to the point of paranoia with the perceived security and ideological threat the presence of nationalist neighbors poses. The Frontline States, for their part, are convinced of South Africa's implacable hostility and have shaped their actions accordingly.

Four broad policy choices have been open to them: accommodation, containment, disengagement, and confrontation.[45] Accommodation would signify acquiescence—however reluctantly—in South African hegemony and the adaptation of domestic and foreign policies to conform to the constraints imposed by subordination to a hostile environment. Containment would imply resistance to further South African encroachments on the autonomy of the Frontline States but acceptance of the realities of the existing dependent relationships, at least for the present. Disengagement would connote a rejection of dependency and would require determined efforts to overcome it through a systematic reduction in the scope and intensity of positive interactions with South Africa.[46] Finally, confrontation (or intervention) would involve a direct challenge to the apartheid regime with a view to its ultimate overthrow.

These policy choices are not necessarily mutually exclusive. The different political, military, and economic dimensions of the evolving relationship could evoke different responses. In practice, this is what has happened (table 14-4). Despite the common public stance of defiance adopted by the Frontline States, their actual behavior has reflected elements of each of these four alternatives. The precise form in which policy has been expressed in individual cases has varied with the issue, the country's capabilities and vulnerability to reprisals, its prior experiences,

Table 14-4 Frontline State responses to South African policies

Options and actions	Functional Dimensions of Relationship			External intervention
	Political	Military	Economic	
Accommodation		SA covert penetration of defense forces (M, Zi)	Preferential trade agreements (B, Zi) Food imports Trade promotion office (Zi) Proposed rail line (B) Comprador class interests	Military advisers (all) Cuban troops (A) Western diplomatic support (A, B, Za, Zi) Tanzanian troops (M) UN Security Council Rapprochement with Portugal (A, M)
Containment	Rhetorical defiance FLS meetings	Increased defense capabilities (all) Defense agreements (M-T, M-Zi) Counterinsurgency Restrictions on liberation movements (B, M, Za, Zi)	Railway agreements (B, M, Za, Zi) Air service agreements (B, M, Za, Zi) Migrant labor (B, M) Tourism encouraged (B, Zi) Nonparticipation in sanctions	
Disengagement	SADCC (all) Rejection of SA constellation of states (B, Za, Zi)		Nationalization (Za, Zi) Collective self-reliance (all)	World Bank, African Development Bank, Western aid agencies

Options and actions	Functional Dimensions of Relationship			
	Political	Military	Economic	External intervention
	Rejection of ministerial contacts (Zi) Diplomatic break (Zi)		Mozambique rail route (M, Za, Zi) Telecommunications Beira oil pipeline (M, Zi) WENELA expelled (Za, Zi) Sports contacts cut (Za, Zi)	
Confrontation	Rhetoric at OAU, UN External broadcasting (A, M, T, Za, Zi) ANC headquarters (Za) ANC offices (A, B, M, T) SWAPO headquarters (A) SWAPO offices (T, Za) Kaunda-Botha meeting Nonracialism (B, Za, Zi)	OAU Liberation Committee: contributions membership (A, M, T, Za, Zi) Training facilities (A, T) Transit rights (A, M, Za)	Call for UN sanctions	Arms procurements Humanitarian assistance OAU, UN, Commonwealth Western contact groups

Note: A = Angola, B = Botswana, M = Mozambique, T = Tanzania, Za = Zambia, Zi = Zimbabwe.

the courage and character of its leadership, and the extent and reliability of external support.

Accommodation is an option that every FLS government would hotly repudiate and fiercely resist as being totally unacceptable ideologically. On the other hand, academic critics have been quick to assume the inevitability of collusion between the bourgeois governing elites and their comprador business associates, especially in Botswana, Zambia, and Zimbabwe, and their class allies in South Africa. Yet, even if this facile assumption is discounted, it is possible to envisage circumstances when a state in extremis would be compelled to turn to Pretoria simply to survive. Such was the situation in October 1978 when Zambia reopened its border to Rhodesia to permit the importation of urgently needed fertilizer through South Africa. A similar compulsion has led Botswana, Mozambique, and Zambia, when afflicted with severe drought and unable to acquire adequate supplies elsewhere, to purchase South African maize. Even President Nyerere has conceded that he would act no differently if this were the only way to save his people from starvation. Less defensible on grounds of dire necessity perhaps has been the retention of inherited preferential trading arrangements. While Botswana took the dramatic step of breaking with the Rand Monetary Union in 1976, it has shown no disposition to abandon its membership in the Southern African Customs Union. Similarly, the Zimbabwe government heaved a sigh of relief when Pretoria withdrew its politically inspired notice of termination of the 1964 trade agreement between the two countries. Harare is, in fact, actively promoting trade with South Africa and, for this and other purposes, maintains an office in Johannesburg.

The distinction between economic necessity that might justify a temporary retreat into accommodation and realism as an excuse for refusing to challenge the status quo is not easy to draw but would seem to turn on the price a people can reasonably be expected to pay for their principles. The same issue arises in assessing the element of pragmatism associated with a policy of containment. The successful negotiation of air, railway, labor, and tourist agreements with Pretoria, although not absolutely vital to national survival, have all arguably been to the net benefit of the four Frontline States concerned—Botswana, Mozambique, Zambia, and Zimbabwe—and therefore worthwhile. The policy stance of these same states in loudly demanding that others impose comprehensive mandatory sanctions on South Africa, while announcing in advance their intention to opt out on the ground that the sacrifice required would be too great, is also understandable, if not particularly heroic.

If one side of the coin of containment has been economic coexistence, the other is resistance to military intimidation. All the Front-line States have reacted to Pretoria's mounting military adventurism by sharply increasing their defense capabilities. As a result, all of them have been burdened with heavy costs that can only be met by diverting scarce resources from urgent development needs (as South Africa no doubt intended) without, however, enabling them to match the South African Defence Force quantitatively or qualitatively. Much of the armament, equipment, and training acquired (except in the case of Botswana and Zimbabwe) has come from Soviet and East European sources,[47] though recently there has been some evidence of growing disillusionment with the excessive costs and inferior quality of much communist military assistance. Mozambique is turning increasingly to Portugal and, to some extent, France for support,[48] while Zimbabwe appears to have had second thoughts about the North Koreans.[49]

Among the Frontline States, Mozambique has forged military alliances with Tanzania and Zimbabwe, both of which have contributed troops to the war against the South African–backed MNR.[50] To supplement this bilateral collaboration, the FLS summit in March 1982 resolved "to reinforce their coordinated action of defence in order to *stop* the racist regime of Pretoria from continuing its acts of military aggression and economic sabotage against the free and independent states of the region and *force* it to withdraw its occupying forces from the People's Republic of Angola."[51] In addition, several of the Frontline States have sought and received Western diplomatic support to deter South African aggression. In May 1981, Prime Minister Mugabe appealed to President Reagan to intercede with Pretoria to cease and desist in its "bully-boy tactics." (Western intervention was apparently also instrumental in South Africa's decision to extend its trade agreement with Zimbabwe.)[52]

A strategy of disengagement from South Africa has proved politically highly appealing and has occasioned considerable symbolic support. Zimbabwe, for instance, has insisted on maintaining a sharp (and, for Marxists, a curious) distinction between ministerial contacts with Pretoria (which it rejects) and meetings of officials (which are acceptable). "Our view," Robert Mugabe declared in June 1981, "is that we should restrict our hostilities to what is political. We hope that South Africa will also recognize that we have left an area where relations can be harmonious—that is, the economic and trade area."[53]

The most convincing evidence of a commitment to disengagement is the energy and enthusiasm that the Frontline States (plus Lesotho, Malawi, and Swaziland) have, since the independence of Zimbabwe in

1980, devoted to ensuring the success of the SADCC.[54] Although its objectives also include development and regional cooperation, economic liberation remains a central concern of its members as well as being viewed as a prerequisite for the achievement of its other purposes. The major focus of attention in its early years has been the upgrading and restructuring of the southern African transport and communications network. Priority has been accorded to developing alternative railway routes that bypass South Africa and to constructing direct communication links between members. From a disengagement perspective, the most significant project to date has been the reopening of the Beira-Feruka pipeline in July 1982, thus offering the prospect—if MNR sabotage can be contained—of freeing Zimbabwe almost completely from dependency on oil imported through South Africa. Equally encouraging as evidence of SADCC's viability is the financial support it has attracted from Western aid agencies, especially from the European Economic Community (EEC).

Continuing economic dependence on South Africa has served as a major constraint on the ability and willingness of potential FLS host states to involve themselves wholeheartedly in the armed struggle inside South Africa (as opposed to Namibia). Whether, once economic independence becomes more of a reality, they will feel able to commit themselves more completely and confidently to the liberation struggle (as Zambia and Mozambique did during the war in Zimbabwe) or whether they will take advantage of their newfound freedom to turn their backs on Pretoria is still uncertain. For the present, all the Frontline States accord the liberation movements full political and moral support, in addition to financial assistance through the OAU Liberation Committee. Moreover, since March 1982, the ANC leader, Oliver Tambo, has joined SWAPO's Sam Nujoma as a full member at FLS summits.

Beyond these cautious gestures, the risks entailed in more substantial support have been carefully calculated. The most prudent and exposed of the Frontline States has been Zimbabwe. In his public pronouncements and private assurances, Mugabe has been emphatic in categorically denying any intention to host or otherwise help South African guerrillas,[55] or even to permit them an official presence in Harare.[56] There has also been a tendency to deprecate the inactivity and lack of commitment of globe-trotting ANC and PAC freedom fighters.[57] On the other hand, the most intrepid state in defying South African vengeance is Angola. It not only offers hospitality to SWAPO and ANC political leaders, but permits them to maintain training facilities for their cadres and operational bases for their guerrilla incursions into Namibia.

The price it has paid for its temerity has been high. In addition to the widespread destruction and loss of life it has sustained, it has had to put up with the unpopularity of the 20–30,000 Cuban troops retained in the country.

Future Prospects

The conclusions to which this study point are, first, that the Frontline States see their futures firmly tied to the fortunes of South Africa, however much they may attempt to disengage, rather than to the course of events across the broad expanse of the Indian Ocean. Second, only Tanzania, itself a somewhat marginal Frontline State, has evinced any significant interest in Indian Ocean concerns and then principally in developments in the offshore African islands. For the others, what limited interest they have demonstrated has largely come about as a reaction to the skillfully orchestrated campaign Pretoria has conducted to heighten Western awareness of the alleged Soviet menace to the east coast sea lanes and to win acceptance of South Africa as an indispensable ally in their defense. Pretoria's transparently self-serving motives have only served to reinforce FLS fears that Western actions to shore up their Indian Ocean defenses are, consciously or unconsciously, a case of playing Pretoria's game. Consequently, objective assessments of the significance of the growing Soviet presence in the theater tends to be dismissed or disregarded. Third, with the emergence of a number of radical regimes in the offshore islands with shared interests in promoting their political ideologies and pressing their territorial claims in every conceivable international forum,[58] the Frontline States may not find it as easy to continue to ignore Indian Ocean issues to the same extent as in the past. Nevertheless, finally, southern African developments will continue to have a greater effect on the states on the Indian Ocean littoral than vice versa.

If, then, the course of events in South Africa is likely to be decisive in determining developments in neighboring states to the north, what kind of future can we envisage for that unhappy country? Three broad possibilities present themselves: a peaceful transfer of power, a violent seizure of power, and a protracted confrontation ending in a military stalemate. A fourth prospect—the retention of the status quo in some recognizable form—can safely be dismissed as fantasy.

A peaceful resolution of the conflict would be the most attractive outcome for a majority, if not all, Frontline States. Since 1969, they have been committed, under the Lusaka Manifesto,[59] to just such a settlement. Moreover, they would probably be prepared to accept something short of full majority rule, at least initially, provided a formula for meaningful power sharing could be devised. The chances of reason and common sense prevailing are, however, so remote that a negotiated solution seems a utopian hope.

A more probable, if less appealing, prospect is the steadily escalating violence long predicted by Kaunda and other FLS leaders. In this scenario, an ever-widening circle of states within southern Africa and possibly beyond would inexorably be drawn more deeply into the conflict whether they wished to be or not. The bitter clash would culminate ultimately in the forcible overthrow of the white regime, with heavy loss of life and widespread destruction to the economic infrastructure. Such a cataclysmic victory might delight revolutionaries who would not be content with merely capturing the commanding heights of the capitalist economy but would insist on pulling down the pillars of the temple as well in order to make a fresh start. However, this vision is unlikely to engender much enthusiasm within the Frontline States or, more especially perhaps, in Mozambique and Angola which have experienced a taste of it. Inheriting a barren battlefield is not the outcome the Frontline States would welcome.

Finally, it is conceivable that there might be no real end to the conflict. Various reforms might be proffered and concessions granted, but these would prove piecemeal, tardy, and totally inadequate—however radical they might appear to the ruling minority. At most, they could be expected to stimulate fresh demands without satisfying existing ones. Meanwhile, urban guerrilla activity would intensify and spread, achieving notable triumphs without quite succeeding in delivering a decisive blow to the embattled white regime. Moreover, the more protracted the struggle, the greater the likelihood of its being internationalized, with no assurance that the great powers would not intervene on opposing sides. In the meantime, opinions within South Africa would become hopelessly polarized along racial lines.

Which of these alternative scenarios will approximate the shape of the South Africa of the future will largely depend on domestic developments within that country, rather than on the interests or inclinations of the Frontline States. However, the state of their economies and the degree of stability of their governments could exercise some influence on the course of events. The one prediction that can confidently be made is that the almost total absorption of the Frontline States with the unfolding tragedy on their doorstep will continue and, if anything, deepen. Under the circumstances, Indian Ocean concerns will remain a luxury.

15. Beyond Limpopo and Zambesi: South Africa's Strategic Horizons ◢ James M. Roherty

Although it has been in power since late 1978, it is still risky to draw any but the most tentative conclusions about Pieter W. Botha's government and the future course of the Republic of South Africa (RSA). Certainly, in the early years this proved to be a perilous exercise. That Botha, at the outset, should have formally committed his government to a "total, national strategy" is not surprising, however. The undertaking, involving public and private sector alike, is nothing less than the marshaling of all national assets in support of a sweeping agenda of survival. Such an explicit resort to "strategy" to serve high national purposes comes easily to a former defense minister and a *verligte* (reformist) *Afrikaner*. Pragmatism and astute management are established benchmarks of his career and, indeed, of the greater part of the new nationalists who now lead South Africa. Equally important in the context of this chapter is the reality that part of the psychic makeup of the *Afrikaner* and, most assuredly, of Botha is the far horizon, "vision," the long trek. The passage that the prime minister would steer for South Africa must avoid dangerous shoals but it is a passage to a definite, though distant, destination. The great undertaking, in a word, is strategic in character, not tactical.

This chapter examines an emerging school of strategy in South Africa (the contemporary school), an enterprise committed to placing the republic in leadership positions both with respect to the continent of Africa and to the southern hemisphere. The appearance of this school has received little attention from the press or scholarly community, largely because they have been preoccupied with the nation's domestic agenda. Here the purpose is to outline the major themes of an approach that could have an important bearing on the future of both South Africa and the United States, which figures so prominently in the thinking of the school.

The Contemporary School

To think strategically about South Africa in the late twentieth century is to discover that "distance" continues in its traditional, commanding role. Today, the strategic mind set of South Africans is one of distant horizons. It is quite simply a mistake, in this context, to speak of a "*laager* (fortress) mentality"; this is to confuse cultural defense of the *volk* ("white tribe") with politico-military imperatives of the state.

Even more mistaken is the contention that the politico-military thrust of the current administration in Pretoria is toward a "Fortress South Africa."[1] *Afrikaner* nationalist leaders stridently opposed the "wider Africa" impetus of Jan Christian Smuts throughout the distinguished career that ended only with his death in 1950. Yet, three decades later, a new generation of nationalists has made the distant perspectives of the renegade Boer their own. Indeed, it is not too fanciful to suggest that the contemporary school takes as its point of departure a hypothesis from Smuts, namely, that the republic is located at the center of an east-west axis.[2] From this perspective the school takes account not only of a wider Africa but of the whole southern hemisphere.

The new nationalists

Prime Minister Botha first publicly outlined his total national strategy before the National Party Congress in Durban on 15 August 1979. Although the prime minister's "vision" contained a number of elements not germane to the present discussion,[3] the speech as a whole consisted of principles to guide policy formation. It was strategic rather than programmatic discourse and included the following elements of a total national strategy: a "new commitment" to the defense of South Africa, emphasis on the "paramount importance" of a sharper delineation of RSA interests, more effective decision making based on a strong defense force, maintenance of the free enterprise system with an enlarged role for the private sector in national strategy, and movement toward "a constellation of southern African states."

In the years since the Durban Principles were articulated there has been ample evidence (which is not to say that it has been grasped in all quarters) that the new commitment to the defense of South Africa is keyed to the rising cacophony of East-West confrontation in the region and that allusions to neutralism in the speech (much qualified since) represented little more than pique with President Carter's African policies.[4] Without doubt the change of administration in Washington has brought the central theme of the new strategy to the surface more rapidly than otherwise might have been the case. Today, American-Soviet rivalry in the southern hemisphere is the centerpiece of RSA strategic thinking. Denial of continental lodging to the Soviet Union (especially along the western littoral of the Indian Ocean) is fundamental to the long-term security interests of the republic. The strategies being fashioned by the contemporary school to cope with this problem consist of factors both old and new. The constant factor is the indispensable requirement for a major, noncontinental partner, a role heretofore played by Great Britain. Since Harold Wilson's preemptive abrogation (as it was viewed in Pretoria) of the Simonstown Agreement in 1975, the highest priority task has been to fill this role with a new player. Alignment with the United States is the cardinal thread in the new strategic design and the animating thrust of the contemporary school.

Botha has sought to engage a wider community in the national strategy enterprise than any of his predecessors. In its broadest terms this departure rests on a critical assumption, namely, that the "Boer-Brit" fissure that ran through the Smuts era and beyond is no longer the dominating political fact of life in South Africa. While the gap is by no means closed, the significant entry of the Boer into the urban-business life of the nation and the increasing propensity of South Africans of British origin to join with ethnic nationalist Boers in an overarching "South Africanism" provides the basis for a politics of national survival. If anything, the prime minister has found the Anglo-Boer business community an impatient ally not wholly sensitive to the political milieu in which he must function. Nonetheless, he draws heavily on this "progressive" force for advice and essential managerial talent.[5] Always comfortable with the predominantly *Afrikaner* South African Defence Force (SADF) he is disposed to have the triumvirate of generals, Magnus Malan (Minister of Defense), Constand Viljoen (SADF Chief), and Jan Geldenhuys (Senior Army Command Officer) play leading roles in national strategy. The involvement of " 'Pik' Botha's people" (R. F. Botha, foreign minister) in close coordination with the Ministry of Defense is a key objective in a major restructuring of executive offices. A reorganized State Security Council is at the apex of this structure. The changes have turned the Policy Planning Section in the Foreign Ministry (modeled on American and Federal Republic of Germany counterparts) into a valued assignment for young careerists, while the renovated National Intelligence Service (NIS) has a professional aspect under Lukas Barnard that compares favorably with that of the former Bureau of State Security (BOSS) and the *grise eminence* of General Hendrik "Lang" van den Bergh.

The most striking aspect of the prime minister's project has been his recourse to the South African academic community. Prior to his term the relationship between this community and the government was cool and minimal in extent. In the first years of this decade, however, there has been a notable degree of interaction between scholars (social scientists, physical scientists, and engineers) and government officials (both political and bureaucratic). The beginnings of a movement of former government officials to universities and institutes is evident, as well as the (more prevalent) enlistment of academics into government positions.[6] In recent years the growth of a culture along government-university-industrial axes has been indicative of a sufficiently cohesive body of thought that it has come to be called the contemporary school. Diverse rather than monolithic, but altogether South African, the school may prove to be the prime minister's most potent weapon not least because it has directed its gaze, the constraints of the domestic agenda notwithstanding, toward continental and hemispheric horizons.

A Continental Strategy

The "Colonial Struggle"

Since the establishment of the republic "terrorism in southern Africa" and, more recently, the mounting possibility of "internal war" have been focal points of attention for RSA defense planners.[7] The consistently vigorous response to these phenomena on the part of Pretoria has led some observers (mistakenly, in this writer's view) to conclude that RSA strategic horizons did not extend beyond the well-executed campaigns of the SADF. In South Africa, terrorism, whether emanating from external sanctuaries or from within, has never been seen as autonomous. On the contrary, it has always been viewed as integral to the prime security problem posed by Soviet activities on the continent. From the outset, the terrorist phenomenon has had all the aspects of a classic colonial struggle that the Soviets, in turn, have sought to exploit. However, this has not at any stage involved the prospect of large-scale, conventional attacks from across the northern borders of the republic. Today, in Pretoria, there is growing confidence that the military phase of this struggle is nearing a successful conclusion. To put the matter more succinctly, success no longer turns on the military prowess of SADF—if this were the case, the issue would be resolved—but on whether RSA strategists, and SADF in particular, can now make the necessary adjustments to cope with the critical, political phase of the struggle.

Probably the most proficient counterinsurgency force in the world, SADF has undertaken to instruct itself more thoroughly in the political elements of this problem than have most military establishments. At the center of an intensive educational effort is the aforementioned triumvirate, but principally Minister of Defense Magnus Malan, who has had a long and close relationship with the prime minister. The relationship is such that General Malan has considerable latitude to articulate the thinking of the government as to how it will cope with terrorism in all of its facets. Botha clearly takes the view that the strategic acumen of his defense minister is a trump card in this struggle.[8] Geldenhuys, as chief of Southwest Command, prosecuted counterinsurgency warfare against the largely Ovambo South West African People's Organization (SWAPO) with startling effectiveness in an operational area that extended from Windhoek to Luanda. Malan and Geldenhuys complement each other to an extraordinary degree; their direction of the impending political phase of the counterterrorist campaign must be rated as having unique possibilities for success. Malan has emphasized the essentially political character of "internal war"; the military aspects—for which SADF is in a high state of readiness—are secondary, even minor. Although the counterinsurgency campaign had a predominantly military phase at the outset it has now passed and armed combat is to be avoided in all but the most extreme circumstances. The challenge confronting SADF today, in Malan's view, is to evolve a creative role for the army in the concluding and decisive phase of the struggle. Malan's attachment to the French colonial school, especially the Gallieni-Lyautey concept of the army as an instrument of enlightened, politico-social development, is striking.[9] It is equally noteworthy that SADF finds little, if anything, in either the French or the American experience in Indochina to draw upon in their new politico-military campaign.

The transition from military to political phases coincides with military success in the border marches and subtle, but growing, indications of improving relationships with the Frontline States. At the top of the political agenda is the pressing requirement for a satisfactory settlement of "the southwest question." The effort to establish an independent Namibia offers a clear instance of Pretoria aligning its strategy with new American initiatives in the region. The strong supposition now is that a solution will be fashioned out of the workings of the Western Contact Group whose influence over the ultimate disposition of the question has risen markedly since the election of President Reagan. The essential strategic requisite that a new state across the Orange River not constitute a threat could possibly be met. This depends crucially upon what will lie beyond the Cuenene River (the significant "Atlantic extension of the veldt") and that, Pretoria makes plain, is largely up to Washington. If not explicitly on cue from the latter, then on an interpretation of American signals, the prime minister has made withdrawal of Cuban forces from Angola a precondition of any Namibian settlement.[10] Pretoria and Washington now agree that Namibia is more than an internal political issue for South Africa; it is a factor in the broader strategies of both. As emissary for President Reagan, General Vernon Walters has visited both Havana and Luanda for a review of a wide range of topics. These talks, in turn, have led to face-to-face meetings between Angola and South Africa. It is evident that Washington will be able to exert more leverage (both "carrot" and "stick") on Luanda at this juncture than can Pretoria. Against a background of growing American involvement with the Frontline States, South Africa is prepared to indulge a Namibian constitutional arrangement that may well vest SWAPO with the responsibilities of governing. At the same time, however, the challenges faced by a new government in Windhoek are expected to offer South Africa opportunities for political and economic collaboration (e.g., the water dispersion scheme in Ovamboland and technical training schools) that are at the heart of its emerging continental strategy.

The Frontline States

A self-professed Frontline State and claimant to ideological leadership of the liberation movement in Africa, Tanzania possesses a strategic significance for South Africa out of all proportion to its basic resources. As M. R. Sinclair of the contemporary school has argued, this is largely explained by Pretoria's perception of Tanzania. According to Sinclair, "The primary origin of Tanzania's political influence is its political strategic location on the African continent. . . . Tanzania is the most suitably located African state in relation to the southern African region." Strategic location permits Tanzania to exploit a second factor, namely, "the exceptional political influence which President Nyerere wields among fellow African leaders."[11] Taken together the two factors are significant in the minds of RSA strategists. However, in the Pretorian calculus, Tanzania's "control" over its landlocked neighbors (through the major Indian Ocean port of Dar es Salaam) and its placement at the top of the eastern land-sea corridor to the cape are the more enduring realities that will remain after the transient, if exceptional, leadership of Nyerere is gone.

Tanzania's leadership role among Frontline States has not included concrete means to carry on armed struggle or to meet more basic economic needs. Still, its political influence is strong in southern Africa, particularly with Zambia. The basis for this, according to Sinclair, "may be sought in the long-time friendship and intellectual affinity of the presidents of the two states, and the geopolitical relationship between landlocked Zambia and sea-girt Tanzania."[12] While the observation is valid to a point, it must be noted that Nyerere has yet to sit down with a South African prime minister, while Kenneth Kaunda has done so twice (1978 and 1980). This does not suggest so much an imminent break in intellectual affinity between the two presidents as it does the "gravitational power . . . of geographical propinquity" that pulls Zambia toward the Pretorian pole.

One of the most powerful magnets working on Kaunda is the South African Railways and Harbour Corporation (SAR&H). Linked to Zambia via the Rhodesian rail system, the SAR&H draws Zambia's trade to outlets on the sea, south of the Zambesi. This situation will remain as long as alternative routes are unavailable. Of these, the Benguela railway, through Angola to the Atlantic port of Lobito Bay, remains out of commission as a result of political, military, financial, and administrative chaos, while the other possibility, Nyerere's Great Uhuru railway administered by the Tanzania-Zambia Railway Authority (TAZARA), requires new rolling stock if it is ever to be suitable for Zambia's mineral exports.[13] Neither route is likely to become accessible in the immediate future; the Benguela issue is likely to await a settlement in Namibia, while modernization of the TAZARA line may leave unresolved the question of improving port facilities in Dar es Salaam.

Newly independent Zimbabwe finds the Rhodesian rail system a valuable legacy but one that, at the same time, reinforces Pretoria's concept of interdependence in southern Africa. It puts Harare, as well as Lusaka, into the South African net of railways and harbors. Mugabe's dilemma is acutely illustrated by his dual policy of maintaining economic relations with Pretoria while having severed political relations. South Africa remains far in front as Zimbabwe's leading trading partner. RSA strategists, for their part, may find Mugabe's dualism an irritant but, far from wishing to destabilize Zimbabwe, they continue, inter alia, to incorporate the new nation into South African transport services.

Another case in point is the unique relationship between South Africa and Mozambique. Lying in the strategic eastern corridor between the republic and Tanzania, Mozambique is by far the most crucial of contiguous states. Pretoria has not been hesitant to take quite different stances toward two former Portuguese colonies, displaying considerably greater flexibility toward Mozambique than toward Angola. This stems from a number of factors, not the least of which is that such flexibility has been reciprocated by President Machel. A long history of Mozambique labor migrating to the republic (and to Rhodesia/Zimbabwe) is not something either side wishes to disturb to any degree, much less the SAR&H management of the port of Maputo. Under this management Maputo has become the second port in Africa, far exceeding in volume Beira and Nacala. Critical technical help at Maputo, a wide range of imported goods from South Africa, and not least the viability of the Cabora-Basa scheme on the Zambesi make continuing cooperation with Pretoria essential.[14] Perhaps the greatest confirmation of this lies in the extent to which Machel supports the African National Congress (ANC), support that is considerably less than the sanctuary afforded earlier to

Robert Mugabe's Zimbabwe African National Union (ZANU) forces. Still, SADF is not restricted by the closeness of economic ties in taking such steps as are deemed necessary along both Mozambique and Zimbabwean borders.

The stark necessity to move in the direction of politico-economic consolidation in southern Africa (regardless of how a "southern constellation" concept might be received) is as compelling to Frontline leaders as it is to RSA strategists. This, at any rate, is the view of the Botha administration which considers that in this regard its position grows stronger each day. Pretoria confronts southern Africa (indeed, the whole continent) with what Jacques Lesourne has called "the global generation gap," the growing chasm between the (mature) developed countries (the RSA alone on the African continent) and the (fledgling) other four-fifths of the world (including all of black Africa).[15] To the South African eye the fundamental bases for consolidation are obvious. The republic is a center of economic and technological sophistication, a geographically contiguous source of development assistance and collaboration, the logical hub of a southern constellation. Declining per capita agricultural production in black Africa is cited as only one indicator of looming socioeconomic chaos that might ordinarily drive the mature metropoles into isolation. RSA strategists, however, feel compelled to reject "enclave options" and to reach out to "our continent" not alone by dint of geographical propinquity, but out of a sober realization that the fate of the republic cannot be extricated from the fate of the continent as a whole. In sum, a complex continental strategy is mandated on the basis of three premises: the vital importance of a proficient defense force, attended by a recognition of its limits; the still undemonstrated efficacy and waning appeal of solutions proffered by Dar es Salaam; and the harshness of development realities confronting African political leaders.

It is manifest in all of this that Pretoria is searching for alternatives to what it regards as the radical politicization of the entire "moral agenda" in Africa. Again, to employ a phrase from Lesourne,[16] South Africa seeks to devise an "à la carte strategy" consisting of, first, direct approaches to the specifics of development (agriculture, technology, trade, education) utilizing the private sector wherever possible; second, at the politico-military level, treating different Frontline States differently, and, third (as we shall see), appealing to the continent on the high plane of common cause against "foreign intrusion." Nationalist leaders, ultimately, will extend their horizons throughout the southern hemisphere and beyond in a search for partners.

A Hemispheric Strategy

The "Southern Ocean"

South Africa's hemispheric perspective, from the base of the African continent, is dominated by the enormous land mass stretching out to the north; yet, in the final analysis, the continent's ocean flanks (the Atlantic on the west and the Indian Ocean on the east) may play the decisive role in the republic's destiny. The Southern Ocean, divided by the cape, is the vital link between a complex, continental strategy and the farther-reaching hemispheric strategy through which South Africa (the contemporary school at any rate) aspires to find common cause with regional partners and, ultimately, with the United States. Foreign Minister "Pik" Botha reviewed this panoramic prospect in a discourse before Parliament on 17 September 1981 that can only be described as a *tour d'horizon*.[17] He expressed confidence that "the gravitational power . . . of our geographical propinquity [and] economic imperatives" will lead to consolidation in southern Africa, but that this could only be one aspect of a "total, national strategy" that must, perforce, take account of the entire continent and its ocean flanks. In a speech that often had the ring of a plea, Botha told his parliamentary colleagues that South Africa must "establish its credibility and status" as a "necessary," "acceptable," and, indeed, "desirable" partner for other governments on the continent. The foreign minister had an initial prospective continental partner in mind and spoke plainly concerning his, no doubt, longer-term aspirations. "With a little realistic assessment by Nigeria and *certain adjustments* by South Africa, these two important African countries could become a bulwark, in the real sense of the word, against foreign intrusion on our continent"[18] (emphasis mine). The theme is one of grand strategy: two premier African states, separated admittedly by more than geographic distance, must nonetheless join in a transcendent, common cause of working against "foreign intrusion on our continent." The statement directs attention away from the colonial struggle, close at hand, to the farther reaches of what is at bottom a global struggle.

The already mentioned cardinal thread in the RSA strategic design—alignment with the United States—ran throughout the speech. Botha volunteered "key southern support" for what he took to be the American objective of developing at least a tacit alliance structure in the southern hemisphere. Referring to possible new linkages that might emerge below the Tropic of Cancer the foreign minister suggested:

> Among the most important southern powers likely to play an
> important role *outside regional boundaries* will . . . be Brazil
> and Argentina, South Africa and Nigeria, India and Aus-
> tralia. . . . If one looks at the map, it is very interesting to
> note how Nigeria and South Africa, on the African continent,
> and Brazil and Argentina, on the South American continent,
> straddle the Atlantic Ocean. It is almost as though the ocean
> invites the four of them into closer cooperation.[19] (emphasis
> mine)

This time the reference to a South Africa–Nigeria relationship is cast
in the larger context of maritime-oriented states of the southern hemisphere. The turn to the Atlantic is a call for a "South Atlantic Alliance"
of sorts; more important, it is a turn to the Americas and to the United
States.

The "congruence of U.S., Latin American, and South African interests" that Pretoria subsumes in its (southern) hemispheric strategy
will be questioned by some and urgently opposed by others.[20] Not the
least of the difficulties, in the view of some observers of the pan-Ameri-
can concept, is the present status of western hemispheric solidarity. One
highly regarded scholar has suggested that "the spread of the Third
World myth in Latin America has just about completed the dissipation
of that other myth, the Western Hemisphere idea."[21] The conjunction
of Fidel Castro and black Africa, insofar as this constitutes a functional
enterprise, embodies the effort to overcome the western hemisphere
idea with the Third World idea and, most assuredly, any southern
hemisphere idea based on a congruence of U.S., Latin American, and
South African interests. At this level the crux of the Washington-
Havana confrontation is competition between revolutionary ideas. The
United States, for its part, is endeavoring to formulate a new western
hemisphere idea attuned to the politico-military exigencies of the late
twentieth century. Among those exigencies is an "unprecedented" military effort in the western hemisphere on the part of the Soviet Union,
compelling the United States to make the hemisphere an integral part
of its current strategic reappraisal.[22] South Africans today see America
newly committed to reestablishing primacy in the western hemisphere
and are putting forward their own southern hemisphere concepts as
timely reinforcement of the American resurgence.

South Africa's "economic penetration" of Latin America, coupled
with a steady effort to increase diplomatic presence there, has been
characterized as contrary to Third World interests.[23] Pretoria recognizes

that this argument must be countered and will rely on the mutual benefits of increased commercial and technical ties to carry the day. However, the basic impetus for a South Atlantic Alliance, formal or informal, stems out of regional security considerations. In this light, the "cone countries" (Argentina, Brazil, Chile), none of which may qualify as Third World countries, are central.[24] Brazil is at once the most essential and the most difficult to enlist, given its leanings toward West Africa and Nigeria in particular. The Anglo-Argentine clash over the Falkland Islands may prove a timely spur for Brazilian consideration of South Africa's strategic concepts. For both countries the conflict served to underscore the significance, and vulnerability, of the maritime commerce lanes to North America and Europe; the South Atlantic is not a low-threat area removed from the global struggle. Soviet naval, hydrographic, and intelligence vessels along with continuing TU-95D Bear reconnaissance flights out of Luanda now loom larger than a persistent eastern bloc fishing fleet in the South Atlantic.[25] All of this reinforces the basic issue South Africa continues to put to Latin America: Cuba as Soviet proxy in the Third World. If the Soviet-Cuban enterprise on the two continents is, in fact, a threat, then there is basis for common action at a number of levels in the southern hemisphere.

The Indian Ocean with its critical strategic zone along the western littoral is the most important variable in South Africa's developing hemispheric strategy. Its prominence will very likely persist for the balance of the century. Quite apart from the significance attached to the Indian Ocean by the United States (a matter that weighs heavily with the contemporary school), a number of other factors explain its priority. Consistent with a worldwide pattern, recent data show the European share of South Africa's total trade declining and the Asian share growing rapidly. Japan is currently the republic's second trading partner after the United States. The new facilities at Richard's Bay (currently seeing 28 million tons of coal exported per year) and close at hand (two hundred miles south) Africa's greatest port, Durban, combine with East London and Port Elizabeth to give Indian Ocean sea lines of communication (SLOC) to Asia and the Pacific a new prominence.[26] Pretoria has not been able to expand its air network throughout the hemisphere to any comparable degree. South African Airways (SAA) does operate over routes from Latin America in the west to Australia in the east and north, via Mauritius, to Hong Kong. Political relationships with two key littoral countries, India and Australia, are recognized as critical to a growing Indian Ocean regional role for South Africa. Recent steps to incorporate Indian and "colored" constituencies into the political process as well as movement toward a Namibian settlement may help with New Delhi and Canberra.[27]

The western islands, "the Great Island" (Madagascar) in particular, have always been sensitive points. Smuts underscored the significance of Madagascar and the Mozambique Channel with his insistence to London in 1942 that he occupy not only Diego Suarez but the entire island.[28] Japanese naval activity in the Indian Ocean that same year has since been assessed as insignificant (from the standpoint of affecting the outcome of World War II), but it did impress on South Africans that they were not out of reach of a major naval adversary. The British withdrawal from "east of Suez" (1968–71) and the abrogation of the Simonstown Agreement (1975) again heightened those sensitivities; a continuing French presence at Réunion and in the Comoros, construed as serving French interests only, would not suffice. The appearance in force of the Soviet navy in the Indian Ocean in the 1970s, which entailed not only passage around the cape to and from the Pacific station but establishment of an *eskadra* (squadron) in the region and extensive use of facilities from Aden to Maputo, was a dramatic development in the minds of RSA strategists. There was more than a naval dimension to the Soviet effort on the African continent; it was the opening up of the Indian Ocean to a global scenario that would absorb local conflicts.[29] The catalytic events at the end of the decade came as compelling confirmation of this view.

Strategic collaboration: South Africa and the United States

The Soviet invasion of Afghanistan and the collapse of the shah of Iran combined in the turning-point year of 1979 to expose a vast new area of vulnerability for the West. Washington's response was to initiate a wholesale strategic review that would issue in the first basic reorientation of the post–World War II period. Southwest Asia was the new crisis point but it was soon evident that American planners were thinking in the broader terms of a security regime encompassing the Indian Ocean region. In Pretoria the moment was propitious for a new administration and a new strategic posture, especially as this coincided with the far-reaching reappraisal in Washington. RSA strategies were quick to focus on two trends in the American review: "the growing orientation to 'globalist' conceptions of U.S. security interests (as against the primacy of Europe), the chief manifestation of this being the emphasis given to the Indian Ocean region as a new theater of operations."[30] "Accompanying this development was the reaffirmation of the sea as a critical datum in U.S. strategic thought, i.e., the global balance turns on the continuing commitment of the U.S. to naval supremacy across the 'indivisible common main'."[31] This historic departure in American security planning gave unprecedented prominence to the southern hemisphere and also gave Pretoria a linchpin for its own hemispheric strategy.

Two factors, tirelessly proclaimed in South Africa and abroad, had structured the discussion of possible American–South African strategic collaboration up to this point: the strategic minerals of southern Africa and the cape sea route.[32] The contention that for all of the advocacy of the importance of the two factors there has been little analysis can be credited without invalidating either. Both continue to be germane but today this discussion is dominated by a new issue: the value of the South African base-complex. It is widely recognized that "the Indian Ocean . . . offers, to the power that dominates it, potential control over the rimlands of Africa, the Middle East and the Indian subcontinent [and that] it can be dominated only by a maritime strategy—a strategy of ships."[33] It is recognized as well that even in an era of nuclear propulsion for naval vessels and impressive underway-replenishment capabilities, a strategy of ships remains a strategy of bases and long logistic lines. In this respect, if no other, there are valuable lessons to be drawn from the Pax Britannica era in Indian Ocean history.[34]

The Cape of Good Hope is the principal maritime entry way to the Indian Ocean. Roughly at mid-transit between Norfolk, Virginia, and the Persian Gulf, the Republic of South Africa provides a "main base" without parallel in the southern hemisphere. The distinction between "main base" and "facilities" is critical to the current strategic discussion. South Africa provides an extraordinary complex of modern ports, state-of-the-art infrastructure (industry, communications, transport), and operational bases (references merely to Simonstown are barely relevant). Just such a logistical-operational support system defines a main base; India as the great base camp of the Pax Britannica is a historical parallel but not a contemporary one. Since 1979 the United States has diligently upgraded the facilities on Diego Garcia in the Chagos Archipelago. Diego Garcia, however, can only serve as an advance staging area with limited logistical-operational value, and not as a "stand-down," repair-maintenance-overhaul-refit base.[35] This is true to an even greater extent of the recently acquired "rights to facilities" in Kenya, Somalia, and Oman. (However, the fact that these facilities, although limited in scope, are located at the top of the "strategic zone" is not lost on South Africans.)

The efficacy of naval presence is determined by duration (staying power), but even more by an objective capability to prevail in all plausible contingencies, that is, by the make-up of the deployed force. American naval resurgence, after a decade of often bitter force-structure debate, will center on a worldwide projection force of attack carrier battle groups. Their effectiveness will depend on the availability of main base support in critical regions of the world. It is fully appreciated that the current practice of putting a single carrier on "gonzo station" in the Arabian Sea does not suffice for an Indian Ocean security regime. A main base, available in the twentieth century only at the cape, is required for an adequate regime.

The construction of an Indian Ocean security regime underscores the global extent of U.S. security interests and, conversely, the regional character of the Western alliance. It has been made patently clear to Washington in the last few years that first, NATO members have interests that reach beyond the well-defined jurisdiction of the alliance and, second, those same members have little disposition to support those extended interests on a collective basis. Neither Pretoria nor Washington considers NATO endorsement a precondition for possible bilateral strategic collaboration, however useful this might be. It remains to consider the form this collaboration might take if it is to bring strategy fully into the contemporary political arena.

Conclusion

The distinction in this chapter between "continental" and "hemispheric" strategies of an emergent contemporary school in South Africa rests on what is taken to be a real distinction. But it must be conceded that the distinction is pragmatic as well. The bilateral collaboration that falls within the framework of South Africa's hemispheric strategy and the American effort to devise an Indian Ocean security regime is plausible today, so long as collaboration that has the appearance of reinforcing South Africa's continental strategy is abjured. If there is to be any possibility of joint U.S.-RSA measures at the hemispheric or global level (no matter how vital or how transcendent the interests at stake), it will be necessary to maintain this distinction in order to contend with the assertion that joint measures taken to deal with the "external threat" will aid and abet South Africa's campaign against the "internal threat."[36] This analysis has not proceeded in terms of internal or external threats, but in terms of converging strategies designed to support mutual interests. In these terms naval collaboration in the Southern Ocean that takes account of the value of the South African base-complex is the most immediate and likely candidate for initiating strategic collaboration. It would appear to be resistant to the charge that it is a counterinsurgency measure.

No longer in partnership with the Royal Navy after 1974, the South African Navy (SAN) recognized that it could not, alone, maintain a "blue-water" role. A prompt retrenchment followed, explained, according to some observers, not just by genuine limitations on SAN capabilities but rather more by Pretoria's judgment that the relinquishment of the blue-water role below the Tropic of Cancer (both by the Royal Navy and the SAN) must be dramatized for Washington. Today, the SAN main force is considerably reduced. Two aging President-class frigates are scheduled for retirement. (The *President Kruger* was lost at sea in April 1982.) This leaves three, French-built (Daphne) diesel-electric submarines (acquired in the 1970s) and, at the end of 1982, eight (missile) strike craft. The latter will be augmented by additional minister-class boats armed with the South African derivative (Scorpion) of the Israeli Gabriel missile. The implications of this force reduction and the consequent constriction of roles and missions continue to be laid before Washington.[37] The Maritime Patrol Group (under SADF rather than SAN control), consisting of Avro MR-3 Shackletons will continue to be useful for a time but, inexorably, the fate of the maritime reconnaissance mission is coming to a head. (In 1982, the twenty-fifth anniversary year of the Shackletons, the force was reduced to five).[38] The Joint Maritime-Air Surveillance Center at Silvermine (under Constantia Ridge behind Simonstown) had functioned as part of the NATO maritime intelligence system but was removed from NATO programming at the end of the decade. The drama Pretoria wished to convey to Washington about declining naval capabilities in the Southern Ocean was heightened by the catalytic events of 1979. It is precisely those circumstances and America's own developing strategic response to them that has been decisive in moving Washington to consider the specifics of naval collaboration with South Africa.

Some indication of the measures that might logically be taken up by the two sides is sufficient for our purposes. Discussion items could be expected to include: naval operating rights or status-of-forces agreements (Simonstown, Durban, Walvis Bay); logistic support-system agreements (including POMCUS arrangements),[39] overhaul-maintenance-repair agreements (Cape Town, Port Elizabeth, East London, Durban), state-of-the-art technology upgrade of Silvermine and its incorporation into the U.S.'s Naval Ocean Surveillance Information System (NOSIS),[40] replacement of the Shackleton force,[41] SAN acquisition of frigates,[42] SADF acquisition of a strike fighter optimized for the maritime environment,[43] and the reverse flow of technology from ARMSCOR.[44]

Needless to say, any consideration of such measures would represent a major turning point not only for the two parties but for the global balance as a whole. This, however, does constitute an important near-term objective for a growing number of strategic analysts in both countries. Such discussions will take place as Washington progressively develops its new policy position, one that attaches importance to maintaining a global balance, in part through a commitment to naval supremacy involving collaboration with South Africa. This policy does not require the United States to modify a long-established position with regard to the resolution of the colonial struggle in Africa, much less its position with regard to the internal politics of South Africa. It is inescapable that Washington must record some degree of democratic progress on the part of all non–eastern bloc countries with whom it would collaborate even for the most transcendent of purposes. While Pretoria will have to satisfy Washington on this score, it is clear that strategic collaboration will also be assessed against the most fundamental security interests of the United States. There is basis for the conclusion that some degree of strategic convergence between South Africa and the United States is on the horizon.

16. Offshore Politics and the Security of Southern Africa ☎ Peter C. J. Vale and Michael Spicer

A cursory survey of the rich literature on the Indian Ocean area reveals that the strategic dynamic of the offshore islands has been, comparatively speaking, a neglected theme. This is not altogether surprising. In an ocean that extends over roughly 30 million square miles, the western islands cover only approximately 371,455 square miles; the total population of the islands is approximately 10.2 million.[1] Such modest statistics, however, are misleading when the affairs of the Indian Ocean are considered. Recent events have pushed the issue of these islands to the forefront of strategic thinking and, as the Falklands crisis so vividly demonstrated, no landmass—however remote—is devoid of strategic significance.

The Subregional Transformation

A little more than a decade ago, the offshore islands (the British Indian Ocean Territory, the Comoros, Madagascar, Mauritius, Réunion, and the Seychelles) could be described with almost quaint simplicity. Of the six, only Madagascar (1960) and Mauritius (1968) had gained independence; the others were all closely tied to either Paris or London. While there were suggestions that new forces and factors might disturb the subregion's tranquility, few could have imagined the extent of the change. Philip Allen's description of the regional situation in 1971 thus explained, "Although traditional forces are changing roles and yielding to new circumstances, the constituent islands have had little opportunity to modify their umbilical relations with the metropoles. A meticulously accommodationist establishment of political leaders, plutocracies, overseas administrators, and *assimilados* still discharges on each island whatever powers the metropoles have decided to transfer during the past decade."[2]

Since the United Nations General Assembly's zone-of-peace resolution (1971), turbulence on the southern African land mass has spilled over to the western islands and has affected their political coloration. Given the long colonial heritage of the southern African subregion, it is perhaps not surprising that it took a major development in Europe— the Portuguese coup of April 1974—to unsettle southern Africa. In the wake of the events in Lisbon, Mozambique and Angola came to independence under governments having links with the eastern bloc. Not only were they antipathetic to a conservative white-dominated southern Africa, but the course of their liberation had been, as they themselves saw it, through the barrel of the gun. Such a perception has had, and will continue to have, a significant impact on the subregion's future and security.

The change in political status in Angola and Mozambique increased pressure on the two remaining white power centers in the region: Salisbury and Pretoria. Since the independence of these two states, the history of the subregion has seen a concerted effort to bring to a close the remaining chapters of settler colonialism and white domination. The replacement of the white minority Rhodesian government with black majority rule after a long and painful struggle has, at least for the interim, contributed new problems for the region's stability. Across the subcontinent, the South African government, having conceded in the wake of the Portuguese coup the necessity for granting independence to Namibia, is currently trying to stave off a nationalist victory in Windhoek that could emulate those in Luanda, Harare, and Maputo. In South Africa, black dissent, after the lull that followed the Sharpeville events of the early 1960s, reemerged in 1976–77 with the massive nationwide uprising associated with the name of Soweto, and was compounded by renewed attempts to suppress emerging black leadership and the death of Steve Biko. The southern African land mass thus remains in a marked state of instability to which the continuing pattern of white wealth and black poverty contributes. However, the white side of this equation is increasingly under threat by the black, which draws succor from the recent political and military successes in Angola, Mozambique, and Zimbabwe.

On the offshore islands, independence has become a reality for all except Réunion and Mayotte (in the Comoros). In this process, political systems that were essentially conservative in nature have given way to socialist-oriented regimes that, in common with the black-ruled states on the mainland, espouse a nascent nonaligned stance in foreign policy. Even in Madagascar, an independent republic for more than two decades, the conservative government of Philibert Tsiranana was replaced by General Ramanantsoa in May 1972; the policy of the new government became fervently nationalist and particularly anti–South African. This departure was confirmed by Didier Ratsiraka, who replaced Ramanantsoa in 1975. In the Seychelles, which achieved independence in 1976, the conservative government led by James Mancham was replaced by a coup after only twelve months. Albert René's party, the Seychelles Peoples' Progressive Front (SPPF), openly espoused a socialist program domestically and began attempts to shape a nonaligned policy in its foreign affairs. In neighboring Mauritius, which gained independence in 1968, the Labour party of Sir Seewoosagur Ramgoolam was replaced in 1982 by a left-leaning coalition comprising the Mouvement Militant Mauricien (MMM) and the smaller Parti Socialiste Mauricien (PSM). This coalition, too, sees itself as socialist in nature and is nonaligned in foreign affairs.

Yet, despite what appears to be a strong wind of change sweeping the western islands, some conservative elements remain in situ, for example, in the Comoros. The people of Mayotte resolutely retained their link with France, with President Ahmed Abdullah replacing the socialist Ali Soilih in May 1978 with the help of the Belgian mercenary, Colonel Bob Denard. Réunion is still under the administration of the French Ministry of Overseas Departments and Territories, while the British Indian Ocean Territory, including Diego Garcia, remains firmly under British sovereignty.

Predictably, perhaps, political independence and the change in orientation in domestic and foreign policy of some of the subregional states has not enhanced regional security. Furthermore, southern Africa, because of the question mark over South Africa's own political future, will continue to be unstable for the foreseeable future. Instability is also apparent elsewhere on the continent. The Angolan Movimento Popular de Libertação de Angola (MPLA) government and the Frelimo government of Mozambique have been unable to consolidate their grip on power, being challenged by resistance movements that have some domestic basis of support aside from South African assistance. The Zimbabwe government has trouble with dissident tribal elements and all governments of the region face economic problems, some of a serious nature. In this regional turmoil, the domestic and foreign policies of the South African government have had sizable impact, also felt strongly in the Indian Ocean's western islands.

The Regional Transformation

Of course, events in the subregion did not occur in a vacuum. The broader Indian Ocean region and considerations of wider security have changed in the past decade; this transformation has seen the same shift from tranquility to turbulence.

The controversial 1968 British decision to withdraw from "east of Suez" can, in a sense, be regarded as a turning point away from the regional tranquility that had prevailed. In the wake of the British decision, the only Western power with a permanent presence in the Indian Ocean was France (in Djibouti and Réunion). But the Soviet Union, then in the process of modernizing and expanding its navy, soon moved into the vacuum created by the British withdrawal. An active policy of cultivating alliances and arms sales resulted in the provision of some anchorages and bases for a small, but permanent, fleet of ships.

The United States moved into the region by leasing the island of Diego Garcia from Britain in 1966. However, they began converting the island into a base only after an interim period, during which Soviet activity in Africa and the Middle East had increased. It was, however, a series of events centered on the gulf and the broader Middle Eastern region that caused significant shifts in global power relations in the Indian Ocean and drew the attention of extraregional powers to the importance of the area. The Arab oil embargo of 1973, the collapse of the shah's regime in Iran in 1979, and the Soviet invasion of Afghanistan at the end of the same year all affected U.S. strategic perceptions of the Indian Ocean area generally. The fear that Muslim radicalism would spread to the whole gulf, destabilizing conservative pro-Western oil producers and providing a fertile field for Soviet intervention, together with Soviet activities in the Middle East, the Horn of Africa, and Angola, also affected U.S. strategic thinking on the broader region and drew attention to the region's enhanced importance. Such attention has come to offend certain of the region's inhabitants deeply.

Under President Carter, one element of America's response to these developments was the creation of the Rapid Deployment Force (RDF).

Although the RDF is built around the concept of airlifting forces from their home bases in the United States, the importance of naval and air supply facilities in East Africa and the Middle East remains. The Reagan administration is unlikely to downgrade its strategic assessment of the Indian Ocean or its presence in the area unless there is considerable progress toward resolving not only the question of Soviet activity in various parts of the region (particularly Afghanistan), but also resolving other indigenous Middle Eastern problems.

On the Soviet side, the paralysis of policy that seems to characterize the ending of the Brezhnev era in the Soviet Union, and the concomitant struggles by his successors to consolidate their positions, does not bode well for the resolution of the foregoing issues, which, it is argued, are responsible for the current state of tension in the broader region. In sum, therefore, the broad context of the region does not provide a stable background for the foreign policy concerns of the western islands.

Subregional Dualism

In the subregional setting, the political relationship that characterizes South Africa's ties with its continental neighbors appears also to characterize the republic's relations with the western islands. This is, generally speaking, a relationship in which the black states are in a position of economic subservience to, but political antagonism toward, South Africa. This situation is markedly different from that of a decade ago when the generally conservative governments on the offshore islands were not openly antagonistic and welcomed the economic patronage South Africa offered. The recognition that Pretoria is deeply involved in shoring up its own security through involvement in the affairs of the subregion, including the islands, has contributed to the rise of socialist-leaning governments in the area.

Mauritius

Mauritius is well ranked among the developing countries of the world with a per capita income of approximately U.S. $650 per year and a high literacy rate. On the negative side, however, unemployment is high with up to 80,000 unemployed in a population of 995,000. Of this number, just under half were unemployed graduates or school leavers. With a high rate of population growth and a high population density, this is a disruptive factor for the islands.

The chief crop of Mauritius is sugar and the current depressed state of the international sugar market has done great harm to the economy. In addition, in 1980 a cyclone caused the worst sugar crop in the last decade.[3] With 28 percent of the labor force involved in growing sugar and the industry generating 75 percent of the country's foreign exchange earnings the implications of poor sugar production are obvious. Despite some benefits under the European Community's Lomé Convention that allows Mauritius to sell 500,000 tons of sugar in Europe above the world market price, profits continue to be low. In recent years, it is thought that they may not have covered production costs. The other major Mauritian industry is tourism, with an average tourist traffic of 100,000 per annum; most tourists come from Europe and South Africa. Tourism alone, however, is probably insufficient to solve the structural problems of the economy. Before the national elections of 1982 other economic indicators were equally discouraging: a national debt estimated at 475 million Mauritian rupees (R), an estimated budget deficit of 1 billion R, inflation running at approximately 50 percent per annum, and further economic complications that are the result of a mandatory 30 percent devaluation ordered by the International Monetary Fund (IMF) as a condition for a loan in 1979. (U.S. $1 equals approximately Mauritian RS 11.)

It is against this background that Mauritius went to the polls in June 1982. As a result of the election the government, under the new prime minister, Anneerood Jugnauth, adopted what should be seen as the new wave of thinking on foreign and domestic policies in the offshore islands. The victorious MMM was founded in 1969 by Paul Berenger, a veteran of the 1968 Paris riots, who became its secretary general. The MMM tried to break the mold of the established politics of communalism and the traditional pattern of ethnic voting. Its general reputation was one of left-wing militancy. In the June campaign, however, the MMM considerably toned down its radical stance—some have even suggested Marxist stance—enabling it to capture the middle ground in Mauritian politics.[4] The electoral platform was broadly based socialism promising increased employment, an increase in the minimum wage, greater welfare benefits, and the nationalization of key sectors of the economy. In foreign policy, the MMM promised a major reorientation, arguing the case for a nuclear-free peace zone in the ocean and the ousting of the United States from the Diego Garcia base. In order to allay fears that it was anti-Hindu, the MMM entered an alliance with the PSM, a small Hindu party that had split from an earlier coalition in 1979. This was an important tactical step, for over half of the Mauritian electorate is comprised of Hindu people. Traditionally, political parties have been based on religion and ethnicity but in the wake of the MMM success it is difficult to assess the importance of that traditional factor.

The defeat of the former prime minister, eighty-two-year-old Sir Seewoosagur Ramgoolam, had been a possibility since the previous general election in 1976. At that time the MMM emerged as the biggest single party with thirty-four out of the sixty-two members of the Legislative Assembly, but it was kept out of government by a coalition of Ramgoolam's Labour party and the Parti Social Democrat Mauricien (PSDM) of Sir Gaetan Duval. However, the last term of the Labour party was marked by a steadily deteriorating economic situation, corruption, ineptitude, and internal squabbling. Toward the end of the election campaign, Ramgoolam attempted to brand the opposition party as Marxist, suggesting close links with the Soviet Union, Algeria, and Libya. Ramgoolam further indicated that the MMM would transform the country into a one-party state, and that it would threaten free enterprise on the islands.

An important issue in the election concerned the Diego Garcia refugees, called "les Ilois," who have been in Mauritius for the past decade.[5] The Ilois had begun to campaign vigorously for increased compensation from Britain and, together with the MMM, had asked the United States to dismantle its naval base on Diego Garcia, thus enabling them to return home. Figures for compensation for the Ilois have differed in relation to the assessment of the number of families involved; for example, the Ilois have claimed U.S. $16 million, maintaining that 940 families were involved. On the other hand, the British claimed that 426 families were involved and proposed to offer only U.S. $3.1 million. The previous Mauritian government wanted Britain to give them U.S. $6 million. The MMM position on the Ilois was quite plain: that the Ilois are the homeless and abandoned Palestinians of the Indian Ocean.

Further pressure was placed on the Diego Garcia issue as a result of the MMM victory; the question of Mauritian sovereignty over Diego Garcia also assumed greater importance. Ramgoolam's position was that "the American presence on Diego Garcia is justified [because] the Soviet Union is making a big, big effort to destabilize the Indian Ocean. . . . My Government is engaged to defend and see that does not take place."[6] The position of the MMM was in sharp contrast to this, and shortly after the coalition took office the foreign minister promised that talks on sovereignty would take place. He also indicated that the party would continue to press the question of Diego Garcia in international forums such as the United Nations and the Organization of African Unity (OAU). Berenger further indicated that he would, together with

Indian officials, seek to take the question of Diego Garcia to the International Court of Justice at the Hague.[7] In early July, the new Mauritian Parliament unanimously adopted a bill formally including Diego Garcia as Mauritian territory. While the government signed an agreement under which Britain paid approximately U.S. $8 million in full and final compensation, it asserted that it would maintain the Mauritian claim to sovereignty over the atoll.[8]

The militant position taken by the MMM on sovereignty and the zone-of-peace question brought the party into line with what was at the time one of the major trends in southern African politics concerning the Indian Ocean, a position close to the policies espoused by both the Seychelles and Madagascar. In addition, the governments of Mozambique and Tanzania had expressed their renewed commitments to the zone-of-peace concept.[9] The extent to which Mauritius will continue to be part of this coalition is now in doubt following the collapse of the MMM-PSM government in March 1983 and the elections held in August of that year.

The immediate cause of the coalition's collapse was the withdrawal of Berenger and several MMM ministers from the government over the issue of official language policy. Jugnauth was expelled from the MMM in April 1983 and then formed a new party, the Mouvement Socialiste Mauricien (MSM), under whose banner he fought and won (with the help of other parties) the August elections. The new government, a coalition of MSM, Labour, and PSDM parties, has distinguished itself from its predecessor by announcing its intentions to amend the constitution to establish Mauritius as a republic within the British Commonwealth. It has also toned down the rhetoric of the former government's position on Diego Garcia, a policy change that may also see a weakening of support for the zone-of-peace concept.

The position of the MMM-PSM alliance government was highly pragmatic with regard to relations with South Africa. Mauritius quite clearly needs the revenue from the thirty thousand South African tourists who visit annually, revenue from South African trade, and revenue from South African transit aircraft. It was noticeable that early in the 1982 election campaign the MMM uttered hostile statements toward Pretoria, but as the campaign progressed the position moderated, probably as a result of the realization of the structural role that South Africa plays in the region's economic affairs. Shortly after the 1982 election, the Mauritian government assured the business community and foreign investors, particularly South Africans, that they would continue to be welcome on the island. The new government has continued this policy, sending a delegation to Pretoria in November 1983 in an attempt to negotiate extra South African Airways services to the island and to increase other economic links.

The version of regional pragmatism, especially the link with South Africa, that has been demonstrated both by the Seychelles and Mauritian experiences, closely resembles the experience of states in southern Africa. This involves cooperation on functional levels with economically dominant South Africa but the maintenance of a degree of hostile rhetoric toward the Pretoria government, especially toward its domestic policies. Where possible, the strategy attempts to lessen the existing dependency on South Africa.

It is interesting to note that opposition groups elsewhere in the Indian Ocean, for example in Réunion, have tended to maintain close links with Mauritian leaders. This trend of increasing links between Indian Ocean islands represents an important new departure, which itself finds some analogue on the mainland. In July 1982, for example, Mauritius and the Seychelles agreed to set up the Indian Ocean Commission (IOC) to promote cooperation among the countries of the subregion. It was reported that the former Mauritian foreign minister, Jean-Claude de l'Estrac, had met Seychelles President Albert René, and that they had discussed "the immense possibilities of developing mutual cooperation in various fields between the Indian Ocean islands."[10] The full extent of the envisaged IOC was revealed a few days later; it would look into the possibilities of cooperation particularly in industry, trade, health, education, and culture. Initially the Seychelles, Madagascar, and Mauritius formed the core of the commission and there are clear signs that they will attempt to coordinate their foreign policy objectives. While the scope of the IOC is not yet clear, it seems possible to suggest that the idea of interregional cooperation parallels the development of the Southern African Development Coordination Conference (SADCC), and in this fashion the Indian Ocean organization follows in the steps of the SADCC's attempts to weaken dependence on South Africa.

The Seychelles

The abortive coup on the Seychelles in November 1981 focused attention on the western islands and particularly on their thorny relations with South Africa. The fact that Tanzanian troops helped repel the invasion was another indication of the close link between Tanzania and the Seychelles, also evident in President Julius Nyerere's earlier backing for the 1977 coup that brought René to power. Prior to the 1981 coup attempt there had been indications that two, if not three, coups had been planned against René's government. In response to these attempts,

René had begun to strengthen the Seychelles' arsenal. It was reported that the Soviet Union had delivered two armored cars, and that Libya had given the government five propeller-driven patrol aircraft. In addition, Chinese vessels were reported to have delivered ten anti-aircraft guns, and the United Kingdom a long-range patrol aircraft. Given the various sources of arms, it is clear that the Seychelles government is pursuing a nonaligned policy in arms procurement and seeking to avoid the liabilities associated with a single source of supply.

René's freedom of movement was initially hamstrung by the state of his economy. In 1979, for example, imports ran at rupees (R) 450 million, while exports amounted only to R 25 million. (U.S. $1 equals Seychelles R 6.5.) But a year later the government's total revenue ran at R 357.8 million, a 68.2 percent increase over the previous year. Britain and France continue to provide the most aid. In recent years major aid assistance from these two countries has developed housing projects, built a tuna quay, and assisted educational and boat-building facilities. The West German government has also provided significant aid. In addition, other assistance to the Seychelles government has come from the Organization of Petroleum Exporting Countries (OPEC) and China. The extent of Soviet assistance is not fully known, although the Soviet Union has trained technicians and helped develop the fishing industry. In 1980, it was announced that Iraq and the Seychelles had planned an extensive joint fishing venture that would run for fifteen years, the major shareholder being the Seychelles government. The other main source of revenue is tourism. The annual tourist traffic, much of it from South Africa, has run at a figure higher than the total population; however, tourism was negatively affected by the 1981 coup attempt.

René's former party, the Seychelles Peoples' United party, transformed itself after the 1977 coup into the Seychelles Peoples' Progressive Front and became the country's only political party. Despite fears that René would pursue a dogmatic left-wing policy, he has been relatively cautious in domestic and foreign affairs. All international commitments, for example, were honored, including the lease to the United States of a satellite-tracking station. His view of tourism and the South African link is similarly pragmatic. He is reported to have said, "The Government realizes that, whatever the future holds, tourists are a bounty, even when they come from South Africa. We do not like apartheid, but we are realistic."[11] Perhaps the major political problem for the René government comes from the very considerable Seychelloise exiled community (some 28,000 people out of a total population of about 93,000), many of them living in Britain but some also in South Africa. They are interested in returning the Seychelles to a more conservative line and this could cause problems for the René government at some time in the future.

The specific case of the abortive coup of November 1981 is an interesting study in the dualistic politics of the region. On the one hand, it seems clear that the coup was linked to the exiled movement most closely associated with the former president, James Mancham. On the other hand, there is compelling evidence to suggest that certain elements within South Africa were involved in the coup itself. The curious behavior of the South African authorities, and the revelations that subsequently emerged from the trial of the mercenaries, together indicate a marked degree of South African complicity in the act.[12] Beyond saying, however, as the South African Supreme Court established, that certain members of the National Intelligence Service and the SADF had known about the planning of the coup, and that members of the SADF had facilitated access of the mercenaries to arms, one enters the realm of speculation. Although the Supreme Court found that the South African prime minister and cabinet had not known of the coup attempt in advance, doubts must remain on this score.

The Future

The southern African region is in a state of political flux, a situation made more complex by the black-white, rich-poor dichotomies previously discussed. Recent political events and the unresolved problems of the colonial period have further complicated the region's endemic instability. Moreover, the aggressive actions of the South African authorities, aimed at preserving South Africa's security, have aggravated the situation. While the underlying political position on the continent has come, as we have seen, to be mirrored on the western islands of the Indian Ocean, it is probable that the political developments on these islands will not unduly influence political events in southern Africa. However, as developments there are played out, they will be increasingly reflected on the islands, with important ramifications for the security both of the Indian Ocean region and the southern African subregion. It is these issues that should be considered in assessing the future of the western islands and southern African security.

The new mood that has come to the fore, particularly in Mauritius and the Seychelles, is tempered with the realization that these islands are economically beholden to the patronage of South Africa and, in a wider setting, to extensive Western largesse. Thus, while the emerging policy is one in which both governments use fairly dramatic language to express their antipathy toward South Africa, they have not taken any steps that will drastically affect their commercial links with the country. This is all the more remarkable in the Seychelles with its continued links with South Africa, particularly in the field of tourism. The November 1981 coup attempt came as a political shock for the René government, and it is not surprising that South Africans should be treated with considerable circumspection on the island. While the figure for tourism is decreasing, this is not the result of any action by the Seychelles authorities but rather a reflection of nervousness on the part of potential South African visitors.

The key to the future security of the subregion will lie in Pretoria's perception of, and response to, developments both on the continent and on the islands. It is clear that at least some, if not all, South African authorities are convinced that considerable mileage is to be gained by a fairly extensive and even ambitious use of Pretoria's influence in the southern African subcontinent. Though the issue continues to be debated in South Africa, it has become the orthodox view in the international community that Pretoria is deeply involved in the affairs of the region and that this involvement is guided by the belief that the country's own security interests are served by keeping its neighbors economically and militarily weak. While the prime focus of attention in terms of South Africa's security is the activity of guerrilla movements such as the South West African People's Organization (SWAPO) and the African National Congress (ANC), there is compelling evidence to suggest that South African support for antigovernment guerrillas in Mozambique, Lesotho, and Angola is aimed at keeping these states economically and militarily weak. The goal is to disrupt the SADCC scheme which is perceived to pose a long-term threat to South Africa's grip over the region.[13]

Much the same reasoning applies in Pretoria's assessment of events on the western islands of the Indian Ocean. This is buttressed by Pretoria's refurbished naval strategy that has recently focused exclusively on limited offshore defense. This development, the single most important maritime strategic departure for South Africa since World War II, was enunciated under the rationale that South Africa, as a result of the UN arms embargo, was not able to obtain the necessary deep-sea maritime equipment for a more ambitious naval defense program. However, the Seychelles affair may have reflected a new dimension to South Africa's naval defense strategy. The hawks among Pretoria's naval strategists may have argued that influence over the offshore islands is an essential part of South Africa's total defense position. Not only would this circumscribe opportunities for Soviet penetration of the islands but, as important, would help facilitate South African access to the land mass from the sea. This position fits neatly into South Africa's general involvement in the region. For example, South Africa would be able to maintain a well-used maritime supply route to the Mozambique resistance movement attempting to topple the Mozambican government of President Samora Machel.

Such access, which might have been secured by a successful outcome to the Seychelles incident, would also have enabled South Africa to pursue certain diplomatic aims in the subregion. One such aim might be to erode Tanzania's influence. It is well known that the Nyerere government is openly hostile to South Africa, and Tanzania has become a linchpin in SADCC. A further diplomatic aim might be to use conservative governments for fairly innovative South African–backed diplomacy in the region, e.g., a rekindling of the "dialogue" with Africa. Therefore, South Africa has more than a passing interest in the affairs of the offshore islands.

Some indications are that South Africa may already have achieved a foothold in the western islands, through its links with the Comoros. A report at the end of 1981 suggested that the ties between the Comoros government of President Ahmed Abdullah and South Africa were strong, and implied that South Africa had played an important role in bringing Abdullah to power.[14] The same report identified five areas of potential association between South Africa and the Comoros government. These included the possibility of a South African telecommunications station on Grande Comore, a loan by the South African government to Abdullah, and South African assistance in building a broadcasting base. Recent information suggests that South African interests also are actively pursuing the idea of building an ambitious hotel and tourist facility on the islands.[15] Of course, the presence of French military personnel on the island of Mayotte is a considerable inhibiting factor for any militant challenge to the Abdullah government. In addition, given the results of the 1982 general election on the Comoros in which Abdullah won thirty-seven of the thirty-eight seats in the Federal Assembly, the president's position appears secure. Therefore, a serious question mark must hang over the real political affiliations of the Abdullah government, despite the close fraternal links that he has rhetorically expressed with other western Indian Ocean islands.[16]

Western strategic interests in the subregion may come to be condemned on the basis of their relations with dominant South Africa and, if this is the case, the islands will have taken their cue from Tanzania. At the current time, the continuing negotiations over the resolution of the remaining colonial problems of southern Africa, particularly the

question of Namibia, may be perceived as a test of the good faith of the
United States and other major Western powers involved in this exercise. If the feeling becomes widespread in Africa that the United States
is involved in retarding the course of Namibian independence through
Washington's current policy of "constructive engagement," the western
islands may respond by intensifying their campaign on Diego Garcia.
Of course this linkage is not an obvious one but, as these issues are
played out in international forums like the United Nations, such linkages come to exist. Pressure from states on the land mass who have concerned themselves with this question may spill over to the islands. On the
other hand, the Western nations are not without considerable influence
in the subregion, such influence arising partially from the even-handed
policy that Madagascar, Mauritius, and the Seychelles have displayed
toward the Western and the Eastern blocs. This policy of even-handed-
ness is underscored by the fact that all three islands are prepared to take
development aid from both blocs. All three are members of the Lomé
Convention and the bulk of their trade is with this major Western
trading bloc. In addition, both Mauritius and Madagascar continue to
be members of the close francophone community of nations.

There is a tendency in some Western strategic circles to misjudge
a policy of nonalignment in the Third World, to presume that every
"new progressive government" represents a fundamental and irrevocable
setback for the West. This one-dimensional interpretation of strategic
reality has become almost the conventional wisdom in South African
policy-making circles. Given that South Africa's assessment of these
issues is crucial for the region's security, a particular responsibility lies
with major Western strategic thinkers and their governments not to
overstate the case one way or the other. In addition, the birth of the
Indian Ocean Commission provides the West with an opportunity to
underscore its obvious strategic interests in the area by active encouragement of this development through providing increased aid to the commission. Some precedent for this has been established by the aid assistance the European Community has given to SADCC. By actively
encouraging these states to become less reliant on South Africa, the
West will have moved somewhat further in securing the Indian Ocean's
future than has hitherto been the case.

The important ingredient for Third World security often neglected
by Western strategic thinkers is the economic dimension. The western
Indian Ocean islands have specific problems, in many cases similar to
those experienced by underdeveloped landlocked countries. However,
the islands also have distinct advantages. One hopeful development in

the western Indian Ocean is recent reporting that indicates the seabed contains minerals that might be exploited. In the wider search for mineral security, Western governments should take note.

At the present time the search for security in southern Africa presents formidable intellectual challenges for innovative diplomacy and sound scholarship. The offshore islands constitute a subsystem of these considerations that also merits serious attention. It is to be hoped that the increasingly rich literature on Indian Ocean problems will no longer be marked by a paucity of attention to developments on the western islands.

South Asia

Since the British withdrawal from the Indian subcontinent in 1947, Indian-Pakistani rivalry has dominated the security issues of the region. War has broken out between the two states on three occasions over the last thirty-seven years but has failed either to resolve the issues that divide them or to enhance their overall sense of security. Following the last of these clashes in 1971, an encounter that led to the dismemberment of Pakistan and the birth of the barely viable state of Bangladesh, there has been evidence on both sides of a desire to improve relations. Building on the spirit of the Simla Agreement of 1972, Pakistan's President Zia proposed talks in June 1982 on a nonaggression pact. Prime Minister Indira Gandhi responded with a permanent joint ministerial commission proposal and in August enlarged the offer to include a treaty of peace, friendship, and cooperation with a no-war declaration. Discussions on these matters, as well as on the perennial problem of Kashmir and a reduction of forces along the states' joint border, took place at several different levels over the years, including during a meeting between Gandhi and Zia in November 1982. These talks served to open the lines of communications between the two capitals but they have yet to show any substantial results. Given the atmosphere of hostility and distrust that continues to persist between Delhi and Islamabad, it seems unlikely that there will be any immediate breakthrough. Gandhi's assassination in October 1984 can be expected to set back the process of normalization.

Since December 1979 the Indian-Pakistani rivalry has been somewhat overshadowed by the Soviets' advance into Afghanistan. This event had its most immediate impact on South-Southwest Asia but has created apprehension among governments throughout the entire Indian Ocean, and necessitated a reappraisal of all regional strategic linkages. As Zalmay Khalilzad argues, the reasons for the Soviet move appear to have had less to do with any long-term Soviet strategic ambitions in

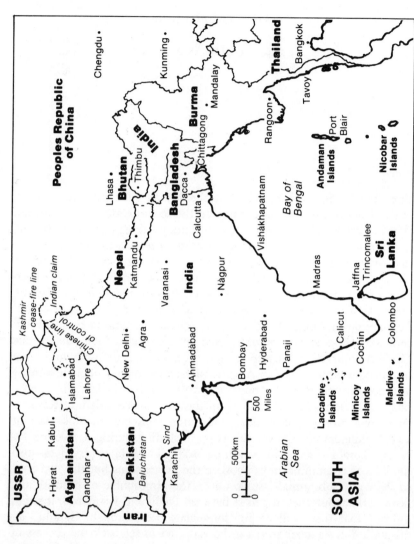

South Asia

Southwest Asia than with the need to stabilize an increasingly troublesome domestic situation in Kabul. Even so, there can be little doubt that if the Soviets can impose their authority on the traditionally independent Afghan people they will have gained an important strategic foothold from which to challenge Western interests in the Persian Gulf and South Asia. It remains unclear whether Moscow can, or will wish to, continue paying the diplomatic and material costs associated with its Afghanistan policy. Reports indicate that the Soviets may be willing to consider a negotiated settlement that would include a withdrawal of their forces. On the other hand, the campaign to impose their authority shows little sign of weakening.

While a resolution of the situation in Afghanistan has yet to materialize, the consequences of the original action continue to reverberate around the region. Apart from Afghanistan itself, the state most directly affected is Pakistan. With hostile forces now poised on both its western and eastern borders, Islamabad has had little alternative but to reinforce its security relationships with its friends within the area and elsewhere. Zia's government has actively encouraged a series of bilateral relationships with Middle East states, reinforcing them with multilateral ties through the Organization of the Islamic Conference and the nonaligned movement while simultaneously making use of his country's long-standing friendship with China to gain much needed economic and military aid. High priority has also been given to reviving Pakistan's once close relationship with the United States, in decline since President Carter made human rights a central theme of American foreign policy. The United States now sees Pakistan as constituting an important link in a strategy to defend Western, particularly American, security interests in the gulf against possible Soviet threats. To this end Washington is to provide Pakistan with a range of military assistance and equipment over the next few years. However, Washington's apprehension that New Delhi might misinterpret the nature of its support for Islamabad, worries about being a party to the development of a Pakistani nuclear capability, continuing reservations, particularly in Congress, over persistent human rights abuses, and Pakistan's chronic domestic instability all serve to qualify the nature of the security guarantee the United States is prepared to provide. The result, as Robert Wirsing carefully points out, is that in the absence of any accord with India that would further reduce the likelihood of conflict, or a settlement in Afghanistan, or both, Pakistan has a security dilemma that will remain unresolved in the foreseeable future.

From India's perspective the Soviet invasion of Afghanistan and the way in which the West (and Pakistan) responded have done little either to improve the security outlook in South Asia or to enhance the prospects for India's own foreign policy objectives. Among the consequences that trouble New Delhi is the effect on Pakistan, in particular the impetus that has been given to pro-Moscow groups within that country to press their campaign to topple the Zia regime. At one level, further deterioration in Pakistan's domestic stability is a cause of concern, at another, there exists the possibility that President Zia might seek to counter it by provoking a conflict with India. The utility of the latter is, of course, something with which India's government is fully conversant. At the same time, New Delhi judges that Islamabad now has more incentive to press on with its nuclear program. As to the wider implications and their impact on India's preferences for a future security regime in the Indian Ocean, the key complicating factor is the revival of U.S. interest. America's support of Pakistan troubles New Delhi but so does the reality that the South-Southwest Asia area has become a part of the frontline of Soviet-American rivalry. With the engagement of superpower interests, there may be an increased danger of conflict; there is almost certainly some restriction on the foreign policy choices available to local states. India, however, will resist any notion, from either East or West, that its horizons should be limited. As Omi Marwah reveals in his account of the ambitious naval development program now under way, New Delhi is seeking the capability to ensure that its options remain open, at least in relation to its maritime environment.

At the root of so much of the political instability in South Asia is the reality of a region beset by complex religious, ethnic, and political cleavages. While the antipathy of Muslims and Hindus is the most visible—and perhaps the most destructive—of these, the tension between Tamils and Sinhalese in Sri Lanka, between Christians and Muslims in Bangladesh, and between Sikhs and Hindus in India, together with the disaffection of Baluchis and Sindhis in Pakistan, all testify to the volatility of the area. Each of the South Asian governments has had to contend with serious outbreaks of ethnic and religious violence, the endemic nature of which has helped to entrench authoritarian military regimes in Pakistan and Bangladesh, and, on more than one occasion, has led to the suspension of the democratic process in India and Sri Lanka. There is little doubt that the stability of every government in the area, and social order more generally, is threatened by the intractability of the issues created by conflicting values and traditions and long-standing perceptions of injustice. Furthermore, the frequency with which these issues overflow rather artificial state boundaries is a recurring cause of interstate tension in the region.

17. India's Strategic Perspectives on the Indian Ocean ☛ Onkar Marwah

The elemental premise of India's strategic policies has been to seek to deny any intermediary role to extraregional powers in the affairs of South Asia. Since the policies of some of its neighbors, such as Pakistan, have often worked in reverse, India has attempted to neutralize the impact of extraregional interference in subcontinental matters. This has proved to be a realistic strategy largely because the South Asian region has not been an area of crucial strategic importance to the two superpowers; their ingress into the subcontinent has been fitful, sporadic, and temporary. Where the policies of one or the other superpower have seriously endangered its independence of action, India has found diplomatic and military means to thwart their onset (e.g., during the Bangladesh war of 1971, and in matching, through counterpurchases, the Western and Chinese supply of arms to Pakistan).

The maritime corollary to the preceding land-oriented premises of Indian strategic policies has been to find a means by which extraregional powers could be persuaded to minimize their physical capacity to intervene with sizable conventional military forces in South Asia. The focus has been on such acts of self-abnegation by the two superpowers, since only they possessed the forces and the incentive to undertake sustained interventions around the world. While India's primary concern was to reduce the chances of a seaborne (or ocean-based) intervention in South Asia, such an objective could be fulfilled only if the waters and islands around the Indian subcontinent could be rendered inviolate to large surface naval flotillas of the superpowers in the Indian Ocean region (IOR). American and Soviet nuclear submarines, as elements of their central strategic forces, were not a means for intervention in the littoral, and hence excluded from the reckoning.

Since India perceived a reduction in superpower intervention as being equally beneficial to other states in the IOR, the Indian objective was generalized, packaged, and presented as the Indian Ocean zone-of-peace (IOZP) proposal. While the proposal was formally put forward in international forums by Sri Lanka, and later by other states of the Indian Ocean littoral, its delineation, articulation, and sustenance as a part of the worldwide debate on strategic issues owed much to Indian design. The high-water mark for the IOZP proposal was reached when the superpowers agreed to engage in the Naval Arms Limitation Talks (NALT) in 1977.[1] Since then a series of autonomous events—particularly the revolution in Iran and the Soviet occupation of Afghanistan—have wrecked the IOZP initiative and, of course, ended prospects for a NALT agreement between the United States and the Soviet Union. India's strategic appreciation of its surrounding seas, therefore, must now take account of all the consequent activities that have been set in motion in the IOR by the two superpowers. Much of that activity has been defined in military-naval terms, so that Indian responses need also to be couched in the same terms, with little scope left for diplomacy.

This chapter will commence with an enunciation of the geostrategic environment that Indian policy makers perceive as enveloping their country in the 1980s. That geostrategic appreciation will be related to certain theoretical considerations about the international strategic system that help to explain the activities of the superpowers in the context of the IOR. Thereafter, the attempt will be to elaborate Indian assessments of the likely course of U.S.-Soviet strategic interaction in the area. This will be followed by a delineation of Indian strategic preferences for the South and Southwest Asia sectors of the IOR. In the next section an assessment will be made of the likely impact on India of superpower policies in South and Southwest Asia. A statement of India's strategic objectives in response to the evolving U.S.-Soviet confrontation in the IOR will then occasion an analysis of the country's capabilities to achieve those objectives. Finally, there will be a definition of the political framework within which India's maritime strategy and capability are to be circumscribed.

The Geostrategic Environment

The littoral states of the IOR contain 30 percent of the world's population, two-thirds of which are located in South Asia. Given the historical record of the past two centuries, the IOR is unalterably the epicenter of the Third World. Yet, at three of the major entry points into the Indian Ocean there exist communities that either deny equal status to non-Europeans (South Africa), have yet to resolve policies that respond to the contradictory pulls of ethnic affiliation and geographic location (Australia), or are engaged in a long-running feud with numerous states of the IOR (Israel). Two of the latter (South Africa and Israel) are suspected of having acquired nuclear weapon capabilities, perhaps in collaboration with each other, and probably with the active but clandestine collaboration of several Western states. It is possible that secret agreements exist for the use of the Simonstown naval base in South Africa by North Atlantic Treaty Organization (NATO) navies in case of need. More overt forms of military-naval arrangements already engage the

United States with Israel and Australia (the North West Cape and Cockburn Sound).[2]

The countries of South Asia cumulatively account for a bare 1.2 percent of world military expenditures. To the west and east of this area are subregions with significantly higher military expenditures, involved in the economic and military web of the superpowers and their respective allies.[3] To the north of the subcontinent lie two major nuclear powers, with one of which (China) India has a disputed boundary and the rankling memory of a military defeat in 1962. China is now not only openly courted in a strategic context by the United States, it has also proclaimed its right to administer "lessons" by military means to its southern neighbors.[4] Nor has the Soviet occupation of Afghanistan left Indian policy makers unperturbed. The manner in which that Soviet move has been interpreted and used, for separate objectives, by Pakistan and the United States, has alarmed India still more. It is felt that, for short-run weapons procurement objectives—which India can and will match—Pakistan has exposed itself to a Soviet riposte at the latter's own time and choosing and, simultaneously, to the risk of no serious support from its American patrons at the moment of crisis. More will be said later on this issue. For the moment, the point is that India is just as concerned about Pakistan's weakness before external powers as it is about Pakistan's strength in relation to itself. The overall Indian assessment is that Pakistan's policies have now exposed the South Asian subcontinent to superpower interference in a manner that had not occurred since the independence of India and Pakistan in 1947.

Perhaps the most prominent land feature of the IOR is the way in which the Indian peninsula juts two thousand kilometers into the sea. This physical configuration brings approximately 50 percent of the Indian Ocean within a thousand-mile arc ascribed from Indian territory. On the positive side, it means that the country has acquired one of the largest exclusive economic zones (EEZs) in the world (approximately two million square kilometers) inclusive of the seas around its island territories. In a strategic context, the implication is that, with the appropriate weapons systems, land-based military power can be projected from and integrated with India's sea-based capability over a wide swath of the Indian Ocean. On the negative side, the country has that many more economic assets to patrol and protect and is that much more exposed to physical ingress along its long coastline.

A final geostrategic concern for India is its currently unprotected island territories (the Andaman and Nicobar group to the southeast of the Bay of Bengal and the Laccadive and Minicoy group to the southwest of the Indian peninsula). A "Falklands Islands syndrome" haunts

Indian military planners, particularly now that massive superpower flotillas traverse the seas close to those islands.[5] An additional if latent worry relates to the defense of small island republics in the IOR, with special emphases on the futures of the Seychelles, the Maldives, and Mauritius. The dubious manner in which Diego Garcia was detached from Mauritius by the British and then handed over to the Americans occasions fear that other major powers may adopt similar tactics to acquire their own Diego Garcias.[6] Should that happen, India would have to reckon with the unhappy situation of being permanently bracketed by two nuclear superpowers to the north and two to the south.

The Superpowers and the International Strategic System in the IOR

For the moment, the northwest quadrant of the Indian Ocean littoral is the focus of major confrontation between the superpowers. Containing 60 percent of the world's proven oil reserves, the region around the Persian Gulf is considered crucial to the future of the world's free-market economies. After the Soviet lurch into Afghanistan, the region stretching from Pakistan to Egypt and from Kenya to Iran has been declared to be of vital importance to the West, in whose defense all means including force would be applied against any aggressors—presumably, the Soviet Union. Beginning in fact earlier than the Soviet invasion of Afghanistan, the United States instituted policies to create a Rapid Deployment Force (RDF) that could, in a relatively short time, introduce upwards of two hundred thousand troops, along with all ground, marine, and air support, into any area of Southwest Asia. The emphasis has been on the rapid and massive application of American military power in the region.[7]

The scale and form of the forward deployment of American power in the IOR raise some interesting questions in relation to classical theories of geopolitics. In the most obvious sense, the Soviet Union is Mackinder's "heartland" and the region in contention Spykman's "rimland," toward which the Americans have adopted a Mahan-style strategy for the forward and flexible application of sea-based power.[8] If the Soviet Union is to be viewed as a naturally expansionist heartland power, then, unable to go east (China) or west (Europe), it must move south. For those who are persuaded by such analyses and assessments, the northern Indian Ocean littoral/rimland becomes of incalculable and permanent importance in the next phase of the struggle of the titans.

Whatever the veracity of theories or motives, the significant point for all the states of the northern and northwestern Indian Ocean littoral/rimland is that one or another from among them, as befits need, is likely to be invited or coerced into collaborative, antagonistic postures by the two superpowers. The organizational framework of the U.S. central command that covers the area, excluding India but including Pakistan in its jurisdiction, should be seen for what it is: a temporary exigency that merely affirms *present* U.S. confrontation objectives, not those that may arise in the future. The overriding reality is to be seen in the massiveness and permanence of U.S. deployments in the IOR. Further, they can only increase, not decrease, in the future. Assuming that the Soviets are not sitting idle, one must reckon with the certainty that they too are marshaling counter-RDF airlift capacities and developing logistical supply lines to their own southern borders. At some future date, the Soviets may also seek a level of deployments in the Indian Ocean capable of neutralizing the U.S. sea-based capabilities.

Future American-Soviet Strategic Interaction

Indian policy makers assess that the cutting edge of the second cold war is going to be the northern Indian Ocean littoral and that India is perilously close to the area of contention.[9] Furthermore, it is felt that the current policies of Pakistan, allied to its Janus-faced search for identity and a role as both a South Asian *and* a West Asian Islamic state, will drag India into more fractious relations with one or another of the superpowers, with unpredictable consequences for the subcontinent's integrity.

Given Western premises for action, Indian analysts realize the importance that the IOR has assumed in American defense planning as a function of the global confrontation with the Soviet Union. They, therefore, view the current level of forward deployments as only the beginning of a much more massive projection of power that will continue to be fleshed out, improved, and honed for the rest of this century.[10] Further, it is felt that Diego Garcia by itself will prove insufficient for burgeoning U.S. needs and capabilities. Other Diego Garcias will be needed and therefore sought. Eventually, the United States will need major military bases and installations on the littoral, preferably in the Persian Gulf–Pakistan area, to counter seriously the natural geographical advantage of land-based Soviet power close to the area of contention.[11] The states of the area will have to contend with all the blandishments, pressures, and interventionism that that need is likely to entail.

Despite its need and massive effort, the United States is still viewed as having to carry the burdens of long-term strategic disadvantage vis-à-vis Soviet power. The most preferred situation for the United States would have been to be able to deploy its power on the northern borders of Iran. That option no longer exists. Indeed, one of the most heavy strategic burdens for the United States is that the largest state in the area of contention is implacably hostile to it. Although, barring a cataclysmic change, Iran is likely to remain hostile to the Soviet Union as well as to the United States, this is less obvious.

Given the Soviet presence in Afghanistan, Pakistan, because of its location, size, population, and efficient armed forces, may be conceived as the best replacement for Iran in American strategic plans for the area. Unfortunately, Pakistan, like prerevolutionary Iran, is a smoldering powder keg. Its centralized, Punjabi-dominated military leadership and armed forces rule without mandate over sullen and rebellious Sindhis and Baluchis and, to some extent, the Pathans. A large segment of the country's political and intellectual elites, as typified by those who participate in the periodic but consistent Movement for the Restoration of Democracy (MRD), remains alienated from the military wielders of power. Within the army itself there appears to be dissent, as signs filter through from the country's censored press of the arrests, transfers, and dismissals of various members of the armed forces.[12] Underlying the whole edifice is a strident streak of anti-Americanism, stoked as much by what is perceived by opposition groups as American support for the military junta, as by Islamic resentment of American support for Israel.

In recent months, some significant members of the Pakistan establishment have called for a modus vivendi with the Soviets over Afghanistan.[13] These voices are likely to grow stronger as more Pakistanis aver the imbalance in dangers from confronting a superpower next door, with the benefits derived from supporting a superpower attempting to extend its power from across the world. Thus Pakistan, despite the shine of its positive attributes, remains inherently unstable, unsure of its attitude toward the Soviet Union, fearful of Indian machinations, and likely to be undependable in a regional emergency. It is perhaps for all the preceding reasons that the Americans themselves have described their new security relationship with Pakistan as a "handshake" and not an "embrace."

The long-term situation in the remaining sector of Southwest Asia is equally troublesome from the American viewpoint. With Iraq totally focused on its hopeless war with Iran, the Arab states of the gulf are akin to a strategic house of cards: empty lands with small populations despite the overt glitter of oil, money, and new weapons. Their anachronistic state structures are likely to be under assault for change; it is unpredictable when they may collapse because of external or internal forces.

As far as the United States is concerned, it is clear that action is better than inaction and that one moves with what pieces one possesses on the international chessboard. It should be equally clear to the Soviets that, in spite of the massive deployment of American power in the region, the U.S. strategic position will remain weak and liable to degradation without warning in the shifting and changing political sands of Southwest Asia. Having made its investment in men, money, matériel, and strategy, the United States will be compelled to protect it and maintain its credibility. At a certain stage, then, the United States will have no option but to buttress its strategic confrontation with the Soviet Union with a deliberate policy of interventionism in the region to secure its power and to keep its allies in line. The stakes, according to Indian analysts, will be too high for the United States to avoid fulfilling such an interventionist role, at least in the area from Saudi Arabia to Pakistan.

In certain respects, this inexorable turn in American policies contains the seeds of its own defeat. The Soviets, safe behind their own borders, could, and probably will, adopt low-cost nonconfrontational tactics that continually bait the Americans and engage them in interventions. With every intervention, implied or real, the American exposure will increase and anti-Americanism will rise. The possible use of surrogate troops instead of their own—for example, from Pakistan— would only partially deflect the increase in hostility. More likely, the surrogate troops would themselves, along with their home state, become the focus of resentment.[14] Indeed, one might surmise that, based on their current and evolving pattern of strategic engagement, the prospects for achievement of long-term American objectives in the area have been rendered more rather than less difficult.

Indian Strategic Preferences

Although irrelevant now in the light of American actions, its remains necessary and perhaps useful as a reminder, to state Indian preferences for the disposition of the region in the aftermath of the Soviet entry into Afghanistan. It would have been more cost-effective in both resources and credibility for the United States to have stooped to conquer rather than run the high risk of rising to defeat. An attempt at a mutually agreed neutralization of the whole area could have been a first step. Along with an agreement under the IOZP proposal, a limit on American naval vessels would have also meant a limit on Soviet squadrons in the IOR. The American refusal to freeze naval deployments in the IOR because of the Soviets' land-based strategic advantage has solved one problem by creating another equally perplexing. The Soviet Union has now the equal right to build its naval forces in the Indian Ocean and, if necessary, to match those of the United States. It also has the right now to coax, to coerce, or to buy for itself a permanent base from one of the island states in the IOR on the model of Diego Garcia.[15] Indeed, if there is any merit in the divination proclaiming the Russian/Soviet long-run drive for a warm-water port, then the incentives for such a push to the south should engage Soviet strategists more now than ever before. The fact is that the Soviets, while continuing to possess their land-based geo-strategic advantage, now also possess a carte blanche to neutralize with a matching capability the sea-based power of the United States in the IOR.

It is possible, of course, that the Soviets will desist from adventurism in the IOR. On the other hand, they may not, so that an aggressive Soviet maritime posture with a permanent base in the IOR could well render the benefits from a Diego Garcia of temporary relevance to the United States. It is on the premises of such, albeit negative, options that the Indian government urged the United States to evolve a strategy of engaging the Soviets in a web of formal international obligations *along with* discreet rather than precipitate military deployments around the IOR. No other state bordering the Soviet Union in the area could be occupied by an overnight putsch spearheaded by a contingent of Soviet para-troops as was Afghanistan—not Iran, not Pakistan. Nor would the Soviets envisage the conquest of Iran or Pakistan with a few thousand border troops detached from their Central Asian forces. A far greater effort would be needed. The marshaling of such forces could be easily monitored and could be made a casus belli at the central strategic level between the United States and the Soviet Union. Low-keyed and, if appropriate, secret military action could have been taken to plug the one potential gap through which Soviet forces in southwest Afghanistan could ostensibly cut through to the Indian Ocean: the Baluchi areas of eastern Iran and western Pakistan.

Simultaneously, a political-diplomatic framework should have been devised, under U.S. auspices, to provide for the early exit of Soviet troops from Afghanistan. The Soviets, then as now, proclaim their intention to leave Afghanistan if the regime installed by them is "guaranteed" and "foreign interference" is stopped. They should have been held to those premises in negotiations on a bilateral basis by the United States, instead of being told that negotiations could take place only after the Soviets vacated Afghanistan. The physical removal of Soviet troops from Afghanistan should have been the first and the overriding priority from a strategic angle. The form and personnel of government should have been a secondary issue. The world is littered with dubiously installed (or self-installed) leaders whose claims to legitimacy could be as tenuous as those of the Karmal regime in Afghanistan.[16] As it is, the Soviets are now embedded in Afghanistan, the heroic resistance of the Afghans notwithstanding. The level and form of aid to the Mujahideen also appears to be finely tuned: enough weapons of a type to keep them fighting and dying but not enough or of a quality to seriously provoke the Soviet forces to escalate the level of the conflict.[17] Meanwhile, the plight of the Afghans, and the bloodletting, continue to recede in memory and appear to have been placed on a back burner in the American-Soviet dialogue.

Finally, it is the Indians' view that closer American consultation and cooperation with their own country—the largest, most powerful, and most stable state in the region—would have been more useful for the realization of long-run American (and Indian) objectives for the area. Instead, the United States initiated the process with Pakistan, which was almost overnight declared a "frontline" state. The Pakistanis, shrewdly enough, saw the opportunity and eventually accepted the status in return for a generous supply of arms. India was, thereafter, asked to fall into line and accept both the American interpretation of events and the courses already proposed for action.

While the quantity, category, and quality of the weapons being supplied to Pakistan have troubled India, they are, in the larger context, of no more than temporary importance in the Indo-Pakistani military equation. India's independent and across-the-board defense modernization program, along with a growing indigenous weapons production capability, is substantially larger than Pakistan's. A portion of that will now be devoted to matching and canceling out the offensive thrust of the new Pakistani acquisitions. It is to be assumed that Pakistani military planners are aware of the essential and widening imbalance in the nature of the threat that their country and India can pose to each other. Some of the items within Pakistan's new weapons systems—the F-16 fighter bombers, the E-2C Hawkeye airborne guidance and control aircraft, the Harpoon sea missiles, and the Vulcan-Phalanx ship-defense system—provide the capability to penetrate deeply toward Indian targets or to resist Indian attack. But the size and quality of Indian capabilities allied with the geography and politics of Pakistan are such as to threaten, at least in conventional terms, the territorial unity of the latter state.

Of greater significance than the weapons in Indian and Pakistani hands is the fact that a momentous opportunity has been lost for engaging the two major states of South Asia in a coordinated venture to maintain the security of the subcontinent. It is known that, in the immediate aftermath of the Soviet entry into Afghanistan, Indian emissaries traveled to Islamabad to offer ironclad guarantees—if necessary, under third-party auspices—against their country creating any problems on Pakistan's eastern borders. Furthermore, India was also prepared to extend such cooperation as Pakistan deemed suitable for shoring up the defenses of the northwest frontier of the subcontinent.[18] Despite a natural Pakistani skepticism of Indian professions, the opportunity existed for the United States to conceive its arms supply in ways that assuaged Pakistani fears without alarming India.[19] Instead, a unifocal and perhaps hastily inspired transfer of weapons to Pakistan—which remain of nominal value against the Soviets—have further divided the subcontinental neighbors.

The Impact of American-Soviet Policies

While the weapons supply to Pakistan may have broadened its tactical military options in the short run, in the long run Pakistan's strategic options have been narrowed. The Indians are bent upon neutralizing Pakistan's newly acquired tactical capabilities, while the latter still needs to contend with Soviet reactions to its rearmament and, even more, with unpredictable Soviet ripostes for the quid pro quos suspected to have been offered the Americans in return for the arms. At the same time, the Pakistanis cannot be sanguine about receiving wholehearted American support. In these constricted circumstances, a Pakistani resort to the acquisition of nuclear weapons seems preordained. India will inevitably respond with a similar move.

The mutual nuclearization of India and Pakistan will have its influence on South Asian affairs but the more crucial impact will be on the politics of West Asia, particularly on the Arab-Israeli dispute. Israeli leaders have frequently affirmed that they would view nuclear weapons in the possession of *any* Islamic state as a direct threat to their own state. So, the responses of Israel to the nuclearization of Pakistan will be an added complicating factor for that country in the total militarization of the Southwest Asia rimland. Pakistanis may feel safe behind their nuclear shield, but they will not be immune to a confusing mix of perceived destabilization threats from the Russians, from the Israelis, and from the Indians. Given the depth of America's rapport with Israel, it seems logical to assume that, over time, U.S. support of Pakistan will remain ambiguous. Indeed, U.S. pressures on Pakistan to stay in line and be more predictable will increase. This raises the possibility of greater internal dissent and greater government-directed repression in Pakistan, with an incalculable impact on India.

The second apprehension in Indian thinking is that the superpowers will resort to a more forthright policy of cross-nuclear targeting all the Southwest Asian rimland states to seek insurance against wayward moves by any of them and to deter those going nuclear from adopting adversarial roles. Considering the stakes judged to be important in the region as a function of their global confrontation, the superpowers will make no distinction in threatening nuclear intervention against both allies and adversaries in South and Southwest Asia.

The third anxiety among Indian policy makers relates to the expected search by the Soviets for their own Diego Garcia in the IOR. The effort, if made, will be directed among islands and island-states in the western Indian Ocean. That puts states such as the Malagasy Republic, Mauritius, the Seychelles, and the Maldives on notice against interventions, coups d'état, bribery, and coercion from both the superpowers—one searching for a base and the other seeking preemption. In this context, states other than the superpowers who have a record or the experience of mounting long-distance mercenary or commando-style raids may get involved in proxy roles, for example, South Africa and Israel.

A final set of dangers is seen to arise in systemic form. With their proximate power and presence in the IOR and the varied incentives to control and to rationalize the situation to their respective advantages, both the superpowers will be prey to invitations for support in the internecine quarrels of the region. As prospective losers seek one superpower patron, their adversaries will invariably run to the other superpower. This happens even now, but the difference will be that with the nearness of their capabilities, the involvements will be deeper, longer, and more provocative in exacerbating the local conflicts. It is feared, for instance, that in addition to facilities in Pakistan, the United States may also be in search of bases for its RDF in Sri Lanka (Trincomalee naval installations) and Bangladesh (Chittagong harbor).[20] Such moves, if undertaken, would create immediate negative repercussions in India–Sri Lanka and India-Bangladesh relations. India's hardened reactions would complicate the settlement of the Tamil problem in Sri Lanka and it would make more difficult a settlement on the issue of illegal emigration from Bangladesh into the Assam province of India.

India's Strategic Objectives

The primary Indian objective will be to prevent the fallout from any of the possible superpower actions from affecting India's economic development, political stability, and flexibility of choices. Second, India's effort will be to preclude, or neutralize the impact of, any whimsical or wayward actions directed at itself from either of the superpowers.[21] The third goal will be to prevent any part of the subcontinent from becoming a bone of contention between the superpowers. Given Pakistan's inclusion in the U.S. Central Command area, this will be a difficult task, but the objective still must be stated. Possibly, Indian diplomacy will seek to convince the Pakistanis that having received American weapons they should now seek a rapprochement with the Soviets.[22] The fourth Indian goal will be to acquire sufficient naval (and land and air) capability so as to raise inordinately the threshold of any threatened superpower military intervention in the South Asia region. The fifth objective will be the acquisition and deployment of such naval/military assets on India's island possessions as will safeguard them from dispute in ownership or a sudden take-over by hostile forces. Allied to the former, the sixth Indian objective could entail an offer to help defend, if requested, some of the island republics in the western Indian Ocean against the threat of mercenary or commando-style invasions or takeovers.[23] (There is no intention to enter into defense pacts or to garrison Indian troops in these islands nor would India act unilaterally in this respect. The purpose would be to improve the channels of communication and the exchange of intelligence with the island states, to designate units of the Indian armed forces for emergency duty, and to act only on the basis of a consensus for such action among a number of the littoral states.) The seventh Indian maritime objective calls for the country's naval and coast guard forces to be able to prevent encroachments upon and to protect the assets of the largest exclusive economic zone in the Indian Ocean. These assets include offshore oil deposits and their attendant installations, seabed minerals and coastal monazite sands, and fishery resources. Finally, Indian naval planners will seek to maintain the rights of peaceful passage for their naval units and mercantile fleet across the Indian Ocean, commensurate with the similar rights of other nations.[24]

India's Capacity to Achieve Its Strategic Objectives

India currently possesses the biggest navy among the littoral states of the Indian Ocean, comprising some eighty vessels of a varied nature— and more, if auxiliaries are taken into account. The Indian navy is also, for the moment, numerically larger than the naval contingents of the United States and the Soviet Union in the IOR. It is clear, however, that the American and Soviet naval capabilities—in the Indian Ocean and worldwide—fall into a class by themselves.

The Indian government, nonetheless, has updated a twenty-year development plan for the Indian navy, first conceived in 1978, for speedier realization. A significant feature of the new thinking is the approval given for the creation of an Indian navy with true blue-water capabilities. Exact details about the number of vessels to be acquired or built in Indian shipyards are not known, but the prospective quality and performance criteria can be gauged from the following general categories that have been mentioned before the Indian parliament. These include long-range guided missile cruisers (Kresta II–class), antisubmarine warfare (ASW) destroyers (Kashin II–class), helicopter-embarked frigates (Godavari-class), and corvettes (Nanuchka II–class); missile- and torpedo-equipped, long-range, fast-attack boats of the Petya and Nanuchka classes; ASW and attack submarines of the Foxtrot, Tango, Kilo, and Type 1500 classes; ocean minesweepers of the Natya class; and attendant auxiliary ships. The Indian navy already undertakes reconnaissance flights up to a radius of a thousand miles with its Ilyushin-38 patrol aircraft. These are being supplemented for longer-range monitoring of the seas with Antonov-32s. Also being negotiated is the purchase (and local production) of sophisticated electronic countermeasure and counter-countermeasure equipment. Furthermore, India is seeking long-range ship-deployable surface-to-surface missiles with over-the-horizon capability, such as the SSN-14, along with radars to locate targets.[25]

India's new naval plans stipulate a speedier indigenization of warship production. Apart from Godavari-class frigates and lesser types of naval vessels, India is embarking on the local construction of Type 1500 submarines under license from a German firm (six to be produced).[26] There have been reports that the Soviet Union has offered to provide the design specifications of their own aircraft carriers and help in the production of one of them in an Indian shipyard. (India already possesses one aircraft carrier, the Vikrant, with Harrier jump-jets embarked.)[27] It is known that, for some years, Indian naval-nuclear teams have been engaged in perfecting nuclear-propulsion systems for undersea craft. A recent news report indicates that the Soviet Union has also offered to supply India with a nuclear-powered submarine.[28]

In terms of support infrastructure for its new naval profile, India will expand its marine bases at Bombay and Cochin on the west coast and at Vishakhapatnam on the east coast. It has been building a large naval base at Port Blair in the Andaman and Nicobar groups of islands, which stretch from the Bay of Bengal to the entrance of the Malacca straits. Plans under review provide for a similar facility in the Laccadive and Minicoy groups of islands, extending from the tip of India in a southwesterly arc toward the Maldives. India has developed the technology of third-generation laser-guided missiles as well as a variety of missiles for air, sea, and ground launches.[29] This technology will also be ap-

314 SUBREGIONAL PERSPECTIVES

plied in a pattern of shore-based parametric missile batteries to guard against seaborne assault and to take advantage of India's long peninsula for offensive-defensive interdiction of hostile forces at sea.

Airborne warning and control system (AWACS) aircraft are to be acquired in India's current phase of defense modernization. These may either be purchased or the "warning and control" systems may be developed in collaboration with another country to specific Indian needs and then provided aboard a suitable aircraft.[30] The AWACS would meet the needs of both the navy and the air force. Indian research teams have also been experimenting successfully with underwater sonar and electronic detection devices and with wire-guided long-range homing torpedoes. These and other parallel capabilities being developed will be integrated into the navy's modernization program.

Early in 1984, it has been learned, the Indian navy began the construction of a very-low-frequency (VLF) communications network at Vijaynarayanam, near Tirunelveli in the southern state of Tamil Nadu. The first of its kind in Asia, the technology for the VLF network was developed indigenously. The venture, code-named Project Skylark, will on completion place India among those few nations that possess such sophisticated means of communication with (and detection of) submarines operating underwater at long ranges. The network will also be able to monitor surface vessels and to distinguish between merchantmen and warships over long distances in the Indian Ocean.[31]

Apart from China's, India's space program is probably the most advanced in the Third World and has provided the country with space-launch capabilities. By 1988, it will have developed booster rockets that will loft a one-ton payload into space. India's current range of satellites, the INSAT/I series, are unique in design and function. They are the first three-in-one satellites in the world, simultaneously offering communication channels, direct broadcasts, and weather-monitoring facilities to users. These satellites can also be used for naval-monitoring purposes along with their civilian functions. High-resolution photography from satellites is bound to be adapted to Indian Ocean surveillance since India is already known to have experimented in this regard over the Tibet region of China.[32]

Supplementing the naval rearmament program, India plans a continuous upgrading of the size, complement, and area of operations of the Indian Coast Guard (ICG). The ICG currently consists of some twenty armed vessels and a helicopter surveillance squadron. It is acquiring a fleet of Dornier 228 aircraft for increasing the area and range of surveillance capability. A $125 million four-year expansion plan now being implemented should bring most of the two million square kilometers of India's EEZ within the country's watch.[33]

As stated earlier, no figures have been released by the Indian government of the expected size or the number of warships that will comprise the Indian navy through the coming decade. Naval experts, however, are quoted as saying that the navy will "double in size."[34] That in itself is not explanatory enough, but one can envisage that, based on current figures, a "doubling" of the units would mean an Indian navy in the 1990s of around 150 modern warships. The latter would include a sizable submarine command and the requisite home-based infrastructure of communications, surveillance, replenishment, and repair facilities.

The Political Framework of India's Maritime Capability

India does not require its refurbished blue-water navy to deal with Pakistan. It is also not needed against any of its close or distant neighbors in the IOR. With the exception of South Africa, India maintains amicable relations with every country in the IOR. It should be clear, therefore, that the naval build-up has been occasioned by the sole objective of contending with the threats, direct and indirect, perceived to arise from the ingress of superpower navies into the IOR.[35]

Fortunately, India's political relations with both the United States and the Soviet Union are good. There is no reason to assume that such relations would deteriorate to the point where hostile naval engagements between India or either of the superpowers would ensue. The prime Indian objective will be to create a stronger, more visible, presence in the IOR, to indicate an active definition and assertion of national interests, and to deny total control of the Indian Ocean stretches by default-in-absence to the superpowers' navies.

In recent years, India has embarked on two major pioneering ventures in and through the Indian Ocean. In the first place, it has developed the technology of extracting minerals from the seabed—one of only six nations in the world and the first in the Third World to have acquired this capability. The country has, therefore, been accredited as a "pioneer investor" under the new international Law of the Sea and has been given the right to select, in the first instance, a 150,000-square-mile area in the oceans to commence commercial seabed mining operations. India's Department of Oceans Development and National Institute of Oceanography are now engaged in mapping and prospecting operations around the IOR to locate a promising lode of mineral nodules.[36] This means India will have important commercial and economic assets to protect, not only within its EEZ limits, but possibly beyond them—and the latter will increase over time.

The second important sea-based Indian venture relates to Antarctica. India has already mounted three successful landings on the southern continent. By 1985 it will have set up a permanently staffed scientific base and extensive satellite communication, weather charting, and research facilities. A 10,000-foot runway for direct flights from India is being constructed to supplement the two-way passage by sea. India was recently accepted as a member of the Antarctic Treaty Parties Consultative Group. That means it will have growing commercial and political interests to guard should plans unfold for the disposition of the wealth and territory of Antarctica.[37]

While India's activities on the seabed and in Antarctica are of commercial and scientific nature, they obviously—as with similar activities of other states—create a political, and perhaps a security, burden.[38] Rights of peaceful passage will have to be guaranteed, interdiction will have to be avoided, and equitable divisions will need to be secured. For all these objectives to be achieved a strong and far-ranging Indian naval capability appears to be a minimal, though not a sufficient, necessity.

Conclusion

India's maritime strategy needs to be visualized in an evolving mode. The decision to embark upon the creation of a sizable blue-water naval force is, at least in timing, correlated with the superpower militarization of the IOR. India preferred and earlier urged a sustained recourse to non-military premises for superpower interaction in the IOR. Since that has not come to pass, it fears that a range of threatening situations and interventionist activities will confront the IOR states as the two superpowers move to assert their respective interests in the region. A substantial arena for the vindication of these superpower interests lies close to India's land and sea territories, and some of the strategic confrontation plans include portions—and may include still more—of the Indian subcontinent.

For the preceding reasons, allied to the need to safeguard the country's growing seabed assets, India has embarked upon a major naval modernization program. When completed, the program should provide the country with the most powerful navy among the littoral states of the Indian Ocean. While the new Indian navy will remain modest in comparison with the total naval assets of the superpowers, its stronger physical presence and strike-power over wider ranges of the Indian Ocean may go some way toward providing the political and military insurance policies sought by India: the means to persuade the superpowers to choose the lesser evil of avoiding encroachments on India's security interests as they mount their new confrontation strategies in the Indian Ocean region.

18. Pakistan's Security Predicament ▰ Robert G. Wirsing

Providing for Pakistan's security has always been a formidable challenge for the country's policy makers. Until the loss of Bangladesh in 1971, they lived uneasily with the militarily perplexing fact that Pakistan's geographically separated eastern wing was virtually indefensible. Even in what remains of Pakistan, efforts to unify its disparate peoples and to consolidate its hold over Muslim majority areas have been frustrated by Afghan rejection of the boundary inherited from the British in the northwest, by the separatist demands of the Baluch tribal minority resident in the southwest, and, above all, by the denial of Pakistan's own claim to the Indian-held portion of Kashmir in the northeast. Having won independence against the will of the subcontinent's Hindu majority, Pakistan's overwhelmingly Muslim population lives with the nagging suspicion that a revanchist India conspires to achieve, if not Pakistan's dismemberment, at least its disablement. Pakistanis look back upon three wars with India, the last of them a humiliating catastrophe, and a major tribal rebellion in Baluchistan. Soviet combat forces are now positioned on their northwestern border; Soviet-equipped Indian combat forces are deployed along their entire eastern border. In view of all this, they have good reason to feel apprehensive about the future.

Despite the worrisome aspects of Pakistan's security situation, there is very little agreement among analysts as to the nature and extent of the threat it faces. Consequently, there is little uniformity in the remedies proposed. Instead, there are seemingly irreconcilable interpretations of Islamabad's situation, each predicated on dissimilar assumptions of threats and the way to meet them. No tidy categorization can do full justice to these rival analytic perspectives for their logic is generally complex and they sometimes overlap one another.

One way to look at them, however, is to distinguish between those analysts who hold that Pakistan's problems are basically internal and those convinced that the difficulties are largely external. The former argue that Pakistan's vulnerability is mainly a reflection of unresolved domestic political and socioeconomic problems, while the latter maintain that it is a reflection of powerful outside pressures that cannot be alleviated without the aid of countervailing pressures also from the outside. At bottom, the internalist perspective places major responsibility for the country's security dilemmas on Pakistan itself, to a large extent on its military elite which has from an early point in the country's history frustrated development of stable parliamentary political institutions and instead served as guardian of a highly inequitable social and political order. In the rulers' strident militarism lies much of the blame for Pakistan's implacable resistance to an accommodation with India, whose own military expansion, according to this perspective, is a reluctant reaction to Pakistan's. Internalists typically maximize the importance of domestic reforms, the restoration of civilian political institutions, and accommodation with the country's religious, ethno-linguistic, and tribal minorities. They customarily plead that the external threat is exaggerated by Islamabad to pacify the military constituency and to divert attention from internal decay. An intraregional and bilateral (India-Pakistan) framework for resolving disputes is preferred by advocates of this point of view over one involving extraregional (superpower) forces in affairs of the subcontinental and Indian Ocean area.

The externalist perspective, in contrast, places the larger burden of responsibility for Pakistan's predicament on the country's foreign adversaries (or on its unreliable allies). It tends to minimize the urgency, utility, or feasibility of domestic reforms while maximizing the severity of the external threat (from the Soviet Union and, at least in some analyses, India). It also emphasizes the degree to which external (extraregional) assistance, especially military assistance, may help to assure Pakistan's security. Pakistan's Islamic identity, its ties to the Middle East, and, ultimately, its "Washington connection" are important elements in this perspective.

Unavoidably, these perspectives on Pakistan's predicament have become entangled in partisan policy debates over global strategic issues. In the United States, the internalist orientation has generally been associated with political doves, the externalist perspective with their hawkish adversaries. The latter view has had the official backing of the Reagan administration, while the former commanded considerable influence among academics and congressmen, as well as throughout the bureaucracy. The externalist perspective, for obvious reasons, has been the one publicly favored in governing circles in Islamabad; the internalist position has naturally been more strongly supported in New Delhi.

This chapter examines the debate over Pakistan's current security situation. It takes the view that events in Southwest Asia in recent years have created a geopolitical environment exceptional not only for the dangers posed for Pakistan's security, but also for its great instability, complexity, and unpredictability. This environment is one in which a deliberately ambiguous, quasi-neutralist policy of conflict avoidance and controlled cooperation with neighbors, potential allies, and adversaries has an appeal to the leaders of a weak and vulnerable state. Neither the internalist nor the externalist camp has taken sufficient account of the pressures exerted on Islamabad to justify unqualified commitment to *either* side. Accordingly, analysis too faithful to one or the other of these perspectives, both of which rest on relatively inflexible geopolitical understandings, may not be much help in assessing Islamabad's perception of the threats to Pakistan's security or in recommending the steps Pakistan's leaders (military or civilian) should take to meet them. This chapter argues the need for a new perspective. Two general problems are considered: the source and severity of the threats to Pakistan's security and the remedy for Pakistan's security predicament.

The Nature of the Threat

According to K. Subrahmanyam, director of the Institute for Defence Studies and Analyses in New Delhi, "Most of Pakistan's security problems, and the haunting sense of insecurity of the country's rulers are inherent in the nature of the Pakistani state and the relationship between rulers and ruled." India, he claims, "can do nothing about it."[1] Onkar Marwah has advanced essentially the same thesis. "The real dangers to the continuance of the Pakistani state are internally generated," he writes, "and they seem to possess a life of their own irrespective of any malicious Indian intent."[2] The "dangers" Marwah points to are the "strong disintegrative forces" at work in Baluchistan, the northwest frontier province, and the Sind, areas that "comprise 70 percent of the territory of Pakistan and 40 percent of its population." Militarized and lacking political institutions routinely responsive to political protest, Pakistan cannot cope with these forces as well as India can. With the Soviet Union now opportunely positioned on the Pakistani border, the probability grows that it "may soon arrogate the incentive to stoke the resentments of strongly disaffected minority communities in Pakistan, beginning with the Baluchis and the Pashtuns." According to Marwah, "India remains, at least territorially with respect to Pakistan, a status quo power." In contrast, "a nuclear-armed Pakistan threatened with disintegration, led by a fundamentalist military leadership, fearful of collusive action by the Soviet Union and India, and suspicious of the staying power of Western states in the region, would be a very unpredictable and therefore a dangerous Pakistan."[3]

Both of these authors appear to be taking the position that Pakistan is itself the greatest threat to its own security. This argument, characteristic of the internalist point of view, implies that whatever the external threat to Pakistan, it can be significantly controlled by taking steps toward internal political liberalization. Selig Harrison, one of the most forceful exponents of the internalist orientation, is especially adamant on this point. He argues that Islamabad could significantly reduce the Soviet threat on its borders by accommodating the demands of disaffected elements of its own population, most especially by granting greater autonomy to the tribal inhabitants of its vast province of Baluchistan. The "steady growth of Baluch discontent in Pakistan and Iran," he reasons,

> offers the Soviet Union an increasingly attractive opportunity. Though not yet disposed to act, Moscow might be tempted to manipulate Baluch nationalism if an anti-Soviet leadership comes to power in Tehran or if Islamabad continues to upgrade its military ties to Beijing and Washington. Moscow can afford to bide its time in deciding whether to play its Baluch card as long as Pakistani and Iranian leaders fail to make meaningful moves toward political settlements with the Baluch. Conversely, *should Baluch leaders reach an accommodation with either Islamabad or Tehran or both, the Baluch issue would no longer tempt Moscow, since the Soviet Union would find it difficult to organize an effective insurgency and legitimate an independent Baluchistan in the absence of strong Baluch nationalist support.*[4] (emphasis mine)

Externalists take a different view of the situation since, for them, the Soviet appetite for expansion exists independently of conditions within neighboring states (indeed, Moscow *creates* the conditions suited to its strategic goals where they do not already exist). W. Scott Thompson, for example, takes the position that Moscow, whether or not it has a "master plan" for territorial aggrandizement, is clearly expansionist and "that it is basic Soviet strategy to reach the warm waters of the Indian Ocean."[5] That being the case, the real question, for him, is not if, but how the Soviets intend to get there. As is commonly supposed, they could choose to lunge directly through Iran. Alternatively, Thompson suggests:

> Perhaps the Soviets would conclude that it was less dangerous—and in some ways more promising—to move south by way of Baluchistan. That region of Pakistan is now isolated, be-

tween a sullen India and Soviet forces in Afghanistan. As long as so much of Pakistan's armor is facing eastward, she cannot promise enough of a fight to deter a Soviet invasion even briefly. Military conquest of Baluchistan—the irredentist Pakistani region lying between Afghanistan and the Indian Ocean—would not be overwhelmingly complicated.[6]

If "it is Soviet policy," as Lawrence Ziring maintains, "to destroy Zia, to pacify Afghanistan, and ultimately to rearrange the political geography of the region,"[7] Islamabad's offer of an olive branch to the Baluch nationalists would hardly suffice to stem the hemorrhaging in Pakistan's security situation.

Very few observers, including those basically sympathetic to Pakistan, would disagree with the judgment that Pakistan is weakened by distrust among its ethnic minorities or that some of its leaders since 1947 have responded to demands for liberal reforms at times with studied indifference, at other times (clearly in Bangladesh) with savage repression, and at still other times with sheer incompetence. There is no doubt a relationship of some magnitude between Pakistan's domestic political malaise and its external security. There is, therefore, substance in the internalist argument that Islamabad's security problems are in some measure of Islamabad's making. Regardless of the degree to which the modern Soviet mentality is ingrained with the ancient Russian imperialist urge to the sea,[8] there is no denying, either, that Soviet-baiting externalists have sometimes squeezed more than the evidence warrants from the "warm water" thesis. On the other hand, the possibility exists that Pakistan's security may be made excessively contingent on internal as opposed to external threats. One wonders, for example, whether the "Baluch card"—the direct or indirect manipulation of Baluch nationalism by Moscow to achieve Soviet strategic objectives—is given more emphasis in the analyses of internalists than it gets in Soviet strategic planning.

Baluchistan, a region of roughly 200,000 square miles overlapping parts of Iran, Afghanistan, and Pakistan, has obvious potential as a Soviet corridor to the Arabian Sea. Occupying the three hundred or so miles between Soviet-dominated Afghanistan and the Makran coast, Baluchistan possesses several natural (though undeveloped) harbors, a 700-mile-long coastline overlooking the vital maritime approaches to the Persian Gulf, and, of equal importance perhaps, a small, but to some extent politically alienated, population of seminomadic tribes.[9] The Pakistani Baluch, the most numerous and politically mobilized element, have mounted at least three insurrections against the central government of Pakistan, the last one (1973–77) being by far the longest, the most widespread, and the costliest, for both the Baluch and Islamabad.[10] The Baluch have deep grievances against the Punjabi elite that rules Pakistan and there are today several thousand armed and trained Baluch guerrillas based in southern Afghanistan who could presumably be used by Moscow to create trouble for the Pakistanis.

As a resource available for Moscow's manipulation, Baluch nationalism is much less useful than is often argued. The nationalist movement is of recent origin, hardly antedating the late 1950s, and it is organizationally weak and fragmented. A sense of common Baluch identity seems to exist but it cannot be said that the fifteen or twenty major Baluch tribes of Pakistan—some of which have engaged in long and violent blood feuds[11]—have been welded into a common political instrument. Two key nationalist leaders are in exile; others have been executed, imprisoned, or harassed into submission. With a great deal of foreign assistance, Islamabad has provided handsome economic incentives (along with titles and political appointments) to those willing to go along with Islamabad. Regular and paramilitary forces are deployed in Baluchistan at a level considerably greater than a decade ago. Almost half a million Afghan (mainly Pashtun) refugees, who are by tradition, religion, and recent experience friendly neither to the Soviets nor to Baluch nationalism, have joined their already numerous coethnics in the northern districts of Baluchistan, forming a rather substantial phalanx against Soviet manipulation of Baluch disaffection. The thesis that Pakistan's internal ethnic discord supplies Moscow with a potent "Baluch card" suffers the additional defect that a significant element of its putative Baluch force—the seasoned Baluch guerrillas located in southern Afghanistan—is highly vulnerable to reprisal from the Afghan *mujahideen*.

Baluch nationalists continue to send out signals that another armed Baluch uprising is imminent and to hint that this time it will have the support of the Soviet Union.[12] So far, however, there are only unconfirmed reports of Soviet-aided activity in Pakistani Baluchistan. The escalation of such activity, especially as a device for relieving the situation in Afghanistan, remains a distinct possibility, of course. Unfortunately, so long as the possibility for Soviet interference exists, the concession of greater autonomy for the Baluch seems very remote. Ironically, the truth of the matter may be that the Baluch are more threatened by Islamabad than a threat to it.

If Pakistan's internal situation seems to me to be relatively less dangerous (to Islamabad) than it appears to others, Pakistan's external environment seems a bit more dangerous. The explanation for this is to be found in the profound political and military transformation of Pakistan's regional environment that has taken place since the loss of Bangladesh. One aspect of this transformation, the fall of the Pahlavi dynasty in Iran at the end of 1978, had at least two negative implications for Pakistan. First, it meant the loss of its former Central Treaty Organization (CENTO) and Regional Cooperation for Development (RCD) partner, an old ally that had buttressed Pakistan with material and moral support in its 1965 war with India and in its struggle against the Baluch guerrillas in the 1970s.[13] Second, it created a vast area of uncertainty to the immediate west of Pakistan, jeopardizing what had been the country's most secure border and generally posing a new threat to Pakistan's security. On the one hand, the turmoil in Iran raised the possibility of a Soviet-backed leftist take-over in Tehran, on the other it created the potential for a religious upheaval that could spread to Pakistan's own right-wing Islamic militants.[14]

The communist coup in Afghanistan in April 1978 and the subsequent Soviet military intervention in December 1979 had even more traumatic consequences for Pakistan's external security environment. On the positive side from Islamabad's standpoint, it meant that American reservations with respect to reviving its former close security relationship with Pakistan were set aside, allowing Pakistan to qualify for major assistance in the modernization of its armed forces. An unwelcome and immediately threatening consequence, on the other hand, was the introduction of Soviet armed forces into the area adjacent to Pakistan and, stemming from that, frequent violations of Pakistani air and ground space by Soviet and Afghan forces.[15] Of greatest significance, however, is the fact that the Soviet occupation of Afghanistan gives every indication of becoming a permanent feature of Pakistan's security environment. While Islamabad can only guess at Moscow's long-range intentions in the area, the reality is that the Soviets have deployed roughly one hundred thousand troops in Afghanistan and are backing them up with some of the most sophisticated weapons in their arsenal.[16] Like India, Pakistan now has powerful and arguably hostile forces on two of its borders and, since those forces are allied by a treaty with potential defense implications, Islamabad faces the prospect of a war on two fronts.

A third aspect of the transformation in Pakistan's security environment stems from London's decision in the late 1960s to relinquish responsibility for guarding the maritime approaches to the Persian Gulf. This decision sparked a competition for naval supremacy in the Indian Ocean between the United States and the Soviet Union. Both now have large naval squadrons permanently on station in the area; both have invested enormously in a whole range of diplomatic, economic, and military initiatives throughout the Indian Ocean and Southwest Asia region designed to acquire naval and air staging bases and support facilities; and both appear to be well along in their efforts to integrate the Indian Ocean region into their global strategic-military planning.[17] U.S. undertakings probably provoke an ambivalent response among the men who rule Pakistan, giving comfort while at the same time reminding them of their country's dependence on and vulnerability to American power. But the fact that Moscow's naval power might one day be used to augment the naval forces of its South Asian ally, India, naturally evokes even stronger misgivings in Islamabad.[18]

Few would dispute that these developments to the north, west, and south of Pakistan pose extraordinary challenges to its security planners. Few would dispute, either, that the military power of Pakistan's large neighbor to the east also contributes to its security problems. About the precise dimensions, dynamics, and trends in the military balance between Pakistan and India there is, however, enormous controversy. The way one resolves that controversy is the real key to a definition of Pakistan's security predicament.

In an article published in May 1982, Mohammed Ayoob, taking a basically internalist position, argued that New Delhi's arms acquisitions have mainly been a reaction to Islamabad's militarization and that Pakistan, in fact, has much less to fear from India than is sometimes alleged. The claim that India has radically altered the balance of power with Pakistan is, according to Ayoob, a myth. While conceding that Indian armed forces have maintained a qualitative edge over Pakistan during the past decade, in the same period, he argues, Pakistan has expanded its forces quantitatively much more rapidly than India. Given that India has a far longer border to defend and much greater distances to cover to move troops to wartime stations, he asserts that "the actual deployable capacity in terms of ground forces of the two sides at the beginning of another round of Indo-Pakistani hostilities would be roughly equivalent. Therefore, New Delhi's current self-image as the preeminent power in the subcontinent and the defender of the status quo in the region, is based on little more than the modest, although fast-eroding, qualitative edge that it possesses over Pakistan in terms of military equipment, and particularly aircraft."[19]

Externalists draw rather different conclusions from their reading of the comparative arms tables. They judge India's arms buildup of the past two decades to have been far less reactive, motivated more by India's own ambitions than by any threat from Pakistan. "It is quite apparent," observes Leo Rose, "that India is already involved in a substantial military modernization program of its own that has little or nothing to do with developments in Pakistan."[20] Furthermore, and in contrast to Ayoob's assessment, externalists find Pakistan quite vulnerable indeed to Indian power. "Indian superiority in conventional arms is unquestioned," writes Shirin Tahir-Kheli, "and Pakistanis believe that in 1981 it stood at approximately fifteen-to-one in India's favor." While conceding that "a more accurate ratio, that can be gleaned from third-party estimates of Indo-Pakistani armaments, is approximately half that, i.e., eight-to-one in India's favor,"[21] Tahir-Kheli leaves no doubt that India, in her view, holds far more than a "modest" edge over Pakistan.

Given the variety and complexity of modern weapons systems; the secrecy and ambiguity that surround their capabilities, transfers, and deployments; the frequent changes in arms inventories; the fact that arms drawn from different foreign suppliers are in many instances not readily comparable; the broad range of variables, from weather and terrain characteristics to the availability of spare parts, influencing military capabilities; and the enormous policy implications of even a slight shift in the perception of a rival's military capability, it is no wonder that estimates of the arms balance in South Asia are invariably controversial. Any number of military and nonmilitary factors, quantitative and qualitative, can plausibly be introduced into the equation either to increase or decrease the magnitude of the disparity between overall Indian and Pakistani military strength.[22]

Though very few would accept Tahir-Kheli's eight-to-one ratio, professional analysts do not really contest the fact that in most categories India at the moment holds an overall quantitative lead in conventional arms.[23] However, India and Pakistan are rapidly moving beyond the point where revealing comparisons of military capability can be made on the basis of a simple count of military manpower or any other readily quantifiable indicator. They both have entered the enchanted and somewhat uncharted world of high-technology weaponry in a major way, considerably clouding the military balance now prevailing between them. Nevertheless, in a technology-oriented race, India, with its growing experience in the manufacture and assembly of sophisticated weapons and weapons components, has some obvious advantages. Under a variety of licensing agreements with foreign governments, it is already producing or is scheduled to produce high-performance combat aircraft, helicopters, tanks, frigates, and submarines. The U.S. $1.6 billion Soviet military assistance package agreed to with India in 1980 reportedly included coproduction rights to the MIG-23. In addition, the Soviets are said to have offered to give India a license to produce indigenously the MIG-27.[24] In October 1982, the Indian Defense Ministry made the portentous announcement that the first Indian-assembled Jaguar had joined the Indian air force.[25] Pakistan, with a comparatively very small domestic arms production industry, can keep pace with India only by importing equally sophisticated weapons, at great cost, from abroad. Its determination in this regard shows no signs of slackening. In November 1982, Islamabad gave a rather stunning display of its intent to contest for each inch of technical advantage when it startled Washington with its much-publicized refusal to take delivery of the first forty F-16s until they were equipped with the vital ALR-69 electronics countermeasures package routinely installed in the NATO version of the aircraft.[26]

What, then, can one safely conclude about the military balance in South Asia? First, there can be no doubt that we are witnessing an intensified arms race between India and Pakistan and that it involves the acquisition of weapons enabling these ancient and predominantly agrarian societies to fight a very modern and lethal species of warfare. At the moment, the competition is largely confined to conventional weapons but India's detonation of a nuclear device in 1974, its progress in the mastery of missile technology,[27] and Pakistan's almost frantic efforts to acquire its own nuclear weapons capability,[28] all point to further nuclearization and an even more radical transformation of the military situation in South Asia.[29]

Second, while India, with its far greater resources and natural advantages, would seem destined to come out ahead, for the moment there can be no precise reckoning of the magnitude of its dominance. In recent years, the opinion has been widely shared among professional observers that "the overall India-Pakistan military balance has grown progressively adverse from Pakistan's point of view since the 1965 conflict," that "on the whole India's forces are better equipped and employ more modern technology," and that, in spite of some qualitative advantages in Pakistan's favor, India currently "seems to be moving towards a qualitative and quantitative break out."[30] Washington's approval of a $3.2 billion force modernization package for Pakistan late in 1981 has raised some doubts about this judgment, for it is quite apparent that Pakistan, in spite of its weaker position, is determined to resist the trend. Indeed, the realization in Islamabad that Pakistan may be losing ground militarily undoubtedly feeds long-held suspicions of Indian intentions and prompts Pakistan's leaders to take even bolder steps to forestall further deterioration in the balance.

None of the foregoing discussion should be understood to imply that Pakistan's security situation might not benefit from domestic political reforms. One thing seems clear, however: Pakistan's external environment has too many patently unhealthy symptoms for it to be judged anything but dangerous. On its northwestern borders, Pakistan houses the world's largest refugee population, the catastrophic result of a long and deadly war to which there is no foreseeable end. Its neighbor to the west, engaged in a vicious war of its own with Iraq, seems to teeter on the brink of political chaos. To the east, the military might of nuclear-capable India seems to be edging toward unchallengeable supremacy. Even the ocean, to the south, presents Pakistan with the specter of in-creasing—and potentially unfriendly—militarization. Against all this, in-ternal political reforms, although unquestionably desirable in their own right, might not go very far to reduce the danger.

The danger to Pakistan can not be waved away by the assertion, so often a part of internalist arguments, that India is a status quo power and poses no military threat to Pakistan.[31] The unpleasant truth is that status quo regimes, when their interests are at stake, do not hesitate to interfere with and, if necessary, to attack their smaller neighbors. De-fensive motivations may find aggressive outlets. A government should not be considered irrational if it steels itself against that possibility.

The Remedy

Externalist and internalist analyses

When it comes to a remedy for Pakistan's security predicament, the basic difference between internalists and externalists is to be found in the emphasis placed on the possibility and desirability of insulating South Asia from global strategic rivalries. Accordingly, while internalists attach great value to the quest for genuine nonalignment and for an autonomous and concerted South Asian role in international politics, externalists profess skepticism over these objectives, seeing in the pattern of Indian policy over the years less a quest for regional autonomy than a drive for regional hegemony. One side sees India and Pakistan as nat-ural allies, with the Muslim suspicion of Hindus having temporarily abated, allowing an accommodation between them; the other, given Pakistan's position in "the sensitive transitional zone which links the Middle East with South Asia,"[32] sees them as almost certain to be com-petitive.

For internalists, the enormous superiority that India enjoys in size, population, resources, and industrial capacity; the extraordinary recep-tivity that India has displayed in both its domestic and foreign policy to the interests of its large Muslim minority and the Muslim Middle East; and the absence of any effort by India, in spite of several opportunities, to recover territory "lost" in the formation of Pakistan in 1947, are all facts that point in the direction of reconciliation between Islamabad and New Delhi. Pakistan's contrary adoption of a confrontationist policy with India, as internalists are prone to see it, frustrates restoration of the natural and historically rooted economic, social, and cultural bonds between them and threatens to reduce them both to the status of dependent pawns in the American-Soviet global strategic competition. As for the danger of Pakistan losing its freedom through an accommodation with its much larger neighbor, Mohammed Ayoob argues that Pakistan's effort to "borrow power" from external (extraregional) sources, far from enlarging its range of options, "has, paradoxically, ended up in curtailing Pakistan's freedom and manoeuvrability in the international sphere." Usually, Ayoob notes, Pakistan "has hitched its star too firmly to one major power or another which has usually failed to come to its rescue in times of dire need, as, for instance, during the events of 1965 and 1971."[33]

From the internalist perspective, Pakistan's leaders are misguided in attempting to orient Pakistan away from India and toward the Middle East. As "attractive and logical as it may seem at first glance," observes Selig Harrison, "the idea of including Islamabad in a Middle East–Persian Gulf strategic consensus is fundamentally flawed because it ignores the ethnic, cultural, historical, and geopolitical ties that orient Pakistan to South Asia. . . . Despite their division into sovereign states, India and Pakistan constitute an interdependent geopolitical and strategic whole, especially in the wake of the Soviet occupation of Afghanistan."[34] Naturally, externalists have a rather different view of Pakistan's Middle East connection. While some of them would hesitate to accept fully the statement that "since 1972, Pakistan has virtually ceased to be a South Asian Power and her orientation has increasingly been towards the Middle East,"[35] few would dispute the judgment that Pakistan's interests—political, military, psychological, and especially economic—have converged with those of Middle Eastern states in recent years, with important implications for Pakistan's security situation.[36]

Even more damaging to prospects for improved India-Pakistan relations, internalists reason, is indiscriminate extraregional (especially U.S.) reinforcement of the Pakistani military. In South Asian Security after Afghanistan, one of the most recent and thorough internalist examinations of subcontinental security issues, G. S. Bhargava argues that the crux of India's security problem and a formidable barrier to a more compromising attitude in Islamabad is Pakistan's unwarranted amassing of military muscle with the assistance of the United States, France, China, and others. "Devoid of external military aid and free of involvement by outsiders," he avers, "Pakistan would be more likely to settle all disputes, including Kashmir, on a realistic basis of give and take."[37]

The U.S. interest, Harrison states, "lies in a scrupulous detachment from the Indo-Pakistani rivalry." U.S. military aid should be "limited and selective" and "for defensive purposes" lest it alienate irretrievably Pakistan's domestic political opposition, provoke an incendiary Indo-Pakistani arms race, and increase Indian dependence on Moscow.[38] Carrying the argument a step further, Ayoob suggests that U.S. military assistance may actually increase Pakistan's vulnerability to Soviet pressures, for it places in jeopardy what is, in fact, the most effective barrier to Soviet support for Baluch nationalism: New Delhi's opposition to any superpower interference in the affairs of the subcontinent.[39]

Internalists see the superpowers' apparent disregard for the UN General Assembly's 1971 zone-of-peace resolution, which sought to enhance the security of all littoral states by excluding superpower rivalries and competition for military bases from the Indian Ocean, looming as yet one more unwelcome intrusion on the natural evolution of a regional security system. Arguing that the projection of military capability is, in the last analysis, a poor palliative for the internal weakness and instability characteristic of most littoral states, Bhargava, for example, points out that neither of the superpowers had "major economic and strategic interests to be served by involvement in the affairs of the region" at the time the zone-of-peace resolution was first advanced in 1971 and that neither has any clear strategic justification for major military presence in the region today.[40] "It was not inadequacy of naval strength or paucity of facilities at bases like Diego Garcia," says Bhargava, "that prevented U.S. action to save the Shah or to preempt the Soviet invasion [since] an impressive U.S. armada was stationed in the Arabian Sea" at the time those events occurred.[41] To this can be added the fact that the military presence of the superpowers, while welcomed by some of the littoral states in the past, has today very few supporters. As mounting opposition to U.S. presence on Diego Garcia attests, the political costs are steadily rising while the military benefits remain limited and uncertain. "Shorn of rhetoric and subject to some changes," observes Bhargava, the zone-of-peace proposal remains "eminently practical and even necessary."[42] Since progress toward demilitarization of the Indian Ocean is contingent on its acceptance by both superpowers, a formula has to be found whereby the basic security interests of each are protected. Thus, one means for deescalating the situation, suggests Bhargava, would be to accept the concept of linkage between Soviet intervention in Afghanistan and militarization of the Indian Ocean and to seek to restore the status quo ante in the area, "including Soviet military withdrawal from Afghanistan and abandonment of its facilities in South Yemen and Ethiopia, in return for the return of Diego Garcia to its original position as a communications facility, coupled with reversal of the series of military measures undertaken [by the United States] during 1980–1981 in Kenya, Somalia, and Oman."[43] In this context, internalists regard few things as more certain to poison the South Asian security climate than the acquisition by the United States of strategic bases or other facilities in Pakistan itself.[44]

For externalists, the Indian Ocean zone-of-peace proposal is "an exercise in futility."[45] It mistakenly tries "to detach the Indian Ocean from the global strategic map, unmindful of the Indian Ocean's strategic importance to global security, and accord it separate treatment."[46] As B. Vivekanandan puts it, "the massive Soviet naval programs and the ever-increasing politico-military activity of the Soviet Union in the Indian Ocean region have made it abundantly clear that the aim of the Soviet Union in the region is to dominate it."[47] That being the case, a more realistic approach would be to forestall any single power from dominating the region, by inviting a balance of naval forces as opposed to their withdrawal.

It has been apparent throughout this discussion that the existence of a Soviet invasion force in Afghanistan has complicated the task of fashioning a remedy for Pakistan's security dilemma that would be consistent with internalist arguments tailored to India-Pakistan reconciliation. Internalists are willing enough to concede that Pakistan's predicament has been worsened by Soviet action in the neighboring state and they generally support external military assistance to Islamabad to the extent that it fills what they can accept as Pakistan's "legitimate defense requirements."[48] But they do not accept the idea that Pakistan's military modernization program should form the centerpiece of Pakistan's response. Indeed, it is their insistence on the urgency and possible fruitfulness of a negotiated political settlement to the Afghan crisis that distinguishes their analysis most clearly from its rivals.

The settlement internalists prescribe for the crisis entails a guarantee to the Soviets for the security of their border with Afghanistan in return for the promise of Soviet military withdrawal from that country. Soviet security is to be assured through the neutralization or "Finlandization" of Afghanistan, a proposal that, as articulated by Harrison, Mehta, Bhargava, and others, rests on assumptions that may be summarized as follows (1) Soviet intervention was largely the result of unforeseen developments in Afghanistan and the Southwest Asian region rather than part of a premeditated grand design for global conquest carefully orchestrated by Moscow; (2) since Moscow now recognizes its intervention to have been reckless and counterproductive, it would welcome the opportunity to extricate itself from an increasingly costly misadventure;

(3) the price of Soviet withdrawal is the restoration of a genuinely non-aligned Afghanistan, neutralized against superpower competition, that will not serve as a hostile base for anti-Soviet forces and that will be sensitive to Soviet interests; (4) the United States, having misread Soviet intervention as a threat to its broad strategic interests, threatens to torpedo the Finlandization remedy by pressing ahead with its plans for the military containment of the Soviet Union in the area; and, finally, (5) Finlandization requires the active collaboration of neighboring states, of Pakistan in particular, in bringing an end to the Afghan insurgency.[49] On this point, some internalists (Harrison and Mehta) go so far as to argue that Afghanistan's neutralization can only succeed if it is part of a larger regional settlement, i.e., if it is accompanied by a reassertion of true nonalignment (what Mehta calls "Swedenization," or "an agreement by which all countries reaffirm their neutrality and detachment from military blocs")[50] in the states located on Afghanistan's southern borders. Others (such as Bhargava), while conceding the long-term desirability of Pakistan's neutralization, suggest that it is presently unrealistic for it to be a precondition for resolution of the Afghan crisis.[51] All seem agreed, however, that present U.S. plans for rearming Pakistan, since they appear bound to invite Soviet retaliation, pose a direct threat to a political solution of any kind.

For those analysts arguing from essentially externalist premises, Islamabad would have little to gain from neutralization. Pakistan's great geopolitical vulnerability to Soviet intervention makes it unlikely that such an accommodation would actually inhibit the Soviet Union in its dealings with Pakistan. Furthermore, Islamabad would have to pay enormous internal political costs to force compliance by the millions of Afghan refugees and Pathan and Baluch tribesmen. "There is no question," argues Leo Rose, "but that the critics of the 'Finlandization' proposal are correct from almost any definition of Pakistan's interests."[52] Externalists observe that "it is questionable whether Moscow's intervention arose out of purely defensive motives in the first place, and that the Soviets would be willing to give up the clearcut strategic advantages toward the Persian Gulf conferred on them by their invasion,"[53] that "Soviet policy in Afghanistan has so far been a success,"[54] and that "the war at its present level is well worth the price being paid as far as Moscow is concerned, . . . Soviet objectives would appear to be well served by keeping the fighting at its present level."[55] In sum, Pakistan's neutralization would simply assure more rapid realization of Soviet expansionist ambitions. What is needed to stem the Soviet tide, according to externalists, is a counterthreat of superior force, which Pakistan can only acquire from extraregional sources.

A critique of existing analyses

Where do these analyses of the remedy go astray? Internalist arguments consistently understate the obstacles to what is clearly the centerpiece of their remedy: normalization of relations between India and Pakistan and a unified approach to regional security issues. To be sure, bilateral and multilateral developments toward South Asian regional cooperation have recently been gaining surprising momentum. Early in June 1982, in an effort that seemed intended to revive the moribund spirit of the Simla Agreement of 1972, Pakistan presented India with a draft non-aggression pact. Later that month, India replied with its own draft of a treaty on the establishment of a permanent joint ministerial commission that would seek to improve ties in economic, commercial, scientific, technical, cultural, and other fields. In mid-August, India dramatically enlarged its offer to include a comprehensive draft treaty of peace, friendship, and cooperation. Movement toward India-Pakistan reconciliation appeared to gain even greater impetus when, on 1 November, President Zia ul-Haq visited Prime Minister Indira Gandhi, a visit that smoothed the way for the signing of the agreement setting up the joint ministerial commission during the nonaligned summit in New Delhi in March 1983.[56] Paralleling and to an extent reinforcing these tentative steps toward rapprochement has been the series of meetings of the foreign secretaries of seven South Asia countries (Pakistan, India, Bangladesh, Nepal, Bhutan, Sri Lanka, and Maldives), which began in Colombo in April 1981, aimed at creating an Association of South-East Asian Nations–styled forum of South Asian regional development cooperation.[57] Though these events should certainly not be dismissed as irrelevant, Pakistan's reluctance to have military and political issues included among the tasks of the joint commission and Prime Minister Gandhi's remarks on the eve of the nonaligned summit demeaning the significance of her November meeting with President Zia, are two of many indications that the process of reconciliation is likely to be drawn out and difficult and that it holds no certain promise of success.[58]

Externalist arguments, on the other hand, tend to understate Pakistan's international isolation and, in particular, count too heavily on Islamabad's Middle East connection to alleviate its security predicament. Of course, its Middle East ties, whether bilateral or multilateral through the Organization of the Islamic Conference (OIC) or the nonaligned movement (NAM) are of immense importance to Pakistan. Since the early 1970s, its contacts with Iran and the Arab states have grown from little more than professions of friendship and communal brotherhood into a substantial and many-faceted relationship. The Middle

East's share of Pakistan's agricultural and industrial export trade, for the nine-month period ending in March 1982, stood at 30.5 percent, a share greater than that of any other global region. For the same period, Pakistan's imports from the Middle East, reflecting its dependence on imported oil for over 90 percent of its domestic consumption, stood at 28.6 percent of total imports, ranking the Middle East second in this category among all world regions. Moreover, Middle Eastern countries have become major sources of loans, credits, and investment funds for Islamabad. For the period from July 1973 to March 1982, total Middle Eastern economic assistance to Pakistan was officially reported at over U.S. $2.16 billion.[59] Saudi credits for arms purchases abroad would considerably enlarge this figure.[60] Also to be taken into account are the huge remittances sent by the 2 million or so Pakistanis working abroad (about 1.5 million in the Persian Gulf region) by the end of 1982. These remittances, amounting officially to over U.S. $2.1 billion (unofficially, closer to U.S. $3.5 billion) in 1981–82, have become a crucial source of foreign exchange, comparing favorably with Pakistan's export earnings (U.S. $2.9 billion in 1980–81) and the amount paid to service its foreign debt (estimated at U.S. $728 million in 1981–82, a figure roughly 27 percent of the country's export earnings).[61] In terms of military ties, Pakistan has become "the third world's leading supplier of military manpower after Cuba."[62] It was providing military assistance in 1982 to twenty-two countries, most of them in the Middle East, and had anywhere from 10,000 to 15,000 members of its armed forces posted abroad.

Impressive as are Pakistan's links with the Middle East, it would be unwarranted to read too much into them, especially insofar as they concern Pakistan's security situation. One reason for this is that Pakistan's economic relations with the Middle East are highly vulnerable to world market conditions and may prove less durable than they now seem. Rice and cotton (raw, yarn, and finished cloth) dominate Pakistan's export trade. While its rice trade with the Middle East is relatively secure, Pakistan's cotton goods have many competitors, not the least of them India. The demand for Pakistani workers, which unquestionably helps to relieve the country's foreign exchange shortage, depends on a steady rate of increase in the ability of the oil-producing states to absorb them. Moreover, the trade relationship between Pakistan and the Middle East is at best slanted in favor of the latter; the current trade balance is weighted more than two-to-one against Pakistan. Pakistan does gain strength from its Middle East connection but the actual substance of this connection may be as much a sign of Pakistan's economic weakness and dependence as of its power and prestige.

A second reason for caution in assessing Pakistan's Middle East links is that whatever role Pakistan plays in Persian Gulf security is going to be sharply limited both by Pakistan's own political weakness and by the suspicion and animosity that mark intraregional relations in Southwest Asia. There are proposals afoot for a form of Islamic "collective security" system,[63] while some analysts envision Pakistan assuming a major role in the defense of Saudi Arabia.[64] If Pakistan's painfully impotent efforts to bring about a ceasefire between Iraq and Iran supply any clue to the future, however, Islamabad is simply not prepared to bear the political burden of "policing" the Middle East, and the Middle Eastern states, deeply divided among themselves, are in no position to come to Pakistan's rescue. None of these states can guarantee continued cooperation. While one can agree that the Middle Eastern connection is vastly greater today than it was a decade ago, one must hesitate to endorse fully Weinbaum and Sen's conclusion, drawn in the more salubrious climate of 1978, that "the Middle Eastern connection, so remarkably strengthened during the 1970s, will not dissolve: it offers Pakistan its best hope for a viable economy and new insurance of territorial integrity,"[65] or another conclusion, reached in 1977 before the collapse of the RCD, that Iran-Pakistan relations "have been the one constant factor in the otherwise fluctuating international and regional events influencing the countries of the Persian Gulf, West Asia, and South Asia."[66]

As already noted, internalists reject outright a remedy for Pakistan's security predicament resting on an enlarged security relationship with the United States. Such a relationship, however, seems to be under development. A formal security alliance would entail upgrading the 1959 Executive Agreement reached between the Eisenhower administration and the government of Ayub Khan. This was given at least passing consideration in the early stages of the Reagan administration's negotiations with Islamabad. But Pakistan's conscious disassociation from CENTO and the South-East Asia Treaty Organization (SEATO) and its disinclination to jeopardize its status in the OIC and the NAM, coupled with Washington's reluctance to press for an agreement that would inevitably arouse strong opposition in both countries, has temporarily eliminated an alliance as a live option.

In reality we may be witnessing the development of an informal security guarantee, which was given initial moral force by the Carter Doctrine and which draws increasing material substance from the steady buildup in U.S. military forces in the Indian Ocean and Southwest Asia. Long-range planning in the Pentagon appears committed to the view that the United States must rebuild the alliance system that existed in the 1960s in order to attain a realistic global war-fighting capability and that it must increase its military presence in areas of strategic interest.[67] From a security standpoint, Islamabad may see advantage in the fact that the situation today is vastly changed from that which prevailed during Washington's earlier courtship of Pakistan in the 1950s and early 1960s. Then, Pakistan's key ally had no more than a token military presence in the Indian Ocean and little interest in expanding it. America now has a large and steadily growing strategic interest that will require close collaboration with friendly—even if not formally allied—regional powers. In spite of all the issues that divide the United States and Pakistan, and in spite of the profound distrust both countries understandably feel toward one another,[68] the emergence of a new U.S. "security regime" in the Indian Ocean may give a surprising attractiveness and durability to what has unquestionably been a very troubled relationship.[69]

Just as internalists tend to exaggerate the negative consequences that would flow from strengthening military ties with the United States, externalists seem to be overly wedded to the thesis that for Islamabad there is little advantage in an accommodation with the Soviet Union over Afghanistan. According to Zalmay Khalilzad, for example, the lesson that all small states contiguous to the Soviet Union should learn from the Afghan tragedy is "that the more they accommodate Moscow, the less likely it is that they will maintain their independence."[70] For Pakistan to abandon the Afghan resistance movement would be an act of appeasement that would only whet the Soviet appetite for further encroachment in the region. While "in the short run accommodation might decrease Soviet pressure, in the long run it would increase substantially Soviet ability to influence and threaten Pakistan."[71]

Pakistanis are of course not blind to the risks inherent in continued support of the Afghan resistance. Nor are they unaware of the dangers implicit in negotiating a political settlement of the situation. They can see, however, the possible benefits of a settlement. These might include amelioration of the refugee burden, a reduced threat of reprisal along Pakistan's vulnerable border with Afghanistan, assurances of noninterference in Pakistan's troublesome tribal nationalist movements, and, by no means least, the promise of very considerable Soviet economic and military assistance. The fact that the Soviet Union may have moved into the neighborhood to stay is certainly an incentive for Pakistan to move in the direction of a settlement.[72] One can hardly speak of a consensus on these matters among Pakistanis but to many of them one thing is clear: Pakistan has more options available to it than either internalists (who basically counsel Islamabad to declare its neutrality and embrace India) or externalists (who exhort Islamabad to supply the manpower for the free world's defense against Soviet expansion in Southwest Asia) seem willing to concede. It would be a remarkable accomplishment, to say the least, but the remedy for Pakistan's security predicament, toward which Islamabad may now be inching, might be to reject both of these alternatives in favor of a strategy that pursued limited collaboration with the United States and offered limited accommodation to the Soviets over Afghanistan. If successful, it would enable Pakistan to maintain independence from New Delhi's dictates, the objective for which the country was founded and to which most of its leaders remain thoroughly committed.

Toward a New Perspective

Regardless of anything done or not done by Islamabad's current leaders, Pakistan is part of a region that is now and shall remain for many years deeply troubled by a whole range of destabilizing and disintegrative forces—Islamic fundamentalism, class antagonisms, nationalism, separatism—all of which render the entire area highly vulnerable to internal collapse as well as to external interference and subversion. Early hopes that South Asia could somehow be insulated from superpower contention have not been realized. The Soviets are now positioned militarily in Afghanistan and the Indian Ocean is increasingly a zone of conflict. No amount of genuflection to more tranquil alternatives will bring them into being. Sudden and violent changes are likely to occur in practically all of the states with which Pakistan shares the southern rim of Asia and these drastic changes are likely to spill over existing borders and threaten governments with disturbing frequency. It is in terms of this great volatility and uncertainty of the environment (internal and external) that Pakistan's security predicament has to be understood.

Lacking adequate indigenous capability to guarantee its own security against any and all potential enemies, Pakistan naturally seeks firm assurances from external allies. The People's Republic of China, while more reliable than most, has not been able to provide the required guarantee. The Soviet Union, for over a decade closely aligned with India, has up until now failed to win the confidence of the men who rule Pakistan.[73] Unfortunately, from Islamabad's perspective, the United States has itself proven to be a very uncertain ally. With strategic interests of its own and a much larger global arena in which to pursue them, the United States has obviously not been willing to underwrite all of Islamabad's concerns or to assume a permanent obligation with regard to them. No matter how much American interests may today converge with those of Pakistan, the inescapable truth is that the overlap could diminish at some point in the near or more distant future. Pakistan has no choice but to seek the friendship of the United States but at the same time there are great pressures to keep other options alive.

One of those options, as Amaury de Riencourt has urged, is for Pakistan to join with India in an effort "to achieve a final and historic reconciliation between the two countries."[74] While it is a most desirable option, it is not, I think, very realistic. Confronted with the immediate and very tangible fact of powerful (and Soviet-equipped) Indian armed forces on their eastern border, Pakistanis cannot be as confident as de Riencourt that they are "facing a nonexistent threat of Indian aggression instead of a much more plausible one coming from Soviet-occupied Afghanistan."[75] They see their predicament as more complex and uncertain and they will tend to pursue a more complex and multipronged remedy. This is likely to include efforts to normalize India-Pakistan relations but it is not likely to exclude simultaneous efforts to keep alive the possibility for compromise with Moscow over Afghanistan; to strengthen the commitment to Islamabad of the United States and the People's Republic of China; to remain faithful to Pakistan's Arab, Islamic, and nonaligned allies; to strengthen substantially its own conventional military forces; and, not least, to create a nuclear weapons capability.

For Pakistan's diplomats, as for its military leaders, the assumption of such tasks poses an evident, some would say impossible, challenge. One wonders how long Islamabad will be able or willing to avoid decisions that would commit it, unambiguously, to one side or another in the struggle for dominance in Southwest Asia and the Indian Ocean. Crafty diplomacy may not be enough to rescue Islamabad from the antagonistic forces of its internal and external environments. For scholars and observers, framing an analytic perspective that responds to the uncertainties and contradictions of Pakistan's security predicament will be an equally difficult project. But as Pakistan strives to cope with the dangerous security dilemmas that clearly lie ahead, it needs to be served (as do all of its neighbors) by a perspective that can be detached from those internalist and externalist premises that time and changed circumstances have rendered inadequate.

19. Intervention in Afghanistan: Implications for the Security of Southwest Asia ✒ Zalmay Khalilzad

The Soviet Union's invasion of Afghanistan was a landmark event in contemporary history. There has been much speculation about reasons for the Soviet move. Some have attributed it to offensive considerations, while others have emphasized defensive ones. It is even possible that the responsible Soviet decision makers favored the invasion for different reasons. Whatever Moscow's motives, the act itself had far-reaching regional and global implications.

While it appears that Moscow's decision to dispatch its armed forces to Afghanistan was the result of a careful and deliberate calculation of risks and opportunities, some of the risks faced by the Soviets there are different from those inherent in other Soviet involvements in the Third World. The substantial Afghan opposition to the Soviet presence puts large numbers of Soviet personnel in danger, provides an opportunity for Soviet adversaries such as China and the United States to raise the need for greater Soviet involvement in a protracted and costly war through assistance to Moscow's opponents, and reduces Soviet capabilities for actions in other parts of the world. The invasion has also undermined the Soviet image in the Third World as a supporter of national liberation movements.

In this chapter an attempt will be made, first, to identify the conditions that appear generally to be conducive to a Soviet invasion by studying the example of Afghanistan and, second, to assess the implications of the Soviet invasion, especially its effect on the relative balance of power in the region. A corollary to the latter is the question of the U.S. response both to the invasion and to its potential consequences. The last section of the chapter deals with Soviet pacification strategy and sketches some likely outcomes of the conflict.

The Setting for the Invasion

Moscow's move against Kabul conforms to the low-risk pattern that has been the general characteristic of Soviet military operations against small neighboring countries. The Afghan case illustrates that the Soviet level of active involvement including military intervention in small countries close to its border increases when ideological relations between such countries and the Soviet Union converge. This is indicative of Moscow's policy of gradual extension of its power and influence around its borders and its commitment to the doctrine of communist "irreversibility" in these areas.

Soviet interest in Afghanistan has been persistent, dating back many years. Before the 1978 coup by pro-Soviet Marxist-Leninist groups (Khalq and Parcham, of which the former became dominant), Moscow had used its leverage in Afghanistan to protect these groups and had given them permission to move against the government.[1] Under the Khalqis, Kabul became an enthusiastic supporter of the Soviet role in international affairs. Khalqi leaders—Nur Muhammad Taraki as president and prime minister and Hafizullah Amin as foreign minister became the most prominent—defended Soviet foreign policy toward the Third World, argued that the Soviets "never attempted to exploit" the developing countries, referred to the Soviet bloc nations as "brother countries," took the Soviet line on every international issue, and referred to their own coup as "the true continuation of the great October Revolution."[2] They broke diplomatic relations with South Korea and recognized North Korea as the only legitimate representative of the Korean people, supported the Ethiopians in the conflict with Somalia, and applauded Cuba for its proxy role in Africa. Afghanistan was one of the first countries to recognize the Vietnamese-installed government in Cambodia and condemned the Chinese attack against Vietnam.

Khalq also intensified bilateral relations with Moscow. The number of Soviet advisers increased. The railroad project that was to link Kabul and the Iranian border, undertaken by Daud and disliked by Moscow, was abandoned, while an agreement was made to construct a bridge over the Amu River linking Afghanistan and the Soviet Union. The two countries signed a number of new economic agreements;[3] Moscow promised to provide $1 billion in aid between 1979 and 1984.[4] An Afghan delegation visited Moscow in June 1979 to participate in the thirtieth anniversary of the founding of the Council for Mutual Economic Assistance (COMECON), while the Afghan government hinted that it might seek associate membership in COMECON. Moscow deferred Afghanistan's payment of all loans and interest for a ten-year period.[5] Kabul and Moscow established a permanent intergovernmental Commission on Economic Cooperation and Soviet advisers were assigned to all Afghan ministries. A high-ranking Soviet official of the State Planning Ministry advised Kabul on its new five-year economic plan. Soviet advisers were attached to the Afghan military units as far down as the platoon level and assisted the regime in establishing party bureaus at all levels of the armed forces. The takeover of the state apparatus by pro-Soviet forces also increased Soviet opportunity for enlarging its influence in Afghanistan's education and mass communication institutions. After the coup, both sides signed an agreement providing for training in Russian language courses at Kabul University and other educational institutions.[6] In September 1979, Amin revealed that fifteen hundred students had been sent to the Soviet Union and that an agreement for sending two thousand to Bulgaria had been reached.[7] Shortly after the coup, the Afghan Press Agency (Bakhter) signed an agreement with Tass for the "exchange of news, information and technical cooperation."[8] Afghan papers, under governmental control, reprinted many articles from Soviet sources such as Tass and *Pravda*. The new director of Afghan television had just returned from fourteen years in Moscow, where he had directed the Afghan Service of Radio Moscow.

An indication of the rapid intensification of relations with the Soviet Union was the signing of a twenty-year Treaty of Friendship and Cooperation between the two countries in December of 1978. This treaty called for the development of "all-round cooperation" between the two countries, including consultation and the introduction of "appropriate measures to ensure the security, independence and territorial integrity of the two countries."[9] Article 4 of the treaty called for the development of "cooperation in the military field on the basis of appropriate agreements concluded between them."[10] It was the provisions of this treaty to which the Soviets were to refer in justifying their dispatch of large numbers of troops to Afghanistan a year later. These changes increased Soviet interest and stakes in Afghanistan, and reduced those of others. They moved Afghanistan decisively closer to Moscow, increased the Soviet presence there, and undermined Afghanistan's role as a nonaligned state.

In expressing support for Moscow's global goals, the Khalqis not only wanted to express their ideological preferences but also to "entrap" the Kremlin into protecting their regime against its internal opponents who were becoming increasingly powerful. Khalqi leaders believed that because of the Treaty of Friendship and Cooperation "the Soviets will protect the Afghan Revolution."[11] Moscow's public statements encouraged this tendency among Khalqi leaders. For example, Brezhnev, referring in June 1979 to the mounting insurgency against the Kabul government, warned, "We will not leave alone our friends, the people of Afghanistan."[12]

Although there is a great deal of uncertainty about the period immediately preceding the December 1979 invasion, the most likely explanation proffers a combination of two important factors. In Afghanistan itself, the invasion was part of a Soviet effort to prevent the possibility of the overthrow of a client regime in Kabul and its replacement by a hostile group. At the international level, the invasion took place after enormous growth in relative Soviet military power vis-à-vis the West; the overthrow of the shah had dramatically weakened the Western position in the region. Therefore the "correlation of forces" in the region favored the Soviets.

At the domestic level, the pro-Soviet regime met with considerable opposition. Khalq favored the establishment of a single-party system and a single command with a centrally directed economy. It had ambitious plans for fundamental change of the country. However, the state apparatus in Afghanistan was not strong enough and Khalq was not in sufficient control of the state apparatus to carry out its plans.[13] Besides, those groups opposed to the regime were quite strong. As the opposition to the government increased, the Khalqis resorted to severe repression.[14] The government measures further fueled the opposition, which in turn led to greater government repression. As the conflict increased, it spread from the countryside to the cities. In March 1979, there was a major uprising in Herat following which Amin replaced Taraki as prime minister, though Taraki continued as president. As the internal conflict escalated, the government began to fall apart. The most important development was a slow disintegration of the army with several defections and mutinies. (The Bala Hissar garrison mutiny in Kabul on 5 August 1979 was the most significant.) The weakening of the state apparatus led to substantial areas of the country falling outside governmental control. Local leaders, both ethnic and tribal, traditionalist and fundamentalist, gained in strength. Rural areas began to refuse to pay taxes; government offices were closed down in a number of areas. Both the gross national product (GNP) per capita and the area under cultivation declined, the former by 19 percent and the latter by 9 percent.[15]

Moscow must have recognized that their local clients had made major errors and faced serious threats. Given the state of Soviet-Khalqi relations, a Khalqi defeat might have dealt a severe blow to Soviet credibility regarding its ability to help allies in a timely fashion. The Soviets were faced with the risk that a client regime might be replaced by groups that were hostile to them and had strong ties with countries and groups unfriendly to the USSR. Such a defeat might have encouraged hostile groups elsewhere and discouraged those who were sympathetic. It would have decreased Soviet abilities to maintain pressure and to influence developments in countries around Afghanistan, especially Pakistan. It could also have meant the loss of many years of economic, political, and military investment in the country.

To avoid such a development, Moscow tried to convince its local clients to reconstitute the government and shift domestic policies rapidly. There are two conflicting accounts of Soviet policy for changing governments in Afghanistan. According to the more convincing account, Taraki, during his 13 September 1979 visit to Moscow, was persuaded that the excesses of previous months should be blamed on the current prime minister, Hafizullah Amin, and as a suitable scapegoat he should be eliminated. A new government with a broader coalition should then be established and abandon or revise those policies that were unpopular. The Soviets might also have promised Taraki that they would increase military assistance, including military personnel, in Afghanistan to protect the new government against its opponents. Upon Taraki's return to Kabul the Soviet-backed plan to eliminate Amin began to unfold on 14–15 September. Apparently, as part of this plan, Moscow deployed some units on the Soviet-Afghan border, and a four-hundred-man airborne unit was sent to the Bagram air base near Kabul.[16] However, Amin apparently received a warning about his intended elimination and acted quickly to preempt Taraki's plan.

After eliminating Taraki,[17] Amin then proceeded to put into practice some of the measures purportedly agreed to between his predecessor and the USSR. He attempted to cast Taraki in the role of the scapegoat, blaming the excesses of the previous government on the cult of personality that the regime had built up around him. To show his displeasure with the Soviet role in the episode, Amin demanded that Moscow recall its ambassador, Aleksander M. Puzanov, and appoint a new envoy.[18] While suspicious of Moscow, Amin believed that the Soviet Union had little choice but to support him and his regime. Moscow tried to deceive Amin by publicly expressing support for his regime while secretly planning his overthrow and the invasion of Afghanistan. Amin had demonstrated his independence of action in a way that did not bode well for Soviet control. A more tractable person was desirable.

To implement their invasion plans, the Soviets took several major steps. First, Moscow gave refuge to military leaders, such as the former defense minister, Colonel A. Watanjar, who had been committed to Taraki and had opposed Amin. Moscow also increased contacts with the Parchami exiles, including Karmal, in Eastern Europe.[19] Second, Moscow attempted to increase its military presence inside Afghanistan by trying to persuade Amin that he needed increased Soviet assistance in his conflict with the Afghan guerrillas. The Kremlin sent several delegations to Kabul to persuade President Amin of the importance of an increased Soviet presence. Two of these delegations were headed by General Ivan Pavolvski, commanding general of Soviet Grand Forces, and Vicktor Semyonivitch Paputin, the first deputy of the Ministry of Internal Affairs. Officially the latter was to help the government with counterinsurgency. His real mission was to mobilize the Parchamis and

Amin's opponents within Khalq. Third, Moscow increased its capability near the Afghan border for massive and rapid intervention. Information about Soviet preparatory invasion measures was available to Western governments and to the public through press leaks.[20]

The other account of what happened, supplied by a Soviet KGB defector, gives a different version.[21] He states that by September of 1979, Moscow had come to a decision that Taraki should be replaced as president by Amin, perhaps because he was judged too weak and ineffective to deal with the mounting crisis. In July 1979, besides the post of premier, Amin had already taken over the Defense and Interior ministries. The Soviet defector does not explain why Amin expelled the Soviet ambassador shortly after the overthrow of Taraki. If his story is correct, which seems doubtful, it is possible that this act was jointly agreed to by Moscow and Amin to provide the latter with greater domestic legitimacy. According to the Soviet defector, Moscow subsequently began to doubt Amin's sincerity and his ability to deal with opposition forces. In its search for alternative solutions Moscow decided on the invasion of Afghanistan and the installation of Karmal at the helm in Kabul.

At the international level, the invasion took place at a time and in a place where the relative configuration of military and political factors favored Moscow. The Soviet move came after the overthrow of the shah of Iran, an event that dealt a devastating blow to the American security framework for the region. After the British withdrawal from the Persian Gulf in 1971, Washington adopted the Nixon Doctrine consisting of security cooperation with key states in the region, Iran and Saudi Arabia (the "two-pillar policy"). Of the two pillars, Iran was far more important since the United States relied heavily on Tehran to protect American interests in the region. Iran adopted a low profile as far as its own presence in the area was concerned. Although after the oil price increase of 1973–74 there was greater recognition of the need for a higher level of American military presence in the area, the policy remained fundamentally the same.

The revolt in Iran not only undermined the two-pillar policy in the gulf, it also led to the disintegration of the Central Treaty Organization (CENTO), conceived as a *cordon sanitaire* between the Soviet Union and the Persian Gulf. Iran, formerly a Western ally, became hostile to the United States, amply demonstrated when the American diplomats were taken hostage on 4 November 1979. By the time of the Soviet invasion, the United States did not even have an embassy in Tehran. Pakistan, too, had been an American ally but chose to become nonaligned and, because of its nuclear efforts, was in fact subjected to an American embargo on military sales and economic aid. Although these changes did not mean greater immediate Soviet influence in Iran and Pakistan, the decline in America's position in both countries must have been recognized as a major positive development by the Soviet Union. In Moscow's hierarchy of preferences, nonaligned states, even hostile ones, are preferable to those allied with the West.

Although there are many difficulties in assessing both the relative American and Soviet military capabilities and their influence on the outcome of particular conflicts, the Soviet invasion clearly took place after dramatic changes favorable to the Soviets had occurred. At the global level, past American strategic superiority had been replaced with parity or essential equivalence. As far as relative capability to project power into the region is concerned, the Soviet position had improved significantly. This change was the result of several factors. First, regional shifts in policy and in power constellations, such as the upheaval in Iran, and infrastructural changes in the area favored Soviet power projection capabilities. One illustration of the shift is the change in Soviet airlift paths. In the 1950s and 1960s, the Soviet overflight route to the Persian Gulf lay across Yugoslavia (and even that was doubtful for much of the period). Iran, Turkey, and Pakistan objected to Soviet overflights. Now, however, Soviet overflight of these countries, especially Iran, has become more frequent. Second, there has been a major increase in Soviet power projection capability through expanding its airlift, building up an overseas "base structure," and strengthening its airborne troops.[22]

With little information about the internal discussion among the Soviet leaders that preceded the invasion, it is hard to assess what calculation Moscow made about possible American and Western responses. It is clear that in Afghanistan the balance of both relative power and interest favored Moscow. The United States did not have the capability to meet the Soviet threat on its own terms in Afghanistan. It also did not regard Afghanistan as vital to its interests. Washington's responses to various internal changes, with possible Soviet involvement, and reports of possible invasion were rather muted.

On the other hand, Moscow clearly had considerable interest in Afghanistan. With the pro-Soviet coup of 1978, Kabul's relations with Moscow fundamentally changed. As the preceding discussion illustrates, Moscow became highly involved in the country politically, militarily, and economically. Even before the 1978 coup, its interest in Afghanistan had been both greater and more sustained in comparison to the other great powers. The coup further shifted the balance of interest in its favor. Because of these considerations, it is likely that the Soviets discounted the likelihood of an American military move against them in Afghanistan (meeting the threat on their own terms) or escalation either horizontally or vertically. The Soviets probably expected only a limited degree of international condemnation and isolation, similar to that which followed in the aftermath of its moves against Hungary (1956) and Czechoslovakia (1968).[23]

The Soviet invasion, therefore, conformed to the low-risk pattern, the general characteristic of Soviet operations. It is important to keep in mind that a major factor determining the relative risks for the Soviets from their aggression abroad is the relative capabilities of their potential adversaries. The more capable the USSR becomes compared to the West, the less risky its actions become. Moreover, the relative growth in Soviet capabilities makes meeting the Soviet threat more risky to Soviet adversaries. In sum, there has been a major shift in risk distribution between the Soviet Union and the West over the past twenty-five years.

Implications of the Soviet Invasion

Although involving little risk of a military confrontation with the West, the Soviet invasion, nevertheless, had far-reaching implications. At the international level, in one sweep the Soviet invasion of Afghanistan overturned a number of assumptions and significantly changed the situation in the region, between the superpowers, and in American thinking. It eliminated a traditional buffer state long considered important for the security of Southwest Asia, brought Soviet forces to the Pakistani border, and set a new precedent in the massive use of Soviet forces in an area outside its Eastern Europe satellite empire. On the strategic level, it substantially reduced the distance between Soviet forces and the entrance to the Persian Gulf, putting that region within range of a large number of Soviet tactical aircraft; it extended the Soviet presence to within 350 miles of the Arabian Sea, an area of vital significance for the industrial world; it thus increased Soviet capabilities to massively threaten vital NATO and Japanese interests; and it has impressively demonstrated the Soviet capability for rapid deployment of forces. (Table 19-1 illustrates how existing or potential bases in Afghanistan would increase Soviet air capability vis-à-vis several important areas.)

As we have seen, the Soviet invasion took place after a number of developments in or near the region had already negatively affected Washington's interests. These included the 1978 coups in South Yemen and Afghanistan, the revolution in Iran and the frustrating hostage crisis, and Soviet-Cuban intervention in the Horn of Africa. Washington had demonstrated restraint (for whatever reason) in its response to

Table 19-1   Soviet air capability

Combat radii of aircraft in Soviet and Soviet allies' service (in kilometers)	
SU-7 Fitter A	525
SU-17 Fitter B	600
SU-20/22 Fitter C/D	930
MIG 19	390
MIG 21	575
MIG 23	1,050
MIG 25	1,070

Distance from potential base areas in Afghanistan to Persian Gulf targets (in kilometers)		
Helmand Valley	to Hormuz	680
Farah	to Hormuz	795
Kandahar	to Karachi	770

Distance from Soviet air bases to potential Persian Gulf targets (in kilometers)		
Kazi Magimed (near Baku)	to Hormuz	1,760
Askhabad (Turkmenistan)	to Hormuz	1,325
Askhabad	to Karachi	1,595

Source: Charles Fairbanks, "On Possible Soviet Threat to the Persian Gulf," outline paper for the European-American Society Workshop, held at Elvetham Hall, Great Britain, 27 June 1980.

these crises, even when the developments were extremely important (as in Iran). However, Soviet action in Afghanistan demonstrated that Washington's restraint was not only not reciprocated but apparently had the opposite effect. It is possible that Moscow expected another muted response from the United States because of its earlier setbacks and the weakness of its relative position in the region. To Washington, however, the invasion reinforced the growing sense of threat to its interests in the area. The Soviet move was seen as part of a Soviet global challenge to American interests. At the regional level, the Carter administration feared the Soviet action would raise serious questions about American reliability among its friends in the Persian Gulf and could lead to increased regional instability and Soviet expansionism. According to Gary Sick, a staff member of the National Security Council during the Carter administration, even before the invasion it was feared "that key states of the Persian Gulf would conclude that they should accommodate to the rising wave of Soviet influence and power before they themselves were swept away."[24] After the invasion, Washington feared that Pakistan might come to terms with the Soviet Union on Afghanistan because of its vulnerabilities to Soviet pressures.[25]

As a result of these factors, the United States decided that there was a need for a major effort. President Carter decided on a three-pronged policy and the Reagan administration has followed essentially the same policies. First, Washington decided to increase substantially political pressure against the Soviet Union. The United States, aware that it could not meet the Soviet threat on its own terms and forcefully dislodge the Soviets from Afghanistan, adopted a high-keyed rhetoric against Moscow. If the American power position in the region had been different, for example, if the shah had still been in power, Washington's rhetoric might well have been more low-keyed and its ability to punish Moscow in Afghanistan much higher. Thus the Soviet invasion led to a major deterioration in Soviet-American relations. In his State of the Union message, President Carter argued that "the implications" of the Soviet action "could pose the most serious threat to world peace since the Second World War."[26] However, the actions taken to affect the situation in Afghanistan itself were largely symbolic. Carter used the hotline to the Kremlin on 29 December, reportedly to ask for the withdrawal of the Soviet troops and to warn that failure to do so would have "serious consequences for U.S.-Soviet relations."[27] He charged that Moscow's explanation for sending its troops into Afghanistan was unacceptable. He recalled the American ambassador from Moscow and took a number of "punitive" measures: suspending the opening of new consular offices by either side, deferring a number of economic and cultural exchanges under consideration, curtailing Moscow's fishing privileges in American territorial waters, boycotting the Moscow Olympics after efforts to move them to another site had failed, placing an embargo on the sale of 17 million tons of food grain to the Soviets, and suspending consideration of the embattled SALT II treaty and the already moribund Indian Ocean Arms Control talks. The United States encouraged political opposition to the Soviets from the Muslim countries, the non-Islamic nonaligned states, and its own allies. Washington hoped that Afghanistan would become a point of tension between these countries and the Soviet Union.

Second, the United States launched a major effort to shore up its military capability around Afghanistan, a region where American stakes were enormous and where its influence was dwindling. In January 1980, the President declared what has come to be called the Carter Doctrine: "An attempt by any outside force to gain control of the Persian Gulf region will be regarded as an assault on the vital interests of the United States of America and such an assault will be repelled by any means necessary, including military force."[28] By engaging vital American interests, Washington hoped to deter Soviet aggression beyond Afghanistan and to reassure local states in Southwest Asia. Some of the measures taken in Washington to increase its military capability in the area had been under consideration before the invasion, but were largely at the conceptual stage. (It has been learned from Samuel P. Huntington that already in the summer of 1977 a presidential directive officially elevated the Middle East and the Persian Gulf to the level of Western Europe and East Asia as an area of vital interest to the United States. Huntington believes that the Afghan invasion provided an opportunity for public announcement of the 1977 directive.) The American military effort in the region had two elements: seeking limited presence in the area and increasing capability for projecting U.S. forces into the area. These efforts have continued under the Reagan administration.

Third, Washington sought improved relations with regional actors, especially Pakistan, and sustained a low level of Afghan resistance against the Soviets. The Soviet invasion brought a change in American policy priorities toward Pakistan. In April 1979, because of nuclear proliferation concerns, all American military and economic aid to Pakistan had been terminated. In the aftermath of the Soviet move, Washington reaffirmed its 1959 security agreement with Islamabad and offered military and economic assistance to that country. The United States wanted to discourage Pakistani accommodation toward Moscow and to help in supplying weapons to the Afghan resistance forces. Washington's offer consisted of a two-year package worth $400 million and included the sale of F-16s. Pakistan rejected this offer as inadequate in view of the threats the country faced. Negotiation between the two countries continued under the Reagan administration and an agreement was reached on a five-year program of economic aid and military sales. Although following a cautious policy toward the Soviets, Pakistan with U.S. support has led the diplomatic opposition to the Soviet move at the United Nations and at nonaligned and Islamic meetings. In coordination with Pakistan, Egypt, and perhaps some other states, the United States apparently also started a covert operation for helping the Afghan resistance.[29] Since the Afghan program is covert, it is difficult to be confident about the size of the effort. Afghan resistance leaders insist it is very small. Since Washington does not transfer these weapons directly, it is also possible that much of what is intended for the Afghans does not reach them. Pakistan, however, has allowed some SAM-7 surface-to-air missiles, Kalashnikov rifles (AK47s), and antitank weapons to reach the resistance. It also provides regular financial support to the major resistance groups with headquarters in Peshawar. According to several reports, in order to reduce the risk to themselves,[30] Pakistanis have imposed several restrictions on sending weapons to Pakistan intended for Afghan fighters: countries supplying the weapons should give little or no publicity to their role; Pakistan will control the distribution of such weapons to the Afghans, deciding who gets what and how much; the weapons given to the Afghans should move quickly across the border; the quantity of weapons should be limited; and the weapons for the Afghans should be largely of Soviet or East European origin.[31]

It is clear that without cooperation from local actors, especially Iran and Pakistan, there would be severe limitations on the U.S. ability to provide significant military assistance to the insurgents. However, it appears that Washington itself has not sought a dramatic or substantial improvement in Afghan insurgent capability. Washington's policy appears to consist of providing only meager assistance in the hope of keeping low-level resistance alive for an extended period. Washington fears that increased Afghan capability might lead to a forceful Soviet response against the insurgents and/or Pakistan, leading to rapid deterioration in the relative position of the Afghans and a Soviet military victory. Pakistan has similar concerns. It is possible, however, that increased Afghan military capability might increase Soviet incentives to seek a political settlement and withdraw. It is unclear what type of political settlement short of total and unconditional Soviet withdrawal is acceptable to Washington. The United States has expressed support for the European Economic Community proposal essentially suggesting that if the Soviet troops were withdrawn, the independence and neutrality of Afghanistan could be internationally guaranteed.[32]

Soviet Strategy in Afghanistan

Several years have passed since the December 1979 Soviet invasion of Afghanistan. To all parties involved, the occupation has been costly. Although it is difficult to have an accurate picture of the war and of the Soviet strategy, it is nevertheless clear that Moscow has had enormous problems in extending the authority of the center, which it largely controls, over the countryside.

The Soviet invasion marked a major escalation in Moscow's long and persistent involvement with Afghanistan. Once in Afghanistan, the Soviets initiated a multi-pronged strategy for pacification of the country. This has included accommodation of Islamic feelings, a propaganda blitz to win support for the Soviet position both in Afghanistan and abroad, and placing blame for the Afghan crisis on the Americans, Chinese, and Pakistanis. Another element has been attempts at harmonizing relations between the two Communist party factions and broadening the base of government through the formation of the National Fatherland Front, an umbrella organization representing various elements of the population. Moscow is also trying to train hundreds of new cadres who are expected to help not only in maintaining law and order but in running the country in the future. The Soviet-installed regime has also attempted to win popular support by undoing some of the "radical" policies of the previous government. Moscow has tried to build loyal armed forces to turn the Soviet-Afghan war into an Afghan-Afghan war. The Soviet military strategy appears to consist of holding onto major cities and highways and applying force intermittently, at times massively, against the area of resistance in the countryside. This policy aims at minimizing Soviet loss of life, while clinging to the belief that in time they will either discourage the population from supporting the resistance or force the opposition to leave the country.[33] Moscow appears also to be counting on the international community to forget about the Afghan crisis. It has been exploring ways to protect its interests in Afghanistan while reducing the costs of occupation. Agreement to participate in UN-sponsored talks on the Afghan conflict is expected to serve this purpose.

The Soviet strategy has not been successful so far and Moscow is far from pacifying the country. The Soviets have not deployed enough forces to extend permanently the center's control over the countryside in a short time; violent opposition to the occupation has spread all over Afghanistan. The Karmal government controls the country's capital; it also has a presence, at times only symbolically, in major provincial centers and towns, while the Soviets and their allies can often bring "overwhelming" force to bear when a tactical situation demands it.[34] However, even Kabul is not very secure: a 10:00 P.M. curfew continues and often gunfire and explosions can be heard. Serious fighting has taken place continuously in nearby towns such as Paghman, less than seven miles away. Regime opponents using guerrilla warfare and urban terrorism techniques have assassinated party members, Soviet officials, and military personnel in the capital city itself. One analyst has described Kabul as "a city ringed by war."[35] Without major changes in policy and capability of either side, the current situation is likely to continue in the near future. Moscow is unlikely to be capable of extending its control throughout the country and therefore is foreseeing a long struggle. It is developing a capability for an indefinite stay in Afghanistan and is linking Afghanistan more closely to the Soviets. The resistance forces, on the other hand, are unable to dislodge the Soviets from major cities, especially Kabul.

Prospects

Several factors will play critical roles in determining whether the Soviet Union succeeds in liquidating or neutralizing the Afghan partisans. These include the policies adopted by Pakistan toward the insurgents, the extent of external support for the partisans, the success or failure of Soviet attempts to convert divisions among the insurgents into open conflict, the Soviets' ability to establish a government in Kabul that commands a large armed force and has a wide base of support, and the scope and duration of the Soviet military commitment.

There are a number of conceivable outcomes to the Afghan crisis. These include a Soviet-dominated pacified Afghanistan in the near future; a protracted war lasting many years leading to an eventual Soviet military victory; a neutral Afghanistan resulting from a compromise involving some voluntary Soviet withdrawal and international guarantees of Afghan neutrality, either in the near future or after a protracted war; or even the spread of the Afghan war to the neighboring countries, especially Pakistan.

There are varying degrees of uncertainty concerning all the factors affecting the likelihood of each of these outcomes. As long as Moscow believes that it can win the war in Afghanistan and that time is on its side, the Soviets are unlikely to work toward a political compromise. Should Moscow insist on the domination of the Afghan political system by pro-Soviet communist groups, with or without their current leaders, a compromise between the Soviets and the Afghan resistance forces appears unlikely. The success of such a policy would require the abandonment of the resistance forces by their current friends. A "neutrality solution," combined with Soviet recognition of Afghan rights to determine their own political system, would have broad Afghan support, although working out the domestic details of such a solution would be difficult. Moscow would clearly prefer the former solution to the latter one. However, should the Soviets become convinced that the costs of achieving this goal are becoming too high, they might settle for the neutrality solution. Whichever of these possibilities materializes, it will have a significant effect on the security of the entire region.

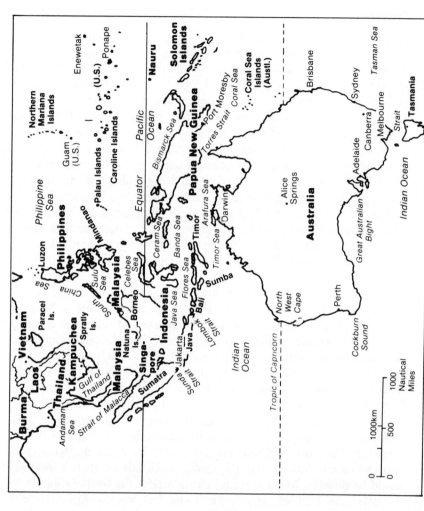

Australia and the Eastern Approaches

Australia and the Eastern Approaches

The withdrawal of the United States from Vietnam in 1975 largely signaled the end of the "colonial" era in Southeast Asia. Free from outside interference in their affairs for the first time in centuries, the states of the region are only now beginning to adjust to this new reality. Signs of stability are evident in the evolution of ASEAN into a more or less cohesive economic and political association and in the carefully managed modernization of the economies of countries like Singapore and Malaysia. Yet the region remains beset by problems. The continuing Vietnamese occupation of Kampuchea, the entrenching of Soviet influence in Vietnam, the expansion of Moscow's naval presence in regional waters, domestic unrest in the Philippines, tension between Hanoi and Beijing, apprehension over the latter's regional ambitions, and uncertainty about the political succession in Singapore as well as in Indonesia, all combine to produce a volatile mix of issues that cause apprehension about security both within the region and outside of it. The way in which these matters develop in the next few years will be of primary importance to the states of the area but their impact is likely to be felt much more widely. The states of the Indian Ocean, and not merely those in the immediate vicinity, are among those most likely to be affected.

An issue of supreme importance to the Indian Ocean region is the extent to which some or any one of the above issues might contain within it the seeds of conflict, whether among the states of Southeast Asia themselves or with outsiders. A particular concern revolves around the possible threat to the free movement of shipping through the area. As Sheldon Simon notes, the sea lines of communication that pass through the area are among the most important in the world. Were they to be put at risk, the cost through disruption to commercial life in the Indian Ocean would be incalculable. No less serious would be the implications for the regular naval deployments that take place throughout the area. While the likelihood of interference with maritime passage presently seems remote, in part because of the vested interest that local states have in its maintenance, a series of credible threat scenarios can be developed, ranging from restriction through the determined action of one state, not necessarily indigenous, to the possibility of a generalized conflict. All gain an element of credibility from the fact that on several occasions when Indonesia and the Philippines were seeking to establish their claim to archipelagic waters in the late 1950s and 1960s, Djakarta sought to restrict the passage of British and Australian warships through the area.

The roles of the superpowers in Southeast Asia, as within the Indian Ocean more generally, are viewed with a mixture of apprehension and reassurance by local states. Both superpowers now have important naval installations in the region from which they make deployments into the Indian Ocean. The Soviet Union's desire to improve its strategic dispositions in the area presented Hanoi with an opportunity to forge a stronger security relationship with Moscow. Although advantageous, reinforcing, for example, Hanoi's hand in its dispute with Beijing, the linkage is not without its costs. In the nature of all such relationships, Vietnam accepts some limits to its independence of action and bears the approbrium of playing host to what many countries see as a force for continued instability in the area. Among those of such an opinion are the members of ASEAN who are disturbed by the Soviet presence both for the reassurance it offers Vietnam and as a manifestation of Moscow's expanding capability to project force into the region. As a response, the ASEAN states have looked, with differing degrees of enthusiasm, to the United States as the one country that can balance the Soviet presence and offer some reassurance of their own security. While the United States has shown some willingness to play the role ASEAN has asked of it, this has largely been a function of protecting America's global security interests. While these may be consistent with an active regional responsibility, the continued application of the Guam (Nixon) Doctrine to the area gives the government of more than one ASEAN member cause for concern.

An issue that has emerged more recently in Southeast Asian politics, and one that serves to reinforce developing interrelationships throughout the Indian Ocean region, is the impact of Islam on Asian society. While Muslims compose about 90 percent of the population of Indonesia, their presence is likely to be more volatile in Malaysia where the figure is around 50 percent and where religion and ethnicity are already socially divisive. Islam serves to reinforce Muslims' perceptions of distinctiveness within Malaysian society, creating demands that have placed yet another item on Kuala Lumpur's already crowded domestic political agenda. The demands of Muslims are also an issue in the attempts of President Marcos to contain civil unrest in the Philippines. Although the extent remains unclear, the emergence of Islam as a more powerful political force in the Middle East seems destined to have an impact on social order in Malaysia and perhaps in Southeast Asia more widely.

On yet another tack, Indonesia retains membership in the gulf-centered Organization of Petroleum Exporting Countries and has seen the revenues from oil decline with the inability of the organization to sustain high crude prices. The result has been a slowdown both in the rate of growth of Indonesia's economy (GDP down from an average of 7.6 percent in 1971–81 to 4.3 percent in 1982) and in ASEAN's plans for greater economic cooperation among members. Even so, the last decade has seen an appreciable expansion in ASEAN's trade with selected Indian Ocean states, notably India, Pakistan, Iran, Iraq, Oman, and Kuwait. If the member countries can regain the momentum of economic growth it is likely there will be a further expansion of this trade.

In recent years, ASEAN has also devoted greater attention to its economic and political relations with the only developed state in the Indian Ocean region: Australia. Much of the impetus for this has come from Australia itself, particularly since the advent of a Labour government in Canberra in March 1983. Thus far the political facet of this drive for closer relations has been something less than an unqualified success, largely because of differences over the Kampuchean problem and Indonesia's takeover of Timor in 1975. However, these and the other issues (e.g., tariff protection) that are irritants to the relationship have been separable from long-standing mutual defense arrangements. Simon makes the point that security cooperation between Australia and ASEAN exists at several levels, giving Australia a modest military role in the area that will persist into the foreseeable future.

The Hawke government's search for a closer relationship with Asia has been accompanied by a recognition of the growing significance of the Indian Ocean region. As Henry Albinski shows, under the Fraser administration political and economic issues were an important facet of Australian policy toward the area, but a high priority was also given to security, largely defined by reference to American interests. Security in the region is an evident concern of the present government, but overall its policy is more broadly conceived. As Australian Foreign Minister Hayden explained in June 1984 in an important speech on the Indian Ocean, the region is undergoing rapid political, economic, and social

356 SUBREGIONAL PERSPECTIVES

change; it is one in which "too much is going on [and] too much is in prospect for it to languish as a token" area of Australian foreign policy. It is an indication of the region's newly perceived importance to Australia that the government has said it will assign the region a higher priority for the receipt of foreign aid, will offer support and technical expertise to the states of the Indian Ocean Commission, will adopt a higher regional diplomatic and cultural profile, will consider extension of the Australian defense cooperation program, will encourage regular exchanges between ministers and parliamentarians, will work to improve human rights, and will encourage efforts to create in the region a zone of peace. At present, these are little more than the first manifestations of a policy that, given the volatility of the Indian Ocean region, could provide Australia with as many challenges as rewards.

20. Australia, New Zealand, and Indian Ocean Security: Perspectives and Contributions from Outlying American Alliance Partners ☎ Henry S. Albinski

When the Australia–New Zealand–United States (ANZUS) alliance was created over thirty years ago, the motives impelling the signatories were a mixture of anxieties about Chinese, Sino-Soviet, and Japanese threats in the Pacific Ocean. Thus, the founding treaty referred solely to members' security in the Pacific. Although the treaty's language has never been altered, in recent years the ANZUS partners' perceptions of their individual and collective interests in the Indian Ocean region and a need for appropriate responses to developments there, have given fresh impetus to the alliance and added another dimension to its activities.

The aim of this chapter is threefold: to relate regional Indian Ocean and ANZUS power interests to the members' security perceptions; to assess Australian and New Zealand assets, debits, and limitations as they affect their capacity to respond to developments in the region; and to examine the extent, the means, and the consequences of the United States, Australia, and New Zealand extending the ANZUS alliance into the Indian Ocean region. The ANZUS alliance is asymmetrical. Australia and New Zealand are the less powerful members, less able to influence wide-reaching, outside events, and thereby more dependent. It is their perspectives that this chapter will feature.

Interests and Perceptions

Both Australia and New Zealand are modern, developed nations, dependent on commerce for much of their national wealth. As island nations, they are inordinately tied to seaborne trade, and the Indian Ocean is the route for much of this commerce. Both, but New Zealand especially, are dependent on the oil that is pumped in the region's littoral and hinterland and then transported across the Indian Ocean itself. A high proportion of Australia's natural resources is found in its vast but underpopulated west. Much of it moves to Japan and elsewhere in Asia over the eastern reaches of the Indian Ocean and through the several Southeast Asian straits that connect the Indian and the Pacific oceans. With the steep decline in importance of the traditional British outlet, Australia and New Zealand have doggedly cultivated, and have been able to establish, lucrative Middle Eastern markets for those primary products that continue as mainstays of their prosperity. It is understandable that, in their own interests and on behalf of friends, trading partners, and allies, Australia and New Zealand highly value their Indian Ocean area markets, sources of supply, and secure lines of communication. From this has followed their considerable sensitivity to issues affecting regional political stability and their version of the region's geostrategic imperatives.[1] Because of their geographic location, Australia and New Zealand constitute the interface between regions, specifically the Indian and Pacific basins.

From 1976 onward, strategic assessments in the three ANZUS capitals have closely resembled each other. On the occasions they have diverged, the differences have been more of degree than of kind. This trend has been upheld by the relative continuity of governments both in Australia (the Liberal-National party coalition) and in New Zealand (the National party) and by prime ministerial continuity in the persons of Malcolm Fraser and Robert Muldoon.[2] All three ANZUS governments have acknowledged that regional stability could be and has been disturbed by national upheavals or subregional enmities that are not an outgrowth of great power rivalry. Nevertheless, the partners have concluded that regional instability has often been fed and exploited by the Soviet Union, which has been perceived as classically imperialist. All three governments have characterized the Soviets as a threat to global security generally, and viewed the Soviet presence and behavior in the Indian Ocean region in particular as mischievous and destabilizing. For all three, the lesson has been that conscious, and indeed conscientious, steps are needed for deterrence and, as required, for crisis management.

The conclusion so often heard in Wellington and Canberra is that the United States must lead with credibility as well as capability. It was the New Zealand prime minister, Muldoon, echoing Fraser's sentiments, who argued that "there is only one power on earth that can resist [Soviet] aggression and that is the power of the United States."[3] Fraser, in turn, in mid-1982 during an American visit devoted a major address to the theme that the Western alliance was losing its sense of coherence and fortitude and must regain its will in the face of a multi-faceted, global Soviet effort. Soviet doctrine, according to Fraser, has not lost its appetite for spoils; it may renounce "adventurism" and urge caution "until the 'correlation of forces' is favourable. But when these forces are favourable it demands that opportunities be seized."[4]

In Canberra and Wellington, this chain of reasoning has led to an affirmation of the ANZUS alliance with the aim of nurturing America's own resolve and averting its isolation. By contributing resources, Australia and New Zealand have sought to reinforce the effectiveness of measures designed to achieve immediate objectives of the alliance, while simultaneously affirming and demonstrating its continued solidarity. Should a traditionally stable, intimate alliance such as ANZUS be viewed by friends and rivals alike as suffering from neglect or denigration, ANZUS's credibility as a regional guarantor would be undercut. Friends would become uneasy and rivals emboldened. Because of the protective American mantle, Australia and New Zealand have interpreted the alliance as a security guarantee and as a channel for access to and influence upon Washington.[5] For its part, the United States has accepted and generally welcomed this interpretation of the conceptual basis for the alliance.[6]

In broad, conceptual terms, what is the ANZUS alliance's application to the Indian Ocean region? ANZUS is a security alliance but not a military alliance; it has no standing forces and no institutionalized secretariat. As noted, the language of the treaty refers only to the Pacific and calls for consultation, followed by unspecified countermeasures, should any member be threatened or should an actual attack be carried out against its metropolitan territory, dependent territories, armed forces, public vessels, or aircraft in the *Pacific*. Strictly speaking, Australia's Indian Ocean littoral and immediate offshore maritime and air space would fall under ANZUS coverage, though the Indian Ocean beyond this perimeter would be excluded. Australia's Indian Ocean exposure is, however, a useful constant if a trans-Pacific, more broadly Indian Ocean–oriented ANZUS application need be "justified." Hence, one writer concluded from his American sources that the origin of a threat to Australia "would make the geographic parameters of the

Treaty esoteric, since it would be in all the parties' interest to meet an opposing force at the Alliance's most advantageous place and time, even if this were in mid–Indian Ocean."[7]

The point is well taken, but it addressed a hypothetical and indeed remote circumstance: an attack or apprehended attack on one of the alliance partners. ANZUS has long been and is likely to continue to be concerned not so much about war fighting as about consultation, planning for contingencies, and the application of various security-reinforcing measures. Such measures can be unilateral, bilateral, or trilateral; they need not be in a formal sense collective ANZUS alliance measures. But if they have an ANZUS dimension or appearance or are felt to contribute to the kinds of alliance objectives outlined earlier, they may be considered alliance measures. In this wide sense, there is a helpful treaty clause (article 2) on which to hang an assortment of activities. In order more effectively to achieve general security objectives, "the parties separately and jointly by means of continuous and effective self-help and mutual aid will maintain and develop their individual and collective capacity to resist armed attack." We will shortly notice how this has resulted, on particular occasions, in the three partners placing a different emphasis on what the alliance should or could do. When doing so, they have never as a group tried to announce that ANZUS has de facto developed an Indian Ocean extension, and they certainly have not contemplated a redrafting of treaty language to that effect.

It has accurately been said that "for much of the alliance's existence there has been a high degree of 'legitimised role differentiation' among the treaty members; the alliance members have generally accepted in practice that each has a very different role to play, and that no common yardstick of performance is appropriate."[8] New Zealand, for instance, the smallest and least powerful member of the alliance, is seemingly the least touched by events in the Indian Ocean and is the least conspicuous actor in the region. But it has not been absent and it has not eschewed some forms of regional ANZUS solidarity. Referring to the Indian Ocean region following the Soviet intrusion into Afghanistan, the New Zealand government reasoned that "a successful alliance is not a simple balance sheet of direct unilateral advantages to members; it is a flexible responsive grouping with common perceptions of danger and able to recognise the significance for each of wider economic and strategic considerations, such as security of trade routes and oil supplies."[9] Hence, when New Zealand has felt constrained from undertaking an active Indian Ocean role, it has nevertheless been able to point to its alliance-supportive contributions in the South Pacific and in Southeast Asia, the strategic gateway to the Indian Ocean.[10]

Australia, an Indian ocean littoral state, with far greater capabilities, a longer international reach, and administrative responsibility for several outlying ocean territories (Cocos Islands and Christmas Island), has been less equivocal about the region's salience and more manifestly assertive there. It has construed the spirit of ANZUS to apply in the Indian Ocean and has on occasion invoked ANZUS in the Indian Ocean context. But Fraser himself denied that "any or all military activity in the Indian Ocean would necessarily occur under ANZUS or that the ANZUS treaty would necessarily cover events anywhere in the Indian Ocean."[11] With these general propositions in mind, we now turn to the capabilities for or limitations on influence that Australia and New Zealand bring to the Indian Ocean region, especially as these may connote alliance purpose and viability.

Economic Dimensions

Australian and New Zealand responses to developments in the Indian Ocean area have been affected by their respective economic circumstances. The relative size and strength of their economies, their trading relationships, the commodities they exchange within the region, their perceived vulnerability to politically inspired commercial pressures of trading partners, and the dynamics of their domestic political systems have all been factors in policy making. These economic considerations have arguably imposed more constraints than opportunities upon Australia's and New Zealand's diplomatic and defense performance in the region.

Of the two nations, Australia has a considerably larger, more diverse, and more resilient economy. New Zealand, rather than Australian, representatives have time and again alluded to the submergence of their nation's foreign policy to its overseas trading concerns. According to the New Zealand minister for foreign affairs, Warren Cooper, only if the issue is great and a foreign customer's actions especially reprehensible will "our foreign policy come to the front more strongly than our trade policy."[12]

Defense spending in Australia and New Zealand has of course been influenced by economic conditions. Both relatively and absolutely New Zealand has allocated less for defense and therefore produced less. Yet after the Soviet occupation of Afghanistan in December 1979, both New Zealand and Australia began programs of real-term increases in their defense spending. However, progress has been uneven, mostly because of deteriorating economic conditions in both countries. For 1982–83, the defense budget in Australia was to rise to A $4,622 million and in New Zealand to NZ $668 million. The New Zealand figure represented a rise of about 2 percent in real terms over the previous financial year, the Australian under 1 percent. With adjustment for the relative value of the two currencies, Australia, with a population five times that of New Zealand (15 million vs. 3 million), is spending nearly nine times as much on defense. This reflects between 2.8 and 2.9 percent of Australia's gross domestic product, not quite 1 percent more than the New Zealand figure. From the perspective of Canberra and Wellington, especially the latter, modest defense expenditures, while in principle regrettable, have been possible in part bcause of ANZUS. Thus, after his mid-1982 meeting with Fraser, Muldoon said they had agreed that "if ANZUS was destroyed it would have major repercussions both in terms of the security of Australia and New Zealand and the amount that Australia and New Zealand might have to spend on defence."[13]

The Soviet move into Afghanistan was viewed with dismay in all three ANZUS capitals and interpreted as potentially destabilizing for the whole Indian Ocean region. The partners agreed that concrete ripostes were necessary and a number were carried out. As reprisal against the Soviets, the Carter administration blocked grain shipments and tightened considerably transfers of high-technology equipment. Australia, which had developed highly lucrative grain sales to the Soviets, promised not to make up the shortfall created by the American ban and suspended fisheries agreements. While Australia did not technically breach its promise on grain, it actually sold more grain to the Soviet Union in the year following than the year preceding Afghanistan, and generally enlarged its export trade with Moscow.[14] The New Zealanders agonized. Burgeoning trade with the Soviets, especially in meat and wool, was paying off handsomely, with a massive trade balance in New Zealand's favor. Thus Wellington decided to reduce Soviet fishing privileges in New Zealand waters but not to go beyond that. Labour party opposition calls for stronger measures were dismissed as irresponsible, and the government undertook to explain its position to United States officials and congressmen. When doing so, mention was made of the protectionist policies of the United States and other Western governments that had forced New Zealand to seek and then protect other markets, including that of the Soviet Union. Moreover, the maintenance of a viable New Zealand export trade was argued to be directly related to the scale and quality of its international commitments, as under ANZUS.[15] Overall, the Americans accepted New Zealand's position.

Just before the Soviet entry into Afghanistan came the seizure of American embassy personnel and their sequestering by Iran's revolutionary regime. Australia and New Zealand plainly disapproved of the

Khomeini regime and shared Washington's concern over the implications for the spread of instability in the Persian Gulf region and the reaping of Soviet advantage. They deplored the hostage taking and understood President Carter's efforts to bring pressure on Tehran to free the captives. As Carter embarked on a program of sanctions against Iran, he asked America's friends and allies to ban all exports save food and medicine. Australia and New Zealand appreciated the emotion with which the United States regarded the hostage issue, as well as the broad significance of exhibiting solidarity with the senior ANZUS partner during its time of anguish. They concluded that the United States should not be left isolated and disappointed. While neither was entirely persuaded that economic sanctions would have their intended effect on Iran, both decided that alliance cohesion might dampen any American inclination to become obsessed with Iran and behave too impulsively, and therefore counterproductively, with regard to essential and longer-term allied interests in the region.

Accordingly, Australia and New Zealand were rhetorically and indeed diplomatically supportive of the U.S. position on Iran but on economic steps they divided. Australia scrupulously observed the recommended guidelines even to the point of canceling some relatively important wool, iron, and steel sales opportunities. But since its exports to Iran were mostly grains, the net economic loss to Canberra was slight.[16] Although their trade with Iran was mostly in foodstuffs, the New Zealanders elected against any commercial sanctions, employing arguments similar to those brought out in regard to post-Afghanistan sanctions against the Soviets: "We have said [to the Americans] we would not adopt self-damaging policies. I think they would understand if we did not change our minds."[17] New Zealand's only apparent exception to this rule was to refuse permission to Iranian military aircraft to land in New Zealand and to fly urgently needed lamb to Iran.

The response of Canberra and Wellington to the events in Afghanistan and Iran reflected their concern that the region not suffer from additional political dislocation and that regional customers not have cause to reconsider their trading relationship with the two ANZUS partners. The latter was particularly important since the Middle East had become the single fastest-growing market for Australian and New Zealand products. Both governments had done much to cultivate the promise of an expanded trade relationship based on the region's rapid development, oil-derived wealth, and strong demand for foodstuffs.

Concerns about the disruption of commercial relations were also at play over the issue of Australian and New Zealand participation in what became known as the Multinational Force and Observers (MFO), created to oversee the Sinai following its reversion from Israel to Egypt. Virtually the entire community of regional nations was flatly opposed to the Camp David Accords under which the restoration was to take place. The Australian and New Zealand fear was that their participation in the MFO would be regarded as a diplomatically partisan act, legitimizing the regionally unpopular settlement. This could result in Middle Eastern nations retaliating against them, either by turning down the oil tap or, far more likely, by restricting Australian and New Zealand access to hard-won Middle Eastern markets.

The United States lobbied long and hard to bring Canberra and Wellington to the Sinai peacekeeping party, but they took their time. Their official advice on possible economic liabilities was divided. National party electoral support in New Zealand was substantially dependent on the rural constituency that would suffer most in the event of retaliation, and a national election needed to be held by the end of 1981. In Australia, the National Country party (later renamed the National party) portion of the coalition was especially skeptical. Doug Anthony, the party leader and minister for trade and resources, had exerted himself to build commercial bridges to the region and had no heart for having them burned. New Zealand and Australia took elaborate soundings among Middle Eastern states to determine whether there was a real prospect of commercial retaliation. Eventually, despite continuing Middle East opposition to the Egyptian-Israeli settlement and the international machinery devised to oversee it, Australia and New Zealand satisfied themselves that no commercial reprisals were likely.[18] They decided to contribute to the MFO in late 1981 and deployed their forces early the following year.

The economic circumstances of Australia and New Zealand, as interpreted by the two governments, have for the most part constrained the latitude of their individual and alliance-related policies in the greater Indian Ocean region. On the diplomatic side, a rather different calculus and pattern of behavior has appeared.

Diplomatic Dimensions

The Australian and New Zealand decisions to participate in the Sinai MFO were predominantly governed by diplomatic considerations, which in turn bore on the American connection and on the ANZUS alliance. These decisions were taken against a background of disquieting factors, of which potential commercial damage was only one. Political and public opinion, especially in Australia, was on balance negative. The contemplated force would lack the reassuring auspices of the United Nations or the commonwealth, under which the two nations had previously committed forces to peacekeeping or supervisory roles. There was unease about assigning forces for a period of years, far from their normal operational areas, and to a region of only indirect political interest to the two countries. Neither wished to be associated with an American component of the MFO that might be detached for regional Rapid Deployment Force (RDF) duty and both were disturbed that their own MFO forces could find themselves caught in the middle of a harsh diplomatic or shooting exchange in that extremely volatile part of the world. Moreover, a scenario could be imagined in which the quality of relations with the United States and, in fact, ANZUS could adversely be affected. Hence, a New Zealand academic's question: "Can you imagine what would happen to the credibility of ANZUS if the Australians and New Zealanders had to say to the U.S. in the event of crisis [in the Middle East] that they were simply going home—that anti-Soviet posturing could only be meaningful when confined to the South Pacific or Indian Ocean regions?"[19]

The antipodean force that was deployed was significantly less elaborate than originally envisioned by the United States. It was composed of ninety-nine Australians and twenty-nine New Zealanders forming a helicopter transport support unit, and a few of each nationality attached to MFO headquarters. Very careful conditions were extracted regulating their noncombat use and right of disengagement.[20] But the decision to participate, and most of the reasons behind it, were in fact alliance related and, more broadly, diplomatic and security related. Australia's decision to join in principle, predicated on the participation of other Western nations so as to ensure breadth and representativeness within the MFO, did have a positive effect on the decisions of the British, New Zealand, and selected Western European governments. In Fraser's view, "The failure of Australia and other Western countries to participate would require the United States to bear the burden itself and would be seen as a failure by the West to support United States policies in the Middle East," one consequence being a gift of propaganda opportunities to the Soviets.[21] While the United States had lobbied Australia and New Zealand heavily, it avoided the explicit argument of a helping hand being requested in the interest of alliance solidarity. The notion of support for the alliance did, however, animate Canberra and Wellington, and was especially important for Fraser and Muldoon personally. The two governments did not allow themselves to be rushed and obtained firm conditions for their protection. Afterward, this was presented as evidence of alliance soundness: "The alliance is strengthened by our insistence on taking our own independent decisions. In this instance, the time taken in reaching a decision reflected a determination by the Government to make our own decision in the light of our own national interest."²² Both vis-à-vis the United States and domestic political considerations, New Zealand and Australia concluded that alliance workability and acceptance must appear to be, as well as be in fact, a matter of judgment independently arrived at on the basis of professed New Zealand and Australian interests.

Australian and New Zealand participation in the MFO was of course measurably influenced by their wish to contribute to the longer-term, Arab-Israeli peace process throughout the Middle East. It was an objective that coincided with the economic and strategic interests of the ANZUS nations and many others as well. While the point has not been expressed by them in its full conceptual implications, Australia and New Zealand have increasingly felt that the Middle Eastern peace process can best be advanced by discouraging the principal regional states from embarking on rash, destabilizing ventures; by ensuring that the United States, as the key extraterritorial actor, is constructively engaged; and by New Zealand and Australia adopting a fairly low profile, a constructive and, as far as possible, an impartial and evenhanded approach. Several rationales have been attached to this last proposition. One is the two nations' need to foster their own commercial and related regional interests. Another is to convey an impression to regional Arab and other Muslim states that there is no Western conspiracy to embrace Israel at the expense of others. A third is that because of their excellent connections with the United States and their pro-American gestures such as MFO membership, Australia and New Zealand might be better able to reinforce those American regional policies they believe to be correct and cause a reconsideration of the policies found to be flawed.

These various perspectives can be seen in operation with regard to Israel. Australia and New Zealand have consistently defended Israel's right to exist behind secure and defined borders. But they have rejected what they have interpreted as Israel's excessive claims and have been urging a more accommodationist approach toward Palestinians and toward Israel's neighbor states. Hence, in 1980 New Zealand abstained, rather than oppose a United Nations resolution calling on Israel to withdraw from all Arab territories occupied during the 1967 war.²³ A year later, Muldoon made it very clear that New Zealand's decision to join the MFO should in no way be construed as an endorsement of any particular approach to the regional peace process or as prejudicing his nation's attachment to evenhandedness.²⁴ Similarly, in late March 1982, during a Middle Eastern tour, then Australian Foreign Minister Tony

Street emphasized, both in Egypt and in Israel, the reality and in certain respects the validity of Palestinian aspirations, including a homeland alongside Israel with direct participation by the Palestinians in the fashioning of their own future.[25]

Australia and New Zealand in public and even more in private were angered by Israel's bombing attack on the Iraqi nuclear facility in mid-1981 and then by its decision to enforce Israeli law on the Golan Heights territory claimed by Syria. Such actions were seen as complicating the assembly of an MFO and, more generally, as counterproductive to regional confidence building. But if Australia and New Zealand were angry in these contexts, they were furious with Israel for its massive 1982 invasion of Lebanon and the protracted siege and bombardment of Beirut. New Zealand called Israel's response "frighteningly disproportionate to the provocation" and urged Israel to withdraw from Lebanon "forthwith and unconditionally."[26] The Australian reaction was also blunt. Fraser used the occasion of the continuing siege of Beirut not only to urge United States special envoy Philip Habib to persevere in his efforts at fashioning an agreement for disengagement but also to remind the United States of its responsibilities to exert its influence with Israel to full effect. Again, as on other occasions, Fraser understood the crisis as a "significant test of Western resolve and unity of purpose."[27] His comments brought together the strands of evolving Australian and New Zealand Middle Eastern policy noted earlier: restraint by the regional principals, American engagement, and evenhandedness in Wellington and Canberra.

Middle Eastern issues have projected Australia and New Zealand well into the hinterland of the Indian Ocean and in both subtle and overt ways have affected ANZUS alliance relations. One facet of the diplomacy to which Middle Eastern issues have given rise has been Australia's and New Zealand's willingness to distance themselves from the United States, although in ways that the Pacific countries have felt would actually fortify security for others and invigorate their sense of what the alliance is about.

A variant on this theme appeared in the way Australia and New Zealand dealt with the new Law of the Sea treaty. They understood but were disappointed with the Reagan administration's 1981 decision to review the painstakingly cobbled draft treaty. They both labored to avert an American disengagement from the negotiating process and then to persuade other states to allow the United States sufficient time to carry out its review. In 1982, both joined a group of middle powers that attempted—and nearly succeeded—in devising a formula under which the United States could associate itself with the draft treaty.

Australia's chief United Nations Conference on the Law of the Sea delegate, Keith Brennan, was especially active and constructive throughout the complex proceedings. But the United States eventually declared itself against the draft, mostly on the basis of its objections to seabed mining provisions.

The significance of this diplomacy for our analysis lies beyond the fact that Australia and New Zealand exerted themselves to assist the United States and most members of the international community to come to terms, in order to avoid America's international isolation and opprobrium. A most important reason for both nations was that the draft treaty contained strategically significant provisions. These provisions established a liberal regime for the transit of aircraft, surface vessels, and submerged craft through international straits, such as those connecting Southeast Asia and the Middle East with the Indian Ocean. The rules for passage would have substantially facilitated American operations in the Indian Ocean and the protection of lines of communication generally—a highly desirable Australian and New Zealand objective. The draft treaty was seemingly the only significantly dissonant note at the June 1982 ANZUS Council meetings in Canberra. The frustration felt in Canberra and Wellington was that the convention was a package, a stitching together of compromises, which could easily come unraveled if any highlight were removed or any major power chose to dissociate itself.[28] Australia and New Zealand were not convinced by the American rejoinder that the United States could continue to rely on "customary law" to enjoy the treaty's transit passage provisions.[29] Their diplomacy during the negotiating sessions had been prompted in part by a desire to ensure unhampered American, and indeed their own, naval access to the Indian Ocean basin. For both, the effectiveness of American forces and of the ANZUS alliance writ contributed directly to their, and especially Australia's, crafting of their diplomacy on regional naval dispositions. To Canberra and Wellington, the United States had cut off the nose to spite the face, misguided about intrinsic security considerations, especially in the Indian Ocean.

The Australian and New Zealand Labour governments of 1972–75 embraced in principle the zone-of-peace concept. New Zealand concentrated on fostering a nuclear-free zone in the South Pacific, and Australia focused on a zone of peace in the Indian Ocean. While both nations disapproved of American plans to upgrade facilities at Diego Garcia, the Australian Labour government undertook diplomatic contacts with the United States and the Soviets to urge the cause of Indian Ocean naval limitations. Changes of government both in Wellington and Canberra meant changed perceptions regarding the implications of the Soviet naval presence in the Indian Ocean and the need for American responsiveness, with Australia being the more vocal and active protagonist. Both governments accepted the desirability of a regional zone of peace, but described it as premature and impractical, mostly because they saw the then-prevailing American presence there as inadequate. Their nominal acceptance of an Indian Ocean naval balance at the lowest practical force level actually translated into a "balance" characterized by de facto United States superiority.[30]

The diplomatic upshot of these changed perceptions took several forms. Both nations quickly made their views about an enhanced American naval capability known to Washington. They supported efforts to build up Diego Garcia and in fact the Ford administration thought that Australian anxiety about the Indian Ocean was overdrawn.[31] When, in his early months in office, Carter declared an objective of a "demilitarized" Indian Ocean, both Australia and New Zealand were deeply unsettled. They made concerned inquiries and were relieved by assurances that the expression had been used as a rhetorical gambit to induce the Soviets to negotiate seriously on Indian Ocean as well as other issues.[32] In the United Nations Ad Hoc Committee on the Indian Ocean, of which it is a member, Australia under the Fraser government supported moves for American membership, so as to strengthen Western representation there, and eventually the United States did join.[33] When the U.S. did increase its Indian Ocean deployments, Australia undertook to persuade Third World countries at the United Nations that its own objective of a "lowest practical" force level was really an exercise designed to reduce force levels and that this was the American objective as well. Through a series of diplomatic maneuvers, some of it charade, Australia endeavored to demonstrate that while lowest-practical-level force balance was good value, demilitarization and zone-of-peace notions were unattainable. After Afghanistan, Australia supported additional American deployments in the Indian Ocean and, for a time, continued to endorse the concept of balance at the lowest practical level. But, as Fraser explained, with the New Zealand government's concurrence, the original Australian comments "were made, I think, in happier days and we now look to changed circumstances."[34]

When the United States and the Soviet Union agreed to undertake Indian Ocean naval arms limitation talks, Australia, with sideline support from New Zealand, was able to use the occasion for bilateral diplomacy with the Americans. Canberra was kept closely briefed by the United States and made several representations to the Americans, persuading them to retract and to ask the Soviets for redrafting of some provisions previously agreed upon. The provisional package that emerged can be interpreted as a major Australian diplomatic success since the points of agreement met Australian as well as United States criteria regarding the integrity of American installations and force levels, and included moves for a supreme national interest clause along with the exemption of Australia itself from the naval limitations. For Australia, the overall effect was a strengthening of its claim to set its own terms for Indian Ocean security plans and the underscoring of the ANZUS alliance's regional interests generally.[35]

Finally, the ANZUS partners undertook a series of cooperative diplomatic moves following the Soviet invasion of Afghanistan. Australia and New Zealand imposed their own forms of economic sanctions against the Soviets. Beyond these, New Zealand expelled the Soviet ambassador to Wellington on the grounds that he had arranged transfer of funds to a radical-left New Zealand political party. But the timing of the action was broadly construed as being in keeping with a deliberate cooling of relations with Afghanistan's invader. The Australian and New Zealand governments both tried to dissuade their athletes from competing at the Moscow Olympics, and many Australians and New Zealanders did not in fact participate. Muldoon later remarked that while the United States had worked to organize an international boycott of the games, New Zealand's own official response was taken independently of any pressure.[36] Fraser met Carter in late January of 1980, and a week later reported to the president on his consultations with European leaders regarding the international implications of Afghanistan. His role was genuinely appreciated by Carter and generally interpreted as a plus for American-Australian relations.[37] At Australia's suggestion, an extraordinary ANZUS Council meeting was convened in Washington in February 1980. At the meeting, the entire Indian Ocean security picture was reviewed and individual member and collective alliance responses were considered.

We have noted some of the opportunities that have enabled Australia and/or New Zealand to practice diplomacy affecting Indian Ocean and more broadly littoral hinterland issues. All of these issues have in some manner featured the United States. A dominant objective of the antipodean partners' diplomacy has been the promotion of an interested, capable, and credible American presence in the region. In the aftermath of Vietnam, the two non-Labour governments worried about American reticence to assume a necessary and sustained leadership role. This in part was the rationale of their prime ministers for the agitated manner in which they pictured conditions and invoked the language of will, strength, and alliance solidarity.

Military Dimensions

On this note we proceed to assess Australian and New Zealand military contributions to the security of the Indian Ocean region, especially as they have been impelled by alliance considerations. While complex, the subject is divisible into the following categories: the activities of Australian and New Zealand armed forces, the opportunities for United States forces to transit or otherwise utilize Australian or New Zealand territory, and the availability of Australian and New Zealand sites for command, control, communication, and monitoring functions.

Some prefatory comments will help to set the stage. We already have examined Australia's and New Zealand's general appreciation of Indian Ocean regional security. It is now useful to underline the perceptions they hold about their own military/strategic roles in the region. Australian and New Zealand doctrine has emphasized defense planning that concentrates on their respective surroundings rather than on an openly "forward" defense policy. Their reasons for this include a natural, middle-power focus on the immediate neighborhood, limited military and related resources, little likelihood of "another Vietnam" overseas ground operation, political cross-pressures at home, and United States acquiescence in a form of geographic division of defense activity labor. At the same time, both governments have made it clear that a continuing element of their defense policy is operations farther afield. Such operations need not be in tandem with the United States or under ANZUS aegis as such. But Australia's and New Zealand's commitment to the alliance, their pleasure that the United States has recovered its confidence since its withdrawal from Vietnam and is prepared to supply international leadership, as well as their assessments of interregional security linkages, have colored the rationale for their extraregional involvement.[38]

With regard to the Indian Ocean region, it is understandable that Australia more than New Zealand has been and will likely continue to be more disposed to undertake direct or supportive defense activities in the area. Its Indian Ocean coastline, the pattern of communications lines, its considerably greater military resources, and its suitability as a site for American defense-related activities that bear on Indian Ocean security, are among the factors responsible. Indian Ocean issues have been mooted at ANZUS Council meetings since 1976. New Zealand has not tried to avoid such consultations or to back away when, as in 1980 following Afghanistan, trilateral pledges for enhanced defense measures were drawn up. It succeeded in having the language of the final communiqué softened, agreeing to be involved but "naval and air support will be given by New Zealand as resources permit."[39]

New Zealand's military capabilities are considerably more modest than Australia's, and Wellington has no military facilities on or near the Indian Ocean. It maintains no on-station vessels in the Indian Ocean, though Royal New Zealand Air Force P-3s intermittently fly surveillance sorties from Australia or Singapore. Until recently Australia's military facilities or forces on or near its Indian Ocean side were very slight but the situation has been improving. Air base facilities in the west and northwest of the country are being upgraded, a squadron of F-18s will be stationed in northern Australia, and P-3 surveillance in the eastern Indian Ocean has been increased. While the P-3 Orion aircraft mainly operate out of Australia, they also stage out of the Malaysian base at Butterworth and deploy in and out of Diego Garcia. A Royal Australian Navy (RAN) patrol boat base will be established at Port Hedland and, more significantly, HMAS *Stirling*, the RAN base at Cockburn Sound south of Perth/Fremantle, is about to home-base destroyers and frigates. The facility is also able to sustain submarine operations.[40]

To what extent have New Zealand and Australia been willing to involve themselves in Indian Ocean military planning, exercises, or operations? Two illustrations of their reaction to tense international situations are instructive, especially for New Zealand, the more distant power. Following the outbreak of hostilities between Iraq and Iran in late 1980, New Zealand and Australia entered into contingency consultations with the United States about possible naval contributions to a multilateral force designed to protect the Persian Gulf (ultimately no such force needed to be formed).[41] In mid-1982, at its own initiative, New Zealand placed a frigate at the Royal Navy's disposal for Indian Ocean patrol, to free a British frigate for duty in the Falkland Islands.[42] Thus, while the Falklands conflict had no direct bearing on the Indian Ocean, New Zealand was not averse to an extensive Indian Ocean naval deployment on behalf of what it felt to be a significant political/strategic interest: defeating aggression and rallying round a historical friend and ally.

Another facet of the two states' military involvement in the region is to be found in various exercises in the Sandgroper and Beacon Compass series that have been conducted in the Indian Ocean. In addition, RAN and U.S. Navy sea and air units have carried out binational exercises off the Australian coast; in 1982 a major exercise was undertaken with regular Australian forces.[43] Australian vessels have been carrying out independent Indian Ocean deployments as far as the western reaches of the ocean. With regard to all of these activities, there has been a reluctance to denominate them openly as falling under ANZUS alliance auspices. For instance, the 1982 ANZUS Council communiqué took notice of the measures followed by the United States and Australia "on an independent national basis, commensurate with the threats to security in the area."[44] In 1981, following Beacon Compass exercises, Muldoon observed that ANZUS made no reference to the Indian Ocean and that New Zealand had not been involved in any "military presence" outside the treaty area. There had been some limited cooperation with the United States and Australia in the Indian Ocean but not under ANZUS sponsorship.[45]

Australia, New Zealand, and indeed the United States have been reluctant to stir up unnecessary domestic and international controversy over whether ANZUS has been or should be extended de facto into the Indian Ocean. In some respects, as suggested earlier, the question of extended ANZUS coverage need not be answered, although the reality of military collaboration in the Indian Ocean region exists. For New Zealand especially, where the ANZUS alliance per se is a lively object of partisan debate, it is imprudent to admit to an extension of the alliance to an area so far from New Zealand's strategic environment and its conventional diplomatic and defense focus. When the Australian government authorizes "independent" Indian Ocean deployments, it can point for political purposes to having a mind and a capability of its own, without in any material way snubbing or detracting from the value of the alliance. Muldoon's down-playing comment about an Indian Ocean presence was made at a time when Wellington was fearful of adverse Middle Eastern nations' commercial reactions to possible New Zealand participation in a Sinai force—a force of which the United States was the principal sponsor. Similarly, Australia's decision to withdraw from scheduled western Indian Ocean exercises in late 1980, while more complex, contained an element of wishing not to jeopardize commercial and political ties in the adjoining region.

Australian and New Zealand sensitivities and cautions are a very slight price for the United States or the alliance collectively to pay. Indeed, such qualifications as are imposed by Australia and New Zealand on their Indian Ocean activity actually make it easier for them to defend and in real terms to support the alliance and its objectives, thereby helping to underwrite, not undercut, regional security. Their contributions are manifested in the form of contingency planning, the sharpening of all the partners' capabilities through training and exercises, and the demonstration to others of alliance resolve and bona fides. Especially since American naval strength has been severely stretched because of increased Indian Ocean deployments, modest yet highly professional Australian and New Zealand cooperation in the region matters. Conversely, the continuing Australian and New Zealand naval concentration in the Pacific enables the United States to release more elements for Indian Ocean service.[46]

Australia and New Zealand demonstrate collateral support for the United States, for alliance well-being, and for Indian Ocean security by close and continuing defense association with Malaysia and Singapore. Through the Five Power Defense Agreement, the two states enjoy access to the two Southeast Asian nations and to their facilities that for historical and other reasons are unavailable to the United States. Yet Malaysia and Singapore are Indian Ocean gateway states. For years American military air traffic has been transiting through Singapore between the Pacific and the Indian Oceans. To avoid local political problems, the servicing of American aircraft has been carried out by Royal Australian Air Force personnel normally posted to Tengah air base. By 1978, it became politically possible for the United States and Australia to conclude a public agreement to formalize the support services.[47]

The Singapore case draws attention to another category of military means by which Canberra and Wellington are able to underpin security objectives in the Indian Ocean: the provision of a multiplicity of facilities for American forces operating in and out of Australian and New Zealand territory. Since its landmass fronts the Indian Ocean, Australia is of preeminent importance in this regard, though the New Zealand scene is not irrelevant to this discussion.

Shortly after entering office, the Fraser and Muldoon governments lifted prevailing bans on the entry of nuclear-powered vessels into their ports. The United States welcomed these steps, which were intended by Canberra and Wellington to have a solidifying effect on the alliance while also enhancing American naval mobility. The United States has no naval base or staging presence either in Australia or New Zealand and, in reality, only occasionally brings a warship into New Zealand. But in the past several years there has been very substantial American naval traffic, including aircraft carriers and attack submarines, moving in and out of Australia. This traffic has been directed overwhelmingly into the state of Western Australia, particularly Cockburn Sound. Thus in 1981, twenty-nine United States surface ships and eight submarines visited Western Australia. The ship visits have at times been made in conjunction with United States–Australian or United States–Australian– New Zealand Indian Ocean exercises, or as stopovers on regular Indian

Ocean deployments. They have been highly useful for reprovisioning, for minor repairs, and for the morale of seamen taking rest and recreation in convivial Australian surroundings.[48]

A problem has arisen in that visits from nuclear-powered and nuclear-armed vessels have become a bone of partisan contention in both Australia and New Zealand. The debate has been especially pointed in New Zealand where the New Zealand Labour party (but not its parliamentary leadership) has advocated withdrawal from ANZUS. The leadership is, however, committed to a ban on all nuclear-powered and -armed craft, in the latter instance, air as well as naval. Despite serious intraparty differences, the Australian Labour party is willing to accept nuclear-powered and -armed vessels, but it rejects home basing or home porting for them, as well as the storage of nuclear arms in Australia. Since the United States continues to adhere to a policy of neither confirming nor denying that its vessels carry nuclear weapons, an imposition of bans against nuclear-armed craft would effectively bar all United States visits to New Zealand and could impose highly deleterious consequences on the ANZUS alliance at large. The Fraser and Muldoon governments were able to realize a measure of political capital from their stand on this issue but at bottom have been persuaded that the maintenance of existing opportunities for the U.S. Navy invigorates regional security, keeps the alliance viable, and indeed enables Australia and New Zealand to raise the level of their own access and influence vis-à-vis the United States.[49]

American utilization of Australia's Indian Ocean region and approaches could in time become much more extensive. As noted, amphibious exercises are already being held in Western Australia, while American aircraft have long had transit access to the Australian Cocos Islands in the eastern Indian Ocean. Western Australia could be developed into a secure logistical and staging area as backup for Diego Garcia, not subject to interdiction as could affect movements through Southeast Asian straits. There was a standing offer from Fraser for the United States to further develop Cockburn Sound and transform it into a major naval base. Such a base would suffer from various shortcomings, including Labour party opposition to its presence. The United States has in any event declined to pick up the option, mostly because it wishes as far as possible to home port its carrier task forces in the United States. Moreover, the U.S. Navy is more eager to allocate its resources to vessels than to bases.[50] But the fact remains that such a base offer was extended within the ANZUS alliance spirit. In principle, such a base could provide unimpeded access to the volatile northwest quadrant of the Indian Ocean with hardly any difference in steaming time than from Subic, and would be an alternative should political conditions render Subic less tenable.

Had the Fraser government's post-Afghanistan offer of Cockburn Sound to the United States Navy been accepted, it would have encountered turbulent political weather in Australia. It is arguable that in the interest of insulating the American connection from excessive strains, it is well that the offer of Cockburn was not exercised. On the other hand, Australia demurred when the United States inquired about its interest in contributing to the RDF early in 1980. Any such contribution would have been marginal as Australia would have been the only non-American component of the force. Furthermore, the gesture would have been resented by the several Asian and Middle Eastern littoral states that Australia wished to cultivate politically and commercially. Finally, an RDF contribution would have been most difficult to sustain politically within Australia, especially because of its connotation of a distant, ground troop commitment. In any event, when it was announced that Australian defense would remain a basically independent, national effort, Washington took no umbrage.[51]

Australia's permission to allow the transit of U.S. Air Force B-52s through Darwin on training and Indian Ocean surveillance flights further illustrates the value of the alliance connection, as well as the constraints that affect the antipodean ANZUS partners. Although by agreement unarmed, the flights are of considerable operational utility and are construed as a demonstration of United States force projection capabilities and of resolve for the alliance. But the Australian government was not rushed into agreeing to the flights and made it plain that the B-52 deployments were designed to contain a regional Soviet threat. But, again for a mixture of political and commercial reasons, neither in fact nor in appearance did Australia wish the deployments to be directed at indigenous Persian Gulf and Middle Eastern disputes. In an attempt to make the deployments as domestically palatable as possible and to avert major reverberations against the alliance, it pressed for a formula that would give Australia knowledge of, and technically veto power over, any future *armed* B-52 flights, despite U.S. policy of nondivulgence of nuclear armament on its weapons platforms. Despite continuing Labour party dissatisfaction with the adequacy of terms under which Australia's sovereign rights were to be protected, the negotiated agreement, together with informal understandings, suggested that both Canberra and Washington were able to achieve their basic requirements.[52]

Significant as much of U.S. military access to Australia and New Zealand may be, it is arguable that Indian Ocean and indeed global security are supported at least as much by static facilities, especially in Australia. These installations perform an array of navigational, monitoring, intercept, and communications functions, the very stuff of modern military capabilities and in some respects of conflict deterrence. Some are dominantly civilian/scientific in purpose, using equipment and products that are wholly unclassified, but with military spin-offs. Examples are the Omega navigational station in Gippsland, Australia, and the transit circle astronomical equipment being installed on Black Birch Mountain near Blenheim, New Zealand. Others, such as the naval communication station at Northwest Cape, Western Australia, and the facilities at Pine Gap and Nurrungar, in Australia's interior, are avowedly military. Nominally, Pine Gap and Nurrungar's very functions are classified.[53]

Installations such as these take advantage of the unique geographic situation of Australia and New Zealand. These nations also are friends and allies of the United States, share various strategic perspectives, are themselves technologically advanced, and are politically stable. Most of the facilities have been the objects of domestic political or technical/scientific criticism over how they allegedly implicate Australia and New Zealand in America's strategic designs, serve to undermine the central balance, lower the threshold of nuclear war, expose host countries to Soviet nuclear attacks, or simply derogate from their sovereignty.[54] Demands have been raised for their abolition or renegotiation. It is not possible within the ambit of this study to examine the political milieu in which the debates have been conducted or the plausibility or validity of particular criticisms. What should be said, with emphasis, is that taken as a whole the various facilities are critical, even indispensable, for Western regional and global security interests. The United States wishes to protect them and their integrity. In Australia, where they are numerous, varied, and especially strategically salient, the government has defended them against criticism on familiar grounds: they count for their security value, they tighten the ANZUS alliance, and they help to keep the United States engaged and capable. We have previously mentioned such Australian and New Zealand official arguments, arguments often made with an eye to political capital. But the familiarity of the arguments, or their partisan presentation, does not detract from the wider, strategic conclusions.

Conclusion

Australia's and New Zealand's respective locations, resources, special diplomatic and economic interests, domestic politics, and other variables preclude an identity of interests and policies with the United States or indeed with one another. But the ANZUS alliance under which the three have worked for over three decades has proved to be an exceptionally pliable and efficient instrument. Its application in the Indian Ocean region has never been firmly defined. However, whether functioning independently, bilaterally, or all together, the ANZUS partners have on balance accomplished much.

In an article called, "The Case for the Alliance," an Australian academic has concluded that ANZUS has in fact found new health in its new Indian Ocean orientation: 'Given its recent re-interpretation in the light of contemporary anxieties which centre . . . round the Indian Ocean [the alliance] seems to . . . have acquired a new dimension of usefulness in the auspicious circumstances of the unfolding decade."[55]

21. ASEAN and the Indian Ocean: Maritime Issues and Regional Security ✒ Sheldon W. Simon

The states of the Association of South-East Asian Nations (ASEAN)— Indonesia, Malaysia, the Philippines, Singapore, and Thailand—dominate the eastern approaches to the Indian Ocean. Linked by geography, a history of anticolonialism, culture, and more recently common economic purpose, they form a continuous land-sea chain stretching over two thousand miles from north to south and approximately thirty-five hundred miles east to west at the southeastern tip of Asia. Located at the juncture of the Indian and Pacific oceans, they are astride one of the world's great maritime crossroads and are a region of crucial strategic and commercial importance.

The Southeast Asian region is composed mainly of seas, among them the Andaman, the South China, the Banda, and the Java, all of which are linked by a series of maritime corridors, straits, and passages. Given these geographic realities, it is hardly surprising that maritime issues figure prominently in ASEAN's calculations of security, being manifest in the ASEAN states' desire to maintain the integrity of their coastal zones and territorial waters as defined at the Third United Nations Conference on the Law of the Sea (UNCLOS III), and in the need to monitor international shipping through the waters of the region. The policies pursued by the ASEAN countries to protect their maritime interests and concerns have the greatest immediate impact in the region itself. Yet they have a salience that extends far beyond, touching the security concerns of all states whose ships ply the sea lanes of the region.

The security of local and external states is also affected by the impact of outside issues. Issues such as American-Soviet rivalry in the Indian Ocean, the advent of militant Islamic fundamentalism, the continued Soviet occupation of Afghanistan, and proposals to declare the Indian Ocean a zone of peace, all have implications for Southeast Asian security. But equally, ASEAN's policies on these matters affect its relations with external powers. Thus the divergence of views between ASEAN and the superpowers toward proposals for a zone of peace in the Indian Ocean (and in Southeast Asia) offers the potential for policy disagreements, if not conflicts, over the passage of military vessels through the straits of the region.

This chapter aims to achieve three things: to examine the nature of the security challenges faced by the states of ASEAN in the light of their maritime environment and location astride an important geostrategic crossroad, to analyze the responses to those challenges, and to relate both challenges and responses to the political and security issues in the Indian Ocean region.

Maritime Issues

Foreign trade is the lifeblood of the five ASEAN states whose economic success stories are based on export-led growth. The ratio of foreign trade to gross national product (GNP) within ASEAN ranges from 33 percent in the Philippines to 89 percent in Singapore. For the ASEAN states combined, trade accounts for approximately 75 percent of regional GNP.[1] The bulk of this trade is with the United States, Japan, and Western Europe, but it is perhaps an indication of growing economic integration among the states of the Indian Ocean that in recent years ASEAN's trade with certain littoral states has shown steady if unspectacular growth. Thus by the early 1980s economic transactions between ASEAN and the Persian Gulf were in the range of $6.7 billion annually.[2] All this trade must move by sea, a reality that renders ASEAN naval planners highly sensitive to the potential for sea-lane disruption. It is in the context of such a danger and its potentially disastrous consequences that we turn to a discussion of several troublesome issues.

The three maritime issues that dominate Southeast Asian, especially ASEAN, politics arc: rival Indonesian and Malaysian claims to the Malacca Straits as national waters, Indonesian and Philippine declarations of jurisdiction over archipelagic waters, and competing Chinese, Taiwanese, Philippine, Malaysian, and Vietnamese claims to several groups of islands in the South China Sea. To these may be added the general difficulty of drawing maritime boundaries as a consequence of the new Law of the Sea treaty.[3] In such a confined area as Southeast Asia, it can be envisaged that the determination of 12-mile territorial seas, 24-mile contiguous zones, and 200-mile exclusive economic zones (EEZs) will be a complicated process that may well create tensions between neighboring states and affect the politics of the region for some time to come.

The Malacca Straits as national waters

The Malacca Straits (actually the straits of Singapore and Malacca) lie between the southern tip of the Malaya peninsula (and Singapore) and the island of Sumatra. Although only two of the several important straits used for commercial and military passage through the region (the others include Lombok and Sunda), Malacca has always been the focal point of maritime transit through the area. More than half of the world's petroleum products pass through the straits en route from the Persian Gulf, with most of it destined for Japan. Malacca is also the principal place for entry to and egress from the Indian Ocean for American and Soviet naval ships deployed there. Their relatively narrow width and their length make the straits prime candidates for use as "chokepoints" in any generalized or local conflicts.

By the early 1970s, strong nationalist regimes in Indonesia and Malaysia had led both countries to assert claims to the Malacca Straits as national waters.[4] Pursuant to the claims, vessels using the straits were required to transit according to the rules of innocent passage. Although never enforced, such a stricture would have placed the operation of commercial and military vessels under the control of the littoral states. Submarines, for example, would have had to navigate on the surface, while all naval craft would have had formally to request passage from local authorities before entering the straits. The stands taken by the Malaysian and Indonesian governments did not command the support of the Singapore government. Concerned that the international trade upon which it depends might be jeopardized, Singapore merely "took note" of its neighbors' declarations.

The potential for tension inherent in these competing claims and approaches has now been diffused somewhat by the new Law of the Sea treaty. Although the new treaty does not specifically incorporate either Indonesian or Malaysian aspirations to use of the straits as national waters, it does establish a regime in which vessels transiting certain international straits (of which Malacca and Singapore are two) must do so according to the rules of innocent passage. Only when the new treaty comes into force will it be possible to see whether the new rules will operate to the littoral and user countries' satisfaction.

Archipelagic waters

For well over a decade the Indonesian and Philippine governments have been attempting to gain international recognition for the concept of archipelagic waters, whereby the waters surrounding the multiple islands that comprise their territory are defined as national waters under their sole jurisdiction. Initially the archipelagic principle met with strong opposition from maritime states like the United States, Great Britain, the Soviet Union, and Australia, who feared that it would place substantial restrictions on their right of transit through the waters of the region. At the same time, the concept caused political difficulties for the Indonesian and Philippine governments within ASEAN.

In recent years several developments have helped to defuse the issue as a source of irritation both within ASEAN and in relation to outside states. First, the new Law of the Sea treaty gives explicit recognition to the concept and establishes a set of provisions to apply to vessels transiting what have now become, in essence, territorial waters. As with the new innocent passage rules applicable to international straits, it is still too early to know how this new regime will operate. The international consensus that built around the concept at UNCLOS III helps to dispel fears in this regard but the refusal of the United States to be associated with the treaty does create a large question mark over future arrangements.

Second, in February 1982, Malaysia's opposition to Indonesia's archipelagic claim was dropped in favor of an agreement in which Kuala Lumpur acknowledged Jakarta's rights over the sea and air space bounded by its extreme territories. In return, Indonesia has acknowledged Malaysia's right to unhindered sea and air access routes across the South China Sea from the Malayan peninsula to East Malaysia. Indonesia has also agreed to honor Malaysia's fishing grounds even though they are located in Indonesian-claimed waters.

Despite the agreement, reservations have been expressed as to whether Kuala Lumpur will in fact be able to maintain adequate access to East Malaysia. Some Malaysian analysts fear that their country has conceded in principle its right to move freely within its own territory. In order to stake out a legal position, the Malaysian government is printing maps showing Malaysian boundaries that include the access lanes between east and west, despite the fact that the recent treaty seems to concede them to Indonesia.

The Malaysian navy is reportedly unhappy over what it believes to have been poor performances by Foreign Minister Ghazalie Shafie and the army during the negotiations. The navy took almost no part in the talks, an illustration of its relatively low status in Malaysian politics.[5] There has been some soft pedaling by the prime minister over the issue of Malaysian ability to defend its sea lines of communication (SLOC), but the acquisition of new aircraft and missiles, along with fast patrol boats, provides enhanced security capability.[6] This would probably not be sufficient if there were to be a confrontation between Malaysia and Indonesia over the former's rights of access, but this seems an unlikely possibility since Kuala Lumpur is inclined to defer to Jakarta's preferences over bilateral matters and issues affecting regional security.

Territorial claims in the South China Sea

While maritime and territorial disputes within ASEAN have generally been resolved amicably,[7] those between an ASEAN state and an outsider have proved more difficult to settle. There are now several unresolved claims in the region, most involving contested land and sea territories in the South China Sea.[8] Given the area's rich potential for undersea oil, natural gas, fishing, and mineral exploration, the stakes in the dispute are not inconsequential.[9] Moreover, the area's strategic location in the context of bellicose Sino-Vietnamese relations enhances the possibility that, at least between these two disputants, and perhaps others, armed conflict may yet be a part of the process by which the claims are settled. If conflicts were to break out, the impact would be felt far beyond the immediate area and would almost certainly involve other states. Traffic in the shipping lanes that criss-cross the area would be disrupted, seriously affecting the international needs of Japan, Australia, and the United States among numerous others. Beyond this, in a conflict the possibility cannot be ruled out that the disputants would attract outside support for their causes. Even if this did not come to pass, a protracted conflict in the area would seriously affect vital Soviet and American interests related, for instance, to the deployment of naval vessels in the Indian Ocean.

The disputes in the South China Sea focus on competing claims to several island groups. In one, Vietnam and the People's Republic of China have both laid claim to the Paracel Islands; in the second, China, Vietnam, Taiwan, the Philippines, and Malaysia all claim either the whole or a part of the Spratly group; and in the third, Vietnam and Indonesia contest the right to explore a wedge of sea north of the Natuna

Islands. The first and second of these disputes became linked in 1974 when China, which had previously occupied the western portion of the Paracels, also occupied the eastern group and simultaneously laid claim to the Spratlys. In recent years China has augmented its air and naval forces on the Paracels and conducted regular overflights.[10] While Beijing probably has the capability to occupy the Spratlys, it seems unlikely to do so, given the attendant dangers. The Philippines government, for instance, has been building up a military force that would enable it to defend the islands it presently occupies and it has consistently sought an American guarantee of support for its claim as part of its overall security relationship with the United States.[11] Although Vietnam would have difficulty defending its garrison on the islands of the Spratly group it occupies, any attack would be a costly one for the Chinese. Furthermore, there would be a distinct danger that Moscow, which supports Hanoi's claims to both the Paracels and the Spratlys, would intervene in the conflict.

Indonesia's dispute with Vietnam over waters to the north of Natuna Island is also one of volatility. There have already been reports of contacts between the naval vessels of the two countries in the 400,000-square-kilometer disputed waters. Further exacerbating the dispute is a recent undertaking by French and American firms to engage in oil exploration under Indonesian auspices. Jakarta's strategy seems to be to offer to negotiate with Vietnam while continuing to survey the region's mineral potential and to build up its naval and air power in the Natuna area.[12] Indonesia's naval bases on the Natunas at Ranai put it in a good position to assert its authority over the disputed waters but this is unlikely to be enough to resolve the differences with Vietnam.[13] These may well have to await detailed negotiations on maritime boundaries.

Maritime Security and Military Capabilities

Military capability

For the foreseeable future it is unlikely that any of these jurisdictional disputes will lead to outright hostilities. This reduces the pressure upon the ASEAN partners to undertake an immediate expansion of their military forces but in recent years the danger inherent in their environment has stimulated a steady increase in defense spending from U.S. $2.85 billion in 1975 to U.S. $5.46 billion in 1981.[14] As a consequence of this increase in spending, the states of ASEAN have become more confident of their capacities to contain internal security threats, particularly since China has reduced its support to local communist revolutionaries.

Nevertheless, ASEAN continues to resist plans for a formal military alliance. Member states believe that such a development would only exacerbate military tensions in Southeast Asia and further accelerate the region's polarization that began with Vietnam's invasion of Kampuchea and China's subsequent incursion into northern Vietnam in late 1978 and early 1979. By refraining from a formal collective military effort, ASEAN demonstrates to Hanoi that it has not organized against Vietnam and provides an opportunity for Hanoi to back away from its close embrace with the Kremlin.

Abjuring ASEAN-wide arrangements and joint commands, the five have adopted a framework of bilateral security agreements that seek to redress single-country weaknesses in naval and air patrols as well as to improve intelligence coordination. In this context, all of the ASEAN countries have been devoting resources to upgrading their naval and air capabilities. The emphasis has been on the acquisition of vessels that can maneuver easily among the numerous islands, shallow straits, and small bays that comprise much of their maritime environment. Thus the concentration has been on patrol boats equipped with surface-to-surface missiles. While the air forces of several of the ASEAN states have respectable fighter forces, in recent times much attention has been paid to increasing surveillance and air transport capability.[15]

All ASEAN militaries are upgrading their naval and air forces but they are still far from possessing a capacity to provide comprehensive maritime security. As currently configured, they are deployed primarily in the performance of tasks associated with coastal security: fisheries protection, the prevention of smuggling and illegal immigration, and inspecting offshore oil and gas interests. More demanding tasks, such as the maintenance of open sea lanes throughout the region, continue to be viewed as the responsibility of the U.S. Seventh Fleet in conjunction with Australian forces. Of the navies of the region, only Indonesia's is moving in the direction of acquiring equipment that might conceivably take over this responsibility, but even this will be a long time coming and, so far as other states of the region are concerned, may not be an entirely welcome development.

A zone of peace, freedom, and neutrality

The members of ASEAN have not only been relying on increased military capability as a means of guaranteeing their security. The association has now endorsed a proposal originally formulated by Malaysia in 1972 that Southeast Asia be declared a zone of peace, freedom, and neutrality (ZOPFAN). The concept has much in common with India's concern for establishing a zone of peace in the Indian Ocean. Both proposals have two essential aims: to ensure that the states of each region have primary responsibility for their own security and to exert political pressure on outside powers, particularly the United States and the Soviet Union, to remove naval and air forces from the regions. Unlike the Indian Ocean proposal, however, ZOPFAN provides a role for the great powers in guaranteeing each other's behavior. In short, should one great power violate the zone by, for instance, the deployment of military forces, countervailing forces could be invited in by ASEAN.

Because ASEAN is essentially pro-Western in its political and economic orientations, the Soviets have viewed ZOPFAN with considerable skepticism and have not endorsed it even conditionally as they have the Indian Ocean peace-zone proposal. Given the American need to station elements of the Seventh Fleet in the Indian Ocean/Persian Gulf area, neither South nor Southeast Asian waters will be free of great power navies in the foreseeable future. These realities leave both proposals at the level of little more than vague ideals in the minds of their sponsors. While this may be seen by some as regrettable, there is, at least as far as the Indian Ocean proposal is concerned, a considerable disparity between the public and private positions of most of the region's littoral states. As Leo Rose has pointed out, in such international forums as the United Nations, endorsement is virtually a ritual performed to maintain Third World public solidarity against great power domination.[16] In private counsels, however, the littoral leaders emphasize the necessity of maintaining an American presence to balance Soviet naval power and its ground and air presence in Afghanistan. The continuation of this situation could well lead to what India most fears: a competitive naval arms race that would bury both the Indian Ocean peace zone and Southeast Asia's ZOPFAN forever.

ASEAN and External Powers

The states of ASEAN live daily with the reality that their geographic location across a major international maritime crossroad brings them face-to-face with the security interests of other countries. Survival in such a potentially volatile environment might conceivably necessitate a strategy of attempting to strike a balance between protecting national interests and the often antithetical, frequently ambiguous, concerns of the international community.

In the context of these East-West relations, ASEAN, as already noted, has generally been less intent on striving for balance than anxious to identify with Western (broadly American) strategic perspectives on issues affecting regional security. Although their response to security issues in Southeast Asia and the wider Indian Ocean region have not been uniform, overall the ASEAN countries have held to a line of argument asserting that Soviet activities in the region tend to be destabilizing and may ultimately become a direct threat to their long-term security. In recent years support for this viewpoint has been building, following the strengthening association between Hanoi and Moscow. No ASEAN state has been at ease with Vietnamese policies since unification in 1975 and all have condemned Hanoi's continued occupation of Kampuchea.[17] In conjunction with Beijing, ASEAN has put its support behind a coalition formed around Prince Sihanouk (which includes the infamous Pol Pot), to oppose Vietnam's presence. While the members of ASEAN continue to see Vietnam as a belligerent power in the region, not only will an accommodation of interests not be possible, but Hanoi will continue to be viewed as the most demonstrable threat to peace in Southeast Asia. It is with these perspectives in mind that attention can now be turned to an examination of ASEAN responses to superpower policies in Southeast Asia and beyond into the Indian Ocean region. At the same time it will be useful to focus on the growing level of defense cooperation between ASEAN and another Indian Ocean littoral state: Australia.

ASEAN and American deployment

ASEAN's views about the presence of the U.S. Navy in its vicinity are mixed. Singapore and Thailand welcome it as a deterrent to a growing Soviet-Vietnamese naval combination. By contrast, Indonesian strategists interpret the presence of any great power as an opportunity for that power's adversary to become involved, especially since each invariably backs local opponents as proxies.[18] Nevertheless, for ASEAN there is no alternative to reliance on the U.S. Seventh Fleet and Thirteenth Air Force for blue-water protection. No ASEAN state has the financial resources to build an ocean-going fleet sufficient to challenge the Soviet Union. As previously noted, the protection of international commercial routes remains an American responsibility. Indeed, Singapore, Malaysia, and Thailand all provide refueling facilities for Philippine-based American P3-CS on surveillance missions over the Indian Ocean.[19] In effect there is a security trade-off between the United States and the Philippines (as ASEAN's representative). Bases at Clark and Subic provide the United States with facilities for projecting military power to East Asia and the Indian Ocean. In exchange, ASEAN commercial routes are protected and no political pressure is exerted against the Americans in order to effect ASEAN's long-term goal of a zone of peace, freedom, and neutrality.

Despite the Reagan administration's modernization of the Seventh Fleet, and the expansion of Diego Garcia's capacity to supply a Rapid Deployment Force (RDF)—all to extend American military muscle in the Indian Ocean–South China Sea area—ASEAN leaders remain skeptical about American support in the event of regional hostilities. They fear that the United States perceives its interests in protecting specific regimes in the region to be tertiary. Hence, American decision makers may be unwilling to accept the risks and costs of military intervention in the event of Vietnamese (or Soviet) aggression. Were the Soviets, for example, to provide the Vietnamese navy with precision-guided missiles, the consequence would be to endanger the Seventh Fleet in the event of a maritime confrontation. Whether the United States would be willing to risk this to assist any of the members of ASEAN is unclear and this worries the association.

On balance, however, the Soviet invasion of Afghanistan, the necessity of balancing a growing Soviet land and naval presence in the Persian Gulf, and the need to maintain SLOCs from that region to East Asia have reassured the ASEAN states that the U.S. Navy will remain in South and Southeast Asia indefinitely, perhaps through the creation of a new Fifth Fleet. Indeed, by emphasizing South Asia, U.S. naval deployments since 1979 have actually been augmented in the ASEAN region at a time when friendly militaries are generally seen as a welcome balance to Soviet-Vietnamese activities. Finally, Indonesia's Ombi-Wetar and Lombok-Makassar straits are important to the United States (as well as to the Soviet Union) in that they provide the most secure routes for submarines transiting between the Pacific and Indian oceans. Several naval experts believe that the Indian Ocean will be the main patrol area for the new Trident strategic submarines, all of which are likely to be based in the Pacific.[20]

By balancing the continued growth of the Soviet Pacific Fleet, American forces allow ASEAN and other Asian states to resist involvement in the Sino-Soviet-Vietnamese imbroglio and to avoid joining either China's antihegemony front or the Soviets' Asian collective security system. By contrast, any pull-back of American military forces from the ASEAN area to the mid-Pacific in the Asian strategic environment of the 1980s would degrade Washington's ability to project and to sustain naval and air power in the South China Sea and the Indian Ocean. Any such reduction of force would reduce the United States' utility to ASEAN and would be opposed by ASEAN members so long as the Soviet-Vietnamese alliance continues and Soviet ships and planes are based in Indochina.

ASEAN and Soviet deployment

Over the past three years, the expansion of Soviet Pacific Fleet strength has been remarkable, beginning with military force buildups on the southern Kuriles in the wake of the 1978 Sino-Japanese Treaty of Friendship and Cooperation and continuing through the use of Vietnamese bases in the aftermath of the early 1979 China-Vietnam border war. The southward deployment of Soviet forces is explained in part by the relationship between East Asia and the Indian Ocean as theaters vital for the maintenance of commerce between the European and rapidly growing Asian extremities of the Soviet Union. Because the Soviet Union lacks extensive road and rail systems to span its continental land mass, ocean lanes for domestic economic purposes are vital.[21] Indeed, the Pacific Fleet and its Indian Ocean squadron are charged with the task of protecting Soviet shipping.

From bases in Vietnam, the Soviets can sustain their fleet in both the Pacific and Indian oceans, thus demonstrating a capacity to sit astride the Straits of Malacca permanently. With access to Indochinese bases, the Soviets are able to flank China in both northern and southern waters, thus monitoring China's coastal activities and its fledgling blue-water fleet whenever it leaves port. The Soviets use Danang regularly for reconnaissance flights and have constructed naval and air electronic monitoring and communications facilities at both Danang and Cam Ranh Bay.[22] In the autumn of 1980, a pier for nuclear submarines was completed in Cam Ranh. From these Vietnamese ports and airfields, the Soviet Pacific fleet can bunker and provision naval and air forces, allowing them to double their time on station in the Persian Gulf–Indian Ocean–South China Sea region as compared with the pre-1979 period. In sum, the foothold that the Soviets have established in Southeast Asia has extended the operational capabilities of their military forces to a level that was difficult to envisage ten years ago.[23]

Reactions of specific ASEAN states to the Soviet military buildup and increased transit through the region's straits vary. Thailand is among the most negative, having closed off its airspace to Soviet transport flights from Tashkent and Bombay to Hanoi in 1979 as the Soviets resupplied the Vietnamese People's Army during its invasion of Kampuchea and its defense against China.[24] Singapore is the most outspoken about a long-term Soviet threat to Asian waters, particularly in combination with Vietnam. This concern has led to informal Singaporean discussions with its ASEAN partners about the possibility of regional defense collaboration—at least among Indonesia, Malaysia, and Singapore—to monitor and control the strait. Such collaboration could appeal to Jakarta and Kuala Lumpur as a form of recognition for their claim that the strait is national waters. From Singapore's perspective, collaboration on defense of the strait would provide an opportunity to integrate its small defense establishment into those of its larger neighbors, while linking the Five Power Defense Agreement indirectly to Indonesia.

Indonesian leaders could well be attracted to this arrangement since they have long been concerned that the failure of the countries of the region to organize their own security arrangements will result in their being drawn into the global Soviet-American contest for influence. As one prominent Indonesian analyst put it recently, "Southeast Asians could not fail to draw the lesson from the cold war that siding with one power will inevitably invite reaction from that power's rival. . . . This will never make them master in their own house or ensure peace and stability in the area."[25]

While ASEAN's regional capabilities are certainly adequate to defend against Vietnamese naval forces, they are still no match for the Soviets. But the danger from the growing Soviet Pacific Fleet operating from Southeast Asian bases lies less in the prospect of a military showdown than in the political influence that attends the projection of naval force. With Soviet naval and air forces regularly moving through ASEAN waters and testing their defense communications, an intimidating political atmosphere could develop unless countervailing American and regional forces are created. In the absence of such forces, ASEAN leaders could well conclude that accommodation of Soviet interests would be a better means of preventing Soviet interference in regional affairs than a policy of resistance.

ASEAN-Australian security cooperation

Australia and New Zealand are becoming increasingly prominent in South and Southeast Asian defense activities. Both are extensively involved in training members of ASEAN defense forces; the majority of trainees in Australian and New Zealand staff and command schools— over a thousand per year—are from Southeast Asia.[26] Stressing the continuing importance of Southeast Asia to Australia under the new Labour government, the foreign minister, Bill Hayden, has stated that the region's stability and development have as high a priority as relations with the United States because "the developments here . . . are going to pretty much determine the course of events in Australia."[27]

Because of Indonesia's importance as Australia's "near north," Canberra maintains particularly supportive relations with Jakarta. It has assisted in the negotiation of Law of the Sea provisions for unencumbered U.S. naval transit through Indonesian straits and has lent its good offices to help defuse tensions on the Papua–New Guinea/Irian Jaya border.

Australia's Defence Cooperation Program (DCP), in addition to the provision of training to upgrade the military skills of ASEAN officers from low to medium technology, has also led to spin-offs for Australian defense contractors. Both Indonesia and the Philippines have purchased Nomad aircraft for coastal surveillance. Under the DCP there are now more Philippine servicemen training in Australia than in the United States.[28]

The Australian military presence in Southeast Asia is significant less for its relatively modest current level than for its potential for growth and general political acceptability in the region. During a visit to Malaysia shortly before losing office, the former Australian prime minister, Malcolm Fraser, found that Kuala Lumpur would welcome a continued Royal Australian Air Force presence in the area following the retirement of the Mirages currently stationed at Butterworth.[29] The benefits of a continued Australian presence are not only to be seen in relation to retained air defense capability. Because Australian and New Zealand forces are politically acceptable, their presence has significantly enhanced Malaysian-Singaporean defense coordination, something especially notable in light of the delicate ethnic-political relations between the two countries. Furthermore, from a purely political perspective, the presence of Australian forces in Malaysia complicates the calculations of any potential aggressor, as the involvement of Australian forces in hostilities would probably trigger Australia–New Zealand–U.S. alliance (ANZUS) consultations about possible American assistance.

By the mid-1980s, Australia will have twenty P-3C Orion maritime patrol aircraft periodically using Singaporean and Malaysian bases for refueling. In this connection it is worth noting that Australians are training Malaysians to fly these antisubmarine warfare (ASW) planes to increase the level of surveillance over the Indian Ocean and the Andaman and South China seas.[30] This will help to fill a noticeable gap in America's regional surveillance capability, which is limited by the absence of U.S. basing rights between the Philippines and Diego Garcia.

Finally, in the context of ASEAN's need to find regional partners to reinforce its defense capability, Australia is likely to be much more acceptable than Japan. Southeast Asians are generally uneasy over, if not outright opposed to, a Japanese naval role in their region. Although alternatives, such as Japanese funding for Southeast Asian militaries and joint patrols involving the United States, Japan, and Australia have been suggested, it is quite conceivable that Japan will have a naval role in the region by the end of the decade, simply because petroleum trade routes are so vital. If a Japanese naval presence is inevitable, ASEAN would prefer it to be in tandem with other friendly naval powers whose motives are less suspect and whose historical behavior in the region is less tainted. Australia fulfills these criteria so, provided ASEAN-Australian relations are not derailed (as is possible) by political differences over issues such as Kampuchea or by economic matters such as protectionism, the future is likely to see the development of a closer defense relationship.

The Impact of Islam

For the member states of ASEAN, the implications of East-West confrontation have always been at the forefront of all calculations of regional security. While this will likely continue to be so for the foreseeable future, in recent years the specter of Islamic revivalism has added another dimension to their security concerns. With several ASEAN countries having large Muslim populations, the impact of this movement could well be substantial.

At present the most striking feature of Islamic revivalism is its failure to make a significant mark on the politics of the most directly affected states: Indonesia, Malaysia, and the Philippines. Geographical distance and secular political leaderships in these three ASEAN states have served to insulate them against most of the excesses experienced in Iran, Iraq, and other Arab states. Having stated this as a general principle, however, it is necessary to point out that Islam's impact varies considerably from country to country within ASEAN.

Islam exerts considerable influence on the Malaysian government of Prime Minister Mahathir. Concerned about the rise of fundamentalism in the major opposition party, which advocates a theocratic state, Mahathir has initiated pro-Islamic policies in the National Front government to preempt the fundamentalists and undercut their support base. Thus, Mahathir has announced plans for an International Islamic University in Malaysia and in 1983 opened Southeast Asia's first Islamic bank. With paid-up capital of M $100 million, it is one of the country's largest financial institutions.[31] In addition to isolating fundamentalists in the domestic arena, Mahathir's "look east" policy is also designed to orient Malaysia away from the internecine squabbles of the Arab world and toward the economic successes of countries such as Japan and Korea. Nevertheless, Malaysia has participated in international Islamic political groups since 1969. The Islamic Secretariat's first secretary-general was Tunku Abdul Rahman. Malaysia has taken a strong position against the Israeli occupation of Jerusalem and in 1981 accorded full diplomatic recognition to the Palestine Liberation Organization. Kuala Lumpur's opposition to the Soviet invasion of Afghanistan is couched in Islamic terms: the invasion is condemned as the actions of "godless communism" and an "affront to Moslems."[32] Finally, then Prime Minister Hussein Onn served as a member of an Islamic mission to mediate between Iran and Iraq in October 1980.

In contrast to Malaysia, the situation with regard to Muslims in the Philippines is far less stable. For over a decade Manila has been attempting to suppress the Moro rebellion in the southern Philippines. Although Muslim resistance against the majority Christian community in the Philippines can be traced back several centuries to the early period of Spanish colonialism, its most recent manifestation began only in 1969. Supported at that time by Libya's Colonel Qadhafy and the Islamic Conference of Foreign Ministers, the rebels also received aid and sanctuary from Sabah, partially in retaliation for the Philippine claim to that Malaysian state. Although the use of ASEAN's good offices has led to a reduction in Malaysian-Philippine tensions over the issue, the Marcos government still faces a serious problem in attempting to deal with the rebels.

Ironically, the country least susceptible to Islamic fundamentalism is the one with the largest nominal Muslim population, Indonesia. Because the majority communities of central and east Java are *abangan* (secularized and somewhat pre-Islamic in their beliefs), the political and military leaderships, drawn disproportionately from these regions, resent and fear the orthodox Muslims of west Java and the outer islands. Indonesia's political leaders, therefore, have little to do with Middle Eastern Islamic revivalism, seeing it as irrelevant to the country's aspirations toward regional leadership and potentially damaging to its modernization.

No ASEAN political leader is attracted to Khomeini or his Arab adherents. Yet in the past this has not prevented Islam from being a source of conflict among members of the association. While no points of tension exist on this issue at present, all of ASEAN's leaders realize that if Islamic fundamentalism were to take hold in Southeast Asia, the results could be highly destabilizing. In the Philippines it would intensify the southern resistance movement, while in Malaysia and Indonesia it would cause unrest and perhaps conflict between the Chinese and

Muslim members of society. Ultimately, relations among the member states of ASEAN could be affected as each country adopted policies that attempted to contain the threat. To avoid these dangers, all member governments of ASEAN will try to deal swiftly and directly with any manifestations of Islamic fundamentalism within their borders.

Conclusion

ASEAN's situation astride the principal eastern maritime approaches to the Indian Ocean region makes it extremely difficult for members of the association to insulate themselves from even the most remote events of the area. The linkage is partly by way of the superpowers, each of which has vital interests in the region and each of which continues to see it as an arena for East-West competition. As long as the deployment of naval forces is used as an instrument of this rivalry, access to the straits of Southeast Asia will continue to be a matter of the utmost strategic significance. Beyond this, the importance of the straits of Southeast Asia as major international commercial waterways, linking outside states such as Japan with vital resources such as Persian Gulf oil, or even Australian iron ore, makes the political stability of the area a matter of concern to many more governments than just those in Moscow and Washington. With so many states having vested interests, however indirect, in Southeast Asia, signs of political instability, especially if they should focus on maritime issues, are apt to be a cause of considerable alarm. For at least some outsiders, the temptation to meddle, either to maintain the status quo or to adjust it to more favorable circumstances, might well be irresistible.

At present, ASEAN has only a limited capability to resist outside interference in members' affairs. In the circumstances, it is hardly surprising that over the past several years, as ASEAN's economic growth has proceeded in ever more impressive increments, a greater proportion of resources has gone to defense. Strengthening national defense capabilities is deemed essential for the promotion of "regional resilience," that is, ASEAN's ability to function independently of great power pressures and to cope unaided with security problems common to the five. It is in this context that ASEAN seeks a solution to the Kampuchean issue, which ideally would combine a modus vivendi with both China and Vietnam as well as stable (if cool) relations with the Soviet Union. By effecting a united front, the members of ASEAN minimize opportunities for outsiders to meddle in intraregional conflicts while strengthening their collective ability to respond to outside pressures. Among the five, there is general agreement that American, Japanese, Soviet, and Chinese regional activities can sustain a regional balance, at least for the foreseeable future, until ASEAN can develop adequate political and military capabilities to exercise a greater degree of control over their own regional affairs.

The time frame for this strategy is indeterminate. The general global economic recession of the past few years has slowed ASEAN's economic performance and reduced allocations to the military. Insofar as economic conditions continue to stagnate, ASEAN militaries will grow slowly, constraining the development of defense structures and forestalling the evolution of strategies that could be expected to accompany them. In effect, ASEAN will continue to rely on the forces of friendly outsiders (the United States, Australia, New Zealand, Great Britain, and possibly Japan) to balance Soviet, Vietnamese, and Chinese military activities. Naval deployments by Western industrialized states will remain primarily responsible for maintaining open SLOCs until the end of the century, while ASEAN states gradually build their own capacities to effect their long-awaited ZOPFAN.

PART FOUR

Interests of External Powers

Introduction ⌖

Since the end of the fifteenth century the history of the Indian Ocean region has been one of competition between and the imposition of successive hegemonies by external powers. In this sense the contemporary rivalry between the superpowers for influence among the states of the ocean's littoral and for facilities to project power into the region is but the continuation of a long-standing pattern. The one element in the present phase of external power activity that distinguishes it most clearly from the past is the extent to which the main protagonists regard their vital national interests being affected by developments in the region. For the United States and the Soviet Union, the Indian Ocean is secondary only to Europe as an arena for the conduct of their global rivalry.

American interests revolve around the need to ensure access to Persian Gulf oil for itself and its allies. The magnitude of U.S. dependence on gulf oil has never been as great as that of Western Europe and Japan, which approximated 75 percent and 90 percent of consumption, respectively, at the time of the 1973–74 embargo. The most portentous result of the embargo was not the damage to Western economies (which was considerable), but the serious bickering and back-stabbing that occurred in the Atlantic alliance as NATO partners and Japan scrambled for favored access to unembargoed oil and for future access to Arab oil. A sustained denial of Persian Gulf oil to the West is an eventuality that the United States is therefore keen to avoid for reasons of alliance solidarity as well as economic health, a fact underlined by the Carter Doctrine and the development of the Rapid Deployment Force. Despite the current glut in worldwide oil supplies and falling prices, Persian Gulf oil—about 55 percent of the world's proven reserves—will remain of vital strategic importance to the West through the end of this century. A related but distinct interest is the concern of the United States to maintain sea lines of communication, particularly through vital choke points such as the Straits of Malacca, Bab el-Mandeb, and Hormuz.

For years, as Larry Bowman and Jeffrey Lefebvre make clear, the United States depended on local states to act as regional surrogates to defend its core political, economic, and strategic interests in the Indian Ocean area. But in the wake of the events that began to shake the region in the late 1970s, Washington developed a new approach to its security interests in the region. By actively seeking to enhance its access to areawide naval, air, and communication facilities, by upgrading the operational capability of British-owned Diego Garcia, by increasing the level of Indian Ocean naval deployments, and by creating the Rapid Deployment Force, the United States has substantially improved its capacity to project power into the Indian Ocean and has thereby declared its intention to take a more active role in the region's affairs.

Foremost among Soviet interests is a preoccupation with the maintenance of stability on its borders and a measure of influence, if not control, over its neighbors. This standard dimension of Soviet behavior is most clearly manifested in its relations with the states of Eastern Europe but it also has relevance throughout Soviet Asia where ancient cultural and ethnic traditions tend to undermine Moscow's political authority and to create natural communities of interest with people outside the Soviet Union. The Iranian Revolution and the Iraq-Iran war are particularly worrisome to Moscow because they could give rise to unstable or anti-Soviet regimes on the border. Apart from the proximate territory to the south, the Indian Ocean itself is of importance to Soviet security interests. It offers one alternative means of linking Soviet Europe with Soviet Asia should the trans-Siberian railroad be rendered inoperable either in peace or in war. At the same time, the Indian Ocean offers a back door to China by which the Soviets could relieve pressure along their common central Asian border if necessary. Thus, like the Americans, the Soviets have an abiding interest in maintaining sea lines of communication throughout the region. The Indian Ocean is also seen from Moscow as a potential operational area for American strategic missile submarines that cannot be allowed to go unchallenged. Finally, the Indian Ocean is an arena in which the Soviets compete for influence with the United States as part of the global search for strategic advantage. Consistent with these interests Moscow has pursued policies directed toward building its influence among the Third World states of the ocean's littoral and neutralizing the threat posed by the projection of American power into the region. Overall, these policies have met with mixed success over the last decade. As Oles Smolansky points out in relation to the gulf in particular, Moscow's efforts to gain a foothold of influence have generally failed to materialize. On the other hand, the increase in Soviet naval capability and the augmentation of an already existing air defense and strike capability in the vicinity of the gulf have greatly improved Moscow's military dispositions throughout the region.

European states were once the dominant outside influence on Indian Ocean politics. Today, while Britain and France continue to assert an independent presence in the region, Western Europe's collective political and economic interests are beginning to be represented by multilateral entities like NATO and the EEC. The changing fortunes of external powers in the Indian Ocean are no more evident than in the decline of Britain's role in the region. Little more than a decade ago the Indian Ocean was virtually a British lake. Now little remains but remnants of London's presence in the form of the British Indian Ocean Territory and a commitment to the five-power defense of Malaysia and Singapore supported by irregular naval deployments to the area. While there has also been a contraction in the French presence, Paris retains what could prove to be, in the event of conflict in southern Africa, important strategic territories in the southwest quadrant. Both to protect these interests and as a function of its status as a world power, France is still able to deploy an impressive naval capability in the region. The development of a collective European economic policy toward the Indian Ocean is evident in, among other things, the extension of Lomé Convention benefits to local states and the special relationship between the EEC and ASEAN. Similarly, there have been signs of the emergence of a more coherent Western security policy to protect vital interests in the gulf. Planning for contingencies in the area has been proceeding within NATO for some years, but 1984 saw a manifestation of cooperation in the form of a joint American-European naval deployment in the Arabian Sea at a time when the Iraq-Iran war threatened to close the Persian Gulf to shipping. It is rather too early to know whether those deployments are for NATO the first stage in the evolution of a coherent maritime strategy outside the treaty area. Ferenc Váli makes the point that if they are, NATO will face new dilemmas as it enters the second half of its fourth decade.

Finally, it is necessary to mention Japan and China in relation to the region. Neither has yet displayed an interest in or a capability for projecting power into the Indian Ocean; yet, for quite different reasons, both see it as important to their security. In his chapter, Taketsugu Tsurutani draws attention to Japan's dependence on the maintenance of sea lines of communication through the region for its commercial shipping. The apparent paradox is that Japan's security policy toward the area seems "quiescent and ambiguous." Strong domestic and international forces work both for and against the maintenance of this policy, not the least of them being that Japan's role in preservation of Western security remains unclear. Until such time as this role is identified, and in the absence of conditions that may necessitate independent action, Japan seems unlikely to become an active participant in the military defense of Western interests in the region.

It is also unlikely that Chinese interests in the Indian Ocean region will soon demand an active military presence there. Beijing claims a strong ideological affinity with the Third World states of the region and has provided many with economic and military aid, but has been careful about being drawn into local disputes. Aside from a limited capability for projecting power, for Beijing a military role in the area would likely mean replicating the kind of superpower conduct that has so often been the object of its condemnation. This said, it remains possible that China will once again see the need to teach the Vietnamese "a lesson" and Beijing's strong commitment to Pakistan will bear watching should the latter's security become any more tenuous because of outside threats. These, however, are matters within Beijing's neighborhood. Overall China's leaders judge that their ideological and political interests are best served by continuing the cautious and pragmatic approach to Indian Ocean affairs that has characterized their policy since the early 1970s.

22. Projection of Force by External Powers ◢
Michael MccGwire

If anything useful is to be said about the Indian Ocean in strategic terms, it must first be broken up into manageable areas reflecting the two basic reasons for wanting to project military force into some distant quarter of the globe. One reason is to influence events on land and there are five (or perhaps six) main focuses of power and/or conflict around the littoral of the Indian Ocean. The other reason is to prevent the use of the sea or to secure its use against obstruction and there are six main axes of maritime movement through the area. Bringing these factors together, the region divides naturally into the four quadrants defined by latitude 10° south and longitude 75° east. The southwestern one, through which pass the shipping routes to the Atlantic, is dominated by South Africa and its attendant problems. The southeastern quadrant is the "empty quarter," with Western Australia in the bottom right-hand corner, five thousand miles from Cape Town. The north-eastern quadrant covers the Bay of Bengal, with three of the five members of the Association of South-East Asian Nations (ASEAN) on its littoral; it includes the routes through the Indonesian archipelago. India looms large in both northern quadrants but it is the northwestern one that is the present focus of interest as it has been since the end of the nineteenth century. It takes in the Arabian Sea, the Red Sea, and Persian Gulf areas and the adjoining states of the Horn of Africa and the Arabian Peninsula, plus Iraq, Iran, and Pakistan.

The Utility of Distant Force Projection

Before turning to consider each quadrant separately, there are some general points to be made about the utility of projecting force into distant quarters of the globe. First to be considered is the question of military intervention ashore, which can be categorized under four main headings: supporting a state against an external military threat, coercing a state or regime, affecting the balance of an internal struggle for power, and securing the lives and property of one's nationals. These generate different types of military requirements, the major distinction being between supportive and coercive intervention. In the case of supportive intervention, the requirement is the contribution of some additional capability to redress the military balance. A measure of cooperation by the country being supported is assumed, including the use of facilities on land.

Coercive intervention (actual or threatened) requires the capability to deliver preponderant military force, the scale of which will differ within three main categories. At the bottom end of the scale is the *coup de main*, which relies on surprise and shock, and is suitable for a cutting-out operation (e.g., the *Pueblo* in 1967), evicting a government that has already lost support, or rescuing one's nationals (e.g., the Entebbe raid). At the top end of the scale is coercion by military occupation. Between these two extremes there is coercion by the threat (or application) of punishment, such as punitive expeditions, air strikes, or gunnery bombardment.

Although it has its dangers, supportive intervention appears to have maintained a fair measure of political utility and the failures have stemmed mainly from an inability to judge the local political situation correctly. Coercive intervention is another matter and there are widespread doubts about its continuing value. Indeed, it can be argued that in the post–World War II period, coercive intervention by a major state has only been successful within its contiguous national security zone,

402 INTERESTS OF EXTERNAL POWERS

where power gradients and political imperatives are high. However, this generalization does not apply to the two ends of the spectrum of force. The value of *coup de main*, or the short, sharp, small-scale rectifying operation, has been clearly demonstrated. At the other end of the spectrum, where the scale of force turns military intervention into invasion and occupation, there is no reason to believe that the use of sufficient force, applied with sufficient persistence and determination, would not achieve the desired results. The problem here is the vast amount of force required and the political will needed to sustain such an operation.

In other words, it is not coercion per se or, for some physical goal, a sustained use of preponderant force that has lost its utility. What has lost its former effectiveness is the use of force to intimidate or punish, which was an important means of imperial control in the colonial era. The main reason for this change has been the emergence of nationalism as a global ideology and the proliferation of nation-states that do not "respond" to the threat of violence in the formerly expected manner. Supporting this process has been the acquisition by these newly independent states of sophisticated weapon systems, requiring a much greater scale of force even to threaten punishment. There has also been a change in general attitudes toward the acceptability of coercive force, particularly when used by external powers.

This does not mean that coercive force will not be used; a credible threat of punishment is likely to introduce some element of short-term deterrence into the target country's political considerations. But coercive intervention of this kind tends to be counterproductive in the longer run and we have to recognize that gunboat diplomacy relied on a political servility that is now a thing of the past.

Accentuating the distinction between supportive and coercive intervention is the Soviet definition of the international status quo as a dynamic process of change toward a predetermined end, whose inevitable progress may be delayed or deflected (but not prevented) by reactionary forces. By contrast, the West has a static perception of the status quo, whose stability tends to be disrupted by undesirable revolutionary forces. The West is beginning to recognize the inevitability of change in the international system but there is no consensus as to the shape of an acceptable future status quo. These different attitudes provide different spurs to military intervention outside their respective national security zones. Soviet perceptions predispose them to a policy of exploiting emerging situations on an opportunistic basis and their intervention has so far always been supportive.[1] Western perceptions prompt a series of rearguard actions, or fire-fighting operations, that results in a generally more active overseas policy of trying to prevent unfavorable change. This often involves coercive intervention. Furthermore, the West tends to intervene directly while the Soviets have developed a policy of limiting their direct involvement to the provision of advisers (often at the highest level), weapons, and logistic support. The combat role is usually delegated to the Soviet-equipped forces of "revolutionary" states such as North Korea, Vietnam, and, of course, Cuba. The major exception to this limited Soviet involvement has been the manning of air defense systems (supportive intervention par excellence), until such time as indigenous forces can take over the weapons themselves.

So much for intervention ashore. The other reason for projecting force into some distant quarter of the globe is to secure the use of the sea in the face of attempts at obstruction or to prevent an opponent from using the sea. As a general rule it is easier to prevent the use of the sea than to secure it, although this of course depends on the maritime geography and the type of use involved. Narrow waterways, where ships must pass close to shore-based weapons, are relatively easy to obstruct, particularly if they are shallow and hence mineable. It is far more difficult to prevent passage across an ocean waterway out of range of land and with opportunities for evasive routing. It is also easier to interrupt a flow of merchant shipping than to prevent the passage of a naval task force.

This could be taken to imply that there is a latent threat to passage through international straits, but, in practice, the straits' states have a vested interest in the continuous flow of trade and shipping through such waters, and their economies would be damaged by a prolonged diversion. The closest precedent is the blocking of the Suez Canal by Egypt in 1956 but this was in response to the Anglo-French assault and control of the canal was the issue in dispute. In general, the diffuse nature of international seaborne trade is its own best protection in peacetime, since most nations have an interest in the principle of safe passage. Meanwhile, as the number of national merchant fleets grows, so too does the extent to which all ships are in hostage to each other.

What of the much vaunted threat to the seaborne flow of oil in the Indian Ocean? The argument is that because the West is so dependent on this oil, the Soviet Union will be tempted to attack the line of supply. This is but the latest variant of the more venerable bogey that because Europe depends on imports, it would be in Russia's interests to initiate submarine warfare against commerce in the North Atlantic. It is a classic example of the fallacy that what hurts one's enemy must help oneself, and can be shown to be implausible for a whole host of reasons. Outside the circumstances of world war, it is nearly impossible to identify circumstances when it would be in the Soviet Union's interests to initiate commerce war, least of all in the Indian Ocean. The reasons range from comparative military capabilities, through political and economic costs, to alternative instruments of policy, and include Russia's own interest in maritime stability and freedom of the seas, factors largely remaining the gift of the West.

Finally, we need to establish how the main external powers are placed in relation to the area. For the United States, the Indian Ocean is literally on the other side of the world. By sea, the shortest routes pass through straits and/or canals; by air, overflight rights have to be negotiated. For the People's Republic of China (PRC), the Indian Ocean is relatively close and direct air access is available across Burma. Britain and France are a quarter of the way around the globe from the Indian Ocean; their air access is more limited than America's since they do not have the relatively unhampered approach from the east. The Soviet Union's Black Sea ports are closer to the Indian Ocean than the Western powers but, when approaching the area from the east, its ports lie beyond those available to Washington and Beijing. However, Soviet access to the northwestern quadrant of the Indian Ocean by air and by land is unmatched by the other four external powers. The USSR is, of course, Mackinder's "heartland," sprawled across the Eurasian land mass from Europe to Japan. It spans 170 degrees of longitude and looks down on about half the globe; about 85 percent of the world's population lives within 3,000 nautical miles (NM) of its borders, which is air transport range. The Middle East and the Indian subcontinent are all within 2,000 NM of the Soviet Union. This is almost the exact reverse of America's position, isolated in the Western hemisphere, with 3,000 NM of sea to the east and 5,000 or more to the west.

The Southwest Quadrant

Turning now to the separate quadrants, the southwestern one is primarily of interest because of the possibility that, at some future date, the African states might somehow contrive for the United Nations to declare mandatory sanctions against the Republic of South Africa. If the Western powers supported such a resolution, the sanctions could be enforced by administrative means. But it is equally likely that the Western powers would abstain or even oppose such a motion and decline to regulate their shipping, leading to the need for a maritime blockade. In such circumstances, it is conceivable that the Soviet Union might volunteer its navy's services, either to enforce the blockade directly, or as a backup to African forces. With South Africa being so far away from the areas of vital interest to either superpower, and with so much to be gained in terms of goodwill throughout the African continent, it is possible (if not very likely) that the Soviet Union might seize such an opportunity for supportive intervention on the side of the United Nations and the Third World.

The southwestern quadrant also includes the "cape route," whose vulnerability is usually exaggerated. The very term invokes the image of a continuous thread running from the Persian Gulf to the North Atlantic, which seems at its weakest where it bends round South Africa and can there most easily be "cut," as if by a simple snip of the scissors. In fact, there is no need for the Cape of Good Hope to be a focal point for shipping, since there is lots of sea room to the south. Meanwhile, this part of the route is the farthest away from bases in the Soviet Union (one can assume that forward bases in Africa would be neutralized at the outbreak of war), and it is also covered by South Africa's (limited) antisubmarine capability. In a general war, there would be simpler and more effective ways of stopping the flow of oil from the Middle East than sinking ships at sea and the reason why there is no significant threat to shipping in peacetime has been outlined above. Much of the emphasis on the cape route was fostered by friends of South Africa, the latter seeing this as a way of binding the country to the Western alliance by preserving the naval links established in World War II. Until the mid-1960s the South African navy was configured to contribute to the general Western antisubmarine effort in defense of sea lines of communication (SLOCs).

The Southeast Quadrant

The "empty quarter" of the southeast is important to the United States because in it is located a rear base for American naval forces. This is situated in a stable democracy with shared cultural roots and it gives directly onto the Indian Ocean. This southeastern quadrant also includes a major shipping route carrying bulk minerals from Western Australia northward to Japan through the Indonesian archipelago. However, in the event of conflict, this shipping can be rerouted south around Australia, avoiding the narrow waters through the islands and the threats in the China Seas.

The Northeast Quadrant

The northeastern quadrant is primarily important as an SLOC, linking the Pacific with the Indian Ocean. For Japan, about two-thirds of its oil comes from the Middle East and about 40 percent of all Japanese imports pass through this quadrant. For the United States, it provides access to the Indian Ocean from its Pacific bases, particularly from Subic Bay in the Philippines. For the Soviets, this SLOC is a primary means of shipping goods in peacetime from western Russia to their Far Eastern provinces. In the event of war with China, it would be the primary means of supplying the Far Eastern front, since the Soviets must assume that the trans-Siberian Railroad would be put out of action.

The economic consequences of disrupting this SLOC through the Indonesian archipelago need not be very serious. Experience with the closure of the Suez Canal suggests that the flow of trade would adapt rapidly to new circumstances, possibly with unforeseen beneficial results. For a country such as Japan, diversion around Australia would increase the length of passage by 30–80 percent (depending on port of origin), but this would be unlikely to add more than 5 percent to the total cost of imports from all sources, well within normal fluctuations in the terms of trade. The political-military consequences of disruption could be more serious. For American forces based on Subic Bay, such a diversion would more than double the distance to the central Indian Ocean and a carrier force would be twelve to fourteen days in passage. But the penalties of such delay are relatively small compared to what could be at stake for the Soviet Union, namely victory or defeat in a conventional war with China. In such circumstances, a regular flow of supplies to the Far Eastern front must be established before stockpiles in the area are exhausted. Diversion around Australia could increase transit time by as much as 80 percent, a delay that could be critical.

The Northwest Quadrant

It will help to understand the development of Soviet interests in the northwestern quadrant if we adopt a historical approach. Although Russian interest in northern Persia was formally acknowledged by the British in 1907, the first event of contemporary relevance was the shipment of substantial military supplies to the USSR during both world wars via the Persian Gulf and overland across Iran. In the 1950s, the Anglo-Saxon partners sought to tighten the drawstring of containment around the Soviet Union in this area, first with the aborted Middle East Defense Organization (MEDO) and then with the slightly more successful Central Treaty Organization (CENTO). In response, the Soviets tried to overleap this barrier; the supply of arms to Egypt in 1955 was the first breakthrough, followed by the links with Syria and then Iraq. In other respects, Soviet involvement in the northwest quadrant was merely part of a general policy of trying to increase Moscow's influence and decrease Western influence among nonaligned states. It was not particularly focused, except in the sense of seeking to impose constraints on Western military intervention, either by supplying newly independent states with arms or by persuading them to deny Western naval units access to their ports. Soviet strategic interests were not engaged.

The first indication of a strategic interest in the northwest quadrant of the Indian Ocean was the deployment of Soviet naval hydrographic units to the Arabian Sea in the spring of 1967. This was at a time when Prime Minister Wilson was still asserting Britain's unshakable resolve to remain east of Suez. Since the Soviet decision to deploy would have been taken at least a year before, this development cannot be tied to the subsequent withdrawal of British forces, which was not decided until the economic crisis in the fall of 1967. Rather, it was part of a larger and quite different pattern, the result of decisions taken in response to the buildup in U.S. strategic forces in the first months of the Kennedy administration in 1961.

From the Soviet viewpoint, a significant aspect of this buildup was the apparent shift in emphasis from land-based to sea-based systems, evident in the rapid buildup of Polaris units coinciding with the entry into service of the large attack carriers ordered in the wake of the Korean War. These units could be expected to survive an intercontinental nuclear exchange and could therefore be held back in order to influence the outcome of the war. In particular, these forces could deny the Soviet Union the use of Western Europe as an alternative socioeconomic base in the event of a world war leading to a nuclear exchange.

As part of their response to this new development, the Soviets decided that the maritime defense perimeter would have to be pushed outward from the Soviet periphery, a process that took place in two stages. The first stage (lasting five years) extended this outer defense zone to the 1,500 NM circle from Moscow, which covered the immediate threat from carrier strike aircraft as well as the early Polaris systems and encompassed the Norwegian Sea and the eastern Mediterranean. The second five-year stage, starting in 1967–68, began the slow process of consolidating the newly established defense zones, while extending the area of concern to take in the 2,500 NM circle of threat; this included the northwest part of the Arabian Sea. Thus, in 1967, the hydrographic precursors were at work in the Indian Ocean (in the same way they preceded the Mediterranean deployment in 1963). In 1968 came the first deployment of combatants and by late 1969 Somalia had been chosen as the main *point d'appui* for sustained forward deployment in the area, with Aden being developed as a lesser alternative.

It is sometimes argued that the decision to move into the Indian Ocean could have nothing to do with the war-related task of developing a counter to the threat from Polaris submarines. The latter were never deployed in the area and, even if they had been, Soviet countermeasures would have been ineffective. But, from the Soviet point of view, the critical issue was whether Polaris could be deployed at some future date, bearing in mind that the Arabian Sea would open up a completely new arc of threat. (It happens to be the best area in the world from which to cover both the Soviet Union and China from a single platform carrying missiles with a range of 2,500–3,000 NM.)

The evidence that the Americans were developing an option to deploy in the Indian Ocean was strong. In 1963, an agreement was reached to build a very low frequency (VLF) radio station (of the kind used to communicate with submerged submarines) at North West Cape in Western Australia. In 1965, the British detached the Chagos Islands from Mauritius before granting the latter independence and entered into an agreement with the United States to develop Diego Garcia as a base. A submarine tender could be deployed there and Polaris patrols instituted within six months of the decision being taken in Washington. As to the question of effectiveness, it should be recalled that it took the Soviets more than fifteen years to develop something approaching a capability against the carrier, and they have never been deterred from embarking on a seemingly impossible task if the threat is serious enough. Something is better than nothing, and a presence in the Indian Ocean at least increased the possibility of attacking at source, while gaining operational experience in the area and seeking to develop other options.

In any case, this is now a dead issue, because by the early 1970s a series of developments had shifted priorities in the area away from the counter-Polaris role to a primary concern with the SLOC to the Far Eastern front in the event of war with China. Developing a counter to Polaris still remained a long-term objective but it was clear that the traditional methods were having little success, while the hoped-for new developments in nonacoustic methods of detection had yet to materialize. Furthermore, the Indian Ocean arc of threat lost much of its significance with the agreement to halt development of anti–ballistic missile (ABM) systems. Meanwhile, overall naval priorities had been reordered as a result of the decision in the late 1960s to place a major element of the national strategic reserve at sea in ballistic missile submarines, which would be deployed close to home in defensible bastions. Protecting these bastions in the Northern and Pacific Fleet areas became the primary mission of the navy's general purpose forces.

On the other side of the account, deteriorating relations with China in the late 1960s prompted a buildup of Soviet forces in the Far East and a new concern for supplying that front in the event of war. Although the Soviets were steadily increasing the availability of the Northern Sea route, primary reliance still had to be placed on the southern route across the Indian Ocean. Ideally, this would run out of the Black Sea via the Suez Canal and through the Red Sea. But if that route were denied to them, the Soviets would have to use the overland route across Iran and ship out of the Persian Gulf. They would also have to be prepared to secure the use of this SLOC against attempts to obstruct it. China, with the world's third largest submarine force, was an ally of Pakistan's, and the United States might be tempted to engage in covert interdiction.

This shift in priorities was made evident by Marshal Grechko's visit to Somalia in February 1972 and the serious buildup in Soviet support facilities that took place thereafter. This was five months before the eviction of Soviet air defense forces from Egypt in July 1972, which was certainly not unexpected and may even have been secretly welcomed by the Soviets. The fact that the Soviets were prepared to use Somalia in this way reinforces the argument that strategic rather than political factors were the primary determinants of policy in this area. By becoming heavily committed to Somalia, the Soviet Union inevitably found itself on the opposite side to Kenya and Ethiopia, the latter still influential in the Organization of African Unity. This involvement provoked adverse reactions from the many francophone states that identified with French-Ethiopian interests in northeast Africa, Malagasy being the most outspoken against Soviet activities in Somalia and in the Indian Ocean generally. It also generated widespread doubts about the Soviet Union's aspirations in the Arabian/East African area, which the Chinese were only too ready to confirm. These were heavy political costs that could only be justified by strategic imperatives.

Soviet requirements to project force into the northwest quadrant of the Indian Ocean are therefore fairly clear-cut. In the event of war with China and/or the West, the primary requirement is to secure the SLOC across the Indian Ocean and in particular to be able to secure passage through the choke points of the straits of Bab el-Mandeb and Hormuz. In the event of world war, or limited war in the Persian Gulf area, the Soviets would also wish to interpose naval forces to the east of the Straits of Hormuz, in order to counter intervention by U.S. carrier forces against land operations out of the Caucasus.

There is also the peacetime mission of deterring "imperialist aggression," both against the Soviet Union itself and against friendly states in the area. As a general rule, Soviet naval forces have responded directly to the deployment of U.S. attack carriers in the area, but with air bases in Afghanistan extending the reach of shore-based air by about three hundred miles, this requirement may be modified. As for deterring imperialist aggression against friendly states, there is considerable doubt that Soviet forces would persist in interposing themselves if it actually came to a showdown. Finally, there is the doctrinal requirement to "prepare" theaters of military operations in peacetime. (There is even a separate entry for this in the military encyclopedia.) On its own, this objective goes a long way toward explaining the Soviet pattern of involvement in the northwestern quadrant of the Indian Ocean. Once deployed, Soviet forces will of course be used to further state interests. For example, Soviet naval units were used to ferry Dhofari rebels to Oman and they continue to protect the shipment of supplies from Aden to Ethiopia against third party intervention. But, in the main, supportive intervention in the area conforms to the principles outlined in the first part of this chapter, with direct Soviet involvement limited to advisers (a task shared with certain of its Warsaw Pact allies) and the provision of training, arms supplies, and logistic support. Meanwhile, war-related requirements will continue to be the primary determinant of Soviet activity in this quadrant and will shape their political objectives.

So much for the Soviet side of the problem, which is fairly well defined. Western requirements for projecting force into the area are much less clear-cut because the primary interest is to secure the flow of oil, an interest that applies in peace as well as war. The chain of supply involves a range of different activities—engineering, industrial, commercial, and transportation—all of which are vulnerable to disruption. Possible threats to these activities cover a broad span, starting with administrative action, and the most probable threats are not amenable to military solutions. Indeed, the major problem that faces the Western countries is how to avoid triggering the latent political contingencies that mine the area, as they seek to develop the capability to handle possible military contingencies.

In the wake of the Iranian crisis and the invasion of Afghanistan, the threat that leapt to the forefront of U.S. attention was a Soviet thrust to the head of the gulf. As time went by, less alarmist perceptions prevailed and, while the Soviet threat remains the most serious, it is also the least likely. It is not that the Soviets do not have the underlying capability, if they set their minds to it, to mount an offensive down through Iran and Iraq. Rather, it is hard to identify the interests that would be served by such action, whereas the costs and the difficulties are all too apparent. Certainly, the Soviet Union is not postured militarily for such an operation and several aspects of its military doctrine argue against such an initiative. If, in the future, the Soviets did decide to move toward the gulf, it is likely that their initial move would be to consolidate their hold on the area three hundred miles to the south of their borders. This would allow them to establish a nominally autonomous Kurdistan, provide direct access to Syria and Iraq, and, most important, bring the head of the gulf within tactical air range of their forces. Once in this position, they would be well placed to pursue a variety of options at some future date, while the West would be hard pressed to check them militarily. This implies that the West must concentrate on deterring the Soviets from moving south in the first place, by the threat of effective military action in northwest Iran, a requirement that cannot be met from the northwestern quadrant of the Indian Ocean.

Although U.S. concern about the Soviet threat in the area has abated, preparations for the contingency of projecting force into the general area have steadily progressed. As Larry Bowman and Jeffrey Lefebvre point out in their chapter, planning had already started in 1977, but Afghanistan instilled a new urgency into the process, with particular emphasis being placed on the means of bringing ground forces to bear. It was projected that between 1982 and 1987 airlift capacity would be increased by 60 percent and the pre-positioning of weapons and equipment by 300 percent. A new thirty-knot, one-division sealift capability would also be provided. Together these measures represent an investment of some $20 billion. At the same time, steady progress has been made in the delicate process of securing access to bases and staging rights in the area. At the beginning of 1983, a new unified Central Command was established with operational responsibility for the area; seven divisions have been earmarked for its use, plus ten tactical air wing equivalents, three carrier battle groups, and one surface attack group. In practice, all these forces have other commitments and, realistically, one can think in terms of bringing three to four divisions to bear within thirty days. It should also be noted that, whereas it was originally planned that maritime pre-positioning ships (MPS) carrying weapons and equipment for three marine amphibious brigades (MAB) would be based on Diego Garcia, the U.S. Navy now talks in terms of deploying only one MAB-worth of MPS in the Indian Ocean, the remainder being available for other theaters.

Clearly, the United States is severely handicapped by its geographical location in matching the scale of ground forces the Soviets could rapidly deploy into the area, but this may be a blessing in disguise since it encourages the use of other means. America's comparative advantage

lies in its ability to swing tactical air units around the world, using in-
flight refueling. This capability is considerably enhanced if the terminal
areas have effective air defense and adequate fuel supplies, and it is
even better, of course, if the host country operates the same kind of aircraft, thereby greatly simplifying the support requirements. Something
of this situation already exists in the states of the Arabian peninsula and
the United States is working to improve it. Carrier air can add to this
capability in three ways. The most usual contribution is by flying aircraft from carrier decks but their usefulness will depend on how close
the carriers can approach to the combat zone, a factor that may be
limited either by maritime geography or by unacceptable risks to the
carrier. An alternative is to redeploy the carrier aircraft to airfields
ashore so as to increase their reach. A third option is to use the carriers
to establish command of the air over a particular area for long enough
to allow the U.S. Air Force to fly in its air defense and fighter support
systems. This could be particularly relevant to exploiting the large civilian airfields in the United Arab Emirates. It would require the carrier
to venture into the heel of the gulf, establish command of the air and
the surface for forty-eight hours or so, and then withdraw to the open
sea and relative safety.

Conclusion

In closing, it is worth stressing the relative importance and the asymmetry of Soviet and Western interests in the northwestern quadrant of
the Indian Ocean. The friction that results from this reality is often
dismissed by onlookers as superpower competition, while the United
States tends to deny that the Soviet Union has any legitimate interests
in the area at all. In fact, the Soviet Union has clearly defined strategic
interests that are directly related to the security of the state and the defense of the homeland, and, failing a radical change in the international
climate, they are unlikely to foreswear them. What is interesting, however, is the relatively small military investment they have made in securing these interests. Clearly this is contingency planning, "preparing" the
theater of military operations against some future need, rather than
maintaining a full-scale capability.

Much the same goes for the West. The United States and its allies
are faced with a more difficult problem, since they have to prepare for
multiple military contingencies, rather than for the fairly simple ones
facing the Soviets. But the West also has advantages. There are the
long-standing administrative and commercial links that provide a form
of de facto infrastructure throughout the region. There is the diversity

of the Western alliance: the members compete economically with each other, which is less oppressive than the Soviet approach, and this fosters the possibility of breathing space, despite the pursuit of common strategic goals. Perhaps most important of all is the political (but not military) advantage of being located far away on the other side of the world. This means that Arab states can think of bringing the Western nations into play as a counterbalance to Soviet and other military threats in the area, without fear of being gobbled up in the process. The sure way of destroying the last advantage is for the West to indulge its penchant for coercive intervention when political developments look as if they are moving off some narrowly defined track.

23. The Indian Ocean: U.S. Military and Strategic Perspectives ☚ Larry W. Bowman and Jeffrey A. Lefebvre

In March 1977, early in the Carter administration, an offer was made to the Soviet Union to proceed with discussions toward the complete demilitarization of the Indian Ocean. Though quickly amended to discussions about the stabilization of military forces there, each proposal represented Carter administration aspirations that the Indian Ocean region would be one place where superpower rivalry could be muted. From mid-1977 until early 1978, four rounds of discussions were held between the United States and the Soviet Union on naval arms limitations in the Indian Ocean. Although they seemed promising at the start, they were hindered by the Soviet Union's massive arms shipments to Ethiopia at the end of 1977. Eventually, the interest of both sides waned for various reasons and the talks were quietly put on the shelf after February 1978, never to be resumed.[1]

The collapse of the naval arms limitation talks was quickly followed by the escalating pace of the Iranian Revolution, which led to the fall of the shah in early 1979. With the shah's ouster, a central component of America's strategic posture in this region collapsed as well. The Nixon Doctrine of securing American strategic interests through the support of regionally influential actors had lost its key element in Southwest Asia or the northwest quadrant of the Indian Ocean.

The fall of the shah and, in particular, the seeming inability of the United States to do anything about it, brought an air of crisis to Washington. This mood was further exacerbated throughout 1979 by the conflict between the two Yemens, by petroleum shortages and the second major surge in prices, by the seizing of American hostages in Iran in November, and, finally, by the Soviet invasion of Afghanistan in December. Each of these events, and others left unmentioned, contributed to a growing debate and a broad strategic reappraisal of U.S. interests and military capabilities in the Indian Ocean region.

In January 1980, in an important and much-quoted passage from his State of the Union address, President Carter replaced the moribund Nixon Doctrine with a doctrine of his own: "Any attempt by any outside force to gain control of the Persian Gulf region will be regarded as an assault on the vital interests of the United States of America and such an assault will be repelled by any means necessary, including military force." No one needed to be reminded that Carter's views had changed markedly from those expressed in 1977. Instead of demilitarization, the Carter Doctrine was expressing the American government's determination to secure its interests by the direct use of its own forces if necessary. This signaled a change in America's strategic posture; it was the first time since the end of the Vietnam War that the United States had declared its intention to increase its military forces and security commitments in a distant region.

This chapter traces the reevaluation of America's strategic posture and its military presence in the Indian Ocean/Southwest Asia region, first under the Carter and then under the Reagan administrations. There are many aspects of this tale, not all of which can be fully recounted here. For instance, the rebuilding of the U.S. fleet—while potentially important for Indian Ocean commitments and deployments—will not be fully accomplished for years. The Camp David process, American efforts to build an anti-Soviet consensus among both moderate Arab states and Israel, the search for solutions to the tangled politics of Lebanon, and concerns about Persian Gulf security caused by the Iraq-Iran war are all matters of real concern to American strategic planners but cannot be fully dealt with here. Instead, this chapter isolates what appear to be four distinct U.S. responses to the crisis brought on by the horn, Iran, oil, the hostages, etc. They are the quest for access facilities, the upgrading of Diego Garcia, the expansion of fleet rotations into the Indian Ocean, and the formation of the Rapid Deployment Force (RDF). Taken together they represent a substantial American response to altered circumstances and a substantially escalated political and military commitment to a distant region of the world.[2] Although obviously interrelated, each will be examined in turn in order to grasp the full extent of the U.S. response.

The Quest for Access Facilities

Since the Second World War overseas bases have played a major role in U.S. defense strategy. The strategic mobility and logistic support an overseas base network can provide has been viewed by American defense planners as indispensable to a nation whose military responsibilities are worldwide and where rapid reaction to local events is deemed crucial.

In the immediate post–World War II period Washington focused the buildup of its military forces and development of a strategic infrastructure in the North Atlantic region and the Pacific basin.[3] Because allied wartime strategy had highlighted the significance of maintaining bases in North Africa from which to launch a counterinvasion of southern Europe, to provide logistic support for military operations in the European theater, and to preempt opportunities to outflank Europe from its southern rimlands, the North Atlantic Treaty Organization's (NATO) charter defined its theater of operations as extending as far south as the Tropic of Cancer. But as the 1958 U.S. intervention in Lebanon demonstrated, rapid American deployment into the Middle East would draw upon U.S. forces and equipment based in the Mediterranean and would rely upon a NATO strategic infrastructure to support operations. The Indian Ocean, sub-Saharan Africa, the Arabian peninsula, and Iran were all essentially ignored as potential bases for operations.

Through the 1960s, the narrow strategic focus of American interests in Southwest Asia (oil) and the absence of a serious threat to Western interests from its southern flank (because of Britain's naval and political domination of the Indian Ocean) combined to relegate the region to backwater status. Moreover, with the enunciation of the Nixon Doctrine in 1969, American policy makers apparently saw little need to build a base network in the region since the need for direct U.S. intervention seemingly would decrease as Iran assumed the role of regional policeman. By the mid-1970s Ethiopia, Iran, and Israel were the only countries in the region that Washington could reasonably count upon to permit U.S. access to their military facilities in the event of a crisis. Even so, the use of these facilities in a Middle East intervention would be extremely complicated and limited by regional political realities: Arab-Israeli hostility, the Arab-Persian and Sunni-Shi'ite Muslim splits, and mutual suspicions and animosity between the Arab (Muslim) world and Christian Ethiopia. With the rupture in U.S.-Ethiopian relations in the spring of 1977 and then the overthrow of the shah of Iran in 1979, only Israel and a partially completed Diego Garcia comprised the foundation for any kind of U.S. strategic infrastructure in Southwest Asia.

Thus, in the wake of the Iranian and Afghanistan crises, the Carter administration found the Indian Ocean region essentially devoid of any infrastructure with which to conduct forward operations. The situation confronting the United States at the time was bluntly stated by the undersecretary for policy in the Defense Department, Robert Komer:

> In order to support forward deployed forces better and introduce the RDF faster, it is imperative that facilities in the region be made available for U.S. use. Logistic support is critical to the success of military operations. Unfortunately, in the Indian Ocean, the U.S. lacks the logistic facilities needed to support operations, especially during crisis. Access to regional air- and port-facilities, storage facilities . . . and assured host nation support help to overcome this shortfall.[4]

Following the seizure of the American embassy in Tehran in November 1979, President Carter ordered a full report on what could be done quickly to provide emergency operating access to the region. At a 4 December 1979 National Security Council (NSC) meeting it was decided that exploratory talks would be initiated with potential host governments to acquire military facilities so as to be able to sustain American forces in the region—an option that the Joint Chiefs of Staff had begun considering in late November.[5] After initially deciding against seeking such outposts in Egypt and Israel, the American search focused upon concluding formal base rights agreements with the governments of Kenya, Oman, and Somalia. Rather than following the post–World War II pattern of establishing U.S.-owned and -operated foreign military bases, the administration instead sought to gain access to already existing facilities. A recognition of the force of Third World nationalism, the wisdom of maintaining a low profile in a politically sensitive region of the world, as well as the need to do, and to be seen to be doing, something quickly to acquire flexibility for military deployment in the area, dictated this course of action.

Within two weeks of the NSC decision the Carter administration set in motion the initial phase of the operation to secure access to facilities in Kenya, Oman, and Somalia. In mid-December the White House sent a joint Pentagon/State Department team to the region, led by Robert J. Murray (deputy assistant secretary of defense specializing in Middle Eastern problems) and Reginald Bartholomew (director of political-military affairs at the State Department), to test the political waters and to take a preliminary look at the potential sites. The group received a very favorable response to the American request in all three countries.[6] Then a team of Pentagon specialists visited the three countries again in January 1980 to assess the potential of their facilities for handling American warships and aircraft.[7] Aware of what each country had to offer and sensing a propitious political climate in the prospective host nations, the Carter administration prepared to enter negotiations in early February.

The first step of this second phase, however, involved conferring with the Saudis. Although Washington could not predicate its Southwest Asia strategy and military posture in the region upon Saudi Arabian approval, the Saudis were too important to ignore. One did not go into the Saudis' own backyard without at least consulting them, especially when a good bit of the logic behind the strategy had to do with protecting them. On 4 February 1980 National Security Adviser Zbigniew Brzezinski and Deputy Secretary of State Warren Christopher met with Saudi Foreign Minister Saud Faisal and Crown Prince Fahd Abdulaziz in Riyadh to discuss Washington's plans. The Saudis would not allow an American presence in their country but they proved to be favorably disposed toward the idea of an increased U.S. presence in the region.[8] It also seemed likely that Riyadh would prove useful in persuading Oman and Somalia, both Islamic nations and members of the Arab League, to accede to the American request.

Upon the return of a high-level American political delegation from the region near the end of February it became clear that U.S. access to the facilities would be linked to aid. The Carter administration initially was prepared to ask Congress to appropriate $100 million in military and economic assistance for the three prospective host countries over a two-year period—a figure that would soon sharply increase.[9] In return, Washington sought access to a total of ten sites in the three nations: Kenya's port at Mombasa and the airfield facilities located in Nairobi and Nanyuki; the airports at the Omani cities of Thumrait and Salalah, the former British air base on Masirah Island, as well as the port/airfield facilities in Muscat and Seeb; and in Somalia the joint port/airfield facilities at Berbera and Mogadishu. The most important of these were Mombasa, Masirah, and Berbera. Moreover, the importance attached by military planners to the concept of base redundancy, particularly given the shifting political winds in the region, demanded that agreement be reached with all three countries.

It seemed that the main obstacle to securing access to facilities in the region involved the publicity surrounding the American effort; this exposed the host governments to a variety of Third World and Soviet bloc criticism. Statements denying that Washington was being given bases and that the host countries were not relinquishing their non-aligned status emanated from all three capitals. The word "base" quickly was replaced by the term "facility." But in April 1980 word leaked that American c-130 transport planes had used Masirah airfield on the way in and out of Iran during the abortive hostage rescue attempt, putting Sultan Qaboos in a politically embarrassing position.[10] Although the U.S.-Oman basing agreement reportedly had been reached in diplomatic notes dated 9 April, the sultan broke off negotiations for a short time.[11] Then, rather quietly in early June, Washington publicly announced it had reached agreement with Oman. This was followed near the end of June with the announcement of the U.S.-Kenya accord.

Publicity seemed to be the least of Washington's worries in striking a deal with Somalia. President Siad Barre essentially wanted an "Israeli" package. Mogadishu's initial asking price was reportedly for U.S. $1 billion in advanced military equipment and U.S. $1 billion in economic aid.[12] This exorbitant demand was in the best bargaining tradition of a Middle Eastern bazaar, but it was also a reflection of the relatively extravagant expectations created by the huge Soviet military aid program that had tipped the balance on the horn in Somalia's favor in the mid-1970s, and which now set a bench mark for what the Somalis expected from Washington. Eventually Barre's price came down to U.S. $1 billion and then to several hundred million dollars. After the successful conclusion of access negotiations with Kenya and Oman, Barre was forced to give way even more since Washington had less incentive to rush into a military relationship that it viewed as full of traps.

Of utmost concern to American officials, particularly to the State Department's Africa Bureau which had been generally suspicious of Somalia, was the risk involved in having Somalia as a military client. On two previous occasions, in the early summer of 1977 and in the spring of 1978, the Carter administration had sent signals to Mogadishu indicating it was interested in establishing a military relationship, only to back down both times because of continued Somali involvement in Ethiopia's Ogaden region. But following the Soviet intervention in Afghanistan, officials who had previously opposed sending any military equipment to Somalia unless it renounced its claims on the Ogaden became resigned to an arms relationship.[13]

Mogadishu, however, as part of its initial asking price sought an accord implying U.S. recognition of Somali claims to the Ogaden. Even more disconcerting to State Department officials was Mogadishu's initiation in the early summer 1980 of a "second" Ogaden war. Although willing to supply "defensive" arms to Somalia, the Carter administration still had no appetite for being drawn into a proxy war with the Soviet Union on the Horn of Africa. Thus, as part of the access agreement, Washington insisted that the Somali government agree in writing that it would not use American-supplied equipment in Ethiopia and give firm verbal assurances that it would not use its regular military forces in the Ogaden. However, only a week after the U.S.-Somali agreement was signed on 21 August 1980, in direct contradiction of State Department statements, the Central Intelligence Agency (CIA) told a secret session of the House Foreign Affairs Africa Subcommittee that elements of three Somali regular battalions were still in the Ogaden, along with 300–1,000 Somali regulars serving as volunteers with the Western Somali Liberation Front (WSLF) guerrillas.[14]

Thus, in little more than six months the United States had moved to establish security connections with Kenya, Oman, and Somalia. The initial agreements called for Washington to provide Kenya with $53 million, Oman with $100 million, and Somalia with $40 million in arms through fiscal year (FY) 1980 and FY 1981 security assistance programs.[15] Although no formal security commitments were made, security assistance on a continued basis was implied as part of the agreements. During FY 1981 the United States also allowed Oman to purchase approximately $50 million, Somalia $41 million, and Kenya $25 million worth of arms through cash or commercial sales.[16] The proposed total security assistance packages for FY 1982 and FY 1983 called for the provision of approximately $110 million ($57 million Foreign Military Sales [FMS] financing program) to Kenya, $100 million ($70 million FMS financing program) to Oman, and $95.5 million ($40 million FMS financing program) to Somalia. For the same two-year period cash or commercial sales were estimated to reach $65 million for Kenya, $60 million for Oman, and $50 million for Somalia.[17] In fact, Washington was actually paying a relatively low price for access since most of the arms were provided on a cash basis or were guaranteed on credit loans provided through the FMS financing program, which would have to be repaid with interest.

A crucial aspect of the access agreements, however, required the United States to bear the full capital costs of upgrading facilities in the host countries. Perhaps one reason Kenya, Oman, and Somalia were so willing to come to terms with the United States at less than optimum terms with regard to security assistance was because Washington would fund the cost of military construction at the sites, while the host governments retained sovereign rights over all facilities and real property. Initial estimates projected approximately a $250 million American investment to upgrade the facilities. This figure proved to be a close approximation. Through FY 1982 military construction funds totaled $167 million for Oman, $45.1 million for Kenya, and $24.4 million for Somalia.[18] In FY 1983 the Reagan administration requested and Congress authorized another $60.4 million for construction at three airfields (Masirah, Seeb, and Thumrait) in Oman, $30 million for port/airfield expansion at Berbera, and $8.3 million for base support facilities and harbor improvements at Mombasa.[19] The U.S. military construction investment now totals over $332 million in these three countries.

This base facility network across the Indian Ocean not only served as a short-term response to the events in Iran and Afghanistan but provided a new dimension for longer-range strategic planning. Although Kenya's facilities are approximately twenty-five hundred miles from the Strait of Hormuz, they will be valuable in supporting local sea control operations. Mombasa will continue to provide an attractive shore leave for American sailors and fleet support for deployed carrier battle groups—a function it has performed for years. Facilities in Somalia will also provide fleet support as well as support for sea control and maritime air operations, particularly in the vicinity of Bab el-Mandeb. Somalia provides an extra dimension since it is a thousand miles closer to the Persian Gulf than Kenya and Diego Garcia, and Berbera's fifteen-thousand-foot concrete runway can handle American B-52s. Oman's facilities are seen as the most important because of their strategic location near the mouth of the Persian Gulf. Not only are they valuable for sea control and maritime air operations in the gulf and the Strait of Hormuz but they also provide convenient support for tactical air operations and can serve as a staging area for the RDF. Besides being well situated for pre-positioning supplies, the sparsely populated Masirah Island offers political and security advantages.

This strategic network does have several rather unavoidable drawbacks. The facilities are not under direct U.S. control and Washington is required to consult the host governments concerning major exercises or deployments that use the facilities. Valuable time, often a critical factor during a crisis, could be lost. Although the access agreements are secret, reportedly they are in effect for ten years, at the end of which time the United States may have to renegotiate.[20] The host governments are also subject to local political constraints. For example, Oman and Somalia certainly would not allow their facilities to be used by the United States should another general Arab-Israeli war break out. Finally, the logistic support these facilities can provide is less than that of a permanent U.S. base.[21] In fact, of all the facilities available in the three countries, the Pentagon plans only to use Masirah Island as a pre-positioning spot for American equipment and as a staging area for the RDF.

In the last two years, however, the Reagan administration has made Ras Banas, Egypt, the focus of an American effort to establish a rear staging facility for the RDF. American facilities in Oman would be a likely and vulnerable target for attack in the event war broke out and American intervention seemed forthcoming. The Pentagon felt uncomfortable putting "all its eggs in one basket" by relying exclusively upon Diego Garcia as a rear staging area for the RDF. Pentagon officials also claim Ras Banas is more centrally located to support the full range of contingencies that might require U.S. forces.[22] It would, therefore, serve as the primary American forward staging area in certain contingencies. At Ras Banas the United States will also be able to deploy its forces before they are actually committed to combat, an action that current politics in Southwest Asia prohibits countries such as Oman, who are supporters of U.S. intentions in the area, from permitting prior to the outbreak of hostilities.[23]

Except for Diego Garcia, Ras Banas will be the most expensive U.S. military construction project near southwestern Asia. If the Pentagon has its way, expenditures are projected to total $522.7 million by the end of FY 1985.[24] Priority has been given to building staging facilities and enhancing its air and sealift capacity. Plans include dredging its port harbor, construction of a concrete pier, and modifying its airfield so it can handle B-52s and C-5 aircraft.

The proposed Pentagon military construction program for Southwest Asia at present calls for a total expenditure of over $850 million in Kenya, Oman, Somalia, and Egypt. This estimate does not even include the substantial investment already in, and future funding requests for, Diego Garcia and Lajes field in the Azores, the latter of which is also considered essential to deployment in the area. There is no doubt that the construction of this strategic infrastructure will enhance tremendously American power projection capabilities, particularly the ability to support the RDF and a peacetime naval presence in the region. In addition, Sudan, now the recipient of the largest U.S. security assistance package in sub-Saharan Africa, has offered to provide the United States with access to military facilities, including Port Sudan, and has suggested the possibility of allowing the pre-positioning of equipment and supplies.[25]

In the final analysis, access to these facilities for any given contingency is dependent upon host government approval. Washington has a very real stake in the survival of these regimes. The American security connection, however, also offers a potential rallying point for domestic opposition. It has been suggested, for example, that it may prove to be a double-edged sword for the Qaboos regime. While U.S. security assistance has enhanced Oman's military potential, it may contribute in the long run to domestic instability.[26]

Turmoil is evident throughout much of the rest of the strategic network. In Mogadishu, the Barre regime has been beset by protest resignations by top government officials concerned about the direction of internal policies, it has seen the emergence of a vocal opposition by Somalis living abroad and the coalescence of groups opposed to the regime under the banner of the Democratic Front for Somali Salvation, and it has come under armed attack by guerrillas operating out of Ethiopia (who receive substantial financial assistance from Libya). Egypt, after the 1981 assassination of Anwar Sadat, must seek to cope with an Islamic fundamentalist revival. And, as George Shepherd discusses elsewhere in this book, even that pro-Western bastion of stability in East Africa, Kenya, displays elements of instability.

All of this points to a certain reality of which American policy makers do seem cognizant. Although the access agreements have certainly enhanced the U.S. geostrategic position in Southwest Asia, each access agreement hangs by a somewhat thin political thread. No matter how low a profile America maintains in the region, the socioeconomic-political dynamics underlying internal and regional instability will not dissipate overnight. It is no wonder the Pentagon is so obsessed with the concept of base redundancy in this volatile region of the world. As Lieutenant General Paul X. Kelley, the first commander of the Rapid Deployment Joint Task Force, noted, "When you talk about projecting combat power 7,000 miles and then sustaining it over the long haul, it boggles the mind. That's why it's absolutely essential that we have access to facilities in the region."[27]

The Upgrading of Diego Garcia

The success of the Carter and Reagan administrations in gaining access to facilities in Kenya, Oman, and Somalia was but one part of their overall strategy for upgrading American ability to project power into the Indian Ocean region. Another was large new increases in funding for Diego Garcia, the small but increasingly important base in the middle of the Indian Ocean. The renewed U.S. interest in Diego Garcia after something of a hiatus during the first Carter years marked an increased appreciation of the base's value to the U.S. military, an appreciation that was reflected in new developments there.

Over the years, Diego Garcia has steadily accumulated more and more functions on behalf of the U.S. military. Begun as an "austere communications facility," by the mid-1970s it was being used by P-3 Orions for antisubmarine reconnaissance throughout the Indian Ocean region. In addition, fuel, munitions, and other supplies were being stored for the use of the intermittent American naval operations that ventured into the ocean. As of 1978, housing was available for up to eight hundred men on the island.

The regional developments of 1979–80 led to a reevaluation of the role that Diego Garcia could play in the overall expansion of U.S. force projection into the Indian Ocean. Before long, extensive new funding for construction on Diego Garcia was approved and several new missions were either in place, or planned, for the island. The budget for construction on Diego Garcia for FY 1981 was $131.9 million, for FY 1982 $237.8 million, and the proposed figure for FY 1983, $117.2 million. There has been speculation that the sum could go over $1 billion by the mid-1980s.[28] That is a lot of money to spend on a tiny island of 10.5 square miles, averaging but 7 inches above sea level.

There are several major components of the expanded activities on Diego Garcia. Taken together, they will make Diego Garcia, according to Rear Admiral William M. Zobel of the Naval Facilities Engineering Command, "a spearhead for logistic support of power projection into the Indian Ocean."[29] J. Clementson, in the best article on the 1980–81 buildup, similarly acknowledges that Diego Garcia has been transformed into a "major logistical support base."[30] What exactly has been done?

Diego Garcia is shaped roughly like the letter V. The arms are long and narrow and they enclose a lagoon that varies in width from approximately six to eight miles. A dredging contract for $17 million was let to a Japanese firm and part of the lagoon has been dredged to forty-five feet.[31] This will allow Diego Garcia to anchor America's largest aircraft carriers. The dredging was also useful for another new responsibility for Diego Garcia. In addition to the storage facilities for oil (capacity is 640,000 barrels), munitions, and other supplies that were already in place, since July 1980 as many as seventeen fully loaded cargo ships have been permanently pre-positioned at Diego Garcia. This pre-stocking at Diego Garcia is in place to support an eighteen-hundred-man Marine amphibious unit that is now permanently stationed in the Indian Ocean. On the pre-positioned ships are heavy equipment such as tanks and artillery, as well as sufficient supplies and stores to keep a twelve-thousand-troop brigade operational in battle for a month.[32]

The point of this pre-positioning of ships and stores at Diego Garcia must be understood in conjunction with the other forward planning that has been taking place. By pre-positioning supplies at Diego Garcia, a deployable sealift capability was being established. In any future Indian Ocean/Southwest Asia crisis, the United States will have the capability to airlift Marines or other manpower assigned to the RDF to the crisis area where they would be met by their equipment sent from Diego Garcia. The pre-positioning of supplies was thus a central element in speeding up the U.S. ability to respond to regional contingencies.

Another new development at Diego Garcia has been the decision to expand and widen the runways and provide new ramps and parking aprons so that B-52s can land on the atoll. Heretofore, Diego Garcia had been able to handle the P-3 Orion antisubmarine warfare (ASW) planes; most manpower and equipment had been ferried in by C-5AS and C-141 cargo planes. After January 1980, President Carter ordered B-52 surveillance missions to be run from Guam (the American B-52 base in the Pacific) over the Indian Ocean. Without a base en route, however, the round-trip flights from Guam to the Persian Gulf area required about thirty hours and several mid-air refuelings, a tiring mission for the crews. While there appear to be no plans at present to make Diego Garcia a permanent B-52 base, landing capability there would make missions out of Guam much easier and would, of course, give this primary U.S. bomber much closer striking range to the gulf area.[33]

These various developments have, of course, meant something of a housing boom on Diego Garcia. It was reported in 1981 that some three thousand men were on the island, doubling, if not tripling, the number who were normally there during the 1970s. Admiral Zobel describes their responsibilities: "There is a naval support facility of about 800 people. . . . Primary tenants are a communication squadron, a security group, an anti-submarine warfare patrol squadron, and a re-con [reconnaissance] squadron, totaling about 900 people. . . . The Air Force detachments, a carrier beach detachment, and others total about 450 . . . and there are about 850 Seabees."[34] In addition to these men, of course, there are from time to time visiting air crews and ships' companies who are on Indian Ocean exercises and stop at Diego Garcia.

The remoteness of Diego Garcia (1,000 miles from the nearest land, 2,660 miles from the head of the Persian Gulf) and its small size necessarily will limit just how completely it can or will be developed. Nevertheless, there is little doubt that for the foreseeable future, Diego Garcia will be used as a major staging base for a wide variety of communications, intelligence-gathering, and pre-stocking functions in the Indian Ocean region. Clementson reminds us "of the central military truism that operations of war can only be conducted within the limits of logistical support." For this, "Diego Garcia affords flexibility of function and a wide range of short-notice options to military planners

[and] as such, it is of incalculable strategic significance."[35] When linked with the sharply augmented fleet rotations into the Indian Ocean, the U.S. naval capability in the region has grown markedly.

Expansion of Naval Forces in the Indian Ocean

Certainly the most immediate and the most tangible expression of heightened American concern about developments in the Indian Ocean/ Southwest Asia region came in the form of rapidly augmented naval deployments to the region. Until the 1970s, the only U.S. naval presence in the Indian Ocean was three destroyers that operated out of Bahrain. As the decade proceeded, the navy began to rotate task forces into the Indian Ocean about three times a year, but there was still no permanent presence of any consequence. This remained the situation until 1979.

With the fall of the shah, the issue of American naval deployments into the Indian Ocean/Southwest Asia region became another part of the overall U.S. strategic reappraisal that was taking place. Two things happened more or less simultaneously in 1979. On the one hand there was a steady increase in U.S. naval forces in the northwest quadrant of the Indian Ocean to the point where, in early 1980, there were briefly three aircraft carriers (the *Nimitz*, the *Midway*, and the *Kitty Hawk*) with their battle groups in the Indian Ocean.[36] Throughout 1980 and well into 1981 there were always two carrier battle groups on station near the Persian Gulf; generally this meant approximately twenty-four men-of-war and supply ships were always in the region with additional supply ships anchored at Diego Garcia.[37] With approximately 170 jet fighters aboard the two carriers, not to mention the fighting capability of the carriers, their escorts, and the Marine amphibious unit deployed after March 1980, a considerable arsenal had been massed in the region. There was a report that one of the two carrier battle groups was withdrawn from the Indian Ocean in October 1981; if true, this would mean the "virtual cutting in half of the task force former President Carter sent steaming into the Indian Ocean after the 1979 Soviet invasion of Afghanistan."[38] Still, one or two carrier battle groups remain permanently deployed in the Indian Ocean.

Alongside this tangible evidence of U.S. military concern about the region, there were also explicit changes made with respect to the American strategic posture vis-à-vis the Indian Ocean and the Persian Gulf. President Carter's January 1980 pledge to defend the Persian Gulf was, of course, a key statement of strategic resolve but it is best seen as but one of a series of steps that together have redefined the U.S. national interest in this area.

By the middle of 1979, a clear decision had been made that the United States would henceforth sustain a "permanent naval presence" in the Indian Ocean.[39] Given the lack of American bases in the region and the uncertainty surrounding overflight rights, it is scarcely surprising that the American buildup would feature the navy. Rear Admiral Robert J. Hanks has noted that "seapower increasingly offers the only assured method of getting U.S. armed prowess from here to there in a crisis [and] short of all-out nuclear war, seapower will remain a predominant implement in the bag of international, crisis-management options."[40]

In July 1980, the supreme allied commander, Atlantic, Admiral Harry D. Train, explicitly stated that the purpose of U.S. naval forces in the Indian Ocean was to maintain access to energy resources; to retain access to the region for political, economic, and military reasons; and to support NATO by providing support for the allies' sources of energy.[41] The current secretary of defense in the Reagan administration, Caspar Weinberger, has reiterated similar themes. With respect to the Persian Gulf, he has stated that "the umbilical cord of the industrialized free world runs through the Strait of Hormuz into the Arabian Gulf and the nations which surround it." As a consequence of this energy dependency "our vital interests are involved there as are the vital interests of our allies [and] we have to be there in a credible way."[42]

There can be little doubt that major new military commitments have now been undertaken by the United States in the Indian Ocean/ Persian Gulf region. Naval force is central to maintaining these commitments through the power it projects, the sea lanes it protects and keeps open, and the support it potentially provides for ground forces through its sealift capabilities. Yet these new commitments and deployments have not come without costs and these need to be briefly mentioned.

One major concern has to do with the ability of the U.S. Navy to undertake these new commitments. In order to maintain two carrier battle groups on station in the Indian Ocean, the carriers have to be withdrawn from either the Sixth or Seventh fleets in the Mediterranean or the Pacific, respectively. In a much-quoted remark during the Indian Ocean buildup, then chief of Naval Operations, Admiral Thomas Hayward, stated that "the U.S. Navy is a one-and-a-half ocean navy with a three-ocean commitment."[43] Hayward's comment reflects the general naval view—a view shared by many defense commentators and the Reagan administration as well—that there is a serious shortage of both ships and manpower to carry out the U.S. Navy's perceived duties.

There is little question that the naval forces deployed in the Indian Ocean suffer severe morale problems. The aircraft carrier *Nimitz* was at sea at one point for over one hundred days and for the first time in sixty-five years the navy allowed beer to be brought on ship. There are various other reports of serious drug problems both on ships and at Diego Garcia.[44] Such problems cannot be quickly solved. The current administration sees the solution in increasing the size of the navy from 450 ships and 12 carriers to 600 ships and 15 carriers. While this may help in time, it is in reality a buildup that will take nearly the rest of the century to complete, and that is only if the commitment to do so remains unflagging.[45] As far as drug and morale problems are concerned, there is little reason to anticipate that the navy will be any more adept at solving these problems than the rest of American society. In the short term, morale problems apparently played a major role in the decision to cut back Indian Ocean deployments in October 1981.[46]

Another concern has to do with the response of regional powers and the Soviet Union to the U.S. buildup. As the access agreements suggest, some regional powers have welcomed the American moves. But other regional powers continue to support the zone-of-peace idea which endeavors to keep the superpowers out of the Indian Ocean. Although any exodus of the superpowers from the Indian Ocean is certainly unlikely at the present time, changed political circumstances in Britain and Mauritius could threaten U.S. access to Diego Garcia, as Joel Larus points out in this volume, and that in turn could call the whole U.S. Indian Ocean strategy into question. As far as the Soviet Union is concerned, it has not markedly altered its Indian Ocean deployments in light of American moves. The Soviet Union, as it has for more than a decade, keeps approximately twenty ships in the Indian Ocean, although many of them are noncombatants.[47] At least for now, U.S. naval superiority in the Indian Ocean seems established.

In just over three years, the United States certainly improved its capabilities in the Indian Ocean region. Through its words and actions, it has upgraded its commitments. But the nature of the region as a whole must continue to be seen as one in which conflict and instability are likely to be persistent. It is unlikely that the new naval commitments can do much about this and, as a result, "the purpose of naval commitment must essentially remain one of crisis management rather than crisis suppression or crisis prevention."[48] If any group can take on the latter tasks, it will have to be the Rapid Deployment Force.

Formation of the Rapid Deployment Force

Since World War II, American defense planners and policy makers have envisioned and prepared for scenarios requiring the rapid introduction of American troops abroad. Since the Korean War, contingency plans have existed for the deployment of a marine amphibious force (MAF) of fifty thousand men to overseas theaters of operation within thirty days of mobilization.[49] In 1962 President John F. Kennedy created the U.S. Strike Command, which designated army units located in the United States to be deployed rapidly overseas. This led the Johnson administration to press Congress in 1966 to approve a new class of fast deployment logistics (FDL) ships and C-5A cargo aircraft that would allow the United States to transport troops and equipment worldwide without the need for intermediate servicing stops.[50] The "rapid deployment" scenario itself was set in motion during the October 1973 worldwide military alert ordered by the Nixon administration when the Eighty-second Airborne Division was readied for intervention in the Middle East.[51] But it was not until the aftermath of the Iranian Revolution in 1979 and the acknowledgment later that year of the presence of a Soviet combat brigade in Cuba that the United States made a concerted effort to create a large, quick-reaction force specifically for intervention in non-NATO contingencies.[52]

Within the Carter administration the notion of forming a quick-reaction force originated in mid-1977. National Security Adviser Zbigniew Brzezinski advocated the creation of a rapid deployment force for possible use in Third World crises. President Carter approved the general idea in August 1977 when he issued Presidential Directive 18. This directive called for the creation of a quick-reaction force that would be comprised largely of light infantry units backed up by expanded strategic airlift and sealift capabilities. Until early 1979, however, there was little incentive either at the White House or within the bureaucracy to move ahead and establish a Third World intervention force. The Carter administration had essentially adopted the Nixon Doctrine—by which the United States looked to the shah of Iran to protect Western interests in the Persian Gulf—as the cornerstone for its regional policy. At the State Department the creation of such an intervention unit was viewed as politically provocative.[53] Pentagon officials were reluctant to take on this mission because it would divert resources from the military's primary mission of defending Western Europe. Defense budgets through the first two years of the Carter administration reflected a continuing preoccupation with U.S. Army, tactical air, and other NATO-oriented forces at the expense of surface naval forces, the Marine Corps, and other forces associated with intervention in areas where American forces were not pre-positioned ashore.[54] With the overthrow of the shah, Washington recognized it would have to develop its own capacity to respond to crises in the Persian Gulf.

Under pressure from the White House, the joint chiefs of staff accelerated plans for the RDF. By the summer of 1979 the joint chiefs started to identify the individual units that would comprise the force. Since no new combat forces were to be created, the RDF would consist of existing forces, most of which already were earmarked for a NATO defense contingency.[55] Rather than being a cohesive unit drawn entirely from one branch of the armed forces, it would be an integrated force composed of units from the various armed services. The Pentagon, therefore, had to identify the specific units that could be drawn upon for any given contingency in varying terrains and weather conditions. Given the proposed force's integrated nature, in December 1979 the administration established a Rapid Deployment Joint Task Force and appointed as its commander U.S. Marine Corps Major General Paul X. Kelley.

Since originally conceived, the RDF has undergone major redefinitions of purpose. Whereas the Carter White House initially viewed it as a fast-reaction force with a global orientation, following the Soviet invasion of Afghanistan in late December 1979 and the pronouncement of the Carter Doctrine in January 1980, the RDF became focused on the Persian Gulf region. In the early spring of 1981 Ronald Reagan's secretary of defense, Caspar Weinberger, announced plans to turn the RDF into a unified command.[56] It would have a defined geographic area of operations, consist of forces from all four services, and report directly to the secretary of defense. Rather than being merely a planning task force, it would assume operational as well as planning control over all American forces that might be ordered to defend the Persian Gulf.

On 1 January 1983 the RDF officially became a full-scale military command, the first to be established in more than twenty years. In the words of its new commander, Lieutenant General Robert C. Kingston, it has been given "clear authority and responsibility for United States military activity within the region of the Persian Gulf and Southwest Asia." American military personnel stationed in the region (including those flying the Airborne Warning and Control System [AWACS] aircraft in Saudi Arabia as well as military advisers) now report to the new command, headquartered at MacDill Air Force Base in Tampa, Florida. Its responsibilities also include recommending which of the approximately twenty countries (excluding Israel) within its area of operations should be allowed to buy what weapons.[57]

The current force level of the RDF numbers 222,000, including three-and-a-half army combat divisions, three aircraft carrier groups, one amphibious ready group, seven air force tactical fighter wings, and one-and-a-third Marine Corps marine amphibious forces.[58] Its power capability is viewed as perhaps adequate to deter a Soviet invasion of Iran but it would likely be unable to stop a concerted Soviet invasion. A Soviet invasion of Iran is viewed by the Reagan administration as the most serious threat to Southwest Asia since, if successful, it would give the Soviet Union the ability to control the oil flow at the Strait of Hormuz. The Reagan administration, therefore, plans to counter this worst-case threat by almost doubling the size of the RDF to 440,000 troops by adding almost two full army combat divisions, three air force tactical fighter wings, and two-thirds of a Marine Corps MAF.[59]

In the event of an RDF deployment, the U.S. airlift capacity would carry the immediate short-term burden of introducing and supporting American combat troops. The United States currently operates a fleet of 70 large c-5 transports and 234 smaller c-141FS, and can draw upon 350 commercial transports to supplement its airlift capacity. Over the next five years the administration plans to procure 56 KC-10 tanker aircraft and 50 c-5s. The Defense Department has also allocated $2.9 billion for the development and procurement of the c-17 advanced cargo transport, with a goal of buying 6 in 1987 and 12 in 1988.[60]

Due to the financial cost and limited capacity of airlift, sealift is also viewed as an essential part of the U.S. total rapid mobility capacity. An RDF contingency in Southwest Asia will be able to draw upon four sea fleets: Military Sealift Command Controlled Fleet, Ready Reserve Fleet, U.S. Merchant Marine, and the National Defense Rescue Fleet. During 1981 and 1982 the navy purchased eight high-speed SL-7 container ships to increase its early-deploying sealift capacity. The navy intends to convert all of these ships to a roll-on/roll-off ("ro-ro") configuration to improve their military utility, although as of FY 1982 Congress had appropriated monies to convert only half of the SL-7s. The Defense Department also plans to increase the number of cargo ships in the Ready Reserve Fleet from twenty-nine to sixty-one by the end of FY 1988 in order to improve the RDF's sealift sustainment (rather than rapid reinforcement) capacity.[61]

Pre-positioning forms the third of the three major deployment programs. The Carter administration viewed the development of a sea-based pre-positioning capacity in the Indian Ocean as the quickest way to demonstrate a commitment to security in the region and to send a clear signal of U.S. resolve. At the present time, the United States maintains an eighteen-ship near-term pre-positioned force in the region: seventeen are pre-positioned near Diego Garcia and one in the Mediterranean. These ships will serve as an interim force until probably 1987 when pre-positioning improvements are expected to be complete. As outlined in the FY 1981 defense budget, under the Maritime Pre-positioning Ship Program the Marine Corps plans by 1987 to pre-position equipment for three marine amphibious brigades plus supplies for thirty days of combat. To support this concept the navy plans to charter, rather than procure, thirteen vessels specially designed for pre-positioning use; the first four were to be available in FY 1984, the next eight in FY 1985, and the thirteenth ship is to be delivered in FY 1986. In terms of developing a land-based pre-positioning capacity, so far only Oman and Egypt have offered sites for the United States to pre-position combat equipment.[62]

Since the creation of the RDF, American forces have participated in three major exercises in Southwest Asia. In November 1980, in conjunction with Egyptian forces, fourteen hundred American troops conducted desert maneuvers in Egypt to familiarize them with Middle Eastern desert terrain and to test the logistics for rapidly deploying combined units from the different services into a joint task force. The most ambitious U.S. exercise to date was held a year later and given the code name Operation Bright Star '82. Whereas the 1980 maneuver lasted only ten days and was confined to Egypt, Bright Star '82 involved five thousand American troops in a six-week exercise in four countries. The Eighty-second Airborne Division parachuted into Egypt, followed by a B-52 bombing run nonstop from Minot Air Force Base in North Dakota to a target range in the Egyptian desert; a Special Forces guerrilla warfare exercise was held in the Sudan; an engineer and medical logistic exercise was conducted at Berbera, Somalia; and a two-thousand-man U.S. Marine Corps force conducted an amphibious landing along the Arabian Sea north of Muscat in Oman. Early in December 1982, about twenty-five hundred U.S. soldiers conducted maneuvers in Oman, under the code name Jade Tiger, aimed at testing defenses in the event of a Soviet or other foreign attack on the Persian Gulf region.[63]

The RDF represents the most significant manifestation of the Pentagon's search for a revitalized overseas posture beyond the bounds of the NATO area.[64] Its creation is a departure from past military strategy which focused upon shoring up defenses in Western Europe. Unlike NATO, however, political sensitivities in Southwest Asia can hamper the injection of even a small American force into the region. Reportedly, Egypt and other countries prohibited maneuvers during 1982 to protest U.S. support for the Israeli invasion of Lebanon.[65] There was practically no publicity concerning the Jade Tiger exercise because Oman wanted to play down its links with the United States to avoid criticism from Arab countries opposed to American policy in the Middle East.[66] Although its use may well be inhibited by political constraints, the RDF has emerged (along with strategic deterrence, American NATO forces, and the navy) as one of the "four pillars of U.S. military power."[67]

Conclusion

There can be little doubt that the Iranian Revolution and the Soviet invasion of Afghanistan, together with other regional developments too numerous to mention, triggered a crisis for the U.S. government in 1979–80. The prevailing American strategy in the Southwest Asia/Indian Ocean region, based on the use of regional surrogates to defend core interests, had failed and there was no obvious consensus on what should take its place. It was from this base of uncertainty and not a little alarm that the developments described in this chapter unfolded.

The policy that emerged was the four-pronged approach to crisis management that has been analyzed. It was, as is obvious, essentially a military response to the political crises that were observed. Insofar as any political analysis underlay these American moves, it rested primarily on the desire to build an anti-Soviet consensus in the region. But this political-cum-diplomatic effort clearly played a secondary role to the unilateral military buildup. At the heart of all these actions was a belief that the United States could no longer depend on regional or other allies to defend its interests in the Indian Ocean. Therefore it had to develop an intervention and sea-control capability of its own.

To a considerable extent this has been accomplished. Access facilities have been arranged and are being rapidly improved; the modernization and upgrading of facilities at Diego Garcia has moved forward quickly. Although not without organizational and other difficulties, sustained fleet deployments to the Indian Ocean have taken place, and the RDF-cum-Central Command for Southwest Asia has been formed. These developments, taken together, mean that the United States now possesses far greater intervention capability in the Indian Ocean region than it did in 1979 and planning for the future looks toward even greater capability.

R. B. Byers argues in this book and elsewhere that "military-strategic competition in the naval environment will increase during the 1980s and that both superpowers will consider augmenting their sea-control/sea-denial forces and their capabilities to project power ashore."[68] The United States has already committed billions of dollars for new cargo vessels, container ships, and a new generation of cargo planes to provide both airlift and sealift capabilities for any American strike force dispatched into an area of crisis. If all goes as planned, by the mid-1980s the United States expects to be able to transport a hundred thousand men, with heavy equipment, to the region within thirty-five days. There, of course, the units will find forward and rear staging areas, pre-positioned supplies, and naval power. This type of capability was simply unavailable to the United States in 1979–80; the movement of a hundred thousand equipped men overseas would have taken at least six months.

Three questions seem important when finally reflecting on these new American capabilities: How persistent are the security concerns that prompted this buildup? What is the regional response to American power projection into the Indian Ocean? How relevant are the strategic steps taken to the crises that are likely to emerge?

The two most prominent U.S. security concerns in the region are about the reliability of oil access and supply and Soviet penetration of key states. Both concerns are likely to persist and thereby give weight to the arguments of those who favor heightened American military capabilities. Some questions come to mind, however. Oil dependency does seem to be a core concern now and for the indefinite future. Better conservation efforts and new energy sources may in time lessen this pressure but these will be distant developments at best. What is less clear is any probable scenario in which the Soviet Union would attempt to cut the flow of oil to the West that would not quickly escalate to a major international crisis. If this is true, then it is not entirely obvious how relevant the arms buildup described would be to the conflict that might ensue. It could even be argued that having ships, men, and matériel deployed to a region so remote from the United States would leave their supply lines dangerously vulnerable in a major crisis. Clearly, proponents of the current buildup would argue that having our current new military capabilities in place will provide the necessary military muscle to back up appropriate diplomacy and forestall any Soviet-led threat to oil access or distribution.

With respect to the regional response, it is obvious that some nations in the region—notably Egypt, Kenya, Oman, and Somalia—have been favorably disposed toward American actions in the region. Other nations no doubt approve as well. But it needs to be remembered that these are uncertain allies. The access agreements have been cut to ameliorate their doubts and fears but the result is some degree of uncertainty over who will define the circumstances in which access is allowed. Beyond this nagging problem one finds continued regional interest in the Indian Ocean peace zone idea. However unlikely it is that this concept will come to fruition, it has exercised a powerful influence over many leaders of the Indian Ocean littoral for the past decade. Both superpowers are likely to find a cool reception from many local states as they increase their arms buildup.

Another aspect of the regional environment that is important to observe is the extreme volatility of the region's politics and the considerable instability of many regimes. The revolution against the shah, the current Iraq-Iran war, the assassinations of Sadat and Gandhi, and many other incidents remind us that little in this region is certain. This very instability, of course, provides a rationale for the recent U.S. buildup. Weak regimes in Afghanistan and Iran provide an excuse and serve as a catalyst for military action. What needs to be asked, however, is whether this response is appropriate to the situation being addressed.

This leads to our final concern: how useful are these new capabilities likely to be for crises the United States might face in the future? Does the United States have an overall strategy that informs its choices or are the decisions that have been made so ad hoc that there is little clarity as to how the new forces in place can or will be used in the future?

In 1979 American policy makers felt that they had few options with which to respond to developments and they have sought to remedy this problem. In the situation of crisis that they perceived, decisions were forced out that had long been on the back burner of the State Department and the Pentagon. As Charles Hermann has noted, sudden changes in the international environment in terms of the balance of power often can act as a stimulus to action.[69]

Certainly the United States today has more regional options. The hardware now in place will necessarily contribute to the range of options that are perceived to be available in any future crisis. This may all be to the good, but it may not be if the available options do not fit the needs of the crisis or if inappropriate means are used. Are, for instance, pre-positioned supplies and a RDF really the vehicles for stemming Soviet moves in the region? Are oil fields and sea lanes really likely to be kept open by aircraft carrier diplomacy and actual intervention?

There is always the predisposition in U.S. foreign policy to attribute instability to Soviet meddling when, in fact, there may be other more important causes. The ability to use military options in future crises may seem to offer advantages but short-run gains may turn into long-range costs. The situation that policy makers perceive may not be the actual one that exists. The new options and flexibility may prove to be illusory if they are not linked to a proper analysis. The militarization of political conflict may seem satisfying in that it responds to the need to "do something," but this response may often be inappropriate.

Internal regime instability, rather than outside intervention or the possibility of severed sea lanes, is the primary source of crisis in the Indian Ocean and Southwest Asia. By applying the wrong analysis, intervention may occur that will deepen commitments in places where America actually has little ability to shape events. The danger of substituting military options for diplomacy (or indeed for doing nothing) is always a real possibility in international relations. Possessing multiple capabilities and numerous options need not ensure good outcomes. In the Indian Ocean/Southwest Asia—a region where the stakes are high but the regimes are weak—any tendency to substitute military solutions for political ones must be carefully modulated in order to avoid turning smaller regime or regional problems into larger global ones.

24. Diego Garcia: The Military and Legal Limitations of America's Pivotal Base in the Indian Ocean ⌦ Joel Larus

Diego Garcia currently is the primary naval/air base of the United States in the Indian Ocean. It has become one of America's essential military installations in the world, the hub for its strategic operational plans to deal with any future crisis in the Middle East/Persian Gulf area. Reportedly at anchor in the lagoon of the island are seventeen ships of the Rapid Deployment Force (RDF), fully loaded with sufficient military equipment, supplies, fuel, lubricants, and water to meet the combat requirements of one Marine brigade of eighteen thousand men. Diego Garcia's airfield has undergone expansion and strengthening so that B-52s can land and take off on a regular basis, thus facilitating U.S. air surveillance of Southwest Asia and eliminating the need for in-flight refueling. An expanded tank farm, a highly sophisticated communications center, enlarged warehouses, new barracks, and improved recreational facilities for military personnel all point to the importance the Pentagon accords the base. Unconfirmed reports suggest that nuclear weapons are stored there. In short, Diego Garcia is not a secondary, temporary military installation. It is as fundamental and indispensable to America's military posture throughout the Indian Ocean as is Subic Bay to the deployment of ships and aircraft in the Pacific Ocean or as is Guantanamo in the Caribbean.

Diego Garcia, one of several island atolls making up the Chagos Archipelago, became part of a new crown colony created by the British in 1965, designated the British Indian Ocean Territory (BIOT). Almost immediately after creating BIOT, London leased Diego Garcia to the United States for joint military purposes. Despite the island's strategic importance and the Defense Department's belief that it has an ironclad legal agreement insuring access and use of Diego Garcia until well into the coming century, there are reasons for believing that the U.S. rights to the facility are less secure than is recognized.

Three interrelated sets of problems have arisen that could nullify the British-American lease agreement. If such developments occur, it could result either in the forced withdrawal of American personnel and closing of the base or, alternatively, in the imposition of severe restrictions on the type of American military equipment and arms that could be landed and stored. This chapter will examine the three dangers to America's extended, unobstructed use of Diego Garcia. The first problem has a legal basis: what is the scope and duration of British sovereignty over the Chagos Archipelago? That is, how legally sufficient and efficacious is London's assertion of sovereignty over the archipelago based on its 1965 agreement with Mauritius?

The second complication is strategic in nature. It concerns the continued commitment of British naval power in the Indian Ocean now that the admiralty must deploy a greater number of warships than heretofore in the South Atlantic, a consequence of the Falklands War. Here attention needs to be given to the announced plans of the Thatcher government to reduce substantially the size of the Royal Navy's surface fleet and to how these cutbacks will affect Britain's strategy in the Indian Ocean. Another dimension of this issue requiring examination is the impact of the proposal by the militant left-wing faction of the Labour party to carry out unilateral nuclear disarmament.

Finally there is the independent island state of Mauritius, which traditionally had jurisdiction over the Chagos Archipelago. Its newly elected, left-wing, nonaligned government is committed to a global campaign to pressure British and American officials to restore the sovereignty of Mauritius over the Chagos, to close down Diego Garcia, and to help bring about a zone of peace in the Indian Ocean.

Background

Diego Garcia, the largest atoll in the Chagos chain, is 10.5 miles long and the most remote, least inviting naval/air installation leased by the United States since World War II. Situated in the middle of the Indian Ocean, it is approximately 3,400 miles from the Cape of Good Hope, 2,200 miles from Berbera, Somalia, 1,900 miles from Oman, and 2,600 miles from North West Cape, Australia. It is equidistant from the major East or West Coast American ports, an awesome 10,000-mile sea voyage. The climate of the island is wretched, its off-duty recreational diversions pathetically limited. Today, except for the military, Diego Garcia is uninhabited.

Traditionally, the Chagos Archipelago was under the jurisdiction of Mauritius, the island country nearly 1,500 miles to the southwest. Following the Napoleonic Wars, Mauritius became a colonial possession of Great Britain and for more than 150 years was ruled by a governor-general appointed by Whitehall, who resided at the capital city of Port Louis. During these decades, the Chagos interested no Western states and even Mauritius itself was inattentive to its development. Beginning in the first part of the present century, an indeterminate number of seminomadic men and women began settling on Diego Garcia, sometimes fishing local waters or working the coconut plantations on the island, sometimes moving to other atolls where opportunities to obtain food and work were somewhat more promising. These people came to be known as the Ilois.

Throughout the nineteenth century and the first half of the twentieth, Great Britain dominated the political-military affairs of the entire Indian Ocean. Following World War II, Britain was forced by financial limitations and political considerations to begin the process of withdrawing from its east-of-Aden empire. Beginning in 1947 with the division of the Indian subcontinent, all former British colonial possessions in the region became independent states.

In 1947, Mauritius achieved its long-awaited goal of self-government. Sir Seewoosagur Ramgoolam, an outspoken supporter of British values and beliefs, emerged as leader of the National Alliance party, a center-right coalition of landowners, professionals, and economically secure groups. The party's goal was independence. In 1963–65, Ramgoolam, then the head of a crown colony with complete internal autonomy, and British diplomats began negotiating the several questions that had to be resolved before independence could be granted and before the British would withdraw. At some point during the talks, Whitehall informed the Mauritians that a condition precedent to independence was cession of the Chagos Archipelago so that it could be included in the new crown colony that London was planning, the BIOT. It appears that Ramgoolam and his government readily and without objection agreed to surrender whatever territorial claims and legal rights Mauritius had in the Chagos to Great Britain.

No formal, written instrument of separation and transfer was drafted setting out precisely the terms and conditions of cession. The arrangement was handled in the best nineteenth-century colonial tradition: a verbal understanding between a colonial representative and the local head of government. Subsequent developments reveal that the parties paid little, if any, attention to the legal complexities of such a land transfer and were only secondarily concerned with the future well-being of the Ilois. The British did not reveal their strategic plans for the Chagos. There was no public protest in Mauritius even while rumors of the pending transfer were circulating. Independence from Great Britain was considerably more important to the Port Louis government and the people of Mauritius than a group of small remote atolls and their impoverished residents. The payment of £3 million that London agreed to make to Mauritius for the Chagos helped clinch the deal.

Whitehall has never offered an explanation as to why an instrument of cession was not drafted and signed by officials of the two governments. At the time negotiations were taking place, Mauritius was a dependency of Great Britain, under the administrative supervision of the Foreign Office and subject to the decisions of the Privy Council. However, the 1895 Colonial Boundaries Act and its subsequent Act of Interpretation were cited by the Privy Council when the formation of BIOT was announced.[1] Unofficially, representatives of the Foreign Office concede that they did not anticipate the legal and political problems that have arisen with Mauritius as a consequence of the cession. In any event, the failure to put in writing all the specific rights and limitations of both parties has immeasurably complicated post-1965 British-Mauritian relations.

On 8 November 1965, the Privy Council issued the order creating BIOT.[2] Originally it was made up of four separate island-chain components, each of which had been detached from a former British possession. In addition to the Chagos Archipelago, BIOT then consisted of the islands of Aldabra, Desroches, and Farquhar. The last three units were detached from the Colony of Seychelles. Two days later in the House of Commons, the secretary of state for the colonies announced formation of the new crown colony. Formalizing what earlier had been indicated, the secretary also told the Commons that "the islands will be available for the construction of defence facilities by the British and United States Governments."[3] His statement was the first public indication that Washington was evaluating the strategic value of sites in its developing plans to become actively involved in Indian Ocean affairs following the British withdrawal. Throughout most of 1966, personnel from the U.S. Defense Department inspected and evaluated the islands.

On 30 December 1966, Great Britain and the United States signed an agreement whereby all BIOT territory was made available to the Pentagon for "the defense purposes of both Governments as they may arise."[4] The duration provision of the 1966 agreement is of fundamental importance since it sets forth the term of the lease. According to article 11, the island(s) eventually selected as the site for the joint military facility was to be available to the United States for an initial period of fifty years, plus a twenty-year extension if needed. Read literally and without regard to subsequent, less generous duration clauses, the article appears to give the United States access to BIOT until well into the twenty-first century. Eventually, Diego Garcia was chosen by American military leaders for the joint defense project, and initially Washington announced it was constructing a "communications center" on the island.

A second British-American agreement regarding Diego Garcia was concluded on 24 October 1972.[5] By this time, the island was being designated as a "limited naval communications facility," the upgrading being a consequence of Washington's greater involvement in the Middle East/Persian Gulf/South Asia region. With one exception this supplemental agreement, which sets out in detail the operational procedures to be followed by the British and American military contingents based on the island, is not unique and does not merit any special consideration here. Article 20 of the 1972 agreement, however, the so-called duration and termination provision, is significant. As worded, it could at some future time bring about the forced closure of the American base. It reads, "This Agreement shall continue in force for as long as the BIOT Agreement continues in force or until such time as no part of Diego Garcia is any longer required for the purpose of the facility, *whichever occurs first*" (emphasis mine).[6] Read literally and interpreted narrowly, the first part of the provision means that if a British government decides sometime in the future to disestablish its crown colony of BIOT, America's access to and use of Diego Garcia could legally terminate. As of this date, significantly, of the four original units that made up BIOT all three former Seychelles possessions have been returned to that state's sovereignty. Only the Chagos Archipelago remains within the original design of BIOT. Stated in a somewhat different fashion, the island of Diego Garcia today is for all intents and purposes BIOT. If Britain surrenders control of this atoll, there is in fact no BIOT.

On 25 February 1976, a third Anglo-American agreement was signed.[7] Under this one, Washington was authorized to upgrade Diego Garcia from "a limited naval communications facility" to "a support facility of the United States Navy," the latter phrase being a diplomatic euphemism for a full-scale American naval/air base. The duration and termination provision remained unchanged from the earlier version but, for the first time, a consultation clause was added. Article 3 states that "as regards the use of the facility in normal circumstances," the senior British and American officers stationed at the base are required as a matter of routine to keep each other informed of ship dockings and plane landings. The clause then continues, "In other circumstances the use of the facility shall be a matter for the joint decision of the two Governments." There is no definition of what constitutes a normal American military movement or operation, that is, when only local notification is needed, or how to define abnormal or exceptional American usage when prior consultation and British approval is mandatory. In 1980, as will be explained, the consultation clause was the source of a British-American diplomatic flurry.

Thus, the American leasehold at Diego Garcia is governed by three separate agreements concluded with Great Britain over a period of nearly ten years. Each defines in somewhat broader fashion the basic nature of the installation and its mission but simultaneously the last two instruments place restrictions and limitations on the rights of the United States to operate from Diego Garcia.

Legal Controversies

Chagos (Diego Garcia) sovereignty

As Peter Vale and Michael Spicer discuss in greater detail elsewhere in this volume, on 11 June 1982, a left-wing alliance of the socialist Mauritian Militant Movement and the smaller, more centrist Mauritian Socialist party won a decisive victory at the polls, electing sixty of the sixty-two members of the National Assembly. The defeated administration of Sir Seewoosagur Ramgoolam had governed for the previous twenty-one years; its pro-Western policies and the failure of its economic programs contributed heavily to its repudiation by the electorate. As the world's press reported, the new government has a clear mandate to bring about fundamental changes in Mauritian domestic and foreign affairs. High on its list are the matters of the sovereignty of the Chagos, the fate of the Ilois, and the future of the base at Diego Garcia.

The chief strategist and theoretician of the coalition government is Paul Berenger, 37, a French-educated ultraliberal. While he is not an official of the new administration, he is its behind-the-scenes secretary-general and is committed to bringing about a political, economic, and social revolution on Mauritius. From speeches made during the last several years while he was working for the defeat of Ramgoolam's administration, as well as from his writings, Berenger appears determined to follow a foreign policy of nonalignment, to develop closer relations with India than have heretofore existed, and to work for acceptance and implementation of the zone-of-peace concept in the Indian Ocean. He is against any policy that can be considered pro-British or pro-American.

In the time that it has been in office, the new government in Port Louis has begun a diplomatic offensive to regain administrative control of, if not sovereignty over, the Chagos Archipelago and to close down the American-British base at Diego Garcia as expeditiously as circumstances permit. The success or failure of these efforts will depend in part on the issue of whether Great Britain has full and unrestricted sovereignty over the Chagos, free of any conditions, limitations, or restrictions, or, alternatively, whether its rights are qualified, conditional, and legally less secure than London originally thought. While the sovereignty issue is a complex one, it is important to the future well-being of the American naval/air base.

Between 1968 and the late 1970s Mauritius did not raise the problem of Chagos sovereignty at international meetings and paid almost no attention to the issue domestically. Not only had Prime Minister Ramgoolam agreed to surrender the archipelago when independence was being negotiated with London, but he had on occasion spoken publicly in favor of cession and the need to set up a Western military outpost in the Indian Ocean to counter Soviet expansion. It was only in early 1980, when there was rising popular resentment against the loss of the Chagos and when Berenger and his colleagues started winning voter support by calling attention to the issue, that Ramgoolam began to express dissatisfaction with the arrangement he had earlier supported so fully. He protested, for example, that he had been duped by the British during the 1964–65 negotiations because no one informed him that a major British-American military facility would be located on one of the islands he was surrendering. He prevailed on the Organization of African Unity to give formal backing to the Mauritian claim of sovereignty. On another occasion when addressing the United Nations General Assembly, he unequivocally argued that Mauritius continued to hold sovereignty over the archipelago, the 1965 agreement and payment notwithstanding. When the British ambassador to the UN challenged his position, Ramgoolam dropped this line of argument and thereafter announced that his government would not challenge the British claim of sovereignty and Mauritius would discontinue its protests concerning Diego Garcia provided the United States paid Port Louis a yearly rental fee for its use. Washington did not respond publicly to the proposal.[8]

Throughout the several years of claims and counterclaims, London's position concerning its rights to the Chagos has not altered. As Sir Anthony Parsons told the General Assembly the day following Ramgoolam's claim of sovereignty, "The United Kingdom has sovereignty over Diego Garcia and has not accepted that the island is under the sovereignty of Mauritius."[9] However, officials of the Thatcher government later qualified his declaration by announcing that Great Britain would "consider" returning (i.e., retroceding) sovereignty to Mauritius once the island base was no longer necessary for Anglo-American defense. The British declined to be any more specific regarding a target date or to offer details of the political-military conditions that would have to prevail in the Indian Ocean before the appropriate ministries would examine the issue.[10]

It is still too soon to determine the specific strategies the new government at Port Louis will employ in its efforts to negate the 1965 cession. There can be no doubt, however, it will be most active and persistent. Within two weeks of taking office, for example, Prime Minister Anerood Jugnauth announced that high up on his government's list of priorities was "the retrocession of the Chagos Archipelago." In mid-July 1982, Foreign Minister Jean Claude del'Estrac was ordered to London to open discussions with British officials but that effort failed to produce any softening of the position of the Thatcher administration. It can be expected that the issue will be raised at upcoming sessions of the United Nations and there also are hints from Port Louis that the government is prepared to submit the case to the International Court of Justice at the Hague for adjudication.

The Ilois

A legal problem related to the issue of the Chagos' sovereignty is the question of the Ilois community and its fate. The exact number of men, women, and children forced to leave Diego Garcia in 1965–66 has been the subject of considerable disagreement among the parties involved. One reliable source has placed the figure at 360 people, while others claim it is nearer 1,200. The key questions that need to be determined are whether they have surrendered permanently their right to return to their former home on Diego Garcia and, if so, how best to compensate them adequately for the ouster.

One issue not in dispute is the postmigration history of these former residents of Diego Garcia and the long indifference of Ramgoolam's government to their situation. After quitting the island, they ended up living in crowded slums at Port Louis, unemployed, depressed, and without a local representative. To help subsidize a program of resettlement on Mauritius, Great Britain in 1968 paid the government U.S. $1.43 million. The money was to be used to set up training programs so that the workers could acquire skills to enter the Mauritian labor force and to help secure and pay for new, permanent homes. For reasons never

explained, the Ramgoolam administration made no distribution what-
soever of the funds, set up no training programs, and was all but in-
different to the socioeconomic trials and misfortunes of the Ilois. Some
died; all suffered grievously.

Eventually the distress of the Ilois attracted the attention of people both on Mauritius and abroad. The first group to become concerned
was Berenger's Mauritian Militant Movement. Both on political and
humanitarian grounds, it decided to take up the Ilois cause, probably
hoping to embarrass the government by calling attention to the injus-
tices forced upon the Ilois, as well as revealing aspects of the 1965 cession deal that had not yet been made public. By the end of the 1970s,
the Ilois were no longer without local defenders and, while their economic situation did not improve, they had become an issue in Mauritian politics.

Under the tutelage of Berenger's party, the Ilois began to hold
demonstrations in Port Louis. They protested their forced exile from
Chagos and demanded the right as British nationals living in a crown
colony to return to their homes. In 1972–73, several of their number
staged a hunger strike in London, an act that for the first time ac-
quainted the English public with the history of the Ilois' forced exile
and the economic hardships they had experienced on Mauritius. Their
activity in England received considerable attention in the press and led
to the formation of the second group working for their betterment, the
Society for Diego Garcians in Exile.[11]

In 1978 Britain responded to the pressure by offering the Ilois an
additional U.S. $2 million indemnity provided they agreed to discon-
tinue their efforts to return to Diego Garcia and agreed to settle down
permanently in Mauritius. The offer was rejected. The Ilois spokesman
stated that the additional compensation was inadequate for the loss of
their island home and their sufferings in Port Louis slums. Furthermore,
they refused to surrender their legal rights to return and reclaim Diego
Garcia. During the next three years, British diplomats and Mauritian
officials attempted to negotiate a compromise solution to the Ilois' future. In 1981, the British offer was raised to U.S. $2.75 million, the same
condition against returning to the island remaining a sine qua non.
Again the Ilois refused to bend. They claimed U.S. $16 million as com-
pensation for the injuries they had experienced in exile, and they emphasized that as residents of the crown colony of BIOT, they were British
nationals who were illegally deprived of their right of residence.

In March 1982, three months before the Mauritian election, Britain
and the Mauritian government struck a deal. London agreed to allocate
U.S. $7.2 million if a Board of Trustees for the Ilois was named by the

government. In return, the Mauritian prime minister also promised that the Legislative Assembly would approve legislation making land available to the Ilois worth approximately U.S. $2.8 million; they were also to be given instruction in modern agrarian techniques. In return, the Ilois were to give up their clamoring to return to the Chagos, particularly Diego Garcia.[12] For several months following the initialing of the Anglo-Mauritian supplementary agreement of 15 April, it appeared that the treaty would not be approved by the Port Louis government. Opposition leaders asked Prime Minister Ramgoolam to delay submitting the treaty for ratification because, they held, the text could be interpreted as surrendering any and all Mauritian claims of sovereignty to the Chagos Archipelago. After the June election and the beginning of the new administration, however, the agreement was approved and became operative. Early in November 1982, Great Britain paid in full the supplementary compensation to the Ilois, thus ending forever whatever claims they might have had to return to their former island home.

While the Ilois problem is now closed, the Chagos sovereignty issue remains a most controversial dispute, one that promises to be around for many years. The new government at Port Louis is determined to establish its legal ownership of the archipelago either by pressuring Great Britain to shift its position or, if unsuccessful, by seeking legal redress in an appropriate legal forum. The clearest statement of the government's position was offered by Foreign Minister del'Estrac after his initial unproductive talks with the British foreign secretary in July 1982. His country, he told reporters, was prepared to use "every possible means, political, diplomatic, and judicial to try to establish the sovereignty of Mauritius over . . . Diego Garcia."[13]

Strategic Controversies

Nuclear weapons deployment in the Indian Ocean

In recent years a spirited debate has arisen in national security circles between strategists who maintain the United States deploys nuclear weapons in the Indian Ocean, intermittently or on a regular basis, and those who contend that there are no good strategic reasons for doing so.[14] Following its long-held practice, the Pentagon will neither admit nor deny the validity of such reports or comment on any such articles. It is, of course, impossible to resolve such a debate here and it is not germane to the discussion to examine the basic premises of the two positions. Yet, regarding America's future use of the naval/air base at Diego Garcia—particularly in a period of severe international tension—

the issue of the right of the United States to introduce nuclear weapons into the facility, unilaterally and without prior consultation with or approval from Great Britain, is of significance.

It is the militant left-wing faction of the British Labour party that is leading a campaign to deny the United States the right to land, store, or service any type of nuclear weapon at Diego Garcia. At the party's 1980 annual conference, a group led by Tony Benn campaigned determinedly for a resolution advocating unilateral disarmament for Great Britain and a policy that committed a future Labour government to restrict or close down all American nuclear bases on British soil or in "its territorial waters."[15] According to the principal proresolution speaker, passage of the proposal would exert considerable pressure on the next Labour prime minister to call upon Washington to remove all American nuclear weapons stored or serviced in the United Kingdom, to deny port facilities to American warships armed with such weapons, and to bar the landing of U.S. planes carrying any type of unconventional armament. It was further noted that the aforementioned phrase in the resolution referring to British territorial waters was intended to preclude the several islands that make up the BIOT from becoming an American nuclear depot.

The resolution secured the support of what one press report called a "large majority" of those present but since it failed to win the necessary two-thirds majority of all Labour delegates attending the conference, it was not included in their manifesto or platform. Not disheartened, the unilateralists remained committed to a nuclear-disarmed Great Britain and to insuring that British soil and British territorial waters would be free of American nuclear arms of whatever type. At Blackpool in August 1982, a similar motion was introduced to the conference, and it carried by a vote of 4,927,000 to 1,975,000, or 71.4 percent to 28.6 percent. For the first time in its history, the Labour party is committed to a no-nuclear defense policy as well as to the removal of all American nuclear weapons on British soil or in British waters.

In Great Britain the cause of unilateral nuclear disarmament attracts adherents from all points along the political spectrum. Tens of thousands are convinced that the government's reliance on nuclear weapons is an irrational policy that must be terminated and they are diligently working to see their views accepted by the majority. Despite the outcome of the 1983 British election, the issue of the role that British and American nuclear weapons should play in the country's defense strategy is not going to disappear. As long as the question remains a lively one, the Diego Garcia aspect of the controversy cannot be disregarded by Washington.

Skeptics may believe that the likelihood of a fundamental policy disagreement arising is slight and that no British government would press Washington on the Diego Garcia issue. Yet Britain's rights under the consultation provision of the 1976 agreement must be considered as a second line of attack if and when there is a British decision to deny to the United States the right to use the base as a nuclear facility in the Indian Ocean.

Consultation

As noted, the 1976 agreement distinguishes between the use of Diego Garcia in normal military operations when pro forma exchanges of information between the senior British and American officers is required and, "in other circumstances," when a joint decision of the governments is a condition precedent. According to the wording of the article, London retains the right to disapprove of any proposed American operation at Diego Garcia provided it is unconventional, irregular, or not customary. Since the consultation provision does not appear in the two earlier agreements, it must be assumed that in the mid-1970s the Foreign Office became apprehensive about how their crown colony might be used by the U.S. Defense Department and the possible entangling consequences to the United Kingdom if Diego Garcia became the base for an operation that they considered outside the joint defense formula.

In the spring of 1980, the U.S. government made use of Diego Garcia in a manner that some observers concluded violated the consultation provision, and a well-controlled yet acrimonious diplomatic furor resulted. In late April, the Carter administration, preoccupied with revolutionary events taking place in Iran and concentrating on ways to bring about the release of American hostages in Tehran, launched a military operation to end the impasse. According to reports, Diego Garcia was used by American troops on their way to the ill-fated rescue attempt. The Pentagon neither notified London beforehand nor sought authorization to use the base in the attempt to upset the policies of the anti-Western government of the Ayatollah Khomeini. In Britain, America's use of the island was categorized as extraordinary, one that fell outside the scope of a "normal military operation," and therefore requiring consultation.

The left-wing British press, along with several Labour members of the House of Commons, raised the issue publicly and vented their anger and resentment that Washington disregarded what to them was a clear, unambiguous obligation. Prime Minister Thatcher declined to confirm or deny reports that Diego Garcia had been a refueling stop for planes carrying equipment used in the rescue attempt, and she also managed to cut off further debate for the remaining days that the Commons was in session. Her parliamentary tactics won her the respect of many, but those resentful of the alleged violation continued to press the government for further details, again without success.

Less than a week later the Diego Garcia consultation issue reappeared and created an even greater rumpus in Britain. This time various British newspapers reported that the Carter administration, acting unilaterally and again without London's concurrence, had dispatched seven fully loaded ships of the U.S. Navy to Diego Garcia as part of its plan for a second try at freeing the hostages. Those frustrated at their earlier failure to open a public debate on the consultation issue used the new information to denounce the government. The *Morning Star,* for example, claimed there was "a panic in Whitehall" after the news of the seven ships was received.[16] The *Guardian* charged that "the Americans appear to have dropped a large diplomatic brick by moving first and informing an ally afterwards." It went on to state that "the Americans have an obligation to inform London of all military operations in the category of 'routine movements,' but anything on a larger scale must, under the treaty, involve advance consultation and the agreement of the British Government." It was the *Guardian*'s position that an investigation was necessary to determine "whether Washington went through the required consultation process with London over the dispatch of the seven ship task force."[17]

No such inquiry took place. Officials in London and Washington released statements that the Thatcher government had acquiesced in the program of pre-positioning ships and supplies at Diego Garcia. Left unclear, and even today unanswered, is the question of whether the United States had received British permission to make Diego Garcia the main base of operation for the Rapid Deployment Force prior to the dispatch of the ships and equipment.

With regard to the nuclear weapons issue, if it is assumed that the U.S. Defense Department deploys nuclear weapons in the Indian Ocean and South Asia intermittently for training purposes and not on a regular basis, the 1976 consultation provision could become troublesome. More specifically, a future British government, seeking to divorce its strategic policies from all direct or indirect reliance on nuclear arms, might decide to apply the consultation provision narrowly and without regard to earlier diplomatic whitewash. By interpreting "normal circumstances" to exclude the use of nuclear weapons in military operations, London could insist that every time an American nuclear weapon of whatever description was headed for Diego Garcia approval had to be secured beforehand. Such a procedure would, in effect, give London the power to determine, limit, or curtail United States military operations in this part of the world, a condition that Pentagon officials could not accept. In peacetime training exercises or regular day-to-day operations, such a limitation would have to lessen the military proficiency of America's armed forces; in a crisis, it could become an oppressive, pernicious limitation.

Continuing British Involvement in the Indian Ocean

In both the 1972 and 1976 agreements the termination provision grants the United States rights on Diego Garcia provided BIOT remains in existence. If for any reason the Privy Council revokes its order establishing the crown colony or the government otherwise disposes of the possession, the joint British-American defense arrangement would exist in name only. Because of Great Britain's newly acquired military responsibilities in the South Atlantic, along with a declining naval capability, the BIOT may be less of a permanent political entity than is generally supposed.

In 1965 when BIOT was established, Great Britain was engaged in withdrawing from its traditional Indian Ocean/Persian Gulf sphere of influence and bringing to a close its military predominance in that part of the world. Its military services, particularly the Royal Navy, remained sizable but markedly smaller and less varied than in former times. In the intervening years, the country's military power has shrunk and, concomitantly, the geographical areas where Britain is able to contribute to Western military efforts to maintain peace have also diminished. Today, the Indian Ocean and South Asia generally must be considered a region of declining strategic importance to the United Kingdom. Thus, according to The Military Balance: 1981–82, Britain's naval power in the Indian Ocean consists of no permanently stationed units, only intermittent deployment of a total of four destroyers or frigates, and two supply ships.[18] Within the near future, even such a minimal naval deployment may be beyond the Admiralty's resources. Certainly the 1981 decision of the Thatcher government to reduce the Royal Navy's surface fleet by approximately one-half in the coming ten years will have global consequences. If the plan is implemented as introduced, London may have sufficient surface naval power to deploy only in areas of high priority, a pattern that will exclude the Indian Ocean.

The plan to shrink the Royal Navy to its smallest size in modern history was formulated before Great Britain and Argentina fought for control of the Falkland Islands. To assemble the shipping necessary to transport and protect the men and equipment needed in the South Atlantic, the Admiralty was forced to withdraw part of its fleet from the North Atlantic and its NATO assignments. Unconfirmed reports also maintain that the British Pacific fleet was cut back during the conflict. Because secure sea lanes in the North Atlantic are a vital consideration and the NATO marine commitment of major importance, Britain's fleet strength there has been returned to its prewar strength or nearly so, but it is questionable whether the same can be said of other areas around the world where British naval power has been deployed.

Britain's decision to retain sovereignty over the Falklands makes substantial logistical demands upon the Royal Navy. Units of the fleet that were formerly on-station elsewhere have been reassigned to the South Atlantic patrol. Having to make up the naval losses that were incurred in regaining the Falklands further weakens the Admiralty's overall naval power. Should the defense of other overseas possessions require the use of Britain's military forces, including the Royal Navy, it would mean a further cutback in British presence in regions that are of only nominal strategic and political importance. Here the Indian Ocean and the crown colony of BIOT immediately come to mind. BIOT is a possession situated in a region that is becoming superfluous to British security needs. Though the same might be said of the Falklands, the BIOT is a luxury that the country may no longer be able to afford. The emerging campaign of the new Mauritian government to regain the Chagos Archipelago could help decide the issue for the British.

Conclusion

The rivalry between the superpowers in the Indian Ocean has continued for more than fifteen years and there is no reason to believe that their campaigns to gain access to a chain of port/air facilities there will abate in the near future. Because both Washington and Moscow have vital interests to protect in the region, their future political-military maneuverings will be no less determined and intensive than in recent years. The efforts of the regional states to win acceptance for the zone-of-peace proposal notwithstanding, the Indian Ocean has become the latest arena of East-West contention and skirmishing. It is a region where territorial conflicts among the littoral and hinterland states remain unresolved and where uncompleted revolutions and increased militarization further complicate and restrict the superpowers' ability to influence regional affairs. Most significantly, the great size of the Indian Ocean makes it a region

450 INTERESTS OF EXTERNAL POWERS

where even one small military installation (one that is legally secure and politically dependable) is of inestimable importance to the maintenance of peace and security.

In 1965 the United States was fortunate enough to lease a mid-ocean site from which to deploy naval and air power, and where it can pre-position units and supplies of the RDF. Diego Garcia today is essential to America's military posture in the Indian Ocean and Middle East/Persian Gulf areas. It is an irreplaceable strategic asset, there being no other location in the region that can be easily acquired with anything approaching the political-military characteristics of Diego Garcia.

The Reagan administration, like Carter's before it, has negotiated with several littoral states to secure the right to station men and equipment in the region but its results to date have not been impressive. In all of the places where the Defense Department has managed to conclude a lease or otherwise gain access, there is the danger of becoming enmeshed in long-standing, seemingly unsolvable internal disputes or being drawn into the domestic affairs of politically troubled states.

On the Horn of Africa, for example, the port of Berbera is a most attractive strategic location for an American naval/air facility, but Somalia's irredentist policies and its unchanging determination to control the Ogaden and to even the score with Ethiopia, reduce significantly the attractiveness of this site. Pakistan is another country that controls strategically important territory, but it is internally unstable and has the added disability of sour relations with India. It would be poor strategy indeed, to lease sites in a country that could break up because of ethnic disharmony or could engage in a war with a more powerful neighbor.

Saudi Arabia has figured prominently in the Pentagon's program to establish a series of regional military facilities, but the government has declined to accept an American presence on its soil. Its neighbor, Oman, has been far less hostile to American plans for a lease of its ports and airfields, but is reported to have placed a series of restrictions and limitations on the use of Masirah Island, Salalah, and Matrah. More recently, there has been speculation about Trincomalee in northeast Sri Lanka, once described as the most glittering strategic port in all South Asia. However, it is most unlikely that the Defense Department will gain access to the port. A recent lease of the British-built oil storage facilities at Trincomalee to a subsidiary of an American corporation with obligations to the Pentagon was canceled by Colombo, apparently after the Indian government pressured Sri Lanka to withdraw. In any event, the eruption in 1983 of ethnic violence involving Sri Lanka's minority

Tamil population has probably served to make Washington wary of pressing for access to Trincomalee.

In sharp contrast, there is Diego Garcia: a British crown colony, despite the uncertainties surrounding issues of sovereignty and London's obligations to the former residents; an uninhabited island that, if kept in that condition, will remain free of coups, countercoups, and political protests; and a naval/air base that needs to be made more secure and less restricted for American military use. To this end, outstanding issues between the United States and Great Britain need to be resolved, specifically the sovereignty question, the permanence of BIOT, the ultimate fate of the Ilois, and the ambiguity surrounding the meaning of consultation. As an alternate course of action, the Pentagon might, after the first three issues have been resolved, determine that it is in America's national interest to purchase outright all the rights and liabilities that Great Britain acquired in 1965 when it took over the Chagos Archipelago.

25. Aspects of United States Naval Deployments in the Indian Ocean ☛ Alvin J. Cottrell

Since the implementation of Britain's decision to withdraw from "east of Suez" in 1971, there has been a steady debate over the size, quality, purpose, and consequences of American naval deployments in the Indian Ocean region. It is the purpose of this brief chapter to discuss certain important aspects of this controversy.

The United States established a naval presence in the Persian Gulf at Bahrain in 1949. Under the command of a rear admiral, this force, known as the Middle East Force (MEF), was established initially for the purpose of intelligence gathering independent of the British intelligence effort. Today, it also serves as a flag-showing mission, paying visits to the countries of the gulf and adjacent areas in an effort to establish cooperative relations with the states and peoples of the region. Although the gulf is the focal point of these activities, the ships making up the MEF deploy in a vast area extending from Pakistan to the East African littoral.[1]

Until 1971, the MEF was maintained at Bahrain with access to facilities used by the Royal Navy. Following the withdrawal of the British forces in November 1971, the United States negotiated an agreement with Shaikh Isa to "home-port" an American command ship and two destroyers at Bahrain. As a consequence of this agreement, the United States brought approximately five hundred naval personnel and dependents to the island.

Following the outbreak of the Arab-Israeli war in October 1973 and the subsequent boycott on the shipment of Arab oil to the United States, there was a change in the conditions of American access to Bahrain. Being practically dry of oil, Bahrain demonstrated its support for the Arab cause by giving notice of termination of its agreement with the United States. While this threatened to interrupt Washington's long-term access to Bahrain's facilities, the United States has since been able to negotiate a new executive agreement—not a treaty—that permits it to maintain a naval presence at the island for four (not necessarily consecutive) months a year. (The MEF is officially home-ported at Norfolk, Virginia, but permanently deployed in the Indian Ocean.) The destroyers or destroyer-type vessels visiting the facility must gain permission for access. Pursuant to the agreement, the U.S. Navy is authorized to maintain as many as five ships in the region and has in fact been maintaining a force of at least four ships over the past few years. In addition, Washington has been required to reduce its personnel on shore with the result that the number of Americans on Bahrain and associated with the facility now totals only about fifty. The Bahrainis have permitted the commander of the MEF to continue to live onshore near the facility and to maintain an aircraft at the Bahrain airport for travel in the region.

While America's relations with Bahrain have preserved the continuity of U.S. naval deployments in the Indian Ocean region, the full extent of these deployments remains, in some quarters at least, a matter of controversy. For over a decade a debate has continued as to whether American strategic submarines have been deployed in the area. Assertions in this direction were often made in the context of Soviet naval deployments into the region, the argument being that these were designed to counter the presence of American A-53 submarines.[2] American officials have never admitted such a presence; as a result, much of the discussion regarding deployments has been based on little more than speculation and conjecture. There is no evidence that the United States has ever stationed Polaris submarines in the Indian Ocean. American officials, in fact, do not acknowledge having Polaris submarines anywhere, although it is obvious that they are serviced by tenders at Rota, Spain, and Holy Loch, Scotland. Official positions aside, it is arguable that the deployment of Polaris submarines in the Indian Ocean is neither a necessary nor a cost-effective means of maintaining America's undersea deterrent posture. There is no American submarine tender in the ocean and this means that the sixty days during which a Polaris or Poseidon submarine can stay on-station is greatly curtailed by travel time to and from Rota or Holy Loch. Furthermore, the United States has sufficient targeting coverage of the Soviet Union with Polaris and Poseidon submarines on-station in the Pacific and the Atlantic and at the entrance to the Mediterranean. As one knowledgeable analyst from the Center of Naval Analysis, Robert Weinland, has written, "Western strategic strike forces are not now, and never have been, stationed in the Indian Ocean; and, given the exigencies of geography and the current and foreseeable strategic balance, there is little incentive for the West to place its offensive capabilities there. It could be done, of course, but it would cost more than it would buy."

In addition to the conjecture over submarine deployments, there has been a debate in the United States over the need for a permanent American naval presence in the Indian Ocean in addition to the modest Middle East Force. Opponents of a permanent presence have consistently argued that it is unnecessary and, more important, that it would bring about a naval arms race with the Soviet Union. On occasion they have gone so far as to say that such an arms race could lead to war between the superpowers. It was the fear of such an eventuality that motivated much of the opposition to establishment in the 1970s of the modest American naval facilities on the British-owned Indian Ocean island of Diego Garcia. With the fall of the shah in Iran and the Soviet invasion of Afghanistan, the debate over the need for an American presence came to an end, to be replaced by a controversy over the nature and purpose of U.S. forces in the region.

The type of American forces needed in the Persian Gulf and the Middle East depends on an assessment of the threat to U.S. interests in the area. Is the threat primarily that of an overt Soviet military attack, or does it come, at least initially, from the deteriorating political stability of the region?

Although the Soviets have large ground, air, and naval forces close to the Middle East and have shown a willingness to use them in the invasion of Afghanistan, it is unlikely they would risk a direct military invasion in the gulf area. Moscow realizes that the West has vital interests in the region and that the exact nature of a Western response to overt aggression cannot be predicted with any certainty. The Soviets would prefer to manipulate events indirectly rather than march to the gulf.

It is the present political instability in the gulf, which has increased rapidly since the shah's demise, that poses the immediate threat to American (as well as to European and Japanese) interests. Any increase in political instability would bring about a situation in which continued

Western access to the region's oil reserves and, therefore, the survival of Western economies would certainly be in danger. This could happen if the Soviet Union exploited regional instability for its own purposes or even if additional local leaders who are anti-Western, such as another Khomeini or Qadhafy, came to power. Much of the inherent instability of the region stems from the many ethnic groups and tribes that abound throughout the area. Iran itself is composed of six different nations, as well as a number of tribes. Regional conflicts such as the Iraq-Iran war, which are largely divorced from the East-West framework, also pose a great danger to Western interests, especially access to gulf oil resources.

How stable are the regimes of the gulf, and how stable are they likely to be in the future? Other contributors to this volume address this issue in detail. In brief, it can be noted that a king rules in Saudi Arabia, a sultan in Oman, and ten shaikhs and emirs in the United Arab Emirates, Qatar, Bahrain, and Kuwait. Until 1979, the shah ruled in Iran. Only in Iraq have nonroyal rulers been in power for very long. But there are many reasons to doubt whether the present state of affairs in the gulf can last. Now that there are nontraditional regimes in both Iran and Iraq, over three-fourths of the population of the gulf are ruled by nonroyal leaders, in other words, about 48 million of approximately 60 million people. In this respect the Iranian Revolution was an important turning point away from traditional methods of rule. The fall of such a powerful monarch and the actions of the regime that succeeded him have contributed significantly to the political erosion and fragility of the gulf. The key state in the Persian Gulf region is Saudi Arabia because of its vast oil resources and the influence it exerts on the smaller gulf states. If it were to shift from royal rule, this might well put continued Western access to oil resources of the area in doubt.

Since the fall of the shah and the Soviet invasion of Afghanistan, America's presence in the region has been massive, certainly in terms of deployed naval forces. On a largely continuous basis the U.S. Navy maintains two carrier battle groups in the Indian Ocean composed of two large attack carriers and thirty or more other surface naval vessels. In addition, steps have been taken to enhance substantially the infrastructure of bases in Kenya, Oman, and Somalia, while four Airborne Warning and Control System (AWACS) aircraft have been deployed to Saudi Arabia.

Much of the impetus for the large increase in U.S. naval deployments was created by the Soviet invasion of Afghanistan. Although there is much evidence to suggest that the Soviets almost certainly intervened to head off the humiliation that would flow from the defeat of a Soviet client state in Afghanistan, the invasion was perceived by many as the harbinger of a larger Soviet thrust into the Persian Gulf. In the United States the fear of such a Soviet push was an important factor in generating widespread support for an enlarged U.S. military presence in the region.

It is symptomatic of a problem that has troubled the making of American security policy for decades that policy makers do not always understand the importance of preventive military deployments. Naval deployments especially can play a key role in undergirding regional stability and inhibiting rapid and destabilizing political change. If the United States had taken this course in the Indian Ocean prior to 1979, it might have slowed down some of the threats to regional stability and halted the process of political erosion before it gained momentum. At the time, those who opposed the projection of American force argued that naval forces carry little political influence. Following the Iranian Revolution and the Soviet move into Afghanistan, however, they seemed to contradict themselves by suggesting that a tenfold increase in America's naval presence would have put an end to the erosion of political stability. If naval forces can help impede the spread of political instability, they should have been used for that purpose before the situation deteriorated. Now the problem is one of countering the erosion of political stability among the gulf states rather than one of reinforcing the more desirable previous situation.

The destruction of the Iranian monarchy has significantly increased the threat to the Saudi monarchy, on which the United States depends for much of its oil supply. The main question now is whether a permanent, large-scale American naval presence can deter the threat to the Saudi regime. While Saudi Arabia is the key to U.S. interests, its protection requires an approach that emphasizes the broad regional context of security. In other words, America's credibility in the eyes of the Saudis can only be established on the basis of a regional military presence, not just as a function of their bilateral relationship. Washington realizes this, as demonstrated by existing efforts to reinforce Western interests in Saudi Arabia and the gulf, not only through the deployment of naval forces but with longer-range plans to establish the Rapid Deployment Force (RDF) and by the search for air and naval facilities capable of providing support for U.S. military actions in the future. The nagging question that hovers over these efforts is whether they will be able to reverse the political erosion in the gulf that has already occurred.

The improvement of basing structures has not only strengthened America's logistics posture in the region but it has increased Washington's political and military credibility with the states of the Arabian Peninsula, especially Saudi Arabia. Given the complex political considerations that determine the Saudis' attitude toward the acquisition of military facilities abroad and/or rights of access to such facilities, it has not been easy for Washington to establish a workable bilateral relationship with Riyadh. Even so, there are signs that the United States has had some success in changing the perceptions of Saudi leaders as to the credibility of the American security guarantee. In the wake of the Iranian Revolution and the Soviet invasion of Afghanistan, the Saudis developed serious reservations over Washington's determination to defend its own and Western interests in the area. In part, the change in attitude can be attributed to the large-scale naval deployment in the Arabian Sea. Reassured by America's conscientious efforts to create a viable security force in the region, the Saudis have been willing to accept closer association with U.S. military policy. One manifestation of this is Riyadh's acceptance of four AWACS aircraft; another is the cooperation that exists between the two capitals in efforts to resolve the complex problems of the Middle East. The U.S. decision to enlarge the Saudi arms program by the sale of five AWACS aircraft and seven KC-135 aerial tankers is still another positive step toward enhancing Saudi acceptance of a greater U.S. military involvement in the defense of the gulf.

As already indicated, the defense of the gulf, and especially of the Kingdom of Saudi Arabia, must be placed in the broadest geographical context. Only the United States has the military capability to confront the Soviet Union with risks so great that they might be expected to act as a deterrent to Soviet adventurism. If this deterrent is to remain credible in the Indian Ocean there is little substitute, at least for the foreseeable future, for the maintenance of a large American naval presence in the Arabian Sea, that is to say, one of about the current magnitude.

The deployment of a sizable naval task force in the Indian Ocean has, however, been carried out at the expense of the navy's commitments in the Pacific and the Mediterranean. Sixty-five percent of the Indian Ocean task force consists of vessels from the Seventh Fleet in the western Pacific, with the balance being drawn from the Sixth Fleet in the Mediterranean. If this situation is permitted to continue for too long it could well undermine the navy's capability to fulfill commitments in these vital areas. In particular, a stretching of resources and a decline in operational levels would challenge the integrity of U.S. commitments in the Far East and the defense of specific interests in Japan, Korea, the Philippines, and perhaps even in the People's Republic of China.

As effective as Washington has been in preparing for military contingencies and in reassuring its friends in the region, it is arguable that more should be done to enhance the capabilities of the RDF in the area, especially by pre-positioning measures. At present, the ships pre-positioned at Diego Garcia consist of six marine roll-on/roll-off ships, three 11,000-ton dry cargo ships, and four tankers for carrying fuel and water. This pre-positioned force of thirteen ships will sustain three Marine brigades for about forty-five days, sufficient time to enable the establishment of suitable supply lines, should this be necessary. However, it leaves unresolved the issue of reaction time. Although nearer at hand than any other American facility, the pre-positioning of forces at Diego Garcia, thousands of miles from the gulf—and for that matter from any other likely trouble spot in the area—still jeopardizes its military value. Pre-positioning enables the United States to accommodate local sensitivities by avoiding stationing of forces on foreign soil. For this reason, it is especially suitable for the extremely sensitive Persian Gulf/Arabian Sea area, particularly during the beginning stages of deploying a permanent presence in the area. It would be wise for the United States to take advantage of this flexibility and attempt to encourage one of the gulf states to allow these floating warehouses to anchor in an area under its sovereignty. This would substantially improve reaction time and ensure the availability of supplies for emergencies anywhere in the northwest quadrant of the Indian Ocean.

The RDF has been widely criticized as the Carter administration's version of the "free lunch" and as a "hollow shell." Yet it is a step in the right direction. The United States cannot rely on the RDF alone and will need to continue with efforts to rebuild its naval forces and logistics capabilities. While the achievement of these goals is still a long way off, they are important priorities if Washington is to be able to demonstrate to its friends and adversaries that it is serious about coping with security problems in the Indian Ocean region. At a minimum, the RDF must be capable of ensuring that the United States does not face a fait accompli in the Persian Gulf/Arabian Peninsula area. In this respect it will be necessary for America to get to the scene of any emergency first and with sufficient force to make the Soviet Union wary of the risks involved in attempting a forced removal. The force that is initially in position will almost always have an inherent advantage as the other side will have to assume the risks of escalating the conflict.

The immediate cry of some academicians to the above will be that it offers a military response to sociopolitical problems. Those arguing this view fail to understand that the navy has two roles, one as a political instrument of foreign policy, the other as a war-fighting instrument. At present the U.S. Navy is being utilized in the Indian Ocean in its peacetime mode as a political instrument, protecting American security interests by encouraging greater political stability in the area.

26. Soviet Interests in the Persian/Arabian Gulf ▰
Oles M. Smolansky

This chapter examines the importance that the Soviet Union has attached to the Persian/Arabian Gulf and, beyond it, to the adjacent Middle East and Indian Ocean regions.

The Historical Record

The historical record of imperial Russian and Soviet policies toward the Persian Gulf and the Middle East is often used to present Russia as an expansionist power that has consistently pursued an aggressive policy designed to gain physical control over the region to its south. In particular, it is often argued that Russia seeks to secure an outlet to the warm-water ports of the Mediterranean (via the Turkish straits) and the Persian/Arabian Gulf.[1] One of the problems with this interpretation is that, in emphasizing the generalities, it tends to overlook the peculiarities of the various episodes of Russian/Soviet involvement in Turkey, Iran, and Afghanistan. Put more directly, such expositions are based partly on fact and partly on fiction.

It is undeniable that Russia's imperial expansion, unlike that of many of the Western powers, was confined to geographically contiguous territories. In the process, vast areas of Asia were incorporated into the empire. Soviet leaders, too, have from time to time given ample evidence of their interest in the Soviet Union's southern neighbors. It must, however, be borne in mind that to have aspirations and to be able to implement them are two very different things. Politics has always been the art of the possible and not of the desirable. This statement applies equally to imperial Russia and the Soviet Union and is just as true today as it has been in the past. Thus, one may well argue that access to and control of the Persian/Arabian Gulf have been viewed by both Saint Petersburg and Moscow as worthwhile objectives, to be sought and, it is hoped, gained in appropriate circumstances. The problem, from the Russian point of view, has been that, with the exception of a few isolated incidents, the prospects of achieving these goals have been either very slim or totally nonexistent. Conversely, on those few occasions when action might have been contemplated seriously, Russia either encountered insurmountable obstacles and, therefore, backed off or found the price it would have to pay to gain its objective unacceptable. The episodes of British and, after 1945, American determination to keep imperial Russia/the Soviet Union out of the gulf fall into the first category; Hitler's 1940 proposal on spheres of influence belongs to the second.

It is also important to note that the historical record—even if it is purged of such "facts" as the alleged aspirations of Peter the Great—serves as a useful but limited point of reference. It does not take into account the entirely different circumstances in which the Soviet Union (along with every other state in the international community) has had to operate after the advent of the nuclear age. Specifically, the availability to the superpowers (and, now, to other states) of nuclear weapons and their means of delivery has totally changed the Soviet leaders' perception of the nature of outside threats to their country's national security. The same is true of Moscow's view of the means at its disposal both to counter perceived threats and to advance its own interests in other parts of the world. For one thing, a major military confrontation with the United States has been ruled out as a viable policy option. This has meant that Soviet determination to compete with Washington and its allies will not be permitted to get out of hand if the Kremlin has any control over the events at all. The same conclusion applies also to the means available to Moscow to secure and advance its interests outside the Soviet sphere of influence. In other words, large-scale and direct military interventions can be undertaken in Eastern Europe but not in regions such as the gulf, long regarded by the West as vital to its survival.

The invasion of Afghanistan does not contradict this basic premise. In the late 1940s Kabul's attempts to join the projected pro-Western security system in the Middle East were turned down by the United States. Since then, and until the communist take-over in 1978, Afghanistan had emerged in the context of the East-West struggle as a political "no-man's land," a characterization that is not intended to justify the Soviet invasion but simply to emphasize the point that, in the Kremlin's evaluation of the situation, the Soviet Union was not treading on any vital Western interests. Moreover, as I have argued elsewhere,[2] Moscow's military intervention in Afghanistan was not the first step on the long march into Iran, Pakistan, and the gulf oil fields, but rather a move to deal with a particular situation that the Kremlin had found unacceptable.

In short, the advent of nuclear weapons, coupled with growing Soviet dependence on Western capital, technology, and trade, have imposed restrictions on the conduct of Moscow's foreign relations that no sane Kremlin leadership is in a position to disregard. The record shows that it has, in fact, not done so. On the contrary, in their dealings with the Western allies, Khrushchev, Brezhnev, and their associates have staked their political reputations on adhering to policies of peaceful co-existence and detente. The latter concept, in particular, is built on three pillars: the absence of nuclear war, continued and widening economic cooperation with the West, and concomitant political competition with the "capitalist system," especially its leading power, the United States. This last Soviet policy has been widely criticized as inherently contra-dictory, if not outright hypocritical. How could the Soviet Union expect to improve economic relations and to negotiate various arms limitation agreements while, at the same time, working to undermine the political interests of those whose economic cooperation Moscow has so eagerly sought? The answer to this question, which the Soviets themselves have explained in terms of the continuing and "inevitable" competition be-tween capitalism and socialism, is not really to be found in Marxist dogma. Rather, the policy of detente reflects the Kremlin's insistence that nuclear parity and the accumulation of substantial conventional military power should be translated into political equality with the United States.

Soviet policies in the Middle East and Africa provide excellent il-lustrations of this proposition. Thus, since the early Khrushchev period, Moscow has persistently sought Washington's recognition of the Soviet Union as a superpower with its own legitimate interests in the Middle East. Time and again, these Soviet overtures have been snubbed by the United States, a state of affairs that the Kremlin leaders find unreason-able, demeaning, and therefore unacceptable.

It is for this reason that various American attempts to "rein in" Moscow have met with failure. One of the more prominent of such ef-forts was Secretary of State Kissinger's "linkage" approach. It rested on the assumption that the Kremlin could be "bought off" by improved economic and trade relations with the West. In the view of Soviet lead-ers, however, business should not be equated with politics. The former is conducted for the mutual benefit of the parties concerned without any regard to their respective politico-military status. Politics, in con-trast, is a relationship between either equals or dominant and subservi-ent parties. An attempt at linking economic cooperation to international behavior *acceptable to the United States* clearly implied that Washing-ton considered itself the dominant power, imposing its will on the weaker Russians. The Soviet leaders, immensely proud of their achieve-ments and highly sensitive about their country's status as one of the world's superpowers, could not accept offers of economic cooperation with political strings attached.

In brief, Moscow's and Washington's respective perceptions of the nature of their relationship leave little room for political compromise, that is, for the establishment of a political climate in which some of their cardinal differences could be resolved to the satisfaction of both parties. This state of affairs is reflected in the superpower rivalry in areas outside their traditional spheres of influence, namely in Asia, the Middle East (including the gulf), Africa, and, to a limited extent, Latin America.

Soviet Interests

For analytical purposes, the Soviets' post–World War II interests in the Middle East as well as in the regions and waters surrounding it can be broken down along both issue (or substantive) and chronological lines. Put differently, the perceptions of interests that, for the sake of convenience, will be classified as military, political, and economic, have been functions of time and space, as well as of the personalities of the various Soviet leaders. For example, although the preoccupation with national security has remained a constant theme in Moscow's post-1945 activities in the Middle East, the nature of the perceived threat has undergone constant change (and has required constant policy readjustments) due to technological advances in the production of strategic weapons systems, rapidly changing political and socioeconomic realities in the region itself, and the different modi operandi of men like Stalin, Khrushchev, and Brezhnev. Needless to say, similar observations apply to Moscow's political and economic interests in the Middle East as well.

Military interests

A major threat to Soviet security developed with the onset of the cold war when, in response to Stalin's demands for the Turkish Straits and other territories in the Mediterranean, his aggressive behavior in Iran, and his presumed involvement in the communist uprising in Greece, the United States established its naval presence in the Mediterranean (1946) and proclaimed the Truman Doctrine (1947). In the ensuing years, the Sixth Fleet, whose strike aircraft were capable of delivering nuclear bombs to Soviet targets, was permanently stationed in the eastern Mediterranean, accompanied by the deployment of Strategic Air Command bombers to Moroccan, Libyan, Saudi Arabian, and Turkish bases. During the Khrushchev period, the U.S. position was further strengthened by the introduction of Jupiter medium-range missiles into Italy and Turkey. Upon their withdrawal in 1962, the United States introduced into the eastern Mediterranean Polaris strategic nuclear submarines.

Combined with overall U.S. nuclear superiority over the Soviet Union, these measures required a concerted Soviet effort to neutralize what to the Kremlin leaders seemed a major threat to their country's national security. Moscow's efforts took various forms, among them the crash development of the Soviet Union's own nuclear arsenal and the revamping of a defensive navy into a modern "blue-water" force capable of neutralizing the U.S. Navy and nuclear underwater delivery systems on the high seas, and of delivering nuclear strikes against enemy targets from the world's oceans. In the context of the Middle East, this meant, above all, the projection of Soviet naval and air power into the Mediterranean and, after the advent of longer-range Polaris 3-A and Poseidon nuclear submarines, into the Arabian Sea and the Indian Ocean generally. To be effective, however, Soviet naval units, deployed at great distances from their home bases in the Black Sea, the Baltic, and the Pacific, required access to naval (and, in view of the initial absence of aircraft carriers, also air) bases in the littoral states. These considerations explain, in part, Moscow's persistent efforts to befriend a number of strategically located developing countries, among them Egypt, Syria, Algeria, Libya, Iraq, the People's Democratic Republic of Yemen (PDRY), Somalia (later replaced by Ethiopia), Mozambique, Angola, Guinea, and Vietnam.

At first glance, it could be argued that some of these far-flung Soviet efforts were crowned with considerable success. By the late 1960s, construction of the new Soviet navy was well under way. Moscow also appeared to be firmly entrenched in the eastern Mediterranean. Although Libya and Algeria refused to open their facilities to the Soviet navy and air force, naval and air bases had been made available by Egypt. A friendly regime in Damascus assured access to Syrian ports. Aerial surveillance and attack capabilities acquired in Egypt, coupled with the presence of Soviet hunter-killer submarines and other antisubmarine warfare systems could, by 1971, be said to have affected American ability to launch nuclear strikes against the Soviet Union from the eastern Mediterranean. In spite of these "encouraging" developments, however, the Kremlin had not moved any closer to its coveted objective of neutralizing U.S. underwater strategic capabilities deployed in the general vicinity of the Middle East. As mentioned earlier, the technological advances that the Polaris 3-A and Poseidon nuclear submarines represented made the Soviet Union vulnerable to strikes from the western Mediterranean, the Atlantic, and the Arabian Sea.

The argument that the United States had not deployed these longer-range strategic nuclear submarines in the Arabian Sea or the

Indian Ocean is irrelevant in the context of this discussion. Military planners, regardless of their political persuasion, must assess an adversary's strength on the basis of his capabilities and not of his intentions. In addition, it was apparent that the United States could have introduced the Polaris 3-AS and the Poseidons into the Arabian Sea and the Indian Ocean at any time it so desired. The necessary communications network, consisting of facilities in northwestern Australia and in prerevolutionary Ethiopia, was well in place by the late 1960s. After the revolution in Addis Ababa and the forced American evacuation of Asmara, Ethiopia's place in the network was taken by Diego Garcia, which has since been developed into a major U.S. naval and air stronghold in the Indian Ocean. Moscow's own frantic search for support facilities finally netted it the Berbera base in Somalia (lost in 1976, as a result of the Kremlin's decision to support Ethiopia in the war over the possession of the Ogaden province), and naval and air bases in the PDRY. Thus, in the 1970s, Aden emerged as Moscow's bastion in the Arabian Sea.[3]

In the Persian Gulf, the Soviets have been far less successful. Among the littoral states, Iran and Kuwait have generally maintained correct relations with Moscow. However, only Iraq has been sufficiently intimate with the Kremlin to be approached with requests for naval facilities. Contrary to many reports circulating in the 1970s, Baghdad has consistently rebuffed these Soviet overtures despite a relatively close political association with Moscow and a heavy dependence on Soviet arms. In the late 1960s and early 1970s, a number of Soviet warships visited Umm Qasr, a practice that has been discouraged by the Iraqi leadership since 1975. This is particularly noteworthy in light of the permanent deployment of a small U.S. naval force from Bahrain.

In the overall context of the Soviet-American rivalry of the post–World War II period, the Soviet Union had achieved nuclear parity with the United States by the early 1970s. It had also made great strides in developing and deploying a modern oceanic navy (including a fleet of strategic nuclear submarines) and in partially neutralizing the older Polaris-type vessels. The latter observation does not, however, apply to America's newer long-range underwater strategic delivery systems or, it would appear, to American surface naval power operating outside the reach of Soviet land-based aircraft. For these reasons, the projection of Moscow's naval power into the Indian Ocean, backed by the bases in the PDRY and Vietnam, may have netted the Kremlin some political benefits but has so far fallen short of the desired goal of neutralizing the U.S. naval presence in that part of the world.

Political interests

After 1953, the Soviet Union undertook a concerted effort to befriend a number of prominent Third World states. Breaking out of the self-imposed isolation of the late Stalin period, Khrushchev waged a relentless campaign to win over to his side those neutralist leaders who refused to tie their countries to what he called the "imperialist chariot." In offering the newly independent nations Soviet military and economic assistance, he attempted to widen the gap between the developing world and the "decaying capitalist West." Khrushchev believed that success in this major undertaking would secure important gains for the Soviet Union. Militarily, the Kremlin expected to acquire naval and air facilities for the use of its armed forces or, at the very least, to deny them to the Western powers. Either way, it was reasoned, the positions of "imperialism" would be greatly weakened. Khrushchev assumed, correctly, that acceptance of Moscow's aid would cause the foreign policies of the "noncommitted" countries to become more anti-Western and pro-Soviet. He was also hoping that the leaders of the developing states would, in time, become convinced of the superiority of the communist socioeconomic model over its Western capitalist counterpart. With this in mind, Stalin's successor never tired of lecturing his bemused (and sometimes annoyed) Asian and African listeners on the advantages of "scientific socialism."

Khrushchev's main achievement, in the context of this discussion, lay in his contribution to the destabilization of Western positions in a number of prominent neutralist states. By providing them with Soviet military, political, and economic assistance, the Kremlin enabled the nationalist leaders of Egypt, Iraq, Syria, and other nations to pursue their interests without undue regard to Western sensibilities. It is equally noteworthy, however, that, prior to 1964, the Soviet Union did not succeed in acquiring military facilities in the Third World or in attracting new converts to Marxism-Leninism. This was not particularly surprising since relations between Moscow and its client states in Asia and Africa were seen by the indigenous nationalist leaders as a marriage of convenience—everyone was pursuing his own interests and was using the other side to protect and advance them. In any event, in the early 1960s Khrushchev came under increasing criticism at home for squandering Soviet resources in the pursuit of ephemeral and intangible gains. Even more significant, Moscow's involvement in the affairs of the Third World had entangled it in regional and local disputes that the Kremlin was ill-equipped to handle, let alone control.

Brezhnev and his associates conducted a more balanced and selective search for possible client states in Asia and Africa. In the Middle East, Soviet attention centered on nations that had well-established anti-Western credentials *and* could be of practical use to the Kremlin. Leading among them were Nasser's Egypt, as well as Syria and post-1968 Iraq, governed by rival branches of the Baath party. In addition, Moscow made a concerted effort to woo Algeria, postrevolutionary Libya, the PDRY, and, in the Horn of Africa, Somalia.

This Soviet involvement, sweetened by generous injections of military and (where applicable) economic assistance, paid off in a number of short-run successes. Thus, in the late 1960s, Egypt placed some of its naval and air bases at the disposal of the Soviets. In the 1970s, such facilities were also made available by Somalia and the PDRY. All in all, however, Moscow's record is far from impressive. The Soviet air force was evicted from Egypt in 1972, followed by the navy four years later. A similar fate befell the Somalian bases, and only the PDRY, economically dependent on the Soviet Union, remains a trustworthy client, having placed its facilities at the Kremlin's disposal. Ethiopia may develop into a major asset in the current decade, but its radical government, beleaguered by serious domestic political and economic problems, is facing an uncertain future.

The Kremlin's most important client in the gulf has been the Baathist regime in Iraq. The checkered history of Moscow-Baghdad relations in the 1970s and early 1980s offers interesting insights into the problems that the Soviets have encountered in their efforts to attract and exploit a leading "socialist," nonaligned, and openly anti-Western Arab state. Having benefited greatly from Soviet economic and military largesse during their early years, while endeavoring to resolve such major economic and political difficulties as the drives to nationalize the country's petroleum industry and to settle the Kurdish question, the Iraqi Baathists in the 1970s moved away from their close association with Moscow. The decision to do so was greatly facilitated by economic independence, achieved after the nationalization of the Iraqi Petroleum Company and the sharp rise in the price of oil, and by the temporary resolution of differences with neighboring Iran. Among other things, the 1975 Baghdad-Tehran accord resulted in the defeat of the Kurdish insurgents.

Its newly acquired wealth, combined with the end of the civil war, made Iraq independent of the Soviet Union economically and politically. To be sure, Baghdad was still dependent on Moscow as a major supplier of arms but, since it could either purchase Soviet weapons or barter petroleum for them, the once one-sided relationship became a mutually beneficial arrangement. In the late 1970s, Baghdad asserted its independence of Moscow in a number of different ways. Domestically, the Baathists initiated a process of liquidation of the Iraqi Communist party, at one point the most powerful Arab Marxist organization. The Kremlin objected but to no avail. Economically, Iraq's massive development program relied mainly on Western technology and expertise, a course of action publicly justified on the grounds that the quality of the "capitalist" goods and services was superior to those provided by the Soviet Union and its East European satellites. Even in its weapons acquisition program, Baghdad made a concerted effort to diversify, purchasing substantial quantities of modern arms from Western countries, especially France.

In its foreign relations, too, while remaining staunchly anti-American, Iraq moved to establish an independent position and did not hesitate to criticize the Soviets publicly for their policy in the horn, their support of Syria, their stand in the Arab-Israeli conflict, and their invasion of Afghanistan. Last but not least, in the context of gulf politics, Baghdad has maintained that the region should be cleared of the presence of all outside powers and has discouraged Soviet naval visits to Iraqi ports. It has been this stand that, more than any other single factor, has prevented Moscow from acquiring a foothold in the Persian/Arabian Gulf.

Little wonder, therefore, that in 1980 and 1981 the Kremlin refused to support Iraq in its war against Iran even though, as early as 1972, Moscow and Baghdad had entered into a twenty-year Treaty of Friendship and Cooperation. Soviet and bloc arms deliveries to Iraq were not discontinued entirely but their quantities remained limited, falling far short of the demands advanced by high Iraqi functionaries during their periodic "business" visits to Moscow. Baghdad's anger was fueled also by the reported transfers to Iran of Soviet-made weapons by Syria and Libya and by the sale of additional arms by North Korea, transactions that, the Iraqis assumed, would not have taken place without the Kremlin's approval. Politically, too, Moscow took great pains to disassociate itself from Baghdad. In his speech before the Twenty-sixth Party Congress, Brezhnev described the war as "fratricidal" and called for its early end. The conflict has since been labeled in the Soviet press as "senseless bloodshed," contrary to the interests of both nations.[4]

In distancing itself from Baghdad, Moscow was not just displaying its disenchantment with the Iraqi leadership. The Soviets were also sending a message to Iran's Islamic leaders: that Moscow was prepared to dump Iraq in favor of the revolutionary regime in Tehran in the manner of the switch from Somalia to Ethiopia effected during the horn conflict of 1977. If this analysis of the Kremlin's intentions is correct, Moscow's gambit, though successful in the horn, failed in the gulf. For one thing, the deeply religious and fervently anticommunist Ayatollah Khomeini was not another opportunistic Colonel Mengistu. Moreover, despite its early setbacks in the war against Iraq, Iran's shaky position could not have been compared to the quiet desperation of Ethiopia at a time when the Somali attack on the Ogaden province coincided with the country's political and economic disintegration.

In any event, considerable Soviet efforts to befriend the Ayatollah, combined with open demonstrations of disapproval of the Iraqi regime, have come to naught. In spite of Moscow's strong political support of Tehran during the hostage crisis with the United States and of concerted efforts to improve economic relations with Iran (they were, in fact, broadened considerably in 1980–82), the clerical regime has refused to discontinue its public attacks on Moscow. Labeled the "second great Satan," the Kremlin has been denounced not only for the atheism of its leaders but also for its invasion of Afghanistan. Backing words with action, Tehran has steadily assisted the anticommunist forces in Afghanistan, much to Moscow's dismay and in total disregard of Soviet pressure to stop aiding the "pro-imperialist bandits." In short, the refusal to adopt a pro-Iraqi stance in the war against Iran greatly angered Baghdad without netting the Kremlin any substantial benefits in Tehran. This state of affairs, coupled with the major change in the course of the war that, in 1982, witnessed the retreat of Iraqi forces from most Iranian territory and the Iranian advance into Iraq proper, prompted the Kremlin once again to alter its position. At the time of this writing, the deliveries of Soviet arms to Iraq appear to have been stepped up.

Elsewhere in the gulf, Kuwait has been the only other state to have established and maintained diplomatic relations with the Soviet Union (1963). In the ensuing years, Kuwait has signed agreements on economic and technical cooperation and, in 1977, made its initial purchase of Soviet arms. The cooperation has proved beneficial to both sides: Moscow has acquired Arab gulf support for some of its diplomatic initiatives while Kuwait has secured a measure of Soviet goodwill. This last commodity came in handy in the 1970s when it became necessary to check its large Palestinian population and, even more important, it has helped in relation to Iraq's periodic claims to parts of Kuwait's territory. The outwardly cordial relations have not, however, netted the Soviet Union access to any of the shaikhdom's military facilities. As far as is known, no such requests have been made. Kuwait, along with Iraq and the other gulf states, is opposed to outside military presence in the region. In the rest of the gulf, Moscow is mistrusted and disliked because of the widely shared aversion to communism and the fear of Soviet ambitions.

In the early 1980s, Western experts have devoted considerable attention to the possibility of the establishment of diplomatic relations between the Soviet Union and Saudi Arabia, the dominant economic and military power on the Arabian Peninsula. Western apprehension over such a development has been heightened by the fact that veiled interest in the idea has been expressed publicly not only in Moscow, which would clearly welcome such a move as a major step in increasing Soviet leverage and diminishing Western influence in the lower gulf, but also in Riyadh. While the Kremlin's motives are quite transparent, the objectives of Saudi Arabia are much more complex. In retrospect, it would appear that statements paying homage to the Soviet Union's leading role in world affairs and alluding to the possibilities of normalizing relations between the two states were aimed not so much at Moscow as at Washington. Specifically, unnerved by U.S. unwillingness to adopt an even-handed approach to the Arab-Israeli conflict, Riyadh has endeavored to exert pressure on the indecisive Reagan administration. It has done so by means of holding out the possibility of reopening diplomatic ties with the Soviet Union and of refusing to associate itself with President Reagan's efforts to attract the conservative Arab regimes to his "strategic consensus" concept for the Middle East. At this time, the Saudis seem to have reached their initial objective: in September 1982, Washington moved to modify its stand on the Arab-Israeli problems and hints at the resumption of Riyadh-Moscow relations are, for now, no longer being heard in the gulf region.

Economic interests

The direct and indirect economic advantages that the Soviet Union has derived from its association with the states of the Middle East appear substantial. In the latter category, the Soviets have long encouraged Arab and other major oil-producing countries to nationalize their respective Western-developed petroleum industries. The successful completion of this task in the 1970s has been hailed by Moscow as an enormous achievement certain to strengthen the economic and political independence of the producer nations and to weaken the "declining" Western capitalist system. However, it would be a mistake to ascribe the nationalization of the oil industries by the Third World governments to Soviet incitement. Instead, the rulers of Iraq, Iran, Saudi Arabia, and other states in and outside the gulf were pursuing their own interests regardless of how anybody else felt about them. It is true that the Kremlin's diplomatic and economic support had indeed been sought and gratefully acknowledged by Baghdad, one of the gulf's pioneers in the drive to nationalize its petroleum industry. But the initiative for this drastic action emanated from Iraq's national requirements as formulated by the Baathist leadership. In addition, the Soviet Union has not benefited greatly from the success of Baghdad's nationalization program. On the contrary, most of Iraq's exported oil has continued flowing to capitalist markets where it has been sold for hard currencies; only limited Soviet and satellite acquisitions have been tolerated by the authorities, usually in exchange for various goods and services. Indeed, the resulting financial gains have obviously served to strengthen Iraq's independence vis-à-vis its Soviet sponsor.

In related developments, the Kremlin also greeted enthusiastically the imposition of an oil embargo against some Western countries in the wake of the 1973 war and the quadrupling of petroleum prices instituted by the Organization of Petroleum Exporting Countries (OPEC) a short while later. Moscow's motives were evident: even a partial embargo was bound to hurt the West economically. The sharp rise in the price of oil could not only be confidently expected to exacerbate the difficulties experienced by the West but was also certain to benefit the Soviets directly, since in the 1970s the Soviet Union had emerged as a major petroleum exporter in its own right. By increasing its supplies to West European markets, where Soviet oil was sold for hard currency at or near the sharply higher market rate, Moscow was able to participate in the bonanza enjoyed by the major petroleum exporters.

It might be noted in passing that the sale of Soviet petroleum in Western Europe evoked considerable resentment in Baghdad. The latter let it be known that Iraqi oil, bartered for Russian arms and other equipment before 1974 at the rate of under $3 per barrel, was subsequently sold at four or more times that price. It was even rumored that Moscow was diverting some Iraqi petroleum to the United States, one of the countries subjected to the Arab embargo. Moscow denied both allegations, countering that only the Soviet Union's own oil had been sold to a number of West European nations. Iraq's petroleum, the Kremlin insisted, had been used strictly to satisfy the requirements of Soviet and satellite domestic consumption. In any case, since the Kremlin was breaching the embargo and simultaneously benefiting financially, its behavior was bitterly resented by the Arab producers.

The Soviets, along with the other major producers, have benefited greatly from the steep rise in the price of oil effected during the past decade. Of importance, in the context of this discussion, however, is the fact that the move to escalate the price of petroleum was initiated and sustained by OPEC not in response to Soviet exhortations but as a result of that organization's determination to exploit favorable market conditions. Moreover, the long-range interests of OPEC and of the other independent producers have consistently run counter to those pursued by the Kremlin. While the latter has publicly welcomed the enormous dislocations that the rise in the price of oil has inflicted on the Western economies, most of the leading OPEC members (above all Saudi Arabia) have endeavored to maintain the economic viability of the West. The motives of the majority of producers are quite plain: their own economic well-being, if not their very survival, depends on the existence of a stable and economically healthy Western community of nations.

No discussion of Soviet economic interests in the Persian Gulf would be complete without a reference to Moscow's alleged designs on the region's vast petroleum resources. Concern about the Kremlin's intentions has been reinforced by the findings contained in a number of reports prepared by the Central Intelligence Agency (CIA) in the late 1970s and early 1980s. Briefly, it has been argued that the Soviet Union's own production will peak sometime in the mid-1980s and then go into a period of slow decline. This state of affairs, combined with the growing energy needs of the Soviet and East European economies, will make it necessary for the Kremlin to supplement its own petroleum production with imports from abroad. The Persian/Arabian Gulf region, situated in geographic proximity to the Soviet Union, would be the primary and logical Soviet target. Such Western apprehensions, reinforced by the Iranian Revolution and Moscow's intervention in Afghanistan, resulted in the proclamation of the Carter Doctrine, subsequently also espoused by the Reagan administration, and in the creation of the Rapid Deployment Force (RDF). The Carter Doctrine stated specifically that the gulf constitutes a zone of vital Western interests and that any attempt at Soviet military intrusion will be met by force of arms. Without getting into a detailed analysis of the case presented by the CIA, it would appear that the Kremlin's ability to satisfy its and the Eastern bloc's energy requirements with oil in the late 1980s and beyond is indeed open to question.

These difficulties will be offset somewhat by an increase in the production of natural gas. In 1981, Soviet output was reported at 465 billion cubic meters, well above the target for that year.[5] A considerable boost to Soviet gas production is expected from the projected pipeline to Western Europe, whose capital and advanced technology are seen as contributing significantly to Moscow's endeavors to remain a major energy exporter for some time to come. These considerations help explain the Reagan administration's efforts to block the construction of the pipeline. The latter will not only facilitate the Kremlin's drive to expand Soviet energy production but will also earn Moscow tens of billions of badly needed dollars.

Critics of this negative U.S. stance have seen the pipeline controversy differently. Not only did Washington openly disregard the interests of its West European allies (with all that this attitude means to the future of the North Atlantic Treaty Organization), but it also demonstrated its failure to come to grips with the fundamental logical issue of future Soviet energy requirements. That is, should the Soviet Union eventually face the twin prospects of a decreased energy production and a correspondingly increased need to satisfy its own and its satellites' demands, would it not then be in the Western interest to assist Moscow in the exploitation of its own resources and, in so doing, to forestall or prevent a possible drive to the Persian/Arabian Gulf?

The pipeline issue aside, it remains to be noted that, although the Soviets' long-range energy future remains uncertain, possible difficulties in the years ahead should not automatically give rise to expectations of Soviet aggression. The latter, in view of the strong stand taken by the United States, could only be undertaken at the risk of an all-out war with the Western alliance, a course of action that the Kremlin, as noted, has ruled out as a viable policy option. This signifies that any possible future imports of petroleum from the gulf or any other region would have to be secured by peaceful means: through barter or outright purchase. In any case, Western efforts to thwart the Kremlin's attempts to maintain its energy independence probably increase the incentive for indirect Soviet "adventurism" in the Middle East.

The most important direct benefit that Moscow has derived from its association with the Middle East stems from the large-scale sales of modern arms to a number of Arab states. Leading among them have been Egypt (prior to its break with Moscow), Iraq, Syria, and Libya. Soviet weapons have also been delivered to the PDRY, the Palestine Liberation Organization, and, in the horn, to Somalia (before 1977) and Ethiopia (after 1977). While the military and political advantages secured by means of such transactions are open to question (with the clear exception of the PDRY), there can be no doubt that, economically, the Soviets have profited from the sale of arms. Having discontinued Khrushchev's practice of bartering modern weaponry for some relatively useless commodities (such as cotton) or of giving it away for nothing, the Brezhnev leadership endeavored to exchange arms for petroleum or to sell them for hard currency.

The magnitude of the Soviet effort is illustrated by the following data. According to the U.S. Arms Control and Disarmament Agency, in 1979 alone, the Soviet Union delivered to its Third World clients arms valued at $9.6 billion, far surpassing American exports of $5.1 billion.[6] Washington has since recaptured some of the market, but the Kremlin is still regarded as the world's leading arms exporter. Whether it will be able to retain this position in the years to come remains to be seen. In the meantime, the Reagan administration's determination to expand U.S. arms sales to developing nations, coupled with the abysmal performance of some of the sophisticated Soviet weapons systems during the 1982 Israeli invasion of Lebanon, cannot but negatively affect the volume of Moscow's arms exports.

Apart from the sale or barter (for petroleum) of military equipment, Moscow's most prominent Middle Eastern trading partner in the 1970s and early 1980s has been imperial and revolutionary Iran. The volume of trade rose sharply during the Tehran-Washington confrontation over the fate of American hostages and has continued its upward spiral since their release. As revealed by Pavel Demchenko, *Pravda's* seasoned analyst of Middle Eastern affairs, Soviet-Iranian trade in 1981 totaled $1.12 billion, compared to $0.94 billion in 1978, the last year of the shah's reign.[7] It is noteworthy, however, that even at the height of Tehran's dependence on the Soviet Union as the trade route to Western markets, the Islamic regime steadfastly refused to accede to Moscow's demands for a resumption of deliveries of Iranian natural gas—a commodity in which the Soviets are keenly interested—in accordance with the agreements negotiated prior to 1979.

The region's major recipient of Soviet economic and technological assistance has been the PDRY. Lacking in mineral resources and politically isolated from the rest of the Arabian Peninsula, the Marxist regime in Aden has developed a situation of almost total military, political, and economic dependence on the Soviet Union, a state of affairs that explains its current status as one of Moscow's staunchest supporters in the Third World. South Yemen's strategic location relative to the Persian Gulf, the Red Sea, and the western part of the Indian Ocean generally no doubt encourages Kremlin leaders to regard the considerable investment in the PDRY as eminently justifiable. Aden's allegiance, however, does not come cheaply. The PDRY has developed into a drain on Soviet resources almost comparable in magnitude to the cost of supporting Castro's Cuba.

In short, during the Brezhnev period, the economic significance of the Middle East to Moscow grew appreciably. Its importance, actual and potential, is not likely to diminish in the years to come.

Evaluation

As demonstrated above, in the course of its post-1945 involvement in the affairs of the Middle East and adjacent areas, the Soviet Union has pursued a number of separate but ultimately related interests, ranging across a broad spectrum of state activities and including military strategy, international politics, and economics. The purpose of many of these initiatives has been twofold: to undermine the positions of the capitalist West and, in the process, to strengthen the military, political, and economic power of the Soviet state. As of the early 1980s, the balance sheet is a mixed one at best. Thus, in the context of the military rivalry between the superpowers, Moscow could point to the projection of Soviet naval power into the Mediterranean and the Indian Ocean. Supported by major bases in Vietnam and South Yemen, the modern Russian blue-water navy can no longer be dismissed lightly in any calculations of U.S. military planners. On the negative side, the Soviets have lost access to the important Egyptian and Somali naval and air facilities. Even more important, the Soviet naval presence in the Mediterranean and the Indian Ocean has not diminished the threat to the Soviet Union's national security emanating from American underwater strategic nuclear delivery systems. Finally, given America's tactical superiority on the high seas, achieved mainly by carrier-launched aircraft as well as by its highly developed hunter-killer submarine capability, Moscow's ability to deny the United States the control of the world's oceans cannot be taken for granted by the Soviet military establishment. Moreover, Soviet advances are primarily responsible for the Reagan administration's decision to strengthen Western military forces in different ways, thus increasing the pressure for new Russian military investments.

Politically, it is undeniable that considerable destabilization of Western positions in Asia and Africa did in fact take place in the post–World War II era. To keep the process in proper perspective, however, the analyst must not lose sight of the following considerations: the Soviet Union was not responsible either for the spread of indigenous nationalism in the developing world—a phenomenon whose origins preceded the communist revolution in Russia—or for its continued growth in the interwar and, especially, the post-1945 periods. Nor did the impetus for self-assertion on the part of the peoples subjected to Western colonialism originate with Marxism or Moscow's own brand of "scientific socialism."

The role that the Soviet Union has played in the affairs of the

Third World after the death of Stalin can therefore be best described as an indirect one. Both Khrushchev and Brezhnev assisted the indigenous nationalist leaders in asserting themselves against the Western powers—militarily, politically, and economically. By providing a counterbalance to the West and by occasionally offering a helping hand, Moscow was able to contribute to the process of decolonization that, among other things, resulted in the destabilization of Western positions in many developing countries.

In this context, it is, however, important to remember that Western losses have not automatically been translated into Soviet gains. As alluded to above, most Asian and African nations seeking Moscow's assistance have been unwilling to tie themselves to the Soviet Union politically or to offer the Kremlin the use of their naval and air facilities. The exceptions to this rule in the Middle East/Horn of Africa regions have been Egypt, Somalia, and the PDRY, and, of the three, only Aden remains in the Soviet camp. Fellow socialist Mogadishu was abandoned in favor of Mengistu's revolutionary regime in Addis Ababa, while Cairo's expulsion of Russian military personnel and the forced retreat from Egyptian naval and air bases stand as some of Moscow's most humiliating political setbacks in the post-1945 period. In short, although some impressive gains were registered during the Khrushchev and Brezhnev periods, many have proved short-lived and some have become a source of considerable embarrassment. Moreover, the acquisition of such clients as the PDRY and Ethiopia has resulted in a drain on the Soviet economy.

Economically, the Soviet Union has benefited considerably from self-assertion on the part of the major petroleum-producing states. In the category of direct gains has been access to Iraqi, Iranian, and Libyan oil and, until its cutoff in 1979, to Iranian natural gas. Most of all, the Kremlin has profited handsomely from large-scale, hard currency sales of weapons to such major customers as Iraq, Libya, and Syria. On the negative side, advanced Soviet arms, as well as technology and capital goods, have proved inferior to Western products with the result that many of Moscow's Third World clients have displayed a clear preference for dealing with the capitalist rather than socialist countries.

The Soviet Union and the Gulf: Present and Future

In assessing the Kremlin's intentions in the gulf, it is imperative to note some of the constraints—international, regional, and local—inhibiting the Soviets' freedom of action. To begin, the Reagan administration, as indicated earlier, has continued to espouse the Carter Doctrine on the gulf. This means that any Soviet decision to gain access to the area's petroleum resources by force of arms would be regarded by the United States as a provocation requiring a military response. Given the Soviet Union's geographic proximity to and local preponderance near the gulf, such a conflict would contain a distinct danger of escalating into a nuclear confrontation between the superpowers. If the assumption that Moscow has determined not to infringe on the West's vital interests is correct, Kremlin leaders are not likely to undertake a military invasion of the gulf.

Equally, the prospects for Soviet penetration of one or several gulf states, beginning with Iran and extending to some of its Arab neighbors, appear to be rather slim. The religious establishment in Iran, although divided on various important issues, seems to be firmly in control and is likely to survive the eventual passing from the scene of Ayatollah Khomeini. The only possible future challenge to the present rulers might arise from Iran's armed forces. But even if the military were to one day overthrow the Islamic regime, there is no reason to believe that the Iranian generals would turn to the Soviet Union as a source of guidance and support. Instead, their natural inclination would be to normalize relations with the West, seen by many as a logical counterweight to the thinly disguised ambitions of Iran's northern neighbor. As to Iraq, regardless of the outcome and political repercussions of its war with Iran, it is difficult to imagine any Iraqi nationalist regime subordinating itself to Moscow's wishes in the manner of, say, the PDRY. Elsewhere in the gulf, barring major political upheavals, opportunities for increasing Soviet influence do not appear promising. For these reasons, it seems unlikely that in the years ahead, the Soviet Union's chances of moving into the gulf will improve significantly.

As Shahram Chubin has noted, Moscow's opportunities for "fishing in troubled waters" have increased substantially due to the strains caused by the process of socioeconomic modernization and by the seeming inability of the United States to implement a coherent Middle Eastern policy.[8] This does not mean, however, that the USSR is likely to be a long-run beneficiary of these unsettling trends. If history is any guide at all, it should be obvious that a zero-sum approach to the process of political and socioeconomic change is a singularly inappropriate yardstick by which to judge "successes" or "failures" of outsiders attempting to manipulate events unfolding in the Middle East. The Soviets, in their public pronouncements, have chosen to disregard this rule; any weakening of the Western position is automatically presented as a gain for Moscow. But while the Kremlin's ideological assumption is quite transparent—namely, the cause of communism is advanced as

Western influence declines—the historical record points to the hollow-ness of these claims. The downfall of the pro-Western regimes in a number of Asian and African countries in the post-1945 period was in many instances followed by the emergence of a new breed of nationalist leaders willing to deal with the Soviet Union. While in a few cases (the PDRY, Ethiopia) the Kremlin has indeed achieved a predominant posi-tion, these gains have usually entailed the paying of a not insignificant economic price. Moreover, many of the erstwhile "progressives" have either been replaced by anti-Soviet elements (Egypt) or have chosen to pursue independent policies that have often brought them into con-flict with Moscow's interests (Algeria, Iraq, Libya, Somalia, Syria). In short, though the West may have lost, the Soviet Union did not neces-sarily gain.

Whether or not one accepts the argument that the political insta-bility in the gulf is bound to lead to violent change and that the Soviets are bound to be the prime beneficiaries of this process because "much of a regime's legacy, including its foreign orientation, is likely to be re-jected by its successor regime,"[9] observers should not lose sight of the fact that the economic realities of the gulf will not be swept away by whatever political upheavals may lie ahead. The economies of the gulf petroleum-producing states are dependent on and closely intertwined with those of the Western nations. No change in leadership or political orientation is likely to alter that. An interesting illustration of this asser-tion can be found outside the gulf. When the United States, for a vari-ety of reasons, chose to stop purchasing Libyan oil, Colonel Qadhafy did not avail himself of the opportunities presented by the Soviet and East European markets. He chose, instead, to attempt to sell more petroleum to Western Europe, which is also a source of most of Libya's nonmilitary imports.

Conclusion

The coming of the nuclear age has had a profound impact on the ability of the superpowers to advance and defend their interests in the outside world. However, the respective positions of the United States and the Soviet Union have been affected in different ways. Washington, initially the only superpower possessing the means to destroy its communist ad-versary, was also able, thanks to its lead in such branches of the armed forces as the navy and the air force, to exert its influence on a world-wide basis. The Soviet Union, in contrast, initially inferior to the United States in nuclear and related technologies and lacking a blue-water navy and long-range aircraft, could utilize its land-power predominance only in areas geographically contiguous to itself. Not content to remain in a militarily inferior and therefore politically subordinate position, Moscow has worked hard to neutralize Washington's lead in nuclear weapons, delivery systems, and certain types of conventional weapons. These defense-related efforts have been supplemented with a far-flung political campaign designed to weaken the industrial West by supporting the aspirations of the developing countries.

The Soviets have since reached what is known as nuclear parity with the United States. They have also significantly upgraded their navy and air force and have acquired a capability to project their power into geographically remote areas. In addition, Moscow has helped a number of Asian and African states, as well as Castro's Cuba, to pursue policies regarded as inimical to the interests of the West. As argued above, however, in many such instances Western "failures" are attributable mainly to the initiatives of the newly independent countries themselves which have used the Soviet Union to attain their own national objectives. The Kremlin leaders, if they so desire, can congratulate themselves on having assisted various Third World states in achieving their, and not Soviet, aims. If Moscow wishes to claim that its interests are identical to those of the developing nations, that, too, is its prerogative. But, as exemplified by the widespread mistrust of Moscow and its ultimate intentions, such assertions have not been taken seriously in many African or Asian capitals. This apprehension has been particularly evident in areas where the Soviets have attempted to supplement their support of indigenous governments with efforts to advance Moscow's own interests. In these situations, with very few exceptions, the Kremlin has encountered serious difficulties and suffered a number of bitter disappointments.

The reception accorded to Brezhnev's plan for "peace and security" of the gulf, presented during the chairman's December 1980 visit to India,[10] is an instructive example. While receiving verbal support from some Asian countries (and, in the gulf, from Iraq and Kuwait), the plan has had no tangible impact on the Western powers and has not resulted in an enhancement of Moscow's prestige or of Soviet positions in or near the Persian/Arabian Gulf. As this episode once again demonstrates, Moscow's ability to advance its interests in the Persian Gulf, the Horn, and the entire Indian Ocean region is subject to serious limitations that no Soviet government is likely to overcome in the current decade and, in all probability, beyond.

27. Western European Interests in the Indian Ocean ≈ Ferenc A. Váli

Since the end of the fifteenth century the Indian Ocean has been dominated by Western Europeans: the Portuguese, the Dutch, the French, and the British. Vying with each other for commercial advantage, these states controlled the ocean and the various narrow sea lanes leading to it. At first, they limited themselves to the occupation of strategically important points and to commercially lucrative trading centers. However, by the end of the eighteenth century, the British had succeeded in restraining their rivals and in establishing a position of predominance in the region. Their dominion extended mainly over the waters of the region but also over much of the adjacent land mass. This dominance ended after World War II. Beginning with India, London gradually gave up most of its possessions in the region. Gradually other Western European powers, the Dutch, the French, and, finally, the very first colonizers, the Portuguese, followed suit.

Since the late 1960s two other external powers, the Soviet Union and the United States, have come to maintain naval units in the Indian Ocean and have thus projected their power into the region. They have not, however, completely replaced the principal colonial powers, Britain and France. London and Paris, directly or indirectly, continue to exert influence in the area. They, along with other Western European nations, retain important, if not vital, interests in the region. Consistent with these interests, the Europeans' collective entities, the North Atlantic Treaty Organization (NATO) and the European Economic Community (EEC), have been taking an increasingly active interest in the region's political and economic affairs. This has involved a departure from these organizations' traditional concerns. At the same time, the evolution of specific Western European approaches to developments in the Indian Ocean region have highlighted the differences in perception between American and European policy makers as to their respective interests in the area.

The Interests of Western European States

Great Britain

In the relatively short period of time from 1947 to 1971, London gave up most of its Asian and African continental possessions and islands in the Indian Ocean. Today, the only remaining British possession is the Chagos Archipelago.

The final decision to withdraw from east of Suez was made in 1968 and implemented by 1971. Eventually this was to entail the abandonment of the Persian Gulf protectorates, departure from Malaysia, and the relinquishment of the bases on Masirah Island along the Omani coast and on Gan in the Maldives Archipelago. But before this decision the British adjusted political and administrative boundaries between the offshore islands for which they were responsible. Thus in 1965 the British Indian Ocean Territory (BIOT) was created by detaching the Chagos Archipelago from Mauritius and uniting it with the islands of Aldabra, Farquhar, and Desroches, which were simultaneously separated from the administration of the Seychelles group.[1] Mauritius, which had yet to gain independence, was compensated by a grant of £3 million sterling, while the Seychelles, also without independence, was awarded the construction of an international airport on Mahé Island.

The BIOT was formed to establish defense facilities within this geographically and strategically important area of the Indian Ocean. As is well known, the island of Diego Garcia in the Chagos group now serves as a naval/military base. It has been leased to the United States for a period of fifty years, with the British having joint access to the facilities.[2] The few, allegedly nonpermanent, inhabitants of Diego Garcia, mainly fishermen and coconut planters, have been removed to Mauritius. But these arrangements and the payment of compensation for the removed islanders have not freed London from troubles and responsibilities with regard to the territory. As Joel Larus discusses elsewhere in this book, unresolved challenges to British sovereignty and claims for compensation continue to plague London and to complicate its relations with several of the newly independent island states of the area.

As Britain's retention of BIOT suggests, London views the Indian Ocean as an important strategic arena. In keeping with this view, Britain, despite having abandoned its vast colonial empire, has not relinquished the potential for projecting military power into the area. A small squadron of Royal Navy ships undertakes regular patrols in Indian Ocean waters and has participated in exercises with ships of the U.S. Navy. The focus for much of this activity is the Persian Gulf but Britain's membership in the Five Power Defense Agreement, which involves a commitment to assist Malaysia and Singapore in the event of aggression, also makes demands on London's military capabilities. Periodic exercises with other outside members of the pact, Australia and New Zealand, and regular visits to other commonwealth countries sustain a British presence in the eastern approaches to the region. This not only preserves

London's links with some of the most strategically important states of
the Southeast Asia area, but also facilitates the maintenance of ties with
the Crown Colony of Hong Kong. Britain's lease of the new territories
upon which the city is situated is to expire in 1997, but it is likely that
London will retain certain rights of access thereafter.

For Britain the projection of power into any but the most western
portions of the Indian Ocean region is fraught with difficulties. Long
lines of supply make heavy demands on Britain's air and naval logistics
capabilities and require ready access to replenishment facilities in foreign countries. Regarding the latter, Britain used to depend upon the
extensive naval and air facilities at Simonstown in South Africa.[3] The
Simonstown Agreement, however, was renounced by the British government in 1975 following pressure from African and Asian members
of the commonwealth opposed to white rule in Pretoria. Since then
Britain has had to make alternative arrangements. These have included
an agreement with the government of Mauritius to use airfields, harbors, and a naval communication station on the island. But even these
may soon be unavailable. Under the agreement, Mauritius may revoke
Britain's right of access on a year's notice and it is likely that the new
government of Paul Berenger will give that notice.

Uncertainty also persists regarding Britain's long-term ability to deploy naval units into the Indian Ocean, notwithstanding the persistence
of its interests in the region. While Britain showed an impressive capability for distant water force projection during the Falklands War,
much of it attributable to naval operations, the declining strength of
the Royal Navy seems likely to make such exercises much more difficult in the future. But the Admiralty's problems are not merely confined to dealing with the next emergency; the Royal Navy now has the
difficult task of performing additional responsibilities with a declining
capability. Naval obligations to NATO, the demands created by the decision to retain the Falkland Islands, and the Thatcher government's apparent determination to reduce the size of the navy, all stretch the
Royal Navy's resources. As a consequence, it is not inconceivable that
British naval patrols in the Indian Ocean will become less frequent, if
not terminate altogether, in the foreseeable future. An alternative scenario is that as a consequence of the lessons and experiences of the
Falklands War, British leaders might now consider the sending of a
task force to the Indian Ocean and to the gulf to protect vital British
interests a more realistic possibility. New shipbuilding programs of the
Royal Navy may be geared to such a possibility. If so, they will have to
include the construction of at least one more carrier as well as more

amphibious ships in order to assure the flexibility that is demanded by the often precarious situations in the Indian Ocean region.[4]

Allied to the military concerns, Britain has a range of political interests in the region. Potentially more enduring, and arguably of more value than periodic naval and air deployments, London's historic ties to its former colonies provide a network of relations serving to maintain Britain's traditional influence in the area. Exercised with subtlety and tact, this influence continues to be used to further British interests in the region, as well as those of the West more generally. Unlike many other former colonial masters, Britain has succeeded in preserving relationships of trust and respect with the people of its former possessions. British administrative, constitutional, and judicial institutions are largely maintained and honored throughout the region, despite the changes that have taken place since the start of movements toward independence. Such legacies are rare and have no easily recognizable parallel.

Britain's trade and navigational interests are still paramount in the Indian Ocean region. At any given time, about one-fifth of the British merchant fleet is likely to be found in the area. British trade with the countries of the region amounts to 22 percent of the United Kingdom's total overseas transactions. About 40 percent of British overseas investments are based in the area. Were it not for the development of its own oil fields in the North Sea, Britain's trade within the region, especially the countries of the Persian Gulf, would be substantially greater. As it is, Britain continues to purchase a significant amount of petroleum from the Middle East but the level of dependency is down sharply and is noticeably less than several of London's partners in Europe.

France

During the eighteenth century, France contended with Britain for supremacy in the Indian Ocean region. At the end of this prolonged struggle, the British had managed to evict the French from their strategic positions in India and, during the Napoleonic Wars, from Mauritius (called by France, Ile de France) and the Seychelles Islands. But during the second half of the nineteenth century, France staged a comeback into the area. Besides the island of Réunion (formerly Ile Bourbon), returned by Britain in 1818, Paris established control over the large island of Madagascar and the Comoro Islands, and set up a colony in the Gulf of Tadjoura, naming it the French Coast of Somali with its capital in Djibouti.

The French decolonization of Africa was followed, with certain hesitations, in the western Indian Ocean region. Madagascar received independence in 1960, and in 1977 the French Somali Coast (known then as the French Territory of Afars and Issas) became an independent state under the name of Republic of Djibouti. In the Comoro Islands, decolonization has proceeded less smoothly. When the four islands of the group declared their independence in 1975, one (Mayotte, now renamed Mahoré) subsequently voted in two referenda held in 1976 to remain with France. Mahoré has a largely Christian population, whereas the other Comoro islands are Muslim-dominated. The Comoro government opposes the secession of Mahoré and is supported in this position by the United Nations General Assembly. Mahoré is now administered as a territorial collectivity of France (a category midway between an overseas department and an overseas territory). In 1979 the French National Assembly extended this status for five years; at the end of this period the island may become an overseas department of France.[5]

In several of these places Paris has attempted to maintain a political-military foothold. For instance, under an agreement with the newly independent Malagasy Republic (now the Democratic Republic of Madagascar), the French were able to maintain an air base and to garrison the strategically important naval base of Diego Suarez. This arrangement continued for over a decade, until 1973, when the French were compelled to withdraw from their facilities following a change of government in Tananarivo. Elsewhere, France has been more successful in preserving its presence. In the strategically important Republic of Djibouti located at the entrance of the Bab el-Mandeb Strait, France has stationed two French infantry (foreign legion) regiments and two squadrons of the French air force. The French navy also uses Djibouti's harbor as a naval base.

In other parts of the Indian Ocean region French links are much stronger. The island of Réunion has been a French overseas department since 1949 and is represented in the French Parliament by three deputies and two senators. It has an ethnically mixed population of half a million comprising French, Indians, Africans, Indochinese, Malays, and Chinese. As in France, there are several political parties: two on the left demanding self-determination, and the others, grouped together as the French Réunion Association, favoring continuation of the present status. Finally, France's determination to hold on in the western Indian Ocean is evident in its continued claim to (or effective control over) several small islands: Tromelin Island off the northeast coast of Madagascar and Europa, Juan de Nova, and the Glorioso Islands in the Mozambique Channel. In some of these cases, France's claim has been challenged by Madagascar.

The key to understanding France's continued presence in and policies toward the Indian Ocean region is to be found in Paris's perception of its status as a great power. As such, France claims to have a global role independent of what French leaders like to call "the condominium of the two superpowers." Paris thus finds it quite natural to have a military presence in the Indian Ocean region next only to that of the Soviet Union and the United States. But this presence is not only justified for reasons of national prestige; Paris is able to point to more tangible and pragmatic motives for its Indian Ocean involvement.

French possessions in the western part of this ocean require protection. These possessions are located along the sea lanes leading to and from the Suez Canal and along the cape route down the east coast of Africa. To protect these sea routes and its sovereign possessions, Paris sees a naval/military establishment as indispensable. Thus, in 1974, following the Arab-Israeli war of 1973 and the Arab oil embargo, Paris formally set up a new naval command to extend over the entire Indian Ocean and the cape route leading to it.[6] The operational headquarters of the commander-in-chief of this naval command is located on one of the larger ships whose base, when not deployed, is the port of Djibouti.

The composition and numbers of the French fleet operating in the Indian Ocean vary a great deal. At any one moment, the French navy may be more powerful than either the Soviet or American squadrons present in the region. At times, one of the Clemenceau-type attack carriers and four or five other surface combat vessels, as well as an unidentified number of submarines, are to be found in those waters. The vessels are routinely rotated between the four naval commands of the French navy, two of them in home waters, one in the Pacific, and one in the Indian Ocean.

In 1974, when the new naval command was established, about 80 percent of French oil supplies came from the Persian Gulf states. Since then this dependence on gulf oil has declined but it is still considerable. Even so, supply lines remain very long since most of the oil passes through the Mozambique Channel and around the cape.

France stations military units in many of its former African colonies. Thus, Senegal, the Central African Republic, Gabon, the Ivory Coast, and, as already mentioned, Djibouti, all have some French military forces on their soil. In what is a highly unstable region of Africa, these forces are intended in part to maintain often precarious levels of internal stability. As events in Chad in 1983 demonstrated, the domestic political fortunes of local leaders can often attract outside attention and lead to dangerous consequences. In France, responding, albeit reluctantly, to such situations is not only seen as a responsibility born of a previous colonial relationship, but is also perceived to be in Paris's best interests given its considerable economic investments in the region.

A sense of the importance France attaches to these interests and to its role in the region can be gained by appreciating that long before the idea of a Rapid Deployment Force (RDF) was conceived in Washington, France had created its own *Force d'Intervention*. Consisting of airborne and airportable motorized units, the force can be employed in practically any part of the world but is intended essentially for use in Africa and in the Indian Ocean region. The socialist government of François Mitterand has confirmed that French forces will remain in Africa and that those units designated for use in emergencies will be maintained at a high level of readiness.[7] The outbreak of fighting between rival groups in Chad in 1983, in which one side was reportedly backed by Libya, provided a test of Mitterand's determination in this regard. On that occasion French forces did go to the aid of the Chadian government but not, it seems, without considerable encouragement from Washington.

American diplomatic intervention in Chad in 1983 is said to have been unwelcome by the French. This attitude appears to typify France's resolution to "go it alone" in the region, largely independent of superpower concerns and, more especially, of American assistance. Thus as regards naval establishments in the Indian Ocean, the close collaboration practiced by the British and American governments generally does not extend to the French. However, the three navies do cooperate in keeping a watchful eye on Soviet naval activities.[8]

France's naval deployments in the Indian Ocean have been hampered by the loss of the excellent base at Diego Suarez. Since the situation on Mahoré is somewhat uncertain and the harbor facilities on Réunion Island are unsatisfactory France now lacks a satisfactory naval base in the waters around Madagascar and the Mozambique Channel. However, the hope that the government of Madagascar might reestablish closer relations with Paris is not unfounded. Besides military aid, France provides considerable economic assistance to its former colonies. In 1974 Madagascar relinquished membership in the Organisation Commune Africaine et Malgache and also left the Franc Monetary group, causing itself considerable economic harm. It is not inconceivable that in an effort to recover from this situation some form of economic cooperation will be reestablished between Tananarivo and Paris. If it is, the question of French access to Diego Suarez may well be reopened.

France is more conscious of the potential of a "cultural imperialism" than most other nations. Both Mauritius (and its dependency, the island of Rodrigues) and the Seychelles are francophone; the majority of their people speak a creolized French. English is the official language of the two countries but the lingua franca is French-creole, making the people open and receptive to French cultural influences. By the dispatch of teachers and books, by radio, and by promoting French tourism (Air France maintains subsidized flights to these islands), Paris has undertaken a "cultural reconquest" of an area that it lost politically to Britain 150 years ago.

Federal Republic of Germany, Italy, and the Netherlands

Among Western European countries, Britain and France are not alone in having direct and important interests in the Indian Ocean region. But as former colonial powers they possess the burden as well as the advantage of a historical relationship with the states of the area. Furthermore, they are the only European states that have a significant capability of projecting power into the region. The Federal Republic of Germany, Italy, and the other major powers of Western Europe (excluding Spain) also have considerable interests in the Indian Ocean but less of a will and a capability to exercise influence among the states of the area.

West German interests are essentially economic. Somewhat less than half of Bonn's oil requirements are met by imports from the Persian Gulf area. Being one of the major industrial countries of the world, West Germany's share in the exchange of goods with the countries of the Indian Ocean is considerable. While exporting industrial and manufactured goods to the region, it imports raw materials from states such as India, Indonesia, Malaysia, and South Africa. More for historic than for tangible reasons, West Germany also maintains an interest in Tanzania, a former colonial possession. Further south, relations between Bonn and Pretoria are underwritten by the many ethnic Germans living in the Republic of South Africa. To the west is Namibia, a former German colony; a sizable proportion of its white population is also ethnically German. These ties to southern Africa have resulted in Bonn taking an active role in the negotiations to bring about a settlement in Namibia. West Germany is a member of the Western "contact group" dealing with the South African government and is acknowledged to have been instrumental in moving this long-standing issue toward a settlement.

Bonn maintains numerous, well-staffed missions in countries of the Indian Ocean and is a careful student of the events and forces of the region. When West German interests dictate a more than usually active role in the area, as in the case of Namibia, it has the advantage of being a former colonial power of a more distant era and, as such, immune from the suspicions that sometimes attach to the activities of more recent imperial states like Britain and France. Yet any West German military or political desire to take a more substantial role in the region is hampered by the legal-constitutional impediments Bonn accepted when acceeding to the North Atlantic Treaty in 1955. Until these impediments are removed, it is unlikely that West Germany's potential of becoming a far more active participant in the affairs of the area will be realized.

Like other Western European countries, Italy also depends on the Persian Gulf states for much of its oil supply. This is reason enough for Rome to take an active interest in the politics of the region but, as with West Germany, Italian interests are wider and relate to the period of colonialism. These interests are concentrated around the Horn of Africa; Eritrea was once an Italian colony. At various times much of Somalia was an Italian possession and for ten years after World War II was administered by Rome as a United Nations trust territory. Of late, Italian business concerns have been particularly active in Third World development projects in Africa and the Middle East.

Among the smaller West European nations, the Netherlands has cherished reminiscences of its former colonial possession, Indonesia, the second largest country of the Indian Ocean region. Although the Indonesians waged a protracted war of liberation against the Dutch, in the last twenty years the Netherlands has developed sound economic ties with the country. Equipped with knowledge of local customs and appropriate language skills, the Dutch are uniquely placed among Europeans to be able to strengthen their burgeoning business and industrial relations with Indonesia. One facet of this relationship is the importance of the Netherlands as a supplier of military equipment. In 1980, for instance, the Dutch supplied Indonesia with three new Fatahillah frigates. It is conceivable that as Djakarta moves to expand its naval capability orders for additional equipment will follow.

The Perspectives of European Organizations

Historically, the states of Europe have competed with one another for influence in the Indian Ocean region. More often than not, their interests in the area were antithetical rather than complementary. Since the end of World War II this adversarial relationship has been transformed, largely as a consequence of the polarization of international politics between East and West, and, more directly in the case of the Indian Ocean, by the process of decolonization. While the interests of individual states may still occasionally compete, the overall movement is in the direction of more cohesive and unified West European policies toward the region. Two international organizations, NATO and the EEC, have been instrumental in developing these policies.

North Atlantic Treaty Organization

NATO, of course, is not exclusively a European organization since the United States and Canada are both members. Yet, being in essence a defense organization with the purpose of preventing and opposing a Soviet advance in Europe, NATO is naturally involved in any question that affects or could affect the security of its members and their defense capabilities. Any interruption in the supply of oil or interference in sea lines of communication (SLOCS) from the Persian Gulf is thus of vital interest to the organization as well as to its individual members. For NATO, the difficulty is that the treaty upon which it is founded limits its activities to areas north of the Tropic of Cancer. It is only here that the territorial sovereignty and security of its members are guaranteed against aggression. But such an artificial division of the Atlantic cannot prevent NATO from being concerned with the flow of energy supplies originating outside NATO's sphere or with the security of the shipping lanes by which these energy supplies reach its members. In fact, NATO seems obliged to be concerned with any question, any development, that affects or may affect the strategic balance between its members and their adversaries.

For these reasons, as early as November 1972, the North Atlantic Assembly called on the NATO Council to authorize plans for the protection of Western European shipping in the Indian Ocean and the South Atlantic.[9] At the NATO Council meeting that took place in Ottawa in June 1974 following the Organization of Petroleum Exporting Countries' (OPEC) imposition of an oil embargo on some members of the alliance, reference was made to the fact that the interests of some members "may be affected by events in other areas of the world." There is little doubt that this was a not particularly well-disguised reference to both the oil crisis and the Soviet naval presence in the Indian Ocean.[10]

In light of Soviet naval activity in the region, the North Atlantic Assembly in November 1976 urged member governments to increase the number of antisubmarine warfare (ASW) vessels in their navies in order to protect shipping lanes leading from the Persian Gulf to Europe.[11] Further reference was made in September 1977 to the vulnerability of NATO's oil supplies from the gulf. Sitting in Paris, the NATO Council again urged member governments to improve their ASW capabilities and to reinforce the authority given to the supreme allied commander, Atlantic (SACLANT) with regard to planning the protection of vital shipping lanes, particularly in the South Atlantic and the Indian Ocean.[12]

The protection of SLOCS is but one dimension of NATO's growing concern for defense in the Indian Ocean region. In May 1980 the NATO Council authorized the United States to divert forces, so far assigned to the alliance, to be used in case of emergencies in the Persian Gulf, that is, outside the defense perimeter of NATO. The integration of European defense with the protection of interests in the gulf was advanced another step in February 1981 when command of the United States Rapid Deployment Force (RDF) was transferred to the supreme allied commander, Europe (SACEUR). As a consequence, SACEUR has responsibility not only for the defense of Europe itself but also for NATO's vital defense interests outside the area and notably in the northwest quadrant of the Indian Ocean region.

Washington would welcome contributions by its European allies to the RDF. To encourage this, the Carter and Reagan administrations have sought an allied consensus on questions of joint planning and cooperative actions. At the outset European governments were reluctant to seriously consider American proposals. Not only was there general skepticism about the expansion of NATO's role but it was also feared that European support might encourage the United States to reduce existing commitments to the defense of Europe. Subsequently, Europeans have come to realize that the defense of the Persian Gulf is as much, if not more, in their strategic interest as in that of the United States.

In February 1981 Britain became the first European country to express interest in adding its forces to the RDF. But, as in the American case, any British deployment east of Suez would diminish forces already earmarked for NATO. London would be obliged to call on its Puma and Jaguar squadrons, on part of its Nimrod force, and on units of Sea Harriers to secure the required air cover for a composite brigade of eight thousand men. Furthermore, the Royal Navy would have to reassign ships to assist Royal Marine commando and amphibious deployments. Today, however, the prospect of Britain contributing to the RDF has virtually disappeared. The continuing decline in Britain's naval capability, the burden of defending the Falkland Islands, and the possibility that by contributing to the RDF Britain might exacerbate its sometimes uneasy relations with Middle East states, all argue against a British commitment. There are few other European members of NATO likely to be interested in giving material support to the RDF.

France certainly has the capability to project naval and land forces into the Indian Ocean region. Indeed, as already noted, France presently maintains sizable military forces in the area. But to increase its military presence, France would need to commit units of its regular army. Paris, however, is reluctant to employ enlisted men overseas as they are not, as a matter of principle, sent in time of peace. The French forces stationed in Africa, or available for use there, are not regular army units but detachments of the French legion. But even more damning to prospects for French participation in the RDF is Paris's opposition to participation in unified military organizations. Having not been a part of NATO's military command structure since 1966, it is highly unlikely that France would become a party to the RDF.

Although Britain, France, and other states of Western Europe are doubtful contributors to the RDF, they have not foreclosed all options of collective action to secure their SLOCs. In June 1981 contingency plans were completed for the creation of a European task force for the protection of SLOCs in the South Atlantic where shipping from the Indian Ocean may face a threat from the Soviet naval squadron almost permanently on-station off the coast of Angola. The proposal is that a task force be formed similar to the Standing Naval Force, Atlantic (STANAVFORLANT). It is contemplated that such a force may eventually become operational in the Indian Ocean. Because the force would be operating outside of NATO's specified geographic perimeter, that is to say it would be operating south of the Tropic of Cancer, the commander or commanders of such a force would only be responsible to the naval commands of the respective participating nations and not to SACLANT or the NATO Council. The drawbacks of a situation in which a multinational task force proceeds without a unified command are obvious. But an amendment to the NATO Treaty extending its geographic sphere of responsibility would be fraught with difficulties and is at this time impractical. Therefore other solutions have to be sought, ones that will allow an efficient and effective force to be established.

Of the proposals that have been under discussion the most promising appears to be use of an existing international institution, namely the Western European Union (WEU). The WEU includes Britain, France, the Benelux countries, and the Federal Republic of Germany. To date its major preoccupation has been to exercise control over West Germany's military establishment, an activity that has already resulted in the strengthening of the West's naval capability through the removal of restrictions on the size of vessels in the West German navy. Beyond this, the WEU has previously shown an interest in defense cooperation outside Europe. In 1977 it acknowledged that member states should be engaged in more extensive consultations with regard to gulf security "to avoid their legitimate interests bringing them into conflict or involving them in differences over which there has been no prior agreement."[13]

Whether the WEU will prove to be an effective institution for the coordination of plans to protect Western European interests in the Persian Gulf and the SLOCs that link the two regions may not be known for some time. The WEU is itself in a state of some disarray and the present glut of oil on the international market tends to reduce the incentive for European states faced by a range of other problems to devote time and resources to protecting against what are arguably remote contingencies. Nevertheless, as Coker and Schulte have observed, the West Europeans "can do much more than they have to help the United States meet the threat to international security that has arisen in recent years."[14] Whatever the likelihood of an actual interruption in gulf oil supplies to Europe, defending against the possibility is something in which Western Europe has a vested interest and which should therefore be an incentive to transatlantic cooperation.

The European Economic Community

The states of Western Europe have reviewed their policies toward the Persian Gulf not only in the context of protecting SLOCs, but they have also been concerned about more than securing oil supplies. More than 44 percent of Arab imports originate in Western Europe and approximately 40 percent of Arab exports, excluding oil, are shipped to Europe. Thus, oil aside, there is a considerable measure of trading interdependence among the states of the two regions. Even so, from the West European perspective, oil serves as the central motif in its relationship with the gulf. In this context the partial oil embargo and the reduction of supplies that followed the 1973 Arab-Israeli war had a sobering effect on the members of the EEC. It served to underline their dependence on the attitudes and goodwill of Arab oil-producing countries, especially those of the Persian Gulf. Consequently, in February 1974 the Council of Ministers of the EEC recommended a "dialogue" with the Arab members of OPEC. The purpose of this initiative was to allay possible Arab resentment and to dissociate Western European governments from any action taken by the United States in retaliation against the oil embargo.

Since then the EEC has moved in the direction of establishing a special relationship with the oil-producing states of the Persian Gulf. The European Council of Ministers has attempted to conclude a series of "cooperation agreements" in the area. Pursuant to these agreements, the parties would engage in a mutual reduction of tariffs and there would be established a framework under which individual member states might enter into import and export agreements, provide financial credits, and offer other forms of economic assistance. Although the EEC has sought agreements with each of the members of the Arab League and with the league itself, arrangements have proved elusive. The first agreements to have been signed were those with Egypt, Jordan, and Syria. The difficulties that have been encountered in negotiating additional cooperation agreements suggest that proposals for a more extensive relationship between the EEC and the gulf states, something approaching an "interregional partnership," may be rather too ambitious, though Iraq and Saudi Arabia have been somewhat favorable toward bilateral arrangements. The Gulf Cooperation Council could be a possible vehicle for multilateral arrangements.

In any event, suggestions that the EEC establish a special relationship with the oil-producing states have not been universally well received in Europe. Members of the European Parliament's Energy Committee, for instance, were highly critical of a report generally supportive of the idea when it was submitted by a German socialist, Wieczorek-Zeul, following a fact-finding visit to the gulf states. The critics tend to believe that independent European political action, not linked with American policies and planning, is undesirable. They suggest that the EEC should try to coordinate its Middle East policy with that of Washington. They point out that the political stability of the gulf area is a prerequisite for peaceful trade and the flow of oil supplies. Furthermore, according to this view, the safeguarding of peace and the security of the oil routes is and must remain a common concern of both the EEC and the United States.[15]

These controversies reflect differing perceptions of the extent to which the EEC, acting independently of the United States, could exert influence on Arab oil-producing states to secure delivery of their oil products. It is characteristic of the decision-making process in the European Parliament that the division on this question has not been along national, but along ideological, lines: the socialist parties favor independent action, while the Christian-socialist and liberal deputies emphasize the necessity and usefulness of policies coordinated with those of the United States.

Before discussing some of the problems associated with transatlantic policy coordination, it remains to conclude this examination of EEC perspectives of the Indian Ocean region by reviewing the community's interests beyond the focal point of the Persian Gulf. Chief among these is the EEC commitment to assist development in the Third World through the provisions of the Lomé Convention. First signed in 1975 and renewed in 1979, the convention gives participating less-developed countries (LDCS) free access to European markets for their exports, stabilizes LDCS' earnings from agricultural commodities and mineral exports, and provides financial aid to assist with development projects. Within the Indian Ocean region, the countries that are signatories to the convention include Kenya, Madagascar, Mauritius, the Seychelles, Somalia, and Tanzania. Elsewhere, in South and Southeast Asia, the EEC has signed a series of economic cooperation agreements, thereby formalizing a framework for trade relations with these regions. In 1973, for instance, an agreement was signed with India and in 1980 another with the Association of South-East Asian Nations (ASEAN).

All of these arrangements reflect the EEC's status as a large, diversified, industrialized trading bloc and differ little in principle from those made with states outside the Indian Ocean region. While this points to the conclusion that the area is not one of special interest to the community, the importance of Persian Gulf oil to the economies of Western Europe clearly belies such a notion. For the foreseeable future, Europe will continue to have a large measure of dependence on gulf oil and this is likely to dictate the EEC's response to political developments there. In other parts of the region, the burden of underdevelopment that afflicts so many of the littoral states seems likely to draw the community into closer economic relations. Accommodating some of the needs of the LDCS in the region would enable the EEC to sustain its reputation for a rather more enlightened attitude toward the problems of Third World countries than appears to exist in some other Western capitals.

Western Europe and the United States

European reactions to American policy in the Indian Ocean region cannot be dissociated from general European attitudes toward U.S. foreign policy or, rather, its handling of foreign policy. Behind the snarls in the relationship are the well-known incompatibilities and inconsistencies between the American system of government on the one hand and those of Western European states on the other. In Europe, American policy is often said to lack continuity, consistency, sophistication, and an understanding of foreign mentalities, as well as to suffer from an absence of secrecy during the decision-making process. In return, Europeans are reproached for wanting cooperation on the "security front" but not on political or economic fronts, for their frequent—often unjustified—complaints about not having been consulted, and for their reluctance to follow the "American lead" after having specifically called for it. These generalizations often prove erroneous when examined in individual cases; nevertheless, they add an atmosphere of suspicion to the relationship.

With regard to the countries of the Indian Ocean, there is no doubt that governments that have had lengthy and traditionally close ties with the region, such as Britain and France, do muster a great many experts on the area. They maintain a network of contacts and have a depth of understanding of the forces at work in the region that may exceed that of the American government, whose interests in and knowledge of the area have developed only comparatively recently. Even so, there are numerous distinguished American academics, foreign service officers, and commentators who are not only cognizant of the affairs of the region but are also insightful when analyzing trends and the impact of particular events. Perhaps the main difference in forming policies and approaches is the tendency for U.S. policy makers to decline the advice of their experts while the general inclination in Europe is to abide by such advice. In any event, in recent years European and American perceptions of developments in the Indian Ocean region have often diverged alarmingly. For example, the declining position of the shah of Iran in 1978–79 was more correctly appreciated by some European chancelleries than by Washington, although the real impact of the Iranian Revolution was not well understood by any; in West European capitals the "Soviet threat" to the Persian Gulf is taken less seriously than in Washington; during the Carter administration, Washington's attempts to come to an understanding with Moscow in order to limit superpower presence in the Indian Ocean were viewed with skepticism in London and with utter suspicion in Paris where fear was expressed of an "American-Soviet condominium" in the region; in Washington, European attitudes toward the Arabs are characterized as opportunistic, while Western European leaders consider the United States to be dangerously biased in favor of Israel; and, finally, the EEC has granted de facto recognition to the PLO, while the United States refuses to do so until the PLO recognizes the existence of Israel.

Of all the issues in the Indian Ocean region, the oil supply (with its Arab-Israeli connection) is the one that affects and interests Europeans most vitally. It is also the issue on which Washington and European capitals have most often disagreed. Washington, for instance, believed that Europeans torpedoed the 1973–74 attempt to set up a common front against the exorbitant increase in the oil price and the embargo by Arab OPEC members. Such matters aside, Europeans recognize that they are much more closely located to the Middle East than the United States is and that they will remain dependent on imported oil from this region far longer and to a greater extent than the United

States will. On the other hand, they see the United States as being in a much better position to ensure the secure supplies of this oil.

The strategic implications of this situation are mixed, both for the United States and for Western Europe. Should the former accord priority to the "coalition strategy," that is, to the defense of Western Europe by conventional forces? Or should it pursue a "maritime strategy," that is, grant priority to securing SLOCS, primarily those that are used for transporting oil from the Persian Gulf? Britain and France may also have to make such a choice. America's RDF will certainly detract from the forces available for the defense of Europe. Similarly, for Britain and France to deploy forces in the Indian Ocean would weaken their contributions to NATO in the European theater. These are dilemmas, the resolution of which the countries of Western Europe and the United States must share. More than the priorities of defense or strategic policies will be affected by these decisions.

28. Japanese Interests in Indian Ocean Security ◾
Taketsugu Tsurutani

The Importance of the Indian Ocean to Japan

One of the most disturbing aspects of Japan's international environment in the last quarter of the twentieth century is the emergence of the Indian Ocean region as the most imminent flash point for a major international confrontation. Until the late 1970s, security-minded Japanese had focused on Europe and the Far East, the two regions that were traditionally viewed as the most likely to pose serious threats to world peace and security. The Indian Ocean region, as one newspaper noted, had remained "outside their security consciousness."[1] But the Iranian Revolution, followed by the Soviet military intervention in Afghanistan, jolted the Japanese out of their indifference toward the region. The jolt was all the more acute because the Japanese were suddenly forced to realize that their nation was far more dependent upon the stability of the region than any other major state and that indeed their survival as an industrialized democracy depended on it. Nearly three-quarters of Japan's oil requirement are supplied through the Indian Ocean region. Fully one-third of Japanese exports and three-fifths of their imports are transshipped through the Indian Ocean. One study recently found that giant freighters head for Japan at intervals of five miles on the ocean's sea lanes.[2] Another estimated that seventy-seven supertankers come out of the Strait of Hormuz every day, one out of every five destined for Japan.[3] Serious disruption of the region's stability would have potentially devastating consequences for Japan. Japan's stake in Indian Ocean security, therefore, is critically high.

This high stake is threatened not merely by the ongoing Iranian Revolution and the continuing Soviet military occupation of Afghanistan. These two major events only attest to the volatility of the region and the unpredictability of the security contingencies that might arise. This volatility and unpredictability are in sharp contrast to the conditions in those two major regions of traditional East-West tension, Europe and the Far East. The possibility of serious instability in Europe cannot be ruled out, of course, inasmuch as the two contending military blocs continue to fear it. The probability of such a contingency, however, remains low despite the exuberant verbal exchanges between the two superpowers. A modus vivendi (and operandi) of considerable resilience in East-West relations prevails there, based in no small measure on each bloc's sound respect for the other's economic utility and military capability. Only gross miscalculation or ideological rigidity would give rise to a violent confrontation in Europe.

A condition of fundamental stability also seems to obtain in the other traditional region of East-West geostrategic focus, the Far East (often referred to as Northeast Asia). The likelihood that Japan would come under serious military threat is extremely low despite the seemingly large Soviet military buildup in the region in recent years. Such a threat would materialize only as part of a horizontal escalation of an East-West confrontation elsewhere. The same may be said of the Korean Peninsula, notwithstanding the still simmering tension between Seoul and Pyongyang. A combination of changes in the relative national capabilities of the two halves of the peninsula, the presence of some twenty-eight thousand American ground combat troops as a trip wire, and the palpable unwillingness of either half's principal ally (or allies) to support its venture against the other, virtually eliminate the probability of a violent eruption there. As for Sino-Soviet relations, Beijing's preoccupation with modernization and Moscow's overriding concerns with the incipient instability of its East European satellites and the quagmire in Afghanistan would likely prevent each from undertaking any serious action against the other. Thus, as one analyst observed recently, in the Far East, "The regional stability the United States has long desired now is an established fact."[4]

All this is not to say, of course, that the dangers of conflict in either Europe or the Far East have entirely disappeared. The point here is that serious security problems in each of these regions are manageable because of the relative clarity of its political topography, the very predictability of any likely contingencies, and the mutuality of restraint that has been tested over time.

The same cannot be said about the Indian Ocean region and this is precisely the cause for Japan's growing, albeit still repressed, fear. Much of the region's political topography is unsettled, in fact, dangerously volatile; contingencies that could arise defy prediction; and this volatility and unpredictability in turn render restraint between adversaries unreliable. It is in this sense that one strategist laments, "We do not know who the enemy may be or where he may attack."[5] Security problems in the region appear unusually intractable and some of them are distinctly worrisome. Indeed, Japanese analysts have identified four general types of potential security threats to the region: a direct Soviet military action against the oil-rich Persian Gulf area, violence between or among states of the region, revolutionary upheaval within one or more of these states, and guerrilla attacks on oil fields and/or coastal waters leading to the Strait of Hormuz.[6] The trouble, as these analysts see it, is that currently there is no effective way to cope with any of these threats should they evolve into more tangible dangers.

Under these circumstances, Japan's objective regarding Indian Ocean security should be clear. One government document concluded in 1980 that the security of the region was "the major premise" for insuring continued supplies of oil for the nation and that, while it was impossible for Japan alone to defend her lifeline stretching through the region, it was imperative that the government give critical consideration to "alternative measures" and to the "sharing of the task of maintaining the security of the region."[7] At about the same time, the newly established Security Policy Planning Committee (SPPC) of the Ministry for Foreign Affairs stated in its first policy review for the 1980s that Japan "should, as a responsible member of the international community and on the basis of a global perspective, endeavor to help maintain and strengthen world peace and security . . . and cooperate in the task of preventing armed conflicts in Asia and elsewhere and reinforce [cooperative international] efforts to contain existing conflicts and seek their early resolution."[8] The Japan Defense Agency (JDA), departing from its traditional indifference to the Indian Ocean region, discussed the area for the first time in its 1980 *Defense White Paper*. The 1982 *Defense White Paper* was particularly emphatic about the security of the region, calling attention to what it termed "the Soviet Union's traditional focus" on the Persian Gulf and Indian Ocean region.[9]

The northern Indian Ocean is some thirty-six hundred miles wide stretching from the Strait of Malacca to the Strait of Hormuz; the Strait of Malacca is another thirty-two hundred miles from southwestern Japan. Japan's Maritime Self-Defense Force (MSDF), with its currently planned contingent of sixty destroyers and sixteen submarines, cannot even defend the western Pacific sea lanes, let alone those in the Indian Ocean. In addition, there is no way by which Japan alone could defend those Indian Ocean sea lanes without the rapid construction of massive naval task forces, including attack submarines and aircraft carriers for antisubmarine warfare, most of which would have to be deployed permanently in the region. Such a proposition is totally impractical and unlikely for an array of reasons, of which only one is fiscal. Moreover, sea-lane security in the Indian Ocean region is only part of the larger security problem. "Sea power would only suffice," notes one expert, "to secure the oil access and routes, of no strategic value if we lose the oil fields themselves."[10] In short, a Japanese naval presence in the Indian Ocean region, however formidable it might look, could not address the types of threats that Japanese analysts fear most.

The Japanese government has never made a clear statement concerning "alternative measures" by which it could share "the task of maintaining the security of the region." Nor can it be expected to do so for the moment. Japan's contribution to this task would have to be predicated upon the formation of an appropriate domestic consensus that, in turn, cannot be shaped in the absence of a unified security arrangement designed for the effective maintenance of stability in the region and clearly sustained by a firm Western alliance. At the moment there is no such arrangement and, consequently, the Japanese government is hard put to shape an appropriate intragovernmental (let alone popular) consensus on what specifically it should do to contribute to the maintenance of Indian Ocean security.

Existing Security Proposals

The absence of a credible Western security arrangement for the Indian Ocean region does not mean that no attempts are being made. Security-minded Japanese, however, are extremely skeptical of the effectiveness or implementability of such attempts as have been made thus far. Of those attempts, the development of an American Rapid Deployment Force (RDF) is the most concrete response to the security crisis in the region and it needs no detailed description here. Japanese analysts tend to contend, however, that there is less to the RDF than meets the eye.[11] They find a wide gap between the RDF's current as well as ultimate capability (a highly integrated 300,000-man, four-service force) and the types of security contingencies they consider most likely. In the case of a Soviet invasion of, say, Iran in the wake of post-Khomeini civil disorder, there would be very little that the RDF could do unless units of sufficient strength were already in Iran—a highly improbable scenario. Not only are Soviet forces already positioned in Iran's immediate vicinity, but they also have far more airborne divisions that could be mobilized than does the United States. As one analysis notes, "Soviet fighter aircraft could be within easy reach of the Gulf from airfields in Afghanistan, while the United States has no bases or airfields in the area at all—and forward airfields would be essential for any military operation to be effective."[12] American aircraft carriers, if they happened to be within sufficiently close proximity, could cause some discomfort to the invading Soviet forces but this would mean their own exposure to Soviet air attack emanating from occupied Iranian airfields or air bases in southern Afghanistan. Airborne counterintervention, in the meantime, would be extremely hazardous without a simultaneous landing on the Iranian shore of massive ground forces, but this would be hopelessly delayed because of the distance these forces and their logistical support would have to be transported. Short of obtaining forward bases in neighboring states for these combat forces, the likelihood of which is remote, quick seizure by the RDF of "the southern oil-producing portion of Iran before the Soviets could establish a viable military presence there" is earnestly to be wished but not seriously to be expected.[13]

The likelihood of intraregional conflict is much greater in Japanese eyes than that of a Soviet military invasion of the region. Indeed, one such conflict has been going on between Iraq and Iran. The fact that the presence in Persian Gulf waters of some thirty ships of the United States Sixth and Seventh fleets, including two formidable aircraft carriers, did not prevent the outbreak of that conflict suggests the rather limited utility of the RDF for the prevention of future intraregional conflict even if RDF units were deployed in close proximity to the contending states. This, however, is not the only problem in such a contingency. "U.S. military intervention to prevent or stop a conflict between states in the area or to support a friendly ruler in trouble would elicit broad-based opposition to the United States," argues Daniel Newsom, a seasoned specialist. Such intervention "would very likely result in exactly what it sought to avoid: severely curtailed oil production."[14]

This pessimistic scenario leads to the third type of security threat viewed as possible by Japanese analysts: internal upheaval in one or more of the major states in the region, especially in the gulf area. America's experience in Iran seems to suggest the high probability that external intervention in a politically unstable state of the region for the purpose of shoring up its incumbent regime would prove to be counterproductive. At the very best, such intervention would amount to a high-stakes gamble unless the RDF were prepared to occupy the country in question. As Newsom contends, "Political upheaval can but need not result in the loss of either production or access [to oil]; outside intervention will almost certainly destroy both."[15] If such an outside intervention turned out to be successful, moreover, it would surely entail enormous political and security costs in the form of resentment and fear by other states in the region. Some of those regimes may desire some form of American military presence in the region, but it should be remembered that such desire is "counterbalanced by fears that such a presence will increase their own political and military vulnerability."[16]

The threat of guerrilla actions against oil fields, pipelines, ports, and sea lanes leading to the Strait of Hormuz could not be prevented by the RDF and, indeed, might well be triggered by the RDF response itself. Such threats could be dealt with only by the local regimes concerned, if at all.

Thus, the general Japanese view is that the RDF, even when fully developed and equipped, cannot serve the purpose expected by its proponents. Instead, it could provoke the Soviet Union into expanding its military presence along the region's periphery and could also aggravate the conflict between pro-Western and anti-Western factions within the region's states.[17] This is part of the reason for the Japanese government's ambiguity toward U.S. eagerness for the full development of the RDF.

In December 1980 a joint Japanese-American study group issued a proposal concerning "the common security interests of Japan, the United States, and NATO." The emergence of a security crisis in the Indian Ocean region commanded its acute concern, and the proposal called for close mutual consultation among industrial democracies and the establishment of a "credible" policy of deterrence in the region. It also recommended as essential the joint contribution of "appropriate military assets" by the United States, France, West Germany, Britain, and Canada "to enhance allied capability and to demonstrate allied solidarity" for the maintenance of security in the region. It further recommended the contribution of "civil assets" by other NATO states and Japan, "including airlift and sealift, to support this allied presence" in the region.[18]

In view of the political topography of the region, the "allied presence" could only be in the form of a multinational Western fleet, with ground combat troops of sufficient strength to be airlifted from Europe, Japan, and the United States only after a serious event had occurred. But an "allied" fleet of sorts, it should be remembered, was already in place when the joint proposal was made—some thirty American ships, France's twelve-ship Indian Ocean Fleet, and some British naval vessels—but its presence did nothing to inhibit the Iranian Revolution, the

Soviet invasion of Afghanistan, or the outbreak of the Iraq-Iran war. The utility of any allied fleet, however large, would be confined to the protection of Indian Ocean sea lanes from naval and air attack, the least likely of potential security contingencies. And deployment of combat troops from Europe, Japan (U.S. Forces, Japan), and the United States in other types of contingencies would face the same difficulties noted earlier regarding the RDF. The joint proposal, in the words of one Japanese analyst, was therefore little more than "idle barber-shop talk."[19]

Another security proposal regarding the Indian Ocean region that caught Japanese attention was one made jointly by the directors of America's Council on Foreign Relations, West Germany's Forschungsinstitut des Deutschen Gesellschaft, France's Institut des Relations Internationales, and Britain's Royal Institute of International Affairs early in 1981. It called for deterrence against Soviet adventurism, the defense of Hormuz, assistance to friendly states calling for help, and quick force deployment to oil fields in an emergency. It argued that "there must be active *European military participation* on the ground and at sea. . . . Arrangements should be based on shared U.S.-European responsibility and truly collective decision making."[20] As had the earlier Japanese-American proposal, this four-nation report recommended closer and sustained consultation among the United States, its major NATO allies, and Japan, calling for the creation of "*new mechanisms* for truly collective decision making." The United States, Britain, France, West Germany, and Japan were to form such a mechanism for "joint assessments and crisis management . . . to deal with developments in the Gulf and Southwest Asia."[21] To the Japanese, however, the exact nature of the specific and workable procedures that were to be established or the strategies that could be worked out remained obscure, even though in principle their Foreign Ministry viewed as proper Japan's participation in multinational consultation and decision making concerning the region's security because of the Indian Ocean's indispensability to its own security.[22]

What inhibits the Japanese government from making clear the manner in which it could contribute to, and thus share the responsibility for, the maintenance of security in the Indian Ocean region? First and foremost is the absence of a clear and consistent policy direction, a concrete and credible strategy, and an unambiguous common commitment on the part of the United States and its NATO allies regarding the issue. Under present circumstances, the Japanese government is unable to shape a proper domestic consensus and, accordingly, is forced to continue evading its share of the burden and responsibility. Given its geostrategic location, the inherent limits of its military capability, and its relations with its neighbors, Japan's role can only be supplementary to a common Western strategy in the region. Despite this basic imperative, however, what the Japanese see is increasing discord between the United States and its major European allies on an array of security issues, including those relative to the Indian Ocean region.[23] This discord constitutes a serious impediment to the formation of the domestic consensus necessary for formulating the specific aspects of Japan's contribution to the common defense of the region.

Japan's Policy Predicament

For the moment, therefore, Japan's security policy toward the Indian Ocean region cannot but seem quiescent and ambiguous. This is not to say, however, that nothing is being done with regard to this critical problem. Indeed, for some time now the Japanese government has been gingerly attempting to create a political climate favorable to the shaping of an eventual consensus that would admit of a more "responsible" security policy. Two phenomena are particularly pertinent here. One is a new governmental vocabulary, the other, an increasingly frequent use of "trial balloons."

Postwar Japanese foreign policy was characterized by judicious politophobic avoidance of anything that would smack of an involvement in realpolitik. As its basic policy orientation, the nation's principal concern in international dealings was economic, under the official principle of separating economics from politics. Insofar as international political and security issues were concerned, Japan was not a part of, but rather was apart from, the community of nations. This traditional seclusionist posture is now undergoing some significant change. For example, in 1980 the newly established Security Policy Planning Committee (SPPC) of the Foreign Ministry (that such a policy body was established was significant in itself) specifically referred to Japan as "a responsible member of the international community" and stressed the need for "a global perspective" as the basis for the nation's external policy.[24] The 1981 *Defense White Paper* contained a section entitled, "The Role of Japan as a Member of the Western Bloc," a reference that had never been made before. The joint communiqué issued by the Japanese prime minister and the U.S. president at their summit meeting in the spring of 1981 called Japanese-American security relations "an alliance," a reference that caused considerable public controversy in Japan.[25] Terms and phrases such as "common defense" and "sharing international responsibilities" are now common currency. And, as if to underscore the putative solidarity with other advanced industrial democracies as "a member of the Western bloc," a suprapartisan delegation of eight members of Parliament attended the 1982 annual session of the North Atlantic Council in London as observers.[26]

In anticipation of the eventual emergence of a credible common Western policy and strategy for the maintenance of Indian Ocean security, the Japanese government is also floating a number of trial balloons to influence popular attitudes and public opinion in the direction it deems ultimately necessary. For example, as early as the fall of 1980, in response to a parliamentary query about international security surveillance for safe passage through the Strait of Hormuz, the Foreign Ministry stated that it considered the nation's sharing of the cost of such an arrangement as "constitutional."[27] In the same year, the government's written response to certain opposition questions contended that existing laws pertaining to the self-defense forces did not forbid their participation in international peacekeeping missions not involving combat or the use of arms in discharging their objectives. It also revealed that the government was reviewing various options for providing personnel and supplies to such United Nations missions.[28] It was the first time that the government officially admitted that it was contemplating direct involvement in such international security activities. As for Indian Ocean security in particular, the first specific and authoritative statement of the need for Japan's participation was made in the summer of 1980 by an influential member of the ruling Liberal Democratic party, a former director-general of the JDA. On the occasion of the twentieth anniversary of the 1960 Japan-U.S. security pact, he stressed in his keynote address that, to the extent that Indian Ocean security was directly linked to Japan's own security, "We can no longer respond [to potential security contingencies in the region] solely within the context of the traditional legalistic interpretation of the security treaty as applicable only to the geographical area of the Far East."[29] More recently, the incumbent JDA director-general publicly argued that Japan was being complacent in its insistence on adherence to the Peace Constitution, the three antinuclear principles (no possession, no manufacture, and no deployment of nuclear weapons on Japanese soil), and the "exclusively defensive posture."[30] The director-general of the Foreign Ministry's Treaties Bureau testified in the Diet that it was the government's view that military actions by the U.S. Forces, Japan (USFJ), are not restricted to the Far East and that in the event of an external attack on the Far East or a threat to its adjacent regions, they may be extended beyond the traditional geographical definition of the Far East.[31] In so testifying, he clearly linked the nation's security (under the existing bilateral security pact) to the stability and safety of such adjacent regions as the Indian Ocean area. Shortly thereafter, it was officially disclosed that the government was considering the adequacy of the self-defense force.[32] In addition, on the eve of his first visit to the White House as the nation's newly elected chief executive, Premier Nakasone told a press conference that "our strengthening of our self-defense capability should allow the U.S. to deploy its resources more effectively for the peace of the world."[33]

These are but a few examples of official government statements that are clearly designed, as critics of the government and of the ruling party suspect, to cultivate the kind of popular climate that would help shape an appropriate policy consensus if and when the United States and its European allies agree on a credible common policy regarding Indian Ocean security. In one sense, therefore, it may be said that the Japanese government is doing all it can under the circumstances, even though the United States and its European allies continue to complain that it is not doing as much as it should. It is precisely because Japan's security is inextricably linked to the security of the entire Western alliance that it cannot do more than it is now doing so long as the basic policy and strategy of the United States and its European allies remain unclear, discordant, or lacking in credibility. For Japan to do more would mean running the risk of becoming involved in ill-conceived security measures of the United States and/or its NATO allies, thus jeopardizing its vastly expanded international as well as national interests.

Japan's Contribution to Indian Ocean Security

It is difficult, of course, to foretell the specific manner in which Japan should and could share the task of maintaining Indian Ocean security, but some general parameters within which it is capable of sharing the task may be identified. These parameters are the function of the nation's particular geostrategic location, the specific capability it is most suited to demonstrate, and its unique domestic and external constraints. The imperative context within which it should and could share the task includes the unity of the Western alliance, the clarity and consistency of its common security policy, and the credibility of its comprehensive strategy.

In the military dimension of Indian Ocean security, Japan's role should best be indirect. As one semi-official Japanese analysis noted, it is essentially the United States, assisted by its major NATO allies, that "can hope to oppose the Soviet Union on any scale" in the region.[34] Geostrategic factors unavoidably confer upon the Soviet Union a significant operational advantage in the region, but, as the same analysis argued, "The cost of Soviet military intervention can nonetheless be made high by a demonstrated capability and a will to resist it."[35] Provided that there is a common and consistent Western policy and a credible strategy of deterrence, Japan can take measures that will enable the United States to divert to the Indian Ocean region a considerable portion of those strategic resources currently devoted to Japan and the Far East. One such measure, obviously, could be an increase in military spending in order to raise the level of its air and naval capability for its own defense and for maintaining the safety of western Pacific sea lanes, tasks that are now underwritten by the United States. Another measure would be to assume the cost of USFJ maintenance so that the United States might divert more financial resources to Indian Ocean security. Yet another measure Japan is capable of undertaking would be logistical, e.g., the use of its sealift and airlift capability for its allies' security efforts as needed. All these measures and others would necessarily increase the government's security-related fiscal burden beyond the traditional limit of 1 percent of gross national product (GNP). As "a responsible member of the international community" and "a member of the Western bloc" with common security interests in the Indian Ocean region, however, Japan should no longer insist on that complacent fiscal limit on security spending. Japan is the second largest economic power in the Western world, yet other industrial democracies have been devoting three to six times more, proportionately, to their common security needs, including, directly or indirectly, Japan's own defense. Equity and fairness demand that, as an economic superpower, Japan make as great a sacrifice in this regard as its security partners.[36]

As noted earlier, no military measure the Western alliance might undertake could effectively cope with intraregional conflict, revolutionary domestic upheaval, or guerrilla attacks against oil fields and ports. These are the kinds of contingencies that can be prevented only by the states concerned. As to the prevention of intraregional conflict, about the only action the Western alliance or any of its members can take is diplomatic (for example, trying to defuse the danger in concert with the region's states by the use of various peaceful means of suasion). Nations in the Indian Ocean region can prevent or deal with revolutionary domestic upheaval or guerrilla action only to the extent that they possess adequate national resiliency, which is a function of internal stability, regime viability, and consequent policy consistency. The principal means to these ends are largely nonmilitary and it is here that Japan can demonstrate its not inconsiderable capability to contribute through economic means. Moreover, this type of contribution is most compatible with the nation's traditional insistence on peaceful means of promoting the stability and security of the world. Indeed, thoughtful foreign observers who recognize the special postwar constraints on Japanese external policy accept the argument that the contribution Japan should make to promoting international stability has to be largely indirect and that "increased Japanese economic aid to threatened countries . . . would free these countries to spend more of their own resources on defense."[37]

The extent to which Japan has been making such contributions is far from impressive, however, and the manner in which they have been made bespeaks of its traditional, myopic, trade-centered external policy. This pattern is evident in Japan's official development assistance (ODA) policy, a policy that has been determined not by any critical political and military security considerations but rather by immediate economic calculus. This is the function of its vaunted principle of separating economics from politics in its international dealings.

Japan's ODA has been rather meager for the second largest economy of the world. ODA constituted only 0.26 percent of Japan's GNP in 1979 and 0.32 percent in 1980. These figures were the third lowest among the major members of the Organization for Economic Cooperation and Development (OECD).[38] In terms of direct governmental policy, even if one adds Japan's ODA and defense appropriations and compares them to similar figures for other OECD nations, Japan's contribution to the stability and security of the world is very low. On a per capita basis, in 1980, the Japanese figure was only $98 ($75 for defense plus $23 for ODA), in contrast to $665 for the United States, $532 for Britain, $469 for West Germany, and $464 for France.[39] The astonishingly low figure for Japan suggests, then, that the country retains an extraordinarily high degree of what is called "commitment capacity,"[40] and it is this capacity that should be utilized. Among the advanced industrial democracies, Japan is now in the best position to make a significant contribution to the common task of enhancing stability in the major geostrategic regions of the world including the Indian Ocean region. As a matter of international fiscal equity, given its extraordinarily low level of defense spending, Japan should be the first major OECD member to budget 0.7 percent of GNP for ODA, a target set some years ago by OECD's Development Assistance Committee.

It is not merely the meagerness of the amount of ODA that Japan provides that causes serious concern. The way in which Japan has thus far distributed its ODA seems highly biased in favor of those states with which it trades heavily, regardless of levels of domestic poverty (as measured, for example, by per capita income). High-income states of the oil-rich Persian Gulf area would hardly seem in need of ODA, yet Japan in 1980 provided them with an average of sixty-six cents per inhabitant.[41]

Another group of nations that is of immediate economic value to Japan is the Association of South-East Asian Nations (ASEAN)—Indonesia, Malaysia, the Philippines, Singapore, and Thailand. Together with neighboring Australia, these states absorb 13 percent of Japan's total exports and provide 20 percent of its imports, including such key materials as oil (Indonesia and Malaysia), iron ore (Australia), bauxite (Indonesia), copper (the Philippines), lumber (Indonesia and the Philippines), and rubber and tin (Malaysia), among others. Japan therefore devotes some 40 percent of its ODA to the ASEAN states, ranging from $1.58 per Singaporean to $4.92 per Malaysian in 1980. (Incidentally, the per capita income in Singapore was $3,820 and in Malaysia, $1,320.) The average ODA per inhabitant from Japan in that year in the ASEAN states was $3.12.[42] It might, of course, be countered that Southeast Asia, together with Australia, is vital to the security of the Indian Ocean in that it constitutes the eastern flank of the ocean and that, therefore, Japan should naturally focus its developmental assistance on the area. That, however, does not appear to be the reason for the aid.

While containing various seeds of potential domestic instability (for example, vast income inequality, racial problems, political corruption) and facing some disquieting regional security problems, including the Vietnamese occupation of Laos and Cambodia backed by the Soviet Union, these ASEAN states are perhaps the most stable among the nations surrounding the Indian Ocean (that is, apart from Australia); they are among the fastest growing economies in the world. In terms of relative criticality of ODA needs, the ASEAN states should rank rather low. In contrast, there are a number of other major nations bordering on the Indian Ocean whose actual or potential instability would pose more direct threat to Indian Ocean security. India and Pakistan in Southwest Asia, and Somalia in East Africa, to cite a few examples, are not only strategically of more immediate importance but also desperately poor. Alleviation of poverty and faster economic development are the first prerequisites for the cultivation of minimally imperative national resilience in these states. Japanese policy has not addressed this most crucial problem. In 1980, for example, Japan's ODA contribution to India amounted to only 5.7 cents; Pakistan received 47 cents per inhabitant and Somalia less than 10 cents.[43] Per capita incomes in these nations were all well below $300.

Indeed, Japan's new security consciousness regarding the Indian Ocean region does not seem to go much beyond the oil fields of the Persian Gulf and the sea lanes over which the oil is transported or beyond the deposits of economic bounty. Apart from the ASEAN states, Australia, and the gulf oil states, the Indian Ocean is surrounded by poverty, that most endemic, most persistent, and most potent of all causes of instability and potential upheaval and violence. But Japan remains remarkably unmoved by those poverty-plagued nations of Southwest Asia and East Africa, a fact quite evident in the general paucity of hard news on these nations and areas in Japanese mass media except for occasional historical, anthropological, anecdotal, touristic, or "human interest" snippets. Government documents and pronouncements are largely devoid of any critical reference to or discussion of poverty and instability of these areas bordering on the Indian Ocean. (For example, there has been no mention of Africa as such in defense white papers and the coverage of Southwest Asia and East Africa in diplomacy white papers has been extremely cursory and superficial.) The low level of serious concern with these areas, in particular Africa, is also evinced in the virtual absence over the years of visits by cabinet-rank Japanese leaders who have otherwise become extraordinarily peripatetic since the first Arab oil shock of 1973. None of the 349 government scholars sent overseas for study in 1980 went to Africa and fewer than 5 percent of the foreign students and trainees to study in Japan in 1980 under the auspices of the Japanese government's technical assistance and cooperation program were African.[44]

Clearly, there is need for Japan to become more critically concerned with the stability and security of Southwest Asia and East Africa, especially as a member of the Western bloc and given its uncommonly high commitment capacity. With a greater utilization of its commitment capacity, together with some needed shifts in regional allocation, Japan could vastly increase its economic assistance to these strategic states and areas, thereby enabling them to improve their domestic economic and social conditions as well as to devote more of their own resources to strengthening their internal and external security.

A Need to Share Responsibility

The security of the Indian Ocean region is vital to Japan's national interests, far more vital than to any other advanced industrial democracy. Japan's deepening concern with the issue may compel it to emerge from its "pacifist," seclusionist shell. The country has hidden in this shell during most of the postwar period in reaction to the devastating and traumatic defeat to which its aggressive external conduct had led. Japan now recognizes the necessity to share the responsibility, in a manner commensurate with its national power, for the maintenance of security in the vital region through which its lifeline extends. It also recognizes that any such sharing of responsibility can occur only within the context of the solidarity of the United States and its European allies, the clarity of their common strategy, and the continuity of their policy direction. In the absence of that context, a critical domestic consensus for Japanese participation in the difficult and sensitive task of protecting the security of the region cannot be formed. How soon those imperative conditions for Japan's participation will be met remains uncertain. "The industrial democracies need to unite and work out a common strategy in the face of threats to their vital interests," observes one senior Japanese Foreign Ministry official, but the fundamental problem plaguing them is "the fact that no international system of sharing responsibilities to ensure global security . . . in response to the diffusion of power has yet been created." He goes on to argue that "the absence of such a system has resulted in what might be called an imbalance between power and responsibility due to the failure of countries to assume responsibilities commensurate with their political or economic strength."[45] In an important sense, then, what appears to be Japan's ambivalence and apparent irresponsibility in the new strategic and political context of the Indian Ocean region is in large measure a function of the continuing inability of the United States and its major European allies to work out this system of sharing responsibilities, that is, an appropriate policy and credible strategy sustained by solidarity and will.

29. The People's Republic of China: Perspectives on the Indian Ocean ⬛ Russell B. Trood

Of the external powers whose interests in the Indian Ocean are examined in this volume, it is the People's Republic of China that can lay claim to the earliest associations with the region. Several centuries before Europeans began their penetration of the area, the Chinese had established a comprehensive network of trading relationships with communities throughout Asia, the Middle East, and, to a lesser extent, East Africa.[1] But despite a period of prolonged contact, the Chinese failed to establish any significant, permanent links with the communities, and later nation-states, of the region. By the middle of this century Chinese interests in the area amounted to little more than some minor trading links and a broad concern for the character of its relations with immediate neighbors in South and Southeast Asia. Only with the advent of a communist government and the formation of the People's Republic in

1949 was there a revival of China's interest in the region and a return to the more active role of an earlier era.

This chapter seeks to examine China's contemporary interests in the Indian Ocean. By way of preliminary observation, it is worthwhile noting that China's leaders and political commentators hardly ever refer to an "Indian Ocean region" and implicitly dismiss the idea of it forming a distinct and identifiable geostrategic arena. Their approach conforms with China's tradition of emphasizing the global and ideological coherence of its foreign policy and is consistent with the view that the concept of regionality contributes little to an understanding of the complex forces that underlie international political life.[2] As one scholar of Chinese foreign policy has noted, "The Chinese apply their particular Sinified Marxist-Leninist yardstick to international developments and formulate their international policies and practices accordingly."[3] In this process certain concepts regarded as universally relevant to international behavior such as class, international contradictions, the struggle against imperialism, and adherence to the principles of coexistence are of greater relevance to the formulation of policy than regional frameworks and designs. Thus, China's response to international events in the Indian Ocean is more likely to be dictated by the broader ideological framework of its foreign policy than by a regional strategy conceived independently thereof.

As a consequence, it becomes difficult to isolate Chinese policies and interests toward a particular region, like the Indian Ocean, from general global interests and the policies they dictate. Yet, as regards the Indian Ocean region, the task of defining and analyzing Chinese interests is rendered more feasible by two realities, the first of which is China's geographic proximity to the region. Like most states, China has a demonstrable interest in events taking place in the areas adjacent to its borders. These in turn dictate policy and define the character of China's relations with its immediate environment. As will become evident from the discussion that follows, the activities of the superpowers, especially the Soviet Union, in areas close to China's borders have had implications for the evolution of Chinese policy toward the whole Indian Ocean region.

Second, most of the states of the region are less-developed countries (LDCs), comprising a substantial proportion of all Third World countries. Since the early 1950s, Chinese foreign policy has emphasized the political, economic, and strategic congruity of interests said to exist between China and other Third World countries. China's leaders have made it a major thrust of their foreign policy to build upon these common interests to achieve a range of international political objectives.

Here again linkages to the region serve to define Chinese interests. However remote the idea of an Indian Ocean *region* may be from the ideological framework of China's policy makers, the social, economic, political, and strategic profile of the area has effectively elevated it to a place of definable and significant, though not perhaps transcendent, interest in the operational conduct of Chinese foreign policy.

The Strategic Dimension

The more dangerous superpower

China's attitude toward a decade or more of expansionist Soviet foreign policy is of central importance to an understanding of the evolution of Beijing's interests in the Indian Ocean region.[4] While Beijing's professed ideological affinity with particular Indian Ocean countries persists and gives rise to interests in the region, until fairly recently the expansion of the Soviet presence and its implications for global and Chinese security tended to define the priorities for China's interests in the area.

Chinese criticism of Soviet foreign policy has been commonplace since the break between the two countries in 1958–59. But until the late 1960s Beijing was as anxious to expose the dangers of American policies as it was to warn against the global ambitions of the Soviet Union. Both had imperialist designs and were seen to be working in collaboration to achieve world domination. So perceived, they both represented threats to international peace and security. From the late 1960s, changes in the ideological framework of Chinese foreign policy produced a reappraisal of Soviet and American policies and resulted in a reevaluation of their international roles. Born of the intense domestic political struggles of the Cultural Revolution and fresh perceptions of the international environment, these changes accompanied the reemergence of Mao Zedong and Zhou Enlai (over Lin Biao) as the principal architects of Chinese foreign policy and were to transform some of the policy's basic tenents. This process and many of its implications has been analyzed extensively in the literature and requires no further elaboration here.[5] It will be sufficient to note that, from about 1967, Soviet policies around the world became the subject of increasing Chinese attention and disapproval. By 1973 the Chinese had reached the conclusion that the two superpowers were no longer colluding to attain world hegemony but were in reality contending for this prize. Further, the Soviet Union was judged to be ahead and clearly the "more dangerous superpower." The threat from the United States had not disappeared but, compared to that now posed by the Soviet Union, in the Indian Ocean as elsewhere, it was less significant. Soviet revisionist social imperialism, according to Beijing, was on the offensive and "engaged in all round striving for hegemony."[6]

While the Chinese regarded Moscow's drive for hegemony as a global phenomenon, the rapid expansion of Soviet military and political contacts throughout the Indian Ocean region led them to view the area as a major arena for the implementation of Soviet policy. Beijing's natural inclination was to try and counter those advances. At the same time, the Chinese were intent upon protecting and promoting their own interests in the region, especially their burgeoning relations with Third World states. Together these imperatives served to raise the level of China's interest in the area and led the Chinese to take a more active and conspicuous role in its affairs.

Initially, Soviet activities attracted critical, but nonetheless restrained, attention from Chinese leaders and commentators. But as Chinese perceptions of the Soviet threat increased and were reinforced by continuing ideological differences Beijing reached for hyperbole to express its rebukes. By the mid-1970s Beijing was consistently accusing Moscow of deception, sabotage, aggression, intrigue, and much more in an attempt to establish its dominance in the Indian Ocean and the countries on its periphery. The Soviets' strategy, according to Beijing, was to place pressure on vulnerable locations in Asia and Africa as they "strive to create a situation [to] outflank Europe from the north and south."[7] Such activities were judged by Beijing to reflect "more realistic opportunities for the expansion of Soviet influence."[8]

During the early 1970s it was Soviet policy in the western half of the Indian Ocean region that provided the stimulus for so much Chinese criticism of Moscow's ambitions. In Asia, where the Americans were the imperialist aggressor by virtue of their war in Vietnam, Soviet policy was at something of a standstill, presenting fewer opportunities for Chinese condemnation. With the collapse of American power in Vietnam, however, the situation began to change. Beijing saw Moscow moving to fill the vacuum and urged the countries of Southeast Asia to be "on guard against the tiger at the back door while repulsing the wolf at the gate."[9]

After 1977 the behavior of the "tiger" was the cause of increasing alarm to Beijing. The spur in large measure was the development of closer relations between the Soviet Union and Vietnam. Faced with this and the deterioration in its own relations with Hanoi, Beijing, in the spring of 1978, refined its interpretation of the strategic situation in Southeast Asia. China's dispute with Vietnam could no longer be seen as being of only local relevance. It now became very clear that "the Soviet leadership is the main backer and instigator of the anti-China and anti-Chinese campaign in Viet Nam." As such it was evident that the Soviet Union was bringing Vietnam "into its strategic framework for world domination."[10] Vietnam's invasion of Kampuchea at the end of 1978 was seen from a similar perspective. Moscow was said to be "using the 'Cuba of Asia,' Viet Nam, as its hatchetman [to] seize the whole of Indochina, to dominate Southeast Asia and South Asia and so edge the United States out of the continent."[11]

Perhaps more ominous than either of these developments was the Soviet advance into Afghanistan in December 1979. It made clear "that the Kremlin ha[d] not changed its strategic tilt towards Western Europe but [was] pressing forward relentlessly." At the same time it "dramatize[d] a recent development—the linking up of the Kremlin's outflanking movement against Western Europe with its drive into the heart of Asia and the Pacific."[12] Thus, the Soviet invasion of Afghanistan confirmed for Beijing the accuracy of a line of analysis regarding Soviet behavior in the Indian Ocean that had been emerging over the past several years. In essence, the whole area was an arena for superpower rivalry. In Africa, throughout Asia, and on the high seas, the United States and the Soviet Union were tangentially competing for mastery of Western Europe as a step toward global hegemony. As part of this struggle Moscow was now moving rapidly, both unilaterally and in conjunction with its allies, to the position of being able to interdict vital Western lines of communication by controlling key choke points: the Red Sea, Suez, and the gulf in the northwest quadrant; Malacca, Lombok, and other straits in the east. Not only would domination of these vital seaways restrict the movement of Western, especially U.S., commercial and military shipping between the Indian and Pacific oceans (Moscow's dumbbell strategy), it would also restrain U.S. allies such as Japan from gaining access to vital resources. Simultaneously, Moscow's control over these vital waterways would facilitate its own naval deployments.

This rich and uncompromising assessment of Soviet strategy was, with minor modifications, to remain the essence of China's view on Moscow's policies over the next two years.[13] In the second half of 1982, however, there was a leavening of Beijing's rhetoric toward the Soviet Union and its policies in places like the Indian Ocean. This was so despite the persistence of most of the factors that had enabled the Chinese to construct their holistic conception of Soviet policy in the first place. In lieu of the frequent tirades opposing Soviet strategy and activities, Beijing began to offer comparatively calm, matter-of-fact reproofs to Moscow's continued presence in places like Afghanistan and its mischievous policies elsewhere in the region. The theme of the Indian Ocean as a place of superpower rivalry persisted but even this was expressed less often and with less hyperbole.[14]

The modification of Beijing's rhetoric can be explained in part by the interest that both Beijing and Moscow have shown in improved bilateral relations. Not since the late 1950s, prior to the split, have the two governments been on such communicative terms with one another. Of course, the present relationship hardly approaches the sometimes turbulent, but often cooperative, alliance that characterized the earlier period. Strong opposition factions in both countries continue to resist rapprochement; Moscow and Beijing remain deeply suspicious of each other's strategic ambitions and continue to be separated by an enormous ideological gulf. For all this, it is evident that a dialogue of sorts is in progress between the two countries that may lead to some form of accommodation of their conflicting interests.[15] While the Chinese are less enthusiastic about this process than the Soviets, they appear, nevertheless, to recognize the possibility that an improvement in relations could be to their advantage on several fronts, perhaps most notably with regard to the Vietnamese problem.

Whatever their intention, the talks now in progress offer little reason to think that there will be an immediate change in Beijing's attitude toward Moscow. Chinese leaders have identified three issues as impediments to improved relations: Afghanistan, Soviet forces on China's borders, and Kampuchea. At present none is within easy reach of resolution.[16] Further, should there be any appreciable expansion of the Soviets' presence in South or Southeast Asia or should they embark on a new military adventure, either in the area or elsewhere, Beijing's long-standing concerns over Soviet policy would quickly resurface and the rhetoric and hyperbole of the past years would almost certainly return. At the same time, the ideological differences that persist between the two communist giants continue to create policy imperatives. In the Indian Ocean region these will continue to be played out partly in the form of competition for influence within Third World countries.

Chinese perspectives on the Soviet Union have also been affected by another consideration: a shift in Beijing's assessment of superpower capabilities. Since 1981 the Chinese have drawn attention to the constraints and obstacles that confront Moscow.[17] They see these as having originated within the Soviet Union itself but do not discount the importance of international forces in frustrating Soviet strategy. The intensity of the USSR's rivalry with the United States, difficulties with Warsaw Pact allies (notably, in recent years, Poland), the unresolved situations in Afghanistan and Kampuchea, and the resolute struggle of the Third World to build a "united front against hegemonism" have all contributed to the Soviets' problems. These constraints imply a weakening of the threat posed by the Soviet Union and have been reflected in Chinese analyses of the contemporary international situation.

Corresponding to the constraints on Soviet behavior is a set of problems that frustrates the Americans' imperialist ambitions. Difficulties in Latin America, differences with European allies, a poor economic performance at home, and the continuing confrontation with Moscow are among the problems most often identified.[18] With both superpowers afflicted by difficulties, Beijing now argues that the military stalemate long evident in Europe is now a much more widespread phenomenon, apparent in all arenas where the two states are in competition, including the Indian Ocean.[19] From a doctrinal perspective at least, the situation offers some prospect that the Third World countries of the region will be able to cast aside the burdens of imperialism, achieve true independence, and, incidentally, develop closer relations with Beijing.

The threat to China

Although the Chinese have viewed the Soviet threat as pervasive, they have resisted the conclusion that China itself is in any immediate danger. In essence, the policy line has followed an analysis offered by Zhou Enlai at the Tenth Congress of the Chinese Communist party as long ago as August 1973. The cause of world "intranquility," according to Zhou, was the rivalry between the superpowers who were competing for global hegemony. The key place of their contention, he argued, was not China, which was "an attractive piece of meat coveted by all, [b]ut . . . very tough." Rather it was Europe where they were scrambling for superiority.[20] This theme of China being attractive to other countries, resistant to foreign domination, and remote from the focal point of world tension—of being, in short, threatened but not immediately endangered—has been articulated more or less consistently since 1973. It reflects the divisions that exist within the Chinese policy-making elite over the issue of the Soviet threat and, more particularly, over whether priority should be given to defense and preparation for war (with the Soviet Union) or, alternatively, to domestic economic reconstruction and development. The equivocal nature of the policy suggests that, while Chinese leaders like Zhou Enlai and, following Zhou's death in 1976, Deng Xiaoping have been able to maintain an emphasis on the domestic economic option, the opponents of this approach remain influential.

At the same time, the persistence of this theme highlights the ambiguous impact of the Soviet threat upon Chinese foreign policy. The principal source of that threat is the deployment of massive numbers of Soviet conventional forces and nuclear missiles along or near the Sino-Soviet border in central Asia. In 1969 the occurrence of several armed clashes in this region was an important factor in calling Beijing's attention to the dangers of Soviet policy.[21] Since then, other incidents have given rise to periods of tension that have, in turn, exacerbated existing problems in the bilateral relationship between Beijing and Moscow. Yet, from Beijing's perspective, having to contend with an external threat from central Asia is not a new development. Historically, the Chinese have always looked upon this exposed frontier as vulnerable to outside attack; the threat posed by the presence of Soviet forces is merely the latest manifestation of a problem that goes back centuries. So viewed, there is an element of predictability about the situation that may not reduce the overall threat but that does ensure a level of vigilance sufficient to give warning of any proposed attack. In addition, Beijing has further neutralized the extant danger by deploying a substantial number of its own forces in the region.[22] China has not, and is unlikely to, become complacent about the threat of the Soviet presence but compared to the uncertainties created by Soviet policy elsewhere, it sees the situation along the Sino-Soviet border as relatively stable and regards a war with the Soviets as only a remote possibility. In Beijing's view, "An armed attack against China, including a nuclear attack, would not prove useful, but would bog the Soviet Union down in a strategically embarrassing position. Therefore, the Soviet Union has adopted a policy of encircling and isolating China."[23]

In contrast, Beijing views the situation in South and Southeast Asia as anything but stable. There, China's differences with Vietnam, the latter's continuing close ties with Moscow and its occupation of Kampuchea, the unrelenting buildup of Soviet naval forces in the area, and Moscow's continued stay in Afghanistan all greatly alarm China's leaders. They regard Southeast Asia as one of the main "hot spots" of contemporary world politics and perceive China as now being surrounded by potentially aggressive neighbors. As one Chinese analyst wrote recently, "Moscow uses its pawn to threaten and attempt to pin down China from the South. . . . Vietnam is the knife the Soviet Union has at China's back."[24]

Given the stringent conditions China has laid down for the resolution of these problems and others, such as the border dispute with India, there is little likelihood the area will become tranquil or be free from "tensions and turmoils" in the foreseeable future. If China were a lesser power in the international system, this situation might conceivably preoccupy the political leadership and limit its foreign policy horizons. Beijing, however, has not become withdrawn as a result of the threats to its security. While the problems are regarded as serious, they have not caused China to curtail its active and ambitious international diplomacy, an important aspect of which is the pursuit of closer relations with Third World countries in the Indian Ocean.

The Political Dimension

Chinese policy toward the Third World owes much of its direction to Marxist-Leninist doctrine and the revolutionary experience of Chinese leaders. Within the context of communist ideology, the prominence accorded to principles such as the struggle against imperialism provided China with a natural link to the emerging and newly independent states of the Indian Ocean in the 1960s and it continues to do so. This ideological imperative is reinforced by a Chinese belief that their country shares, in the words of one scholar, "two important characteristics with the countries of Asia, Africa and Latin America: a common history of colonial and semi-colonial oppression and economies which were relatively backward and non-industrialized."[25] As he goes on to note, this common inheritance has allowed China to press its claim to identity of interest with the Third World in a way that competitors, such as the Soviet Union, cannot.

At the same time Beijing views its relations with Third World countries, in the Indian Ocean as elsewhere, in the context of its own aspirations within the international system. While China's leaders disavow any interest in China becoming the leader of the Third World, seeing it as tantamount to the exercise of hegemony,[26] they have consistently sought to gain recognition of their claim to be a legitimate spokesman for Third World interests on a range of international political, economic, and security issues. These efforts are part of the policy to reinforce China's sense of identity with Third World states,[27] but they also appear to be part of the more ambitious undertaking to establish China as a major international actor with a unique and independent role in the international system. For a country of China's military and economic potential, whose natural inclination is to avoid alliances, the aspiration to a position of prominence in the Third World offers a viable and attractive alternative to an international posture that leans toward either of the superpowers. At the same time, the burgeoning sense of common identity among Third World countries and their increasing inclination to act in concert to achieve international goals signify the advent of a formidable international coalition of states. For the Chinese, the prospect of being able to count on the support of such a grouping or bloc offers the possibility of greater international status and perhaps success in achieving the hitherto elusive goal of an international role comparable to that now performed by the United States and the Soviet Union. For all these reasons, Beijing in recent years has earnestly pressed ahead with a campaign to improve substantially its relations with all Third World countries.[28]

In the Indian Ocean region Beijing has reason to be pleased with the results of its diplomatic efforts; overall, China's standing in the area has improved markedly from the low point reached prior to the Cultural Revolution. In Africa, China's relationships with local regimes have generally transcended the difficulties with which they were plagued during the 1960s.[29] The main cause of those problems, the imperatives created by China's differences with the Soviet Union, has been overcome with changes both in the substance and style of Chinese policy toward Africa. While China's opposition to Soviet ambitions still tended to characterize and dictate the thrust of China's African policy during the 1970s, in general it did not interfere with Beijing's simultaneous drive for improved bilateral contacts. The extent to which relations had improved was demonstrated by Prime Minister Zhao Ziyang's extensive tour of Africa in December 1982.[30] China's diplomacy on the continent has been helped by a modest aid program and Beijing's uncompromising opposition to the policies emanating from Pretoria. The result has been the restoration of close relations between China and Tanzania and closer links with Zambia and Zimbabwe in southern Africa, and with Somalia and the Sudan on the horn.

Similarly, China's bilateral relations with the countries of the Persian Gulf, and the Middle East more generally, have shown a marked improvement over the past decade.[31] Beijing tends to look upon the area as being particularly vulnerable to Soviet pressure and has taken an evident interest in events and countries there largely for this reason. By doing so, China was able to profit from some of the diplomatic setbacks the Soviets suffered in places like Egypt. China has sided strongly with the Arab cause against Israel and has proved to be a consistent champion of the rights of the Palestinians. Chinese policy on the Iraq-Iran war has been cautious and for the most part balanced, although 1981 saw a slight tilt toward sympathy for Iran's position.[32] The Gulf Cooperation Council has received Beijing's consistent support.[33] Egypt remains China's closest friend in the area, while, overall, relations are more cordial with moderate states like Jordan, Oman, and Kuwait than with Syria and Libya, whose connections with Moscow and radical philosophies cause alarm in Beijing. The noticeable shortcoming in this pattern of generally improving Sino–Middle Eastern relations is the lack of any substantive Chinese ties with Saudi Arabia. Although several un-official contacts have taken place and there is movement toward closer relations, Saudi Arabia is diffident about the process and has generally sought to deflect Beijing's overtures.

Among the developing states of Asia, Beijing's attempts to estab-lish closer ties have met with mixed success. In Southeast Asia, an area of primary importance to Beijing, Chinese fortunes have undergone con-siderable change over the past decade. The pattern has been one of de-teriorating relations with the communist countries, notably Vietnam, and steadily improving contacts with the noncommunist states of the Association of South-East Asian Nations (ASEAN).[34] The countries of ASEAN have little enthusiasm for the Soviet Union's attempts to expand its influence in the area and are concerned about Vietnam's aggressive policies in Kampuchea and Laos. They are naturally sympathetic to-ward Beijing's anti-Soviet and anti-Vietnamese position and have joined with Beijing in supporting the Kampuchean resistance headed by Pol Pot. The diplomacy that has been necessary to sustain the coalition, to-gether with contacts on a range of other matters, has resulted in a steady improvement in relations over the past several years, although these have not been uniform among the ASEAN partners; Indonesia remains the most wary. The reticence and the general diffidence that still char-acterize ASEAN's attitude toward China reflect the irritants that continue to affect relations. The large number of overseas Chinese in several ASEAN states remains a source of tension, as does Beijing's reluctance to sever its connections with local communist parties engaged in subversive activities against governments in places like Malaysia and Thailand.

In South Asia, China's long-standing friendship with Pakistan sur-vived the death of former Prime Minister Bhutto and was strengthened considerably by the Soviet invasion of Afghanistan. Similarly, relations with Sri Lanka continue to be most cordial. As regards India, a series of bilateral talks and reciprocal visits of high officials suggest there is now movement toward reconciliation after the split caused by the Sino-Indian war of 1962.[35] Progress in this regard is likely to be slow and may, in any event, be inherently constrained by New Delhi's cordial relationship with Moscow and Beijing's support of Pakistan. Finally, among the remaining countries of the Indian Ocean region the Chinese have succeeded in achieving closer relations with such offshore island-states as the Maldives and the Seychelles.

From about 1972, Beijing's assumption that all Third World coun-tries shared an interest in opposing Moscow's strategic ambitions was both a motivation and a constant theme of China's drive to build bridges to the developing world. Yet the building of a "united front against hegemonism" was not, as already noted, China's only interest in better relations. It also does not account for the overall success of Beijing's Third World diplomacy in the Indian Ocean region. In large part that can be attributed to the cautious, pragmatic approach Beijing now adopts toward issues in the area and the disappearance of the often doctrinaire Marxist-Leninist policy prescriptions that used to accompany Chinese diplomacy. Since the early 1970s Beijing has been wary of injecting its own perspectives into local issues and disputes and generally has not done so, unless China's own interests are directly affected. This has not meant, however, that Beijing has taken little interest in regional problems or that China's leaders and commentators have been silent with regard to them. Chinese analyses of regional issues have often been lengthy and detailed, but they have consistently paid careful attention to local opinions and sensitivities.

Broadly, three lines of policy have emerged regarding Beijing's treatment of contentious regional issues. Where local, Third World opinion has tended to consensus, as in the case of attitudes toward the policies of the South African and Israeli governments, Beijing has offered rhetorical, and occasionally more substantive, support. Similarly, issues of areawide interest, such as the proposal to declare the Indian Ocean a zone of peace, that command broad Third World support, although with varying degrees of enthusiasm, have received Chinese backing.[36] In those cases where regional opinion has been divided, the Chinese have tended to distinguish issues on the basis of Soviet involvement. Where this has been overt, and even though the disputants may be developing countries, as in the case of the Somali-Ethiopian conflict, Beijing has tended to support the anti-Soviet party.[37] On other divisive issues where the Soviets have been less intrusive, as in the Iraq-Iran war, China has generally avoided taking sides, preferring to draw attention to the danger that the prolongation of conflicts will contribute to regional instability and create favorable opportunities for foreign penetration.[38]

Particular issues to one side, Chinese leaders have generally sought to cast their country in the role of a sympathetic friend of Third World states of the region. To this end they continue to reiterate China's status as a member of the Third World and to assert the unity of all Third World people and countries as they struggle against imperialism, exploitation, and the array of other forces that blights their existence.[39]

Before leaving this section it is worthwhile noting that besides its evidently strong ties to the Third World, China has good and improving relations with the only developed country in the Indian Ocean region: Australia. Since the institution of diplomatic relations in 1973, Beijing and Canberra have been able to establish a generally harmonious relationship. At the political level, the Chinese were pleased by the strident anti-Soviet stance of the Fraser government and its support, although uneven, for certain Third World issues. The general cordiality of the relationship has continued under the Labour government, elected in March 1983, made evident by the visit of Zhao Ziyang soon after.[40] Australian and Chinese views on contemporary international issues are not in complete accord, with differences evident on issues like nuclear proliferation, Kampuchea, and U.S. policy. But the difficulty on the horizon may be more economic than political since the balance of trade between the two countries runs heavily in Australia's favor and will prove difficult to correct.

The Economic Dimension

Economic and military aid

For Beijing the provision of foreign aid has proved to be a friutful way of expanding and improving its relations with the Third World countries of the Indian Ocean region. China's experience as a foreign aid donor, however, has not been without its problems. As Beijing itself acknowledges, aid levels have fluctuated quite sharply over the past twenty-five years, reflecting economic and political developments in China and changing attitudes with regard to the costs and benefits of aid.[41] In more recent years China's own commitment to economic modernization and the demands this has placed on the country's resources have greatly impaired its ability to support a substantial aid program. As a result, China now provides considerably less aid than it did during the early 1970s.

China has provided both economic and military aid to the states of the Indian Ocean region. It has placed greater emphasis on the economic component of its program, providing both financial and technical assistance. Thus, from 1954 to 1979, China provided U.S. $4,960 million in financial aid worldwide. Of this amount U.S. $2,995 million or 60.38 percent was made available to states in the Indian Ocean with Pakistan, Sri Lanka, and Tanzania being the principal recipients.[42] In 1979 China provided 12,860 technicians to Third World states around the globe of whom 6,500 or 50.64 percent were located in the Indian Ocean region. This figure is higher than in 1960, 1965, and 1970, but substantially lower than in 1975, clearly indicating the decline in support.[43] Once again, Tanzania was a principal recipient, with substantial assistance also going to Somalia, North and South Yemen, and Sri Lanka.

By comparison China's military aid has been quite modest. This reflects China's inability to compete with Western and other communist suppliers as well as its preference for economic aid as a contribution to peaceful development. Between 1955 and 1979 China trained 1,795 military personnel from Indian Ocean states, 56.98 percent of the total trained.[44] In the same period China concluded agreements for U.S. $1,145 million in military aid. Once again a declining trend is evident, although the figures for 1976 (U.S. $145 million) and 1979 (U.S. $140 million) reveal it to be less precipitous than for economic aid.[45] Within the Indian Ocean region Pakistan has been the major recipient of Chinese military aid, followed by Tanzania. Both are now diversifying their sources of supply and will be reducing their dependence on Beijing.

In common with other countries, China views its aid program as a means of reinforcing the objectives of its foreign policy. In the late 1950s Beijing provided U.S. $150 million in aid in an effort to expand its influence in East Asia but by the mid-1960s the emphasis of the program had turned toward Africa. Beijing began offering large amounts of aid to several African countries as part of a campaign to counter Soviet penetration of the continent. Again in 1976 and 1977, China promised additional aid to Egypt, Somalia, and the Sudan after they had renounced their affiliations with Moscow.[46]

However, while pursuing specific objectives, Beijing has been a careful and discriminating aid donor. It provided U.S. $400 million to Tanzania and Zambia for the construction and outfitting of the TAZARA railway, but this was a grant of unusually high proportions. For the most part, China's economic aid has been provided for projects of a more modest nature. During the 1970s the typical aid package was between U.S. $40 and U.S. $50 million,[47] amounts that not only reflect China's limited capacity to offer aid, but also its perspective on the whole issue of foreign assistance.

In this regard the Chinese draw upon their own experience in the early part of this century. As a result, they view aid as being most effective if it is provided at low cost to the recipient, it contributes to the improvement of the country's economic infrastructure, and it promotes self-reliance.[48] Consistent with this approach Chinese aid has focused on transport, agricultural, and light industrial projects that show early results and contribute to economic and social development, rather than on heavy industrial plants that may be ill-suited to a country's human and technical resources. Within the Indian Ocean region, China has made aid available for road, railway, bridge, and port construction in

Pakistan, Somalia, North and South Yemen, and Tanzania; irrigation and other agricultural purposes in Sri Lanka, South Yemen, and Somalia; medical and educational facilities in the Seychelles; and a variety of light industrial mills in Pakistan, Sri Lanka, Afghanistan, and Zambia. Beyond this, the Chinese have offered aid for such diverse purposes as the construction of sporting arenas, hotels, and theaters, and have granted specific assistance in the form of commodities and foreign exchange.[49]

By tailoring aid packages to the specific needs and resources of Third World countries and by providing support on comparatively generous terms, China has earned a highly favorable reputation as an aid donor. As a consequence, the Chinese have been able to strengthen their relations with the Third World states of the Indian Ocean region with an aid program considerably smaller than that of either the Soviet Union or the states of Eastern Europe.

International trade

Being a state monopoly, China's international trade reflects the policies of the central political leadership to a much greater extent than in market economies. Thus, like China's aid program, the level, direction, and commodity composition of China's trade have been affected by changes and upheavals in the domestic political and economic environment.[50] Within this environment China's economic relations with the rest of the world have been a continual source of controversy. Since the Cultural Revolution the debate has been largely between those who see China as a vulnerable, underdeveloped country that must rapidly transform itself into a modern industrial state, and those who see a continuation of China's tradition of economic self-reliance as a means of forestalling dependence on foreign governments and thus vulnerability to foreign economic "blackmail."[51] For the present this debate has been settled in favor of economic modernization with a view to making China a strong, self-reliant state by the turn of the century. One of the consequences has been an expansion of China's trade relations with both the industrialized world and the Third World, including states of the Indian Ocean region. China's trade with the region in 1977 comprised about 21 percent of all trade, but it seems likely that this figure will increase as modernization proceeds.[52]

China's attempts to expand its trading links with the states of the Indian Ocean began in the early 1970s. As China emerged from the isolation of the Cultural Revolution, trade was regarded as an effective way in which to reestablish links with the international community. Initially,

Beijing's extensive aid program of the same period facilitated and helped to consolidate trade with the Third World states of the region. This interdependence is now less important than the mutual benefits available through an expanding trading relationship.

Since China committed itself to modernization, Third World states, many located in the Indian Ocean, have become increasingly significant as suppliers of crucial raw materials. Beijing's imports from those states now include: copper, cobalt, zinc, oil, cocoa, timber, rubber, cotton, and crude fertilizers. At the same time, the Third World states are growing in importance as export markets for Chinese goods. Machinery and transport equipment, yarn and fabrics, clothing and grain have all been exported. Trade with these Third World markets provides China with an important source of foreign exchange and some of the hard currency it requires to continue trading with the countries of the developed world. In recent years China has also expanded its trading relationship with Australia. Here most of the activity consists of Chinese imports of Australian agricultural products and exports of clothing and fabrics.[53]

From Beijing's perspective the opportunities for increasing trade links with the Third World countries of the Indian Ocean region accord with the desire to establish closer relations. In the circumstances trading activities seem certain to expand, thereby reinforcing the ideological and strategic dimensions of Chinese–Third World relations. The prospects for expansion are not, however, devoid of potential trouble. China's developing economy bears a certain structural similarity to the developing economies of other Third World states, arguably making them natural competitors rather than partners when seeking export markets for goods such as clothing, textiles, and certain foodstuffs. At the same time, both seek import credits and other forms of international financing at a time when there is widespread uncertainty over the wisdom of continuing to support Third World economies at the prevailing level. China's economic potential probably ensures that Beijing will be able to gain access to such developmental funds as it may require. The same may not, however, be true of other Third World countries. To the extent that their economic development may be retarded by a shortage of international finance, the expansion of Chinese trade into specific areas of the Third World may also be affected. Finally, should China's drive toward modernization falter, a development of which there is already some evidence, it is likely that trade with the states of the Third World will also be affected. Although these considerations may not completely overshadow the generally encouraging outlook for China–Third World trade, they justify at least a note of caution being appended to all assessments.

Conclusions

China's drive toward modernization, its search for a more significant role within the international community, and its proximity to the Indian Ocean region, all point to the likelihood of Beijing taking an increasingly active role in the region's affairs. Except insofar as China's leaders may be required to take steps in defense of their country's immediate national interests, perhaps in Southeast Asia, the likelihood of this role assuming a military dimension is presently rather remote.

China will continue to seek closer relations with the Third World for reasons related to its ideological competition with the Soviet Union, its search for a distinctive international role, and its need of raw materials for modernization. In particular, Beijing seems likely to press cautiously for a normalization of its relations with three of the most important states of the region: India, Saudi Arabia, and Indonesia. In all three cases progress appears likely to be slow, with long-term prospects being, from Beijing's perspective, reasonably encouraging. Consistent with Beijing's general approach to Third World issues, China will continue to support those causes on which there is a broad consensus, such as the proposal to declare the Indian Ocean a zone of peace, and will continue to be circumspect where opinion is divided, as over the Iraq-Iran war. While China's policy will continue to display the pragmatism that has been its hallmark for over a decade, Beijing's options will still be constrained by the wider ideological and geopolitical imperatives of Chinese foreign policy. In the Indian Ocean, as elsewhere, those wider policy imperatives will be more important in determining China's response to Indian Ocean events and issues than any perceived need for a coherent regional policy.

PART FIVE ☎

Conclusion

30. Security in the Indian Ocean Arena: Trends and Prospects ☎ Ian Clark

What are the present security trends in the Indian Ocean region? Do future prospects provide cause for optimism or pessimism? This chapter will attempt to provide tentative answers to these questions by analyzing the following five dimensions of Indian Ocean security: general sources of tension and instability, recent superpower activities, specific regional disputes, problems in integrating indigenous and external security perspectives, and prospects for "peace zones" or "demilitarization" in the region.

Such an exercise, by its nature, must be conducted at a general level and carries with it the danger of superficiality. Nonetheless, if the Indian Ocean itself has any value as a framework for strategic analysis, the exercise is mandatory and should prove fertile. Alternatively, if our focus on this strategic arena does not enable us to discern any meaningful trends and prospects, the very framework itself is called into question.

General Sources of Tension and Instability

The Indian Ocean region manifests various symptoms and sources of insecurity, most of which are by no means restricted to that area but many of which are therein present in an especially virulent form. They include the spread of conventional armaments from an ever-eager Soviet Union which has traditionally directed its arms supplies to the Middle East and Indian Ocean regions and from an American administration no longer committed, even in principle, to treating arms sales as an "exceptional" instrument of foreign policy.[1] Such militarization may not be considered entirely negative; it may be thought to contribute to the stability of specific regimes, to create or maintain regional balances of military power, or to stave off pressures for nuclear proliferation (see Ashok Kapur's chapter in this book). Equally, however, on the debit side, regimes stabilized by arms programs in the short term (such as in Iran) may become massively undermined in the longer term; the pursuit of regional balances of power can provide the stimulus to unending regional arms competitions; and the source of supply in the superpowers can lead to the unhealthy polarization of regional states around antagonistic superpower patrons. No subregion of the Indian Ocean has remained immune to such adverse developments.

Likewise, and from competing perspectives, the issue of nuclear proliferation has become firmly placed on Indian Ocean security agendas.

Concern about this phenomenon has been most vocally expressed with regard to southern Africa, the Middle East, and South Asia. But even within a country such as Australia, which has thus far resisted pressures for serious contemplation of the nuclear option, the occasional alarm has been sounded at any prospect of proliferation in Southeast Asia, in general, or in a country such as Indonesia, in particular.

Whether the prospect of increasing nuclearization in the Indian Ocean region contributes to insecurity depends upon overall viewpoints. To some, proliferation is by definition a dangerous thing. To others it may be seen as having a positive side.[2] Apart from such general positions, however, two issues of contention seem to be especially germane to a discussion of the Indian Ocean. First, on the negative side, is the fear that the embryonic stage of national nuclear programs may invite Osirak-style raids (India on Pakistan?). Second, more positive, is the view (expressed with special clarity by Indian representatives) that a regional nuclear capacity would underwrite the autonomy of the Indian Ocean from the superpowers and that such proliferation is necessary to induce serious arms control negotiations between the United States and the Soviet Union.[3]

Another source of regional insecurity and instability can be foreseen in the new ocean regime and the extension of national jurisdiction over economic zones. At the very least, developments in the Law of the Sea and the need for policing new jurisdictions,[4] will certainly make additional demands on the navies of the littoral states (see the chapter by Booth and Dowdy in this book).

Finally, the above specific issues must be looked at in conjunction with persistent sources of conflict in the region deriving from problems of economic distribution, ethnic and religious divisions, secessionism, and internal political instabilities. All of these are a present, and foreseeable, characteristic of the Indian Ocean landscape (or seascape). Whether or not they have been aggravated recently, and whether the trend is toward deterioration, is impossible to assess in a chapter as brief as this. We should note, however, that some optimistic notes have been sounded on the basis of the mellowing of traditional rivalries and beneficial trends in the direction of economic interdependence and regional economic cooperation (see the chapter by Raju Thomas).

Recent Superpower Activities

The recent policies of the Soviet Union and the United States in the Indian Ocean arena, and the exacerbation of relations between the two, have generated considerable concern in the world community. If it is true that we are now in the incipient phase of a second cold war, then the general consensus is that its epicenter is to be found in the north-western segment of the Indian Ocean.

Soviet policies toward the Indian Ocean currently reflect general trends in Soviet security in relation to Asia as a whole and it is within this framework of Asian security, along the USSR's southern periphery, that the analysis should commence.[5] While the intensifying strategic interlinkages between the Middle East, the Persian Gulf, South Asia, the Sino-Soviet frontier, and the waters of the Indian Ocean present the USSR with something of a strategic seamless web, simultaneously there has been throughout the late 1970s a pronounced fragmentation in the Soviet Union's overarching conceptions of security in the region, a drift from *collective* to *selective* patterns of Asian security. Even prominent Soviet columnists like Kudryavtsev have expressed doubts that an Asian collective security system can be created in a short or medium length of time.

This disintegration has occurred as a result of regional conditions that have remained intractable to Soviet preferences and in response to a general deterioration in the USSR's perceived security environment in Asia: its exclusion from the Middle East core, volatile Islamic move-ments in Southwest Asia, renewed American military activities in the region, and Sino-American and Sino-Japanese pressures in South and East Asia. *Pravda* highlighted Soviet misgivings when it referred on 9 April 1979 to the "defense line being created by the Pentagon along the Egypt–Israel–Persian Gulf–Diego Garcia–Australia perimeter," thereby reflecting a Soviet fear of an "integrated" Indian Ocean–wide threat to its security.

The invasion of Afghanistan may have been symptomatic of the disintegration of a Soviet "grand design" for Asia, if for no other reason than that various regional developments have been pressing Moscow to make choices it might prefer not to have to make (see Khalilzad's chap-ter). Just as Ethiopia could be wooed only at the cost of the "loss" of Somalia, so the detente between Iran and Iraq, which Moscow had as-siduously cultivated in the mid-1970s, has also collapsed. Likewise, while the USSR would certainly prefer not to abandon relations with Paki-stan, President Zia's policies (reinforced by Moscow's own actions) have driven the two widely apart. There have been Soviet verbal onslaughts on Pakistan in past years that would have been inconceivable in the pre-vious fifteen, even at the height of the events of 1971.[6] Andrei Gromyko, while in Delhi in February 1980, complained publicly of Pakistan's neg-ative and dangerous policies. In short, the end of the decade witnessed the collapse of the Tashkent policy that Moscow had initiated in the mid-1960s. There have been reports that in 1982 the Soviet Union again broached its nebulous Asian collective security scheme to both India and Pakistan.[7] Nonetheless, it would appear that what is true of Soviet Asian security policies is true also of Soviet Indian Ocean policies generally: namely, that whatever preferred visions of Asian security it might secretly harbor, the Soviet government is responding to its regional security problems on an ad hoc basis.

Superficially, the United States seems to be moving in the opposite direction. If the Soviet Union had a grand security design but has since lost its way, then the United States appears only recently to have developed a coherent, active policy for the Indian Ocean (see Bowman and Lefebvre). In the judgment of two writers, "the Reagan administration . . . sees more geostrategic logic in viewing the Indian Ocean Basin as a strategic entity, linking together the littoral states of East Africa, the Arabian Peninsula, and South Asia."[8]

Not surprisingly, Soviet commentators have taken Washington at its word and they claim to be able to see a coherent (and, of course, mischievous) American policy for the region as a whole. Not only has the Reagan administration ambitions for the Indian Ocean but, according to Soviet reports, it is following up the Carter Doctrine by creating the military and naval infrastructures for their implementation. According to Moscow "with the adoption of the new strategy, plans are being fleshed out for the formation of a U.S. Fifth Fleet in the area."[9] Attacks on U.S. military exercises, such as Bright Star and Jade Tiger (in Oman and Somalia), are expressed in a similar vein.[10] It is also from the perspective of such an "integrated" U.S. Indian Ocean strategy that Moscow has expressed alarm at proposed transfers of American forces from East Asia to the Persian Gulf region and at the renewed U.S. pressure on its East Asian allies (notably Japan) to take up some of the resulting slack.

Unlike the period of the early 1970s, the anxieties generated by present superpower activity do not appear to have arisen from fears of an ongoing, open-ended, naval escalation in the ocean. The "ship-day" approach to Indian Ocean security that dominated Western political debate in the early 1970s is not now so obviously in vogue. In part, this is a direct consequence of the increase in American naval activity in the ocean since 1979 and the decreased political utility of providing ship-day counts that no longer incriminate the USSR as the major naval intruder into Indian Ocean waters. More substantially, however, the shift of attention away from counting ships reflects the facts that while there may be two runners, there is clearly no naval race, and that these naval presences are more a symptom of the security problem than the embodiment of it (see the chapter by Cottrell). This is not to deny the reality of these naval/military forces or the potential threat they might represent either to each other or to littoral states. It is only to emphasize that what people currently worry about is not primarily the prospect of a direct naval race in the ocean.

This assessment reflects the facts of recent deployments in the region. Since 1979, the United States has expanded the size of its overall presence in the Indian Ocean. The Middle East Force (MIDEASTFOR) has been increased to five ships and, with the two carrier battle groups generally in the area, the U.S. presence has remained at between twenty-five and thirty ships. Several supply ships have been pre-positioned at Diego Garcia as part of the Rapid Deployment Force (RDF) support.[11] This Indian Ocean presence has entailed long tours of duty on "gonzo station" for American ships such as the USS *Nimitz* and USS *Constellation*.[12] Associated support activities have taken place at the ports of Mombasa, Ras Banas, and al Masirah. Additionally, via exercises such as Bright Star in late 1981, the United States has tested its force projection capabilities in the area and has simulated them in the California desert through exercises such as Gallant Eagle in March and April 1982.

Activity there has been, but naval race there has not. The Australian Parliament was recently informed, in response to a question on new Soviet naval activities in the Indian Ocean, that in late 1981 a Klaipeda-class dry dock had been introduced to Maputo but that there was no information to confirm significant new developments at Aden or Socotra. On the overall Soviet naval presence in the Indian Ocean, the defense minister stated, "There is no evidence of an increase in the level of presence in the last two years."[13] If this is so, the action/reaction model of arms races would appear not to be applicable to present Indian Ocean deployments.

Paradoxically, however, while there are no signs at present of a naval competition (with both navies having problems maintaining force levels in the ocean), there is even less prospect of a naval standstill agreement. If neither side is currently interested in running the race, neither can they mutually agree to cancel it. There are several reasons for this, but most important are the perceived asymmetries represented by the lack of a Soviet base equivalent to Diego Garcia (from the Soviet perspective) and as a result of Soviet contiguity to the Persian Gulf, now from Afghanistan (from the American perspective). Above all, it is the current U.S. judgment that its interests in the Persian Gulf are vital and require for their defense, among other instruments, the projection of naval power into the area. While these various asymmetries persist, the issue of naval limitations in the ocean must remain nonnegotiable.

Regional Conflicts

Around the Indian Ocean, there are ongoing regional conflicts, some relatively quiescent; others have already erupted into fighting or threaten to do so imminently. Whether the aggregate picture is better or worse than it was a decade ago is not, however, easy to discern.

East and southern Africa continue to live in the shadow of persisting conflicts, indigenous to some extent but with the ever-present danger of escalation via superpower entanglement: territorial disputes, the spillover effects of regime instability, and the overarching confrontation with South Africa rank high on the list of such potential sources of tension.

It is a moot point whether the troubled relations of southern Africa legitimately belong within an Indian Ocean context at all. As Douglas Anglin in his chapter in this volume remarks of the Frontline States, "The Indian Ocean is an occasional diversion; South Africa is a daily obsession." What lends southern Africa's confrontation an Indian Ocean dimension is, on the one hand, the republic's "southern hemisphere" strategic conceptions and, especially since 1979, its renewed efforts to engage a Soviet threat as a means of strengthening its own strategic leverage with potential allies (see Roherty's chapter). On the other hand, the Indian Ocean concerns of the Frontline States have been a direct result of their need to counter South Africa's policy and to "decouple" the status of the republic from the strategic posturings of the superpowers. Neither side, however, can free itself completely from the potential assistance that the superpowers might bring to their respective causes.

In East Africa, lingering territorial disputes remain, periodically punctuated by regime instabilities, as in the case of Tanzania's incursion into Uganda. Moreover, once again, a reorientation of superpower activities has brought to the surface latent regional suspicions. The more prominent role of Kenya in Washington's gulf strategies has caused tremors in Somalia, as well as in Tanzania, at the same time as Kenya's leadership has regarded with anxiety the unpredictability that America's ties with Somalia might lend to Mogadishu's irredentist claims (see the chapter by George Shepherd).

Likewise, the Horn of Africa has enjoyed only a fragile peace since the 1977–78 Ogaden war between Ethiopia and Somalia (see Colin Legum's chapter). Both regimes suffer from chronic internal insecurity and could again convert this problem into international incidents. Indeed, this has happened repeatedly. For example, in June 1982, fighting broke out in Somalia involving the anti-Barré forces of the Somali Salvation

Democratic Front, but it was widely reported in the Western media that the fighting was joined by units of the Ethiopian army and air force that were alleged to have crossed into Somalia.[14] This was strongly denied by Mengistu and by Soviet commentators who asserted that the problem was essentially one of internal opposition to Barré and to his pro–U.S. policy.[15] Nonetheless, the United States was prompted to hasten some arms shipments to Mogadishu. As a State Department spokesman, Rush Taylor, announced, "I can confirm that the United States is airlifting military equipment to Somalia. This is in connection with the recent incursion by Ethiopian and Ethiopian-supported forces."[16] The Soviet press reported air shipments being flown in from Diego Garcia and were quick to denounce the move.[17]

Additionally, if Somalia's regime is vulnerable to internal dissidence (and potentially to its exploitation from outside), then Ethiopia is equally insecure in this respect. Although the Eritrean campaign appears to have been placed on the back burner since 1980, a recent upsurge can perhaps be linked to the volatile international situation in the Red Sea area. As Ethiopia's ties with Libya have been strengthened and as Sudan's anxieties and pro-Western sentiments have increased, so it has been reported that the Sudanese have renewed collaboration with the Eritrean Popular Liberation Front (EPLF), if not with the Eritrean Liberation Front (ELF).[18]

In the Persian Gulf region, the salient security concern has, of course, been the ongoing Iraq-Iran war (Tareq Ismael discusses this in his chapter). Both superpowers have been constrained in their responses to this war by the knowledge that an overt "tilt" might lead to a dramatic polarization of the situation, but neither is blind to the potential repercussions of an extended Iranian push into Iraq and/or the collapse of the Saddam Hussein regime. Washington is, above all, cautious not to drive Tehran to an accommodation with Moscow, whereas the Soviet leaders have all along been perplexed by the uncomfortable choices that the war has presented. Iraq has been a major Soviet client in the region but has, for several years, shown signs of discontent, whether in regard to Soviet arms or in regard to Soviet policy in the Horn of Africa. The Soviet Union has thus discovered that there are very real limits on the influence it can exercise over that country (see the chapter by Smolansky).

Iran, despite its present waywardness, is a state that Moscow would prefer not to alienate. *Pravda*, in making one of its periodic calls for an end to the war, candidly revealed its own dilemma created by a war between its Iraqi ally and a revolutionary Iran that is supported by such other Soviet clients as Syria and the People's Democratic Republic of Yemen (PDRY).[19] At the same time, Soviet authorities realize that the "anti-Iran" motif is an important element in those regional states that Washington currently seeks to court. As *Izvestia* was to phrase the point, the United States has been planting the notion of an "Iranian threat" in Arab states "in hopes of accelerating the formation of a pro-western alliance in the Middle East on the basis of a so-called 'strategic consensus.' "[20] In other words, no matter what the Soviet Union might think of the Khomeini regime,[21] Moscow inescapably shares with it some common strategic interests. It is perhaps from this point of view that we can understand reports that Soviet military equipment has been supplied to Iran during the war through North Korea.[22]

If the Iraq-Iran war embodies the immediate and tangible security threat in the gulf, the more general problem derives from concern with the future of Iranian policy in the region (see the chapter by Ramazani). Can, and will, Khomeini's Iran export its revolution in the gulf? At least two responses can be given to that question. First, Iran will seek to do so as long as the revolutionary regime retains its present character (see Burrell's chapter). Second, there will remain the likelihood of political upheaval in the region as long as so many of its states are marked by gross domestic economic disparities, with or without Iranian instigation (see the chapter by James Bill). In either case, we are presented with a picture of future political volatility; the only debate is over the nature of its source.

The Indian subcontinent is still in the shadow of Afghanistan and superpower policies have had undesirable secondary effects for Indo-Pakistani relations. In other respects, however, an intermittent Indo-Pakistani foreign ministers' dialogue during 1982 was a moderately hopeful sign, as was the November 1982 agreement between Zia and Gandhi to begin discussions on an Indo-Pakistani nonaggression pact.[23] Whether and when Rajiv Gandhi resumes his late mother's moves toward normal relations with Pakistan remain to be seen. Arguably, the worst polarizing effects of the Afghanistan invasion may well be avoided by skillful subcontinental diplomacy toward the major powers and, in this respect, there are also hopeful signs.

The point can be made in the following manner. Current Soviet policy in South Asia differs crucially from that of the other major powers. The United States, however falteringly and with whatever minimal success, has been attempting to "thaw" its relations with New Delhi simultaneously with the renaissance of its military links with Pakistan. Gandhi's visit to Washington in late July 1982 was a public demonstration of this process (see the chapter by Marwah). China, also, while maintaining its traditional links with Pakistan, has moved into a more accommodating relationship with India (see the chapter by Trood). Moscow alone is confined to a single client and this very Indo-centricity of Soviet policy, as argued above, reflects the recession of Moscow's grander variants of Asian security and their substitution by a selectivity in the USSR's subcontinental policy that was more typical of Soviet–Third World diplomacy in the 1950s than in the sixties or seventies. Moscow's Afghan solution has only aggravated this situation by increasing tensions in the entire region and by contributing to the USSR's isolation. Indeed, it could be argued that the Soviet Union can only "solve" its security problems in relation to Afghanistan and Pakistan at the cost of further alienation of India and further erosion of their common strategic interests.

This is not to say that Soviet-Indian relations are in serious decline. There is little evidence to support such a claim. However, there is evidence that India, by balancing its relations with the major powers, may help to insulate the subcontinent from the direct effects of the new Soviet-American cold war. The signs were present in August 1981 when, on the tenth anniversary of the Indo-Soviet treaty, Prime Minister Gandhi sought consciously not to give emphasis to the event. The signs were confirmed in the announcement by the French Defense Ministry in April 1982 that India was to buy 40 Mirage 2000 aircraft, with an option on another 110,[24] despite Soviet Defense Minister Ustinov's visit to India the previous month.[25] Gandhi's visit to Moscow in September 1982 revealed the continuities in the Indo-Soviet relationship but it would be difficult to ignore the changing framework within which that relationship is now viewed by the Indian government. Western leaders of course hope that the new prime minister, Rajiv Gandhi, will loosen India's ties with Moscow. On balance, this would be a desirable development, most assuredly *not* because it would represent a Soviet "loss," but rather because it would hold out the best prospect of preventing Indo-Pakistani relations from being sucked into the maelstrom of Soviet-American confrontation.

Whether such tendencies will ultimately resolve some of South Asia's problems may depend on the nature of the dynamics generating subcontinental tensions. To this extent, the difference between "internalist" and "externalist" interpretations of Pakistan's security environment becomes crucial (see the chapter by Wirsing). If Pakistan's insecurity is seen to derive from external alignments and threats, the scenario described above may be considered hopeful and likely to reduce Pakistani concerns. However, if the diagnosis that Pakistan's insecurity is a product of its domestic problems is at least partially valid, then the final stability of the subcontinent will depend upon much more than skillful diplomacy and an evenhanded management of great power presences. From this perspective, the necessary conditions for regional security can be created only in the much longer term and by means of much radical political readjustment. Such a progress, in itself, is unlikely to be painless.

Integration of Indigenous and External Security Perspectives

The age-old problem of security in the Indian Ocean arena has been that outside presences, whatever they might have done to "solve" regional security problems, have also created new ones or aggravated existing ones for the indigenous states. It is therefore not at all surprising that areawide ideologies, in however articulate or explicit a form, have been centered on a concept of "autonomy" (see Ayoob's chapter).

It is a venerable political maxim that if you are not part of the solution, you must be part of the problem. Unfortunately, as far as great power presences in the Indian Ocean are concerned, it has to be said that the relationship is even more complex; it is precisely because the superpowers are a part of the solution of Indian Ocean security (at the very least from the point of view of weaker regional states seemingly threatened by stronger neighbors) that they are also a part of the problem. This dilemma manifests itself in two main ways.

On the one hand, Soviet and American pursuit of their respective security objectives has provided the solidification of regional—and antagonistic—power blocs. While the hostility among some of these groups would exist in any event because of the policies pursued by indigenous states, it has been "structured" and given prominence by the backing of superpower patrons. The recent alignments in the Horn/Red Sea area demonstrate the point. In August 1981, a summit conference was held in Aden at which Libya, South Yemen, and Ethiopia agreed to sign a treaty of friendship that gave tangible expression to the coalescence of interests that had occurred among these three states.[26] This association has been denounced by the United States. As then Secretary of State Alexander Haig explained, "The new entente between Libya, Ethiopia, and South Yemen—three of the Soviets' closest friends in the area—is only the most recent of many threats to the security of our friends in the region."[27] However, it is also abundantly clear that the emergence of this "axis" in the Horn/Red Sea area is itself in no small measure a product of American policies in the region and specifically of the involvement in these policies of such countries as Somalia, Oman, Sudan, and Egypt. The attempt to reduce one security threat has contributed to the solidification of another.

The second way in which there can be an inconsistency between indigenous and external security perspectives is one pointed to by many commentators. It has been examined most closely in the case of the United States but it has relevance also to the Soviet experience. The substance of the argument is that those steps that are most needed to make effective the military presence of the outside power are precisely the steps most likely to expose indigenous regimes to internal opposition and to pressures from neighboring states. It is thus that Newsom maintains that "the desire of local regimes for an outside presence is counterbalanced by fears that such a presence will increase their own political and military vulnerability,"[28] and Van Hollen suggests, "The inevitable escalation in demands for logistical support for the projected 225,000-member RDF carries the risk of imposing intolerable political strains on the four states—Egypt, Kenya, Oman, and Somalia—which have granted the U.S. military facilities."[29] Quandt well illustrates how Saudi Arabia specifically is caught between these conflicting pressures.[30]

There is a striking contrast between the situation on the Indian subcontinent and that prevailing in the Persian Gulf region in this respect. Mohammed Ayoob has shown that, between 1971 and 1979, the course of Indo-Pakistani relations was substantially insulated from superpower rivalry and his fear was that, in the aftermath of Iran and Afghanistan, this situation would no longer apply.[31] On the other hand, it has been suggested that the worst effects of such polarization are in fact being avoided in the subcontinent, in no small measure as a consequence of Indian policy.

However, by contrast, given the nature of present geopolitics, the option of insulating regional security from superpower rivalry by means of a balanced approach to the external powers is an option that is not available to many states in the gulf region. For them, the problem can only be resolved by keeping the superpower patron at arm's length and not by counterbalancing a major presence of one power by a matching relationship with another. Saudi Arabia, for instance, could not do for the gulf what India is in the process of doing for the subcontinent. To the extent that this analysis is valid, the point would be that the problem of reconciling indigenous and external perspectives on security presents itself in a more intransigent form in the Persian Gulf than it does, for instance, on the subcontinent.

Peace Zones and Demilitarization

To round off this discussion of security trends in the Indian Ocean, it is worth looking at the present state of the question of "peace zones" and at the status of proposals for "demilitarization," although the prospects for either have not been deemed especially bright (see the chapter by Byers). Indeed, Barry Buzan is probably correct in his "negative" explanation for the persistence of the Indian Ocean zone-of-peace proposal in terms of which "the negotiations continue because nobody has any incentive to kill them off. The Non-Aligned have little to lose and something to gain by keeping them going. The Western powers and the USSR do not wish to attract the embarrassment and opprobrium of rejecting a regional arms control proposal out of hand."[32]

The Soviet Union has made very general endorsements of peace-zone and demilitarization proposals.[33] It has also made three public appeals on the matter. First, in December 1980 during a visit to India, Brezhnev made a proposal for a Persian Gulf security agreement. Subsequently, in February 1981 at the Soviet Communist Party Congress, Brezhnev specifically linked Persian Gulf/Indian Ocean matters with a settlement in Afghanistan when he noted that "we have no objection to having questions connected with Afghanistan discussed in coordination with questions of security in the Persian Gulf." Third, Brezhnev, in a welcoming speech for Gandhi during her September 1982 visit to the Soviet Union, again proposed mutual forbearance from military activities in the Indian Ocean.

There has been little advance in the Soviet position in these three proposals and little increase in Western responsiveness to them. Above all, the Western reaction has been unsympathetic because it believes that the proposals, given strategic asymmetries, would favor the Soviet Union and because the linking of the matter to Afghanistan is seen to have been offered merely to legitimize the Soviet presence in that country. Accordingly, recent demilitarization proposals have been made, and rejected, in an increasingly ritualistic manner. There is no cause for optimism on this particular score.

This leads to a rather dismal conclusion. If it is true that a salient feature of Indian Ocean security is to be found in the structural relationship existing between indigenous concerns and external presences, and if it is also accepted that the superpowers have a Janus-like quality, being both part of the solution and part of the problem, then it is unlikely that this structural problem can be overcome while the superpower relationship itself remains tense and strained. If the superpowers cannot reach some tacit agreement upon the nature and extent of their presence in the region (and a pact restraining military or naval presences would be only one possible expression of such an agreement between them), then it is scarcely to be expected that the more deep-seated difficulty of accommodating the superpower relationship to a volatile Indian Ocean setting can even begin to be tackled.

Notes ⚊

Notes to Chapter 1

The author gratefully acknowledges the substantial contribution made by Russell B. Trood to this chapter, particularly to the economic analysis of the "Internal Perspectives" section. I also wish to thank Professor James Eayrs, editor of the special "Ocean Politics" issue of *International Journal* 38 (Summer 1983) for permission to use portions of an article coauthored with Russell B. Trood that appeared under the title, "The Indian Ocean: An Emerging Geostrategic Region."

1 Michael Banks, "Systems Analysis and the Study of Regions," *International Studies Quarterly* 13 (December 1969): 343.

2 Donald C. Hellmann, "The Emergence of an East Asian International System," *International Studies Quarterly* 13 (December 1969): 423. Jorge I. Dominquez also predicted a "long-term structural trend toward international fragmentation— *a breakdown into subsystems.*" ("Mice That Do Not Roar: Some Aspects of International Politics in the World's Peripheries," *International Organization* 25 [Spring 1971]: 178). Emphasis mine.

3 Leonard Binder, "The Middle East as a Subordinate International System," *World Politics* 10 (April 1958): 408–29.

4 Michael Brecher, "International Relations and Asian Studies: The Subordinate State System of Southern Asia," *World Politics* 15 (January 1963): 213–35. See also Brecher, *The New States of Asia* (London: Oxford University Press, 1963), and Brecher, "The Middle East Subordinate System and Its Impact on Israel's Foreign Policy," *International Studies Quarterly* 13 (June 1969): 117–39.

5 William Zartman, "Africa as a Subordinate State System in International Relations," *International Organization* 21 (Summer 1967): 545–64.

6 Larry W. Bowman, "The Subordinate State System of Southern Africa," *International Studies Quarterly* 13 (September 1968): 231–63.

7 Hellmann, "Emergence of an East Asian International System," 421–34.

8 Louis J. Cantori and Steven L. Spiegel, *The International Politics of Regions— A Comparative Approach* (Englewood Cliffs, N.J.: Prentice-Hall, 1970). See also Cantori and Spiegel, "International Regions: A Comparative Approach to Five Subordinate Systems," *International Studies Quarterly* 13 (December 1969): 361–80, Cantori and Spiegel, "The International Politics of Regions," *Polity* 2 (Summer 1970): 397–425, and Cantori and Spiegel, "The Analysis of Regional International Politics: The Integration Versus the Empirical Systems Approach," *International Organization* 27 (Autumn 1973): 465–94.

Using Cantori and Spiegel's analytical framework, the author of this chapter first stated and examined the proposition ten years ago that there was an incipient regional identity in what he called the "Indian Ocean area" ("Politics of the Indian Ocean Area and Its Persian Gulf Core: A Subsystemic Analysis," M.A. thesis, Tulane University, 1974). That perspective was further developed in the author's Ph.D. dissertation ("International Politics of the Persian Gulf States from a Subsystemic Core Perspective," Tulane University, 1982), from which portions of this chapter have been derived.

9   In considering disintegrative and conflictual dimensions of regional affairs, the subsystemic approach parts company with the neofunctionalist approach of Ernst Haas and others. Other approaches to regional studies in political science literature distinguishable from the subsystemic tradition have been the aggregate data analysis of Bruce Russett and others, the transactional analysis of Karl Deutsch and others, and the eclectic approaches of Joseph Nye and others. (See Banks, "Systems Analysis and the Study of Regions," 351–52.)

10 Hellmann, "Emergence of an East Asian International System," 423. Andrew M. Scott explains the former lack of interest in regional-global linkages as follows: "Many areas of the world were politically irrelevant as far as the functioning of the system was concerned. They were irrelevant in the sense they lacked the capacity to generate systemwide disturbances" (*The Functioning of the International Political System* [New York: Macmillan, 1967], 12). "If many geographical areas were once politically irrelevant, now scarcely any area may be said to be so" (ibid.).

11 William R. Thompson, "The Regional Subsystem—A Conceptual Explication and a Propositional Inventory," *International Studies Quarterly* 17 (March 1973): 101.

12 The thirty-six independent Indian Ocean states from southwest to southeast around the perimeter are: South Africa, Mozambique, Tanzania, Kenya, Somalia, Djibouti, Ethiopia, Sudan, Egypt, Israel, Jordan, Saudi Arabia, the Yemen Arab Republic (North Yemen), the People's Democratic Republic of Yemen (South Yemen), Oman, the United Arab Emirates, Qatar, Bahrain, Kuwait, Iraq, Iran, Pakistan, India, Bangladesh, Burma, Thailand, Malaysia, Singapore, Indonesia, and Australia; the independent island-states are Madagascar, the Comoros, the Seychelles, Mauritius, the Maldives, and Sri Lanka.

13 Cantori and Spiegel, *International Politics of Regions*, 20. The term "core" is used with similar meaning by Brecher ("The Middle East Subordinate System") and Binder ("The Middle East as a Subordinate International System"). Zartman's "subregional constellations" ("Africa as a Subordinate State System") seem to have analytical referents similar to the other theorists' "cores."

14 Oran R. Young has discerned two alternative orientations under the rubric of general systems theory. On the one hand, "general systems theory appears as an integrated and generalized set of concepts, hypotheses, and (hopefully as time passes) validated propositions." On the other hand, it "may be seen as . . . a framework for a systematic process of analysis. In this instance it is not so much the specific principles and propositions of the theory that are of ultimate interest; rather it is the suggestions that the theory offers for analyzing and organizing data." It is the latter version of systems theory, namely, as a framework for analysis, that is proposed in this chapter as useful for thinking about the politics of the Indian Ocean. Indeed, Young notes that "general systems theory in its extended and well-integrated form has rarely been applied to the analysis of

political phenomena" (Oran R. Young, *Systems of Political Science* [Englewood Cliffs, N.J.: Prentice-Hall, 1968], 19, 21).

15 Banks, "Systems Analysis and the Study of Regions," 346.

16 "A Systems Approach," in *Approaches and Theory in International Relations*, ed. Trevor Taylor (London: Longman, 1978), 187.

17 The definition of "system" as "a set of objects together with relationships between the objects and their attributes" also suffices as the definition for "subsystem" since a subsystem "is internally a system" (A. D. Hall and R. E. Fagen, "Definition of System," *General Systems Yearbook* 1 [1956]: 18, and Charles A. McClelland, *Theory and the International System* [New York: Macmillan, 1966], 21, respectively).

18 Kenneth N. Waltz, *Theory of International Politics* (London: Addison-Wesley, 1979), 39.

19 Peter Nettl, "The Concept of System in Political Science," *Political Studies* 14 (October 1966): 321.

20 M. B. Nicholson and P. A. Reynolds, "General Systems, The International System, and The Eastonian Analysis," *Political Studies* 15 (February 1967): 14.

21 "Studies in Political Geography," Report of the Ad Hoc Committee on Geography, Division of Earth Sciences (Publication 1277, 1965), in *The Structure of Political Geography*, ed. Roger E. Kasperson and Julian V. Minghi (Chicago: Aldine, 1969), 64. One of the principal motivating factors behind development of contemporary systems theory was the perceived need for a central organizing concept and related principles that could serve to integrate knowledge across different academic disciplines.

22 See, for example, the "pattern variables" approach of Cantori and Spiegel, *International Politics of Regions*, esp. pp. 1–41.

23 See, for example, J. D. Singer, S. Bremer, and J. Stuckey, "Capability Distribution, Uncertainty, and Major Power War, 1820–1965," in *Peace, War, and Numbers*, ed. Bruce Russett (Beverly Hills: Sage, 1972). See also W. H. Ferris, *The Power Capabilities of Nation-States* (Lexington, Mass.: Lexington Books, 1973), and M. Wallace, *War and Rank Among Nations* (Lexington, Mass.: Heath, 1973).

24 Auguste Toussaint has noted that the ocean's history has traditionally been divided into two periods—"pre-Gaman" and "post-Gaman"—with Vasco da Gama's voyage around the tip of southern Africa in 1498 as the dividing line between the ancient and modern histories of the Indian Ocean ("Shifting Power Balances in the Indian Ocean," in *The Indian Ocean: Its Political, Economic, and Military Importance*, ed. Alvin J. Cottrell and R. M. Burrell [New York: Praeger, 1972], 3). Ferenc Váli has observed that at least "the Indian Ocean *has* a history, whereas no comprehensive history of the Atlantic or the Pacific has yet been written. . . . This may be a reflection of the 'closed' character of the Indian Ocean, the continuum of its historical development, and the interrelations and interactions between events in its various corners, which provide a centrality that better permits a consistent narrative and pertinent analysis of its multimillennial story" (*Politics of the Indian Ocean Region: The Balance of Power* [New York: Free Press, 1976], 1).

25 Toussaint, "Shifting Power Balances in the Indian Ocean," 7.

26 For a detailed analysis of the U.S. approach to the region, see Larry W. Bowman and Jeffrey A. Lefebvre, "The Indian Ocean: U.S. Military and Strategic Perspectives," in this volume.

27 *Department of State Bulletin*, October 1981, 14, and June 1981, 43, respectively.

28 See Ken Booth and Lee Dowdy, "Soviet Security Interests in the Indian Ocean Region," in *Soviet Armed Forces Review Annual* 6, ed. David R. Jones (Gulf Breeze, Fla.: Academic International Press, 1982), 327–77.

29 Quoted in Jonathan D. Pollack, "Chinese Global Strategy and Soviet Power," *Problems of Communism* 30 (January–February 1981): 62.

30 See the chapters in this volume by Ferenc A. Váli, Taketsugu Tsurutani, and Russell B. Trood.

31 "The Indian Ocean as Seen by an Indian," *United States Naval Institute Proceedings, Naval Review* issue (May 1970): 181.

32 For an interesting collection of essays on the cultural history of the Indian Ocean, see H. Neville Chittick and Robert I. Rotberg, eds., *East Africa and the Orient—Cultural Syntheses in Pre-Colonial Times* (New York: Africana Publishing, 1975). The editors write in their introduction (p. 1) that "the Indian Ocean basin has an intrinsic cultural and economic unity which has always been shared by the peoples of the East African coast. They, like others living on the eastern and northern shores of the basin, have long enjoyed the similar climatic and ecological conditions which facilitated unity and comparable perspectives."

33 The following discussion of "regional strategic linkages" owes much to an unpublished paper by Ian Clark, "Security in the Indian Ocean Region: Trends and Prospects," presented to the conference on "The Indian Ocean: Perspectives on a Strategic Arena," sponsored by Dalhousie University's Centre for Foreign Policy Studies, 14–16 October 1982. A later version of the paper, "Security in the Indian Ocean Arena: Trends and Prospects," appears in this volume.

34 Váli, *Politics of the Indian Ocean Region*, 235.

35 Clark, "Security in the Indian Ocean Region," 18.

36 Ibid.

37 Quoted in P. R. Chari, "The Indian Ocean: An Indian Viewpoint," *Iranian Review of International Relations* 8 (Fall 1976): 175.

38 Barry Buzan, "Naval Power, the Law of the Sea, and the Indian Ocean as a Zone of Peace," *Marine Policy* (July 1981), 196.

39 *World Development Report 1981* (Washington, D.C.: World Bank, August 1981), 134–35.

40 The Republic of South Africa is often described as industrialized but such a description ignores the economic condition of the black majority in the country. The World Bank classifies South Africa as an LDC.

41 *World Development Report 1981*, 134–35 and 138–39.

42 The World Bank categorizes oil production in the CSOES as industrial activity. However, since most of the oil exported is unrefined, it could arguably be considered part of the primary production sector of the CSOE economies and therefore analogous to the agricultural sector of the LDCs.

43 The members of ASEAN are Indonesia, Malaysia, Thailand, Singapore, and the non–Indian Ocean state of the Philippines. Brunei joined in 1984.

44 On the formation and prospects of the GCC, see R. K. Ramazani, "The Gulf Cooperation Council: A Search for Security," in this volume.

45 United Nations, *Yearbook of International Trade Statistics 1, Trade by Country*, 1974 and 1981. See also Raju G. C. Thomas, "The Economic and Strategic Interdependence of the Indian Ocean Region," in this volume, and Dieter

Braun, "New Patterns of India's Relations with Indian Ocean Littoral States," in *The Indian Ocean in Global Politics*, ed. Larry W. Bowman and Ian Clark (Boulder, Colo.: Westview, 1981), 21–39.

46 The impact of escalating oil prices was somewhat ameliorated, however, by discounts offered by the oil-producing states to various Indian Ocean trading partners.

47 One of Australia's most interesting ventures involves an agricultural product. "Australian wool comes to Mauritius to be transformed into sweaters for European department stores. In such a way, small, tropical Mauritius has become one of the world's leading exporters of knitwear" (Bart McDowell, "Crosscurrents Sweep a Strategic Sea," *National Geographic* 160 [October 1981]: 440).

48 In a review of Bowman and Clark, *The Indian Ocean in Global Politics* in *Survival* 24 (January–February 1982): 44.

Notes to Chapter 2

1 It was this inability to distinguish the "essence" from the "trappings" in the ideology of the Iranian Revolution that led to the distorted, often uneducated, reports and analyses in the Western press about Iran during the period 1978–80. For details see Edward W. Said, *Covering Islam* (New York: Pantheon, 1981), esp. pp. 74–125.

2 David E. Apter, "Introduction: Ideology and Discontent," in *Ideology and Discontent*," ed. David E. Apter (New York: Free Press, 1964), pp. 16–17.

3 Clifford Geertz, "Ideology as a Cultural System," in Apter, *Ideology and Discontent*, p. 64.

4 *The International Encyclopaedia of the Social Sciences* 7 (1968), p. 68 (emphasis in the original); s.v. "Ideology: The Concept and Function of Ideology," by Edward Shils.

5 *International Encyclopaedia of the Social Sciences* 7:68.

6 Ibid.

7 Peter Willetts, *The Non-Aligned Movement* (London: Frances Pinter, 1978), pp. 244–45.

8 Wang Gungwu, "Nationalism in Asia," in *Nationalism: The Nature and Evolution of an Idea*, ed. Eugene Kamenka (London: Edward Arnold, 1976), p. 89.

9 Jawaharlal Nehru, *India's Foreign Policy: Selected Speeches, 1946–61*, p. 242. Quoted in David Kimche, *The Afro-Asian Movement: Ideology and Foreign Policy of the Third World* (Jerusalem: Israel Universities Press, 1973), p. 21.

10 See Basil Davidson, *Africa in Modern History: The Search for a New Society* (London: Allen Lane, 1978), p. 143.

11 According to Davidson, "A party or movement with mass support is one in which a self-chosen leadership can rely upon a wide audience of followers who are prepared to demonstrate or otherwise act in support of its leadership, but who are otherwise uninvolved in the leadership's policies, plans, or intentions. A party or movement with mass participation is one with mass support which becomes organically involved in political life, and is organized and organizes itself for political discussion, activism and control within the movement's life and programme" (Ibid., p. 227).

12 *Jawaharlal Nehru's Speeches*, vol. 1, p. 2, quoted in A. P. Rana, *The Imperatives of Nonalignment* (Delhi: Macmillan, 1976), p. 54.

13 G. H. Jansen, *Afro-Asia and Non-Alignment* (London: Faber and Faber, 1966), p. 404.
14 Ali Mazrui's Foreword to Willetts, *The Non-Aligned Movement*, p. xiii. Emphasis in original.
15 William LeoGrande, "Evolution of the Nonaligned Movement," *Problems of Communism* 29 (January–February 1980): p. 51.
16 Ibid., p. 52. Emphasis in original.
17 Willetts, *The Non-Aligned Movement*, p. 29.
18 Calculated on the basis of the list of participating countries included in the "Political Declaration" of the summit. See *Documents of Gatherings of the Non-aligned Countries, 1961–1979* (New Delhi: 1981), p. 359.
19 For details, see my chapter, "Oil, Arabism and Islam: The Persian Gulf in World Politics," in *The Middle East in World Politics*, ed. Mohammed Ayoob (London: Croom Helm, 1981), pp. 118–35.
20 Fouad Ajami, *The Arab Predicament* (Cambridge: Cambridge University Press, 1981), p. 181.
21 For details see Mohammed Ayoob, ed., *The Politics of Islamic Reassertion* (London: Croom Helm, 1981), particularly the concluding chapter, Ayoob, "The Discernible Patterns."
22 Mohammed Ayoob, "Two Faces of Political Islam: Iran and Pakistan Compared," *Asian Survey* 19 (June 1979): pp. 535–36.
23 Bernard Lewis, *The Middle East and the West* (London: Weidenfeld and Nicolson, 1968), p. 114.
24 Michael C. Hudson, "Islam and Political Development," in *Islam and Development*," ed. John L. Esposito (Syracuse, N.Y.: Syracuse University Press, 1980), p. 12.
25 Zeine N. Zeine, *The Emergence of Arab Nationalism*, 3d ed. (Delmar, N.Y.: Caravan, 1973), pp. 130–31.
26 Sylvia Haim, ed., *Arab Nationalism: An Anthology* (Berkeley: University of California Press, 1974), p. 27.
27 For details see Abd al-Rahman al-Kawakibi, "The Excellences of the Arabs," in ibid., pp. 78–80.
28 Ibid., p. 62.
29 For a discussion of Afghani's use of Islam as an ideology, see Nikki Keddie, *An Islamic Response to Imperialism* (Berkeley: University of California Press, 1968); for parallels between Afghani and Khomeini, see Nikki Keddie, *Roots of Revolution* (New Haven, Conn.: Yale University Press, 1981).
30 Ajami, *The Arab Predicament*, p. 70.
31 It is no wonder, therefore, that the Saudi regime has reportedly so far underwritten Saddam Hussein's war against Iran to the tune of U.S. $20 to $25 billion.
32 Mohammed Ayoob, "Autonomy and Intervention: Super Powers and the Third World," in *New Directions in Strategic Thinking*, ed. Robert O'Neill and D. M. Horner (London: George Allen and Unwin, 1981), pp. 104–16.

Notes to Chapter 3

1 See K. P. Misra, "The Indian Ocean as a Zone of Peace: The Concepts and the Alternatives," *India Quarterly* 23 (January–March 1977); T. T. Poulose, "Indian Ocean: Prospects of a Nuclear-Free Zone," *Pacific Community* 5 (April

1974): 323–52; T. T. Poulose, ed., *Indian Ocean Power Rivalry: A Study of Littoral State Perspectives* (New Delhi: Young Asia Publishers, 1974).

2   The following is a limited selection of studies on the Indian Ocean that display a variety of perspectives on security issues: Alvin J. Cottrell and R. M. Burrell, eds., *The Indian Ocean: Its Political, Economic, and Military Importance* (New York: Praeger, 1972); Ferenc A. Váli, *Politics of the Indian Ocean: The Balance of Power* (New York: Free Press, 1976); Kim C. Beazley and Ian Clark, *Politics of Intrusion: The Super Powers and the Indian Ocean* (Sydney: Alternative Publishing, 1979); Larry W. Bowman and Ian Clark, eds., *The Indian Ocean in Global Politics* (Boulder, Colo.: Westview, 1981); Philip Towle, *Naval Power in the Indian Ocean* (Canberra: Strategic and Defense Studies Centre, Australian National University, 1979); and Alvin J. Cottrell and Associates, *Sea Power and Strategy in the Indian Ocean* (Beverly Hills, Calif.: Sage 1981).

3   There is a wealth of literature on the concept and policy of regional economic integration. See, in particular, Joseph S. Nye, ed., *International Regionalism: Readings* (Boston: Little Brown, 1968); Minerva M. Etzioni, *The Majority of One: Towards a Theory of Regional Compatibility* (Beverly Hills: Sage, 1970); Louis J. Cantori and Steven L. Spiegel, *The International Politics of Regions* (Englewood Cliffs, N.J.: Prentice-Hall, 1970); Amitai Etzioni, *Political Unification: A Comparative Study of Leaders and Forces* (New York: Holt, Rinehart and Winston, 1965); and Ernst B. Haas, *The Uniting of Europe* (Stanford, Calif.: Stanford University Press, 1958).

4   See Kim C. Beazley, "The October War, the 1973–74 Arab Oil Embargo, and U.S. Policy on the Indian Ocean" in *The Indian Ocean in Global Politics*, ed. Bowman and Clark, p. 120.

5   See Raju G. C. Thomas, "Energy Politics and Indian Security," *Pacific Affairs* 55 (Spring 1982): pp. 32–53; Richard K. Betts, "Incentives for Nuclear Weapons: India, Pakistan, Iran," *Asian Survey* 17 (November 1979): pp. 1053–72; and "Nuclear Proliferation and Regional Rivalry," *Orbis* 23 (Spring 1979).

6   For some critiques on this proposal to promote peace through economic interdependence, see Ivan Illich, "The Delinking of Peace and Development," *Alternatives* 7 (Spring 1982): pp. 409–16. On the broader impact of economic interdependence on Soviet-American relations and global stability, see Jock Finlayson and Paul Marantz, "Interdependence and East-West Relations," *Orbis* 96 (Spring 1982): pp. 173–94.

7   Shirin Tahir-Kheli, "Iran and Pakistan: Cooperation in an Area of Conflict," *Asian Survey* 25 (May 1977): pp. 474–90; and Dileep Padagaonkar, "India and the Arab World: A Dramatic Growth in Trade Ties," *Times of India*, 25 November 1977.

8   See Peter H. Lyon, "Reconciling Variable Roles, Regional Leadership and Great Power Intrusions," in *The Great Power Triangle and Asian Security*, ed. Raju G. C. Thomas (Lexington, Mass.: Lexington Books, 1983), pp. 97–101.

9   For a detailed study of economic cooperation in South Asia, see T. K. Jayaraman, *Economic Cooperation in the Indian Subcontinent* (New Delhi: Orient Longman, 1978).

10 See Chimelu Chime, *Integration and Politics Among African States* (Uppsala: Scandinavian Institute of African Affairs, 1977); Joseph S. Nye, *Pan-Africanism and East African Integration* (Cambridge, Mass.: Harvard University Press,

1965); and I. William Zartman, "Africa" in *World Politics: An Introduction,* ed. James N. Rosenau, Kenneth W. Thompson, and Gavin Boyd (New York: Free Press, 1976), pp. 569–94.

11 See Zuhayr Mikdashi, "Oil Prices and OPEC's Surpluses: Some Reflections," *International Affairs* 57 (Summer 1981): pp. 407–27; and Rehman Sobhan, "OPEC's Political Options: Case for Collective Self-Reliance within the Third World," *Alternatives* 7 (Summer 1981): pp. 43–60.

12 For a detailed analysis of recent developments toward economic and security cooperation within the gulf area itself, see R. K. Ramazani's chapter in this volume on the Gulf Cooperation Council.

Notes to Chapter 4

1 Barry Buzan, in *Survival* 24 (January–February 1982); p. 44. For arguments in favor of the concept of an Indian Ocean region, see William L. Dowdy and Russell B. Trood, "The Indian Ocean: An Emerging Geostrategic Region," *International Journal* 38 (Summer 1983): pp. 432–58.

2 Martin Wight, *Power Politics,* ed. Hedley Bull and Carsten Holbraad (New York: Penguin, 1978), chap. 15.

3 Strategy refers here to the *external* strategy of a state. It is a technique or method to exploit international divisions and to organize international divisions of power. Culture is defined as a set of political symbols—adopted by a group of people in relation to other groups—that asserts concepts of reality, human destiny, and global order. Culture expresses a system of beliefs and values derived from historical experiences or images of history that calls for action: to resist, to induce, or to force change. Material means include scientific, technological, economic, and military capabilities of a state that can be used in interstate conflict.

4 Wight, *Power Politics,* pp. 63–65.

5 Ibid., p. 42.

6 Ibid., chap. 3, passim.

7 Ibid., p. 160.

8 G. H. Jansen, *Militant Islam* (London: Pan Books, 1979).

9 Saul B. Cohen, *Geography and Politics in a World Divided,* 2d ed. (New York: Oxford University Press, 1973).

10 Ibid., pp. 64–66.

11 E. Kaufman, *The Superpowers and Their Spheres of Influence* (London: Croom Helm, 1976).

12 Irving L. Horowitz, *Beyond Empire and Revolution: Militarization and Consolidation in the Third World* (New York: Oxford University Press, 1982), p. vii.

13 For an extended discussion of this concept, see A. Eide and M. Thee, eds., *Problems of Contemporary Militarism* (London: Croom Helm, 1980).

14 Sources of data indicating a steady growth in Third World military expenditures include the annual Stockholm International Peace Research Institute (SIPRI) yearbooks, *World Armaments and Disarmament,* the United States Arms Control and Disarmament Agency's *World Military Expenditures and Arms Transfers* series, and Ruth Leger Sivard's *World Military and Social Expenditures* annual series.

15 For data on the increasing incidence of military conflict, see L. Kende, "Local

Wars 1945–76," in Eide and Thee, *Problems of Contemporary Militarism*, chap. 15.

16 For a full development of the perspective introduced in this chapter, see Ashok Kapur, *The Indian Ocean—Regional and International Power Politics* (New York: Praeger, 1983).

Notes to Chapter 5

1 Unless stated otherwise, the raw data for this chapter is taken from the annual "International Navies Issue" of the *U.S. Naval Institute Proceedings* (hereafter referred to as *USNIPs*) (March 1981, 1982, and 1983), particularly William L. Dowdy III, "Middle Eastern, North African, and South Asian Navies," 1982 and 1983.

2 Samuel P. Huntington, *The Common Defense* (New York: Columbia University Press, 1961), pp. 3–4.

3 For a general discussion of the neglected subject of the domestic sources of naval policy, see K. Booth, *Navies and Foreign Policy* (London: Croom Helm, 1977), chap. 8.

4 In January 1979 the 19,500-ton *Vikrant* was decommissioned for a major refit. Extensive work took place, including the updating of all sensors and weapons systems, in the hope that its life would be extended for ten years. It was recommissioned in January 1983. In mid-1983 the ship was scheduled to be decommissioned once more, this time to be fitted with the equipment necessary to fly Sea Harriers, including a ski-jump.

5 In 1982 Pakistan attempted to meet its needs by adding one former British and one former United States destroyer to its inventory. In the first case, a nineteen-year-old destroyer replaced a thirty-eight-year-old cruiser.

6 Jon Connell, "Nott—'Badly Misunderstood'," *Sunday Times*, 5 September 1982.

7 For an account of Oman's rather remarkable little navy, see Lieutenant Colonel Thomas M. Johnson and Lieutenant Commander Raymond T. Barrett, "Omani Navy: Operating in Troubled Waters," *USNIPs* (March 1982), pp. 99–103.

8 For discussions of the Australian navy's options, see Rodney Cowen, "Australia Considers Alternatives to HMS Invincible," *Times* (London), 18 September 1982, and A. W. Grazebrook, "Australia's Maritime Air Power: Where Next?" *Pacific Defence Reporter* (July 1982), pp. 8–12.

9 Robert L. Scheina, "African Navies South of the Sahara," *USNIPs* (March 1982), p. 56.

10 "We May Create an Arms Industry," interview with Abdulla Bishara, secretary-general of the Gulf Cooperation Council, *Newsweek*, 11 April 1983.

11 John Kane-Berman, "S. Africa Launches 'World Beater' Arms Exports," *Guardian*, 18 November 1982.

12 The problems encountered by the Indian navy in its relations with foreign arms suppliers can be traced in Ravindra Tomar, *Development of the Indian Navy: An Overstated Case*, working paper no. 26 (Canberra: Australian National University Strategic and Defense Studies Centre, 1980). For an alarmist view of the Soviet connection see Arroj Taha, "Indo-Soviet Co-operation at Sea," *Naval Forces* 3, no. 1 (1981), pp. 44–49.

13 See William L. Dowdy III, "Naval Warfare in the Gulf: Iraq versus Iran," *USNIPs* (June 1981).

14 See James M. McConnell and Anne Kelly Calhoun, "The December 1971

Indo-Pakistani Crisis," in *Soviet Naval Diplomacy*, ed. Bradford Dismukes and James M. McConnell (New York: Pergamon, 1979), pp. 178–92.

15 See Barry Buzan, "Naval Power, the Law of the Sea, and the Indian Ocean as a Zone of Peace," *Marine Policy* (July 1981), pp. 194–204.

16 Commander Dennis R. Neutze, "Whose Law of Whose Sea?" *USNIPs* (January 1983), p. 48.

17 Sir James Cable, "The Fashion for Island Grabbing," *Daily Telegraph*, 5 May 1982.

18 Barry Buzan, "A Sea of Troubles? Sources of Dispute in the New Ocean Regime," *Adelphi Papers*, no. 143 (London: International Institute for Strategic Studies, 1978), p. 22.

19 Ibid., p. 34. A list of regional disputes can be found on pp. 31–34.

20 See Johnson and Barrett, "Omani Navy: Operating in Troubled Waters."

21 Quoted in *Time*, 20 September 1982, p. 12.

22 Peter Lewis Young, "Navies of ASEAN," *Navy International* (September 1981), pp. 520–22. See also Sheldon Simon, "ASEAN and the Indian Ocean: Maritime Issues and Regional Security," in this volume.

23 Commander Geoffrey Evans, "America's Ally 'Down Under,'" *USNIPs* (March 1981), p. 85.

24 Lee Dowdy, "Third World Navies: New Responsibilities, Old Problems," *Marine Policy* (April 1981).

25 Dismukes and McConnell, *Soviet Naval Diplomacy*, pp. 130–33.

26 Ken Booth and Lee Dowdy, "Soviet Security Interests in the Indian Ocean Region," in *Soviet Armed Forces Review Annual* 6, ed. David R. Jones (Florida: Academic International Press, 1982), pp. 327–77, esp. 337–41.

27 See Joel Larus, "India: the Neglected Service Faces the Future," *USNIPs* (March 1981), pp. 77–83.

28 To put spending on the Indian navy into perspective, it should be noted that the U.S. Navy was allocated approximately 30 percent of an estimated defense budget for 1982–83 of $215.9 billion. In 1981 the Indian navy received less than 10 percent of the defense budget of $5.26 billion.

29 Quoted in S. W. Roskill, *The War at Sea*, vol. 1 (London: HMSO, 1954), p. 419.

30 "Dispute" refers to "an overt difference of opinion between states over rights or boundaries relating to law of the sea." On the other hand, "conflict" refers to "situations in which at least one party pursues the dispute by nonpeaceful means." The distinction is Buzan's ("A Sea of Troubles?" p. 4).

31 On the new suppliers of arms in the world see Rodney Cowton, "Boom Time at the Bazaar," *Times* (London), 22 March 1983; and "Arming the World," *Time*, 26 October 1981.

32 The military implications of the changing law of the sea are examined at length in Ken Booth, *Law, Force, and Diplomacy at Sea* (London: George Allen and Unwin, 1985).

Notes to Chapter 6

1 *New York Times*, 30 May 1982.

2 United Nations, *Disarmament Yearbook* 6 (New York: 1981), p. 306.

3 United Nations, Final Document of the Assembly Session on Disarmament, 23 May–1 July 1978.

4 Ibid., pars. 60 and 61.

Notes to Chapter 7

1 Iranian President Abol Hassan Bani Sadr was dismissed in June 1981 and fled secretly to Europe. Sadegh Ghotbzadeh, former Iranian foreign minister, was tried and executed in September 1982. Both men had been among the closest of Ayatollah Khomeini's advisers during his period of exile in France.

2 Many of Khomeini's writings, including his important lectures on Islamic government, have been translated and annotated by Hamid Algar, *Islam and Revolution: Writings and Declarations of Imam Khomeini* (Berkeley: Mizan Press, 1981). See also N. Calder, "Accommodation and Revolution in Imami Shi'i Jurisprudence: Khumayni and the Classical Tradition," *Middle Eastern Studies* 18 (January 1982): 3–20; A. R. Kelidar, "Ayatollah Khomeini's Concept of Islamic Government," in *Islam and Power*, ed. A. S. Cudsi and A. E. Hillal Dessouki (London: 1981); and Ayatollah Yahya Nuri, "The Islamic Concept of State," in *Strategic Digest* (November 1979), pp. 701–15.

3 On the origins and development of Islamic political theory see A. K. S. Lambton, *State and Government in Medieval Islam: An Introduction to the Theory of Islamic Government: The Jurists* (London: 1981). For a survey of recent writings see H. Enayat, *Modern Islamic Political Theory* (London: 1982).

4 According to the tenets of that variety of Shi'ite Islam which is followed in Iran, the true leader of the community of believers is the imam, an individual who possesses special knowledge and whose rule is absolute. The twelfth holder of that office disappeared from human sight in A.D. 873 when he was still a young boy. In his absence all forms of political authority are, strictly speaking, illegitimate because they are usurped. Iran's Shi'is believe that the imam will return one day to fill the earth with justice and equity.

5 On 19 August 1982 Ayatollah Khomeini declared that all Iranian laws that ran counter to Islam should be abolished, and within a week the Supreme Court in Tehran had declared that all such laws were revoked. *Times* (London), 24 August 1982.

6 See, for example, a speech delivered by Ayatollah Khomeini to workers in Tehran on 19 January 1981 as quoted in *Islamic Revolution* 3 (March 1981): 2.

7 Translations of the 1979 and 1980 messages are included in Algar, *Islam and Revolution*, pp. 275–79 and 300–306.

8 Those arrested in September 1982 included Hojat al Islam Kho'ini, a religious figure who had played a leading part in the seizure and detention of the U.S. embassy hostages. *Times* (London), 25 September 1982.

9 There is already a considerable body of literature on that war. For a concise survey of the historical background and a useful collection of documents including the text of the 1975 Algiers Treaty, see Tareq Y. Ismael, *Iran and Iraq: Roots of Conflict* (Syracuse, N.Y.: Syracuse University Press, 1982). Further details on the course of the conflict are provided by Stephen R. Grumman, *The Iran-Iraq War: Islam Embattled*, Washington Papers no. 92 (New York: 1982).

10 On the background to Shi'ite political activities in Iraq see Hanna Batatu, "Iraq's Underground Shi'i Movements: Characteristics, Causes and Prospects," *Middle East Journal* 35 (Autumn 1981): 578–94.

11 *Financial Times* (London), 19 June 1982.

12 Estimates of the size of that community are as disparate as those for the total population of Saudi Arabia. A recent report put the number of Shi'ites at around two hundred thousand. *Economist* (London), 12 June 1982.

13 Estimates of the amount of money provided for Iraq in the form of loans and grants vary, but in March 1982 it was reported that Baghdad may have received as much as $22 billion over the previous six months. *Financial Times* (London), 26 March 1982.

14 In June 1982 it was reported that Iran had demanded war reparations amounting to $150 billion. *Financial Times* (London), 11 June 1982. Other reports have quoted different, but still very substantial, figures.

15 On his arrival in Syria in late August 1982, George Habbash, leader of the Popular Front for the Liberation of Palestine, denounced the "impotence and treason" of certain Arab states and predicted that "the Arab region will see from now on one earthquake after another" *Observer* (London), 30 August 1982.

16 After taking action against the Mujahidin and Fedayin groups, the Iranian government ordered the arrest of many leading members of the communist Tudeh party in February 1983 on the grounds that they had acted as spies for Moscow. A number of executions, including that of the party's secretary general, Nur al Din Khianouri, followed in June.

17 See, for example, Azar Tabari, "Iran: Year One of the Islamic Republic," *Issues* (May 1980), pp. 13–17 and 30.

18 The Iranian government might also decide to reawaken issues concerned with the demarcation of undersea boundaries. Those at the head of the gulf, disputed among Iran, Iraq, and Kuwait are among the most sensitive. See W. D. Swearingen, "Sources of Conflict over Oil in the Persian Gulf," *Middle East Journal* 35 (Summer 1981): 314–30.

Notes to Chapter 8

1 Crane Brinton, *The Anatomy of Revolution*, was first published in 1938. A revised edition appeared in 1952, and a revised and expanded edition was published in 1965. Page references in parentheses in the text are from the 1965 edition. I have explored the relevance of Brinton's typology to the Iranian case in very preliminary fashion in "Cromwell, Napoleon, and the Iranians," *Christian Science Monitor*, 9 September 1981, p. 23; and in "The Unfinished Revolution in Iran," *International Insight* 2 (November–December 1981): 6–9.

2 The term "Thermidor" refers to the fall of Robespierre on 27 July 1794, the ninth of Thermidor of the second year of the revolutionary French calendar. From this date onward, French historians refer to the slow return to normalcy as the Thermidorian reaction.

3 See Brinton, *Anatomy of Revolution*, p. 139, for a fuller discussion of the moderates.

4 *Tehran Times*, 13 February 1982, p. 3.

5 *Foreign Broadcast Information Service*, 17 August 1981, pp. 1–13.

6 *Iran Times*, 11 September 1981, p. 1.

7 These figures on the violence of the French and Russian revolutions are drawn together from various classical sources and are presented in Carl Leiden and Karl M. Schmitt, *The Politics of Violence: Revolution in the Modern World* (Englewood Cliffs, N.J.: Prentice-Hall, 1968), pp. 34–35.

8 *Iran Times*, 25 September 1981, p. 1.

9 The important concept of relationships of emanation as they are manifested in

Shi'i Islam has been introduced in the theoretical investigations of Manfred
Halpern. See also James A. Bill and Carl Leiden, *Politics in the Middle East*
(Boston: Little, Brown, 1979), pp. 150–61.

10 For the best analysis of these factional divisions, see Gregory Rose, "Factional
Alignments in the Central Council of the Islamic Republican Party of Iran,"
paper to be published by Woodrow Wilson Center, Smithsonian Institution,
Washington, D.C.

11 *Iran Times*, 24 September 1982, p. 15.

12 "We are facing many problems which are not a secret to the nation because
the nation is of the government and the government is of the nation. All the
government officials are servants of the people and the nation supports the
government. So long as this coordination exists this Islamic Republic will not
be harmed" (Ayatollah Khomeini, quoted in *Tehran Times*, 26 July 1982, p. 1).

13 Much of the data presented in this paragraph have been drawn from the writings of Fereidun Fesharaki. See F. Fesharaki, "Iran's Petroleum Policy: How
Does the Oil Industry Function in Revolutionary Iran?" (Paper to be published
in a book edited by Haleh Afshar).

14 The split between the Majority and the Minority factions can be traced to 10
and 11 June 1980 when each group published its own edition of the party's
newspaper, *Kar*. Both editions were presented as number 62. See *Kar*, 20 and
21 Khordad 1359.

15 *Tehran Times*, 3 February 1982, p. 1. In September 1982, the official voice of
the IRP, *Jomhuri-ye Islami*, sharply attacked the Tudeh party and accused it
of "throwing a mouse in the soup of the revolution" (*Iran Times*, 1 October
1982, p. 1).

16 "The History of the PMOI, 1965–1971," *Mojahed—The Organ of the People's
Mojahedin Organization of Iran* 1 (May 1980): 20.

17 "The Content of the Islamic Republic," ibid., p. 24.

18 For a detailed analysis of Khomeini as political strategist, see J. A. Bill, "Power
and Religion in Revolutionary Iran," *Middle East Journal* 36 (Winter 1982),
esp. pp. 41–45. The most complete and authoritative collection of Khomeini's
ideas is *Islam and Revolution: Writings and Declarations of Imam Khomeini*
translated and annotated by Hamid Algar (Berkeley: Mizan Press, 1981).

19 *Tehran Times*, 10 February 1982, p. 6.

20 Ibid.

21 *Tehran Times*, 19 September 1982, p. 1.

22 *Tehran Times*, 26 July 1982, p. 1.

23 Ibid.

24 *Tehran Times*, 21 September 1982, p. 4.

25 *Tehran Times*, 6 September 1982, p. 3.

Notes to Chapter 9

1 The dispute is actually centuries old but this chapter examines only the contemporary period. For a historic overview, see Tareq I. Ismael, *Iraq and Iran:
Roots of Conflict* (Syracuse, N.Y.: Syracuse University Press, 1982).

2 Amil Toma, *Siton 'Aman 'ala al-Haraka al-Qawmiyah al-Arabiyah al-Filastiniyah*,
2d ed. (Beirut: Dar Ibn Rushd, 1978), p. 246.

3 *The 1968 Revolution in Iraq—Experience and Prospects* (London: Ithaca
Press, 1979), pp. 130–31.

Notes to Chapter 10

1 See the text of the final statement of the Supreme Council of the Gulf Co-operation Council as read by the GCC secretary general 26 May 1981 in *Foreign Broadcast Information Service* 5, no. 219 (hereinafter referred to as *FBIS*), Middle East and Africa, 13 November 1981.

2 See the text of GCC Working Paper in *FBIS* 5, no. 107, Middle East and Africa, 4 June 1981.

3 Personal interviews by the author suggested that at this point in the war GCC leaders really wished, at least in private, "a plague on both houses" of the warring countries.

4 A good example of a sympathetic account of the GCC that may appear to be condescending is James Tyson's caustic characterization of the organization as the "Society for the Preservation of Obsolescent Emirs" in his otherwise perceptive article, "The Gulf—Evolution or Revolution," *Middle East International* (7 May 1982), pp. 10–11.

5 See *New York Times*, 12 October 1980.

6 See Rouhollah K. Ramazani, "Iran's Search for Regional Cooperation," *Middle East Journal* 30 (Spring 1976): 173–86.

7 For details see R. K. Ramazani, *The Persian Gulf and the Strait of Hormuz* (The Netherlands: Sijthoff and Noordhoff, 1979), pp. 107–12.

8 For an excellent and brief discussion of this question see *Economist*, 11 December 1982, p. 55.

9 See David B. Ottaway in *Washington Post*, 25 November 1982.

10 See *Washington Post*, 8 January 1983.

11 See *New York Times*, 28 March 1982.

12 Ibid.

13 For example, in a statement to the Qatari newspaper *Ar-Rayah*, the secretary general of the GCC reportedly said on 16 January 1982 that all gulf countries have become a basic party to this war "and how can we be mediators in an issue in which we are a major party?" See *FBIS* 5, no. 013, Middle East and Africa, 20 January 1982.

14 The resolution was adopted during the Fez summit on 9 September 1982. Reportedly it stated at the outset, "The Arab presidents and kings have announced their readiness to carry out their commitments to Iraq in accordance with Article Six of the Arab League Charter and Article Two of the collective Arab defense pact in case Iran fails to respond to the peace efforts and continues its war against Iraq." See *FBIS* 5, no. 176, Middle East and Africa, 10 September 1982.

15 For details see *FBIS* 5, no. 219, Middle East and Africa, 12 November 1982.

16 I treated this subject in a paper entitled, "Khumayni's Islam in Iran's Foreign Policy," delivered on 13 July 1982 to a conference on Islam and foreign policy held by the Royal Institute of International Affairs in London. It is published as a chapter in the proceedings of the conference.

17 See *FBIS* 5, no. 244, Middle East and Africa, 21 December 1981.

18 See *FBIS* 5, no. 026, Middle East and Africa, 8 February 1982.

19 Ibid.

20 See *FBIS* 5, no. 028, Middle East and Africa, 25 February 1982.

21 For the text of the draft agreement see *FBIS* 5, no. 225, Middle East and Africa, 22 November 1982.

22 *Al-Nahar*, 25 August 1978.
23 *Arab News*, 3 April 1979.
24 For details of a major statement by the Hojatoleslam Khoiniha on the functions of the *hajj*, see the Iranian newspaper *Ettela'at*, 24 August 1982.
25 See R. K. Ramazani, *The United States and Iran: The Patterns of Influence* (New York: Praeger, 1982).
26 See, for example, *FBIS* 5, no. 029, Middle East and Africa, 11 February 1982.
27 As reported in *Washington Post*, 25 January 1983.
28 Ibid., 26 January 1983.
29 For details see *FBIS* 8, no. 244, South Asia.
30 On the oil emergency meeting held in Manama, see *FBIS* 5, no. 011, Middle East and Africa, 17 January 1983.

Notes to Chapter 11

1 See Mordechai Abir, *Oil, Power and Politics: Conflict in Arabia, the Red Sea and the Gulf* (London: Frank Cass, 1974); and William Nurthen, *Soviet Strategy in the Red Sea Basin* (M.A. thesis, Naval Postgraduate School, Monterey, Calif., 1980).
2 U.S., Department of Commerce, *A Statistical Analysis of the World's Merchant Fleets* (Washington, D.C.: Government Printing Office, 1979).
3 See P. M. Holt, *The Mahdist State in the Sudan* (London: Oxford University Press, 1970); and Haim Shaked, *The Life of the Sudanese Mahdi* (New Jersey: Transaction Books, 1978).
4 Statement made by Chairman Mengistu Haile Mariam to the Conference Organizing the Peoples and Workers of Ethiopia (COPWE), Addis Ababa, 3 January 1983.
5 See Colin Legum and Bill Lee, *Conflict in the Horn of Africa* (New York: Africana Publishing, 1977); and Legum and Lee, *The Horn of Africa in Continuing Crisis* (New York: Africana Publishing, 1979).
6 Bereket Habte Selassie, *Conflict and Intervention in the Horn of Africa* (New York: Monthly Review Press, 1980); Othman Saleh Sabby, *The History of Eritrea* (Beirut: Dar Al-Masirah, n.d.); G. K. N. Trevaskis, *Eritrea* (London: Oxford University Press, 1960).
7 Statement to COPWE, 3 January 1983.
8 Ethiopia, Foreign Ministry, Statement of 1 March 1982.
9 *Libya International Report* (London), September 1981.
10 Ibid.
11 See Colin Legum, "Angola and the Horn of Africa," in *Diplomacy of Power*, ed. Stephen S. Kaplan (Washington, D.C.: Brookings Institution, 1981).
12 Edward Wilson, *Russia and Black Africa Before World War II* (New York: Africana Publishing, 1972).
13 *Pravda*, 26 July 1960.
14 Radio Moscow, 8 March 1977.
15 See interview given by Cuba's vice-president, Carlos Rafael Rodriques, to Hugh O'Shaughnessy, in the *Observer* (London), 26 February 1978.

Notes to Chapter 12

1 For the purposes of this chapter, the term "state" refers to either the YAR or PDRY, while "nation" embraces the population and territory of all of Yemen.

"National" (as in "national politics"), however, is more narrowly defined to apply only to either the YAR or the PDRY.

2 Some of the more informative and reliable sources on domestic politics in the Yemens include the following books and monographs: Mordechai Abir, *Oil, Power and Politics: Conflict in Arabia, the Red Sea and the Gulf* (London: Frank Cass, 1974); Fred Halliday, *Arabia Without Sultans* (New York: Vintage, 1975); Halliday, *Threat from the East? Soviet Policy from Afghanistan and Iran to the Horn of Africa* (Harmondsworth: Penguin, 1982); Richard F. Nyrop et al., *Area Handbook for the Yemens* (Washington, D.C.: Government Printing Office, 1977); Robert W. Stookey, *Yemen: The Politics of the Yemen Arab Republic* (Boulder, Colo.: Westview, 1978); Stookey, *South Yemen: A Marxist Republic in Arabia* (Boulder, Colo.: Westview, 1982); J. E. Peterson, *Conflict in the Yemens and Superpower Involvement* (Washington, D.C.: Georgetown University, Center for Contemporary Arab Studies, 1981); and Peterson, *Yemen: The Search for a Modern State* (Baltimore: Johns Hopkins University Press, 1982).

3 The loss of President Ibrahim al-Hamdi through assassination has been particularly unfortunate for the YAR. His success resulted from a combination of widespread acceptance because of his neutral background, his well-known commitment to development, and his ability to see the long-range needs of the country and to devise ways in which to accomplish his goals. Of course, all this was in addition to his skillfulness in shifting key supporters into strategic positions and maintaining a fragile balance between competing factions.

4 Muhammad is the quintessential survivor of PDRY politics. During the long period of triumviral leadership (1971–78), Muhammad carried a reputation as the weak link, the political nonentity who kept his position through his ability to maintain careful relations with all competing factions. These skills have apparently served him well in keeping his balance on Aden's tightrope.

5 The National Democratic Front, while formally organized only in the late 1970s, has its origins in the ouster of the YAR's radicals from the North Yemen government and army in the latter days of the civil war (1962–70). NDF ranks were later swelled by followers of President Hamdi after his assassination and by the defection of militant Shafi'is with the tightening of Zaydi control over the state in recent years.

6 Rather irrationally, many Yemenis are also convinced that substantial oil reserves have been discovered in various parts of the YAR and that the Saudis have deliberately prevented the oil companies from exploiting these fields in order to keep Yemen poor and dependent on Riyadh.

7 The population of North Yemen is approximately 6 million. Over 0.5 million adult males work outside the country, following the tradition of their fathers and grandfathers. While the largest number by far work in Saudi Arabia, significant communities also exist in Aden, on the other side of the Red Sea, in the smaller gulf states, in Britain, and in the United States.

Notes to Chapter 13

1 Samir Amin, *Unequal Development, Essay on the Social Formation of Capitalism of the Periphery* (New York: Monthly Review Press, 1976); Terence K. Hopkins, Immanuel Wallerstein, and Associates, *World Systems Analysis,*

Theory and Methodology (Beverly Hills: Sage, 1982); and Andre Gunder Frank, *The Development of Underdevelopment* (New York: Monthly Review Press, 1966).

2 The author's first use of the tributary state concept was in "Demilitarization Proposals for the Indian Ocean," in *The Indian Ocean in Global Politics*, ed. Larry W. Bowman and Ian Clark (Boulder, Colo.: Westview, 1981).

3 Carl G. Rosberg, Jr., and John Nottingham, *The Myth of Mau Mau* (Stanford, Calif.: Hoover Institution Publications, 1966), pp. 320–48.

4 Alan E. Amey and David K. Leonard, "Public Policy, Class, and Inequality in Kenya and Tanzania," *Africa Today* 26 (1979).

5 Steven Langdon, *Multi-national Corporations in the Political Economy of Kenya* (New York: St. Martin's, 1981), pp. 41–43.

6 In 1972–73 a survey showed that twenty multinational corporations largely dominated the Kenyan economy providing 69 percent of employment, 84 percent of the turnover, and 86 percent of the capital in key manufacturing industries (ibid., pp. 32–34). See also Colin Leys, *Underdevelopment in Kenya* (Berkeley: University of California Press, 1974).

7 See Langdon, *Multi-national Corporations in Kenya*, pp. 41–42.

8 See Armed Mohiddin, *African Socialism in Two Countries* (Totowa, N.J.: Barnes and Noble, 1981), pp. 105–7.

9 The *Matajiri* have been particularly active in the tourist industry. See "Countdown for Kenya's Rhino," *Africana* (Nairobi) 6, no. 12 (1979).

10 International Labour Organization, *Employment, Incomes, and Equality, A Strategy for Increasing Productive Employment in Kenya* (Washington, D.C.: World Bank, 1972).

11 Academics and members of the press are among those who have suffered most from repressive measures. These have involved violations of political rights ranging from censorship to detention and assassination. *See* Amey and Leonard, "Public Policy, Class, and Inequality," p. 16.

12 The "Mzee" was elusive about who should succeed him, but Moi as the vice president and one of the very few non-Kikuyu leaders was seen as a compromise. With the assistance of then Attorney General Charles Njonjo, Moi was able to foil a concerted effort on the part of the Kenyatta family to ensure that one of their own succeed to the presidency. Having taken over after Kenyatta's sudden death, Moi subsequently gained the unanimous nomination of KANU for the presidency.

13 *Africa News*, 9 August 1982.

14 *Africa Contemporary Record* 14 (1981–82): B187–88.

15 Ibid., B203.

16 "Kenya: The End of an Illusion," *Race and Class* (Winter 1983): 237.

17 *Africa Contemporary Record* 14: B202.

18 L. L. Matthews, "Kenya," in *World Armies*, ed. John Keegan (New York: Facts on File, 1979), p. 402.

19 "The Image Cracks," *South* (London), August 1982.

20 *Africa News*, 9 August 1982.

21 See J. F. Rweyemamu, "Introduction," in *Industrialization and Income Distribution in Africa* (Dakar: Codesvia, 1980).

22 Roy Preiswerk has defined the self-reliance strategy as involving more than nineteenth-century capitalist ideas. See Johan Galtung and Peter O'Brian, "In-

troduction," in Galtung and O'Brian, ed., *Self-Reliance: A Strategy for Development* (London: L'Ouverture Publications for the Institute of Developmental Studies, Geneva, 1980), p. 12.

23 See Julius K. Nyerere, *Freedom and Socialism—A Collection from Writings and Speeches 1965–67* (London: Oxford University Press, 1968).

24 For a discussion of the various facets of this dependence see Okwudiba Nnoli, *Self-Reliance and Foreign Policy in Tanzania* (New York: Nok Publisher, 1978), p. 205.

25 Julius Nyerere, "Freedom and Development," reprinted in the *Nationalist* (Dar es Salaam), 18 October 1968.

26 Julius K. Nyerere, "South-South Option," *Third World Quarterly* 4 (July 1982).

27 The criticism comes from both the right and the left, in the West and East as well as in Africa. Among Nyerere's most scornful African critics are the *Matajiri* from Kenya who oppose state-directed economies. At home Nyerere's strongest critics are Marxists. See for example, Issa Shivji, *Class Struggles in Tanzania* (New York: Monthly Review Press, 1976).

28 Dean McHenry, "The Struggle for Rural Socialism in Tanzania," in Carl Rosberg and Ian Callaghy, ed., *Socialism in Sub-Sahara Africa* (Berkeley: Institute of International Studies, 1978). Also see Roger Yeaker, *Tanzania: An African Experiment* (Boulder, Colo.: Westview, 1982).

29 See Amey and Leonard, "Public Policy, Class, and Inequality."

30 For a discussion see Zaki Ergas, "Why Did the Ujama Policy Fail?" *Journal of Modern African Studies* 18, no. 3 (1980–81).

31 Under the program over 90 percent of Tanzania's rural population was transferred from individual huts and plots to *Ujama* villages between 1970 and 1980. In the villages, which were to establish links among themselves, families were to be encouraged to own their own plots but the primary occupation was to be that of working communal land and establishing related cottage industries. For discussions of the program, its achievements and shortcomings, see Zaki Ergas, *The Tanzania Economy: What Went Wrong?* (Jerusalem: Truman Research Institute, Hebrew University, 1981); David J. Vail, *Technology for Ujama, Village Development in Tanzania* (Syracuse, N.Y.: Syracuse University Press, Foreign and Comparative Studies, African Series 18, 1975); Louise Fortman, *Peasants, Officials and Participation in Rural Tanzania's Experience with Villagization and Decentralization* (Ithaca, N.Y.: Center for International Studies, Cornell University, 1980); and Jannik Boesen, Birgit Storgard Madsen, and Tony Moore, *Ujama—Socialism from Above* (Uppsala: Scandinavian Institute of African Studies, 1977).

32 Nevertheless, increased agricultural productivity is the critical issue for *Ujama* and unless it succeeds the whole system will collapse. See the conclusions of S. S. Mushi in "Tanzania, Foreign Relations and the Policies of Non-Alignment, Socialism, and Self-Reliance," unpublished paper, University of Dar es Salaam, 1979.

33 Major initiatives have been left to parastatels financed by various government banks and central agencies. See Mohiddin, *African Socialism in Two Countries*, p. 145.

34 *Critical Phase in Tanzania, 1945–68: Nyerere and the Emergence of a Socialist Strategy* (Cambridge: Cambridge University Press, 1976).

35 Nnoli, *Self-Reliance and Foreign Policy*, p. 324.

36 Tanzania's own defense forces are quite small, though the army is now battle seasoned as a result of its intervention in Uganda. For the most part, the Tanzanian military has been standardizing on Chinese equipment. See *World Military Expenditures and Arms Transfers, 1970–79* (Washington, D.C.: United States Arms Control and Disarmament Agency, 1980), table 3, p. 127; and L. L. Matthews, "Tanzania," in *World Armies*, ed. John Keegan (New York: Facts on File, 1979).

37 Robert S. Jaster, *A Regional Security Role for Africa's Front Line States: Experience and Prospects*, Adelphi Paper no. 180 (London: International Institute for Strategic Studies, 1983), p. 11.

38 Julius Nyerere, "The Second Scramble," *Freedom and Unity: A Selection from Writings and Speeches, 1952–65* (London: Oxford University Press, 1967), p. 208.

39 *Africa Contemporary Record* (1981–82): p. B284.

40 Ibid., p. B285.

41 See Mohammed Babu, *African Socialists or Socialist Africa* (London: Zed Press, 1981); and Shivji, *Class Struggles in Tanzania*.

42 *Africa Contemporary Record* (1981–82), p. B283; *Africa News*, 7 December 1979.

43 UNDP, Country Programme for United Republic of Tanzania, 1978–81, Dar es Salaam, DPGC/URT/R-2, 9 October 1978. The total aid projected was $29,290,205.

Notes to Chapter 14

1 Rough estimates of the Asian (citizen and noncitizen) populations of the Frontline States in the early 1970s are as follows: Tanzania, 130,000; Mozambique, 20,000; Zambia, 12,000; Zimbabwe, 10,000; Botswana, 500; Angola, insignificant; or a total of over 172,000.

2 President Nyerere implicitly admitted this when he declared in India in January 1971, "We must treat the Indian Ocean as the link it can be, not the barrier others would like it to be!" (*Freedom and Development* [Dar es Salaam: Oxford University Press, 1973], p. 258).

3 Ronald T. Libby, "The Frontline States of Africa: A Small Power Entente," University of Zambia, 18 May 1977, mimeo; *The Front-Line States: The Burden of the Liberation Struggle* (London: Commonwealth Secretariat, 1978); John Marcum, "African Front-Line States: Forcing the Pace," *Nation* 225 (12 November 1977), pp. 492–95.

4 The Lusaka Agreement ending the war in Mozambique and establishing a transitional government comprising *Frente de Libertação de Moçambique* (FRELIMO) and Portuguese nominees pending full independence was signed on 7 September 1974. As a result, Tanzania technically ceased to be a Frontline State in the sense of providing launching pads for guerrillas operating across its borders. However, its commitment to the cause of liberation distinguished it from Malawi, Swaziland, and Lesotho.

5 Initially, during 1974–75, Zaire also attended on occasion. Since 1976, Nigerian representatives have participated (somewhat irregularly) in several sessions as an honorary Frontline State; and, since 1980, the current OAU Chairman has occasionally been invited to attend. The leaders of southern African liberation movements—ZANU and ZAPU, SWAPO, and, since March 1982, the South African

558 Notes

ANC—have also participated as observers when their specific interests were under discussion.

6 A combined Seychelles-Malagasy-Tanzanian military exercise was held in June 1977 (*Africa Contemporary Record* [1979–80], p. B301).

7 See John A. Marcum, *The Angolan Revolution* (Cambridge, Mass.: MIT Press, 1978), 2:231; *Africa Diary*, 1967, p. 3489.

8 "Economic Cooperation among Developing Countries: The Case of India and Southern Africa," International Workshop on Research Priorities in Southern Africa, Roma, Lesotho, November 1981, mimeo.

9 Indira Gandhi has visited Tanzania (in 1961 and 1976), Zambia (in 1970 and 1976), Zimbabwe (in 1980), and Mozambique (in 1982). India has received visits from Kaunda (in 1958, 1961, 1967, 1975, 1980, and 1981), from Nyerere (in 1971, 1974, 1976, 1981, and 1982), from Khama (in 1976) and Masire (in 1981), and from Mugabe (in 1981). All six FLS leaders attended the Seventh Non-Aligned Conference in New Delhi in March 1983.

10 Saudi Arabia is the major source of oil for Zambia, Mozambique, and (along with Iraq) Tanzania. Iran was the principal supplier to Zambia until 1974 and to Tanzania until 1978, as was Iraq to Mozambique until 1977 (IMF, *Direction of Trade States Yearbook*, 1982). Iraq appears to have been alone in selling oil to the three countries on "solidarity" terms (*African Research Bulletin* [EFT] (1979), p. 5364; ibid. (1980), p. 5596; ibid. (1982), p. 6511).

11 Zambia's close ties with Iraq began with Kaunda's meeting with President Hussein in Havana in September 1979. Subsequently, he visited Baghdad in November 1979, in September 1980 (a week after the invasion of Iran), and in May 1982. An Iraqi trade commission visited Lusaka in September 1980 (*Africa Contemporary Record* [1980–81], p. B907). Iraq is now the largest single market for Zimbabwe tobacco (*Standard Bank Review*, July 1982, p. 3).

12 *Times of Zambia* (Lusaka), 7 August 1981, p. 1.

13 In Jiddah, Prime Minister Nalumino Mundia appealed to Arab nations to give aid bilaterally rather than through the IMF (*Times of Zambia*, 23 June 1982, p. 1). On the occasion of Kaunda's visit to Saudi Arabia in August 1981, Lusaka was compelled to deny rumors in financial circles that he was seeking Saudi support to counter American moves to block Zambia from receiving additional IMF loans (in retaliation for its expulsion of two American diplomats accused of spying) (*Zambia Newsletter* [London] 11 September 1981, p. 4).

14 *Times* (London), 25 May 1982, p. 20. SADCC embraces the Frontline States plus Malawi, Swaziland, and Lesotho. Since Malawi and Lesotho maintain diplomatic relations with Israel, the Arabs boycotted SADCC conferences in Blantyre in November 1981 and, to a lesser extent, in Maseru in February 1983.

15 *Sunday Times of Zambia*, 16 February 1975, p. 1. The Khomeini regime has retained Iran's 17.5 percent interest in the South African National Petroleum Refinery (*Financial Times* [London] 12 February 1981, p. 24).

16 The Arabs, on the other hand, seem to have experienced no serious problems in ensuring that their oil does not reach Israel. Of fifty tankers delivering Saudi Arabian oil to South Africa between January 1979 and March 1980, only fifteen had "end-user" certificates (Gwendolen M. Carter and Patrick O'Meara, ed., *International Politics in Southern Africa* [Bloomington: Indiana University Press, 1982], p. 117). See also, Shipping Research Bureau, Amsterdam,

"Oil Tankers to South Africa" (1981); *Observer* (London), 18 January 1981, p. 8; *Financial Times*, 12 March 1981, p. 20; *Times of Zambia*, 8 May 1975, p. 6.

17 Oye Ogunbadejo, "Diego Garcia and Africa's Security," *Third World Quarterly* 4 (January 1982), pp. 104–20; Larry Bowman and Ian Clark, ed., *The Indian Ocean in Global Politics* (Boulder, Colo.: Westview, 1981); Raymond W. Copson, "East Africa and the Indian Ocean: A 'Zone of Peace'?" *African Affairs* 76 (July 1977), pp. 339–58; Philip M. Allen, "The Indian Ocean: A New Area of Conflict or a Zone of Peace?" *Africa Contemporary Record* (1980–81), pp. A72–79.

18 "Statement on the United Nations," NAC/CONF.3/RES.12, Lusaka, 10 September 1970; UN General Assembly A/RES.2832 (XXVI), 16 December 1971; "A Synthesis of the Arguments Adduced for and against the Proposal for the Establishment of a Zone of Peace in the Indian Ocean," A/AC.187/70, 6 October 1977; "Report of the Ad Hoc Committee on the Indian Ocean," UN General Assembly, *Official Records: Twelfth Special Session*, Supplement no. 5 (A/S-12/5), 1982; OAU Council of Ministers, Resolution CM/Res. 790 (XXXV), February 1981. Tanzania and Zambia have been members of the ad hoc committee since its inception in 1972; Mozambique joined in 1977. All three states plus Botswana participated in the Meeting of the Littoral and Hinterland States of the Indian Ocean held in New York in July 1979.

19 "What We Are, and Are Not Saying," 1 November 1970, *Africa Contemporary Record* (1970–71), p. C27.

20 The latent anti-Americanism in several of the FLS has been revived since Reagan's election to the presidency. In 1981, both Zambia and Mozambique expelled American diplomats following accusations of spying. Botswana is an exception; it is the only FLS to admit U.S. Peace Corps volunteers.

21 Zimbabwe, however, appears to have been the first FLS to raise the zone-of-peace issue in the course of the UN Second Special Session on Disarmament, June–July 1982 (Zimbabwe Government, *Press Statement* 549/82, 21 June 1982). Following Gandhi's visit to Mozambique in August 1982, Machel pressed the case for a zone of peace, notably at the New Delhi Non-Aligned Conference in March 1983.

22 P. W. Botha's Carlton Center address, 22 November 1979, in *Towards a Constellation of States in Southern Africa* (Pretoria: South Africa Information Services, 1980).

23 In warning Zimbabwe that South Africa would "hit back hard," its minister of police stated, "I wish to confirm our standpoint once more, namely, that we are not prepared to cooperate with a country which harbours terrorist forces against the Republic and that we will attack and destroy such bases, as in Maputo, without regard if need be" (*Times* [London], 9 May 1981, p. 6).

24 Among the victims have been: Onkgopotse Tiro in Botswana (1 February 1974), John Dube in Lusaka (12 February 1974), Joe Gqabi in Harare (31 July 1981), and Ruth First in Maputo (17 August 1982). In each case, South Africa hotly denied any responsibility for the killings (*Africa Research Bulletin* [PSC] (1974), pp. 3134–35; ibid. (1981), p. 6133; ibid. (1982), p. 6565). On 14 March 1982, a bomb wrecked the London Office of the ANC (ibid., [1982], pp. 6392–93).

25 See, for example, UN doc. S/10352, 6 October 1971; S/12821 and S/12822,

25 August 1978; *New African* (London), no. 113 (April 1981), p. 53; *Times of Zambia*, 28 April 1982, p. 8; "Zambia: South African Military Attacks," *Focus* (London), no. 40 (May–June 1982), p. 12.

26 *Africa Research Bulletin* (PSC) (1981), pp. 5921–23 and 5956–57; "South Africa's Lebanon," *Foreign Report*, no. 1741 (26 August 1982), pp. 4–6.

27 "Botswana: Military Destabilization Reviewed," *Focus*, no. 41 (July–August 1982), p. 12.

28 *Times*, 26 July 1982, p. 1; 28 August 1982, p. 1, 9; 8 September 1982, p. 5.

29 *Financial Times*, 14 August 1982, p. 2. Earlier large-scale combined operations included the incursions of March 1982 (Operation Super), November 1981 (Operation Daisy), August 1981 (Operation Protea), June 1980 (Operation Smokeshell), and May 1978 (the Kassinga massacre).

30 14 August 1982, p. 29.

31 In August 1982, *Expresso* in Lisbon published "documentary proof" of a South African-backed operation, Kubango, intended to overthrow the Angolan government (*Guardian* [London], 17 August 1982, p. 3). Kaunda alleged initially that the October 1980 coup plot in Zambia involved the South Africans; that charge appears to have been quietly dropped (*Africa Research Bulletin* [PSC] (1981), p. 6088; ibid. (1980), pp. 5834–35). The Zimbabwe government reported in March 1982 that General Peter Walls, the Rhodesian defense chief, had sought South African intervention to frustrate Mugabe's electoral victory in February 1980 but that Pretoria refused the request (*Africa Research Bulletin* [PSC] (1982), pp. 6396, 6427; *Times*, 2 March 1982, p. 6).

32 *Africa Confidential* 23 (4 August 1982), pp. 5–7; Paul Fauvet and Alves Gomes, "The 'Mozambique National Resistance'," supplement to *AIM Information Bulletin* (Maputo), no. 69 (March 1982).

33 Adamson Mushala, along with other Zambian dissidents, was allegedly trained, armed, and financed by South Africa. He conducted a low-level insurgency operation in northwest Zambia from 1976 until his death in November 1982 (UN doc. S/PV. 1944, 27 July 1976, pp. 16, 26–28; *Africa* [London] no. 69 [May 1977], pp. 41–42; *New African*, no. 185 [February 1983], pp. 32–33).

34 The Beira-Feruka oil pipeline (which was shut down shortly after the Unilateral Declaration of Independence [UDI] in 1965) was sabotaged within a month of its reopening in July 1982 (*Times*, 14 August 1982, p. 5). This is less serious than it sounds as eight days' operation a month is adequate to meet Zimbabwe's needs.

35 See n. 22 above.

36 *Financial Times*, 13 April 1982, p. 3.

37 J. G. H. Loubser, *Transport Diplomacy: With Special Reference to Southern Africa* (Sandton: Southern African Editorial Services, 1980). Loubser, general manager of South African Railroads (SAR), defines transport diplomacy as "the art of enabling the transport potential of a country to perform a maximum role in that country's relations with other countries" (p. 5).

38 Zimbabwe House of Assembly, *Parl. Deb.* 3(29), 26 August 1981, cols. 1317–53 and 3(33), 2 September 1981, cols. 1560–84; *Times*, 17 July 1981, p. 4; *Financial Times*, 10 September 1981, p. 5.

39 *Financial Times*, 4 August 1982, p. 4; *Times*, 14 August, 1982, p. 5; *Economist*, 12 June 1982, p. 26.

40 In March 1981, South Africa unilaterally embargoed all oil traffic to Maputo, allegedly in protest against the nonreturn of wagons, but more likely (in the

aftermath of Matola) in retaliation against Mozambique's (verbal) support for international sanctions against South Africa (*Financial Times*, 10 March 1981, p. 4). South Africa has had great difficulty overcoming the reluctance of South African exporters to make full use of the Maputo route (ibid., 30 January 1978, p. 3; 28 February 1979, p. 3).

41 *Financial Times*, 19 March 1982, p. 6; R. C. Riddell, *Zimbabwe's Manufactured Exports and the Ending of the Trade Agreement with South Africa* (Harare: Confederation of Zimbabwe Industries, December 1981). The South African notice of termination of the agreement was Pretoria's third hostile act (along with the recall of its locomotives and the imposition of visa requirements) directed against Zimbabwe during 1981 (*Economist*, 16 January 1982, p. 43).

42 "The Ultimate Bargaining Lever," South African Forum *Position Paper* 4 (Johannesburg: 1981).

43 Shortly after independence, Zimbabwe, like Tanzania and Zambia, closed down the WENELA (Witwatersrand Native Labour Agency) recruiting offices in the country. Pretoria retaliated by deporting thousands of Zimbabweans who were long-term residents of South Africa (*Sunday Mail* [Harare], 18 July 1982, p. 6; *Herald* [Harare], 27 January 1982, p. 1).

44 MNR sabotage of the power line interrupted the supply of electricity to South Africa on four occasions during the first eight months of 1982, causing "brownouts" and power failures in a number of cities. Evidently, Pretoria considers this an acceptable price to pay for the damage MNR is inflicting on Mozambique and Zimbabwe. Maputo imports its electricity from South Africa rather than directly from Cahora Bassa.

45 For alternative schemes for categorizing foreign policy behavior, see James N. Rosenau, *The Study of Political Adaptation: Essays on the Analysis of World Politics* (New York: Nichols, 1981), pp. 58–79; Kenneth W. Grundy, *Confrontation and Accommodation in Southern Africa: The Limits of Independence* (Berkeley: University of California Press, 1973), pp. 293–98.

46 Douglas G. Anglin and Timothy M. Shaw, *Zambia's Foreign Policy: Studies in Diplomacy and Dependence* (Boulder, Colo.: Westview, 1979), p. 173.

47 Mozambique (in 1977) and Angola (in 1976) signed formal military assistance agreements with the Soviet Union; Tanzania turned down a similar offer (*Africa Contemporary Record* (1977–78), pp. B509 and C19–21). Following the Matola raid, two Soviet warships promptly paid well-publicized visits to Maputo and Beira to underscore Soviet military interest (*Times*, 23 February 1981, p. 1).

48 *Financial Times*, 29 April 1982, p. 4; 2 July 1982, p. 4; *Foreign Report*, no. 1741 (26 August 1982), p. 7.

49 *Africa Confidential* 23 (4 August 1982), p. 8.

50 Ibid.; *Africa Research Bulletin* [PSC] (1980), p. 5823; ibid. (1981), p. 5921. Earlier, Mozambique, Tanzania, and Zambia had concluded an agreement on the exchange of security information (ibid. [1976], pp. 3987, 4117). In July 1981, in an attempt to secure Banda's cooperation in the suppression of MNR and other guerrillas, Maputo established diplomatic relations with Malawi (despite its continued diplomatic relations with South Africa).

51 Zimbabwe Government *Press Statement* 197/82 8 March 1982, p. 2. The Zimbabweans have tended to be critical of the energy with which the Mozambicans are prosecuting their counterinsurgency campaign against the MNR—

much as the Rhodesians were contemptuous of the failure of the Portuguese to crush FRELIMO.

52 *Economist*, 16 January 1982, p. 43; *Financial Times*, 11 May 1982, p. 2; *Observer*, 20 December 1981, p. 4.

53 *Financial Times*, 24 September 1981, p. 2.

54 Reginald Herbold Green, "Southern African Development Coordination," *Africa Contemporary Record* (1980–81), pp. A24–34; Richard F. Weisfelder, "The Southern African Development Coordination Conference (SADCC): A New Factor in the Liberation Process," in Thomas M. Callaghy, ed., *South Africa in Southern Africa* (New York: Praeger, forthcoming); Aloysius Kgarebe, ed. *SADCC2—Maputo* (London: SADCC Liaison Committee, 1981); *SADCC Blantyre 1981* (Blantyre: SADCC, 1982).

55 *Sunday Times* (Johannesburg), 9 March 1980, pp. 1, 2; *Herald*, 18 April 1980, p. 7; *Times*, 23 June 1981, p. 7; *Financial Times*, 24 September 1981, p. 2. Following the 1980 elections but before the results were announced, Mugabe met the South Africans secretly in Maputo to assure them that the new Zimbabwean government would not interfere in their domestic affairs. There is some uncertainty whether the South African contact was Foreign Minister Roelof Botha or Army Chief Magnus Malan (*New York Times*, 31 March 1980, p. 12; *Africa Research Bulletin* [PSC] [1982], p. 6427). In May 1980, Mugabe dispatched the former head of the Rhodesian Special Branch to Pretoria to reiterate the assurances.

56 The ANC maintains an unofficial office in Harare. ANC leader Oliver Tambo paid an official visit to Harare in 1982. PAC leaders have also been welcome in Zimbabwe, more so (for historical reasons) than in any other FLS.

57 "The people of South Africa are now ready for a revolutionary change. What might not be ready is the leadership of both liberation movements, who seem to be spending most of their time galloping from one capital to another" (*Herald*, 10 July 1982, p. 6).

58 A Conference of the Progressive Parties of the South West Indian Ocean met in the Seychelles in April 1978 and May 1979. The present ruling parties in Madagascar, Mauritius, and the Seychelles and opposition parties in Réunion and (in 1978) the Comoros attended (*African Contemporary Record* [1978–79], p. B370; ibid. [1979–80], pp. B255, 300).

59 Fifth Summit Conference of East and Central African States, *Manifesto on Southern Africa*, Lusaka, 14–16 April 1969 (*Africa Contemporary Record* [1969–70], pp. C41–45).

Notes to Chapter 15

Reactions to developments in South Africa since 1979 have varied greatly around the world. Among the most perceptive, in my view, are those from France where an awareness of South Africa's extended horizons is displayed. The title of this chapter carries this theme somewhat farther. For a review of French opinion, see *The Constellation of States* (Pretoria: South Africa Foundation, 1980), pp. 66–69.

I should like to thank James D'Amato, Ph.D. candidate in International Studies at the University of South Carolina, for his assistance in the preparation of this study.

1 The contention stems, for the most part, from research done prior to the administration of P. W. Botha. See, for example, Robert S. Jaster, "South Africa's Narrowing Security Options," *Adelphi Papers*, 159 (London: International Institute for Strategic Studies, 1980); J. E. Spence, "South Africa: Reform versus Reaction," *World Today* 37 (December 1981): 461–68; and John Seiler, "A South African Threat to Regional Security?" *Africa Report* 27 (July–August 1982): 64–65. On the "mentality of the *Afrikaner*" an outstanding research effort is Theodor Hanf, Heribert Weiland, and Gerda Vierdag, *South Africa: The Prospects of Peaceful Change* (Bloomington: Indiana University Press, 1981). Also recommended are T. Dunbar Moodie, *The Rise of Afrikanerdom: Power, Apartheid, and the Afrikaner Civil Religion* (Berkeley: University of California Press, 1975), and Heribert Adam and Hermann Giliomee, *Ethnic Power Mobilized: Can South Africa Change?* (New Haven, Conn.: Yale University Press, 1979). For an explicit rejection of the "fortress" concept from the South African Defence Force see, Vice Admiral A. P. Putter, SAN, "South Africa's Maritime Policy," *Contemporary Maritime Strategy*, ed. M. Hough (Pretoria: Institute of Strategic Studies, University of Pretoria, August 1982), pp. 45–46.

2 The premise of South Africa at the center on an east-west axis, rather than on the periphery of a north-south axis, derives from Smuts's extensive investigations into botany and geology. He felt that he had found sufficient evidence for a hypothesis in which "Africa assumes a central position among the continents; it becomes in fact the great 'divide' among the continents of the Southern Hemisphere. It appears as the mother-continent from which South America on the one side and Madagascar, India, Australia and their surrounding areas, on the other, have split off and drifted away." Smuts, of course, appreciated the analogous character of the proposition with its implications for politico-military strategies as well as the comparative study of natural history. A later generation, as we shall see, would pursue this logic with precision. W. K. Hancock, *The Fields of Force, 1919–1950*, vol. 2 of *Smuts* (Cambridge: Cambridge University Press, 1968), pp. 173–75.

3 *Rand Daily Mail* (Johannesburg), 16 August 1979.

4 Jaster, "South Africa's Narrowing Security Options"; and Christopher Coker, "South Africa and the Western Alliance 1949–81: A History of Illusions," *Journal of the Royal United Services Institute for Defense Studies* 127 (June 1982): 34–40.

5 See Hanf, Weiland, and Vierdag, *South Africa*. The seconding of John D. Maree from Barlow Rand to be the chief executive officer of Arms Corporation of South Africa, Ltd. (ARMSCOR), 1979–82, is possibly the most conspicuous example of drawing upon the business sector.

6 For an editorial comment on this see Deon Geldenhuys, *International Affairs Bulletin* 4 (1980): 1–2. Geldenhuys is one of a growing group of academicians with informal ties to the Botha administration. Among them are Michael Hough, director of the Institute of Strategic Studies at the University of Pretoria and one of the principal academic spokesmen of the contemporary school; Lieutenant General H. V. duToit (SADF, ret.) who moved from the Intelligence portfolio on the SADF staff to the National Strategy Chair at Rand Afrikaans University; and University of Witwatersrand faculty members such as Peter Vale, Colin Vale, Dirk Kunert, and Michael Sinclair. Institutionally the Africa

Institute of South Africa under the direction of Erich Leistner is, perhaps, the best established research entity contributing to the "wider Africa" thinking of the current regime.

7 *The 1979 White Paper on Defence and Armaments Supply* (Pretoria: Department of Defence, 1979), pp. 1–3. The succeeding white paper (1982) placed this phenomenon more in the context of the global threat reflecting the growing impetus to align with the United States.

8 Gerard Chaliand has noted that under Malan the army is not only playing a determining role in South African politics but that "this role is innovative because its *vision* springs from a global analysis and not purely local considerations" (emphasis mine) (*La Monde*, November 1979).

9 See Jean Gottman, "Bugeaud, Gallieni, Lyautey: The Development of French Colonial Warfare," in *Makers of Modern Strategy*, ed. Edward Meade Earle (Princeton, N.J.: Princeton University Press, 1971), pp. 234–59. On the French school, see Lyautey, "Du Role Colonial de l'Armee," *Revue des Deux Mondes* 157 (15 February 1900): 308–28. For a nonmilitary perspective on the school's influence, see A. duPlessis, "Diplomacy or Military Force? Theoretical Perspectives of a Southern African Policy Dilemma," *Strategic Review* (February 1982): 2–12.

10 *Rand Daily Mail* (Johannesburg), 6 July 1982.

11 *The Strategic Significance of Tanzania*, Publication no. 4 (Pretoria: ISSUP, 1979), pp. 74 and 79.

12 Ibid., p. 77. See also Sinclair's *The Strategic Significance of the Horn of Africa*, Publication no. 6 (Pretoria: ISSUP, 1980).

13 For two useful if somewhat tendentious studies produced in the mid-1970s, see Guy Arnold and Ruth Weiss, *Strategic Highways of Africa* (New York: St. Martin's, 1977), and Richard Hall and Hugh Peyman, *The Great Uhuru Railway* (London: Gollancz, 1977).

14 Since the February 1979 Transportation Agreement between South Africa and Mozambique nearly one-fifth of South Africa's total trade passes though Maputo. This is a major factor in SAR&H's construction of the largest railmarshaling yard in the southern hemisphere at Benoni in the Transvaal (*South African Digest* [Pretoria: Department of Foreign Affairs and Information, 2 July 1982], p. 9). Regarding Cabora-Basa see Hanf, Weiland, and Vierdag, *South Africa*, p. 72; Theodore Malan, "Mozambique and Zambia's Economic Relations with South Africa," *Strategic Review* (January 1981), pp. 2–13; and Keith Middlemas, "Independent Mozambique and its Regional Policy," in John Seiler, ed., *Southern Africa Since the Portuguese Coup* (Boulder, Colo.: Westview, 1980), pp. 213–34.

15 See the interview with Sophie Lannes excerpted from *L'Express* (Paris) in *World Press Review* (July 1982), pp. 32–34.

16 Ibid.

17 *South African Digest* (9 October 1981), Special Supplement. Compare with his *Address to Members and Guests of the Swiss–South African Association in Zurich* (7 March 1979), press section: RSA Embassy, Berne. See also *South African Yearbook of International Law* 5 (1979): 210. Again, it is instructive to point to a paper by Michael Hough, "The Strategic Importance of South and Southern Africa: The Pretoria View," Publication no. 9 (Pretoria: ISSUP, 1981). This paper, presented a few months prior to the foreign minister's par-

liamentary address, continued to reflect some of the Zurich speech but clearly anticipated the broader horizons offered later in the year.

18 *South African Digest* (9 October 1981).

19 Ibid.

20 *ISSUP Bulletin* (November 1981), p. 3; see also *ISSUP Bulletin* (March 1982).

21 Arthur P. Whitaker, "America in the Western Hemisphere," *Orbis* 20 (Spring 1976): 20, as quoted by Edmund Gaspar, *United States–Latin America: A Special Relationship?* (Washington, D.C.: American Enterprise Institute, 1978). Gaspar, however, suggests that a new "mature partnership" is possible between the United States and Latin America, one that will involve a stronger security system (pp. 89–90).

22 LTG Wallace Nutting (commander in chief, U.S. Southern Command), Testimony before U.S. Senate, Committee on Foreign Relations, 3 August 1982; also see *Cuban Armed Forces and the Soviet Military Presence* (Washington, D.C.: U.S. Department of State, August 1982).

23 Edward Kannyo, "South America/Africa: The Latin Balancing Act," *Africa Report* 27 (July–August 1982): 52–59.

24 Pretoria has added Chile to the list because of the latter's "easy access" to the Atlantic. Following General Malan's visit to Santiago in 1981 his former deputy, Lieutenant General Jack Dutton, was established as the rsa's first resident ambassador.

25 *Aviation Week and Space Technology* 117 (26 July 1982): 106.

26 For 1981 data see *Sunday Business Times* (Johannesburg), 9 May 1982; also Desmond Colborne, "South Africa and East Asia," *South Africa International* 12 (July 1981): 261–81.

37 Prime Minister Botha has taken a step that may well improve South African–Australian relations. He has dispatched Denis Worral, highly effective "anglo" voice for the Nationalist party (MP for the Gardens–Cape Town and with a Ph.D. in political science from Cornell), to Canberra as ambassador.

28 See Deon Fourie, "South Africa: The Evolving Experience," in *Defense Policy Formulation, Toward Comparative Analysis*, ed. James Roherty (Durham: Carolina Academic Press, 1980), pp. 98–99.

29 For a typical view of the Soviet role in Africa from the contemporary school, see Dirk Kunert, " 'Windows of Perils': Africa, The World and the 1980s," *South Africa International* 11 (July 1980): 1–20; also Kunert, *Wars of National Liberation, The Superpowers and the Afro-Asian Indian Ocean* (Johannesburg: South African Institute of International Affairs, 1977).

30 See Helena P. Page, "Long Range Forecasting in the Pentagon," *The World Today* 38 (July–August 1982), pp. 274–81. Page outlines a model that American strategic planners increasingly credit ("World D"), one in which traditional alliances are declining, new focuses of power are emerging, and the United States is searching for new allies. This is the thesis that underlies my own work with emerging "defense communities" among a range of middle powers of concern to the U.S. See my *Defense Policy Formation*, chap. 1. On the developing Indian Ocean security regime, see Robert G. Wirsing and James M. Roherty, "The United States and Pakistan," *International Affairs* 58 (Fall 1982).

31 This is succinctly formulated in B. Mitchell Simpson III, ed., *The Develop-*

ment of Naval Thought: Essays by Herbert Rosinski (Newport: Naval War College Press, 1977), pp. 130–39.

32 There is an extensive literature but, for a competent assessment by a naval professional, see Rear Admiral Robert J. Hanks, U.S.N. (ret.), *The Cape Route: Imperiled Western Lifeline* (Washington, D.C.: 1981); also Richard E. Bissell, "How Strategic is South Africa?" in *South Africa into the 1980s*, ed. R. E. Bissell and C. A. Crocker (Boulder, Colo.: Westview, 1980), pp. 209–32.

33 Hanson W. Baldwin, *Strategy for Tomorow* (New York: Harper and Row, 1970), p. 231.

34 Philip Darby, *British Defense Policy East of Suez* (London: Oxford University Press, 1973).

35 See United States Naval Institute, *Proceedings* 105 (August 1979) for various pieces on the Indian Ocean, and Joel Larus, "Diego Garcia: Political Clouds Over a Vital U.S. Base," *Strategic Review* 10 (Winter 1982): 44–55.

36 See Glen St. J. Barclay, "In Defense of South Africa: A Western Dilemma and its Resolution," *Strategic Review* (June 1982): 20; also Barclay's statement in *Pacific Defense Reporter* (July 1982), p. 4. For other perspectives on strategic collaboration, see Edward Heath, Speech to the SAIIA International Outlook Conference, Johannesburg, 31 August 1981; and Peregrine Worsthorne, *Sunday Telegraph* (London), 6 September 1981. In the scholarly community the discussion ranges from the contention that the end of apartheid is "in sight," that historic change has already occurred (Colin Legum, "The End of Apartheid," *Washington Quarterly* [Winter 1982]: 169–82), to the view that the "colonial struggle" in South Africa must be understood as "unique" and admitting only of a "unique" resolution (William Gutteridge, "South Africa: Strategy for Survival?" *Conflict Studies* 131 [June 1981]: 1–32).

37 For what can only be regarded as an "official" statement on this matter, see Putter, "South Africa's Maritime Policy." An anonymous SAN official may have been wondering whether the effort to dramatize the changed situation was working: "We find it difficult to understand why Western nations ignore the importance of the Cape Sea route and make no provisions to protect that shipping choke point" (*Aviation Week*, 21 June 1982, p. 44). As early as May 1974 the then chief of SAN, Rear Admiral Hugo Bierman, visited the United States to discuss the implications of the imminent break with the RN. His visit produced a reaction similar to that of the visit of the SADF Intelligence chief, Lieutenant General P. van der Westhuizen, in 1981.

38 See David M. North's series on "Aerospace in South Africa," *Aviation Week*, 7 June 1982, 21 June 1982, and 19 July 1982.

39 Prepositioning of material configured to unit size. This is already in effect in Europe, the Pacific, and Indian Ocean sites.

40 NOSIS has two components: the Sonar Surveillance System (SOSUS) and the Signals Intercept System (Bullseye Network). Data are fed to the Naval Ocean Surveillance Information Center (NOSIC) at Suitland, Maryland, an element of the Directorate of Naval Intelligence (DNI) from five correlation centers around the world. There is, however, no correlation center in the southern hemisphere. NOSIS is tied to the National Security Agency (NSA) through the Naval (Communications) Security Group component and to the Worldwide Military Command and Control System (WWMCCS) through the Defense Satellite Communication System of the Defense Communications Agency (DCA). This elaborate network does not have facilities between Ascension Island and Diego

Garcia. For an Australian debate on this issue see Desmond Ball, "The US Naval Ocean Surveillance Information System (NOSIS)—Australia's Role," *Pacific Defense Reporter* (June 1982), pp. 40–49, and in the August 1982 number a response by Harry Gelber (pp. 2–4). The SAN Operations Command Center is colocated at Silvermine (with the Joint Air-Maritime Surveillance Center) with "satellites" at Durban and Walvis Bay.

41 An obvious replacement is the Lockheed P-3C (Orion) now being equipped with the McDonnell-Douglas Harpoon air-to-surface missile. Presumably, it could operate from Walvis Bay (the "bare base" at Rooikop) to Durban. This aircraft has been made available to maritime allies such as Japan and Australia through the Defense Security Assistance Program (DSAP).

42 The obvious model in this instance is the DSAP sale to Australia of Perry-class FFG frigates.

43 Any upgrade of the SADF tactical fighter force would, perhaps, be the most sensitive item. The suggestion of a long-range bomber is hardly plausible (Barclay, "In Defense of South Africa," p. 19). Again, the sale to Australia (and most recently, Spain) of the McDonnell-Douglas F/A 18 (Hornet) provides a model.

44 Arms Corporation of South Africa. ARMSCOR work in recent years on propellants, explosives, and electro-optics (among other things) is of considerable interest to the United States.

Notes to Chapter 16

1 Madagascar, Mauritius, the Seychelles, the Comoros, Réunion, and the British Indian Ocean Territory (most significantly Diego Garcia) are included.

2 Philip M. Allen, "New Round for the Western Islands," in *The Indian Ocean: Its Political, Economic, and Military Importance,* ed. Alvin J. Cottrell and R. M. Burrell (New York: Praeger, 1972), p. 309.

3 *New York Times,* 13 December 1981.

4 *Baltimore Sun,* 11 June 1982.

5 This and other issues relating to Diego Garcia are fully analyzed in Joel Larus's chapter in this volume.

6 *Washington Post,* 26 March 1981.

7 *New York Times,* 20 June 1982.

8 *Rand Daily Mail* (Johannesburg), 9 July 1982.

9 In relation to Mozambique's view of the zone of peace, see "Indian Ocean as a Zone of Peace; India–Mozambique Concern Over Worsening Situation," *Indian and Foreign Review* 19 (15–30 April 1982): 4–5.

10 *Foreign Broadcast Information Service,* Daily Report, Middle East and Africa 14 (14 July 1982): R.2.

11 Cited in *Brief Report,* no. 35 (Johannesburg: SAIIA, December 1981).

12 See Peter Vale, "South Africa's Regional Foreign Policy: A Search for the Status Quo Ante," *New Zealand International Review* 7 (September–October 1982): 18.

13 See Deon Geldenhuys, "Recrossing the Matola Threshold: The Terrorist Factor in South Africa's Regional Relations," *South Africa International* 13 (January 1983): 152–71.

14 *Star* (Johannesburg), 21 December 1981.

15 *Rand Daily Mail* (Johannesburg), 21 December 1981.

16 *Foreign Broadcast Information Service,* Daily Report, Middle East and Africa 5 (3 December 1981): U.3–U.4.

Notes to Chapter 17

1   For an understanding of the larger dimensions of the zone-of-peace proposal, see George W. Shepherd, "Developing Collective Self-Reliance in the Zone of Peace," *IDSA Journal* 15 (New Delhi) (July–September 1982): 19–33.

2   For a systematic rendering of the Israeli–South African military connection—which could not, in Indian assessments, be beyond the knowledge of Western governments—see James Adams, *The Unnatural Alliance* (London: Quartet, 1984), and "Joint N-blasts by S. Africa and Israel," *Times of India*, 10 July 1983, p. 1, quoting the American journal *Defence Electronics* (*sic*) to the effect that the two states had jointly conducted two nuclear tests overground "on trajectory parameters. The launch site was identified as being in Zululand."

3   See the *SIPRI Yearbook 1984* (Stockholm: Stockholm International Peace Research Institute, 1984). South Asia's defense expenditures on a regional comparison basis are the lowest in the world.

4   At the commencement of China's border invasion of Vietnam in 1979 Premier Deng Xiao-Ping stated that a "lesson" was being administered to Vietnam similar to the one administered to India in 1962. Recently, the Chinese again carried out a short military incursion and bombardment of Vietnam's frontier areas, presumably as a second "lesson" to that country.

5   The two groups of Indian-owned offshore territories consist of some thousand islands, most of them uninhabited. They extend in two different directions and are separated by long distances from each other and the Indian mainland. For an assessment of the Falklands War and its implications from an Indian viewpoint, see H.M.L. Beri, "The Falklands Crisis," *IDSA Journal* 14 (New Delhi) (April–June 1982): 539–80.

6.   See, in this respect, Onkar Marwah, "Superpower Rivalry in the Indian Ocean: Indian Perspectives," in *Navies and Arms Control*, ed. George H. Quester (New York: Praeger, 1980), pp. 169–80.

7   For a detailed discussion of American policy, see Bowman and Lefebvre in this volume. As regards American plans involving Pakistan and India, see Lawrence Lifschultz, "Ring around the Gulf," *Far Eastern Economic Review* (11 December 1981), pp. 17–18; and Special Correspondent, "Zia's New Role in the Gulf," *Middle East* (April 1983), pp. 33–34.

8   References are made to the following: H. J. Mackinder, "The Geographical Pivot of History," *Geographical Journal* 23 (1904): 421–37; N. J. Spykman, *America's Strategy in World Politics* (New York: Harcourt Brace, 1942); and Admiral T. Mahan, *The Influence of Sea Power upon History* (Boston: Little Brown, 1919). See also N. B. K. Reddy, "The Emerging Geopolitical Patterns of the Indian Ocean Region," in *The Indian Ocean Region*, ed. Alex Kerr (Boulder, Colo.: Westview, 1981).

9   For a succinct presentation of Indian views concerning the new problems developing for the littoral states of South and Southwest Asia in the context of the second cold war, see K. Subrahmanyam, "Present and Likely Developments in South and Southwest Asia," *Strategic Analysis* 7 (New Delhi) (November 1983): 589–608.

10   Current reports speak of 250,000 American troops being designated for RDF duty. However, there are indications that the eventual numbers might involve some 450,000 U.S. troops for the IOR.

11   Indian strategists are strongly convinced that, in due course, plans will unfold

for the creation of such a landward naval/military base under joint American-Pakistani auspices at Gwadar on the Makran coast of Pakistan's Baluchistan province. The Pakistanis are already developing this small fishing port into a large naval installation, although they deny that it is for the Americans.

12 For a summary of Pakistan's internal politics and problems of governance over the past three decades, see Samuel Baid, "Pakistan: Crisis Is Inherent," *IDSA Journal* 15 (New Delhi) (July–September 1982): 85–135. Also see Robert Wirsing's chapter in this book.

13 See the papers and discussions relating to the First International Conference on the Strategy for Peace and Security in South Asia, held in Islamabad, 28–30 November 1982. See also Bhabani Sen Gupta, "Scrambled Strategic View," *India Today* (15 November 1982), pp. 68–69.

14 Pakistan has military liaison-and-training missions in twenty-two (mostly Islamic) states of the Persian Gulf, Middle East, and North Africa. It is known that, since 1981, approximately thirty thousand Pakistani troops have performed garrison duty in Saudi Arabia in lieu of an undisclosed sum of money. The sorts of problems that such a foreign praetorian guard can create may be gauged from John Eastman, "Saudi Clash with Hired Troops," *Sunday Times* (London), 4 December 1983, p. 14.

15 It is known that the Soviets have sought facilities for their fishing fleets—and perhaps for other types of naval vessels—in the Seychelles, Mauritius, the Malagasy Republic (Diego Suarez), and the Maldives (Gan Island). See "For Rent: Furnished Air Base on a Quiet, Lush Maldive Island," *New York Times*, 24 December 1977, p. 2.

16 By the yardsticks demanded of the Karmal regime in Afghanistan, the Pakistani leadership itself does not qualify to be in power.

17 Indian strategic analysts now believe that the Afghans are being used in cynical fashion by both the superpowers to their own separate and conflicting purposes. While the Soviet objective of imposing a communist regime on the Afghans seems obvious, the question is why, if the Afghan resistance is really to be supported by the United States, more lethal weapons have not been funneled to the Mujahideen. For example, the American Redeye portable and hand-held anti-air missiles could destroy the lumbering but lethal Hind helicopter gunships used by the Soviets in Afghanistan.

18 From interviews with senior Indian policy makers.

19 Prior to the Soviet entry into Afghanistan, the U.S. had little interest in supplying any weapons to Pakistan. After the Soviets moved into Afghanistan, the weapons systems were ostensibly supplied to deter the Soviets from threatening Pakistan. However, these weapons (and aircraft) appear too few in numbers to trouble the Russians. Indian analysts assume, therefore, that the United States was not worried about a Soviet threat to Pakistan but supplied the weapons in return for as-yet-undisclosed Pakistani quid pro quos, e.g., the provision of secret bases for the RDF in the future.

20 See "Site-Seeking," *Far Eastern Economic Review* (17 November 1983), p. 15.

21 One of the seminal naval threats in this respect from an Indian viewpoint was the sending of U.S. Task Force Seventy-four into the Bay of Bengal during the 1971 Indo-Pakistani war. See James M. McConnell and Anne M. Kelly, "Superpower Naval Diplomacy: Lessons of the Indo-Pakistani Crisis, 1971," *Survival* 15 (November–December 1973): 289–95.

22 It seems that important sections of Pakistan's political-bureaucratic establish-

ment are now advising such a course to their military leaders. See the series of articles alluding to the issues involved by Sajjad Hyder in the *Muslim* (Islamabad), 3, 5, and 7 November 1983. Hyder is a former ambassador from Pakistan to the Soviet Union.

23 See P. K. S. Namboodiri, "India and the Security of Indian Ocean Islands," *Strategic Analysis* 6 (New Delhi) (September 1982): 381–85.

24 The Indian merchant fleet consists of about four hundred ships with a deadweight tonnage of 10 million tons. It is the second largest in Asia after Japanese mercantile registries and is slated to double in size and tonnage by the end of the decade.

25 "Plans to Enhance Strike Power of Navy," *Times of India*, 19 March 1984, p. 7.

26 "India to Buy More Subs from W. Germany," *Times of India*, 15 February 1984, p. 9.

27 William L. Dowdy III, "Middle Eastern, North African, and South Asian Navies," *U.S. Naval Institute Proceedings* (March 1983), p. 52.

28 Anthony Mascarenhas, "Russian Nuclear Sub for India," *Sunday Times* (London), 22 April 1984, p. 21; and "India Has Open Option on N-subs," *Times of India*, 6 April 1983, p. 1.

29 "Laser-guided Missiles Being Developed," *Times of India*, 28 March 1983, p. 1. Indian naval defense research teams are also working on bringing the production of sea-skimmer missiles to local factories.

30 "India Looks for Early Warning Plane," *Times of India*, 20 April 1983, p. 1.

31 "Navy to Start Major Project in Tamil Nadu," *Times of India*, 5 February 1984, p. 13.

32 "India: All-purpose Spies in the Sky," *Economist* (London), 14 April 1984, pp. 54–55.

33 "Coast Guard Completes 7 Years Today," *Times of India*, 31 January 1984. p. 7.

34 "Long-term Plans to Strengthen Navy," *Hindustan Times*, 19 March 1984, p. 7.

35 See K. C. Khanna, "Indian Navy in Rough Seas," *Times of India*, 8 November 1983, p. 8.

36 G. V. Joshi, "Diving for Treasure: India Shapes Up to Capture Exclusive Seabed Mining Rights with Its First Deep Sea Company," *South* (London) (September 1983), p. 59. For an idea of India's unfolding plans and long-term economic interest in the oceans, see B. Ramachandra Rao, "Man and the Ocean: Resources and Development," presidential address at the Seventieth Session of the Indian Science Congress held at Tirupathi, January 1983, *Strategic Digest* (New Delhi) (September 1983), pp. 587–624.

37 See Joel Larus, "India Claims A Role in Antarctica," *Round Table* (London), no. 289, pp. 45–56; and "Indian Eyes Set on Antarctica," *Pakistan and Gulf Economist* (24–30 December 1983), pp. 13–14. India's permanent base in Antarctica has been named *Dakshin Gangotri*, that is, "southern (source of the) Ganges."

38 For a summary of the complex hotbed of political, economic, and security concerns emerging for the international regime in Antarctica, see Deborah Shapely, "Antarctica: Up For Grabs," *Science* 82 (November 1982): 75–78.

Notes to Chapter 18

1   K. Subrahmanyam, *Indian Security Perspectives* (New Delhi: ABC Publishing House, 1982), p. 178.

2   Onkar Marwah, "India and Pakistan: Nuclear Rivals in South Asia," *International Organization* 35 (Winter 1981): 179.

3   Ibid., pp. 176–77, 179.

4   Selig S. Harrison, "Fanning Flames in South Asia," *Foreign Policy* 45 (Winter 1981–82): 89–90.

5   W. Scott Thompson, "The Persian Gulf and the Correlation of Forces," *International Security* 7, no. 1 (Summer 1982): 159.

6   Ibid., p. 176. For alternative views on the Soviet military threat in Southwest Asia, see Keith A. Dunn, "Constraints on the USSR in Southwest Asia: A Military Analysis," *Orbis* 25, no. 3 (Fall 1981): 607–629; and Thomas L. McNaugher, "The Soviet Military Threat to the Gulf: The Operational Dimension," paper prepared for the Biennial Conference of the Section on Military Studies, International Studies Association, held at the University of New Hampshire, 5–7 November 1981, esp. pp. 12–13 and 29.

7   Lawrence Ziring, 'Soviet Policy on the Rim of Asia: Scenarios and Projections," *Asian Affairs* 9, no. 3 (January–February 1982): 141.

8   For an argument that it is deeply ingrained, indeed, see Rebecca V. Strode and Colin S. Gray, "The Imperial Dimension of Soviet Military Power," *Problems of Communism* 30 (November–December 1981): 1–15.

9   For additional discussion of the Baluch situation, see Selig S. Harrison, *In Afghanistan's Shadow: Baluch Nationalism and Soviet Temptations* (New York: Carnegie Endowment for International Peace, 1981); Robert G. Wirsing and James M. Roherty, "The United States and Pakistan," *International Affairs* 58 (London) (Autumn 1982): 588–609; Wirsing, *The Baluchis and Pathans*, Report no. 48 (London: Minority Rights Group, March 1981); and Wirsing, "South Asia: The Baluch Frontier Tribes of Pakistan," in *Protection of Ethnic Minorities: Comparative Perspectives*, ed. Wirsing (New York: Pergamon, 1981), pp. 277–312.

10 According to one estimate, in addition to noncombatants, at least thirty-three hundred Pakistani troops and fifty-three hundred Baluch guerrillas were killed in the four-year conflict (Selig S. Harrison, "Nightmare in Baluchistan," *Foreign Policy* 32 [Fall 1978]: 137).

11 The Karachi daily *Dawn* reported (19 September 1982) that one of the longest running and bloodiest feuds—between the large Marri and Bugti tribes—had formally been brought to an end. If true, it would represent a major development in the history of the Baluch nationalist movement (*Foreign Broadcast Information Service*, South Asia Series, no. 184 (1982), p. F4 (hereinafter referred to as *FBIS-SAS-82*).

12 See Anthony Mascarenhas's interview in London of Sardar Ataullah Menghal in *Times of India* (Bombay), 29 August 1982, in *FBIS-SAS-82*, no. 176, pp. F2–4.

13 See Shirin Tahir-Kheli, "Iran and Pakistan: Cooperation in an Area of Conflict," *Asian Survey* 17, no. 5 (May 1977): 474–90.

14 From Islamabad's standpoint, another and perhaps equally important consequence of the shah's collapse was to raise the possibility that Pakistan, in spite

of its professed nonalignment, might substitute for Iran as the West's principal military ally in the Persian Gulf region.

15 Islamabad has reported over four hundred violations of its airspace since April 1978.

16 These appear to include the MIG-27 long-range fighter-bomber, the advanced SAM-8 missile, and the SU-25, the Soviet reply to the American A-10 close support plane. See *New York Times*, 26 September 1982, p. 13Y, for a report on the SU-25. On other weapons developments, see Gordon Brook-Shepherd's comments in *Sunday Telegraph* (London), 8 August 1982, in *FBIS-SAS-82*, no. 154, p. C1.

17 For one discussion, see the article by M. V. Pradhan, "Indian Ocean and the Superpowers," *Indian Express* (New Delhi), 15–17 September 1982, in *FBIS-SAS-82*, no. 185, pp. E1-4.

18 For background on the Indian naval buildup, see Raju G. C. Thomas, "The Politics of Indian Naval Re-Armament, 1962–1974," *Pacific Community* (April 1975): 452–74.

19 Mohammed Ayoob, "India, Pakistan and Super-Power Rivalry," *World Today* 38 (May 1982): 196.

20 Leo E. Rose, "Pakistan's Role and Interests in South and Southwest Asia," *Asian Affairs* 9 (September–October 1981): 64.

21 Shirin Tahir-Kheli, *The United States and Pakistan: The Evolution of an Influence Relationship* (New York: Praeger, 1982), p. 137.

22 For a more extensive discussion of the India-Pakistan arms balance, see Robert G. Wirsing and Wilbur R. Snyder, "The Military Balance in South Asia," forthcoming.

23 See, for example, *The Military Balance, 1981–1982* (London: International Institute for Strategic Studies, 1981).

24 It has apparently not been finally decided, but the Mirage 2000 agreement with the French in late 1982 (for 40 aircraft) may be expanded to include assembly under license of an additional 120 aircraft (New Delhi, 18 October 1982, in *FBIS-SAS-82*, no. 201, p. E1.)

25 New Delhi, 2 October 1982, in *FBIS-SAS-82*, no. 192, p. E3.

26 *New York Times*, 30 November 1982, p. 1Y. See also *Far Eastern Economic Review*, 3 February 1983, p. 30 (hereinafter referred to as *FEER*).

27 India's space program, which has important military implications, has already accomplished indigenous launchings of space satellites and is, without question, the most advanced in the Third World. *Aviation Week and Space Technology* (29 June 1981) pp. 18–19. For background, see Onkar Marwah, "India's Nuclear and Space Programs: Intent and Policy," *International Security* 2 (Fall 1977): 96–121.

28 See David K. Willis, "On the Trail of the A-Bomb Makers," *Christian Science Monitor*, 30 November–4 December 1981. See also *FEER*, 4 December 1981, pp. 21–22.

29 See Onkar Marwah, "India and Pakistan," pp. 165–79.

30 Richard P. Cronin and Douglas D. Mitchell, *Issues Concerning Pakistan's Possible Acquisition of the F-16 Fighter Bomber Aircraft*, Report no. 81-225F (Washington, D.C.: Congressional Research Service, Library of Congress, 5 October 1981), p. 5.

31 Subrahmanyam, *Indian Security Perspectives*, p. 213.

32 Zubeida Mustafa, "Pakistan and the Middle East," *Pacific Community* (July 1976): 608.
33 Ayoob, "India, Pakistan and Super-Power Rivalry," p. 199.
34 Harrison, "Fanning Flames in South Asia," pp. 98–99.
35 Mustafa, "Pakistan and the Middle East," p. 619.
36 M. G. Weinbaum and Gautum Sen, "Pakistan Enters the Middle East," *Orbis* 22 (Fall 1978): 595–96.
37 G. S. Bhargava, *South Asian Security after Afghanistan* (Lexington, Mass.: Lexington Books, 1983), p. 123.
38 Harrison, "Fanning Flames in South Asia," p. 95.
39 Ayoob, "India, Pakistan and Super-Power Rivalry," p. 201.
40 Bhargava, *South Asian Security*, pp. 149–68.
41 Ibid., p. 165.
42 Ibid., p. 161.
43 Ibid., p. 164.
44 Ibid., p. 166.
45 B. Vivekanandan, "The Indian Ocean as a Zone of Peace: Problems and Prospects," *Asian Survey* 21 (December 1981): 1248.
46 Ibid., p. 1244.
47 Ibid., p. 1243.
48 Andrew J. Pierre, "Arms Sales: The New Diplomacy," *Foreign Affairs* 60 (Winter 1981–82): 279.
49 See, for example, Selig S. Harrison, "Dateline Afghanistan: Exit Through Finland?" *Foreign Policy*, no. 41 (Winter 1980–81): 163–87; Jagat S. Mehta, "A Neutral Solution," *Foreign Policy*, no. 47 (Summer 1982): 139–53; and Bhargava, *South Asian Security*, pp. 169–85.
50 Mehta, "A Neutral Solution," pp. 148–49.
51 Bhargava, *South Asian Security*, p. 183.
52 Rose, "Pakistan's Role and Interests," pp. 60–61.
53 Francis Fukuyama, *The Future of the Soviet Role in Afghanistan: A Trip Report*, RAND/N-1579-RC (Santa Monica: Rand Corporation, September 1980), p. 25.
54 Shirin Tahir-Kheli, "The Soviet Union in Afghanistan: Benefits and Costs," in *The Soviet Union in the Third World: Successes and Failures*, ed. Robert H. Donaldson (Boulder, Colo.: Westview, 1981), p. 229. Tahir-Kheli writes, "Soviet objectives—to keep Afghanistan out of the Western orbit, to use the country to legitimize Soviet concern with Asia, to demonstrate to Pakistan the need for Soviet friendship—have now largely been realized."
55 Nearby Observer (pseud.), "The Afghan-Soviet War: Stalemate or Evolution?" *Middle East Journal* 36, no. 2 (Spring 1982): 160–61, 163.
56 For the text of the agreement, see *FBIS-SAS-83*, no. 049, pp. E1-2, New Delhi, 11 March 1983.
57 Karachi/New Delhi, 5–8 August 1982, in *FBIS-SAS-82*, no. 153, pp. A1-3. See also the illuminating interview with President Zia ul-Haq in the *Bangkok Post*, 26 September 1982, in *FBIS-SAS-82*, no. 188, pp. F1-7, 28 September 1982.
58 *New York Times*, 24 December 1982, p. 3Y. In an interview with the London *Financial Times*, Gandhi dismissed the meeting as "a drawing room chat" (London, 25 February 1983, in *FBIS-SAS-83*, no. 041, Annex 2–3).
59 Government of Pakistan, Finance Division, *Pakistan Economic Survey 1981–82* (Islamabad: Printing Corporation of Pakistan Press, 1982), p. 121.

60 But the report that Saudi Arabia had alone contributed a total of U.S. $7.5 billion to Pakistan by fall 1980 and was committed for some $5 billion more is almost certainly exaggerated (*Economist*, 13 September 1980, p. 40).

61 *Pakistan Economic Survey 1981–82*, p. 116.

62 *New York Times*, 6 February 1981, p. 4Y.

63 Karachi, 31 August 1982, in *FBIS-SAS-82*, no. 169, p. F1.

64 Shirin Tahir-Kheli and William O. Staudenmaier, "The Saudi-Pakistani Military Relationship: Implications for U.S. Policy," *Orbis* 26 (Spring 1982): 155–71.

65 Weinbaum and Sen, "Pakistan Enters the Middle East," p. 612.

66 Tahir-Kheli, "Iran and Pakistan," p. 490.

67 *New York Times*, 1 November 1982, p. 11Y.

68 The suspect nature of U.S. intentions in the region is a common media topic in Pakistan. For example, see the editorial comments in the *Muslim*, published in Islamabad, on establishment of the new U.S. Central Command, 4 January 1983, in *FBIS-SAS-83*, no. 009, pp. F1-2.

69 For an illuminating discussion of the issues between the two countries, see Thomas P. Thornton, "Between the Stools?: U.S. Policy Towards Pakistan During the Carter Administration," *Asian Survey* 22 (October 1982): 959–77. On the significance of the emergent security regime, see Wirsing and Roherty, "The United States and Pakistan."

70 Zalmay Khalilzad, statement to the Subcommittees on International Security and Scientific Affairs, on International Economic Policy and Trade, and on Asian and Pacific Affairs, Committee on Foreign Affairs, U.S. House of Representatives, *Security and Economic Assistance to Pakistan*, 23 September 1981, p. 268.

71 Ibid., p. 233. See also Khalilzad's comments in a letter to *New York Times*, 16 December 1982, p. 28Y.

72 Bhabani Sen Gupta reports the judgment of a Pakistani strategic expert who mused that " 'it is absolutely necessary for Pakistan to find working relationships with its neighbours, who, acting in collusion, can once again dismember Pakistan. . . . Like it or not, the Soviet Union is a next door neighbour, after what has happened to Afghanistan. This is the supreme reality that Pakistan's external and even internal policies must reckon, and I cannot say that this has happened yet' " (*The Afghan Syndrome: How to Live With Soviet Power* [New Delhi: Vikas, 1982], p. 159).

73 In a rather candid interview that appeared in the *Guardian* (London) on 22 October 1982, President Zia ul-Haq is reported to have said that the Soviets had invited Pakistan to join them in a security pact, to which he says he replied "nothing doing, not so long as I am living, over my dead body" (Islamabad, 26 October 1982, in *FBIS-SAS-82*, no. 207, Annex 2–3). For a suggestion that a Soviet-Pakistani alliance is not so farfetched, see Stephen P. Cohen and Richard L. Park, *India: Emergent Power?* (New York: Crane, Russak, for the National Strategy Information Center, 1978), pp. 68–70.

74 Amaury de Riencourt, "India and Pakistan in the Shadow of Afghanistan," *Foreign Affairs* 61 (Winter 1982–83): 437.

75 Ibid., p. 433.

Notes to Chapter 19

1   *Time*, 22 November 1982, pp. 33–34.
2   Amin's speech on the sixty-first anniversary of the Soviet Revolution, distributed by the Afghan embassy in Washington.
3   *Communist Aid Activities in Non-Communist Less Developed Countries* (Washington, D.C.: Director for Public Affairs, CIA, 1978).
4   *New York Times*, 28 April 1978.
5   *Foreign Broadcast Information Service*, MENA, no. 161, 17 August 1979, p. S-3 (hereinafter referred to as *FBIS*).
6   Ibid.
7   *FBIS*, MENA, no. 78, 12 September 1977, p. S-1.
8   *Christian Science Monitor*, 30 November 1979, and *New York Times*, 16 June 1978.
9   The text of the treaty as released by the Soviet mission to the United Nations, December 1978.
10   Ibid.
11   See n. 2 of this chapter.
12   *Pravda*, 10 April 1979, and the *Kabul Times*, 12 June 1979.
13   For a sympathetic description of the Khalqi program, see Beverly Male, *Revolutionary Afghanistan* (London: Croom Helm, 1982).
14   For a description of the Khalqi policies and the opposition to them, see Zalmay Khalilzad, "The Struggle for Afghanistan," *Survey* 26 (Spring 1981).
15   *Anis*, 28 February 1980, and *Kabul New Times*, 28 February 1980.
16   Jiri Valenta, "The Soviet Invasion of Afghanistan: The Difficulty of Knowing Where to Stop," *Orbis* (Summer 1980): 201–18. Also see Valenta, "From Prague to Kabul: The Mode of Soviet Invasions," *International Security* (Fall 1980): 114–41.
17   According to a postinvasion Afghan government account, Taraki was killed on 8 October 1979 after he had been placed under arrest on 14 September (*The Truth About Afghanistan* [Moscow: Novesti Press Agency Publishing House, 1980], pp. 85–88).
18   The new ambassador is Fikryat A. Tabeyev.
19   There have been reports that Moscow arranged a meeting between Taraki and Karmal during the former's visit to Moscow in September 1979. Karmal, however, has denied this.
20   Interview with U.S. government officials.
21   *Time*, 22 November 1982, pp. 33–34.
22   For a detailed discussion of this problem, see Albert Wohlstetter, "Meeting the Threat in the Gulf," *Survey* 25 (Spring 1980).
23   William E. Griffith, "The Superpower Relations After Afghanistan," *Survival* (July–August 1980), pp. 146–51. In the case of Czechoslovakia, according to President Johnson, the only course open to the U.S. had been to "watch and worry" (Lyndon Johnson, *The Vantage Point* [New York: Holt, Rinehart and Winston, 1971], p. 486). In fact, there are even indications that NATO took measures to reassure Moscow that it would not exploit Soviet difficulties there. Washington did not want to interfere in the Soviet sphere of influence. According to Philip Windsor, "At no time was any form of sanction discussed among Western leaders" (Philip Windsor, "Yugoslavia, 1951, and Czechoslovakia,

1968," in *Force Without War*, ed. Barry M. Blechman and Stephen S. Kaplan [Washington, D.C.: Brookings Institution, 1978], p. 411).

24 Gary Sick, "The Evolving U.S. Strategy toward the Indian Ocean and the Persian Gulf," unpublished manuscript, p. 31.

25 Based on interviews with many Carter administration officials including Zbigniew Brzezinski, Gary Sick, and Thomas Thornton. There was some hope that Iran might follow a less hostile policy toward Washington because of an increased perception of the Soviet threat.

26 *New York Times*, 24 January 1980.

27 Ibid., 30 December 1979.

28 Ibid., 24 January 1980.

29 President Sadat of Egypt disclosed in September 1981 that Washington was buying Soviet arms in Egypt for use by Afghan insurgents (*New York Times*, 23 September 1981).

30 Carl Bernstein, "Arms for Afghanistan," *New Republic*.

31 Ibid. and personal interviews.

32 *New York Times*, 24 February 1980.

33 On Soviet strategy see Zalmay Khalilzad, "Soviet Occupied Afghanistan," *Problems of Communism* (November–December 1980).

34 Nearby Observer (pseud.), "The Afghan-Soviet War: Stalemate or Evolution?" *Middle East Journal* 36 (Spring 1982): 151.

35 Ibid., p. 154.

Notes to Chapter 20

1 For summaries of Australia's interests in the Indian Ocean region, but with a measure of application to New Zealand as well, see Parliament of Australia, *Australia and the Indian Ocean Region*, Report from the Standing Committee on Foreign Affairs and Defence (Canberra: Australian Government Publishing Service, 1976), pp. 169–93; Parliament of Australia, *The Gulf and Australia*, Report from the Joint Committee on Foreign Affairs and Defence (Canberra: Australian Government Publishing Service, 1982), pp. 11–26; Kim C. Beazley and Ian Clark, *The Politics of Intrusion. The Super Powers in the Indian Ocean* (Sydney: Alternative Publishing Cooperative, 1979), pp. 127–30.

2 The Australian Labour party under Robert Hawke entered office following elections in March 1983. During its first several months, the Hawke government demonstrated considerable foreign and defense policy continuity with its predecessor. No new constraints were imposed on American ship visits, on the b-52 transit flights, or on various American facilities in Australia. The Sinai troop contribution was left undisturbed and consideration was being given to basing some f-18 aircraft at Butterworth once the aircraft entered the inventory. While Labour definitely decided not to acquire an aircraft carrier, plans continued to enhance Western Australia–based naval strength. Labour did not insist on a formal limitation of anzus treaty application to the Indian Ocean and Foreign Minister Hayden even proposed a program of Australian political and economic initiatives around the eastern African littoral as well as increased, although "independent," naval deployments in the area.

3 Robert Muldoon, address of 7 April 1976, cited in *New Zealand Foreign Affairs Review* 26 (April–June 1976): 11 (hereinafter referred to as NZFAR).

4 Malcolm Fraser, address in New York, 18 May 1982, "The Western Alliance: Perceptions and Reality."

5 For representative, official expositions on the meaning and value of ANZUS, see Hugh Templeton, New Zealand deputy minister of finance, address of 6 June 1980, in *New Zealand and ANZUS—A Defence Policy for the 80s* (Wellington: Ministry of Foreign Affairs, 1980), Special Bulletin 1980/2, pp. 2–12; A. A. Street, Australian foreign minister, address of 24 March 1981, in Department of Foreign Affairs *News Release*, M25, 24 March 1981. For an official American perspective, see Evelyn Colbert, "The Alliance: A Dialogue," *New Zealand International Review* (November–December 1980) (hereinafter referred to as NZIR). For an assessment of ANZUS alliance dynamics, see Henry S. Albinski, "American Perspectives on the ANZUS Alliance," *Australian Quarterly* 32 (August 1978): 131–52.

6 On United States–New Zealand compatibility and mutual value, see Richard Kennaway, "New Zealand and the United States: The Bilateral Relationship," paper delivered at the Conference on the United States and Oceania West, held at Massey University, Palmerston North, August 1981; and Henry S. Albinski, "New Zealand and ANZUS: A United States Perspective," in *Beyond New Zealand: The Foreign Policy of a Small State*, ed. John Henderson, Keith Jackson, and Richard Kennaway (Auckland: Methuen, 1980), pp. 46–51. On United States compatibility with Australia, see the present author's *The Australian-American Security Relationship. A Regional and International Perspective* (St. Lucia: University of Queensland Press, 1982).

7 Thomas D. Young, *ANZUS in the Indian Ocean: Strategic Considerations*, memoir presented for the Diploma of the University Institute of Advanced International Studies, Geneva, 1982, p. 64.

8 Kennaway, "New Zealand and the United States," pp. 6–7.

9 *Report of the Ministry of Defence* for the year ended 31 March 1980 (Wellington: Government Printer, 1980), p. 3.

10 See the comments of Denis McLean, secretary, Ministry of Defence, "New Zealand: Isolated but Not Isolationist," paper delivered at the International Studies Association Conference, Philadelphia, March 1981.

11 Fraser, answer to question upon notice provided by Attorney General John Carrick, *Commonwealth Parliamentary Debates*, Senate, 19 August 1980, p. 84 (hereinafter referred to as *CPD*). Also see Andrew Peacock, foreign minister, *CPD*, House of Representatives, 30 April 1980, p. 2479, and commentary in Parliament of Australia, Senate, Standing Committee on Foreign Affairs and Defence, *Transcript of Evidence* for the report, *Australia and the Indian Ocean Region*, Annexure A., pp. 10, 30.

12 Interview with Bruce Wallace, NZIR (May–June 1982).

13 Muldoon, cited in *Dominion* (Wellington), 11 June 1982.

14 See the useful analysis by Marian Wilkinson, *National Times*, 24 May 1981.

15 See relevant accounts of the visit to the United States by Foreign Minister Brian Talboys in *Star* (Christchurch), 29 February 1980, and in *Dominion*, 1 March 1980. On trade issues growing out of New Zealand–Soviet relations, see Barry Gustafson, "New Zealand and the Three Bears," NZIR (January–February 1980), and "The Kiwi and the Bear," NZIR (September–October, 1980).

16 On Australia and the Iranian crisis, including the economic sanctions issue, see Albinski, *Australian-American Security Relationship*, pp. 147–50.

17 Muldoon, cited in *New Zealand Herald* (Auckland), 18 April 1980. See also *Star*, 19 April 1980, and *Press* (Christchurch), 12 May 1980.

18 On the Australian side, see Michelle Grattan, *Age* (Melbourne), 2 July 1981,

and David Balderstone, *Age*, 4 March 1982. On the New Zealand side, see *Evening Post* (Wellington), 26 November 1981.

19   R. R. MacIntyre, letter to the New Zealand government, cited in *Star*, 27 April 1982. For a good summary of Australian (and, in large part, New Zealand) official concerns about participation, see Street's letter to Haig of 27 April 1981, reproduced by Alan Reid in *Bulletin*, 16 June 1981.

20   On the conditions, see Street, *CPD*, House of Representatives, 17 March 1982, pp. 1066–67. For a description of the ANZAC Sinai force, see Ian Hamilton, "The ANZAC Contingent and its Role," *Pacific Defence Reporter* (April 1982).

21   *Sydney Morning Herald*, 6 November 1981.

22   Street, *CPD*, House of Representatives, 29 October 1981, p. 2746.

23   See accounts of New Zealand's behavior at the United Nations in *Press*, 1 August 1980, and in *Evening Post*, 2 August 1980. See also Gordon Parkinson, "The Palestine Problem: An Evenhanded New Zealand Approach," *NZIR* (September–October 1982).

24   Remarks of 25 November 1981, cited in *NZFAR* 31 (October–December 1981): 39.

25   Street, Tel Aviv address of 28 March 1982, in Minister of Foreign Affairs *News Release*, M35, 31 March 1982, and address in Cairo of 31 March 1982, in *News Release*, M37, 1 April 1982.

26   H. H. Francis, New Zealand ambassador to the United Nations, cited in *Dominion*, 28 June 1982.

27   Statement of 9 August 1982, cited in Department of Foreign Affairs *Backgrounder*, no. 345, p. 6. Also see Sam Lipski's analysis in *Bulletin*, 24 August 1982.

28   ANZUS Council communiqué, Canberra, 22 June 1982. For major ANZAC nation expressions touching on the value of the right of naval and air passage, see Talboys, article in *NZIR* (July–August 1981); and for Australia, *Backgrounder*, no. 31, esp. p. 12.

29   *New York Times*, 2 February 1982.

30   See for instance Peacock, "Defence and Diplomacy in the Indian Ocean," *Australian Foreign Affairs Review* 7 (November 1976): 598–600; Muldoon, radio interview with Cris Turver, 30 January 1976, in *NZFAR* 26 (January 1976): 42–43.

31   See, for example, the comment by the United States ambassador to Australia, James Hargrove, in an Australian television interview of 4 July 1976, with Alan Reid and Gerald Stone, transcript.

32   See, for instance, Stephen Barber, *FEER*, 8 April 1977; Fraser's London press conference of 31 May 1977, transcript; Fraser's Washington press conference of 22 June 1977, transcript. The suggestion that Australia, and Fraser in particular during his June 1977 visit to Washington, may have been directly responsible for dissuading Carter from following a demilitarization objective has been made by Rear Admiral Robert J. Hanks (U.S.N., ret.), in "The Indian Ocean Negotiations: Rocks and Shoals," *Strategic Review* 6 (Winter 1978): 25. In my view, however, the argument is not substantiated by available internal evidence.

33   For a summary of Australia's approach to the work of the committee, see remarks by United Nations Ambassador David Anderson to the First Committee, 19 November 1979, contained in text issued by the Australian mission to the United Nations, *Backgrounder*, no. 275, p. 5.

34   *Canberra Times*, 10 January 1982.

35 This account is a digest of Albinski, *Australian-American Security Relationship*, pp. 127–30.

36 Interview with Bruce Wallace, NZIR (September–October 1981).

37 See Carter's remarks following Fraser's European consultations in Prime Minister and President Carter, *Joint Statement*, Press Office transcript, 7 February 1980. For examples of Australian press comment, see Creighton Burns, *Age*, 31 January and 9 February 1980, and Russell Schneider, *Australian*, 9 February 1980.

38 For recent expositions see, for Australia, W. B. Pritchett, secretary, Department of Defence, paper delivered at the Australian Institute of International Affairs Conference, Sydney, May 1982, and Sinclair, address of 25 July 1982, cited in *Commonwealth Record* 7, no. 29, pp. 938–40. On the New Zealand side, see David Thomson, minister of defence, "Introduction," in *Report of the Ministry of Defence* for the year ended 31 March 1982 (Wellington: Government Printer, 1982), pp. 3–6.

39 ANZUS Council communiqué, Washington, D.C., 28 February 1980. On New Zealand's position at the council meeting and on ANZUS and the Indian Ocean generally, see John Henderson, "The Burdens of ANZUS," NZIR (May–June 1980), and Bruce Wallace, "Which Way the Alliance?" NZIR (November–December 1980).

40 For summaries of Australian facilities and force activities in the west and northwest, see Deborah Snow, *Australian Financial Review*, 16 June 1982; Patrick Walters, *Sydney Morning Herald*, and Stephen Mills, *Age*, both of 18 June 1982; John Stackhouse, *Bulletin*, 22 June 1982. For a description of HMAS *Stirling*, see "General Information–Notes–HMAS Stirling," mimeo, Australian Defence Department publication.

41 See Anne Summers, *Australian Financial Review*, 29 September and 2 October 1980; Creighton Burns, *Age*, 18 October 1980; on New Zealand, see *Press*, 3 October 1980, and *New Zealand Herald*, 3 October and 6 October 1980.

42 See *Star*, 29 May 1982, and *New Zealand Herald*, 4 June and 29 July 1982, and an account of the actual deployment in *Press*, 26 August 1982.

43 In late 1980 Australia withdrew from scheduled exercises with British and American forces in the Indian Ocean. For a discussion of the factors that induced Australia's withdrawal, see Henry S. Albinski, "The U.S. Security Alliance System in the Southwest Pacific," in *U.S. Foreign Policy and Asian-Pacific Security*, ed. William T. Tow and William R. Feeney (Boulder, Colo.: Westview, 1982), pp. 146–47.

44 ANZUS Council communiqué, Canberra, 22 June 1982.

45 Parliamentary remarks of 10 July 1981, cited in *Press*, 11 July 1981.

46 Especially in the New Zealand context, see Young, *ANZUS in the Indian Ocean*, p. 170.

47 For the agreement, see *Defence News Release*, no. 71/78, 18 May 1978. For background, see Michael Richardson, *FEER*, 14 February 1978.

48 On ship visits to Western Australia, and their reception, see Graeme Atherton, *West Australian* (Perth), 30 January 1982, and Chris Evans, *Australian Financial Review*, 30 July 1982.

49 For a typical Australian defense of port visits, see Fraser, statement of 10 June 1982, in *Backgrounder*, no. 337, pp. 3–4. [Editors' note: U.S. Navy access to New Zealand ports has been put in doubt by the new Labour government of David Lange because of the nuclear issue.]

50   See the report in *Washington Star*, 24 April 1981, and transcript of remarks by
     Admiral Thomas Hayward, U.S. chief of naval operations; remarks of Admiral
     James Watkins, commander in chief, U.S. Pacific Command, in *West Australian*
     (Perth), 5 May 1982. For a forward-looking assessment, see Peter Samuel,
     Australian, 11 June 1982.

51   See Michael MacKellar, acting foreign minister, statement of 2 March 1980,
     cited in *Age*, 3 March 1980. For media assessments, see Brian Toohey, *Aus-
     tralian Financial Review*, 29 February 1980, and John Edwards, *Bulletin*, 18
     March 1980.

52   For the agreement, see Fraser, *CPD*, House of Representatives, 11 March 1981,
     esp. pp. 666–67. For the American interpretation of the agreement, see United
     States Embassy, Canberra, *Press Release* of 30 March 1981, "U.S.-Australian
     Agreement on Transit of Darwin by USAF B-52 Aircraft on Training and Sea
     Surveillance Missions." For a summary of the recent debate regarding United
     States disclosure policy and Australian entitlements, see, for instance, Geoff
     Kitney, *National Times*, 27 June 1982.

53   On the Blenheim facility, see Brian Whitehead, *Press*, 20 December 1981;
     Owen Wilkes, "Why the US Military Needs Another NZ Mountain," *New
     Zealand Monthly Review*, August 1981; and remarks by U.S. official James
     Hughes, cited in *Star*, 30 January 1982. The most elaborate study of American
     installations in Australia is in Desmond Ball, *A Suitable Piece of Real Estate:
     American Installations in Australia* (Sydney: Hall and Iremonger, 1980). Also
     see Ball, "The US Naval Ocean Surveillance Information System (NOSIS)—
     Australia's Role," *Pacific Defence Reporter* (June 1982).

54   For a succinct balance sheet of dangers and advantages to Australia in hosting
     various defense facilities, see Parliament of Australia, *Threats to Australia's
     Security—Their Nature and Probability*, Report from the Joint Committee on
     Foreign Affairs and Defence (Canberra: Australian Government Publishing
     Service, 1981), esp. pp. 15–19, 23–29.

55   Coral Bell, "The Case for the Alliance," paper delivered at the Conference on
     Australian Defence Policy for the 1980s, held at Australian National University,
     May 1981.

Notes to Chapter 21

The author wishes to thank his colleague, Robert Youngblood, for helpful comments on the original version of this chapter and to express his gratitude to Dundee
Kelbel, graduate assistant in political science, for the preparation of material
related to ASEAN's economic performance.

1   These figures are cited in Agerico O. Lacandale, "Domestic Instability and
    Security of Sealanes in Southeast Asia," *Asia Pacific Community* 16 (Spring
    1982): 27.

2   The value of ASEAN's imports from selected Indian Ocean states (India, Paki-
    stan, Iran, Iraq, Oman, Qatar, and Kuwait) between 1977 and 1980 shows an
    increase from U.S. $1.9 billion to U.S. $3.5 billion, while ASEAN's exports to
    those countries over the same period show an increase from U.S. $0.8 billion to
    U.S. $1.4 billion (ASEAN figures do not include Malaysia for 1980). By contrast,
    ASEAN's trade with the United States presently exceeds U.S. $20 billion, and
    trade with Japan is even greater. For details, see Annual Papers, Commodity
    Trade Statistics, United Nations Publishing Service.

3 For a brief enumeration of the major provisions of the new draft Treaty on the Law of the Sea, see Edward J. Lacey, "A New Law of the Sea," *International Studies Newsletter* 9 (June 1982): 7.

4 For a discussion of the background to the conflict, see Daniel P. Finn, "The Marine Environment and Maritime Security in Southeast Asia: Controlling Oil Tanker Traffic in the Strait of Malacca," *Naval War College Review* (November–December 1981), pp. 71–72.

5 The foregoing analysis draws extensively on discussions between the author and Chandran Jesherun of the University of Malaysia during his visit to Arizona State University, 23 August 1983.

6 Malaysia is to buy eighty-eight reconditioned A4 Skyhawks from the United States as well as Exocet missiles. On the other hand, economic conditions have forced a slowdown in the construction of new military bases on the east coast. See Robert L. Rau, "The Role of the Armed Forces and Police in Malaysia," paper presented to Naval Postgraduate School Conference on the Role of the Armed Forces in Asia, held in Monterey, California, 4–6 August 1982; and *Asian Wall Street Journal Weekly*, 8 March 1982, p. 9.

7 For a recent discussion of these, see "ASEAN '82," *Far Eastern Economic Review*, 13 August 1982, pp. 66, 68.

8 For a general discussion of these disputes, see Barry Buzan, "A Sea of Troubles," Adelphi Paper (London: International Institute for Strategic Studies, 1978).

9 In 1965 Southeast Asia produced very little offshore crude oil. Ten years later production surpassed 14 million tons annually. Fishing catches in the South China Sea amount to between 2 and 2.5 million tons annually, making it one of the world's richest fishing grounds. Ibid., p. 68.

10 See ibid.

11 Corolina Hernandez, "Trends and Problems in Philippine-American Relations 1972–1980," paper presented to Second International Philippines Studies Conference held at University of Hawaii, Honolulu, 27–30 June 1981, p. 9; discussions between this author and Major William Berry, U.S.A.F., Naval Postgraduate School, 5 August 1982, and with a U.S. official in the Philippines, 1 May 1982.

12 Vietnam has warned foreign oil companies about conducting operations in the contested area. Hanoi Domestic Service, 25 August 1982, *Foreign Broadcast Information Service*, Daily Report Asia-Pacific, 26 August 1982, p. K1 (hereinafter referred to as *FBIS*, A-P).

13 Agence France Presse (Hong Kong), 27 August 1982; in *FBIS*, A-P, 30 August 1982, p. N1; and my discussions with a U.S. Air Force officer. For a discussion of the expansion of the Indonesian navy, see Peter Lyon, "Indonesia," in *Security Policies of Developing Countries*, ed. Edward Kolodziej and Robert Harkavy (Lexington, Mass.: Lexington Books, 1982), p. 168.

14 For an extended discussion of ASEAN's defense buildup, see Sheldon W. Simon, *The ASEAN States and Regional Security* (Stanford, Calif.: Hoover Institution Press, 1982), esp. chap. 3.

15 For details of new weapons acquisitions by ASEAN members, see Robert L. Rau, "ASEAN Security in the 1980s: The Maritime Dimension," paper presented at the Twenty-second Annual Meeting of the International Studies Association, held at Philadelphia, March 1981, pp. 22–24. Also see James A. Hazlett, "Strait Shooting," *U.S. Naval Institute Proceedings* (June 1982): 71.

16 Leo E. Rose, "US Policy in Asia: The India Factor," in *A US Foreign Policy*

for Asia: The 1980s and Beyond, ed. Ramon Myers (Stanford, Calif.: Hoover Institution Press, 1982), p. 45. Also see Robert C. Horn, *Soviet-Indian Relations: Issues and Influence* (New York: Praeger, 1982), p. 198.

17 In the summer of 1982 the Vietnamese-backed Kampuchean regime issued a decree on territorial seas that claimed the waters through which Chinese and Thai vessels have been transporting arms for Kampuchean resistance. Should the Kampuchean government of Hen Samrin be contemplating naval action against Thailand or China, they have a legal claim on which to justify it. See *FBIS, AS*, 9 August 1982, pp. H1-H3; and *FBIS, AS*, 23 August 1982, p. H3.

18 See William T. Tow and William R. Feeney, eds., *US Foreign Policy and Asian-Pacific Security*, Special Study in National Security and Defense Policy (Boulder, Colo.: Westview, 1982), p. 9.

19 Interviews by author in ASEAN capitals, April–May 1981.

20 Michael Richardson, "Missile Maneuvers," *Far Eastern Economic Review*, 30 April 1982, pp. 15–16.

21 See Lt. Commander James T. Westwood, U.S.N., "The Soviet Union and the Southern Sea Route," *Naval War College Review* (January–February 1982), pp. 54–57.

22 On an average day, according to U.S. Deputy Assistant Secretary of Defense Richard Armitage, four Soviet reconnaissance flights leave from Vietnamese bases and up to ten naval vessels cruise Southeast Asian waters (*Asian Wall Street Journal Weekly*, 14 June 1982, p. 12).

23 Vietnamese officials insist that the Soviets do not possess bases in Vietnam and have not engaged in building significant onshore facilities with the exception of communications. All maintenance and resupply work for Soviet vessels is said to be carried on from a Soviet support ship moored in the harbor. See Nayan Chanda, "Snake in the Grass," *Far Eastern Economic Review*, 7 May 1982, p. 25.

24 *Far Eastern Economic Review*, 5 October 1979, p. 16, and 29 February 1980, p. 10.

25 Lie Tek-tjeng, "Southeast Asian Regional Security in the 1980s: A View from Jakarta," in *International Security in the Southeast Asian and South-west Pacific Region*, ed. T. B. Millar (St. Lucia: University of Queensland Press, 1983), p. 272.

26 Henry Albinski, "The US Security Alliance System in the Southwest Pacific," in Tow and Feeney, *US Foreign Policy*, p. 140.

27 *Bangkok Post*, 4 July 1983.

28 Warwick Beutler, "On Parade Down Under," *Far Eastern Economic Review*, 21 July 1983.

29 Michael Richardson, "A Nest for the Hornets," *Far Eastern Economic Review*, 20 August 1982.

30 Remarks by Deputy Secretary of State Walter J. Stoessel, Jr., to U.S. Senate, Foreign Relations Committee, 10 June 1982, *Current Policy*, no. 403; and my discussions with U.S. officials in Kuala Lumpur in May 1981 and with Robert O'Neill, former director of the Strategic and Defence Studies Centre, Australian National University, July 1982.

31 Diane Mauzy, "The 1982 General Election in Malaysia," *Asian Survey* 23 (April 1982): 502; and Raphael Para, "Malaysia's Moslem Faithful Flock to New Islamic Bank," *Asian Wall Street Journal Weekly*, 11 July 1983.

32 *Malaysian Digest*, 31 January 1981.

Notes to Chapter 22

1 The invasion of Afghanistan is not an exception to this rule, since it comes within the Soviet national security zone (as does Finland), whereas this discussion focuses on activity outside that zone. The Soviets' response in Afghanistan paralleled their behavior in similar crises in Hungary and Czechoslovakia.

Notes to Chapter 23

1 For two quite disparate views of these talks see Rear Admiral Robert J. Hanks, "The Indian Ocean Negotiations: Rocks and Shoals," *Strategic Review* 6 (Winter 1978): 18–27; and William Stivers, "Doves, Hawks, and Detente," *Foreign Policy*, no. 45 (Winter 1981–82): 126–44.
2 Two excellent journalistic reviews of the policy debate that culminated in these actions are Don Oberdorfer, "The Evolution of a Decision," *Washington Post*, 24 January 1980, and Richard Burt, "How U.S. Strategy toward Persian Gulf Region Evolved," *New York Times*, 25 January 1980.
3 Admiral Thomas H. Moorer and Alvin J. Cottrell, "The Search for U.S. Bases in the Indian Ocean: A Last Chance," *Strategic Review* 8 (Spring 1980): 31.
4 *Department of Defense Authorization for Appropriations for FY 1981*, part 1, Hearings before the Committee on Armed Services, U.S. Senate, 96/2 (Washington, D.C.: Government Printing Office, 1980), p. 484.
5 Oberdorfer, "Evolution of a Decision."
6 Henry S. Bradsher, "Three Nations OK U.S. Request to Use Bases," *Washington Star*, 4 January 1980.
7 This involved checking the depths of harbor channels, the lengths of airport runways, and sites for storing U.S. equipment (Drew Middleton, "U.S. Sending Experts to Seek Persian Gulf Military Sites," *New York Times*, 11 January 1980).
8 Stuart Auerbach, "Saudis Termed Responsive to U.S. Military Needs," *Washington Post*, 6 February 1980.
9 Michael Getler, "U.S. Would Link Aid to Access to Bases," *Washington Post*, 28 February 1980.
10 Michael Getler, "Oman Again Receptive to U.S. Use of Its Bases," *Washington Post*, 12 May 1980.
11 "U.S. Announces Pact with Oman on Access to Air Bases and Port," *New York Times*, 6 June 1980.
12 See Richard Burt, "U.S. Wins Bases in Oman and Kenya," *New York Times*, 22 April 1980; and "U.S. Reassesses Need to Use Somali Base," *New York Times*, 16 July 1980.
13 As one American official commented, "Once a decision is made that you need greater access for ships and aircraft in that part of the world, Somalia becomes a logical candidate. . . . If you look at the map you find that you don't have a lot of choices" (Graham Hovey, "U.S. Moving Toward Military Ties with Somalia, Recognizing Risks," *New York Times*, 10 February 1980).
14 George C. Wilson, "Indian Ocean Bases Plan Hits Snag," *Washington Post*, 28 August 1980.
15 See Henry S. Bradsher, "U.S., Kenya in Accord on Allowing Greater Use of Port Facilities," *Washington Star*, 28 June 1980; Gregory Jaynes, "The U.S.

Finds High Prices on East Africa's Bargain Bases," *New York Times,* 14 September 1980; and Don Oberdorfer, "Somalia Agrees to Let U.S. Use Ports, Airfields," *Washington Post,* 22 August 1980.

16 *Congressional Presentation: Security Assistance Programs, FY 1983.*

17 Ibid. There are four components of a security assistance package: Foreign Military Sales (FMS) Financing Program, Economic Support Fund, Military Assistance Program; and International Military Education and Training Program.

18 U.S. House of Representatives, *Military Construction Appropriations for FY 1983,* part 5, Hearings before the Committee on Appropriations, 97/2 (Washington, D.C.: Government Printing Office, 1982), p. 265.

19 See ibid., and Congressional Budget Office, *Rapid Deployment Forces: Policy and Budgetary Implications,* February 1983, p. 60.

20 Jeffrey Record, *The Rapid Deployment Force and U.S. Military Intervention in the Persian Gulf* (Cambridge, Mass.: Institute for Foreign Policy Analysis, February 1981), pp. 58–60.

21 Richard Halloran, "U.S. Looking to Leasing of Bases for Easier Access to Crisis Areas," *New York Times,* 20 January 1980.

22 U.S. House of Representatives, *Military Construction Appropriations for FY 1983,* part 5, pp. 267 and 275.

23 Congressional Budget Office, *Rapid Deployment Forces: Policy and Budgetary Implications,* p. 59.

24 Estimate as of 26 March 1982. See U.S. House of Representatives, *Military Construction Appropriations for FY 1983,* part 5, p. 278. Congress, however, authorized only $91 million of the $193.6 million requested for construction at Ras Banas for FY 1983 because Egypt refused to sign an agreement giving the United States a guaranteed right of access there. See Richard Halloran, "Special U.S. Force for Mideast Is Expanding Swiftly," *New York Times,* 25 October 1982; and Congressional Budget Office, *Rapid Deployment Forces: Policy and Budgetary Implications,* p. 60.

25 *Congressional Presentation: Security Assistance Programs, FY 1983.* It has also been reported that Turkey has agreed to let the United States improve ten air bases that could support operations in the Persian Gulf. See Halloran, "Special U.S. Force for Mideast."

26 Dale F. Eickelman, "U.S. Interests in Oman," *New York Times,* 16 April 1983.

27 "Preserving the Oil Flow," *Time,* 22 September 1980, p. 29.

28 *Military Construction Appropriations for FY 1983,* part 5, p. 265. Also see Richard Halloran, "U.S. Studying $1 Billion Expansion of Indian Ocean Base," *New York Times,* 6 April 1980. One of the ironies of this construction upsurge is that laborers are being recruited in Mauritius; however it has been stipulated that no Ilois, the displaced islanders from Diego Garcia, are to be allowed to go. See Pranay B. Gupte, "Dispossessed on Mauritius are Inflamed," *New York Times,* 14 December 1981.

29 *Persian Gulf/Indian Ocean Military Construction Program and Defense Posture in the Pacific,* Hearings before the Subcommittee on Military Construction Appropriations of the Committee on Appropriations, House of Representatives, 97/1 (Washington, D.C.: Government Printing Office, 1981), p. 211.

30 Squadron Leader J. Clementson, "Diego Garcia," *Journal of the Royal United Services Institute* 126 (June 1981): 33.

31 *Persian Gulf/Indian Ocean Military Construction Program,* p. 193.

32 On the prestocking program for Diego Garcia, see Robert S. Dudney, "A Year

After—New U.S. Role in Mideast," *U.S. News & World Report*, 3 November 1980; Charles W. Corddry, "U.S. Deploys 7 Shiploads of Gear in Indian Ocean," *Sun* (Chicago), 6 March 1980; Clementson, "Diego Garcia," pp. 36–38; Halloran, "Special U.S. Force for Mideast"; and Robert A. Manning, "Gearing Up for the 'Quick Strike,'" *Boston Globe Magazine*, 21 November 1982.

33 See "U.S. Expected to Seek B52 Use of Indian Ocean Isle," *Washington Post*, 4 March 1981; and Halloran, "U.S. Studying $1 Billion Expansion."

34 *Persian Gulf/Indian Ocean Military Construction Program*, p. 211. The Seabees are a construction battalion.

35 Clementson, "Diego Garcia," pp. 38–39.

36 See Richard Burt, "How U.S. Strategy toward Persian Gulf Region Evolved"; "U.S. Increases Ships in Indian Ocean Area," *Sun* (Chicago), 18 January 1980; and Drew Middleton, "The President Draws the Line: In Persian Gulf," *New York Times*, 25 January 1980.

37 See Halloran, "U.S. Studying $1 Billion Expansion"; Jay Ross, "U.S. Navy Flotilla Adapting to New Mission in Indian Ocean," *Washington Post*, 3 February 1981; and Michael T. Kaufman, "U.S. Naval Buildup is Challenging Soviet Advances in Asia and Africa," *New York Times*, 19 April 1981.

38 Patrick J. Sloyan, "Mombasa: U.S. Presence Unsubtle," *Hartford Courant* (Conn.), 10 March 1982.

39 Richard Burt, "President, Under the Pressure of Crisis, Looking to New Foreign Policy Goals," *New York Times*, 9 January 1980.

40 Rear Admiral Robert J. Hanks (ret.), "A Fifth Fleet for the Indian Ocean," *U.S. Naval Institute Proceedings* 105 (August 1979): 98.

41 "Navies and Foreign Policy: SACLANT's Views," *Navy International* 85 (September 1980): 570. A related article that urges greater allied support and assistance for U.S. actions in the Indian Ocean is Dov S. Zakheim, "Of Allies and Access," *Washington Quarterly* 4 (Winter 1981): 87–96.

42 *Hearings on Military Posture*, before the Committee on Armed Services, House of Representatives, 97/1, part 1 (Washington, D.C.: Government Printing Office, 1981), p. 995.

43 Quoted by Admiral Harry D. Train II, "NATO—Global Outlook?" *Navy International* 86 (January 1981): 9. Also see Drew Middleton, "Navy's Plight: Too Many Seas to Cover," *New York Times*, 1 February 1981.

44 See "Indian Ocean Fleet is Posing Problems," *New York Times*, 15 April 1980; and *Persian Gulf/Indian Ocean Military Construction Program*, pp. 142–43.

45 James W. Abellera, Roger P. Labrie, and Albert C. Pierce, "The FY 1982–1986 Defense Program," *AEI Foreign Policy and Defense Review* 3 (1981): 63–66.

46 Sloyan, "Mombasa: U.S. Presence Unsubtle."

47 See Norman L. Stone, "An Indian Ocean Fleet—the Case and the Cost," *U.S. Naval Institute Proceedings* 107 (July 1981): 56; and Kaufman, "U.S. Naval Buildup."

48 Peter L. Young, "Naval Balance in the Indian Ocean," *Navy International* 85 (December 1980): 721.

49 Major Maxwell Orme Johnson, "U.S. Strategic Options in the Persian Gulf," *U.S. Naval Institute Proceedings* 107 (February 1981): 57. The U.S. Marine Corps has traditionally served as America's primary long-distance, general-

purpose amphibious intervention force, a role codified by Congress in the 1947 National Security Act. See U.S. Congressional Budget Office, *The Marine Corps in the 1980s: Prestocking Proposals, the Rapid Deployment Force and Other Issues* (Washington, D.C.: Government Printing Office, May 1980), p. xi.

50 See Record, *Rapid Deployment Force*, p. 45; and Zakheim, "Of Allies and Access," p. 89.

51 Michael Klare, "Gunboat Diplomacy, Lightning War and the Nixon Doctrine: U.S. Military Strategy in the Arabian Gulf," *Race and Class* 17 (1976), pp. 303 and 306.

52 Congressional Budget Office, *Rapid Deployment Forces: Policy and Budgetary Implications*, p. 4.

53 On this debate, see Burt, "How U.S. Strategy toward Persian Gulf Region Evolved"; and Record, *Rapid Deployment Force*, p. 46.

54 Johnson, "U.S. Strategic Options in the Persian Gulf," p. 54; and Record, *Rapid Deployment Force*, p. 46.

55 Some of these forces would also be drawn off U.S. forces committed to northeastern Asia (Korea). See Congressional Budget Office, *Rapid Deployment Forces: Policy and Budgetary Implications*, p. 1.

56 See Richard Halloran, "U.S. Plans Persian Gulf Command," *New York Times*, 25 April 1981; and Halloran, "Deployment Force Seeks Permanent Mideast Post," *New York Times*, 18 December 1981.

57 Halloran, "Special U.S. Force for Mideast."

58 Congressional Budget Office, *Rapid Deployment Forces: Policy and Budgetary Implications*, p. 12.

59 Ibid.

60 Ibid., pp. 31–35.

61 Ibid., pp. 35–37.

62 Ibid., pp. 37–39.

63 On these exercises see Manning, "Gearing Up for the 'Quick Strike'"; Loren Jenkins, "U.S. Forces Airlifted to Egypt for Joint Maneuvers," *Washington Post*, 10 November 1981; Richard Halloran, "U.S. Starts Deploying Troops for Maneuvers in Four Mideast Nations," *New York Times*, 3 November 1981; and Richard Halloran, "U.S. Rapid Deployment Operation in Egypt Shows Readiness Problem," *New York Times*, 21 November 1980.

64 Zakheim, "Of Allies and Access," p. 87.

65 American officials claimed no exercises were planned. See Halloran, "Special U.S. Force for Mideast."

66 See "2,500 GIS Held Maneuvers in Oman," *New York Times*, 6 December 1982.

67 Statement made by former Secretary of Defense Harold Brown, quoted in Kenneth Waltz, "A Strategy for the Rapid Deployment Force," *International Security* 5 (Spring 1981): 50.

68 R. B. Byers, "Seapower and Arms Control: Problems and Prospects," *International Journal* 36 (Summer 1981): 502.

69 Charles Hermann, "International Crisis as a Situational Variable," in *International Politics and Foreign Policy*, ed. James N. Rosenau (New York: Free Press, 1969), pp. 409–21.

Notes to Chapter 24

1 Great Britain, Privy Council, Orders in Council no. 1920, *British Indian Ocean Territory Royal Instructions* (8 November 1965).
2 Ibid. Also see Colony of Mauritius, *A Collection of Proclamations and Governmental Notices, 1965* (1966).
3 Great Britain, 720 Parliamentary Debates (Commons) 2.
4 TIAS 6196.
5 TIAS 7481.
6 Ibid., p. 3094.
7 TIAS 8230.
8 *Times of India*, 15 and 28 June 1980.
9 United Nations, General Assembly, A/35/PV.33 (12 October 1980).
10 Ibid. Also see *Times of India*, 8 and 9 July 1980.
11 See John Madeley, "Diego Garcia: An Indian Ocean Storm-Centre," *Round Table* 283 (July 1981): 253–57.
12 *New York Times*, 14 December 1981, and 20 June 1982. See also *Times* (London), 15 June 1982.
13 *Times* (London), 22 July 1982.
14 See, for example, Rodney W. Jones, "Ballistic Missile Submarines and Arms Control in the Indian Ocean," *Asian Survey* 20 (March 1980).
15 *New York Times*, 3 October 1980.
16 *Morning Star*, 29 May 1980.
17 *Guardian*, 30 May 1980.
18 *The Military Balance: 1981–1982* (London: International Institute for Strategic Studies, 1981), p. 29.

Notes to Chapter 25

It is with a deep sense of regret that the editors acknowledge the death of Al Cottrell in the spring of 1984. This chapter represents one of his last contributions to scholarship on the Indian Ocean region. Al was instrumental in arranging publication of this volume, and he provided early encouragement for our plans to organize the Dalhousie conference.

1 For a discussion see Emile A. Nakhleh, *Bahrain* (Lexington, Mass.: Lexington Books, 1976), p. 112.
2 See, for example, Oles Smolansky, "Soviet Entry into the Indian Ocean," in *The Indian Ocean: Its Political, Economic, and Military Importance*, ed. A. J. Cottrell and R. M. Burrell (New York: Praeger, 1972), pp. 337–53.

Notes to Chapter 26

1 For a succinct and balanced refutation of this theory, see Ken Booth and Lee Dowdy, "Soviet Security Interests in the Indian Ocean Region," in *Soviet Armed Forces Review Annual* 6, ed. David R. Jones (1982): 334–36.
2 Oles M. Smolansky, "Soviet Policy in Iran and Afghanistan," *Current History* 80 (October 1981): 321–24, 339.
3 For an excellent summary of the disagreements among Western specialists concerning the reasons for the establishment of the Soviet naval presence in the Indian Ocean, See Booth and Dowdy, "Soviet Security Interests," pp. 330–34.

4   Text of Brezhnev's speech in *Pravda*, 24 February 1981. Other comments are from Iu. Glukhov, *Pravda*, 31 May 1982.
5   The information on Soviet energy production is based on Foreign and Commonwealth Office, *Background Brief—The Soviet Economy 1981–1982* (London: 1982), p. 2.
6   Quoted in *New York Times*, 29 April 1982.
7   *Pravda*, 9 March 1982, as quoted in *New York Times* of the same date.
8   Shahram Chubin, "Gains for Soviet Policy in the Middle East," *International Security* 6 (Spring 1982): 122–52.
9   Ibid., p. 129.
10 The text of Brezhnev's 10 December 1980 address to the Indian Parliament is in *Pravda*, 11 December 1980.

Notes to Chapter 27

It is with a deep sense of regret that the editors acknowledge the death of Ferenc Váli at the end of 1984. His legacy to friends and colleagues is a rich one.

1   These islands were returned to the Seychelles at independence in 1976.
2   For a discussion of the U.S. lease, see Joel Larus's chapter in this book.
3   On the Simonstown Agreement, see C. J. R. Dugard, "The Simonstown Agreement: South Africa, Britain, and the United Nations," *South African Law Journal* 85 (May 1968): 142–56; and G. G. Laurie, "The Simonstown Agreement: South Africa, Britain, and the Commonwealth," ibid. pp. 157–77.
4   *Economist*, 3 July 1982.
5   See Arthur S. Banks and William Overstreet, eds., *Political Handbook of the World* (New York: McGraw-Hill, 1981), p. 191.
6   *Christian Science Monitor*, 27 February 1974.
7   President Mitterand has also announced that the name of the force is to be changed to *Force d'Assistance*. See the *Economist*, 29 May 1982.
8   Parliament of the Commonwealth of Australia, *Australia and the Indian Ocean Region*, Report from the Senate Standing Committee on Foreign Affairs and Defence (Canberra: 1976), p. 153.
9   *Economist*, 16 December 1972.
10 *New York Times*, 20 June 1974.
11 Ibid., 26 November 1976.
12 Ibid., 12 September 1977.
13 Document 754, Assembly of the Western European Union, Twenty-third Ordinary Session, 3 November 1977, par. 76.
14 Christopher Coker and Heinz Schulte, "A European Option in the Indian Ocean," *International Defense Review* 15 (1980): 34. Much of the foregoing analysis of NATO's interests in the Indian Ocean region draws upon the work of Coker and Schulte.
15 See *Debates of the European Parliament*, 18 November 1980, pp. 84–94; ibid., 16 September 1981, pp. 101–3; "Resolution on Trade Relations between EEC and the Gulf States," *Official Journal of the European Communities*, 10 December 1981; Alan R. Taylor, "The Euro-Arab Dialogue: Quest for an Inter-regional Partnership," *Middle East Journal* (1979), p. 429.

Notes to Chapter 28

1   *Asahi Shimbun*, 19 June 1981, p. 3.
2   Ibid.
3   Koichi Tsutsumi, "Chuto no antei to Nihon no yakuwari," *Kokusai Mondai*, no. 263 (February 1982), p. 66.
4   Edward A. Alsen, "Changing U.S. Interests in Northeast Asia," *World Affairs* 143 (Spring 1981): 349.
5   Stansfield Turner, "Toward a New Defense Strategy," *New York Times Magazine*, 21 June 1981, p. 16.
6   See, for example, Sogo Anzen Hosho Kenkyu Gurupu, *Sogo Anzen Hosho Senryaku* (Tokyo: Okurasho Insatsukyoku, 1980), p. 69; *Asahi Shimbun*, 24 June 1981, evening edition, p. 3; and Yatsuhiro Nakagawa, "Nihon ga seibi subeki boeiryoku towa," *Chuokoron*, September 1981, pp. 110–18.
7   *Sogo Anzen Hosho Senryaku*, p. 66.
8   A summary text published in *Nihon Keizai Shimbun*, 28 July 1980, and reprinted in *Shimbun Geppo*, no. 405 (August 1980), pp. 69–70. The SPPC is a top policy group created in the wake of the Iranian Revolution and the Soviet invasion of Afghanistan and chaired by the administrative vice minister, the highest career ministry official.
9   Boeicho, ed., *Showa 56 nen ban Boei Hakusho* (Tokyo: Okurasho Insatsukyoku, 1982), pp. 63–64.
10 Robert W. Komer, "Maritime Strategy vs. Coalition Defense," *Foreign Affairs* 60 (Summer 1982): 1139.
11 See, for example, *Asahi Shimbun*, 24 June 1981, p. 3.
12 *Asian Security 1980* (Tokyo: Research Institute for Peace and Security, 1980), pp. 165–66.
13 Turner, "Toward a New Defense Strategy," p. 16.
14 Daniel D. Newsom, "America EnGulfed," *Foreign Policy*, no. 43 (Summer 1981), p. 21.
15 Ibid. See also *Asahi Shimbun*, 26 July 1981, p. 1.
16 Ibid. See also *Asahi Shimbun*, 24 July 1981, evening edition, p. 3.
17 *Asahi Shimbun*, 24 July 1981, evening edition, p. 3.
18 Joint Working Group of the Atlantic Council of the United States and the Research Institute for Peace and Security, Tokyo, *The Common Security Interests of Japan, the United States and NATO* (Washington and Tokyo: Atlantic Council of the United States, December 1980), p. 35.
19 Sharakusai (pseud.), "Iken kanken: seiji gakusha ni okeru gakumon to jissen," *Keizai Hyoron* (January 1981), p. 142.
20 See the summary of the report published as Winston Lord, "Western Security: What Has Changed? What Should Be Done?" *Atlantic Community Quarterly* 19 (Summer 1981), p. 170.
21 Ibid., pp. 171–72.
22 *Asahi Shimbun*, 10 April 1981, p. 1.
23 For this discord, see a cogent analysis by Eliot A. Cohen, "The Long-Term Crisis of the Alliance," *Foreign Affairs* 61 (Winter 1982–83).
24 *Shimbun Geppo*, no. 405 (August 1980), p. 69.
25 For this controversy, see Taketsugu Tsurutani, "Old Habits, New Times: Challenges to Japanese-American Security Relations," *International Security* 7 (Fall 1982): 175–79.

26   *Asahi Shimbun*, 14 November 1982, p. 2.
27   Ibid., 10 April 1981, p. 1.
28   Ibid., 28 October 1980, p. 1.
29   Ibid., 10 April 1981, p. 1.
30   Ibid., 22 October 1982, p. 2.
31   Ibid., 8 October 1982, p. 2.
32   Ibid., 26 October 1982, p. 1.
33   As quoted in *New York Times*, 16 January 1983, p. 3.
34   *Asian Security 1980*, p. 166.
35   Ibid.
36   Japan accounts for only 4 percent of the total Western alliance's military spending (*Far Eastern Economic Review*, 3 February 1983, p. 11).
37   Komer, "Maritime Strategy vs. Coalition Defense," p. 1140.
38   UNCTAD, *Handbook of International Trade and Development Statistics: Supplement 1981* (New York: United Nations, 1982), p. 331.
39   Computed from Gaimusho, *Showa 56 nen ban Waga Gaiko no Kinkyo* (Tokyo: Okurasho Insatsukyoku, 1981), pp. 567–69 and 592–93.
40   The term is borrowed from Coral Bell, "Security Preoccupations and Power Balances After Vietnam," in *Conflict and Stability in Southeast Asia*, ed. Mark W. Zacher and R. Stephen Milne (Garden City, N.Y.: Doubleday, 1974), p. 478.
41   Computed from *Showa 56 nen ban Waga Gaiko no Kinkyo*, pp. 539 and 582.
42   Ibid., pp. 536, 578, and 580.
43   Ibid., pp. 536, 540, 580, and 586.
44   Ibid., p. 634.
45   Takakazu Kuriyama, "Japan's Foreign Policy in the Reagan Era," *Japan Echo* 8 (Summer 1981): 64–65.

Notes to Chapter 29

1   An overview of the history of China's relations with communities in the Indian Ocean region can be gained from Edwin O. Reischauer and John K. Fairbank, *East Asia: The Great Tradition* (Boston: Houghton Mifflin, 1958). For a history of China's maritime tradition, see Bruce Swanson, *Eighth Voyage of the Dragon: A History of China's Quest for Seapower* (Annapolis: Naval Institute Press, 1982). For a general discussion of Chinese interests in the Indian Ocean, see Ferenc A. Váli, *Politics of the Indian Ocean Region, The Balance of Power* (New York: Free Press, 1976), pp. 192–96.
2   This is not to deny the quite frequent Chinese practice of using the word region as a shorthand means of identifying a specific geographic area. Occasionally Chinese commentators even refer to an "Indian Ocean region." See "Soviet-Australian Relations," *Beijing Review*, 16 March 1981, p. 10.
3   Greg O'Leary, *The Shaping of Chinese Foreign Policy* (Canberra: Australian National University Press, 1980), p. 12.
4   For an analysis of the evolution of Chinese perceptions of the Soviet threat, see Jonathan D. Pollack, "Chinese Global Strategy and Soviet Power," *Problems of Communism* (January–February 1981), pp. 54–69. Discussions also appear in the general works on Chinese foreign policy, among them, Michael B. Yahuda, *China's Role in World Affairs* (New York: St. Martin's, 1978); and Wang Gungwu, *China and the World Since 1949: The Impact of Indepen-*

dence, Modernity and Revolution (London: Macmillan, 1977). My discussion closely follows that of Pollack.

5   See, for example, O'Leary, *The Shaping of Chinese Foreign Policy*, chap. 3; Wang Gungwu, *China and the World Since 1949*, chap. 7.

6   "The World Advances Amidst Great Disorder," *Renmin Ribao*, 31 December 1973, p. 5.

7   Cited in Pollack, "Chinese Global Strategy," p. 62. For other examples of China's assessment, see "Soviet Contention for Straits," *Peking Review*, 8 July 1977, pp. 25–26; "Soviet Social-Imperialism—Most Dangerous Source of World War," *Peking Review*, 15 July 1977, pp. 4–10, 21; and Chu Ya, "From Angola to the Horn of Africa," *Peking Review*, 21 April 1978, pp. 9–11.

8   Pollack, "Chinese Global Strategy," p. 62.

9   "Guard Against Tiger at the Back Door while Repulsing Wolf at the Gate," *Peking Review*, 9 January 1976, p. 20.

10 *Renmin Ribao*, commentator, "Who is the Instigator?" *Peking Review*, 23 June 1978, p. 24.

11 "Social Imperialist Strategy in Asia," *Beijing Review*, 19 January 1979, pp. 13–16.

12 "Moscow's Dumb-bell Strategy," *Beijing Review*, 25 February 1980, p. 8. For discussions of China's reaction to the invasion of Afghanistan, see Pollack, "Chinese Global Strategy," pp. 65–66; and Jaacov Vertzberger, "Afghanistan in China's Policy," *Problems of Communism* (May–June 1982), pp. 1–23. An analysis that emphasizes the ambivalence of Chinese policy to the invasion is to be found in Gerald Segal, "China and Afghanistan," *Asian Survey* 31, no. 2, pp. 1158–74.

13 Despite this, it is evident that within China there were conflicting views on the implications of the Soviets' Afghanistan adventure. See Pollack, "Chinese Global Strategy," and Segal, "China and Afghanistan."

14 See, for example, "Soviet Aggressors Sink Deeper Into Afghanistan Quagmire," *Beijing Review*, 27 September 1982, pp. 12–14; Zhang Zhen and Rang Zhi, "Some Observations of Soviet Detente," *Journal of International Studies* 4 (1982), reprinted in *Beijing Review*, 18 October 1982, pp. 16–22; and interview with Chen Zhongjing, *Renmin Ribao*, October 1982.

15 For discussions of and references to this process, see *Times* (London), 25 March, 22 May, 29 September, 3 and 14 December 1982, 6 June 1983; *Weekend Australian*, 26-27 March, 11–12 September 1983; *Canberra Times*, 5 October 1983; *China Quarterly*, Chronicle and Documentation, Soviet Union, vols. 90–97; Kenneth Lieberthal, "China," *Asian Survey* 23, no. 1, pp. 26–33.

16 See "The Kampuchean Issue and Sino-Soviet Consultation," *Beijing Review*, 14 March 1983, p. 4; Pei Monong, "China's Future Position in Asia," *Beijing Review*, 18 April 1983, pp. 15–19; "China's Views on World Situation," *Beijing Review*, 10 October 1983, pp. 13–17 and 25.

17 See Li Ning, "1982, a Year of Mounting Troubles," part 1, *Beijing Review*, 3 January 1983, pp. 18–24; and Xinhua News Agency, *Daily Report*, 2 June 1983, p. 54.

18 Li Ning, "1982, a Year of Mounting Troubles," part 2, *Beijing Review*, 10 January 1983, pp. 21–26.

19 Ibid., p. 26.

20 Cited in Pollack, "Chinese Global Strategy," p. 57.

21 For a discussion of this point, see Donald H. McMillan, "China and the Con-

tending Barbarians: Beijing's View of the Contemporary World Order," Working Paper 41, Strategic and Defence Studies Centre, Australian National University, p. 4.

22 A recent Western assessment of Chinese forces deployed in the border areas of the Shenyang, Lonzhou, and Urumqi military regions in the northeast, north, and east put the total divisional strength at four armored, thirty-two infantry, and twenty-two local forces. See *The Military Balance 1983–1984* (London: IISS, Autumn 1983), p. 84. For a discussion of the situation in the Urumqi military region, see Donald H. McMillan, "The Urumqi Military Region: Defense and Security in China's West," *Asian Survey* 22, no. 8, pp. 705–31.

23 Jiang Yuanchum, "Soviet Strategy for East Asia," *Beijing Review*, 23 March 1981, p. 20.

24 Tang Shan, "Source of Southeast Asian Tension," *Beijing Review*, 14 November 1983, p. 9.

25 Yahuda, *China's Role in World Affairs*, p. 114.

26 *Renmin Ribao*, commentator, "China Will Never Seek Hegemony," *Beijing Review*, 7 February 1983, p. 17.

27 As Deng Xiaoping explained to the United Nations in 1974, the developing countries of the Third World "constitute a revolutionary force propelling the wheel of history and are the main force combating colonialism, imperialism and the superpowers." See Special Supplement to *Peking Review*, 12 April 1974, p. 2. For a discussion, see Yahuda, *China's Role in World Affairs*, pp. 238ff.

28 For a general discussion of recent Chinese policy toward the Third World, see Lillian Craig Harris, "China's Third World Courtship," *Washington Quarterly* 5, no. 3, pp. 128–37.

29 The shortcomings of Chinese policy and their consequences are discussed in Alan Hutchison, *China's Africa Revolution* (London: Hutchison, 1975), pp. 103–32.

30 China's relations with Africa are discussed in Hutchison, ibid.; George I. Yu, "Peking's African Diplomacy," *Problems of Communism* (March–April 1972); and Harris, "China's Third World Courtship." For Western accounts of Prime Minister Ziyang's African tour, see *Christian Science Monitor*, 22 December 1982; *New York Times*, 3 January 1983; *Times* (London), 18 January 1983. For Beijing's account, see *Beijing Review*, 31 January 1983.

31 For discussion of China's relations with the Middle East, see Victor Shichor, *The Middle East in China's Foreign Policy 1949–1977* (Cambridge: Cambridge University Press, 1979); Hashim S. H. Benbehani, *China's Foreign Policy in Arab World, 1955–1975* (Henley-on-Thames: Kegan Paul International, 1982); Harris, "China's Third World Courtship," pp. 133–35; Areyeh Y. Yodfat, "The P.R.C. and the Middle East," parts 1 and 2, *Asia Quarterly* (1977 and 1978).

32 In general the policy has been that continued hostilities only provide opportunities for outside exploitation; as a consequence, Beijing has consistently urged Tehran and Baghdad to settle their differences. See "Iran and Iraq Still Fighting," *Beijing Review*, 6 April 1981, pp. 10–11. For references to the "left," see Quarterly Chronicle and Documentation, *China Quarterly* (January–March 1981), vols. 86 and 89.

33 For a commentary typifying the support, see "Gulf States' Third Summit Backs Fez Resolution," *Beijing Review*, 22 November 1982, pp. 10–11.

34 Sino–Southeast Asian relations are discussed in Yahuda, *China's Role in World*

Affairs, pp. 260–66; Harris, "China's Third World Courtship," pp. 132–33; and Takashi Tajima, *China and South-East Asia: Strategic Interests and Policy Prospects*, Adelphi Paper no. 172 (London: IISS, Winter 1981).

35 For developments in Sino-Indian relations in recent years, see Chronicle and Documentation, *China Quarterly*, and Harris, "China's Third World Courtship," pp. 133–35.

36 See "Huang Hua Visits Sri Lanka And the Maldives," *Beijing Review*, 13 July 1981, pp. 6–7.

37 The Chinese position regarding the Somali-Ethiopian conflict is set forth in "Somalia Protests Soviet Intervention," *Beijing Review*, 2 August 1982, pp. 11–12.

38 See n. 32 of this chapter.

39 See Xinhua News Agency, *Daily Report*, 20 May 1983, pp. 42–44.

40 For Chinese accounts of the visit see *Foreign Broadcast Information Service, Daily Report, People's Republic of China*, 20–26 April 1983.

41 See "China and the Third World," *Beijing Review*, 27 April 1981, p. 3. For an analysis of the fluctuations in China's aid program, see John A. Kringen, "Allocating Foreign Affairs Resources: Chinese Policy Toward the Third World in the 1970s," paper prepared for the Annual Meeting of the International Studies Association, held in Los Angeles, March 1980.

42 See *Communist Aid Activities in the Non-Communist Less Developed Countries 1979 and 1954–1979* (Washington, D.C.: National Foreign Assessment Center, 1980), pp. 18–20.

43 Ibid., pp. 10 and 21.

44 Ibid., p. 16.

45 Ibid., p. 13.

46 See Carol Fogarty, "Chinese Relations with the Third World," in *Chinese Economy Post-Mao*, papers submitted to the Joint Economic Committee, Congress of the United States, Washington, D.C., 1978, pp. 851–59.

47 Ibid., p. 855.

48 In 1964 Zhou Enlai declared that China would provide aid in accordance with Eight Principles of Providing Economic Aid; see "Premier Chou En-lai, Revolutionary Prospects in Africa Excellent!" *Peking Review*, 14 February 1964, p. 8.

49 See Fogarty, "Chinese Relations with the Third World" and, for a more extensive but now somewhat dated discussion of China's aid activities, Udo Weiss, "China's Aid to and Trade with the Developing Countries of the Third World," *Asia Quarterly*, no. 3 (1974) pp. 202–13, and no. 4 (1974), pp. 263–309.

50 For an analysis of the patterns of China's trade, see Richard E. Batsavage and John L. Davie, "China's International Trade and Finance," in *Chinese Economy Post-Mao*, pp. 707–41. For an interesting comparison of China's imperial and modern trade policies, see Udo Weiss, "Imperial China's Tributary Trade and the Foreign Trade Policy of the People's Republic of China: A Comparison of Attitudes," *Asia Quarterly*, no. 1 (1976), pp. 34–68. For a Chinese analysis of Third World trade, see Chen Muhua, "Developing Trade with other Third World Countries," *Beijing Review*, 19 September 1983, pp. 15–18.

51 See Batsavage and Davie, "China's International Trade and Finance," p. 721.

52 *China: International Trade 1977–78* (Washington, D.C.: National Foreign Assessment Center, 1978), pp. 12–13. For a discussion of Beijing's expectations

for trade in 1983, see Chen Muhua, "Prospects for China's Foreign Trade in 1983," *Beijing Review*, 7 February 1983, pp. 14–17.

53 See Batsavage and Davie, "China's International Trade and Finance," pp. 726–31; Fogarty, "Chinese Relations with the Third World," p. 858; and *Weekend Australian*, 24–25 September 1983.

Notes to Chapter 30

1 On Soviet arms transfer policy, see the discussion in my "Soviet Arms Supplies and Indian Ocean Diplomacy," in *The Indian Ocean in Global Politics*, ed. Larry W. Bowman and Ian Clark (Boulder, Colo.: Westview, 1981), pp. 149–72. For details of President Reagan's directive on arms sales of 8 July 1981, see *Department of State Bulletin*, September 1981, p. 61.
2 See, e.g., Kenneth Waltz, *The Spread of Nuclear Weapons: More May Be Better*, Adelphi Paper no. 171 (London: IISS, 1981).
3 Sri K. Subrahmanyam, director of India's Institute for Defence Studies and Analyses, is an inveterate proponent of this point of view.
4 See, e.g., Barry Buzan, "Naval Power, the Law of the Sea, and the Indian Ocean as a Zone of Peace," *Marine Policy* (July 1981).
5 The following argument was originally presented by the author in "South Asian Security and the Soviet Union," paper presented to the Conference on Security in South Asia, International Institute for Strategic Studies, held in London, July 1981.
6 See, e.g., the attack in *Izvestia*, 25 January 1983.
7 Regarding India, see *Overseas Hindustan Times*, 1 April 1982. As to Pakistan, see *Sunday Telegraph* (London), 11 April 1982.
8 Sharin Tahir-Kheli and William O. Staudenmaier, "The Saudi-Pakistani Military Relationship: Implications for US Policy," *Orbis* (Spring 1982), p. 157.
9 *Pravda*, 22 July 1982.
10 *Izvestia*, 18 December 1982.
11 See, e.g., Capt. A. Jampoler, "America's Vital Interests," *U.S. Naval Institute Proceedings* (January 1981), p. 30.
12 *US News & World Report* (22 February 1981), p. 32.
13 Sinclair, minister of defence, answer to question upon notice of 6 May 1982, *Commonwealth Parliamentary Debates* (House of Representatives), 24 August 1982.
14 See, e.g., *Backgrounder* (Australian Department of Foreign Affairs), 4 August 1982, p. 3.
15 *Izvestia*, 14 July 1982.
16 *Herald Tribune*, 26 July 1982.
17 *Pravda*, 28 July 1982.
18 *Africa* (February 1982), p. 44.
19 *Pravda*, 14 May 1982.
20 *Izvestia*, 14 May 1982.
21 During March 1982, for instance, *Pravda* was openly critical of the regime.
22 See, e.g., *International Herald Tribune*, 20 December 1982.
23 See, e.g., *Washington Post*, 2 November 1982.
24 *New York Times*, 18 April 1982.
25 *International Herald Tribune*, 22 March 1982.
26 *Africa Research Bulletin*, 31 August 1981, p. 6161.

27 *U.S. Department of State Bulletin,* October 1981, p. 13.
28 D. Newsom, "America EnGulfed," *Foreign Policy* (Summer 1981), p. 21.
29 C. Van Hollen, "Don't Engulf the Gulf," *Foreign Affairs* (Summer 1981), p. 1066.
30 William Quandt, "Riyadh between the Superpowers," *Foreign Policy* (Fall 1981), p. 39.
31 "India, Pakistan and Super-Power Rivalry," *World Today* (May 1982), p. 194.
32 Buzan, "Naval Power, the Law of the Sea, and the Indian Ocean," p. 201.
33 See, typically, *Pravda,* 2 October 1981, on the occasion of the visit to the USSR by President Ratsirata of Madagascar.

Index ✒

Association of South-East Asian Nations
(*Cont.*)
with Australia, 51, 355, 388–89, 390,
393; relations with Bangladesh, 52,
58; relations with Britain, 393; relations with Burma, 51, 52, 62; relations
with China, 518; relations with EEC,
399, 492; relations with Japan, 390,
393, 506; relations with Soviet Union,
387–88, 392; relations with Sri Lanka,
52; relations with United States, 92,
385, 393; relations with Vietnam, 49,
385, 386, 388, 392; and Soviet presence in Afghanistan, 386, 391; territorial disputes within, 62, 381; trade
of, 355, 378, 580 n.2; and United
Nations Conference on the Law of
the Sea III, 377, 380; and Zone of
Peace, Freedom, and Neutrality
(ZOPFAN), 58, 383–84, 386, 393. *See
also* Khomeini
Australasia: economic cooperation in,
51, 52; subregion of Indian Ocean, 5,
39
Australia, 5, 82; attitude toward Rapid
Deployment Force, 364, 375; and
"boat people," 89; economy of, 17,
357–60; and Five Power Defense
Agreement, 373; interests in Indian
Ocean region, 357, 362, 365, 367,
370; military capability of, 101, 360–
61; military facilities of, 371; and
Naval Arms Limitation Talks (NALT),
368–69; naval deployments and exercises in Indian Ocean region, 371–72,
479, 579 n.43; navy of, 83, 84, 86,
88, 354, 383; policies in Indian Ocean
region, 355–56, 360–73 passim; policy
toward Multilateral Force and Observers (MFO), 362–63, 364; relations
with China, 5, 20, 523; relations with
Iran, 362; relations with Iraq, 366;
relations with Israel, 366; relations
with Japan, 506; relations with South
Africa, 277, 565 n.37; relations with
Soviet Union, 357, 358, 361; relations
with Third World, 368; relations
with United States, 358–77 passim,
389; and Soviet presence in Afghanistan, 15, 361, 368, 369; trade of, 21,
84, 357, 362; and transit of B52

bombers, 11, 375; and United Nations
Conference on Law of the Sea III,
366–67, 389; and United States in-
stallations, 376, 408; views of Diego
Garcia buildup, 367–68; visits of
American ships, 373–74, 375. *See
also* ANZUS, Association of South-East
Asian Nations, Indian Ocean Zone of
Peace
Ayoob, Mohammed, 324, 325, 328,
329, 537
Aziz, Tariq, 177

Bab el-Mandeb, Straits of, 10, 193,
201, 206, 409, 420, 482
Baghdad Pact, 159–60
Bahrain, 167, 454; and American access
rights, 452; arrest of Iranian "sabo-
teurs" in, 128, 179–80; member of
Gulf Coopoation Council, 170; se-
curity agreement with Saudi Arabia,
180, 187. *See also* Saudi Arabia, Gulf
Cooperation Council
Bakhtiar, Shapour, 142, 143, 148
Bandaranike, Prime Minister, 16
Bangladesh, 8, 17, 20, 39, 332; do-
mestic politics in, 300, 339, 340, 341,
342, 343; navy of, 84, 89. *See also*
Association of South-East Asian
Nations, India, Indian Ocean Zone
of Peace
Bani Sadr, Abol Hassan, 142, 143,
148, 157
Banks, Michael, 6
Barre, Siad, 199, 235, 418, 422, 532,
533
Bazargan, Mehdi, 142, 182
Berenger, Paul, 287, 288, 289, 440, 441,
443, 480
Bhargava, G. S., 328, 329, 330, 331
Bhutan, 111, 332
Bhutto, Zulfigar Ali, 518
Binder, Leonard, 4
Bindra, A. P. S., 14
Botha, Pieter W. (South African prime
minister), 242, 267, 268, 270
Botha, R. F. (Pik), 269, 275
Botswana, 19, 60, 246, 258, 262. *See
also* Frontline States
Brazil, 95, 277

Ocean region, 105, 110, 200, 201, 206, 251, 311, 329, 409, 462, 463, 473, 531; naval modernization by, 205, 463, 473; nuclear targeting of, 103; and Persian Gulf, 299, 458, 473, 474–75, 476, 477, 498; projection of force into Indian Ocean, 99, 344, 409–11, 462, 493; relations with Third World, 36, 77, 245, 535; response to Zone of Peace, Freedom, and Neutrality proposal (ZOPFAN), 384; sea lines of communication (SLOC) in Indian Ocean, 12, 386, 402, 403, 405, 406, 409; strategic outlook of, 459–60; and test ban treaty negotiations, 107; trans-Siberian railroad of, 12, 398, 406. *See also* Afghanistan, Australia, Egypt, Ethiopia, India, Indian Ocean Zone of Peace, Iran, Iraq, Kenya, Libya, Mauritius, Mozambique, Pakistan, People's Democratic Republic of Yemen, People's Republic of China, Republic of South Africa, Somalia, Syria, Tanzania
Spiegel, Steven, 4, 5
Spratly Islands: claims to, 381, 382
Sri Lanka, 16, 17, 29; and Association of South-East Asian Nations (ASEAN), 52, 58; internal unrest in, 300; possible US base, 450; proposes Indian Ocean Zone of Peace, 301; relations with China, 518, 520, 521; relations with South Asian states, 332
Subrahmanyan, K., 319
Sudan, 5, 191, 194; aid recipient, 61; and Eritrean independence, 199, 201; relations with China, 517, 521; relations with United States, 194, 202, 421, 536
Suez Canal, 9, 191, 193, 406, 483
Superpowers: and Afghanistan, 345–46; chemical weapons talks by, 107; China's view of, 511, 513–14; disarmament negotiations by, 106; future relations in Indian Ocean region, 499, 531, 538; impact of rivalry between, 109, 378, 536; Indian Ocean rivalry of, 8, 9, 12, 45, 397, 413, 453, 528–29, 531; interests in Southeast Asia, 354, 392; naval competition between, 323, 473, 530–31; relations with

"middle powers," 77; rivalry in Persian Gulf, 161, 411, 456, 471, 476–77; rivalry in Southwest Asia, 304, 306–7; status of, 66, 67, 91, 99. *See also* France, Indian Ocean Zone of Peace, Soviet Union, United States
Syria, 79; Baath socialism in, 41; alliance with Egypt, 160; alliance with Egypt and Iraq, 163; and Eritrean independence movement, 198; and European Economic Community (EEC), 491; Gulf Cooperation Council support of, 178; member of Steadfastness Front, 183; relations with China, 517; relations with Soviet Union, 462, 464, 465, 471, 474

Tahir-Kheli, Shirin, 325
Taiwan, 378, 381
Tanzania: as aid recipient, 244–45, 249; and Arusha Declaration, 238, 240; economy of, 19, 239–41, 248, 556 n.31; as Frontline State, 5, 246; incursion into Uganda, 532; interests in Indian Ocean region, 250, 265; member of East African Community, 59; Muslim population in, 39; policy on bases in Indian Ocean region, 110; relations with China, 244, 517, 520, 521; relations with European Economic Community, 492; relations with other Frontline States, 241, 245, 263; relations with India, 248; relations with offshore islands, 247, 265, 290; relations with South Africa, 242, 254, 256, 272, 294; relations with Soviet Union, 229, 241, 243–44; relations with United States, 243; self-reliance policy in, 237, 241, 245; and superpower rivalry, 243, 244; Tanganyika African National Union, 239; TAZARA railway, 257, 273, 521; as tributary state, 230, 245. *See also* Frontline States, Indian Ocean Zone of Peace
Taraki, Nur Muhammad, 339, 341, 342, 343
Thailand, 15, 99, 506
Thatcher, Margaret, 241, 442, 446, 448, 480

Doctrine, 461; and Western Pacific, 92. *See also* ANZUS, Association of South-East Asian Nations, Australia, Diego Garcia, Egypt, Ethiopia, Iran, Iranian Revolution, Islam, Israel, Japan, People's Republic of China, Republic of South Africa, Saudi Arabia, Sudan, Tanzania

Váli, Ferenc, 15
Vietnam, 33; and Association of South-East Asian Nations, 52, 62, 392; maritime claims, 378, 381; present in Kampuchea, 382; relations with Soviet Union, 387, 462. *See also* People's Republic of China
Vivekanandan, B., 330

Warsaw Treaty Organization, 78, 410
Weinberger, Caspar, 100, 429
Western Europe: perception of Indian Ocean region, 492–94
Western European Union: defense cooperation in Indian Ocean, 489–90. *See also* European Economic Community, North Atlantic Treaty Organization
Wight, Martin, 65–66, 71
Willets, Peter, 31, 37
World Bank, 17, 61, 244

Yemen Arab Republic (YAR, North Yemen): as aid recipient, 61, 92, 193, 209; people of, 209–10; relations with China, 521; relations with Red Sea states, 218; relations with Saudi Arabia, 209, 213, 214, 216, 217, 221, 222; relations with Soviet Union, 221,

222, 224–25; relations with United States, 221, 222, 224–25. *See also* Libya, Oman, People's Democratic Republic of Yemen
Young, Oran, 540 n.14

Zambia, 19; dissidents in, 255; as Frontline State, 246; dependence on gulf oil, 248; loans recipient, 248–49; relations with China, 517; relations with India, 247; relations with South Africa, 60, 258, 262, 272; relations with superpowers, 243, 244; and TAZARA railway, 273; South West African People's Organization (SWAPO) loss in, 254. *See also* Frontline States
Zeine, Zeine N., 42
Zhao Ziyang, 517, 520
Zhou Enlai, 514
Zia, ul Haq, 297, 299, 300, 321, 332, 529, 534
Zimbabwe: aid receipts of, 249; air force attacked, 254; dissidents in, 215; as Frontline State, 19, 246; economic dependence on South Africa, 248, 258, 262, 264; landlocked, 37; railways of, 273; relations with China, 512; relations with India, 248; security relations with South Africa, 255, 263; Soviet interest in, 243. *See also* Frontline States
Ziring, Lawrence, 321
Zobel, William M., 423, 424
ZOPFAN (Zone of Peace, Freedom, and Neutrality). *See* Association of South-East Asian Nations, Malaysia, Soviet Union, United States

Contributors ▄

Henry S. Albinski is professor of Political Science, and director, Australian Studies Center, Pennsylvania State University.

Douglas G. Anglin is professor of Political Science, Carleton University, Ottawa, Canada.

Mohammed Ayoob is associate professor of Political Science, National University of Singapore.

James A. Bill is professor of Government and Middle Eastern Studies, University of Texas, Austin.

Ken Booth is senior lecturer in International Politics, University College of Wales, Aberystwyth.

Larry W. Bowman is professor of Political Science, University of Connecticut, Storrs.

R. M. Burrell is lecturer in Contemporary History of the Near and Middle East, School of Oriental and African Studies, University of London.

R. B. Byers is director, Research Programme in Strategic Studies, York University, Ontario, Canada.

Ian Clark was senior lecturer in Politics, University of Western Australia. He is now Teaching Fellow in Defence Studies, Selwyn College, University of Cambridge.

Alvin J. Cottrell was, until shortly before his death in 1984, executive director, Maritime Policy Studies, Center for Strategic and International Studies, Georgetown University.

William L. Dowdy was research associate, Centre for Foreign Policy Studies, Dalhousie University, and visiting fellow, Centre for the Study of Arms Control and International Security, University of Lancaster, England. He now holds the Chair of Military and Strategic Studies, Acadia University, Nova Scotia, Canada.

Tareq Y. Ismael is professor of Political Science, University of Calgary, Alberta, Canada.

Ashok Kapur is associate professor of Political Science, University of Waterloo, Ontario, Canada.

Zalmay Khalilzad is assistant professor of Political Science, Columbia University.

Joel Larus is professor of Politics, New York University.

Jeffrey A. Lefebvre is a doctoral candidate in Political Science, University of Connecticut.

Colin Legum is editor of *Africa Contemporary Record* and the author of numerous studies on Africa.

Michael MccGwire is senior fellow, Brookings Institution, Washington, D.C.

Onkar Marwah is joint director, Asian Centre, Graduate Institute of International Studies, Geneva.

John E. Peterson was the 1983–84 Thorton D. Hooper Fellow, Foreign Policy Research Institute, Philadelphia and has taught at William & Mary.

R. K. Ramazani is Harry F. Byrd, Jr., Professor in the Woodrow Wilson Department of Government and Foreign Affairs, University of Virginia.

James M. Roherty is professor of Government and International Studies, University of South Carolina, Columbia.

George W. Shepherd, Jr., is professor of International Relations at the University of Denver.

Sheldon W. Simon is professor of Political Science, and director of the Center for Asian Studies, Arizona State University.

Oles M. Smolansky is professor of International Relations, Lehigh University, Pennsylvania.

Michael Spicer is director of Programs at the South African Institute of International Affairs.

Raju G. C. Thomas is associate professor of Political Science, Marquette University, Milwaukee.

Russell B. Trood was affiliated with the Centre for Foreign Policy Studies, Dalhousie University, and is now lecturer in Political Science, Australian National University.

Taketsugu Tsurutani is professor of Political Science, Washington State University.

Peter C. J. Vale is director of research at the South African Institute of International Affairs.

Ferenc A. Váli until his death in 1984 was professor emeritus of Political Science, University of Massachusetts, Amherst.

Robert G. Wirsing is associate professor of Government and International Studies, University of South Carolina, Columbia.

Library of Congress Cataloging-in-Publication Data
Main entry under title:
The Indian Ocean: perspectives on a strategic arena.
(Duke Press Policy Studies)
Bibliography: p.
Includes index.
1. Indian Ocean—Strategic aspects—Addresses, essays,
lectures. 2. Indian Ocean Region—Strategic aspects—
Addresses, essays, lectures. I. Dowdy, William L.,
1944-   . II. Trood, Russell, B. III. Series.
UA830.I545 1985   355'.03301824   85-20606
ISBN 0-8223-0649-2
ISBN 0-8223-0691-3 (pbk.)